Multicultural
Commonwealth

RUSSIAN *and* EAST EUROPEAN STUDIES

Jonathan Harris, Editor

Multicultural Commonwealth

POLAND-LITHUANIA *and* ITS AFTERLIVES

Edited by Stanley Bill and Simon Lewis

UNIVERSITY *of* PITTSBURGH PRESS

Published by the University of Pittsburgh Press, Pittsburgh, Pa., 15260
Copyright © 2023, University of Pittsburgh Press
Manufactured in the United States of America
Printed on acid-free paper
10 9 8 7 6 5 4 3 2 1

Cataloging-in-Publication data is available from the Library of Congress

ISBN 13: 978-0-8229-4803-2
ISBN 10: 0-8229-4803-6

Cover art: Main exhibition of the Museum of the History of Polish Jews in Warsaw. Reconstruction of the synagogue in Gwoździec, Ukraine. Museum of the History of Polish Jews. Photo by Magdalena Starowieyska, Dariusz Golik. CC BY-SA 3.0 PL.

Cover design: Alex Wolfe

CONTENTS

      Oskar Halecki, Lewis Namier, and the Burden of History   181
          Robert Frost

9   Whose Grand Duchy? Contesting the Multicultural Past
      in Lithuania and Belarus   205
          Rūstis Kamuntavičius

10   Polish-Belarusian Encounters and the Divided Legacy of
      the Commonwealth   220
          Simon Lewis

11   Jewish Heritage Revival in the Polish-Belarusian-Ukrainian
      Borderlands and the Myth of Multiculturalism   241
          Magdalena Waligórska, Ina Sorkina, and Alexander Friedman

12   A New Multiculturalism in Poland: Memory of the Past
      and Migration from Ukraine   266
          Ewa Nowicka

      Notes   291
      List of Contributors   365
      Index   371

ACKNOWLEDGMENTS

Acknowledgments pages often glow about editors, but Peter Kracht of the University of Pittsburgh Press is truly in a class of his own. The extraordinary level of informed engagement that he brought to the project both helped to drive it forward and made the finished product significantly better. We thank him for his enthusiasm, knowledge, good judgment, and patience.

The book passed through a rigorous peer review process, involving multiple scholars with specific expertise scrutinizing each chapter under the auspices of the "Recovering Forgotten History" conference series. We extend special thanks to Andrzej S. Kamiński and Eulalia Łazarska for leading this process as well as all the individual experts who made key contributions to improving the book: Ihar Babkoŭ, Maria Cieśla, Anna Engelking, Tomasz Hen-Konarski, Maciej Janowski, Igor Kąkolewski, Adam Kożuchowski, Natalia Królikowska-Jedlińska, Andriej Moskwin, Andrzej Nowak, Andrii Portnov, Maciej Ptaszyński, Hienadź Sahanovič, Bożena Szaynok, Jan Szemiński, Wojciech Tygielski, Michał Wasiucionek, Marek Wierzbicki, and Anna Wylegała. Thanks also to Oleksandr Avramchuk and Ekaterina Kolb for their logistical support in Warsaw.

Finally, we warmly thank the three anonymous reviewers who played an important part at an earlier stage in the project's development, giving very helpful guidance on the overall shape of the volume.

Any remaining deficiencies and errors, of course, remain ours alone.

NOTE ON PROPER NOUNS, PLACE NAMES, AND TRANSLITERATION

Undoubtedly among the greatest challenges we faced in compiling this book was the question of what to do with names. The very raison d'être of the project is to explore the rich diversity of the Polish-Lithuanian Commonwealth, a composite entity inhabited by people who spoke (dialects or older versions of) Polish, Lithuanian, Belarusian, Ukrainian, Yiddish, German, Armenian, Kipchak Turkic, and other languages. Various liturgical and literary languages—including Latin, Church Slavonic, Hebrew, and Arabic—were also in use to varying degrees at different times. This diversity inevitably leads to the existence of a multitude of different names for the same places and people. The capital of modern Lithuania has been variously known as Vilnius in Lithuanian, Wilno in Polish, Vilne in Yiddish, Vilnia in Belarusian, and so forth. A historical figure associated with the same city, the Grand Chancellor of the Grand Duchy of Lithuania from 1589 to 1623, is known as Lew Sapieha in modern Polish, Leonas Sapiega in Lithuanian, and Leŭ Sapieha (Леў Сапега) in Belarusian. He himself would have been equally comfortable in Chancery Ruthenian, Polish, and almost certainly Latin—though in his case, probably not Lithuanian. The spelling of his name in accordance with one modern national orthography or another may appear to suggest that he should be considered a forerunner of modern Polish, Lithuanian, or Belarusian national state identities. Thus, any specific choice of how to spell a historical personal or place name is fraught with political implications; however inadvertently, such decisions may imply an anachronistic belief that this person or place "belonged" to a given linguistic community in its modern form.

In a book with over a dozen contributors and a temporal focus extending from the early modern period to the present day, it makes no sense to impose a single, monolithic spelling system. When discussing political events in, say, sixteenth-century Danzig or Breslau (now Gdańsk and Wrocław, Poland), it is intuitive to use the German names. This is not to say that *only* German was used in these cities at this time, but it was clearly the dominant language of administration, culture, and everyday life. Yet if we are talking about modern times, the Polish names must be used; both cities are today indisputably part of a sovereign Polish state.

On the other hand, it would be difficult to impose a rule of thumb that the most commonly used spelling "at the time" be employed on each occasion. Many urban spaces were culturally heterogeneous. In this context, what would be the most appropriate name for, say, the now-Belarusian city of Viciebsk? The politically dominant culture may have been Polish toward the end of the eighteenth century (Witebsk); numerically speaking, Yiddish was widely spoken (וויטעבסק, Vitebsk); Belarusian (Viciebsk) and Russian (Vitebsk) were also in use, especially by the nineteenth century. Consistently favoring Polish over Yiddish may suggest that Polish was somehow "more important"; choosing Russian lends legitimacy to Russian imperial dominion over the city after the partitions of the Commonwealth; insisting on modern Belarusian for periods preceding the existence of a Belarusian state would be anachronistic. Such dilemmas offer no easy solutions.

Therefore, readers of this book will encounter different spellings of certain proper nouns throughout the volume. In many instances, alternatives will be offered in parentheses in order to signal that more spellings have been in use: for example, the sixteenth-century clergyman Ioannes Dantiscus (1485–1548) is spelled initially in the Latin manner, given that he wrote and published in Latin under this name, but the parenthesis on first mention (*Pol.* Jan Dantyszek, *Ger.* Johannes Dantiscus) indicates that he is referred to in many Polish and German sources using alternative spellings. Place names likewise are rendered as, for example, Iŭje (*Pol.* Iwje, *Yid.* אייוויע) or Lwów (now Lviv, Ukraine) on first mention within a chapter. At the same time, such parenthetical elaborations cannot and do not exhaust the possibilities of equally legitimate spellings. In each case, the authors and editors claim discretion in making informed decisions about the most relevant variants in the given context. Analyzing the Belarusian former shtetl of Iŭje in the context of local Holocaust memory, the Yiddish spelling is clearly of interest; in other instances in the volume, however, Yiddish spellings of towns are often not given— this does not imply a denial of historical Jewish presence in a particular locality, but merely assumes that in the given context under discussion other variants may be more directly relevant. This practice is applied, above all, for reasons of legibility—if every proper noun had five or six variants in parentheses throughout the volume, the text would soon lose clarity amid the thicket of names. Furthermore, there is no hierarchy implied in the order of variants: if a Polish spelling is listed outside the brackets, and a Ukrainian spelling first within the parenthesis—say, in the case of Konstanty Ostrogski (*Ukr.* Kostiantyn Ostrozkyi; *Bel.* Kanstantyn Astroski or Astrožski; *Lit.* Konstantinas Ostrogiškis; ca. 1460–1530)—this should not be taken as a value judgment that Polish takes precedence over Ukrainian, which is in turn more important than Belarusian and Lithuanian.

There are some exceptions to this very loose system. The names of rulers of the Polish-Lithuanian Commonwealth are rendered consistently in anglicized form, with many of those derived from Latin: for example, Sigismund I the Old (1467–1548) rather than a listing of all the possible local variants (*Pol.* Zygmunt, *Lit.* Žygimantas, *Bel.* Žyhimont, *Ukr.* Syhizmund, etc.). This also extends to a few somewhat awkward collocations, such as the multilingual naming of John III Sobieski (r. 1674–1696; rather than *Pol.* Jan III Sobieski or *Lit.* Jonas III Sobieskis, etc.) and Stephen Báthory (r. 1576–1586; rather than *Hun.* István Báthory; *Pol.* Stefan Batory, etc.). The names of some of the earliest Lithuanian Grand Dukes have no ready English equivalents, and thus are rendered using alternatives in parentheses—for example, Vaišvilkas (alternatively Vaišelga; *Bel.* Vojšalk, *Pol.* Wojsiełk; Grand Duke 1264–1267).

Cities with standard forms in English are also consistently spelled in this way, such as Warsaw and Moscow. We prefer Kraków to Cracow or Krakow, Kyiv to Kiev. In some instances, it is debatable whether a city has a standardized form. Minsk is spelled in a similar way in most European languages (Minsk in both Russian and Belarusian, Mińsk in Polish, etc.), but some activist circles in Belarus prefer the archaic Belarusian form Miensk (pronounced M-yen-sk), arguing that "Minsk" is the colonial, Russified form; while acknowledging this fact, we stay with the more familiar Minsk. Vilnius may also arguably be already "standard" English, but especially when talking about the early modern period, we consider it expedient and consistent with the practices outlined above to allow Wilno (now Vilnius, Lithuania); a similar argument can be made with respect to Lviv/Lwów.

Polish is spelled consistently using modern standardized Polish orthography—with the exception of citations, where original archaic forms can be preserved. The same is true of Lithuanian and German. Belarusian is transliterated into Roman script using the UN-approved "National System of Geographic Names Transmission into Roman Alphabet in Belarus" (2007–2008); however, towns such as Polatsk (*Rus.* Polotsk; *Pol.* Połock) remain an exception—we spell it with a "tsk" rather than as "Polack," assuming that most anglophone readers would find it counterintuitive to read the "-ck" ending as anything another than a hard /k/. Ukrainian is transliterated using the UN-approved "Romanization System in Ukraine" (2011–2012). Russian is romanized using the Library of Congress system, without diacritics.

None of the thorny linguistic issues mentioned above can be resolved in a way that will please all readers in all instances. However, we consulted widely on these questions throughout the writing process, and thus all the final decisions have been made from a position of deliberative compromise.

Multicultural
Commonwealth

Introduction

Diverse Histories and Contested Memories

Stanley Bill and Simon Lewis

The title of this book—*Multicultural Commonwealth*—is something of a provocation. The phrase might easily be followed by a question mark, or the key term "multicultural" suspended within scare quotes. The book does not seek to define the Polish-Lithuanian Commonwealth (1569–1795) as a multicultural state in any contemporary sense. Instead, it presents a range of perspectives on how cultural diversity functioned during its existence and how this diversity has been represented or remembered since its destruction. Our aim is not to idealize the Commonwealth as a uniquely tolerant land of harmonious relations between groups—though we will show that this view has formed an attractive way of presenting its legacy for some of its modern inheritors. At the same time, we do not dismiss the existence of a deep political tradition of relative toleration in its institutions and social practices. Diversity became a fact in the late medieval union of the Kingdom of Poland and the Grand Duchy of Lithuania from its very inception in 1385. This fact led to the establishment of various political and legal norms, and perhaps even a kind of ideology, to sustain an internally differentiated, composite state. The Commonwealth, as the union became in 1569, was literally "multicultural" to the extent that its territory was home to Poles, Lithuanians, Ruthenians, Germans, Jews, Tatars, Armenians, and others. This book is concerned with the ideas, norms, and practices that regulated this diversity, and with the later imaginative and political uses of its memory.

The first half of the book examines the historical diversity of the Commonwealth through six chapters focusing on different groups and cultures. Individual chapters are devoted, respectively, to: the development of Jewish communities; multiconfessionalism in the Commonwealth's Prussian and Ruthenian lands; Muslim Tatars in the Grand Duchy of Lithuania; the evolution of Ruthenian identities in Kyiv; the overarching "Sarmatian" mythology that united various elites; and the role of religious diversity in the Commonwealth's final phase before the late eighteenth-century partitions that finally wiped it off the map of Europe. All these chapters reveal the complexity of group and individual identities, and the often vexed relations between them, while also explaining some of the legal norms and informal practices that supported and codified coexistence. The second half of the book discusses the memory and afterlife of the Commonwealth's diversity in six chapters looking at cultural and political reconstructions of the past, from the nineteenth-century period of the partitions through to the contemporary nations and states that may lay claim to the Commonwealth's legacy. The respective chapters examine: nineteenth-century Polish Romantic visions of Ukraine; conflicting historical interpretations of past diversity during the interwar period of the twentieth century; the disputed legacy of the Grand Duchy of Lithuania in modern Lithuania and Belarus; Polish-Belarusian literary dialogues on the afterlife of the Commonwealth; reconstructions of the Jewish past in contemporary Belarus, Poland, and Ukraine; and the new "multiculturalism" being created in present-day Poland by the mass immigration of Ukrainians. The chapters all demonstrate the fundamentally contested nature of the memory of the Commonwealth's historical diversity, which has been perceived and utilized in multiple ways by diverse actors from its late eighteenth-century demise until today.

In this introduction, we outline the historical and theoretical foundations of the volume. First, we summarize what the Polish-Lithuanian Commonwealth was and how it has been understood in existing scholarship. Second, we explore the applicability of concepts of "multiculturalism" to the Commonwealth, differentiating between multiple meanings of the term and briefly considering the legal, political, social, religious, and linguistic dimensions of the Commonwealth's internal heterogeneity. Third, we examine the challenges and specificities of analyzing memories of that multicultural past in contemporary central and eastern Europe—a region in which more

recent histories of mass violence and atrocity have led to dramatic rearrange-
ments of political boundaries and national demographics. Throughout this
introduction, we also offer glimpses into what the rest of the book will offer,
drawing parallels and lines of comparison between its constituent chapters.
In the multiplicity of the book's interpretations and approaches, we hope to
capture some of the rich diversity of the Commonwealth's history and legacy.

What Was the Polish-Lithuanian Commonwealth?

The Polish-Lithuanian Commonwealth was the product of a union treaty
signed on July 1, 1569, in Lublin that brought together the Polish Crown
and the Grand Duchy of Lithuania under a single monarchy, with a common Sejm (parliament) and currency, but separate treasuries, ministries,
and armies. A dynastic union between the two states had existed since the
Union of Kreva (*Pol.* Krewo, *Lit.* Krėva) in 1385, when Jogaila, grand duke of
Lithuania, agreed to marry Jadwiga, queen of Poland, and take up the Polish
throne after converting to Christianity—he thereby became known in Polish as Władysław II Jagiełło (*Lat.* Ladislaus). The 1569 Union of Lublin was
therefore a renewal of a nearly two-century-long alliance between Poland
and Lithuania, as well as the birth of a new political entity.[1] As the third article of the Union treaty put it, the agreement created "an undivided, single
and uniform Commonwealth [*Rzeczpospolita*] that has come together from
two states and peoples and created one people."[2]

The Commonwealth is usually known in Polish as *Rzeczpospolita Obojga
Narodów*—the Commonwealth (or Republic) of Both Nations.[3] But it was not
only the two titular "nations" that made it a diverse polity. As the Vilnius Jesuit Jakub Olszewski (ca.1586–1634) proclaimed in 1631, the Commonwealth
was "a bird of many colors: Poles, Lithuanians, Masovians, Samogitians,
Prussians. As for the diversity of its estates [it is also] a bird of many colors:
senators, nobility, and commoners. As for the diversity of religions, [it is] a
bird of many colors: there are Roman and Greek Catholics, there are Protestants, Saxons, and dissenters."[4] Throughout its existence—until its partitioning by the Russian Empire, the Kingdom of Prussia, and the Habsburg
Monarchy in three stages between 1772 and 1795—the Polish-Lithuanian
Commonwealth was a multiethnic and multiconfessional entity. In addition
to the groups mentioned by Olszewski, there were significant communities
of Ruthenians, Jews, Karaites, Tatars, Armenians, and Roma, among others.
Scholars have estimated that at the time of the first partition, if one anach-

ronistically projects modern ethnolinguistic categories onto the premodern past, "ethnic 'Poles' constituted 40% of the Commonwealth's population, or 5 million inhabitants. From this ethnolinguistically slanted perspective the rest of the populace was composed of 'Lithuanians' and 'Ruthenians' (that is, today's 'Belarusians' and 'Ukrainians') amounting to 0.7 million (5%) and 5.7 million (45%), respectively, alongside 1 million Jews (8%), and the rest made up of 'Germans,' Armenians and Tatars."[5]

This diversity has prompted some historians to prefer the label *Rzeczpospolita Wielu Narodów*—a Commonwealth of *many* nations.[6]

The many communities of the Commonwealth were dispersed unevenly across the realm, and were also socially differentiated.[7] One major dividing line was the internal border between the Polish Crown and the Grand Duchy—the latter already a cultural composite of Baltic Lithuanians and East Slavic Ruthenians, whose lands of the medieval Kyivan Rus' the originally pagan Lithuanians had absorbed in the fourteenth century in the wake of Mongol invasions. The Commonwealth's two constituent parts initially used different chancery languages (Polish and Ruthenian) in addition to other vernaculars and dialects; and the separate political cultures were also enshrined in the maintenance of different legal codes, the legislation of the Grand Duchy of Lithuania being codified in the Lithuanian Statutes of 1529, 1566, and 1588. Some groups were mostly represented in specific regions— such as the Baltic Lithuanians, who were concentrated in Samogitia (*Lit.* Žemaitija, *Pol.* Żmudź) and Aukštaitia (*Pol.* Auksztota; also known as "Lithuania Proper"), loosely corresponding to the territory of the modern-day Lithuanian state. The central, southern, and eastern regions of the pre-Lublin Grand Duchy were populated above all by Eastern Orthodox—and later also Uniate—Ruthenians, as well as settlements of Tatars, Jews, and Armenians. Importantly, the Union of Lublin transferred the large southern Ruthenian palatinates from the Grand Duchy to the Polish Crown, thus dividing the Ruthenian lands and contributing to the divergent development of what would eventually become separate Ukrainian and Belarusian national identities.[8]

"Ethnic" Poles were originally concentrated in the regions of the pre-1569 Polish Crown—in Wielkopolska (Greater Poland), Małopolska (Lesser Poland), and Mazovia, although the Polish language quickly became the lingua franca of the Commonwealth. From 1696 onward, it was the only language of administration in the Grand Duchy, replacing chancery Ruthenian; and in 1697, courts of the majority-Ruthenian areas in the southern and southeastern regions of the Polish Crown were ordered to keep official records in

Polish only.[9] Thus, early examples of Ruthenian and Lithuanian literary culture, such as Francišak Skaryna's biblical translations (e.g. his *Biblija Ruska*, printed in Prague in 1517–1519) and Martynas Mažvydas's *The Simple Words of the Catechism* (*Catechismusa prasty Szadei*, printed in Königsberg in 1547), remained relatively unknown until their "rediscovery" in the nineteenth century.

The spread of Polish was one factor that led to a complex overlapping of social divisions with language and culture. As the once-pagan Lithuanian elites of the Grand Duchy assimilated first to the Ruthenian and then Polish languages, the remaining speakers of Baltic Lithuanian were predominantly peasants dwelling in rural regions; as Ruthenian went out of high political use, it also gradually became a peasant vernacular in the lands of the Commonwealth, only later to be "revived" by Romantic poets and national "awakeners" (including as separate Belarusian and Ukrainian languages).[10] Jewish communities, on the other hand, were more often urban, settled in towns and shtetls throughout the Polish Crown and the Grand Duchy. This was partly because Jewish identity was circumscribed by a separate legal status "as a second urban group, with rights and duties parallel to (though not the same as) those of the non-Jewish burghers."[11] German was another language that was confined to specific regions—above all Royal Prussia (*Pol.* Prusy Królewskie, *Ger.* Königlich-Preußen) and Livonia (*Pol.* Inflanty; *Ger.* Livland).[12] Like their counterparts in the Grand Duchy, German-speaking nobles in these provinces gained the same privileges and liberties as the Polish nobility under the Union of Lublin, while also retaining distinctive local identities.[13] Thus, while the Polish language was the standard medium of communication between different social and regional groups—and some communities actively polonized in linguistic terms—local, regional, and religious identities remained strong markers of diversity and difference.

One of the main points of departure for this volume is that the cultural diversity of the Commonwealth was a defining feature of the polity, but also one that has often been eclipsed in memory, at least until recently. In both academic and popular discourses, the Polish-Lithuanian Commonwealth has often been understood as simply "Poland," reflecting a long-standing orthodoxy in Polish historiography that one critic, the historian Andrzej Sulima Kamiński, has called a "historical imperialism" that "disfigures the truth about our common past."[14] The Polish ethnonationalist master narrative is reflected in the numeration of historical incarnations of "the Polish state," with the Commonwealth referred to as the "First Republic," the interwar

republic—also a multicultural entity—as the "Second Republic,"[15] and the
current state that emerged after the collapse of state socialism as the "Third
Republic." In this way, a continuity between the multinational Commonwealth and modern Polish national sovereignty is established at the level of
everyday language.[16] Yet the Polish-Lithuanian Commonwealth was not by
any measure a Polish nation-state; it was a union between two states, the
Polish Crown and the Grand Duchy of Lithuania. Several modern nations
may lay claim to its heritage: Belarus, Poland, Lithuania, and Ukraine, among
contemporary sovereign nations, in addition to numerous ethnic and religious communities with historical roots in the region.

The Polish-Lithuanian Commonwealth's diverse heritage poses problems
for both contemporary historiography and memory politics between the successor nations. Andrzej Sulima Kamiński appeals to a hidden "truth about
our common past," but such a normative position is also fraught: stretched
too far, it can be construed to mean that modern nationalities had ready
equivalents in the time of the Commonwealth itself. Yet *whose* common past
is "ours"?[17] Does history "belong" to nations? The Grand Duchy of Lithuania,
for example, is regularly discussed in terms of whether it was a "Lithuanian"
or "Belarusian" state, or alternatively a "Balto-Slavic" or "Lithuano-Ruthe-
nian" entity.[18] Such debates reveal the extent to which the very concepts of
identity, language, and culture that we use to analyze a premodern entity
such as Poland-Lithuania are circumscribed by modern modes of thinking.
In some ways, it is easier to define what the Commonwealth was *not*: it was
not a nation-state—in fact, it was not a unitary state at all; it was not (only)
Polish, Lithuanian, Ruthenian, Belarusian, Ukrainian, Slavic, Catholic,
Christian, or Jewish. And while the Commonwealth certainly hosted many
cultures within its borders, it was clearly not a polity with an ideology of
diversity or multiculturali*sm* in any modern sense.

A further problem is that a focus on the diversity of cultures within the
Commonwealth may mask very real inequities in the representation of those
cultures, historically speaking. As Andrzej Leder puts it, the many-culturedness (*wielokulturowość*) of the Commonwealth had little in common with
contemporary egalitarian multiculturalism (*multikulturalizm*), because its
society was characterized by a "profound, fundamental inequality . . . with
such deep divisions between religions, ethnies, and estates that in essence
there was no anthropological unity."[19] Another name commonly given to
Poland-Lithuania is the "Noblemen's Commonwealth" (Pol. *Rzeczpospolita
szlachecka*), reflecting the fact that it was in political terms "above all a nation

of nobles."[20] The incremental polonization of the Grand Duchy's Lithuanian and Ruthenian nobility and institutions—along with the partial assimilation of the German-speaking elite—created a majority Polish-speaking ruling class, which remained "multicultural" only in origin and regional identity. By the time the belatedly reformist Constitution of May 3, 1791, was declared on the eve of the final partition, the Commonwealth had become for all intents and purposes "Polish," with hardly a mention of the Grand Duchy, let alone other minorities, as Richard Butterwick's textual analysis of the Constitution shows: "In other places where 'the Commonwealth' might ordinarily have been used, we find *naród*—the nation—thirty-one times, *Ojczyzna*—the Fatherland—twelve times, *kraj*—the country—six times, and *Polska*—Poland—six times. . . . This choice of language, significantly different to the phrasing of prior and subsequent laws, would facilitate the future evolution of the political community. The Polish-Lithuanian noble estate, associated by long usage with the term *Rzeczpospolita*, could thus expand into a common Polish nation composed of all inhabitants and defenders of a shared Polish Fatherland and country."[21] Thus, a significant feature of the multicultural Commonwealth was that its key institutions and political elites increasingly denied its multiculturality.

It is not only the mainstream of Polish historiography and everyday discourse that renders the Commonwealth "Polish." In addition to the terminological lethargy of Western scholarship that until recently parroted the polonocentric perspective, the national master narratives of the other successor nations—perhaps more surprisingly—have also tended to disown the Commonwealth. From a Lithuanian perspective, the country's Golden Age is considered to be the era before cultural polonization gathered pace after the Union of Lublin; the seventeenth and eighteenth centuries are for Lithuanian historiography an "epoch of noblemen's anarchy and polonization, whose essence fits the image of a decadent and moribund state."[22] The Ukrainian scholar Andrii Portnov goes so far as to suggest that the Commonwealth has come to play the role of an "external enemy and oppressive power" in the national historiographies of Ukraine, Belarus, and Lithuania.[23] The very naming of the Commonwealth in various languages is symptomatic of the mutual polonization of its legacy. On the one hand, the word "Rzeczpospolita"—a calque of the Latin *res publica*—denotes only the Polish state in Polish (other republics can only be *republika*, e.g., *Republika Słowacka* for Slovakia); on the other hand, the old Commonwealth is rendered as *Žečpospolita* in Lithuanian, *Reč Paspalitaja* in Belarusian, and *Rich Pospolita* in Ukrainian—which, in each case, has a distinctly foreign, Polish sound.[24] Whereas *Rzeczpospolita Polska* is the official name of the modern Polish state, no one would speak of a *Reč Paspalitaja Bielaruskaja*.

Only in the past decade or two has the Commonwealth begun to be gradually "depolonized," both among critical circles of Polish intellectuals and elsewhere. Historians and literary scholars have explored the heterogeneity, multilingualism, and polycentrism of Poland-Lithuania's culture and history—for example, in the complex coexistence of religions in its towns, or through close readings of early modern Ruthenian-language literature that the canon of Polish philology (*polonistyka*) had previously marginalized.[25] Polish scholarship and publishing have also paid considerably more attention to Belarus, Lithuania, and Ukraine in recent years: in the early 2000s, the Lublin Institute of East-Central Europe published a pioneering series of histories of the Commonwealth as a multicultural realm, including separate treatments of the successor nations;[26] since then, the presence of Poland's eastern neighbors in its intellectual and cultural landscape has continued to grow.

For instance, in literature, authors such as Ziemowit Szczerek have contributed to a debunking of polonocentric myths about Ukraine, while Żanna Słoniowska's novel *The House with the Stained-Glass Window* (*Dom z witrażem*, 2015) is a rare example of "migrant literature" in Poland, written by a Ukrainian in her nonnative Polish and set in Lviv.[27] These and multiple other examples show that Belarus, Lithuania, and Ukraine have increasingly become recognized in Poland as sovereign nations, rather than as spaces of Polish past cultural presence. At the same time, scholars in those countries are also moving away from metanarratives that reject the legacy of the (especially latter-day) Commonwealth as "too Polish." In Belarus, for example, recent studies of Latin-language literature of the Grand Duchy of Lithuania have sought neither to nationalize that heritage nor to polonize it, instead analyzing it on its own, pre-national terms.[28] Contemporary Ukrainian historians have reassessed the significance of the Commonwealth and the Union of Lublin in the early development of Ukrainian identity.[29] Lithuanian historians have also begun to examine the legacy of the Grand Duchy with a greater focus on the Ruthenian elements that played a substantial role in its development.[30]

Meanwhile, international scholarship has also exhibited a growing interest in the region and an expanding conceptual apparatus with which to interpret the diverse connections between nations and ethnoconfessional groups. Historians in particular—including several contributors to this volume—have taken the initiative in researching the Polish-Lithuanian Commonwealth as a multicultural polity, rather than as a monolithic state.[31] The Commonwealth has been analyzed in detail in the context of its entanglements with other polities, such as the Kingdom of Sweden and the Ottoman Empire.[32] At the same time, interpretations placing the Commonwealth within broader frameworks, such as that of the Jagiellonian dynasty that ruled in vast lands covering huge swathes of central and eastern Europe over two centuries,[33] have helped shed new light on the diversity of the region from inter-dynastic and comparative perspectives.

While acknowledging and taking inspiration from the insights of the existing literature, we hope that the provocative framing of our discussion through the concepts of "multiculturalism" and "the multicultural" will offer some new perspectives. Moreover, the very evocation of these modern terms—variously understood and always accompanied by critical acknowledgment of their limitations—immediately foregrounds the much broader problem of the imposition of contemporary norms, values, and political exigencies on the past. This problem is directly relevant to analysis of the various political uses of the Commonwealth's legacy discussed in the second part of the book, but it also remains a key consideration in attempts to characterize its historical diversity in the first part. The book aims to grapple with retrospective fantasies and polemics about the Commonwealth's history, while also examining aspects of the real cultural diversity of that history in its own terms. In this sense, the chapters of the two parts of the book—on history and memory—reflect and inform one another.[34] By adopting an explicitly contemporary conceptual framework in a self-reflexive mode, the book draws attention to the writing of history as a fundamentally interpretive act. In our own interpretation, we must begin by defining some of the specific ways in which we will understand the terminology of "multiculturalism."

Types of Diversity in the Historical Commonwealth

Theories of multiculturalism have distinguished two main uses of the term. The first is purely descriptive, meant to convey the presence of cultural diversity within a particular territory, region, or state. The second is normative, often referring to an ideology or a set of state policies promoting or celebrating cultural diversity.[35] In some English-language contexts, adjectival and nominal uses of the term may serve partly to clarify this distinction, so that "multicultural" implies description, while "multiculturalism" suggests a normative idea.[36] In Belarusian, Lithuanian, Polish, and Ukrainian, separate nouns helpfully distinguish between the social fact of "many-culturedness" (Bel. *šmatkul̇turnaść*; Lit. *daugiakultūriškumas*; Pol. *wielokulturowość*; Ukr. *polikultur'nist'*) and the ideology of "*multykul̇turalizm / multikultūralizmas / multikulturalizm / multykulturalizm.*"

The primary sense in which we use the term in this book is firmly adjectival or descriptive. The Polish-Lithuanian Commonwealth was indisputably a "multicultural"—or "many-cultured"—entity in this delimited meaning. Yet its elites did not espouse a specific ideology of "multiculturalism" or celebrate diversity for its own sake. At the same time, we by no means wish to do away with the normative dimension. Indeed, one of the book's central purposes is to consider whether, to what degree, and in what specific spheres some variant of the normative definition can be applied to the Commonwealth. In other words, to what extent was its factual diversity lived and understood in structured or even affirmative ways, both institutionally and informally?

Before giving some provisional responses to these questions, we must first clarify what we mean by "culture." For if this is a book about the interaction of different "cultures," then what are those "cultures"? Scholars of culture have repeatedly underlined the fundamental dynamism and indeterminacy of the term, noting its shifting meanings across time and in different academic disciplines.[37] Among other approaches, culture can be understood semiotically, normatively, societally, or in terms of group identity and practices. In influential interpretations, it denotes coherent systems or "webs" of symbolic meaning and communication, embracing language, beliefs, moral codes, customs, art, artifacts, dress, architecture, and food.[38] Culture can overlap or intersect with a range of other identities formed on the basis of nationality, ethnicity, kinship, religion, geographical location, shared history, and political affiliation. Individual identities, especially in diverse societies, inevitably involve combinations of different elements from these categories, all of which are themselves fluid and difficult to define.[39] The parameters of "culture" are thus deeply ambiguous, and the borders between discrete "cultures" equally so.

In this book, we assume an anti-essentialist view of culture from the outset, taking as a moniker Edward Said's succinct claim that "all cultures are involved in one another; none is single and pure, all are hybrid, heterogeneous, extraordinarily differentiated, and unmonolithic."[40] From this point of view, there is a fundamental paradox inherent in the very notion of a "multicultural" Commonwealth, since it implicitly imposes "culture" as an essentialized, countable object—that is, plural cultures as "distinct worlds of meaning" that are "logically consistent, highly integrated, consensual, extremely resistant to change, and clearly bounded."[41] Despite often being employed in the service of open, tolerant, or even cosmopolitan ideals, concepts of "multiculturalism" and "many-culturedness" thus may function to delimit, categorize, and draw boundaries. In the premodern world of the Commonwealth itself, such boundaries do not reflect the internal diversity of groups and the often mixed identities of individuals—especially among elites—who could activate different aspects of these identities in different contexts. Linguistic, ethnic, and confessional pluralism in the Commonwealth did not necessarily translate into a multiplicity of readily identifiable "cultures." Indeed, one might argue that "multiculturalism" only becomes a thinkable category at all with the onset of modernity and political nationalism, with their rationalized impulses to divide social groups into cohesive cultures, nations, and ethnic groups.

Despite these limitations, the book does tacitly accept the existence of putative identities coalescing around culture, language, religion, geographical location, political tradition, and history. The Commonwealth was inhabited by people who were called—or who called themselves, though with diverse meanings—Poles, Lithuanians, Ruthenians, Germans, Jews, Tatars, Armenians, and so on. The meanings of these terms were unstable and subject to change, and at no point did they signify "ethnic" identities in a modern sense. A "Lithuanian" member of the nobility was often a Polish speaker with no knowledge of the Baltic Lithuanian language—although he or she might well have also spoken Ruthenian. A "Pole" in Ukraine could be bilingual, while simultaneously identifying as "Ruthenian"—a "two-layered" identity combining a Polish civic-political identity with a Ruthenian "ethnic" one, as captured in the formula *Gente Rutheni, Natione Poloni.*[42] In other contexts, "Ruthenian" identity may be viewed as an early modern precursor to divergent "Ukrainian" and "Belarusian" modern identities, both of which terms are anachronistic when retrospectively applied with contemporary meanings. Other terms, like "Sarmatian"—an overarching, mythical identity uniting diverse members of the nobility—are rarely used today. In all cases, these terms and the "cultures" heuristically associated with them throughout the book must be treated as dynamic, unstable, porous, and intertwined with one another.

With these caveats established, it is useful to examine how the Commonwealth became diverse or multicultural. Unlike many contemporary multicultural states in Europe, the Commonwealth's diversity was not

primarily the result of immigration, though this was also a factor—for instance, in the case of Jewish, German, Tatar, and Armenian communities in
certain periods. Neither was imperial expansion, in its strict sense, the main
driver of diversification, as it was for the Russian Empire, although—as we
shall see—some interpretations have raised the question of an "imperial"
or "colonial" dimension to the Commonwealth's later development. The
Commonwealth initially became diverse through the consensual and negotiated processes of union that lay at its foundations in the Union of Kreva.
This moment began the process of joining together the Kingdom of Poland,
with its majority population of Polish-speaking Roman Catholics, with the
Grand Duchy of Lithuania, itself already a composite of pagan Lithuanian
and East Slavic Orthodox Ruthenian populations. Later, in the fifteenth and
sixteenth centuries, the majority German-speaking regions of Royal Prussia
voluntarily joined the union. By the time the Commonwealth was formed in
1569, the diversity of this composite entity had long since been established.
Indeed, the very concept of the union implied this diversity, and thus the
Commonwealth was "multicultural" from its inception and by definition.

The first half of this book is devoted to various accounts of what this
"multiculturalism" meant in specific times and places during the Commonwealth's existence. Focusing on different communities and identities within
the Commonwealth, the chapters reveal various normative dimensions of
the union's diversity. In chapter 1, Magda Teter discusses the legal rights,
privileges, and responsibilities enjoyed by Jewish communities in the Commonwealth, emphasizing that their "separateness" was not exceptional, but
rather typical of the pluralist legal frameworks that governed premodern,
estate-based polities. In chapter 2, Karin Friedrich describes the role of
self-government of the mostly German-speaking and Protestant cities of
Royal Prussia in the broader context of the Commonwealth's interconfessional dialogue. In chapter 3, Dariusz Kołodziejczyk shows that the formal
legal rights accorded to Muslim Tatars settled in the Grand Duchy of Lithuania were not equal to those of other nobles, but that informal practices
often disregarded the letter of the law to accord Tatars a kind of equality. In
chapter 4, Olenka Z. Pevny examines early modern conceptualizations of
an autonomous Ruthenia-Rus' nation under the auspices of the Commonwealth's pluralist political idea. In chapter 5, Tomasz Grusiecki argues that
the unifying mythology of "Sarmatia" and "Sarmatians" allowed Polish, Lithuanian, Ruthenian, and Prussian members of the nobility to imaginatively
occupy the same geographical, political, and cultural space, while preserving

the differences between them. Finally, in chapter 6, Richard Butterwick asks whether the multiconfessionalism of the Commonwealth—and its declining normative basis, as Roman Catholicism decisively gained the ascendancy in political and legal structures—contributed to the Commonwealth's downfall in the late eighteenth-century partitions.

The image of the Commonwealth that emerges from these chapters suggests the existence of a strictly limited politics and practice of normative "multiculturalism"—at least at certain points in time and in relation to certain groups. This did not imply the positive embrace of diversity that characterizes modern varieties of multiculturalism, but rather sprang from the pragmatic need to regulate relations between groups in a diverse polity so as to avoid conflict—a "multiculturalism of fear," to apply a term used by Jacob T. Levy in contemporary contexts. Modifying Levy's modern typology of rights claims, we may note several distinct varieties of normative regulation of the Commonwealth's diversity: separate legal codes for different regions and groups; special exemptions; rights to self-government; representation in government bodies; and symbolic claims acknowledging the worth or equality of different groups.[43]

To offer but a few examples: the Union of Lublin guaranteed that chancery Ruthenian would be the legal language on Ruthenian lands—including both the rump Grand Duchy and the southern, "Ukrainian" palatinates newly annexed to the Crown—and that the Second Lithuanian Statute, written in Ruthenian, would be its legal code (chapter 4); Jewish communities governed themselves through the Council of the Four Lands in the Polish Crown and the Council of Lithuania in the Grand Duchy (chapter 1); Lipka Tatars in the Grand Duchy of Lithuania enjoyed specific tax exemptions in return for their military service (chapter 3); the Union of Brest (1596) established—at least in theory—that the Ruthenian Uniate Archbishop would have a designated seat on the Senate (chapter 6); Protestant control was so well established in Royal Prussian cities that Roman Catholics were formally excluded from key offices (chapter 2); sixteenth-century maps clearly distinguished the different regions of the Commonwealth, sometimes using the neutral, overarching appellation of "European Sarmatia" to describe the whole (chapter 5); multiple documents and declarations specifically affirmed the equal dignity and rights of Lithuanian and Ruthenian nobles—though admittedly the reality was often different.

None of these norms created "group-differentiated rights" in the modern sense.[44] Their purpose was not specifically to recognize, validate, or accommodate difference. Instead, they were the result of negotiation and compromise, or simply constituted pragmatic measures designed to avoid conflict. Importantly, many of these norms were never fully implemented, or were substantially eroded over time. For example, the designated Senate seat of the Uniate Archbishop was never actually granted until as late as 1790, shortly before the final partitions, when it was offered as part of a series of conciliatory measures prompted by fears of a Ruthenian rebellion (chapter 6). More generally, Orthodox Ruthenian nobles were barred from holding key offices throughout most of the existence of the Polish-Lithuanian union, and the Eastern Orthodox Church always endured a lower political and legal status than the Catholic Church.

As the examples above reveal, the diverse cultures that overlapped in the Commonwealth were very often defined by religion, both by their own adherents and by others. The separate rights of Jewish communities flowed from their status as a religious other. Muslim Tatars were denied access to noble privileges on the basis of their religious identity. Lutheranism was defined as a distinctly "German heresy" in Polish Catholic polemics. Roman Catholicism was viewed as the "Lach," or "Polish," faith by Ruthenian adherents of Eastern Orthodoxy.[45] In this sense, the multiculturalism of the Commonwealth was partly a form of multiconfessionalism, and its normative dimension was therefore closely related to the shifting application of rights and privileges to adherents of different faiths and confessions. Some of the key moments in the Commonwealth's multicultural history were agreements on religious toleration and access to political power—for instance, the 1563 decree of King Sigismund II Augustus (r. 1548–1572) lifting political restrictions on Orthodox nobles, or the Warsaw Confederation of 1573, with its general provisions of religious toleration and freedom for members of the nobility.[46]

While religious boundaries frequently coincided with linguistic, ethnic, geographical, and social markers of identity, they sometimes cut across these lines. Both "Poles" and "Lithuanians" (Polish- and Lithuanian-speaking varieties) were usually Roman Catholic in most periods. Many Polish/Lithuanian Catholic and Ruthenian Orthodox nobles joined their German compatriots in converting to various denominations of Protestantism during the sixteenth century. Most nobles who identified as Ruthenian later converted to Roman Catholicism, a process that was often interpreted as polonization by definition. This trend reveals once again the key point of the growing ascendancy of "Polish" and Roman Catholic identities over time, especially from the seventeenth century. In fact, one might argue that this domination—at least in the sphere of religion—had existed from the beginning of the Polish-Lithuanian union.

The very condition for the personal union in 1385 was the Lithuanians' abandonment of their original pagan faith for Catholic Christianity. Over time, the newly Catholic Lithuanian nobles gained access to the rights and privileges enjoyed by their Polish counterparts, while the Orthodox Ruthenians of the Grand Duchy were regularly excluded (chapter 2). The elites of the whole Grand Duchy managed to preserve key aspects of their separate political, legal, and linguistic identity, but various processes of polonization steadily eroded these differences over the centuries.[47] A key moment was the law of 1696 that replaced Ruthenian with Polish as the administrative language of the Grand Duchy.[48] By the time of the partitions, the Commonwealth was indeed a very diverse entity, but one in which most of the elites were functionally "Polish"—that is, speaking Polish and adhering to Roman Catholicism, in spite of diverse ethnic origins and distinct regional identities. In practice, this meant a polity in which Polish-speaking Roman Catholic nobles had a monopoly on power, dominating a space also inhabited by Ruthenian-speaking Orthodox peasants (probably the largest single group), Polish-speaking Catholic peasants, Lithuanian-speaking Catholic peasants, Jews, German Protestants, and Muslim Tatars. The diversity or multiculturalism of the Commonwealth was thus fundamentally hierarchical.

This notion of "hierarchical pluralism" brings us back to the interpretive question as to whether the Commonwealth's diversity included a quasi-imperial dimension.[49] Multiculturalism has often been tied to empires and imperialism. From the ancient Achaemenid and Roman Empires to the more recent Ottoman, British, Habsburg, Russian, and Soviet Empires, imperial realms have been fundamentally "multicultural" in the descriptive, nonnormative sense of this term.[50] At the same time, the ethnic, cultural, linguistic, and religious diversity of these empires usually necessitated some level of negotiation, compromise, or power sharing, even if one cultural group remained dominant.[51] These processes could sometimes verge on more normative understandings of multiculturalism, involving some degree of formal recognition of diversity or the accordance of particular rights to groups. Institutionalization of group identities within imperial structures could even contribute to the rise of autonomist or, later, nationalist movements—as the case of the Habsburg Empire in the late nineteenth century shows.[52] Though the Polish-speaking, Roman Catholic nobles of the Commonwealth did not set about building an empire by conquest, they did become the dominant group within the polity, effectively ruling over a vast and diverse territory of "others," some of whose elites they gradually assimilated.

In summary, the Polish-Lithuanian Commonwealth was normatively multicultural in some dimensions, especially in its pluralist legal and political traditions and relative religious tolerance at certain points in time. Different communities enjoyed political rights, sometimes on a basis of equality, though more often differentiated and hierarchized. Diversity and difference were not generally celebrated in or for themselves, as they often are in contemporary multiculturalist polities.[53] Instead, they were regulated and controlled in the interests of stability, and increasingly under the auspices of a dominant culture of Polish language, political institutions, and Roman Catholicism. Even the Warsaw Confederation of 1573 was not a statement embracing religious diversity as such, but rather a pragmatic agreement among nobles to keep the peace, in spite of religious differences, against the background of contemporary religious violence in France and a dangerous period of interregnum in the Commonwealth itself.[54] Even so, the Confederation still represented a key moment in the institutionalization of existing diversity and in the consolidation of a distinctive political culture of toleration.

Contested Memories of the Commonwealth

After the partitions that dismembered the Commonwealth at the end of the eighteenth century, the multicultural union lived on in political and cultural discourse. From Adam Mickiewicz's famous 1834 invocation to "Lithuania, my homeland!"—written in Polish in yearning for the former Grand Duchy—to movements such as the *krajowcy*, political conservatives who campaigned (unsuccessfully) for Polish, Lithuanian, and Belarusian forces to unite for the multinational revival of the Grand Duchy in the early twentieth century, identity narratives that appealed to the pre-national and cosmopolitan legacy were plentiful throughout the partition period.[55] When sovereign nation states emerged in the aftermath of the First World War—in Poland and Lithuania, though not in Belarus and Ukraine—the new polities were multiethnic societies riven by intergroup tensions.[56] In the aftermath of the Second World War—when genocide, deportations, and major territorial shifts eviscerated these multicultural societies—the new socialist states downplayed the significance of the former Commonwealth,

placing a greater ideological emphasis on class struggle and the internation-
alist bond with Moscow. Thus, the fall of communism in 1989–1991 marked
the beginning of a multifaceted reckoning with the past, including what the
Lithuanian-born Polish-language poet Czesław Miłosz warned would need
to be a "working through of an entire heritage"—the heritage of the multicultural Commonwealth.[57]

In the Commonwealth's successor nations, memory and multiculturalism
have been aligned in a cardinally different way than in Western societies. In
western Europe after the Second World War, multiculturalism in the normative sense, as an ideology both recognizing and affirming cultural diversity,
came into being in the wake of the disintegration of empires. Large numbers
of people from former imperial possessions in Africa, the West Indies, and
South Asia migrated to countries like Britain, the Netherlands, and France,
creating unprecedented levels of ethnic and cultural diversity, often driv-
en by the needs of labor markets.[58] As western European societies became
increasingly "multicultural" in this descriptive sense, various normative
ideologies of "multiculturalism" began to emerge to remake ideas of the
nation in the image of the gathering plurality.[59] These ideologies have taken
different forms in different countries, and since the 1990s have increasingly
faced contestation and even a radical backlash in many of them.[60]

Thus, in the postcolonial societies of western Europe, memory and
multiculturalism are above all connected by the histories of imperial injury
and the present need for postcolonial reparation. Societies are "many-
cultured" not because of significant historical diversity, but rather because of
the postwar "return" of colonial subjects—the logic of "we are here because
you were there."[61] Until recently, scholarly and popular discourses tended
to marginalize these colonial legacies.[62] In the past decade or so, however,
debates about historical responsibility for colonial atrocities have become
increasingly mainstream. For instance, the subject of the return of looted
artifacts from European museums is ongoing in earnest, with key objects
such as some "Benin Bronzes" having been transferred to their countries of
origin and many more pledged.[63] At the same time, a growing number of
recent scholarly analyses have begun to uncover lost stories of multicultural
interaction and to critically examine the postcolonial amnesia at the heart of
national and pan-European identity discourses.[64]

In central and eastern Europe, on the other hand, the relationship between memory and multiculturalism is inversed. While the postimperial
centers of western Europe were becoming more diverse, the lands of the for-

mer Polish-Lithuanian Commonwealth in postwar Poland, Soviet Lithuania, Soviet Belarus, and Soviet Ukraine had become less diverse than they had been for centuries. By the middle of the twentieth century, the combination of the Holocaust, local ethnic cleansing, border shifts, and postwar population exchanges had led to the partial realization of earlier integral visions of nations "reconstructed" along ethnic lines.[65] The previous diversity of these countries, especially in their border regions, was reduced or destroyed, thus erasing one of the remaining legacies of the early modern multicultural Commonwealth. In 2004, when Poland and Lithuania joined the European Union, they entered a community of multicultural states espousing an official motto of "united in diversity," while themselves remaining ethnically and culturally more homogeneous (less so in the case of Lithuania, with its Polish and Russian minorities). Especially in Poland, this disjuncture prompted a search for the country's own dimensions of diversity or multiculturalism, necessitating a turn to the past.[66] This turn has often involved idealized visions of a "multicultural" utopia within an anachronistically "Polish" framework.[67] Accordingly, it has remained bound up with old notions of hierarchical pluralism in the service of new forms of national self-assertion.[68]

A common thread of the second part of this book is the premise that memory and multiculturalism in central and eastern Europe have been shaped by a specific constellation of sensitivities, traumas, and nostalgias. Accordingly, traditional postcolonial approaches to the memory of historical diversity can be both a help and a hindrance. As we have already suggested, the Polish-Lithuanian Commonwealth was not an imperial entity in the way the British, French, or Russian Empires were: it did not continuously expand through military conquest; there was no clear spatial division into a ruling metropole and exploited periphery; and there was no racialized division between ruler and ruled.[69] Indeed, the Commonwealth was eventually conquered by "real" empires during the partitions. Nevertheless, the development of ethnic divisions and cultural hierarchies—with Polish-speaking Roman Catholics making up the core political and cultural elites in both the Polish Crown and the Grand Duchy of Lithuania by the eighteenth century—led to the emergence of a pseudocolonial configuration of cultural difference; or, at the very least, to the retrospective perception of such a configuration by some sections of certain groups, such as Belarusians and Ukrainians.

In other words, the Polish-Lithuanian Commonwealth is the subject of a mnemonic colonialism: it is colonized (or framed as a colonizing project) in and through remembrance—for instance in the Polish myth of the "Kresy

Wschodnie," which constructs a polonocentric vision of the former "Eastern Borderlands" as a lost arcadia of Polish glory.[70] It has also been contested as a colonial realm in Belarusian and Ukrainian thought, as well as in critical examinations by some Polish scholars. Polish cultural hegemony in the latter-day Commonwealth and in the partitioned lands, together with Polish political dominance in the interwar period, are thus construed as evidence of imperialism, with Belarusian, Lithuanian, and Ukrainian resistance interpreted as manifestations of an anti-colonial liberation struggle.[71] Therefore, although the Polish-Lithuanian Commonwealth may not, strictly speaking, have been an empire, its cultural power imbalances and its mnemonic afterlife have turned it into one in the eyes of many.

Combining both postcolonial injury and nationalizing nostalgia, memories of the Commonwealth's multiculturalism tend to mix two contrasting modes: what Dirk Uffelmann calls "traumatic" and "idyllic" memory.[72] Traumatic memories foreground conflict and confrontation. They tend to frame ethnic others as perpetrators of crimes, or as oppressors or traitors. Such memories—divided along national lines—frequently clash with one another. Idyllic memories, on the other hand, envision the past as harmonious and conflict free: ethnic others are represented as "safe" and "harmless" members of the community, though often with a marginalizing or appropriating effect. For example, in her study of the klezmer revival in contemporary Poland and Germany, Magdalena Waligórska argues that "Klezmer becomes incorporated into the narrative of Poland's past multi-ethnicity and is granted the status of a heritage that is not extraneous but our own and familiar. Such absorption of the other is a means of abolishing distance, and a way to venerate the similarities between the two cultures. Jewish music is presented here as belonging to a common superordinate category of Poland's folklore, and as such it feeds into the myth of prewar Poland as a multicultural arcadia."[73] Thus, in both "traumatic" and "idyllic" modes of remembering, the multicultural past is tinged with ideologies of the present—in culture, politics, and popular representation. Neither mode is value free, and the extent to which they interact and compete has colored the dynamics of remembrance in the aftermath of the Commonwealth's demise.

Yet memories of the Commonwealth can also be dialogical and multidirectional, rather than competitive or mutually antagonistic.[74] An interesting example of this third way is the international success of the Lithuanian writer Kristina Sabaliauskaitė's novelistic tetralogy *Silva Rerum* (2008–2016), which chronicles the history of several generations of the Vilnius-based Narwoysz family in the seventeenth and eighteenth centuries.[75] With their microcosmic focus on a single family and a host of other characters that showcase the multilingualism and multiconfessionality of historical Vilnius, the books are devoid of any sanitizing impulse to nationalize the past or to idealize interethnic relations. Their recognition through multiple literary awards and best-seller status in Lithuania, as well as the warm reception of the Polish translations,[76] points toward the cosmopolitanization of the memory of the Commonwealth: remembrance beyond ethnolinguistic national "containers" and across political borders appears to be gaining ground.

The second part of this volume explores multiple ways in which memories of the Commonwealth have had an impact on culture, politics, and society at different points over the centuries since the third partition of 1795. All the studies foreground transnational entanglements, showing how nascent and then established national(ist) discourses have influenced, interacted with, and competed with one another, while drawing on the heritage of the multicultural Commonwealth. In chapter 7, Stanley Bill explores some canonical works of nineteenth-century Polish literature, coining the term "Ukrainian sublime" to capture the often contradictory ways in which Polish-language writers subsumed Ukraine under a polonizing gaze, while also endowing the Ukrainian "other" with particular kinds of subjectivity and agency. In chapter 8, Robert Frost compares the lives and works of two historians, Oskar Halecki (1891–1973) and Lewis Namier (1888–1960), whose different approaches to the history of the Commonwealth led them to very different visions of the future of the European continent after the First World War. In chapter 9, Rūstis Kamuntavičius analyzes the contrasting ways in which Lithuanian and Belarusian national historiographies have idealized the Grand Duchy of Lithuania and marginalized the Polish Crown, while rarely seeing eye to eye on the mutual commonalities of the Grand Duchy's legacy. In chapter 10, Simon Lewis traces the history of literary interactions in the Polish-Belarusian borderlands, in which authors such as Tadeusz Konwicki (1926–2015), Sakrat Janovič (1936–2013), Marta Pińska (pseudonym—true identity unknown), and Ignacy Karpowicz (born 1976) have engaged in a sustained dialogue over shared memories. In chapter 11, Magdalena Waligórska, Ina Sorkina, and Alexander Friedman compare memory initiatives in three former Jewish shtetls in Poland, Belarus, and Ukraine, showing that at the local level it is the specific history of discrete locations within the Commonwealth that gains most attention, but that, ultimately, national frames of appropriative memory remain dominant in all three countries. In chapter 12, Ewa Nowicka explores the "new multiculturalism" of contemporary Poland with reference to its largest minority, the Ukrainians who have arrived in large numbers in search of economic and educational opportunities—and, more recently, as refugees—showing that memories of the past have played only a limited role in their ongoing integration into Polish society.

Taken together, these chapters show the continuing importance of remembrance of the Commonwealth in various national discourses, as well as the divisions and tensions that result from the cleavages in memory between them. The coexistence of traumatic, idyllic, and dialogical memories creates both conflict and (potential) reconciliation in a set of multilateral dynamics that will continue to evolve and change. The social and political importance of memory notwithstanding, it is also crucial to emphasize that remembrance of the Polish-Lithuanian Commonwealth is far from the only driver of contemporary discussions of multiculturalism in the region, as Nowicka highlights in chapter 12. All the successor states are becoming, in different ways, multicultural societies in the present day, affected by the in- and out-migration of people and the globalization of culture and consumption. While the multicultural legacy of the Commonwealth can provide historical inspiration, it need not be remembered by local communities at all, and it often has no bearing on real-life interaction between, say, Poles and Ukrainians, or Belarusians and Lithuanians.

As this book goes to press, the Russian Federation, with support from the Belarusian dictatorship, has renewed its military onslaught on Ukraine, creating a humanitarian catastrophe of massive proportions and displacing millions of Ukrainians. At the time of writing, Poland is the country that has accepted by far the largest number of refugees from Ukraine, while Lithuania has also offered extensive support. The solidarity shown by Polish civil society has made news around the world, showcasing deep reserves of empathy for a neighbor locked in a struggle against Russian imperialism—a struggle also still encoded in Polish collective memory. Whether the specific legacy of the Commonwealth has played a significant role in this outpouring of goodwill cannot be established at this point, though some sense of a shared historical and geopolitical fate has clearly been salient. In the years to come, international solidarity in the face of Russia's invasion may bring increased political, social, and cultural attention to the common histories that tie the societies of central and eastern Europe together, including to the legacies and memory of the Commonwealth.

Open Questions and Diverse Approaches

This book inevitably raises more questions than it can definitively answer. How far-reaching was the proverbial "tolerance" of the Commonwealth, and how did it shift over time? To what degree was this tolerance expressed through concrete legal frameworks, and how close did they ever come to establishing political equality between groups? To what extent did the Commonwealth become a "Polish" state oppressive to its other inhabitants? Was the Commonwealth's diversity—or the management of this diversity—ultimately a source of strength or weakness? Does the memory of the Commonwealth unite or divide the contemporary states, nations, and groups that may connect its history to their own? How has this history been instrumentalized for political purposes? Does it make sense at all to link contemporary national identities directly to antecedent group identities within a premodern or early modern composite state? What really connects the Poles, Lithuanians, Belarusians, and Ukrainians of today with the "Poles," "Lithuanians," and "Ruthenians"—variously understood—of the Commonwealth? How can the Commonwealth's history be presented so as to respect these differences, together with the subjectivity and agency of modern national communities on often difficult paths to self-determination, especially in this time of war?

Through its diverse chapters, the book offers multiple answers to these questions. It does so from a suitably wide set of disciplinary perspectives, with its contributors drawing on expertise in the fields of history, literary and cultural studies, art history, and sociology, among others. In a work of only twelve chapters treating over five hundred years of history of a multicultural polity and its successor nations, we are keenly aware of the many gaps, silences, imbalances, and deficiencies in coverage. Indeed, the book itself may also be situated within the framework of the cultural and political hegemonies discussed in its chapters. There are many ways to frame the Commonwealth's "multicultural" dimensions, and thus we see our contribution as one moment in an evolving discussion rather than as a comprehensive treatment of the subject. Nevertheless, we hope that the volume offers enough diversity in its wide scope and multiple approaches to do some justice to the complexity of its theme. In the end, we will be satisfied if both its successes and failures serve to inspire or provoke new attempts to capture the multifarious history of one of Europe's most fascinating polities and its many afterlives in contemporary memory.

PART I

THE COMMONWEALTH IN HISTORY

1

How Jewish Is the History of
the Polish-Lithuanian Commonwealth?

Magda Teter

When a new statue of Roman Dmowski (1864–1939) was unveiled in Warsaw in 2006, around two hundred people gathered to honor the founder of the National Democracy movement (Narodowa Demokracja, ND) and leading proponent of ethnonationalist visions of a Polish state: "Poland for Poles."[1] The monument was later regularly defaced, but also became a locus of Polish nationalist circles. The commemoration of Dmowski became a catalyst for yearly marches across Warsaw on November 11, the anniversary of Poland's regained independence in 1918. Since 2011, the nationalist "March of Independence" has gone mainstream, becoming an annual fixture of Polish public life and attracting thousands of participants claiming "Poland for Poles" and sometimes chanting far-right and antisemitic slogans.[2] Every year a new theme is chosen for the march, each focusing on a nationalist message often framed in terms of "tradition" harking back to the imagined history of the Polish-Lithuanian Commonwealth. Some participants have even appeared as winged hussars riding their horses through the streets of contemporary Warsaw, evoking the memory of battles in which the hussars vanquished Poland's enemies. The memory of the premodern past has been flattened and simplified in these nationalist circles. "From Sobieski to Dmowski," some signs proclaimed, connecting Dmowski to seventeenth-century John III Sobieski (r. 1674–1696), the king of the multiethnic Polish-Lithuanian Commonwealth best known for his victories over the Ottoman Turks at Khotyn (1673; *Pol.* Chocim) and Vienna (1683).

The "Poland" of yesteryear that today's Polish nationalists conjure up in the figure of King John Sobieski did not exist. The slogan "Poland for Poles" articulates a monolithic ethnocentric vision that only became a reality after the Second World War. For the current Polish nationalists, Sobieski defended Christian Europe from Islam. But they conveniently forget that John Sobieski's Polish-Lithuanian Commonwealth was a multiethnic and multicultural republic of nobles. The king was indeed fighting the military forces of an Islamicate empire; but on his side were also Muslim Tatars, deeply rooted inhabitants of the Polish-Lithuanian Commonwealth, whom the king rewarded with privileges and land—such as the village of Kruszyniany in the Podlachia region, where there is still an active mosque to this day.[3]

While this memory of "Polish" history and tradition is patently false and full of forgetting, its roots lie in nineteenth-century national historiographies. The modern study of history that emerged at this time was supposed to offer a new objective "scientific" method of studying the past. However, the writing of history was placed at the service of newly emerging national states, identities, and ideologies. This political purpose resulted in the sharpening of ethnic understandings of history. German, Polish, and other national histories thus tended to exclude groups that were not part of a given ethnonational conception of the nation. This was, as Sebastian Conrad has argued, a "birth defect" of "modern academic disciplines."[4]

In Polish historiography, until recently, minority groups—such as Ukrainians, Muslim Tatars, Jews, Scots, and Armenians—often had little place. When they did appear, they were generally presented as outsiders, or, in the case of Ukrainians, even as enemies. But while Scots assimilated, Muslim Tatars remained a tiny minority, and Ukrainians eventually succeeded in creating their own state, the dominant historiographical framework effectively excluded Jews as foreign, "alien," and peripheral to national narratives. As a result, the history of the Jews in Poland-Lithuania was long confined to Jewish scholars writing for Jewish readers. And when nineteenth- and twentieth-century Polish historians did write about Jews, their writing was often permeated with hostility and a sense of separation, as in Władysław Smoleński's late nineteenth-century description of Jews as *corpus in corpore, status in statu*—an idea that persisted for many decades.[5] But were Jews indeed so alien and insular as the popular opinion and some scholarly analyses have claimed? This chapter presents evidence to the contrary, arguing that

Jews and Jewish communities—in spite of their differences and conflicts with Christian neighbors—formed an integral part of the composite social structures of the Polish-Lithuanian Commonwealth.

Whose History?: Discourses of Otherness

In the early modern period, the period often venerated today by the participants of the nationalist March of Independence, the Polish-Lithuanian Commonwealth was home to the largest Jewish community in the world. By the mid-eighteenth century, an estimated 750,000 Jews lived there, amounting to over 5 percent of the total population of the vast state.[6] But while 5 percent may not seem like a lot, Jews enjoyed greater prominence than their proportion in the population would suggest. The historian Gershon Hundert has questioned the very notion that Jews in eighteenth-century Poland-Lithuania constituted a "minority," arguing that there was "no majority, as we now understand the term," in the ethnically and culturally diverse cities and towns of the Commonwealth.[7] Although the urban population in the early modern period composed only some 20 percent of the total, the majority of the Jewish population was urban. In small towns, which were considered urban in the overwhelmingly rural Commonwealth, Jews were often a dominant group, and by the end of the eighteenth century even occasionally a majority. But beyond the numbers, Hundert has argued, the term "minority," which denotes "vulnerability, dependence, and marginality . . . can only be applied to Polish-Lithuanian Jewry with elaborate qualification."[8] While commenting on the historian Shmuel Ettinger's assertion that "at no period in their history have Jews barricaded themselves against social and cultural developments of other nations," Moshe Rosman has asserted in his book—aptly titled *How Jewish Is Jewish History?*—that "Jews were always part of the social, cultural, and political context in which they lived."[9] And that included the Polish-Lithuanian Commonwealth, where Jews were not marginal, but rather played an important role in its history. Rosman later went on to ask "How Polish Was Polish History?" thus perhaps inviting the question "How Jewish was Polish History?"[10] This is not a new question. Indeed, Polish Jewish historians of the interwar period were determined to demonstrate that Jews belonged to the narrative of Polish history.[11]

But mental habits of thinking about history are difficult to break. Although in the past few decades scholars of Polish history have begun to incorporate discussions of Jews into their histories of Poland, the language was initially somewhat awkward—Jews have still sometimes been called "Israelites" or "Old Law" believers (*starozakonni*), or "adherents to the law of Moses" (*ludność wyznania mojżeszowego*).[12] Sometimes, as late as the 1990s, Jewish sections of towns were described as "ghettos."[13] In some works, the discussion of Jews in Poland is framed within the scholarly discourse of diaspora studies, presenting Polish Jews as a "diaspora."[14] But this too otherizes Jews as foreign, since "diaspora" implies a disconnect from, perhaps even a loss of "a homeland"; diaspora also signifies dispersion, "powerlessness, longing, exile, and displacement."[15] Yet, though Jews are often seen as a paradigmatic diaspora, the term is not unproblematic when applied to them, for it raises fraught questions about the meaning of homeland and belonging, and the depth of theological concepts of exile.[16] As Barbara Kirshenblatt-Gimblett points out, "Diasporic discourse . . . is strong on displacement, detachment, uprooting, and dispersion—on disarticulation."[17] All these categories imply that places where diasporic peoples, including Jews, made their homes were ultimately not their "homelands," but merely "hostlands." But that was not necessarily how Jews, including Polish Jews, perceived the places where they lived with their families for many centuries. Diasporic discourse undermines their sense of belonging, effectively representing a translation of theological discourse about Jewish exile into a modern scholarly framework. Indeed, even scholars who have otherwise been very careful in their research and language, occasionally slip into that discourse, stating, for example, that Jews found a "refuge" (*azyl*) in Poland, rather than a permanent home—conceptually, then, Poland as "azyl" remained a "hostland."[18]

Jews in the Polish-Lithuanian Commonwealth, like Jews everywhere else, indeed had a relationship with "Eretz Israel," the historic Jewish homeland, praying each Passover for "Next Year in Jerusalem," or contributing alms to Jews in the region.[19] But the Polish-Lithuanian Commonwealth was nonetheless their "homeland," and Jews were intrinsic to and inseparable from the country's social, political, and economic landscape. Their distinct identity as Jews did not necessarily imply "alienation" or insularity, even as they still connected with Jews and Jewish communities beyond the Polish-Lithuanian Commonwealth, and even if some Christian writers denigrated them in their works.[20]

But much is at stake in promoting this narrative of Jewish alienness, separatism, and insularity, especially after the Second World War. History is a contested territory. How history is told is shaped by questions of the present, but the telling of history also shapes the future. The importance of *how* Polish history is told is evidenced by the extent to which it has been politicized: Is "Polishness" built around a Polish history that is multicultural, multiethnic, and inclusive? Or is Polish history the history of an ethnically Polish nation that acted as a tolerant "host" to those who were not its members? In both visions, the idea of "tolerance" plays a role, but with different resonances and ramifications for understandings of belonging.

"Assimilation" has often served as a test of patriotism and belonging. Scots, as one scholar phrased it, "had fewer troubles assimilating," while Jews, in some modern scholars' telling, were an insular minority, always turned away from their Christian neighbors.[21] The expectation of Jewish "assimilation" in the writings of modern historians is a manifestation of a deeply ingrained Christian habit of thinking about Jews and Judaism. Jewish "assimilation," by implication, was only possible if they converted to Christianity—otherwise they remained, as Smoleński noted a century and a half ago, "a state within a state," a foreign element that did not belong. Some contemporary scholars have also described towns and neighborhoods in which Jews lived in ways that signal their exclusion, even when they lived intermixed with Christians or engaged in similar businesses.[22]

In classic modern historical studies, Jews in the Commonwealth were presented as an "alien ethnic element," standing "outside the social ladder," and despite shared professions were usually considered separately, or as competition to Christian burghers.[23] For example, a study of Sandomierz discussed the royal city's position in regional trade and the reach of the town's merchants across the region, including at the famous Lublin fair. After listing by name the Christian merchants found in Lublin registers, the authors added "and also Jews."[24] In local histories, Jews are often discussed not as a native population—even when they indeed had lived there for centuries—but as alien competitors engaged in "expansion" and a "persistent and long-term struggle" with local Christians.[25] This type of language is used even when the evidence shows business partnerships between local Jews and Christians, and the participation of Jews in civic duties, including the provision of night guards.[26] Moreover, sometimes historians have erased Jews altogether—for instance, presenting the country's "population categories" as "peasants, burghers, the clergy, and the nobility [*szlachta*]."[27] Such persistent patterns of thinking about the history of the Commonwealth have had a profound impact on the acceptance of Jews as part of a shared past.

Yet approaches focusing more constructively on the shared dimension of this history are also possible, as multiple Polish scholars have already demonstrated in recent studies breaking with the earlier exclusionist tendencies.[28] Here, what Sebastian Conrad saw as one of the inherent problems of the early years of modern historiography—territoriality—might be a useful, if perhaps counterintuitive, tool in rethinking national histories.[29] When exploring the history of the Polish-Lithuanian Commonwealth as a territory inhabited by a multitude of groups and cultures—a *multicultural* commonwealth—the past looks very different from later nationalist visions of it. Moreover, this way of looking coheres more closely with historical sources, which show Jews—and many others—as part of the social and political fabric of the country, more central than national histories have hitherto allowed.

The Legal Status and Socioeconomic Roles of Jews in Poland-Lithuania

In his 1669 biography of Giovanni Francesco Commendone, the sixteenth-century papal nuncio to Poland-Lithuania, Antonio Maria Graziani described the Commonwealth of Commendone's time as a place where:[30]

> One still finds a great number of Jews, who are not despised like in many other places. They do not live miserably off the lowly profits of their usury and services, though they do not refuse these kinds of gain, but they have land, engage in commerce, and even apply themselves to studying literature, particularly in medicine and astrology. . . . They possess a considerable wealth; and not only are they among the honest people, but sometimes they lead them. They have no mark that distinguishes them from Christians; they are even allowed to wear the sword and arms. Finally, they enjoy all the rights of other city dwellers [*citoiens*].[31]

Even if Graziani's description, attributed to Commendone, might be exaggerated, other accounts also suggest that Jews were indeed valued and considered integral to the economy of cities, individual estates, and royal domains. In fact, visitors to the Polish-Lithuanian Commonwealth often remarked on the position of the Jews as being distinctly *not* "marginal."[32]

The significance of a proper understanding of Jewish life and Jewish-Christian daily interactions in the Polish-Lithuanian Commonwealth, but also more broadly in Europe, lies not just in demonstrating that these interactions did take place, but rather in counteracting the impact that the political and legal transformations of modern nation states have had on our understanding of both modern and premodern historical realities. Indeed, the charge that Jews were "a body within a body, a state within a state" only gained negative connotations because of changes to how the state itself was understood: away from estate and corporate legal structures, and toward individual citizenship in a nation-state. In the premodern period—in the Polish-Lithuanian Commonwealth and elsewhere in Europe—communal and judicial autonomy were part of the broader political system. Jews were granted royal and then private privileges that outlined the framework for their legal status within the state: their fiscal responsibilities, their place in the political and judicial system, and their communal autonomy. In an era of estates and legal pluralism, this was not unusual, but it came to be seen as such when states transformed away from these corporate estate structures. Jewish communal structures and adherence to separate laws came to be seen as incompatible with the new form of state, and this judgment was projected backward to claim that Jews had never fitted in—thus, the phrase "a state within a state" was born.

In the context of the legal framework of premodern states such as the Polish-Lithuanian Commonwealth, organized into distinct legal estates and corporations, "Jews" were not just a religious or even "ethnic" group, but also a separate legal category. And although there were legal differences between the Polish Crown and the Grand Duchy of Lithuania in terms of fiscal structures and jurisdictions, the larger legal framework in which Jews were subject to distinct privileges accorded to them was similar.[33] According to these legal and political structures, different populations were subject to different jurisdictions and different laws. The nobility (*szlachta*) was subject to the land law (*prawo ziemskie*); the clergy was subject to ecclesiastical jurisdiction, and in mixed cases to the Crown tribunal; Christian town dwellers were subject to the municipal or Magdeburg law; peasants were subject to rural law (*prawo wiejskie*); and Jews were subject to Jewish law in cases involving Jews or royal courts for cases involving Jews and Christians, and, after 1539, also to the private jurisdiction of town owners. Thus, references to "Jews" in premodern documents do not necessarily designate otherness or hostility, but, as the historian Adam Kaźmierczyk put it, a "religio-legal" category.[34] As such, Jews and the Jewish community were integrated into the political system of the Polish-Lithuanian Commonwealth, though such divisions of jurisdiction also influenced the dynamic of life in towns and interactions between residents. So, too, were Armenians, who also had distinct laws and privileges, though their impact was far less felt because it was geographically circumscribed.[35]

Jews in the Polish-Lithuanian Commonwealth developed what came to be seen as the quintessential body of Jewish communal autonomy—the Council of Four Lands. It became, to quote the historian Jacob Goldberg, an "integral part of the state's fiscal apparatus."[36] This supracommunal body has often been caricatured by non-Jewish scholars as another example of the "state within a state," and idealized by Jewish scholars as evidence of Jewish political autonomy and a model of Jewish self-government. Such framings of the Council of Four Lands fit into the dominant notion, accepted by both Jewish and non-Jewish scholars, that Jews in premodern times were insular, refusing or unable to integrate into broader society. But a closer look at the institutions of Jewish autonomy demonstrates that not only the council but also the Jews were an integral *part of*, not *apart from*, the complex legal and political structures of the Polish-Lithuanian Commonwealth.

Known in Jewish historiography as the *Va'ad Arba'a Arazot* (*Heb.* ועד ארבע ארצות,), the Council of Four Lands was sometimes known as the "Jewish Sejm" (*Sejm Żydowski*) in Polish documents, using the same word as that used for the nobles' parliament.[37] That the council was part of the state fiscal apparatus is evidenced not only by its Polish name but also by the terminology applied to its officers and by its composition. At its head was a *marszałek*, and its order mimicked the composition and order of senators in the nobles' Sejm, with the community of Kraków at its head, followed by Poznań, and then by other communities in order of importance.[38] Just how much the *Va'ad* was considered part of the Polish-Lithuanian state structures is also suggested by the presence of representatives of the Polish authorities at the council's meetings.[39] The Council of Four Lands was thus both a Jewish institution *in* the Polish-Lithuanian Commonwealth—that is, an institution representing the Jewish community and dealing with internal Jewish matters—and *of* the Polish-Lithuanian Commonwealth, functioning entirely within its broader legal and political structures.[40] Indeed, just as there were legal distinctions between the Polish Crown and the Grand Duchy of Lithuania, so too were divided the institutions of Jewish governance: the Council of Four Lands functioning in the Crown and the Council of Lithuania in the Grand Duchy.[41]

A similar dynamic of integration into political structures also applied at the local level in the *kahal*, the local Jewish community board. As Moshe Rosman has argued, "For the Polish authorities, the *kahal* was an extension of their administration."[42] In Kraków, for example, each year, elected Jewish leaders had to take an oath before the palatine court to uphold the law.[43] Archival sources also show the Polish-Lithuanian authorities affirming and revoking the authority of rabbis, urging Jews to respect the existing communal structures and administrative divisions and to obey the decisions of Jewish community leaders, as well as intervening at the behest of Jews. In 1746, for example, Jan Tarło, the palatine of Sandomierz, approved one David Szmelka for the position of rabbi in the Kraków-Sandomierz region.[44] The previous rabbi, Józef Icko Jonowicz, was ousted after Jewish lay leaders protested against his failure to administer justice. In 1753, Karol Sedlnicki, the treasurer of the Crown, appointed Abram Chaimowicz, "a merchant from Lublin, as the *marszałek*, or speaker, of the Crown Jews."[45] Some documents indicate conflicts between "private" and "royal" Jews, pitted against each other and seeking arbitration from non-Jewish authorities—with similar conflicts and competition between Christians in royal and private towns. These documents undermine the notion of Jewish autonomy, idealized by Jews and derided by Christians, as they underscore the integration of Jews into the political structures of the Polish-Lithuanian Commonwealth. The fact that Christian officials intervened in the appointment of community rabbis and participated in the council is an indication that the council and rabbis were seen as performing roles important to the proper functioning of the Polish-Lithuanian Commonwealth, and this contradicts the notion of Jewish communal insularity.

As Maria Cieśla has observed in her studies of Jews in the Grand Duchy of Lithuania, Jews were an integral part of the Commonwealth's fiscal apparatus as tax and duty collectors. In this capacity, they functioned effectively as officials of the state, sometimes even representing the state in court.[46] As Cieśla has noted, by leasing the collection of duties and taxes, Jews, as "professional employees with appropriate qualifications, usually supported by many years of experience," played an important part in the functioning of "the state and royal treasury" as well as "in local tax administration."[47] By tracing the role of Jews in the fiscal structures of the Grand Duchy of Lithuania in the seventeenth and eighteenth centuries, Cieśla was also able to capture broader political and cultural shifts in the Polish-Lithuanian Commonwealth, thereby demonstrating that understanding the role Jews played in the fiscal system of the Commonwealth helps us understand the way the Commonwealth, both as a whole and in its separate parts, functioned as a state.

The same can be said of Jews in urban spaces across the Commonwealth. While many scholars have tended to discuss Jews' place in urban spaces and economies in alienating and adversarial terms by focusing on competition,

Adam Teller has argued that small towns, which made up the majority of urban spaces in the Commonwealth, were in fact "arenas of Polish-Jewish integration." Teller has demonstrated that Jews and Christians divided crafts and trade so as not to compete directly with each other, with each filling a specific economic niche.[48] In Sandomierz, for example, there seems to have been a division of trade areas among Jewish and Christian merchants. While Christians dominated the food trade, Jews engaged in trading textiles, leather, wax, wood, and to some extent also wine.[49] This division sometimes even led to partnerships, though there were also conflicts and complaints about competition.[50] Often Jews from other cities provided Sandomierz Christian craftsmen with necessary supplies—for instance, a Jew from Opatów named Gabriel, who became a purveyor of leather for shoemakers in Sandomierz in the second half of the sixteenth century.[51] Nevertheless, when they faced competition, Sandomierz burghers complained about the loss of income, as they did, for example, at the beginning of the seventeenth century, when Jews apparently began to dominate the mead trade.[52] A similar dynamic has been shown in Żółkiew (now Zhovkva, Ukraine)—though archival sources tend to focus on conflict, they also show Jews as playing an integral role in the town's economy, defense, and even politics.[53]

The geography of the Jews' dwellings in towns also demonstrates that Jews were part of the urban fabric, with domiciles and synagogues established in proximity to market squares. Privileges granted to Jews typically allowed them to own houses and land, and placed no restrictions on where Jews could purchase property.[54] Indeed, archival records show how intermixed many neighborhoods were.[55] In Przemyśl, for example, testimony about structural damage inflicted on a town house owned by Salomon Markowic and his wife Dwora reveals that it was nestled between two houses owned and inhabited by Christians.[56] And although, at times, Jews did find themselves relegated to peripheral backstreets abutting town walls—for example, in Sandomierz—even then the location was central, one block from the market square. This was also true in Poznań, where Jews' residential rights were more restricted. In many private towns, the location of synagogues often mirrored, in relation to the main square and the town hall, the location of churches. In Tarnów, for example, the Catholic church and the synagogue were both located near city walls at each end of the town, approximately the same number of steps from the main square and the town hall. This was also true, in Zamość and in private towns established in Ukraine after 1569. In Sharhorod (*Pol.* Szarogród), founded by Jan Zamojski in 1585, the synagogue was built in 1589, just a year after royal privileges were granted to the town and six years before the Catholic church of Saint Florian.[57] In the small town of Janowiec, near Puławy, Lord Jerzy Sebastian Lubomirski allowed Jews to build a synagogue with adjacent structures on the main square.[58]

Even in towns where there were "Jewish Streets," the population living there was often mixed. In Sandomierz, though there was a named "Jewish Street" (ulica Żydowska), the street had a mixed population of Jews and Christians living together. It also had one of the two municipal public bath-houses, which was probably used by all Sandomierians. According to a census of 1567, Jews appear to have owned twelve houses, and by 1569 they had also built a synagogue.[59] In 1603, according to a census taken a year after a major plague had decimated the city, there were eighteen houses on the street, with Jews owning about fourteen, and by 1611 sixteen.[60] But ownership of houses by Jews was not limited to this street. In 1635, a house on the main market square was co-owned by a nobleman, Zygmunt Paszyński, and a prominent Sandomierz Jew, Joachim Wolfowicz.[61] Such social mixing on a "Jewish" street was also evident in Poznań.[62]

As residents of towns and cities, Jews frequently shared the same rights and tax exemptions as their Christian neighbors, and were also expected to share resources and responsibilities with other burghers, including the use of fields, meadows, or orchards, and to contribute to the safety and sanitation of the towns.[63] In 1676, two years after his election to the throne, King John III Sobieski, the hero of today's Polish nationalists—desiring to "resuscitate from ruins our ruined city of Kazimierz and to bring it back to past perfection"—granted the Jews of Kazimierz Dolny a generous privilege.[64] Jews were granted the same "freedom as other burghers and citizens." They were given the right to engage in any economic activity and trade, and "to buy plots and buildings on the main square, to renovate old ones, and to build new ones." No one, the king stressed—neither the magistrate nor the guilds—should take away any of these freedoms. Admittedly, while subject to specific privileges accorded to the Jewish community, Jews could not be elected to city councils, which were governing bodies of towns settled on the Magdeburg law.

Nevertheless, Jews continued to be perceived as assets to the towns, to the point that, as Gershon Hundert has noted, in the 1750s one magnate remarked that the town "declined significantly" when Jews married their children off to families in other towns or countries.[65] There is no question that competition existed, and Christians, especially Christian guilds, often sought to limit Jewish business activities. Yet some of the modern scholarship has effectively marginalized, or even delegitimized, the presence of Jews in Polish towns to an extent incompatible with the historical record. As the privileges granted to Jews and as various court records demonstrate explicitly, Jews were not a marginalized group; they were considered a major force in the towns' prosperity, to the extent that they needed to be supported and protected.[66]

In the same year that John Sobieski granted the generous privilege to Jews in Kazimierz Dolny, the Sejm issued a decree concerning the obligation to defend the royal city of Lwów (now Lviv, Ukraine), described as "the first rampart of the Kingdom," against "the enemies of the Holy Cross"—that is, Tatars or Turks.[67] This decree, issued while the Polish–Ottoman War (1672–1676) was still raging, offers a telling illustration not only of Jews' responsibilities within cities and towns as part of their right to conduct business but also of their position as an integral part of the city's population. All people, Jews and non-Jews, living in the city and its suburbs, in all jurisdictions—municipal, noble, or ecclesiastical—shared the responsibility to contribute to the city's defense. So, too, "Jews, municipal and suburban, are obliged to help according to an old custom in cannon defense of the fortifications."[68] However, the decree's significance comes from the use of the phrase "enemies of the Cross" in reference to the enemies posing a danger to Lwów. In Christian anti-Jewish literature, it was Jews who were often so described, but here, in the context of war against the Ottoman Turks, Jews were among the defenders of the city—here they were unquestionably seen as members of the local polity, in which they had both rights and obligations.

Polish-Lithuanian Jews' role in trade, both local and international, was so important that kings sometimes intervened on their behalf, as did King Ladislaus IV (r. 1632–1648) in 1638, when he wrote to the city council of Breslau (now Wrocław, Poland), following complaints that Jews were defrauded at the fair there.[69] The centrality of the Jews to the economy of the Polish-Lithuanian Commonwealth can be further attested by the fact that Catholic clergy, despite prohibitions within church law, welcomed Jews into their possessions and engaged in business relationships with them, sometimes causing outrage among higher church officials.[70] In 1749, one parish priest in a small town in Poland was punished by an episcopal court for not expelling a Jewish lease-holder of a brewery in the village belonging to the church, despite previous orders to do so.[71] Another example shows a Jew from a town near Kraków who held the lease of a brewery in a nearby village belonging to the Cistercian monastery, and who was admonished under penalty of arrest by the bishop's decree not to take up leases of ecclesiastical properties or anything prohibited by canon law in the future.[72] Further instances of business relations between Jews and Catholic clergy can be found in the minutes of the Council of Four Lands, which often list communal expenses, among them payments resulting from debts owed by Jews to the Jesuits and Dominicans.[73] The prominent role played by Jews in Poland-Lithuania was also a reason for Pope Benedict XIV's promulgation of an encyclical letter, A Quo Primum, in 1751, in which he condemned their economic position and the closeness of Jewish-Christian relations.

Just how important Jews were in the country's life and economy, and how much we might be missing by ignoring them, emerges also from their role in the magnate economy. As Adam Teller has shown, even the magnates' rise and power in the post-1648 Polish-Lithuanian Commonwealth cannot be fully understood without the role Jews played in their estates.[74] Power, Teller claims, was related to money, and the Jews helped improve the profitability of the magnates' estates, and, thus, to increase their influence. If there is a quintessential characteristic of both the historical and the romanticized image of the Polish-Lithuanian Commonwealth of this era, it is the power of the magnates. In this sense, within the limits of their own distinct social roles, Jews remained closely tied to the political and economic power base of the Commonwealth.

Intimacy and Belonging in Everyday Life

The Jews' religious identity and their distinct legal status were obvious to all in the Polish-Lithuanian Commonwealth, but this did not mean that they were considered "aliens." In court, they had to swear on "the law of Moses."[75] Sometimes they signed court documents in Hebrew. The separate rhythms of their religious life were visible to their Christian neighbors.[76] Jews went to synagogues, not churches, celebrated the Sabbath, not Sunday, and observed Passover, not Easter. Especially in small towns, these differences played a role in social interactions. In 1632, for example, a civil case was brought to court over spoiled fish in Lublin. The barrels arrived in town on Friday and a Christian merchant was trying to sell them quickly. Christian buyers did not want to buy because "the gills were white as if sprinkled in ashes," but when the barrels were brought to a Jewish merchant, he refused even to have the barrels opened to look at the fish "saying that it was Sabbath."[77] The tone of the document is matter-of-fact, suggesting there was nothing unusual about this exchange.

Daily interactions are exceptionally difficult to document—when nothing out of the ordinary took place, nothing was recorded. Glimpses into daily life have to be gleaned from documents of conflict or those focused on unrelated issues. Archival records dealing with contracts and property transfers offer one such glimpse at the level of "normal" engagement. Jews appear in similar situations to those of Christians. They sued and were sued for debts, and took part in the legal system as anyone else.[78] They appear as lenders and borrowers, as buyers and sellers of homes and land plots, from and to Christians.[79] Sometimes they even sought enforcement of internal communal disciplinary sanctions from palatinate courts. In Poznań, local Jews appear to have sought enforcement of the *herem*, an act of communal ostracism, in a palatine court, which issued decrees of infamy against Jews in cases where the first instance was the judgment of the Jewish authorities.[80]

Jewish-Christian interactions in the premodern era have also typically been portrayed as merely expedient, grounded in economic exchange. However, this was not necessarily the case. Even in the context of economic exchange, there were venues for contact, conversations, and also intimacy, as Jews and Christians shared carriages traveling from town to town, or as they shared lodging or enjoyed a drink at an inn. There is no doubt that there was pleasure in these interactions.[81]

Daily interactions, in friendships and in business, required a shared language. Indeed, language has been at the center of the modern perception of Jewish social insularity in Christian Europe. Jews were said to speak a "jargon," in and of itself a modern notion, and, contrary to historical record, not to know local vernaculars. Jews did speak Yiddish with each other, and the language served as a lingua franca of Ashkenazi Jews, but they were at home in Polish as well as in other vernacular languages. Surviving court documents, especially in criminal cases where formal statements written by competent scribes are less frequent, suggest that Jews spoke Polish. When translation was needed, this fact was noted in the documents, but in the majority of records involving Jews, no such remark exists. The assumption that they did not know Polish is a modern one, shaped in part by the period of partitions, which greatly complicated language politics in the region, and in part by modern understandings of national languages, which demeaned dialects as "jargons." This common perception of linguistic otherness is another product of the modern process of excluding Jews from belonging to modern nations.

But in the early modern period, Jews themselves felt they belonged. In 1667, a Polish rabbi named Moses Rivkes found himself a war refugee in Amsterdam. He expressed his longing for his home in Wilno (today Vilnius, Lithuania), and his desire to return there, as the news of peace in the

Commonwealth reached Dutch shores. In a language deeply inflected with religious meaning, he expressed his feeling of being "exiled" from his home in "the holy community of Wilno . . . [the] longing of his soul."[82]

Still, although Jews and Christians closely intermixed, sometimes even living in the same houses and drinking together, the religious identities they each held meant that tensions existed and that boundaries between the two groups were both guarded and transgressed. One conflict arose between a Jewish and a Christian bookbinder in Lublin over whether the Jew could bind Christian religious books such as breviaries and other devotional books.[83] In another case noted in Jewish sources, a rabbi was asked if it was permissible to lend clothes to Christians who then wore them to church on Christian holidays.[84] The questioner's concern was whether by doing so Jews were contributing to idolatry. The rabbi answered that he could allow the practice "for the sake of peace," remarking that Christians did not require fine clothing for worship, and thus that lending clothes to Christians for that purpose did not contribute to idolatry. Notably, he did not question the social aspect of the practice.

Eating and drinking, whether in taverns or private homes of non-Jews, were prohibited by rabbis and church authorities alike. The sixteenth-century Polish rabbi Solomon Luria (known as the Maharshal) called it "shameful" that some Jews stayed in the inns of non-Jews, drank forbidden wine, and ate food cooked in their nonkosher pots.[85] However, some decades later, another Polish rabbi, Benjamin Slonik, conceded that this situation was unavoidable. Specifically, he allowed the practice of using the utensils of non-Jews to soak meat for salting when "a Jew lodges in the house of a non-Jew and he does not have kosher utensils."[86] And even anti-Jewish writers revealed matter-of-fact interactions. Sebastian Śleszkowski, one of the most virulently antisemitic authors of the seventeenth century, remarked that until he read anti-Jewish stories in books he encountered when traveling abroad, he had not known anything about any dangers coming from Jews. Indeed, as a student in Kraków, he used to frequent Jewish establishments in Kazimierz, where he would eat and drink, without any sense of danger or suspicion.[87]

These examples clearly illustrate the existence of intimacy in Jewish-Christian interactions bound together with awareness of both separate identities and religious hostility. The exchange about borrowing clothes shows also that Jews and Christians shared aesthetic values. The fact that Christians apparently desired to wear clothes borrowed from Jews to church demonstrates that there were no "Jewish" clothes, or at the very least that Christians did not consider wearing clothes borrowed from Jews to church offensive. Other examples also suggest that in the Polish-Lithuanian Commonwealth Jews and Christians may not have looked that different.

In 1716, two Christian women were tried for apostasy from Christianity to Judaism in the town of Dubno (now in Ukraine). One, Maryna Dawidowa, hailed from Witebsk in the northeastern part of Poland-Lithuania (today Viciebsk, Belarus) and the other, Maryna Wojciechówna, from Mielec and Jędrzejów in Małopolska.[88] After Maryna Dawidowa's husband died, she "connived to abandon the Christian faith and to accept the Jewish faith." Having converted, apparently on her own without anyone's aid, Dawidowa took her horse and left. After about fifty miles, she was "provided transportation from town to town by Jews," telling them that she was Jewish. It was only in Dubno, just over 450 miles away from Witebsk, that she was discovered and imprisoned. Since Dawidowa was unwilling to repent and return to Christianity, the court, "basing its judgment upon common law and the legal codex, in particular on article 79 of the Carolina and the Speculum saxonicum, Book I, that all apostates have to be punished by fire (speculum lib. 6.)," ordered "that for this scandalous deed of abandoning the holy Christian faith, this Maryna Dawidowa, a widow, be burned alive at the stake of wood; but before she goes to the stake of fire, three pieces from her body should be first ripped off with pincers and they should be thrown into the fire and only then should she herself be put at the stake and burned alive."

The other woman, Maryna Wojciechówna, had more people involved in her affair. Wojciechówna was arrested at her wedding, marrying a Jew. During the interrogation, she said: "I am from the town of Mielec, and I served there for three years in the house of a certain Jew, and then I was hired by Jews in Leżajsk, and so in Leżajsk I became Jewish and accepted the Jewish faith upon the persuasion of a Jew, Pasternak, and other Jewish men and women." Five Jews from the wedding, including the groom, were also arrested. During her interrogations under torture, Wojciechówna expressed "disgust" with Judaism and returned to Christianity, while the five Jews, also interrogated, "first voluntarily, then under torture . . . all said the same: that we did not know, none of us, that this maiden was Christian." In this case, the court ruled that Wojciechówna, because she "returned to the Christian faith, and regretting her scandalous deed, again wants to be a Christian," was to be spared the gruesome death to which Dawidowa was sentenced. However, the court ruled, she was still, "according to the commonly accepted laws, to be decapitated first and her body is to be burned at the stake like those of other faithless people and apostates."

The five Jews escaped the death penalty, after "the maiden, Maryna, herself admitted under torture that 'I do not know whether or not the Jew, Froim Jakubowicz [whom she was marrying], knew that I was a Christian.'" That neither woman had any problem entering the Jewish community—one during her travels, the second by marrying a Jew—is striking. Maryna Dawidowa's ability to pass herself off as a Jewish woman and the court's acceptance of the claim that the Jews involved in Wojciechówna's wedding did not know she was a Christian demonstrate that social distinctions between Jews and Christians in the Commonwealth were not as clear cut as modern historians (and activists) have imagined. The case of the two Marynas is not unique, although admittedly much rarer than Jewish conversions to Christianity and marriages between Jewish converts to Christianity with Christians.[89]

The rootedness and integration of Jews in the Polish-Lithuanian Commonwealth did not, of course, mean a utopian coexistence or lack of any distinctions between Jews and Polish Christians. The fact that Jews and Christians sharing clothes provoked anxiety among some Jewish leaders, and the fact that both Marynas lost their lives for converting to Judaism suggests that friendly, casual Jewish-Christian interactions did not always preclude conflict.[90] Indeed, they sometimes ended at the stake.

Exploring a Shared History of a Multicultural Commonwealth

The history of the Polish-Lithuanian Commonwealth includes Jews. It is not a story of an interfaith utopia or of a state without stakes, but it does constitute a shared history. How that history is told matters greatly. Jews have often been omitted from the writing of the Commonwealth's history and from the common memory of that past, but very clearly not from the historical evidence itself. However, as nationalism intensified in the nineteenth century and beyond, Jews were increasingly excluded from the imagined Polish nation—as they were from the German nation—and, as a corollary, also from narratives of Polish history, which began to emphasize the military and royal past and to examine the causes of the Commonwealth's collapse. It is this romanticized and glorified image of the Polish-Lithuanian Commonwealth—shaped more by nineteenth-century historical and literary imagination than by the historical record—that has been on display in the nationalist demonstrations of recent years in Poland.

As Polish nationalism developed and the post-partition history created new political, linguistic, and cultural divisions, the past that Jews and Christians shared in the vast territories of the Polish-Lithuanian Commonwealth was forgotten and the former connections between them weakened. Now, Jews, too, began to feel alienated and excluded, and, with the dominance of Hasidism in eastern Europe, many turned inward. In the nineteenth century, Jews increasingly came to be seen as foreign and alien, unable to "assimilate"—with "assimilation" becoming a secular version of conversion. With the rise of modern ethnocentric nationalism, which eschewed any difference and expected "assimilation," retaining any aspect of Jewish identity, even modernized and acculturated, disqualified individuals from belonging to the modern nation and state. It was in this context that new national histories were written to exclude Jews, or, if their presence was noted, to paint them as foreign, insular aliens.

This exclusion of Jews from modern history books was not just a result of modern nationalism. It was also built on the theological concept of Jewish exile, accepted by both Jews and Christians. The idea of exile implied that Jews were sojourners wherever they lived—a notion internalized by modern historians, who continued to perceive Jews as "foreigners" in the lands where they had lived for centuries, thus excluding them from historiographies of modern nation-states. The effective exclusion of Jews as a foreign diasporic people from national narratives not only resulted in the confinement of the history of the Jews to Jewish scholars writing for Jewish readers but also helped modern nationalists, who often espoused antisemitic views, whether consciously or unconsciously, to justify the promotion of policies that would exclude Jews from the social fabric of their new nations. After all, if Jews had always been foreign and thus peripheral, they did not deserve to be part of the nation, and their equal citizenship could be questioned.

Accordingly, this (mis)understanding not only of Polish but also of wider European history, with its tendency to see Jews as an insular minority, had ramifications beyond historiography. Yet historical evidence clearly shows that Jews were "part of the social, cultural, and political context in which they lived." In the context of Polish history, understanding the role Jews played in society, politics, economy, and culture prompts the question: "How Jewish is Polish history?" and how much have we missed by seeing Jews as an "alien ethnic element," standing "outside the social ladder"? As Jacob Goldberg famously said, "There is no history of Poland without the history of the Jews, and no history of the Jews without the history of Poland."[91]

2

Multiconfessionalism and Interconfessionality

Religious "Toleration" in Royal Prussia, Lithuania, and the Ruthenian Lands

Karin Friedrich

When, in 1582, the Catholic Church adopted the Gregorian Calendar, the Lutherans in Vilnius (*Pol.* Wilno) had no objections. The Jesuit Stanisław Grodzicki described their reaction: "I know what the heretics of the Saxon faith say, both in Germany . . . and also here, that this [adherence to the new calendar] is a voluntary matter."[1] The Lithuanian Lutherans accepted the new rule as part of religious adiaphora—indifferent matters—not worth fighting over. Another Jesuit, Marcin Łaszcz, praised such interconfessional understanding in 1594 with a pinch of sarcasm, when he wrote to Simon Teofil Turnowski, a member of the Bohemian Brethren: "I certainly have cause to praise you, in that you have received our dear St Wojciech and St Stanisław into your Church and, as I hear, have written them into your calendar. What is more, you have converted these saints to your faith." Łaszcz, however, was more overtly critical of the Protestants' habit of eating meat on fast days: "Poles have not eaten meat on Saturday for 600 years; it has only been during the time of you Lutherans that such gluttony has begun."[2] In a variation on the anticlerical critique of priests living the good life, Łaszcz then turned against the Vilnian Lutherans, telling the story of a minister who, while looking into a henhouse to choose his roast dinner, had fallen from the ladder and broken his neck. Nationalizing his insults, the Jesuit wished the Lutheran minister to go "to hell, where a third of all devils already speak German."[3]

Strikingly, this Catholic author, while identifying himself as a Pole, de-
nies Turnowski—wrongly identified as a Lutheran—the same nationality.
Łaszcz's implication is that all Lutherans are Germans, identified by their
"Saxon faith." This assumption was not uncommon at the time. Ioannes
Dantiscus (*Pol.* Jan Dantyszek; *Ger.* Johannes Dantiscus, 1485–1548), bishop
of Warmia (*Ger.* Ermland) and Chełmno (*Ger.* Kulm), suspected his priests of
Lutheranism because they sang hymns in the vernacular German that many
inhabitants of Royal Prussia still spoke in 1534.[4] Yet, despite such views of the
"Saxon heresy," the Protestant Reformation in Poland-Lithuania was not just
a German import, but rather a "multicultural" event. Adherents of several
versions of the Reformation arrived in Poland from abroad: Lutherans from
Ducal Prussia, Western Pomerania, and Silesia; Scottish, French, and Swiss
Calvinists and Zwinglians; Utraquists and the congregationalist traditions
of the Bohemian Brethren; Dutch Mennonites; Venetian Anabaptists; and
eventually Antitrinitarians following the ideas of Lelio and Fausto Sozzini
(1525–1562 and 1539–1604, respectively).[5] But the Reformation also had native,
Polish-Lithuanian roots: early Lutheran Danzig (*Pol.* Gdańsk); the Humanist
circles and their Erasmian outlook in Kraków; the Philippists in Wielkopolska. After his return from England and Frisia in 1556, Jan Łaski (1499–1560)
helped create the presbyterian-synodal structures of the Calvinist Church in
Poland, while Andrzej Wolan (*Lat.* Andreas Volanus, 1531–1610) supported
the Calvinist Radziwiłłs to do the same in Lithuania.[6]

Poland-Lithuania had a long tradition of the coexistence of different
cultures, languages, and national identities, preceding the Reformation and
intersecting with multiple religious practices—in particular, with Latin and
Eastern Christianity.[7] According to a British traveler to Poland-Lithuania at
the turn of the sixteenth century, its form of multiculturalism and multiconfessionalism had been highly successful: "Religion in thys lande is manifold,
bothe for manyfest opposition and diversity of sectes, which commes, for
that it confynes with nations of most contrary rites, all men drawing by
nature some novelty from theire neighboures."[8] "Foreign" customs became
acceptable in a religious context in which they were considered as irrelevant
adiaphora, or where they turned into new hybrid forms, as in the Lutheran
acceptance of the Catholic calendar or saints' images. Sensitivities varied:
as we have seen, liturgical singing in a foreign language triggered suspicion.
The "nationalization" of heaven and hell went hand in hand with learned
treatises promoting or rejecting the enforcement of religious unity by decrees and punishments.[9] Yet agreements between opposite sides continued

to be struck—for example, in the practice of *Simultankirchen*: churches that offered mass or religious services for different confessional communities and in different languages, albeit subject to strictly defined rules and regulations on how to limit or delimit sacred spaces.[10] One prominent example was Saint Mary's Basilica in Danzig, where both Lutherans and Catholics worshipped from 1572; another was the ecclesiastical space shared between Brethren and Calvinists in the Radziwiłł town of Węgrów in Mazovia.[11] In Vilnius, bi- or multiconfessional ordering of religious spaces presented what David Frick calls a "particularly tenacious and complicated case of parity arrangements."[12]

In the German lands, Thomas Kaufmann has shown that many such practices went beyond a mere sharing of spaces to a mutual borrowing in processes of "interconfessionality."[13] This term can be defined as "conscious imitation which extends beyond one's own confessional traditions and adapts elements of a foreign confessional culture."[14] Examples of interconfessionality included decisions by Protestant parents to seek out education for their children in Jesuit colleges, which offered high standards and a broad curriculum. It also expressed itself in admiration for the achievements of other confessions and religious communities, albeit without support of the theological doctrines behind them. As Susan Karrant-Nun points out, "interconfessionality" in Europe was most prominent "within those territories that, owing to an ineluctable religious plurality, could not be confessionalized in the purest sense ... where power was shared, citizens had religious choices. In such locations, and along geographic boundaries, tolerance-in-practice preceded both its treatment by intellectuals and its elevation to a Christian ideal."[15]

The Polish Kingdom and the Grand Duchy of Lithuania had precisely embodied such religious plurality for centuries, and religious belonging never mapped neatly onto national or linguistic identities. Not all Lutherans were German, not all Bohemian Brethren considered themselves Czech in the second or third generation, and over time, a number of Orthodox Ruthenian families began to adopt Polish, Calvinist, or Catholic identities.[16] Religious conflict and peacemaking played out against the background of a republican political constitution of civic participation that for many citizens—albeit not for all—became the single most important identifier. But how did the fundamental stipulation that civic concord, unity, and equality before the law should preserve citizens' liberties in a well-balanced mixed form of government (*forma mixta*) tally with demands for individual freedom of conscience? If the ruler or magistrate did not act as the main "confessionalizing" force—as in the territorial states of the Holy Roman Empire after the 1555 Peace of Augsburg ("cuius regio, eius religio")—who or what determined citizens' cultural and confessional options?

The following pages suggest that an analysis of the confessional development of early modern Poland-Lithuania can only yield results if the relationship between the individual citizens and their identity (or belonging) as part of a wider civic community is taken into account. This becomes problematic when religious and political loyalties to a group in society do not coincide. An inevitable question then arises as to how political freedoms ("iura et libertates") are linked to liberty of religious choice. This chapter tries to address some of these questions with a focus on several Christian faith groups and communities—Lutherans in Royal Prussia, Calvinists in Lithuania, and the Ruthenian Orthodox—selected from the multinational and multiconfessional kaleidoscope of Poland-Lithuania from the early decades of the Reformation in the sixteenth century to the late seventeenth century, when multiconfessional existence became more problematic. Under scrutiny is not the theoretical definition of toleration,[17] but rather the practical possibility of religious coexistence and interconfessional dialogue in diverse cultural environments.

The 1573 Warsaw Confederation

Historians have traditionally dubbed the sixteenth century Poland-Lithuania's "Golden Age," when "Polish toleration" contributed to the optimistic view of the multiethnic and multiconfessional Commonwealth as a "state without stakes."[18] The English language has the ability to distinguish between "tolerance," a liberal-minded attitude toward religious pluralism, and "toleration," which is associated with legal or other guarantees to "suffer" the existence and rights of those who differ from one's own beliefs. The two can coincide, but what motivated early modern societies was not enlightened tolerance but a grudgingly accepted minimum of practical "toleration"—without using the word—in order to keep the peace. The resulting practices and legal measures could range from absence of expulsion and punishment to the recognition of the right to public worship by other denominations.[19]

The decision to find necessary agreements to keep the peace was at the core of the 1573 Confederation of Warsaw, the culmination of long-standing demands to accommodate a variety of religious groups, as the Kingdom of Poland had been a refuge for non-Catholics long before that. After the suppression of their church in the Habsburg lands under Ferdinand I in 1547, the

Bohemian Brethren settled as religious exiles mainly in Wielkopolska, where they cooperated with the local Reformed (Calvinist) community, with whom they signed the short-lived Union of Koźminek (1555), building their religious and educational center in Leszno. They also found common ground with the Calvinists in Małopolska, where the Brethren settled in Włodawa, protected by the Reformed Leszczyński family. In 1570, a year after the Union of Lublin that formed the Polish-Lithuanian Commonwealth, the Calvinists and the Bohemian Brethren reached an agreement, which was mainly directed against the Antitrinitarians (also called "Arians" or Polish Brethren). The agreement did not contain a consensus on doctrine and church structures, and it did not mean that the Brethren were "Calvinized."[20] This 1570 *Consensus Sandomiriensis* prepared the way for the Confederation of Warsaw, signed three years later, on January 28, 1573, during the interregnum after the death of the last Jagiellonian king, guaranteeing "eternal peace" between the councilors and the nobility of the Polish Crown and the Grand Duchy of Lithuania "inter dissidentes in religione."[21] The call went out for a "process of confederation," aspiring to implement the agreement by giving the believers of all Christian religions (except the Antitrinitarians) the same legal rights and opportunities.[22]

While the Warsaw Confederation entered political discourse in the Sejm and sejmiks,[23] its translation into everyday practice was more difficult. Vilnius can serve as an example, where a great variety of faith communities experienced intense conflict, but at the same time also negotiated hard-won compromises between their religions, languages, and cultural traditions.[24] According to Kazimierz Bem, "The choice between 'Protestant' and 'Catholic' was not a zero-sum game."[25] Where did one confession end and another begin? Did kneeling or standing in church during the Eucharist really separate Calvinists from Bohemian Brethren? What motivated the castellan of Kraków, Spytek Jordan (1518–1568), to take communion in both kinds from his Catholic chaplain? In the Grand Duchy of Lithuania, the catechism of Nieśwież (*Bel.* Niasviž) of 1565 contained many elements of the Antitrinitarian theology that had entered Lithuania under the patronage of Mikołaj Radziwiłł "Czarny" ("The Black," 1515–1565), but there was no alternative available, so the Calvinist and Bohemian Brethren also used it. It was only in 1618 that the Lithuanian Calvinist church adopted the 1563 Heidelberg catechism, which was also acceptable to the Bohemian Brethren. Was the Calvinist Thomas Forbes, who died in Kraków in 1642, still clinging to the Catholic emphasis on good deeds when he left money to the poor of his

Reformed church as well as to Catholics?[26] Could one safely ignore these matters as adiaphora without risking salvation?

The main aim of the Warsaw Confederation was to prevent the religious conflict and war experienced at the time in parts of western Europe, especially in France.[27] Many Catholics also subscribed to the ideal of religious peace. At the Sejm of 1590, Lew Sapieha (*Bel.* Leŭ Sapieha; *Lit.* Leonas Sapiega; 1557–1633), who had recently returned to the Catholic faith, condemned the papal nuncio's campaign against the Warsaw Confederation, proclaiming that although he was a Catholic, "I do not wish my country to suffer what happened in France, and I know many Catholics who do not wish it either, as it would lead to the destruction of the fatherland."[28] Despite Hugo Grotius's verdict that "Poland does not legislate on matters of religion,"[29] it was the strong belief of the citizens in the supremacy of the law that ensured that religious liberties became part of the wider canon of their civic liberties, confirmed by the king and implemented by secular law courts.

During the "confessional age," between 1550 and 1650, churches tried to define their doctrines to discipline their faithful, particularly within political bodies, where rulers often allied with one confessional church to impose a confessional program. The concept of "confessionalization"—the institutionalized coercion by territorial rulers of their subjects in matters of faith—became popular with German historians of state-building in the 1980s.[30] While the paradigm has undergone transformations that take into account grassroot pressures, it is still fruitful for research. Much criticism, however, has been directed at its application to Poland-Lithuania, a decentralized body politic without absolute monarchy.[31] Theories of "confessionalization" find it difficult to cope with interconfessional practices and multicultural societies. Attention also needs to shift away from the well-explored high politics of the bishops and the royal court, whose confessional policies are often blamed for the failure of the Polish-Lithuanian Reformation. Answers to questions as to why and how religious diversity in Poland-Lithuania lasted as long as it did can be found in everyday hybrid religious practices. These are most apparent where the Commonwealth's society was most multicultural: in the borderlands of Royal Prussia, Lithuania, and the Ruthenian lands.

"German Lutheranism" in Royal Prussia

In 1522, the year of Luther's first translation of the Bible into German, Jakub Hegge, a cobbler's son, began to preach Lutheran ideas in the Corpus Christi Church near Danzig. Luther was aware of the success of his message in the city, and wrote to his friend and colleague, Georg Spalatin: "Everywhere they want to hear the pure word of Scripture, and everywhere preachers are sorely needed."[32] In Danzig, an urban protest movement against corrupt magistrates joined the Reformation. While the German Peasants' War raged in Swabia and Thuringia in 1525, the city governments of the Royal Prussian cities of Danzig, Thorn (Pol. Toruń), and Elbing (Pol. Elbląg) were ousted by representatives of the trade and craft guilds who adopted Lutheranism.[33] Although the old Catholic elites were temporarily restored with the help of the Polish king's troops, after the severe punishment of rebellious burghers, a compromise emerged. The *Statuta Sigismundi*, King Sigismund I's (r. 1506–1548) anti-heresy laws of 1526, while fierce, were rarely, if ever, evoked. Reform ideas that had spread among the populace continued to flourish, and the city council eventually accepted Lutheranism. Academic matriculation registers demonstrate the attraction the Protestant hotbed of Wittenberg University had for students from Royal Prussia, despite the king's ban on studying there.[34]

Yet early Reformation ideas arrived in Poland not only across the western border from the empire but also from Baltic Prussia, where Albrecht of Hohenzollern (1490–1568), the last grand master of the Teutonic Knights, officially adopted Luther's teaching in 1525. After a meeting with Martin Luther and Philip Melanchthon in 1523, Albrecht turned the Teutonic Order's state into a secular duchy.[35] Faced with immediate hostility from Rome and the Holy Roman emperor, who opposed Albrecht's conversion, the Duchy of Prussia could only survive under the protection of its powerful Polish neighbor. The duke's envoy and representative at the German Imperial Council, Asverus von Brandt (1509–1559), worked closely with Polish diplomats to fend off demands by the now-exiled Teutonic Order, which called for war against Ducal Prussia.[36] On April 8, 1525, King Sigismund I accepted Albrecht's oath of allegiance, declaring him "dux in Prussia" and a vassal of the Polish crown—a status his descendants were to inherit. Ducal Prussia became a center for the dissemination of Protestant print materials over its borders into Poland-Lithuania.[37]

It was from Ducal Prussia that Lutheran ideas spilled over into Danzig and Royal Prussia, the western part of the former state of the Teutonic Knights, which had seceded from the order in 1454 and was finally incorporated into the Polish Crown after the Second Peace of Thorn of 1466. The first chapters of Protestantism in Poland were indeed written by the urban Reformation of Royal Prussia, sustained by printing presses, the book trade, and guild activism. After the 1530s, the three major Royal Prussian cities hired German preachers to spread the Reformation, which also found resonance in neighboring Wielkopolska.[38] In 1557, Sigismund II Augustus (r. 1548–1572), who was more open than his father toward a modus vivendi, guaranteed by royal edict the freedom of religion for the followers of the Augsburg Confession in Danzig, Elbing, and Thorn.

Despite the Polish Crown's political backing of Duke Albrecht against Rome, the Polish bishops condemned Lutheranism not only for differences in religious doctrine, but in political terms, as a force of sedition and disobedience, "[insulting] to the royal and heavenly majesties," and full of "tumults and errors."[39] The episcopate—which occupied a double position, as high clergy, loyal to Rome, and as noble officeholders in the Commonwealth by royal appointment—was concerned about the influence of Lutheran preachers, but also looked down on them. In particular, they viewed Evangelical pastors' affinity with the "plebeian" element as a threat to church authority. The Polish primate Andrzej Krzycki (1482–1537) warned the Crown in his anti-Lutheran *Encomia Luteri* of 1524 that Lutheranism led to the "insolentia vulgorum." And yet, a year later, Krzycki defended Albrecht of Hohenzollern's oath to Sigismund I against attacks from the papal legate to Hungary, pointing to the late medieval multicultural tradition of Poland's rule over "Ruthenians, Armenians, Jews, and Tatars."[40] Why should a Lutheran prince not be added to the mix? Condemnations continued, however, when in 1560, Cardinal Hosius (*Pol.* Stanisław Hozjusz; 1504–1579), bishop of Warmia and himself of non-noble origins, condemned Luther as a Hussite and a Waldensian—a "rebellious infection" that threatened to spread beyond the German lands.[41] Despite denouncing Luther as a heretic, Hosius did not care or dare to take on Luther's positions in a theological debate. Polish polemics against Luther focused on the reformer's person within the "orbis Wittenbergensis," and less on his theology.[42]

Toward the late sixteenth century, Catholic polemic against Lutherans switched from mockery to more serious attacks. In mass-produced pamphlets against "German heresy," Lutherans were characterized as "German lizards." Such polemic intensified after the Livonian Wars of 1558–1583 and the Polish–Swedish wars of 1600–1629, which saw Swedes and German mercenaries occupy towns in the Commonwealth, where they sided with Lutherans and other Protestants.[43] In private correspondence kept in the archive in Toruń, we can even read narratives of Lutheran martyrdom. One story—unconfirmed by other sources—focuses on a Lutheran merchant who, after an in-

cident brought about by a misunderstanding during his travels, was accused
of causing the death of a Polish official, who had in fact died at the hand
of his own servant. The Lutheran merchant was allegedly incarcerated by
Catholic authorities and unjustly condemned to death by quartering. In the
process that led to the merchant's execution, the name of "Lutry" ("Luthers")
was interchangeably used with an invective meaning "Germans" and "sons
of a whore."[44] Such rhetoric should be taken with a pinch of salt, particularly
after the Tridentine decrees gave free reign to baroque eloquence against
"heretics." The story might have been a piece of Protestant urban counter-
propaganda, although it must have sounded true to some.

According to Michael Müller, the urban Reformation in Royal Prussia
was the only such movement in Poland-Lithuania that established itself
through intense "confessionalization" from above, led by urban authorities.[45]
While Thorn was, for most of the sixteenth century, a center for the Bohemian Brethren, Danzig attracted Calvinists, not least from among the Polish
and Lithuanian nobility who educated their sons at the Danzig Gymnasium,
where the Calvinist theologian Bartholomäus (*Pol.* Bartłomiej) Keckermann
(1572–1609) built his reputation.[46] Among the nobility, it has been estimated
that around 30–40 percent joined Lutheran or Calvinist churches in the Po-
morze and Malbork palatinates, while the Chełmno palatinate and its bishopric remained in the majority Catholic.[47] Well into the early seventeenth
century, the Lutheran movement in Royal Prussia followed the teaching of
Philip Melanchthon (1497–1560). As they disagreed with the *Formula Con-
cordiae* of 1577, a doctrinal statement of the Lutheran faith, Royal Prussia's
Lutherans experienced the censure of the stricter doctrinal line of the Wittenberg theologians. The openness of the so-called Philippists toward the
Calvinists and other denominations was based on a strong civic patriotism in
which burghers and nobles participated equally. At the same time, Protestant
communities could function quite easily even within a wider Catholic environment. Many Lutherans accepted traditional Catholic material culture in
their churches, such as images of the Virgin Mary or highly ornate baroque
altarpieces, as mere adiaphora.[48] As late as 1683, during a visit to Elbing, the
bishop of Warmia, Michał Radziejowski, expressed his surprise and noted
his objection to the practice of shared Catholic and Lutheran funeral processions, intermarriage between denominations, and Protestant ministers
blessing Catholic marriage vows.[49]

After the cessation of cooperation between Lutherans and the other
Reformed denominations during the Synod of Thorn in 1595, the previous

mutual solidarity and support showed signs of decline. The *Consensus Sandomiriensis* became mainly a document to the solidarity of the Protestant Trinitarian churches, directed against the Antitrinitarian Socinians.[50] In the Royal Prussian cities, Protestant theologians became more politically established as they intermarried with families of lawyers who led urban governments. The Lutheran population of Danzig began to resent what they perceived as a Calvinist oligarchy, eventually ousting it from government.[51] As the Bohemian Brethren and Calvinists lost control over the city councils in the 1620s, the Lutherans, with strong support from Wittenberg, outlasted them in ecclesiastical and secular positions. Meanwhile, the strong synodal structures of the Polish and Lithuanian Calvinists continued to be led by the nobility, which intensified alienation between urban and noble society. With minor exceptions, Catholics remained excluded from holding offices in the major Royal Prussian cities, and urban elites found ways to prevent religious parity, despite the best efforts of the Polish king and the bishops of Warmia and Chełmno to change the situation.[52] There were occasional victories for royal policies, such as the return of the Church of Saint Jacob to the Benedictine nuns in Thorn in 1667.[53] The Lutherans nevertheless retained their monopoly over the composition of the city councils, which seriously hampered Catholic attempts to take back control.[54] This was a model that worked in strongly Protestant self-governing cities, but could not be extended to other territories of the Commonwealth.

Multiconfessionalism in the Grand Duchy of Lithuania

Lutheran books from Königsberg (now Kaliningrad, Russia) and Danzig also reached the Lithuanian lands. In many ethnic Lithuanian communities, just emerging from their pagan past, the Roman Church had barely taken root when Protestantism arrived on the map.[55] The links between Protestants in Lithuania and Ducal Prussia across the shared border intensified during the course of the sixteenth century. The Königsberg Reformer Paulus Speratus (1484–1551), who had helped Luther to put together the first Lutheran hymn book for Ducal Prussia, maintained a correspondence with Lithuanian ministers and their noble patrons to organize language training for Lutheran preachers from Prussia.[56] A lively trade in Lutheran print material developed between Königsberg and Vilnius via Memel (*Lit.* Klaipėda), and in 1530 Duke Albrecht of Prussia established stipends for Lithuanian students to prepare for the ministry in Wittenberg. One of these students,

Abraham Culvensis (*Lit.* Abraomas Kulvietis), returned in 1539 to Vilnius to set up a Lutheran school.[57] His *Confessio Fidei* of 1543 was published in Königsberg. These contacts also led to the printing in Königsberg of the first catechism in Lithuanian, in 1547, by Martynas Mažvydas (1510–1563).[58]

Initially dominated by a handful of theologians, the Reformation in the Commonwealth was soon taken over by secular nobles. In 1553, Mikołaj Radziwiłł "Czarny," Lithuanian grand chancellor and palatine of Vilnius, established the first Protestant parish near his castle in Brest (*Pol.* Brześć), conducting correspondence both with Jan Łaski, as leader of the Polish Reformation, and with John Calvin in Geneva, who in six letters between 1555 and 1561 impatiently censured the magnate for taking too long to establish a church organization. Calvin also recommended Lelio Sozzini to Czarny, a decision he soon regretted, as the Italian introduced Antitrinitarianism to Lithuania. Shortly after Calvin's death in May 1564, the Lithuanian magnate embraced Antitrinitarian views, including the denial of the divine nature of Christ. Consequently, Czarny removed pastors who defended Calvinist Trinitarianism from his parishes.[59]

The magnate later became embroiled in a dispute with the Roman nuncio Luigi Lippomano, who had come to Poland-Lithuania to organize resistance against Protestant influences. In an act of defiance, Czarny had his correspondence with Lippomano printed in Königsberg, insulting the pope as the Antichrist.[60] The magnate had political support: in the Polish Sejm of 1550, Protestants were in the majority, and few followed any clear set of religious doctrines.[61] In the Lithuanian council during the 1560s, sixteen of twenty-two senators were Protestants, and in 1591 around two hundred Protestant churches existed in the Grand Duchy.[62] In the Sejm of 1572, among the senators from the Grand Duchy of Lithuania, once again, sixteen were Protestants, three Orthodox, and three Catholics.[63] By the end of the sixteenth century, the Lithuanian Calvinist church was based in six districts, headed by superintendents and a governing body, the Lithuanian Synod, which met annually in Vilnius.[64]

This considerable success depended on the personal engagement and support of the Reformed nobility. The demands on the patrons of the Lithuanian Calvinist church were considerable: landlords appointed teachers to their village schools, selected and paid ministers, maintained buildings and printing presses, and covered legal costs to defend the right of their Protestant subjects to practice their faith. The strong association between personal and civic liberty and the free exercise of religion shows the motivation of

the "dissidents" to translate the Warsaw Confederation into legal and political reality.[65] The Act of Confederation had been introduced during the
interregnum, when the Polish nobility endorsed the free election of all its
members, and the Commonwealth ruled itself for the liberty of the citizens,
as many contemporary voices stressed.[66] It specifically defined the choice
of religion as a private choice for each noble citizen.[67] Since the lands of the
Polish Crown had no codified law, however, the Confederation agreements
passed by the Sejm were no more than an electoral pact, incorporated into
the electoral oath of the king (Henrician Articles and future *pacta conven-
ta*). They could be overturned if a king, who would not confirm them, was
not held to such a confirmation by the Sejm, or if the confirmation became
meaningless rhetoric.

Lithuanian law, in contrast to the situation in Poland, was codified in
three statutes (1529, 1566, and 1588), which provided a more solid legal framework. The last statute incorporated the text of the Warsaw Confederation.[68]
The Calvinist church organization in Lithuania had thus become a legal
public body, and attacks against it could be challenged in court. The "process
of confederation," so desired by the fathers of the Confederation of 1573 in
order to separate political and religious powers, saw some practical progress
in Lithuania: the Statute of 1588 banned the participation of clerics in the
Lithuanian sejmiks, and from 1607 priests who were leaseholders of land were
no longer exempt from taxation.[69] But even Lithuania's statute law was no
iron guarantee against contrary practice: from the seventeenth century, tribunals were increasingly stacked with Catholics, and lawsuits against Catholics were frequently undermined by Catholic tribunal judges and politicians
in the Chamber of Deputies.[70] They eventually recommended that the king
should bar "heretics" from political and judicial offices.[71] It is therefore worth
shifting attention away from the "top-down" model of Reformation and
Counter-Reformation to focus instead on how noble political agency itself
created or hindered a culture of interconfessionality and religious dialogue.

Historiography is particularly divided on the question of whether the
Warsaw Confederation permitted landlords to impose their religion on their
subjects—to "confessionalize them"—and to arrange the religious affairs on
their landed estates as they wished,[72] or how much multi- and interconfessionality was allowed. Toward the end of the sixteenth century, Lithuania's
Calvinists came to be led by a group of powerful families, including the Sapieha, Mirski, Hlebowicz, Dorohostajski, and Zenowicz, and the Birże-branch
(*Lit.* Birżai) of the Radziwiłł family.[73] There were fewer magnate families

in Lithuania than in Poland, but they traditionally held a stronger position within the social hierarchy in the Grand Duchy than the Polish elites in the Crown.[74] Matthias Niendorf has stressed the link between the most powerful Lithuanian magnate families' resistance to the union with Poland at Lublin in 1569 and the choice of Calvinism among these opponents, particularly the Radziwiłłs.[75] This has sparked comparisons between the confessionalization policies of the princes in the Holy Roman Empire and the power of magnate families over their subjects.[76] If the Royal Prussian city fathers had successfully implemented confessional policies, could the Lithuanian magnates do the same?

The act of 1573 confirmed that "with this our confederation we do not derogate the lords' authority over their subjects, *tam in spiritualibus, quam in saecularibus*, and do not abolish the duty of their subjects' obedience."[77] This phrasing seemed to give magnates free recourse to religious coercion of their subjects, just as princes in the Holy Roman Empire had power over their subjects in matters of faith. This parallel, however, does not work well. Magnates' latifundia in Poland-Lithuania were usually scattered far and wide. Even the old Lithuanian and Ruthenian princes of the blood were unable to consolidate their allodial territories sufficiently to follow the German example. Moreover, the Confederation of Warsaw defended liberty of conscience for all *dissidentes in religione*—not a corporate idea of religious territoriality.[78] The idea to extend the right to freedom of religion to individuals even further down the social hierarchy was also not alien to the Sejm. In the Sejm of 1606, the Chamber of Deputies intended to complement the original resolution with the following paragraph: "No plebeian must be prevented from exercising his religion or be coerced to adopt another one against his will, nor be forced to accept baptism, ceremonies, and church liturgies he does not want to exercise."[79] This rule was never implemented, however, because the Sejm, stricken by the outbreak of the Zebrzydowski rebellion (1606–1609) against King Sigismund III Vasa (r. 1587–1632), was not concluded. After that, the moment had passed, and many landlords successfully introduced their own religion on their estates.[80]

Despite the 1588 Statute's protection for dissidents, Lithuanian Protestant communities started to suffer considerable restrictions in the first half of the seventeenth century, similar to their Polish counterparts a generation earlier. Protestant numbers declined, first in the Senate, but also in the Chamber of Deputies. In 1586, 56 percent of Lithuanian state and senatorial offices were in non-Catholic hands; by 1606, only 36 percent; and in 1632, not a single one.[81] The last Calvinist senator was Jan Sosnowski, a Radziwiłł client who had risen to the position of castellan of Polatsk (*Pol.* Połock). He died in 1660 after converting to Catholicism four years earlier.[82] As a response to such pressures, Calvinist social control on the Radziwiłł estates intensified. In 1624, for example, Krzysztof Radziwiłł instructed the starosta in Birże to punish anyone who brought a Catholic priest into their home.[83] Doctrinal matters were refined in the 1634 Synod of Włodawa, near the present-day Polish-Belarusian-Ukrainian border, which tried to prescribe one program of church discipline to all Calvinists and Bohemian Brethren.[84] As in 1595, at the Synod of Thorn, the Lutherans resisted compromise with the Calvinists.

Could non-Catholic magnates, who made it their main business to protect dissidents, have saved interconfessional dialogue in the Grand Duchy? We will not enter here into discussion of the historical role of the magnateria, but examples show that their religious policies reflected a wider trend in Polish noble society. The argument that a citizen's patriotism and virtue depended on his Catholicism was to become a strong political weapon against multi- and interconfessionality during the seventeenth century.[85] Conversions to Catholicism weakened non-Catholic patronage and interconfessional practices.[86] Dissident magnates sought to preserve non-Catholic faith communities on their own estates, but this did not always work. In 1662, Bogusław Radziwiłł decided to move his Antitrinitarian servants and clients across the border into Ducal Prussia, because he could not prevent the confiscation of their properties and attacks on their lives.[87] After Radziwiłł sold Węgrów in 1664 to Jan Kazimierz Kraiński, the Catholic treasurer of the Polish Crown, the Calvinist community of the town dispersed, especially after the burning of their church in 1678.[88] However, we also know that Bogusław Radziwiłł's daughter, Ludwika Karolina, despite her second marriage to the Catholic Charles III Philip of Pfalz-Neuburg in 1688, supported her Calvinist subjects and their churches in the Grand Duchy, as well as the Orthodox institutions on her lands. The alumni fund for the Lithuanian Calvinist church existed until 1868 as a remnant of noble support of Protestantism in Lithuania.[89]

The Orthodox and the Limits of Interconfessionality

The Union of Kreva of 1385 brought together the Catholic Kingdom of Poland with the Grand Duchy of Lithuania, composed of pagan Lithuanians and Orthodox Ruthenians in the former lands of Kyivan Rus'. Medieval Lithuania under the pagan Prince Gediminas (*Bel.* Hiedzimin, *Pol.* Giedymin;

Grand Duke 1316–1341) had attracted communities from various religious backgrounds—Karaites, Armenians, Muslim Tatars, and Jews.[90] According to the Lutheran historian and deputy to the Polish Sejm, Swiętosław Orzelski (1549–1598), there was nothing new about the large number of religions in the Commonwealth: "Next to the Greek religion, pagans and Jews have been known for a long time, and many other, non-Roman Catholics have lived here for centuries."[91] As late as the Sejm of 1615, Jan Herburt (1567–1616) pointed out that "the Commonwealth did not grow as trees grow, but came into being like a wall that was built from different nations"—nations with a variety of religious identities.[92]

Herburt's speech asked the king to respect the equality of the many "nations" in this union, while referring to the metaphor of Poland-Lithuania as the bulwark (*antemurale*) of Christianity. Yet the union's cultural traditions did not find themselves treated equally. In defense against the Teutonic Knights, the Union of Horodło of 1413—which the chronicler Jan Długosz (1415–1480) saw as a further step in the growing together of "the Poles with the Lithuanians and Samogitians"—resulted in forty-seven Catholic Lithuanian princely and boyar families being adopted into the Polish nobility and henceforth sharing their coats of arms.[93] Not included were the Orthodox Ruthenian lords of the Grand Duchy, descended from the princes of Polatsk, Viciebsk, Chernihiv, Smolensk, and Pinsk.[94] In Poland, royal administrators and towns routinely imposed restrictions on guild membership and office-holding by Orthodox candidates.[95]

Nevertheless, negotiations over political equality between Catholics and Orthodox brought some progress during the early sixteenth century. The Jagiellonian dynasty guaranteed the free appointment of Orthodox clergy and self-government over ecclesiastical jurisdiction in 1511, although the metropolitans were still subject to royal nomination. Greater equality was also reflected in the first Lithuanian Statute of 1529, which applied to both Catholic and Orthodox nobles.[96] In 1563, under the threat of war with Moscow, King Sigismund II Augustus sought to lift existing discrimination against the Orthodox in Poland-Lithuania, to prevent restrictions on officeholding and attempts to enforce a Catholic liturgy.[97] Despite the fact that the great majority of the country's population were followers of the Orthodox faith— estimates put the Catholic population between 10 percent and 20 percent of the overall population of the Grand Duchy around 1400—political influence once more shifted toward Lithuania's Catholics after the 1569 Union of Lublin.[98] The Orthodox Church de facto maintained a lower status, and its bishops were barred from taking up seats in the newly joint Senate, just as they had been excluded from the Lithuanian council in the past.[99]

Some among the Orthodox princely families were inspired by religious reform themselves, adopting either Protestant ideas or converting to Catholicism (such as the Chreptowicz, Sanguszko, Massalski, or Czartoryski families), although many continued to support Orthodox Church foundations and brotherhoods.[100] Others, such as the Olelkowicz (*Bel.* Alelkovič) dukes of Slutsk or the Ostrogski family (*Ukr.* Ostrozkyi), defied Catholicization until they either died out or their sons converted in the seventeenth century. Konstanty Wasyl Ostrogski resisted in defense of his faith, creating printing presses, the trilingual Ostroh Academy (teaching in Latin, Greek, and Old Church Slavonic), and Bible translations into Ruthenian (the Ostroh Bible).[101] The most interesting examples are multiconfessional families, such as the Wołłowicz, Holsztański, Chodkiewicz, or Sapieha. There are parallels here to Protestant families that intermarried with Catholics. Like the urban society of Vilnius, they still celebrated and communicated across different festivals, calendars, and theological or doctrinal understandings.

Kazimierz Bem draws our attention to the role of women, many of whom converted to the faith of their husbands, such as the Orthodox Fedora Wołłowicz (d. 1625), who upon her marriage to the palatine of Brest, Krzysztof Zenowicz (1540–1614), adopted his Calvinism, while her Jesuit-educated son later convinced her to join the Greek Catholic Church. Other women were known for steadfastness in their "dissident" faith, even when their husbands and children chose conversion to Catholicism—such as Krystyna Zborowska, the wife of Jan Chodkiewicz (1537–1579). After her husband became a Catholic in 1572, she remained a Calvinist, as did one of her daughters.[102] Bogusław Radziwiłł's cousin Anna Maria, whom he married in 1665, was christened a Catholic, following her mother's faith, but was brought up as a Calvinist by the elector of Brandenburg's sister, the duchess of Courland. Radziwiłł sought a papal dispensation to make sure the marriage was recognized in Catholic circles before he married her in secret, first in a Calvinist ceremony, and a day later in the presence of a Catholic priest.[103]

The religious divisions in the Ruthenian lands were further complicated by the Church Union of Brest of 1596.[104] Michael V. Dmitriev has argued that the union was the result of a fundamental cultural and ideological misunderstanding between Eastern and Latin Christianity, which turned a large part of its original Orthodox supporters into staunch opponents.[105] In the tradition of the 1439 Council of Florence, which had attempted a reunion of the Byzantine Church with Rome, the higher Orthodox clergy had initially supported calls for reform to address dissatisfaction with priests' education, simony, and other grievances against the patriarchs in Constantinople. A majority therefore supported a transfer of authority over the Metropolitanate of Kyiv to Rome, while demanding protection for Eastern-style rituals, liturgy, and theology. Pope Clement VIII and the Roman curia, however, ignored the proposals of the Orthodox to create a union of equals. In the face of the Roman Church's demands for obedience, Dmitriev finds no evidence of meaningful negotiations when the Orthodox embassy arrived in Rome in the autumn of 1595. Ipatiy Potiy (*Pol.* Hipacy Pociej), bishop of the eparchy of Volodymyr-Brest, and Kyrylo Terletskyi (*Pol.* Cyryl Terlecki), bishop of Lutsk and Ostroh (*Pol.* Łuck and Ostróg), signed the act of submission to the pope and a confession of faith that had been prepared for them by Rome, sealing the union of the Orthodox and Roman Churches. The document denounced everything that contradicted the decisions of the Tridentine Councils as heresy and schism.[106]

The synod of Brest in October 1596 confirmed the church union. Instead of healing the tensions within the Orthodox Church, it opened up divisions between the new Uniate or "Greek Catholic" Church and those who now refused to recognize the union with Rome. For its opponents, it was simply not the union they had intended: "unio non est unitas"—these were the words of Petro Mohyla, the later metropolitan of Kyiv, who founded an academy that merged Byzantine and Latin traditions in 1632, thus creating the first institution of higher education among the Orthodox Slavs.[107] In cooperation with Adam Kysil, Mohyla tried to amend the agreement with Rome, but he died in 1646, before he could implement his plans.

The consequences of Brest were far-reaching. Not only did the Orthodox launch an (unsuccessful) attack in 1609 on the life of Potiy, but in 1621 the Uniate bishop of Polatsk, Yosafat Kuntsevych, died at the hands of an Orthodox lynch mob in Viciebsk. The "state without stakes" turned to violence in a hitherto unknown way. While not the only motivation, the discrimination of Orthodoxy also contributed to the grievances of the Cossacks and Ruthenian nobles affiliated with them, paving the way to the devastating Cossack wars from 1648. Despite the 1632 restoration of the Orthodox hierarchy, the abolition of the Union of Brest remained one of the key demands of Bohdan Khmelnytsky (ca. 1595–1657), the leader of the Cossack uprising.[108] During the first half of the seventeenth century, and especially during the Northern Wars, silos of religious intransigence proliferated—and not just on the

Catholic side. The way the Union of Brest was negotiated symbolizes the declining appeal of interconfessionality, a precondition to peaceful multi-confessional coexistence.[109] Many Orthodox priests and bishops continued to support the union with Rome, even at the cost of martyrdom. Ironically, the split between the Orthodox and the Uniates added another denomination, making the Commonwealth even more multiconfessional.

Perhaps the most significant interconfessional cooperation of the first half of the seventeenth century resulted from an alliance between Ortho-dox and Reformed nobility. Prince Ostrogski sent his representatives to the Protestant synods in Thorn in 1595 and in Vilnius in 1599, proposing a confederation under the patronage of the Calvinist branch of the Radziwiłł family and the leader of the Wielkopolska Brethren, Andrzej Leszczyński.[110] The aim was to show solidarity against post-Tridentine Catholicism, against a Uniate Church that the Orthodox considered the usurper of their tradi-tions, and against the claim of papal supremacy. The Orthodox hoped to step up as political partners—as equals among equals—in the confessional conflicts of the age. A promise of mutual political support clinched the deal. While most of the leaders of this cooperative pact were motivated by political pragmatism, some contemplated opportunities for greater religious unity in a multireligious Commonwealth. Ostrogski—always a man of practical deals—gave his daughters in marriage to the Calvinist Krzysztof Mikołaj Radziwiłł "Piorun" (1547–1603) and the Antitrinitarian (Polish Brethren) Jan Kiszka, respectively.[111]

Other interconfessional unions soon followed. Ostrogski was the mater-nal grandfather of Janusz Radziwiłł (1579–1620), who married the Orthodox Sofia Olelkowiczówna (1585–1612). She brought the Belarusian duchy of Slutsk into the family. As palatine of Vilnius, Janusz extended his protection over the city's Orthodox brotherhood, which was embroiled in fierce legal battles with the Uniate metropolitan Potiy. Negotiations led to a written program regulating matters of faith between Orthodox and Protestants in the Grand Duchy's sejmiks, which laid out an agenda of political and juridical equality of all "dissidentes in fide," but failed to gain the approval of the king and the Catholic bishops.[112] In their double roles, here as senators, the bishops could block any legislation in the Sejm. After Janusz's exile and death in 1620, his brother Krzysztof Radziwiłł continued these strong interconfessional re-lations by offering the son of the disestablished Orthodox metropolitan Iov Boretskyi (Pol. Hiob Borecki, 1560–1631) a place at his court for education.[113] Even a generation later, Bogusław Radziwiłł, the last male Calvinist in the family, closely involved himself in the nomination process of Orthodox clergy, including the appointment of a new head of the monastery of the Mother of God in Zabłudów.[114]

This cooperation was not welcomed by Calvinist theologians. The Synod of the Lithuanian Calvinist church banned the construction of Orthodox churches on the land of Reformed nobles, an injunction ostentatiously ignored by the Calvinist Radziwiłłs.[115] In the 1630s, Krzysztof and his son Janusz Radziwiłł (1612–1655)—who through his marriage to Maria Lupula, daughter of the Orthodox Hospodar of Moldavia, had a personal interest in this matter—protected the Orthodox brotherhoods on their properties, not shying away from contacts with the Orthodox Cossacks. The Protestant Radziwiłłs never tolerated Uniates on their estates.

In the 1640s, when the legal position of the Orthodox improved markedly under the reign of Ladislaus IV (r. 1632–1648), Orthodox-Protestant cooperation petered out.[116] Radziwiłł's Calvinist or Antitrinitarian administrators occasionally could not hide their contempt for the local Ruthenian population when they spoke of the "uncivilized" and superstitious "idolomania ruska" (Ruthenian idol mania) of the common people in their correspondence with their patrons.[117] This image of Orthodoxy as a "peasant religion" was also widely shared by Catholics across the Commonwealth.[118] Yet Janusz enjoined one of his clients, the starosta of Birże, not to look down on the Orthodox: "I wish *per gloriam Dei* that in all negotiations you should not forget the dissidents, their liberty of religion and security in the royal and private cities, ours [the Reformed] as well as the Lutherans, Ruthenians, and Antitrinitarians [Ariani]."[119] Notably, he did not call them "prawnosławni" (Orthodox), but rather "Rusini" (Ruthenians), thus referring to their ethnicity rather than to their faith. Multiconfessionalism was closely joined with multiculturalism.

The recognition that the Radziwiłłs afforded the Ruthenian Orthodox led to some interesting hybrid practices. Under Radziwiłł instruction, Calvinist ministers even allowed festivals and celebrations to take place twice, in observance of the Orthodox Church calendar.[120] By 1655, four Orthodox nobles from Ukraine and Belarus still retained seats in the Senate. The last Orthodox senator—Aleksander Ogiński—died in 1667 without being replaced by a coreligionist.[121] At the time of King John Casimir's (r. 1648–1668) abdication, the senate was exclusively composed of Catholics. Henceforth the Sejm demanded that non-Catholic candidates for the Senate had to convert to the Roman or Uniate Church to secure appointment.[122] In practice, despite high expectations, no Uniate bishop gained a seat in the Senate until

1791. Discrimination against Ruthenians would prove costly to the Commonwealth, undermining the expectations awakened by the Union of Lublin and
leading to conflict.

After the Second Northern War (1655–1660), the "process of confederation" was rarely evoked. Increasing unwillingness to "agree to disagree"
undermined the civic spirit of the republic that had animated Bogusław
Radziwiłł's 1645 letter to Petro Mohyla: "As patron and protector in every
place [where there is an Orthodox church], I act as a good citizen."[123] Twenty
years later, it seems, Radziwiłł had forgotten his promise. He opened legal
proceedings against Janusz's widow, Maria Lupula, refusing to recognize her
claim to her husband's starosties and her demands for a return of her dowry.
After her demise in 1660, he contested her bequest to Orthodox convents and
schools in Zabłudów, Slutsk, and Vilnius, accusing her Orthodox confessor
of falsifying her testament.[124] The lawsuit lasted until 1823. The Orthodox
institutions never received the benefices their Moldavian patron intended to
bestow upon them.[125] Interconfessional compromise had gone out of fashion.

Catholicization and Compromise

The Commonwealth's extraordinary multiconfessional nature in the early
modern period was embedded in a multitude of agencies. Confessional policies did not emanate predominantly from a ruler who cooperated with an established territorial or national church, as in the territorial states of the Holy
Roman Empire, in France, or in England. Indeed, Andrzej Sulima Kamiński
has urged us to focus our attention on the politically active citizenry, rather
than the interests of monarch and magnateria.[126] In the absence of strong
church institutions on the German model, this focus should also apply in
matters of faith. Active freedom of religion—not just "toleration"—was the
basis for the dissidents' claim that a free Commonwealth was best secured
when it created a safe space for cultural and religious diversity.

The Vasa kings' (1587–1668) and the episcopate's post-Tridentine agenda
have traditionally come under attack for their support of Catholic confessionalization, discriminatory appointment policies, and inaction in the face
of riots and legal challenges to Protestant property. While they played their
role in the attempt to curb the Commonwealth's multireligious character, the
main work was done by the nobles themselves. In the Sejm and the sejmiks, it
was they who insisted on the execution of the law to expel the Polish Brethren
in 1658 and censured Orthodox-Protestant cooperation; it was the Mazovian

deputies who proposed a ban on Protestants in the Sejm in 1659; and the Sejm passed a prohibition on the ennoblement of non-Catholics in 1673. It was a majority of nobles who expelled Jan Mierzeński from the Chamber of Deputies for his Antitrinitarian views in 1662, and also tried to deny Bogusław Radziwiłł a seat there—while the king, in fact, offered Radziwiłł his protection.[127]

Yet without local interconfessional compromise, the Commonwealth's multiconfessional character, intersecting with its ethnic pluralism and multi-culturalism, would not have survived as long as it did. More research is needed to explore the "stubbornness" of local nobles' opposition to paying the tithe, Protestant burghers' charitable donations to local monasteries, and wives' persistent defiance in the face of their husbands' conversion—all defending their freedom of conscience.[128] At the same time, civic noble society practiced self-government in the running of its religious affairs and "confessionalized" itself in local tribunals and sejmiks. The discourse around the "process of confederation" of 1573 in defense of personal religious choice might have fallen silent under the pressures of the wars of the seventeenth century, but the desire to live and let live according to Orthodox-Ruthenian, Lutheran-German, and Lithuanian-Reformed norms and cultural traditions persisted in niches of local noble and urban agency. While legislation might not have been able to effectively protect interconfessional and multicultural practices over time, it often could not prevent them either.

3

Encounters with Islam within the Commonwealth's Borders and Beyond

Dariusz Kołodziejczyk

After the Second World War, when Poland found itself in its new borders deprived of its large prewar Ukrainian, Jewish, German, and Belarusian minorities, a dominant narrative entered the Polish school curricula that identified the state with the nation as the optimal and "natural" condition. In the following decades, a somewhat unexpected reinforcement of this thesis came from the side of Western academics who linked Weberian bureaucracy, religious uniformity, and enforced social discipline with the rise of modernity, embodied in a nation-state. The Polish-Lithuanian Commonwealth, whose inhabitants had spoken different languages and belonged to different religions and confessions, was thus regarded as an aberration that had been deservedly punished by the partitions for its ineffectiveness as a state and a society.[1] It is only in the late twentieth century, in an atmosphere of accelerating globalization, when the idea of cultural diversity lay at the foundation of the European Union and the notion of cultural uniformity was also challenged in the United States and other postcolonial societies, that historians began to look for inspiration in once despised heterogeneous bodies like the German Reich, Poland-Lithuania, and even early modern empires from Habsburg Spain to Manchu China.[2]

Although many scholars argue that the term "multiculturalism" rather belongs to the present era, as it refers to a genuine acceptance of the other that was unthinkable for early modern humans, the term is nonetheless used in reference to earlier periods, especially in regard to everyday social practice.[3] In an article devoted to Lithuanian Tatars, the young Polish historian Adam Moniuszko defines the Polish-Lithuanian Commonwealth as a "multicultural" state, though he fails to define the term itself.[4]

While not rejecting this term altogether, one must observe that it is open to dispute and that the tolerance of early modern rulers displayed toward heterogeneous subjects was usually articulated in a context of hierarchy and subjection. To invoke an example that is especially familiar to the present author, even scholars who today favorably describe the toleration of Ottoman sultans toward non-Muslim communities admit that this policy merely served to maintain the legitimacy and stability of their empire, and that it was in no way dictated by any moral principles that would imply cultural relativism or an affirmative attitude toward religious dissenters.[5]

This chapter examines the history and development of a Muslim community that has survived under Christian rule in Eastern Europe for several centuries, preserving its religion and identity notwithstanding its ongoing assimilation in many aspects of everyday life and culture. Its history suggests that multiculturalism was possible as a social practice, though it was much less likely to be accepted as a legal concept until the very last years of the eighteenth century and the demise of the Polish-Lithuanian Commonwealth.

Lithuania's Forgotten Heritage

Polish historians have long depicted the history of the Polish-Lithuanian union in terms that can be labeled today as colonial, suggesting a unilateral transfer of institutions and models from the region of a "higher" culture to a less developed one, along with the notion of the Polish *mission civilisatrice* in eastern Europe. However, even if we were to stick to this vision of Polish-Lithuanian relations as colonial, any modern scholar of postcolonialism would suggest that mutual borrowing was inevitable. The Lithuanian Gediminids (later called Jagiellonians) did not arrive in Kraków empty-handed, prepared as a tabula rasa to absorb Polish cultural models after the initial union of 1385. They actively chose what to take and what to reject. The tension between the new rulers and their Polish hosts is perhaps best visible in the monumental chronicle of Jan Długosz (1415–1480), a prominent clergyman and historian from a Polish noble family, who often decried the "stubbornness" of Jogaila (Ladislaus II Jagiełło, grand duke of Lithuania,

1377–1434; king of Poland, 1386–1434), his cousin Vytautas (grand duke of
Lithuania, 1392–1430), and Jogaila's son Casimir IV Jagiellon (grand duke of
Lithuania, 1440–1492; king of Poland, 1447–1492). The latter was Długosz's
own patron, and as ruler he often refused to act in accordance with the expectations of the Polish lords.

After Jogaila's father, Algirdas (grand duke of Lithuania, 1345–1377), extended his realm toward the Black Sea with the tacit consent of the Muslim
ruler of the Golden Horde,[6] Lithuanians had become a pagan minority in the
vast territory of a Grand Duchy peopled mainly by Orthodox Ruthenians.
Religion thus could not serve as a factor cementing the subjects' loyalty to
the dynasty. It had rather to be downplayed, while Lithuanian rulers had to
rely on their personal charisma and the devotion of their closest companions. This model was reminiscent of the neighboring Tatar states of central
Eurasia, whose rulers relied on their Genghisid ancestry rather than on a
common religion shared with their subjects—in this case, Hanefi Sunni
Islam in a "soft," watered-down version. Another parallel can be found in the
early Ottoman state, whose founder, Osman, is depicted by one present-day
scholar as the charismatic leader of a "predatory confederacy," composed of
Muslim and Christian warriors, rather than as a rigid Muslim ruler.[7] When
Jogaila adopted Christianity from Rome in 1386, he maintained—at least in
Lithuania—the dividing line that separated his closest entourage that had
now turned Catholic from the majority of Orthodox subjects. Hence, the
Grand Duchy remained a space in which the ruler did not share a common
confession and faith with his subjects. His authority was rather supported by
dynastic charisma and personal loyalty. In these circumstances, the prominence of Muslim Tatars settled in grand ducal domains, whose service to the
ruler was defined in the categories of group and personal devotion, should
not come as a surprise. A very similar role was played by the Karaites, who
arrived in Lithuania roughly at the same time as the Tatars and were settled
by Vytautas in Trakai at the end of the fourteenth century.

The first major wave of Tatar immigration to the territory of the Grand
Duchy of Lithuania coincided with the invasion of the territory of the Golden
Horde by Timur (1336–1405), in 1395. Tokhtamısh (ca. 1342–1406), its former
khan, found refuge in Lithuania and secured support from Vytautas; yet, after
a failed joint expedition whose aim was to restore Tokhtamısh on the Horde's
throne in 1399, when the allies suffered a crushing defeat on the Vorskla River,
he departed and resolved to try his luck in Siberia. Meanwhile, many of his
supporters settled down in Lithuania, having been granted lands by Vytautas in

return for military service. The fighting between Tokhtamısh's successors over the heritage of the Golden Horde and the control of territories extending from the Volga to the Black Sea continued until the sixteenth century and resulted in further waves of refugees, who found shelter under the grand dukes' protection.[8]

From the very beginning, the legal position of Tatars in the Grand Duchy was different from that in the Polish Crown. Długosz openly lamented that whereas the Tatars who had settled in Poland had cast off the "error of paganism" and become one people with the Poles by accepting the faith of Christ and marrying local women, those who had been settled in Lithuania by Vytautas had remained loyal to the "filthy sect of Muhammad" and lived according to their customs and "detestable rites."[9] The Polish chronicler leaves his reader in no doubt as to which approach he regarded as the right one.

After the defeat of the Teutonic Order at the hands of the diverse Jagiellonian force at the Battle of Grunwald in 1410,[10] Europe became the scene of vigorous polemics in which the order's propagandists accused their enemies of being non-Christian, and certainly non-Catholic. In fact, their accusations were partly true. Apart from Catholic Poles and recently catholicized Lithuanians, the allied coalition consisted of Orthodox Ruthenians, pagan Samogitians, and Muslim Tatars. Prince Djalaleddin (1380–1412), the eldest son of Tokhtamısh, who commanded the Tatar auxiliary troops at Grunwald, was to ascend the throne of the Golden Horde only two years later. The vision of an "ecumenical coalition," consisting of Christians, Muslims, and pagans, who united in order to fight foreign aggressors, may find sympathy in the eyes of a present-day reader, but it was deeply confusing for the royal court in Kraków. In 1414, the best Polish lawyers were sent to the Council of Constance with the task of proving that King Ladislaus II Jagiełło (Jogaila) was a faithful son of the Roman Church. At the same time, they argued that non-Christians and their properties were protected by natural and divine law, meaning that the order's claims to their conquest were null and void. The latter doctrine, developed by Paweł Włodkowic (*Lat.* Paulus Vladimiri, ca. 1370–1435) and formulated in the language of the Roman law taught at Italian universities, in fact expressed the ancient Gediminid tradition.[11]

The Lithuanian Tatars: Their Number, Legal Position, and Socioreligious Organization

In the sixteenth century, the number of Tatars serving in the Lithuanian cavalry had reached 700. Settled in grand ducal estates, they probably numbered, along with their families, around 4,000 people. In addition, around 1,500 Tatars lived in Lithuanian towns, earning a living as craftsmen (especially tanners) and petty traders.[12] Over a dozen mosques had been constructed in Lithuania by 1600, including one in the ancient capital of Trakai and another in a suburb of Vilnius. Their number more than doubled in the following century.[13] In 1569, Lithuania was forced to cede the palatinates of Podlachia, Volhynia, Bratslav, and Kyiv to the Polish Crown, and thus local Tatars found themselves under the direct rule of the Polish kings. Hence, only from this point on can one maintain that Muslims were legally permitted to dwell in Poland.[14] In the seventeenth century, Tatars also began to settle in Podolia, which had belonged to Poland since the fifteenth century.

Muslim Tatars were not only allowed to dwell in Lithuania and build mosques. The members of their highest strata, who enjoyed hereditary rights to their lands that had been granted by the ruler in return for military service, aspired to noble status.[15] They boasted of aristocratic ancestry, often derived from the Genghisid dynasty and the most prominent clans of the Mongol Empire, proudly displaying their coats of arms.[16]

Over thirty years ago, the historian Jacek Sobczak persuasively demonstrated that from the purely legal point of view, Tatar claims to noble status were unfounded. The lands held by the Tatars remained inalienable without the ruler's consent, unlike the lands held by ordinary Lithuanian nobles. In contrast to the latter, who were required to report for war only when a *levée en masse* was formally announced by the monarch with the authorization of noble assemblies, Tatars who served under separate banners were called to arms more frequently, solely upon the ruler's order.[17] The fines for murdering a Tatar were lower than those imposed for the murder of a noble, and testimony provided by a Tatar was not given the same credence as a noble's testimony, even though in the latter two aspects the late seventeenth-century legislation strove to put Tatars on an equal footing with the nobles. Most importantly, the Tatars were deprived of noble political rights and barred from participation in sejmiks, the Sejm, and royal elections.[18]

Andrzej Zakrzewski concurs with Sobczak in regard to political and purely legal aspects, while observing that local practice often differed from the letter of law. In theory, the Tatars were barred from purchasing alienable noble lands, but there is abundant evidence that this prohibition was disregarded. On the other hand, Tatars often sold their lands to noble Christian neighbors without the ruler's consent, and the new owners ignored the special obligations that were linked with their new holdings. Accordingly, the

blurring of the distinction between conditional and unconditional landown-
ership was in the interest of both parties. Tatars also appeared in courts as
witnesses, and their testimony was usually accepted. As long as the relations
between Christian nobles and their Tatar neighbors remained peaceful, the
former regarded the latter as fellow nobles, even if somewhat inferior in rank
and of different religion. However, this attitude would change in the case of
conflicts, and the atmosphere of the Counter-Reformation contributed to
growing tensions from the beginning of the seventeenth century.[19]

Tatars found powerful patrons in the Polish-Lithuanian rulers, who often
disregarded the canon laws that barred "infidels" from attaining elevated
ranks that would give them jurisdiction over Christians. In the sixteenth
century, King Sigismund I (r. 1506–1548) relied heavily on the services of
Ibrahim Tymirčyn (alias Tymirčyc), who was sent on several embassies to
the Great Horde and Crimea. When his position was questioned by members
of other Tatar families who had settled in Lithuania earlier, Ibrahim procured
documents that confirmed his pedigree from the rulers of both neighboring
Tatar khanates, Sheikh Ahmad (r. 1465–1481) and Mengli Giray (r. 1466,
1469–1475, 1478–1515), even though the two were mortal enemies. On the basis of these documents, Sigismund granted land and noble status to Ibrahim
and his descendants.[20] In the late seventeenth century, Lithuanian Tatars
found a powerful patron in the person of King John III Sobieski (r. 1674–
1696), who not only forgave their desertion to the Ottoman Empire during
the campaign of 1672 and induced them to return to the Commonwealth, but,
in 1679, granted them extensive lands in the royal domains of Brest, Kobryn,
and Hrodna (now in Belarus; *Pol.* Brześć, Kobryń, and Grodno). A century
later, in 1766, King Stanislaus II Augustus resolved to nominate a Muslim
Tatar colonel, Józef Bielak, to the post of major general, but the Lithuanian
military commission refused his request on the grounds that the nominee
was not a Catholic. It took the king several years to persuade his opponents,
and the promotion effectively took place only in 1790,[21] just in time to give
Bielak an opportunity to play an important role in the Polish–Russian War
of 1792 and in the uprising led by Tadeusz Kościuszko in 1794.

One might expect that the harshest anti-Islamic measures would have
been instigated by the Catholic Church. Yet the reality was not that simple. Some clergymen indeed opted for a forceful conversion of Muslims or
their expulsion from the Commonwealth—for instance, Benedykt Wojna,
the bishop of Vilnius (*Pol.* Wilno) in the years 1600–1615, whose anti-Tatar
stand was praised by Piotr Czyżewski in his famous anti-Tatar pamphlet.[22]

However, Muslims were also settled in the lands of the bishopric of Vilnius and carried out various policing duties, such as detaining runaway peasants and serving in the bishops' militia. We find them performing these tasks in both the sixteenth and eighteenth centuries.[23]

The construction of a mosque required royal authorization, although initially this rule was not strictly observed. Canon law also required that when constructing a synagogue, Jews needed authorization from a local bishop. This rule was extended to Muslims. In regard to the Tatars settled on the private estates of Lithuanian magnates, such as the powerful Radziwiłł family, the local lord also had a say in this matter. Finally, in 1668, the Sejm passed a new law that explicitly forbade the building of new mosques, only permitting the restoration of ancient ones.[24] This law closely resembled the rule applied to Christian churches in the Ottoman Empire, which also permitted the restoration of ancient churches while forbidding the construction of new ones.[25] In both countries, such restrictions often remained a dead letter.

Each Tatar community (*dżemiat*) elected its imam, who was also locally known as *mołła* or *mołna* (mullah). In larger communities, the imam could have a deputy, who apparently performed the role of a muezzin.[26] Muslim clergymen were provided for by local donations and tithes, and even Christian peasants settled in Tatar villages are known to have paid tithes to maintain the local *mołła*. In the eighteenth century, Tatar mullahs were also formally employed in the Lithuanian army on an equal footing with Christian chaplains.[27] Moreover, in the sixteenth century, we encounter the position of head judge of Lithuanian Muslims, appointed by the grand duke. For instance, in 1586, this post was filled by Dervish Chelebi, who is referred to in a later document of 1594 as "the cadi of all the Tatars of the Grand Duchy of Lithuania" (*kadyj vsikh tatar Velikogo kniazstva Litovskogo*).[28] In their internal disputes, Lithuanian Tatars could also seek justice in the Sharia courts of neighboring Muslim states, the Crimean Khanate and the Ottoman Empire, although this possibility was limited by distance or prevented by military conflicts, especially frequent in the turbulent seventeenth century.[29]

The Impact of Foreign Policy on the Situation of Muslims in Poland-Lithuania

The attitudes of Polish-Lithuanian rulers toward Muslim clergymen were conditioned by external as well as domestic factors. This is clearly visible from a letter that King Sigismund I sent, in 1510, to Hadji Baba Sheikh, the head mullah at the court of Mengli Giray. Fearing that the Crimean khan might break his promise to keep peace, Sigismund appealed to his moral guide in the person of the Muslim sheikh, whom he referred to in another letter as the Crimean ruler's archbishop (*achiepiscopus imperatoris*), asking him to hold the khan and his retinue members to their oath: "I have heard of you as a spiritual person at [the court of] the great khan, Mengli Giray, so that the khan and the princes could not lie to you."[30] The conviction that every human being needed moral guidance in the divine law was almost universal in early modern Europe. Ideally, this guide should have belonged to one's own confession, but apparently the Jagiellonian monarchs believed that even "infidels" would behave better if guided by their own shepherds, and this belief must have applied to their own Muslim subjects as well. Six-teenth-century correspondence between the Jagiellonian and Giray courts also reveals a sound mutual acquaintance with their respective religious calendars and invocations. While the khan could invoke Jesus and the Virgin Mary in his letter addressed to the king, the Lithuanian chancery at Vilnius required that the khan's solemn oath to keep the mutual peace invoke the Prophet Muhammad and contain the standard Arabic formula for such oaths, *vallahi billahi tallahi*.[31]

The Jagiellonian policy toward their Tatar subjects was further mitigated by the presence of a powerful neighbor on Poland-Lithuania's southern border, namely, the Ottoman Empire. A persecution of Lithuanian Muslims might have served as a pretext for Ottoman invasion, just as the persecution of English Catholics contributed to the invasion of the Spanish Armada.

In 1558, three Lithuanian Tatars performed a pilgrimage to Mecca, making a stopover in the Ottoman capital. They were received by Grand Vizier Rustem Pasha (ca. 1500–1561), who asked them to describe the situation of Lithuanian Muslims in a report that was submitted to Sultan Suleyman (r. 1520–1566). The report, penned in Ottoman Turkish with the assistance of Ottoman scribes, was discovered and published in 1858 by Antoni Muchliński, a professor of Oriental languages at Saint Petersburg Imperial University.[32] The very fact of its existence indicates that the Porte was highly interested in the fate of Muslims who lived beyond the Ottoman "well-protected domains." Its content has been analyzed by Michael Połczyński, who observes that by extolling the sultan's patronage over all Sunni Muslims performing the pilgrimage to Mecca, the report served as a tool for internally legitimizing the authority of the Ottoman padishah.[33] Yet Połczyński fails to explain why Rustem Pasha, who—along with his wife Mihrimah—was credited for his efforts to maintain peace with Poland-Lithuania, should have instigated a report that openly proposed its invasion and the extension of Ottoman rule onto the local Tatars.[34] It is nonetheless apparent that the Porte was prepared to use its concern about the fate of Lithuanian Muslims in its negotiations with Kraków and Vilnius, either as a pretext for war or as a condition for maintaining peace.[35]

After the extinction of the Jagiellonian dynasty, the Ottomans consistently supported anti-Habsburg candidates to the Polish throne and maintained peaceful relations with the first elective kings: Henry de Valois (r. 1573–1575) and Stephen Báthory (r. 1576–1586). Sigismund III Vasa (r. 1587–1632) also initially enjoyed Ottoman support, but the first years of his reign brought a crisis in mutual relations.[36] The peace was formally restored in 1591, yet the sultan's solemn treaty document ('ahdname) was accompanied by a separate letter, in which Murad III (r. 1574–1595) required that Sigismund allow his Tatar subjects to build a Friday mosque in a suitable site so that they could perform solemn Islamic prayers on the occasion of religious feasts. From the letter's content, we learn that it was issued on the request of two Lithuanian Tatars who had joined the royal embassy to the Porte. The sultan gave them his formal permission to perform Islamic rites in their settlements and to invoke his name in their prayers, thus acting as their sovereign and—in consequence—as the overlord of the Polish king. We might concur with Jan Tyszkiewicz that this letter, whose tenor was unprecedented, served as an informal appendix to the newly concluded treaty.[37]

If the sultan's letter was intended to improve the situation of Polish-Lithuanian Muslims, it did not bring the desired effect. The reign of Sigismund III brought rising intolerance toward non-Catholics as the king strove to strengthen his power by introducing the policy of the Counter-Reformation. Although this policy was primarily directed against Protestants—regarded as the major obstacle to the royal plans due to their greater numbers, affluence, and political influence—the new measures also affected other religious and confessional groups. In 1605, the situation of Lithuanian Tatars became still worse after the death of Chancellor Jan Zamoyski, known as an advocate of cooperation with the Ottoman Porte.

In 1609, a hostile mob destroyed the mosque in Trakai, and in the same year several Tatar women were accused of witchcraft and executed in Vilnius, whose bishopric was then held by Benedykt Wojna, known for his opposition to the construction of mosques in Lithuania. Soon after the death of Wojna, another mosque was burned down in Salkininkai (*Pol.* Solkieniki) by a local noble.[38] In 1613, Tatars were banned from holding officer ranks in the Polish-Lithuanian army except for their own units, and in 1616 the Sejm not only confirmed an earlier law that forbade the Muslims to keep Christian servants and maids but also declared that a marriage between a Muslim man and a Christian woman would be punished by death, although it does not seem that this law was ever put into effect.[39] The following year brought an infamous anti-Tatar pamphlet by Piotr Czyżewski that was also republished in 1640 and 1643.[40] The author's identity is uncertain, and it is unclear whether he penned the work because his father had been killed by a Tatar neighbor (as he maintains in the preface), or rather that his publication was sponsored by the Jesuits, whose pamphlets were often printed by the same Vilnius publisher.[41] Czyżewski advocated the destruction of all Tatar mosques in Poland-Lithuania. He was also ready to respond to the counterargument that Christian churches were allowed to function in the Ottoman Empire. According to Czyżewski, the Turks were newcomers in lands that had earlier been Christian, so the preservation of the Christian faith in these lands was natural and just, whereas the Tatars had arrived in a Christian land and their mosques should not be tolerated.[42] Czyżewski's pamphlet received a response in a treatise titled *Apologia Tatarów*, published in 1630 by a Lithuanian Tatar named Azulewicz, though this work has not survived to the present day.[43]

During the seventeenth century, numerous Lithuanian Tatars were settled in the southern provinces of the Polish Crown, serving as guards against Cossack rebellions and the raids of Crimean Tatars and Nogays. Tatar soldiers also participated in the campaigns against Sweden (1655–1660) and Russia (1654–1667), some of them even ending up in Russian Siberia as prisoners of war. However, when the war was over, the treasury was unable to pay the arrears, causing great unrest in the army. Tatar soldiers were additionally frustrated by new anti-Muslim measures. In 1666 and 1667, the Sejmik of Halych (*Pol.* Halicz) repeatedly forbade the building of mosques in the Palatinate of Ruthenia, and in 1668 the Sejm outlawed the construction of new mosques in the entire Polish-Lithuanian Commonwealth.[44] These measures coincided with rising tensions between the Commonwealth and its Muslim neighbors, first the Crimean Khanate, and then also the Ottoman Empire. On the eve of the Ottoman invasion of Poland in 1672, a few detachments of Lithuanian Tatars changed sides and joined the sultan's army. One of their commanders, Aleksander Kryczyński, was rewarded with the governorship of Bar in the new Ottoman province of Podolia. The 1672 Treaty of Buchach (*Pol.* Buczacz) provided for a free passage of all Lithuanian Tatars, along with their families and movables, from the Commonwealth to the sultan's lands. Hence, with a little assistance from the noble legislative bodies, the most dreaded nightmare of possible treason by the local Muslims came true, though only a minority chose to emigrate and most of the Lithuanian Tatars remained in the Commonwealth. In the following years, many of the recent emigrants resolved to return, encouraged by the newly elected king John III Sobieski.[45]

After the Treaty of Karlowitz (1699), Polish-Ottoman relations remained peaceful for the entire eighteenth century. The Lithuanian Tatars, who now lived on both sides of the border, could freely maintain contacts with their relatives and travel in both directions. Some of them served alternately in the Ottoman provincial troops under the governor of Khotyn (*Pol.* Chocim) and in the Polish-Lithuanian army, or in the private troops of powerful Polish magnates, especially the Potocki family, thus acting as model cross-cultural and transborder brokers.[46]

The Intellectual life of Polish-Lithuanian Tatars and Their Role in Interreligious Discourse

In a text published in 2004, the present author expressed his skepticism regarding the impact of Lithuanian Tatars on religious discourse in early modern Poland-Lithuania, pointing to the small size and mostly rural character of their diaspora, whose members largely exhibited military rather than intellectual skills. The argument also invoked the Tatars' inadequate command of Arabic, Persian, and Ottoman-Turkish, the major vernaculars of Islamic high culture, and their limited access to higher education. As I then suggested, these conditions had resulted in the rather plebeian character of the Tatars' literary heritage, preserved in the so-called *kitabs*—books of typically religious content in the Belarusian and Polish languages recorded in the Arabic script.[47] This opinion was supported by Andrzej Zakrzewski, who stressed the role of the large distance that separated Lithuanian Tatars from the major centers of Islamic learning and the lack of individuals capable of invigorating their religious life.[48]

However, it seems that this judgment was premature and too harsh. In the same year, 2004, Andrzej Drozd published an article devoted to a recent discovery of the oldest translation of the Koran into Polish, preserved in the library of the Belarusian National Academy of Sciences in Minsk. Its colophon, penned in Turkish and published by Drozd, refers to the date and place where the manuscript was copied, namely, the month of Muharram 1098 AH (November 17–December 16, 1686), in Minsk.[49] The colophon also refers to the Koran's translator—Urjasz ibn Isma'il, the Tatar imam of Minsk.[50] Drozd initially argued that Urjasz did not have to be identical with the manuscript's copyist and that the translation had actually been prepared many decades earlier.[51] However, in a 2017 article, he accepts the year 1686 as the date of its completion.[52] The Minsk manuscript contains the Arabic text of the Koran and its interlinear translation (*tefsir*): the *surah*s nos. 2–18 are translated into Turkish, and the *surah*s nos. 19–114 into Polish, recorded in the Arabic script. At present, it is the oldest extant translation of the Koran into a Slavic language.[53] A comparison with the contents of Tatar religious manuscripts of more recent times indicates that this translation had been in use into the twentieth century, even though a more recent Polish translation of the Koran was published in Vilnius in 1858.[54]

The creation of the *tefsir* in Minsk, one of the major towns of the Grand Duchy of Lithuania, suggests the existence of a vibrant urban Muslim community whose members were apparently active in crafts and horticulture.[55] On the basis of the fragments of the work published so far, one may conclude that the Minsk *tefsir* is a masterpiece of early modern Polish. If we think of the role played by the vernacular translations of the Bible in the development of early modern nations, Protestant as well as Catholic, Urjasz ibn Isma'il should be given due credit for his translation of the Muslims' most holy book into Polish, even if we know nothing of his whereabouts apart from his name, recorded in the colophon. One intriguing aspect is the translator's borrowing from the vocabulary of Polish Unitarians, which is best reflected by his rendering of the Arabic term *mušrikūna* (مشركون), referring to "polytheists," with the Polish term *trójczanie* ("trinitarians"), with which the Unitarians referred to their Catholic, Lutheran, and Calvinist adversaries.[56]

The familiarity of Lithuanian Tatars with the writings of Unitarians, also known in that period as Polish Brethren, Arians, and Antitrinitarians, is best demonstrated by a copy of the Unitarian Bible (the so-called *Biblia Nieświeska* or *Niasvižskaja Biblija* in Polish and Belarusian, respectively), translated into Polish and published in 1572, that is today preserved in the University of Warsaw Library. In its margins, the copy contains numerous comments in the Arabic script, in Polish as well as in Turkish, and several Koranic citations, which altogether suggest that its Tatar owners had seriously studied the Old and New Testaments, looking for analogies as well as differences in comparison with Muslim teaching. Szymon Budny (ca. 1530–1593; *Bel. Sy-*

mon Budny), the translator and editor of the Unitarian Bible, was a Hebraist and a prominent leader of the Polish Brethren, who spent most of his life in the Grand Duchy of Lithuania under the protection of the Radziwiłł family. He was especially active in Kleck, Vilnius, and Trakai, so he may also have maintained personal contacts with local Muslims.[57]

In his painstaking studies on the early modern religious literature of Lithuanian Tatars, Andrzej Drozd has found arguments directed against Saint Jerome and his Latin translation of the Bible, against the Polish Jesuit translation of the Bible penned by Jakub Wujek and published in 1599, and even against Saint Augustine, whom the Tatar authors accused of distorting the Holy Scripture.[58] By questioning the idea of the Holy Trinity and the belief that Jesus was the son of God, and by criticizing the rule of celibacy among Catholic clergymen, the Polish-Lithuanian-Muslim writers followed in the footsteps of radical Protestant theologians. However, their arguments were also based on independent readings, revealing the authors' familiarity with the Koran, the Bible, and with some Polish contemporary authors, including the Renaissance poet Jan Kochanowski (1530–1584).[59]

With the passing of time, Tatar writers gradually adopted the vocabulary of the Polish nobility, including some baroque stereotypes, so that their writings include expressions of admiration for Mars and the Virgin Mary, along with contempt for Mercury, the Jews, and the Lutherans.[60] With the aim of endearing themselves to Polish-Lithuanian nobles, the Tatars represented the Prophet Muhammad as coming from a noble and princely family, while identifying his language—and consequently the language of the Koran—with the Chaldean that was especially venerated by the writers of the Polish Renaissance. In their texts, recorded in the Arabic script, we also find loanwords of Latin and German origin, such as *rejestra* ("registers"), *dekret* ("decree"), *intrata* ("revenue"), and *jurgielt* ("annual salary"), as well as common Polish honorifics such as *Waszmość* ("Your Excellency"), *Mości Panowie* ("Your Excellencies"), and even *Prorok Jego Miłość* ("His Excellency, the Prophet").[61]

The very choice of the language(s) in which the Tatars recorded their literary works reflected their efforts to integrate within the upper strata of the adoptive society. While Ruthenian (Old Belarusian) formally functioned as the official chancery language of the Grand Duchy of Lithuania until 1697, it was gradually replaced by Polish, especially among the upper nobility, followed by middle and lesser nobles and some inhabitants of the towns. Hence, it is symptomatic that while most of the Lithuanian Tatar literature was recorded in Belarusian and Polish almost interchangeably, the Koran was translated solely into Polish, suggesting the more prestigious status of this language.[62]

Multilingualism was a characteristic feature of the culture of Lithuanian Tatars. Although they had lost their original Tatar Kipchak language, probably by the early seventeenth century, they maintained contacts with the Muslim world and retained the Arabic script until the nineteenth century. Some of them knew Arabic and Turkish, also in writing.[63] At the same time, they were adopting the languages of their environment, first Ruthenian and then also Polish.[64]

In his evaluation of the early modern literature of the Lithuanian Tatars, Drozd observes that they were well integrated into Polish-Lithuanian society and that the earlier opinions of their cultural isolation have proved false. He also notes that the era of the Renaissance and Reformation that invigorated social, religious, and cultural life in the Commonwealth also activated and inspired the local Muslims, whose literary products can be classified as oscillating between plebeian and noble culture.[65]

Contacts and mutual inspirations between Christians and Muslims were naturally not limited to Poland-Lithuania, although its territory played a special role in this dialogue. In 1570, a German Unitarian theologian, Adam Neuser, was forced to flee from Heidelberg, finding a temporary safe haven in the Commonwealth. In 1572, he arrived in the Ottoman Empire, where he converted to Islam, having discovered a close relationship between his new religion and the one he had preached at home. In a letter sent from Istanbul to Kraków, addressed to Simon Ronemberg, a prominent Polish Antitrinitarian, he disclosed his new identity by signing his name as *Adamus Neuser nunc Mustafa begh.*[66]

A hundred years later, one of the most important cultural brokers between Christian Europe and the Islamic world, who corresponded with scholars in Leiden and Oxford, recorded Ottoman music, left us a unique description of the Topkapı Palace, and translated the Old and New Testaments into Turkish, was Wojciech Bobowski, a former Polish captive who made a career at the sultan's court.[67]

In their influential monograph stimulated by the idea of the spatial turn, published in 1997, Martin Lewis and Kären Wigen propose that "the cleavage between Christendom and Islam is the shallowest of the major divisions across the ecumene in the premodern world. Professing sibling Abrahamic faiths and sharing a common Hellenic intellectual heritage, Christians and Muslims are historically united by broad social and philosophical common-

alities. . . . While Rome and Mecca represent two distinctive varieties of human culture, both belong to the same phylogenetic order and even the same
family."[68] Formulated shortly after the publication of Samuel Huntington's
Clash of Civilizations (1996), in an atmosphere that would soon produce the
September 11 attacks and the "war on terror," the above thesis might have
sounded odd to many readers at the time. However, it would probably have
been less surprising to many inhabitants of early modern Poland-Lithuania.
Admittedly, anti-Islamic pamphlets, the so-called *Turcica*,[69] were present in
large numbers on the Commonwealth's book market, as was the case in other
states of Christian Europe. Yet, in contrast to propagandist slogans that presented Poland as the "Bulwark of Christianity," frequently invoked in internal discourse as well as in foreign correspondence (especially with Rome and
Vienna), the policy of the Polish court and the attitude of Polish-Lithuanian
nobles toward Muslim neighbors, both domestic and external, were highly
pragmatic. Even the seventeenth century, the age of the Counter-Reformation
and confessionalization, saw only twenty-five years of Polish-Ottoman military conflicts, whereas in the same century the Commonwealth waged wars
with Sweden and Russia that lasted over thirty years each.[70]

The Legacy of the Muslim Diaspora after the Commonwealth

The position of Muslims in Poland-Lithuania, which—with the exception
of Muscovy—did not find any comparison in early modern Europe, was
largely owed to the tradition of Lithuanian statehood. In an article titled
"The Glass Ceiling of Lithuanian Tatars," Andrzej Zakrzewski observes
that it was precisely on the eve of the Union of Lublin, in the years 1563 and
1568, that the Tatars and Orthodox Lithuanian nobles parted ways in regard
to their legal and political position. By passing a series of new laws, King
Sigismund II Augustus lifted the last barriers internally dividing the Lithuanian nobility and granted Orthodox nobles the rights of their Catholic peers.
At the same time, he made them equal with Polish nobles. Yet he could not
do the same for the Tatars because they were not Christians.[71] Hence the
process of polonization of Lithuanian culture, including legal culture, was
not necessarily beneficial for the local Muslims.

In his study on Lithuanian Tatars, published in 1938, Stanisław Kryczyński made the important observation that, in Lithuania, mosques and Muslim
cemeteries were as old as Catholic churches, and sometimes even older.[72]
With its pagan heritage, predominantly Orthodox population, and newly

introduced Catholic institutions, Lithuania formed a loosely defined space between the Catholic, Orthodox, and Muslim worlds—a "middle ground," to invoke the term coined by Richard White in regard to another corner of the world.[73] This space, where neither side could fully dictate its terms to the other, also provided a safe haven for other religious groups, to mention only Karaites and Jews.

The creation of the Polish-Lithuanian Commonwealth in 1569 strengthened the role of the Catholic Church. Yet the Polish nobles' legal freedoms also had an impact on their Lithuanian peers, and the ideas of the Reformation deeply penetrated the new state's eastern provinces. Although the legal position of Lithuanian Muslims worsened and they were never able to fully extend their privileges into the Polish Crown, they nonetheless managed to preserve their faith until the Commonwealth's demise in 1795.

In her recent study on interreligious relations in the Ottoman Empire, Eleni Gara proposed to adopt a bottom-up perspective in order to shed light on everyday social practice.[74] In regard to the Lithuanian Tatars, the same method is applied by Andrzej Zakrzewski, who focuses on legal practice and everyday relations between Muslim and Christian neighbors, concluding that with the latter's consent and cooperation it was possible to bypass many discriminatory regulations.[75] There is ample evidence showing that relations between Muslims and Christians were often quite cordial, not only on the battlefield, where Lithuanian Tatars served side by side with Christian nobles and soldiers, but also in everyday life. One example can be drawn from the court register of Trakai. In 1646, Khava Tamovna Aleevichova, a Tatar widow and local resident, called to her deathbed "her friends and neighbors, Christians as well as Muslims,"[76] so that they might give testimony to her will. Admittedly, the term "friend" (*pryiatel'*) had a somewhat different meaning in seventeenth-century language, but the fact that a Muslim woman used it in reference to her Christian neighbors is nonetheless telling.

Having studied secular sources reflecting the military service, economic activity, and legal lawsuits of Lithuanian Tatars, Zakrzewski confirms the findings of Drozd in his work on Tatar religious literature. Both scholars observe a gradual cultural assimilation of Lithuanian Tatars into local society, reflected in their language, customs, and the syncretic elements entering their religion.[77] This syncretism was perhaps best visualized in the banner of a unit of Lithuanian Tatars that was captured by Swedish troops in the war of 1655–1660: on its black background, we can see a crescent, a cross, and the double bladed sword of the Prophet Muhammad—Zulfiqar.[78]

The most idealized image of the Polish-Lithuanian Commonwealth as a space of peaceful and friendly Christian-Muslim cohabitation can be dated back to the nineteenth century. After the partitions, the writers of Polish Romanticism glorified the common past and depicted the brotherhood that had once united Polish and Tatar nobles in their struggle against external enemies. Ironically, it was precisely in the post-partition era that Tatars actually became full-fledged nobles thanks to the legal reforms introduced by the same Russian Empire that remained the archenemy of Polish nationalists. In the first half of the nineteenth century, Muslim land owners were granted the full rights of Russian nobles, and after the Polish January Uprising of 1863–1864 their legal position became even better than that of Catholic nobles.[79]

Later, in interwar Poland (1918–1939), the authorities exhibited a highly favorable attitude toward the Tatar diaspora, in sharp contrast to their attitude toward the Ukrainian, Jewish, and German minorities. Due to their dispersal and small number, the Tatars did not present a challenge to the territorial integrity of the state; neither were their representatives visible in radical political movements. In fact, the legal protection of tiny minorities considered as innocuous and loyal, such as the Tatars or Karaites, served as a convenient face-saving device, used by the government to demonstrate its tolerance and benevolence.[80] Both before and after the Second World War, the presence of an ancient Muslim diaspora in Poland could also bring image benefits in political and economic relations with Muslim states. Accordingly, the development of these relations positively shaped Warsaw's attitude toward local Muslims.[81]

In present-day Poland, the memory of the centuries-long presence of Muslim communities on its soil is undoubtedly beneficial for deconstructing the negative image of Islam that is sadly omnipresent on the internet and in media. On the other hand, the fact that a group of Muslims could live for centuries in a Christian country without losing its identity and faith flies in the face of those Islamist radicals who argue that the cohabitation of Christians and Muslims in present-day Europe inescapably leads to the latter's cultural uprooting.

Yet there is also a darker side. By uncritically invoking the idealized image of past interconfessional relations, the nationalist politicians and their supporters strive to maintain the image of Poles as being exclusively tolerant and unable to commit any harm, preventing a serious reexamination of Poland's complicated past, including Poles' relations with their neighbors, domestic as well as external. The continued existence of the Tatar diaspora also serves as a convenient excuse whenever the present government refuses to accept refugees and new immigrants.[82] In this vein, a nationalist politician can claim that nobody should lecture on tolerance to the Poles, because centuries ago, when western Europe was a nest of religious persecution, Poland was the cradle of tolerance. Alas, some Polish Tatars have recently entered this game and one can hear voices differentiating between "our own, peaceful Muslims" and "foreign radical Muslims," who should be barred from entering the country. One can only observe that this is a time-honored strategy often used by old immigrants, who tend to forget their own past, against new immigrants, and that it will probably pass with time.

Notwithstanding its current abuse in political debate, the fact that Christians and Muslims lived for centuries in neighborly relations in the territories of Poland-Lithuania, that the Koran was translated into Polish, and that references to the Polish Renaissance poet Jan Kochanowski can be found in the writings of Polish-Lithuanian-Tatar Muslims, indisputably reflect a vivid past multiculturalism, though this should not be confused with myths of equality, harmony, and "tolerance." Perhaps this positive history can help revise the still widespread dark image of the Commonwealth as a failed state and a cradle of fanaticism and anarchy.

4

Art and Transcultural Discourse in the Ukrainian Lands of the Polish-Lithuanian Commonwealth

Olenka Z. Pevny

"For as once one of the Egyptian monarchs said, 'Our Egypt is heaven'; proclaim in a thunderous voice 'Our Kyiv is heaven!'"—so states the second introduction to the 1635 Polish-language publication of the *Paterikon, or the Lives of the Holy Fathers of the Caves* (*Paterikòn abo Zywoty SS. Oycow Pieczarskich*), a collection of stories about the medieval monks of Kyiv's leading monastery.[1] The text, compiled by Sylvestr Kosiv (*Pol.* Sylwester Kossów; d. 1657) at the request of Petro Mohyla (*Pol.* Piotr Mohyła; 1596–1647), the Orthodox Metropolitan of Kyiv, Halych, and All Rus' from 1633 to 1647, positions Kyiv as a center of Christianity and parallels the city with the universe within which all heavenly bodies turn. To begin to decipher the significance of the quoted passage and the importance it assigns to Kyiv, one must grapple with the transcultural discourses that defined early modern Ukrainian culture. This chapter does just that, focusing on the polyvalent, fluctuating, continuous, and overlapping interactions among cultures that both shaped and were shaped by the distinctiveness of Kyiv's early seventeenth-century art and architecture.

At the center of the chapter stands not the *Paterikon*, but the Church of the Savior on the Berestovo Hill in Kyiv (figs. 4.1 and 4.2),[2] built in the late eleventh or early twelfth century and renewed in the 1640s under the patronage of Metropolitan Mohyla. The palimpsest of frescoes and architecture

Figure 4.1. Exterior view of the Church of the Savior on the Berestovo Hill in Kyiv, Ukraine. Photo by Olenka Z. Pevny, 2018.

that constitutes today's Church of the Savior offers insight into various periods of Ukraine's history. However, it is the visual forms of the early modern period, with their locally determined social logic, that this chapter explores. The full spectrum of connotations that the early modern architecture and imagery of the Church of the Savior held for its primary viewers remains inaccessible; nevertheless, architectural and visual parallels, literary sources, archival records, texts, and documents connected with Metropolitan Mohyla, inform us of the cultural and intellectual discourses that conditioned the designs of the patron, as well as the expectations of his inner circle and early modern viewers.

After 1569, at the end of a period of dramatic and rapid political, religious, and cultural change in the Polish-Lithuanian Commonwealth, multiple and fluctuating inflections of Ruthenian-Rus' identity coexisted within regions, communities, and among individuals. The manifestations of these situational

Figure 4.2. Interior view of the sanctuary in the Church of the Savior on the Berestovo Hill in Kyiv, Ukraine. Photo by Ivan Vasylovych Krezhenstovskyi. Reproduced by permission from Olenka Z. Pevny.

identifications involved measures of self-revelation as well as self-concealment expressed and interpreted within arising constellations of cultural and social imperatives. The seventeenth-century renewal of Church of the Savior attests to the kaleidoscopic vigor that characterized Ruthenian-Rus' culture in early modern Kyiv.[3] From the amorphous ruins of a medieval church, Metropolitan Mohyla brought to life a sacred space that linked the contemporary reformation of the Ruthenian-Rus' Church with Kyiv's medieval Christian beginnings. In doing so, Mohyla aspired to advance the status of Eastern Christianity and of the Ruthenian-Rus' nation in the Polish-Lithuanian state, which increasingly identified with Roman Catholicism and was known as the Commonwealth of Both Nations, thus symbolically enfranchising only the "Polish" and "Lithuanian" nations. Mohyla, a descendant of the Movilă boyars of Moldavia, was a member of the Commonwealth's noble nation and held the legal rights and privileges of "Golden Liberty."[4] He was also an Eastern Christian rising through the ecclesiastical ranks of the "non-united" Ruthenian-Rus' Church at a time when this church was prohibited in the Commonwealth as a consequence of the 1596 Union of Brest, which had "united" part of Ruthenian-Rus' Eastern Christians with Rome, thus creating the legally sanctioned Uniate Church.[5] Mohyla's close associate, Adam Kysil (*Pol.* Adam Kisiel; ca. 1600–1653), another nobleman, who was the only Orthodox member from the Kingdom of Poland in the influential assembly of the Senate from 1639 until Mohyla's death, held various key administrative posts in the Commonwealth, and identified as a Ruthenian-Rus' "Sarmatian."[6] While embracing the collective "Sarmatian" ancestry of the Commonwealth's nobility, Kysil traced his familial line to Kyiv's medieval Rus' past, and, like Mohyla, was an Eastern Christian of the "non-united" Ruthenian-Rus' Church.[7] Both men were at once insiders and outsiders in the context of the Commonwealth's different social and cultural milieus and accentuated different aspects of their identity as they deemed appropriate in given situations. Both highly valued their legal entitlements as part of the noble nation, and both were aware of the inequitable status of the Eastern Church with respect to the Catholic Church and of the Ruthenian-Rus' nation in comparison to the Polish and Lithuanian nations of the Commonwealth. Dedicated to the well-being of their collective homeland, they used procedural power to assert the integral position of the Eastern Christian Church and of the Ruthenian-Rus' nation within the Commonwealth. Among the arguments they made in defense of the "non-united" Ruthenian-Rus' Church was that union and uniformity are two very different things. From their perspective, the 1596 royal support of the Union of Brest—effectively outlawing the "non-united" Ruthenian-Rus' Church, which fell under the jurisdiction of the patriarch of Constantinople—was an act that stood against the very foundations and principles of the Commonwealth. They contended that the abolition of the identity and traditions of a people that formed an integral part of the Commonwealth transformed the notion of union into uniformity.[8]

The concerns of Mohyla and Kysil find parallels in present-day contestations of multiculturalism, where essentialized "others" are envisioned as striving to maintain their given identity in the face of a one-sided process of assimilation into a majority culture. To say that the Polish-Lithuanian Commonwealth was "multicultural" applauds the composite nature of this polity, and implies a peaceful coexistence among clearly defined and more-or-less coequal cultural groups. This simply was not the case. Polish-Lithuanian societal ideals carried political goals and implications that resulted in constant, fluid cultural adaptation and contestation among peoples. For Mohyla and Kysil and other like-minded Ruthenian-Rus' noblemen, ecclesiastics, literati, Cossacks, and townsfolk, in suppressing the jurisdiction of the patriarch of Constantinople over the Ruthenian-Rus' Eastern Church, the Polish-Lithuanian Commonwealth came a step too close to cultural homogenization or uniformity. Administrating the "non-united" Ruthenian-Rus' Church and the Chernihiv and Kyiv palatinates of the Commonwealth, Mohyla and Kysil had their finger on the cultural, social, and political pulse of the Ruthenian-Rus' nation they led. From their perspective, their efforts to find an acceptable solution for the position of the Ruthenian-Rus' Church in the Commonwealth were as much about preserving Commonwealth ideals as they were about asserting the presence and equality of a third nation within the Polish-Lithuanian state.

Focusing on the Church of the Savior at Berestovo, this chapter explores the transcultural discourses that sometimes succeeded and sometimes failed to unite the peoples of the Polish-Lithuanian Commonwealth—with "transculturalism" understood here as a tendency to "define shared interests and common values across cultural and national borders," thus allowing for "a chameleon sense of self without losing one's cultural center."[9] The chapter will show that the process of participating in transcultural discourses neither "assimilated" nor "othered" the Eastern Christian community of Ruthenian-Rus' lands. Instead, through visual forms that marked their cultural and historic presence in the here and now of the late sixteenth- to early seventeenth-century Commonwealth, Ruthenian-Rus' Eastern Christians called into question the unproblematized division of Commonwealth culture into center and periphery. To borrow from the cultural theorist Homi Bhabha, they "rendered the canonical center elusive" by expressing difference within the Commonwealth through forms that crossed cultural boundaries.[10] The architecture and imagery of the Church of the Savior combine Western Latin modes of the dominant Polish Catholic culture and of Protestantism with a Ruthenian-Rus' East Christian meta-text to articulate Commonwealth identity from a Kyivan perspective, and to position Kyiv as a center of Universal Christianity.

Kyiv—A Center of Universal Christianity

The *Paterikon*, which envisions Kyiv as heaven, is an early modern, Polish-language remake of a medieval namesake that was composed in the thirteenth century and written in Old Slavonic.[11] The new version recasts the popular and much copied medieval text for a contemporary audience that could include Eastern Christians, as well as Catholics and Protestants, who spoke various languages, but, in some capacity, were all exposed to Polish. Plurilingualism was not unusual among the elite populations of the Commonwealth, and the combination of Latin with vernacular languages, such as Middle Ukrainian and Polish, was popular among the literati of Ruthenian-Rus' lands.[12] Kosiv's *Paterikon* uses Polish intermixed with Latin, contains Greek and Latin neologisms, references classical and humanist literature, and evidences the influence of the Reformation and Counter-Reformation, all in a conscious effort to present Ruthenian-Rus' Christianity in the contemporary framework of Reformation and Commonwealth concerns. In the full title of the *Paterikon* and at the very start of the preface, Kosiv makes clear that he conceives the Rus' past as part of a Universal Christian narrative; he relies on Greek, Slavic, Latin, Rus', and Polish sources to unearth information about the earliest monks of Kyiv's Monastery of the Caves.[13] Although Kosiv repeatedly mentions Rus' chronicles, he assigns priority to Polish chronicles, especially the *Chronicle of Poland, Lithuania, Samogitia, and All Rus'* (*Kronika Polska, Litewska, Żmudzka i wszystkiej Rusi*, 1582) by Maciej Stryjkowski (ca. 1547–ca. 1593); and it is the *Annales ecclesiastici* (1588–1607) of Caesar Baronius (d. 1607) that take precedence over Byzantine sources.[14]

Both the medieval and the seventeenth-century versions of the *Paterikon* relate the founding of the mid-eleventh-century Caves Monastery in Kyiv, telling the stories of the holy brethren who lived and were buried in underground cells, chapels, and passageways excavated in the hills overlooking the Dnipro River. Aboveground, monastic walls with elaborate gateways circumscribe a sacred monastic territory boasting some of Kyiv's great churches. Just outside one of the monastery gates stands the Church of the Savior in Berestovo. According to the *Paterikon*, the Berestovo Hill was the site of the oldest monastic cells in Kyiv. This is where Anthony (d. 1073), one of the founders of the Caves Monastery, first settled in a Varangian cave, and it is where Kyiv's first native metropolitan, Ilarion, dug his monastic cell before agreeing to head the Rus' Church in the 1050s.[15] The stories related in the *Paterikon*, just like the primary structure of the Church of the Savior, belong to the medieval period when Kyiv was the dynastic and ecclesiastical center of the Rus' lands.

Metropolitan Mohyla was a man of his time, and his interest in antiquarianism extended to literary texts and material culture. As in Rome, where between 1400 and 1650 ancient remains of the city were exposed and where from 1578 the subterranean maze of early Christian catacombs became the subject of continuous inquiry, Mohyla took it upon himself to uncover and restore the splendors of the earliest period of Christianity in Kyiv. Aboveground, the Metropolitan engaged in renewing the city's foremost medieval monuments, including the Cathedral of Saint Sophia, the Desiatynna (Tithe) Church, the Church of the Three Hierarchs, the Church of Saint Michael at the Vyduby-chi Monastery, and the Church of the Savior at Berestovo.[16] Belowground, Mohyla searched for the relics of the first Christian rulers of Rus' and for the remains of Kyiv's earliest holy men and women.

The metropolitan devoted considerable attention to rendering visible the relics of Prince Volodymyr the Great (ca. 958–1015). The bodily remains of the Rus' ruler were discovered during work on the Desiatynna Church; Mohyla made plans to transfer Volodymyr's relics to the Cathedral of Saint Sophia, but we do not know the outcome of these intentions.[17] We do know, however, that as part of his 1634 renovation work in the Saint Sophia Cathedral, the metropolitan added a celebratory inscription on the arches of the main dome. The inscription dedicated the renewal of the cathedral to the "glory of God praised in the Trinity," identified Prince Yaroslav the Wise (ca. 978–1054) as the founder of the cathedral, credited the Polish King Ladislaus IV (r. 1632–1648) for the return of the cathedral to the hands of the "non-united" Eastern Christians, and attributed the renovation of the cathedral structure to Mohyla, "the revered Archbishop, Metropolitan of Kyiv, Halych, and all Rus', Exarch of the Throne of Constantinople, Archimandrite of the Monastery of the Caves."[18]

Like Ruthenian-Rus' princes, magnates, and nobility, Mohyla was committed to both his Ruthenian-Rus' homeland and his Commonwealth father-land, and envisioned the renovation of Kyiv's medieval churches within the cultural and political parameters of the Polish Lithuanian-Commonwealth; it was King Ladislaus IV, after all, who appointed Mohyla to the post of metropolitan and who aspired to create a Ruthenia-Rus' Eastern Christian patriarchate in union with Rome within the Commonwealth. Mohyla, the exarch of the Patriarchal Throne of Constantinople, was a prime candidate for the future Kyivan patriarchal seat. In all his undertakings, Mohyla sought to demonstrate that the Ruthenian-Rus' sacred past and religious traditions possessed both the gravitas and the requisite antiquity to form an integral part of the framework of a Universal Church.

In Rome, Counter-Reformation scholars such as Caesar Baronius, the author of the *Annales ecclesiastici* (1586) and *Martyrologium romanum* (1598), and Antonio Bosio, the author of *Roma sotterrane* (1634), studied the paleo-Christian beginnings of their ancient city to reveal the spiritual reality it mediated in the present.[19] Mohyla's priorities were similar; he conducted a census of the sacred to illuminate God's presence in Kyiv and to make visible the parity of Ruthenian-Rus' Eastern Christianity with the Roman Catholic faith. The Metropolitan's search for Kyiv's Christian hallowed beginnings led him to present anew the lives of Rus' saints in the *Paterikon*, but also to commission the Polish text of the *Teraturgema or Miracles* (*Teratourgema lubo cuda*, 1638), a text that collates more recent accounts of miracles associated with the monastics of the Caves Monastery and thereby links the spiritual reality of the present with that of the past.[20] The metropolitan approached visual culture with a similar reformative hand; his extensive engagement with Kyiv's topography distinguished his crafting of Ruthenian-Rus' sacred history from that of his predecessors. As with his written endeavors, the sources for his renovation of Kyiv's built environment referenced the Kyivan Rus' past, late Byzantine developments, the Polish-Lithuanian inheritance, and post-Tridentine practices of Papal Rome. If we consider that the rediscovery and mapping of the catacombs of Rome date back only to 1578, when the underground chambers became the subject of archaeological study after lying undisturbed since the ninth century, and that Bosio's *Roma sotterrane* was published in 1634, only a year before Kysil's *Paterikon*, we can begin to appreciate the contemporaneity and scope of the cultural sources to which Petro Mohyla's blueprint for Orthodox reformation can be traced.

In Rome, Pope Gregory XIII's (1572–1585) reformative projects, such as the *Kalendarium Gregorianum* (1582) and Baronius's *Martyrologium romanum*, linked celestial and terrestrial realms, and positioned Rome as the center of Christian worship. In Kyiv, Mohyla simultaneously emulated and countered these Roman visions of a Christian past. Or, to look at it from another perspective, by confirming the pious traditions and legends surrounding Kyiv, Mohyla and his ecclesiastical cohort were addressing a lacuna that existed in Latin and Polish compilations of the history of the Universal Church—the failure to address Christian history in Ruthenian-Rus' lands. In the second introduction to the *Paterikon*, heavenly planets stand in for the holy monastics of the Kyiv Caves Monastery, and Kosiv emphasizes that even "people of a simple mind can see holy stars [Kyiv's holy men and women] in the churches and caves of the city."[21] A woodcut in the 1661 Church Slavonic *Paterik* renders this idea visually. Here, the Mother of God, flanked by Saints Anthony and Theodosius, the eleventh-century founders of the Caves Monastery, is surrounded by

Figure 4.3. *Wreath of Heavenly Stars of the Mother of God*, engraving from the *Kyiv-Pechersk Pateryk* of 1661. Kyiv, Museum of Book and Print of Ukraine, f. 7621 inv. no. SD-174, fol. 296. Photo by Olenka Z. Pevny.

stars that represent the monastery's numerous brethren, among whom we now see Petro Mohyla (fig. 4.3).

Already from the late sixteenth century, the process of reform in Ruthenian-Rus' Eastern Christianity encouraged the spread of Jesuit models of education, promoted interest in local history and tradition, stimulated the printing of books, brought about the clarification of doctrine and the regularization of liturgical practice, and invigorated confessional and polemical exchange. Mohyla was personally engaged in all aspects of this Eastern Christian reformation.[22] The Kyiv Mohyla Collegium, which he helped establish, was modeled on Jesuit schools.[23] Mohyla reformed and regularized Orthodox doctrine and liturgical practices, publishing his *Book of Services* (*Leiturgiarion si est Sluzhebnik*) in 1639 and his *Euchologion* (*Eukhologion albo Molitoslov ili Trebnik*) in 1646.[24] Like most leading ecclesiastics of the period, he participated in the stream of polemical discourse with his 1644 publication *Lithos* (*Lithos abo Kamien*), which defends the right of the Orthodox to use Latin and Polish—a right challenged by Jesuits, Uniates, and

Figure 4.4. *Vault of Heaven*, wall painting on the ceiling of the naos of the Church of the Savior on the Berestovo Hill, Kyiv, Ukraine. Photo by Ivan Vasylovych Krezhenstovskyi. Reproduced by permission from Olenka Z. Pevny.

Catholics.[25] Nevertheless, although Mohyla is best known for his *Orthodox Confession of Faith* (*Confessio Orthodoxa*), which he probably wrote in Latin in 1640,[26] it is his role in an attempt to bring about a universal union of churches that concerns us here.

An Eastern Christian Patriarchate in Kyiv

Within the Berestovo Church, the imagery of the star-filled heavens in the vault of the naos hovers above the prophets, a dedicatory image, scenes of the miracles and the Passion of Christ, and the standing figures of monastics of the Kyiv Monastery of the Caves, all of which decorate the naos walls (fig. 4.4). This imagery not only links the cosmic and terrestrial realms but aspires to advance the Ruthenian-Rus′ Church within Universal Christianity. The circular mandorla with the image of Christ is inscribed with the words of the prayer of the pontiff from the Little Entrance of the Pontifical Mass (Psalm 80:14–15): "O Lord our God, look from the heavens and behold and

visit this vineyard which thy right hand has planted and perfect it and fill
it with Your Spirit and bless Thy inheritance."[27] While the reference of this
inscription is clearly Eucharistic, these same words were inscribed on the
miter of Iov, the first patriarch of Moscow (d. 1607).[28] The 1589 consecration
of Iov by Patriarch Jeremiah of Constantinople (1536–1595) established the
autonomy of the Moscow Church from Constantinople.

Making his way home from Moscow through the Commonwealth, Patri-
arch Jeremiah confirmed the appointment of Mykhailo Rahoza (*Pol.* Michał
Rahoza; d. 1599) as the Kyiv metropolitan of the Ruthenian-Rus' Church.[29]
Yet this apparent recognition of the separate natures of the Muscovite and
Ruthenian-Rus' Churches did little to strengthen the position of the Eastern
Christian hierarchy in the Commonwealth. For a few years later, in 1595–1596,
Metropolitan Rahoza warily gave his support to the union with the Church
of Rome, exchanging the authority of the patriarch of Constantinople for that
of the bishop of Rome in what became known as the Union of Brest. In doing
so, the metropolitan and most Ruthenian-Rus' hierarchs aimed to equalize
the rights of the Commonwealth's Eastern Christian clergy with those of
the Catholic clergy and to reassert the power of the church hierarchy at the
expense of the laity within the Eastern Church. They were determined to
preserve Ruthenian-Rus' liturgical traditions and practices and to limit the
Latinization of the Eastern Christian rite. In the eyes of the papacy, however, the pro-union Ruthenian-Rus' hierarchs were repenting schismatics,
who were submitting to papal authority and accepting Tridentine canons
and decrees.[30]

The acceptance of union at Brest was not unanimous; two members of the
Ruthenian-Rus' Eastern Christian hierarchy, monastics, magnates, nobility,
burghers, and soon also the Zaporizhzhian Cossacks opposed the union and
chose to remain under the jurisdiction of the patriarch of Constantinople.
From the point of view of the Catholic Church and King Sigismund III
(r. 1587–1632), the Ruthenian-Rus' Eastern Christian Church was now divided in two, those "united" (Lat.: *uniti*) and those "non-united" (Lat.: *disuniti*)
with Rome. Sigismund III formally recognized only the "united" (Uniate)
church; the "non-united" church was now considered illegitimate. The loss
of official status for the "non-united" church carried with it material implications; it was the "united" hierarchy that claimed to hold jurisdiction over
churches, monasteries, and other ecclesiastical properties.[31]

In the Sejm, where the Ruthenian-Rus' nobility presented their case against
the Union of Brest, progress toward legal recognition of the "non-united"

Ruthenian-Rus' Eastern Christian church was incremental. In 1620, with the help of the Zaporizhzhian Cossacks, Patriarch Theophanes III of Jerusalem (d. 1644) consecrated Iov Boretskyi (*Pol.* Hiob Borecki; 1560–1631) as metropolitan of Kyiv, Halych, and All Rus', and appointed several bishops to the hierarchy of the "non-united" church. With these appointments, Kyiv became the center of the "non-united" church, and the city of Navahrudak (*Pol.* Nowogródek) served as the residence of the metropolitan of the "united" church. It took another twelve years and the election of a new monarch, King Ladislaus IV, before the "non-united" church was fully legitimized and the existence of two Ruthenian-Rus' Eastern Christian Churches in the Commonwealth—the Uniate ("united") and the Orthodox ("non-united")—became reality.[32]

At the Election Sejm of 1632, Adam Kysil argued that the "non-united" church was rooted in the beginnings of Rus' Christianity, and that its banning encroached on the religious liberty of the noble estate and therefore threatened the cornerstone of the Commonwealth nation.[33] In that same year, King Ladislaus IV legitimized the "non-united" church and, in 1633, with the strong support of the king, Mohyla, who was then the archimandrite of the Caves Monastery, became metropolitan of Kyiv, Halych, and All-Rus'. Mohyla received from the king the Cathedral of Saint Sophia and all the churches of Kyiv, except for the Vydubytskyi Monastery.[34]

When Ladislaus IV appointed Mohyla to the metropolitan throne of Kyiv, Patriarch Filaret (1553–1633) occupied the Moscow ecclesiastical throne. As the father of Tsar Michael I Romanov (r. 1613–1645), Filaret functioned as co-regent of the tsardom and acted as the effective head of government from 1619 until his death. King Ladislaus IV held pretenses to the Muscovite throne and, until 1634, his royal title included a reference to his 1610 election as grand duke of Muscovy. Within the Commonwealth, Ladislaus IV was concerned to establish peace between the Orthodox and Uniate populations, and to prevent the Ruthenian-Rus' Orthodox from developing bonds with the Muscovite opposition.

In 1635, Prince Oleksandr Sangushko (*Pol.* Adam Aleksander Sanguszko; ca. 1590–1653), the palatine of Volhynia and an Orthodox convert to Catholicism, sought to mediate a new union between the Roman and Ruthenian-Rus' Eastern Churches.[35] The matter was brought before the new Congregation for the Propagation of the Faith in Rome, where it stalled. Ladislaus IV, for his part, was in favor of elevating the metropolitan of Kyiv to patriarchal status on the model of the recently established Moscow Patriarchate. In a proclamation issued on September 5, 1636, the king called on the Uniate and Orthodox

Ruthenian-Rus' Churches to find common ground and create their own
Ruthenian-Rus' Patriarchate independent of Constantinople.[36] Supporters
of the proposed union of the two Ruthenian-Rus' Churches reasoned that,
once formed, this new patriarchate could join Rome in the formation of a
Universal Church.[37] Mohyla was in favor of the proposal and brought it to
the awareness of Orthodox faithful.[38] Due to opposition from both Rome
and the Orthodox led by the former metropolitan of the "non-united"
Ruthenian-Rus' Church, Isaia Kopynskyi (*Pol.* Izajasz Kopiński; d. 1640), the
proposal failed.[39] Kopynskyi informed the Orthodox faithful that Mohyla
had forsaken Orthodoxy, causing some 150 Orthodox monks and nuns with
peasant families from the Trans-Dnipro region of the Commonwealth to flee
to the Muscovite Tsardom.[40] Avoidance of such situations required caution
and involved a degree of concealment of plans on the part of both Mohyla
and Kysil.[41]

Conversations regarding union between Rome and the Ruthenian-Rus'
Orthodox Church continued into the 1640s. In 1643, Pope Urban VIII
(1623–1644) wrote to Metropolitan Mohyla and to Kysil calling upon them
to unite with the Roman Church.[42] Again Mohyla and Kysil were interested,
and in 1644 they drafted a response to the pope titled *Sententia cuiusdam
nobilis Poloni graecae religionis* (*Opinion of a Certain Noble Pole of the Greek
Religion*).[43] The anonymity of the response is indicative of the precautionary
posturing assumed by the drafters of the document, which identifies three
obstacles to union: (1) the lack of proper intention; (2) the lack of an understanding of the political structure of the Commonwealth, specifically the
place of the nobility; and (3) the failure to recognize that unity does not mean
uniformity.[44]

Mohyla and Kysil envisioned a Universal Church union of two equal
parts—Western and Eastern Christianity. At present, only the Ruthenian-
Rus' Church was entering the union, but the hope was that other Eastern
Christian Churches would follow. While the *Sententia* avoids mentioning the
creation of a Kyivan patriarchate, existing correspondence makes it clear that
a patriarchate was expected in Orthodox circles.[45] According to the *Sententia*,
the Kyiv metropolitan was to enjoy patriarchal powers and the nobility was to
play a key role in the union process.[46] In 1644, concurrently with the drafting
of the *Sententia*, Mohyla completed the rebuilding of the Church of the Savior
in Berestovo and decorated the nave ceiling with a celestial image from which
Christ, who appears in a medallion encircled by the inscription associated
with the patriarchal miter, overlooks Mohyla's donor portrait, which reaches

into the heavens from the summit of the east wall of the naos (fig. 4.4). Referencing Ladislaus IV's proclamation on the creation of a patriarchate in Kyiv, following the precedent set by Moscow, the imagery of the Berestovo Church depicts Christ extending his heavenly blessing on the patriarchal powers that were to be assumed by the Kyiv metropolitan. Clearly, Mohyla's imagining of an empowered and united Ruthenian-Rus' Eastern Christian Church within the Commonwealth was not restricted to words; it was advanced through visual culture.

Berestovo and the Many Forms of Ruthenian-Rus' Ecclesiastical Architecture

On January 1, 1647, Petro Mohyla, the archbishop and metropolitan of Kyiv, Halych, and All Rus', and exarch of the Throne of Constantinople, passed away in Kyiv after heading the Ruthenian Orthodox Church for fourteen years. The metropolitan's testament discloses the importance he assigned to the Church of the Savior at Berestovo. It divides his silver and valuable possessions among four entities: the Mohyla Collegium, the Monastery of the Caves, the Berestovo Church, and his brother, Moses. While other restoration projects are mentioned, none are allocated the same prominence as the Church of the Savior.[47] The significance of Mohyla's rebuilding of the Berestovo Church resonated beyond his inner circle. A 1649 polemical treatise informs readers that the zealously Orthodox Zaporizhzhian Cossacks were once ready to drown Mohyla in the Dnipro and put him in his grave (*mohyla*) for restoring the ceiling of the Berestovo Church to resemble a Catholic shrine. It was written in response to a statement, drafted in 1648 after Mohyla's death, probably by Kysil, arguing for amicable relations between the Zaporizhzhian Cossacks and the Commonwealth.[48] As we shall shortly see in more detail, the Cossacks were objecting to the decorative rib vaults framing the Byzantine-style frescoes that form the ceiling over the altar of the church (fig. 4.5). The evidence of Mohyla's testament, of the cited polemical treatise, and of the Berestovo Church speaks to the variety of cultural forms that linked and divided different social groups participating in the fluid discourses of identity that defined Ruthenian-Rus' inhabitants of mid-seventeenth-century Kyiv.

When Petro Mohyla engaged in the rebuilding and redecorating of the Berestovo Church, he was not aspiring to reconstruct a specific medieval monument; rather, through the performance of renewal, he was making palpable the medieval origins of Kyiv's contemporary ecclesiastical culture as he and his compatriots imagined it. Kyiv's medieval Christian past was rooted in a Byzantine inheritance; Kyiv's ecclesiastical present was informed by transcultural discourses that entangled Ruthenian-Rus' culture with that of the broader Polish-Lithuanian Commonwealth and with the intellectual and artistic currents of the Reformation and post-Tridentine Catholic revival. The poor state of preservation of the Berestovo Church, with only significant portions of the west wall of the original narthex standing, provided an opportune occasion for Mohyla to use the rich arsenal of architectural and visual forms that defined the seventeenth-century landscape of Ruthenian-Rus' lands to renovate a monument that dated back to the very beginnings of Kyivan Christianity. The coalescence of past and present in the church structure offered viewers palpable evidence of the continuity between early medieval and early modern Kyiv.

Unlike most medieval Kyivan Rus' structures that followed the cross-dome plan typical of Middle Byzantine churches, Mohyla chose to restore the Church of the Savior at Berestovo as a variant of the rib-vaulted hall church popular in Poland and western parts of Ruthenia-Rus' from the fourteenth through sixteenth centuries.[49] This means that the interior of the seventeenth-century Church of the Savior is not subdivided into numerous bays by heavy piers, but rather consists of a barrel-vaulted naos that opens through a wide arch onto a spacious sanctuary. The sanctuary itself is composed of a rectangular bay crowned by a quadripartite-ribbed vault and a trapezoidal apse with a domical vault segmented by three Gothic ribs (fig. 4.2). It is the Gothic ribbing of the ceiling, unusual for the medieval churches of Kyiv, that, according to the 1649 polemicist, caught the eye of the Cossacks, who interpreted it as an indication of Mohyla's lapse into Catholicism.[50]

Although very different in spatial dimensions and without a central column in the naos, the renewed Church of the Savior is reminiscent of the Chapel of the Holy Trinity in the Lublin Castle. The rib vaulting of the sanctuary of the Lublin chapel and that of the Kyiv church form a compelling visual parallel (figs. 4.5 and 4.6). In 1418, three Ruthenian artists completed the frescoes of the Trinity Chapel, founded by Jogaila (grand duke of Lithuania and Ruthenia, 1377–1381 and 1382–1434; King of Poland, 1386–1434; Ladislaus II after ascension to the Polish throne).[51] Ladislaus II and his son, Casimir IV (grand duke of Lithuania and Ruthenia, 1440–1492; king of Poland 1447–1492), also commissioned Byzantine-style frescoes for several other churches of the Latin rite.[52] The melding of artistic traditions

Figure 4.5. Ribbed sanctuary vault in the Church of the Savior on the Berestovo Hill, Kyiv, Ukraine. Photo by Ivan Vasylovych Krezhenstovskyi. Reproduced by permission from Olenka Z. Pevny.

Figure 4.6. Ribbed sanctuary vault in the Chapel of the Holy Trinity, Lublin, Poland. Photo by Art Media Factory.

associated with both the Byzantine and the Latin Church characterized the culturally fluid areas connecting Polish, Lithuanian, and Ruthenian-Rus' lands of which Lublin was a part. In these buildings, as in the Lublin Trinity Chapel, Gothic structures enclose Byzantine frescoes in the service of the Catholic Church.[53] Mohyla's early modern renovation of the Church of the Savior looks back to the Lublin tradition, where Byzantine-style painting is fused with Gothic architecture, but radically transforms it. Whereas in Lublin, Byzantine images decorate the walls and webbing of a Gothic structure used in the service of the Catholic Church, in Kyiv, Gothic ribs are added as decorative elements to a structure rooted in the medieval Rus' past and used in the service of the reinstated Orthodox Church.

Mohyla spent time in the western regions of Ruthenia-Rus' and in Lublin before ascending to the metropolitan throne of Kyiv. An influential city, Lublin was an important Orthodox ecclesiastical and cultural center. The Lublin Orthodox Brotherhood was established in 1583 and modeled on the Lviv Dormition Brotherhood with which the Mohyla family was associated. The Church of the Lublin Brotherhood served both the local Eastern Christian community and the Eastern Christian nobility that made its way to Lublin for the Sejms of 1566 and 1569 or for cases to be heard by the Crown Tribunal. In the 1630s, this wooden church burned down and was replaced with a masonry structure built at the expense of leading Ruthenian-Rus' noble families, including the Sangushko family, whose member, Prince Oleksandr, mediated the proposed union between the Roman and Ruthenian-Rus' Churches in 1635.[54] On March 15, 1633, in one of his first acts as metropolitan, Mohyla consecrated the newly completed masonry Lublin Church, which like the Berestovo Church was dedicated to the Transfiguration of the Savior.

In 1633, when King Ladislaus IV granted privilege to the Lublin Brotherhood for the Church of the Transfiguration, he concurrently recognized the legality of the seizure of the church by the Uniate bishop Metodii Terletskyi of Chełm (*Pol.* Metody Terlecki; d. 1649). As a result, the possession of the Lublin Transfiguration Church became a major issue of dispute between the Orthodox and Uniate branches of the Ruthenian-Rus' Church. At the Sejms of 1640 and 1641—that is, right before the Berestovo Church in Kyiv was built—Adam Kysil pursued the return of the Lublin Church of the Transfiguration to the Orthodox Brotherhood.[55]

When in Lublin, Metropolitan Mohyla would not have missed the opportunity to visit the Trinity Chapel. In 1569, this very chapel served as the site of the signing of the Union of Lublin, which formalized the centuries-long coexistence of the Grand Duchy of Lithuania and the Polish Crown into the Polish-Lithuanian Commonwealth. The Union of Lublin also involved a re-distribution of lands between the Kingdom of Poland and the Grand Duchy of Lithuania and Ruthenia. The lands of Podlasie, Volyn', Kyiv, and Bratslav, and later, in 1619, Chernihiv—that is, many of the lands that form today's Ukraine—were transferred from the Grand Duchy to the Kingdom of Po-land in accordance with negotiated unions and privileges that both justified Polish incorporation of Ruthenian-Rus' lands and defined the relationship of the palatinates to the Polish Crown. Whereas the Crown saw Ruthenian-Rus' lands as returning to the fold of the Kingdom of Poland and expected Ruthenian-Rus' nobility to adhere to Crown laws passed after 1569 and swear allegiance to the king, Ruthenian-Rus' nobility saw things differently.[56] Nataliia Starchenko has shown that the Union of Lublin was an important step in the conceptualization of a Ruthenian-Rus' nation. Members of the Ruthenian-Rus' nobility understood the incorporation of their lands into the Kingdom of Poland in light of the union between the Kingdom of Poland and the Grand Duchy of Lithuania. They saw themselves as representatives of a Ruthenian-Rus' political entity with its own rights, language, and laws, which the king had guaranteed formally in the negotiation of the Lublin Union. The conceptualizing of the Ruthenian-Rus' nation as a third nation in the Commonwealth can be traced back to Union of Lublin.[57]

The diverse and broadly interconnected architectural monuments ad-dressed here form just a fragment of the built environment in which Metro-politan Mohyla and his early modern Ruthenian-Rus' compatriots dwelled. These structures were both shaped by and gave form to the transcultural interactions and dissonances that characterized the dynamics of Ruthenian-Rus' culture. For members of the Ruthenian-Rus' nobiliary nation and of the Eastern Orthodox hierarchy, the Gothic ribbed vaulting of the Church of the Savior in Berestovo likely mirrored the transculturally marked spaces of the landscapes within which they acted; for disenfranchised and disgrun-tled Cossacks, the Gothic vaulting constituted a Catholic infringement on Ruthenian-Rus' Orthodox identity. Clearly, many aspects of identification were at play in the early modern reception of the architecture and wall paint-ings of the Berestovo Church, not least of which was the tension regarding the ecclesiastical jurisdiction of Ruthenian-Rus' Orthodox Christians in the Commonwealth and the changing conception of just who constituted the Ruthenian-Rus' nation.[58] It is clear that Ruthenian-Rus' culture was not a tightly bound discrete cultural unit, but rather took the form of an entangled discourse that situated Metropolitan Mohyla's restoration of the Church of the Savior in a boundless network of local, regional, and global developments.

Visual Discourse: Sacred Images and Political Meanings

Petro Mohyla began his restoration of the Church of the Savior sometime in the early 1640s, and, following Stryjkowski's *Chronicle*, attributed the foundation to Prince Volodymyr the Great.[59] Scholars have firmly established that Polish and Lithuanian chronicles informed the revitalization of the Rus' inheritance in early modern Ruthenian-Rus' lands of the Commonwealth.[60] However, it is not just such overt references to aspects of the Commonwealth tradition that feature in Mohyla's restaging of the Orthodox past. The Reformation and Counter-Reformation changed the way images were used, viewed, read, interpreted, and contemplated among the Ruthenian-Rus' ecclesiastical elite. The significance of images was no longer limited to their iconic function; in addition to conjuring the holy, they took on an emblematic role and served as loci for memory, meditation, and invention. Interest in dialectic and rhetorical processes, in epistemological tools, and in cognitive operations that linked knowledge and sensory perception informed Jesuit visual culture and formed part of the transcultural discourse of the Counter-Reformation in which ecclesiastics, such as Mohyla, participated.[61]

This new engagement with and reflection upon images encouraged viewers to contemplate the relevance of sacred history to proximate events. Take, for example, the depiction of the vision of Peter of Alexandria that is found on the left side of the sanctuary apse (fig. 4.7). Here, Christ appears to Saint Peter as a twelve-year-old child wearing a robe torn from top to bottom. Saint Peter asks the Savior who tore his garment, and the Savior replies that the heretic Arius has torn it by dividing the Christian faithful. In Orthodox iconography, this image with the motif of the torn garment came to symbolize church schisms and carried liturgical connotations—the tearing of the garment represented the breaking of the Eucharistic bread and affirmed that the Eucharist is the real body and blood of Christ.[62]

In the Kyiv church, we see Peter conversing with the young Jesus who stands on an altar. The inscription reads, "Who tore your chiton, Savior?" and the Savior replies, "Arius the mad and all-evil, Peter."[63] The inscribed dialogue plays on the homonymous relationship between the patron Petro Mohyla and the apostle Peter, evoking an immediate relevance in the

Figure 4.7. *Vision of Saint Peter of Alexandria,* wall painting in the sanctuary apse of the Church of the Savior on the Berestovo Hill, Kyiv, Ukraine. Photo by Nazar Kozak.

context of the Metropolitan's efforts to bring an end to the division of the Ruthenian-Rus' Church. On the first day of the 1629 synod called to discuss the possibility of reuniting the "united" and "non-united" churches, in the presence of Mohyla, Kysil expressed the opinion that the fratricidal religious struggle of the Ruthenian-Rus' nation must stop. He stated:

> We all weep at the sight of the rent coat and precious robe of our dear Mother the Holy Eastern Church. You, Gentlemen, bemoan, as do we all, that we are divided from our brethren, we who were in one font of the Holy Spirit six hundred years ago in the Dnipro waters of this metropolis of the Rus' Principality. It wounds you, Gentlemen, and it wounds us all. Behold! There flourish organisms of commonwealths composed of various nations, while we of one nation, of one people, of one religion, of one worship, of one rite are not as one. We are torn asunder, and thus we decline.[64]

The Passion imagery of the naos also includes references to Metropolitan Mohyla and the Ruthenian-Rus' context by the "double-sided" dedicatory inscription that frames a circular opening over the entrance on both the exterior and interior of the west naos wall (fig. 4.8). The inscription on the interior wall is written in Church Slavonic and reads: "This church was built by the Great Prince and Autocrat of all Rus', Volodymyr, in baptism [named] Basil. After many years and after destruction at the hands of the godless Tartars, [the church] was renewed with God's volition by humble Petro Mohyla, Archbishop Metropolitan of Kyiv, Halych and all Rus', Exarch of the Holy Throne of Constantinople, Archimandrite of the Caves monastery. For the Glory of the Transfiguration of Christ, God the Word, on Mount Tabor, in the year 1643, that is 7151 from the creation of the world."[65]

On the opposite side of the wall, over the entrance leading into the church, the dedicatory inscription is written in Greek (fig. 4.9), and reads:

> Petro Mohyla, God's bishop, built this church for the Lord [*God our Heavenly*] Ruler, having made this illustrious and memorable house of stone having painted it with the hands of the Greeks, returning the glory which You, Eternal, brought to the entire world with your suffering on the Cross and brought for all in the name of God to the temple. You are the firmament and hold the burden of the world in your palm. Strengthen this house, rendering it forever indestructible for the glory of Thy nation. In the year from the birth of Christ 1644, November 16.[66]

Figure 4.8. Church Slavonic donor inscription over the doorway on the west wall of the naos of the Church of the Savior on the Berestovo Hill, Kyiv, Ukraine. Photo by Ivan Vasylovych Krezhenstovskyi. Reproduced by permission from Olenka Z. Pevny.

Figure 4.9. Greek donor inscription over the doorway on the west wall of the naos of the Church of the Savior on the Berestovo Hill, Kyiv, Ukraine. Photo by Ivan Vasylovych Krezhenstovskyi. Reproduced by permission from Olenka Z. Pevny.

In addition to the dedicatory inscription, both Greek and Church Slavonic inscriptions occur throughout the Berestovo Church. The intentional juxtaposition of the Greek and Church Slavonic languages carried an immediate polemical relevance in the mid-seventeenth-century Ruthenian-Rus' lands of the Commonwealth. Contemporary Catholic polemicists, such as the Jesuit Piotr Skarga (1536–1612), often attacked the use of Church Slavonic as a liturgical language, claiming that it constituted an intellectual barrier for the Ruthenian-Rus' population. In his work *On the Unity of God's Church under One Shepherd* (*O jedności Kościoła Bożego pod jednym pasterzem*, 1577), Skarga writes that "no one can ever become learned through the Slavonic tongue," and that only the Greek and Latin apostolic languages with long traditions and stable grammars and lexicons can ensure true understanding and learning.[67] Among the books published by the Lviv Dormition Brotherhood, with which Mohyla was associated, was *Brotherhood: A Grammar of the Good-Sounding Helleno-Slavonic Language* (*Adelphotes: Hrammatika dobrohlaholivaho ellinoslovenskaho iazyka*), the first Church Slavonic–Greek grammar, published in 1591.[68] Prepared by Arsenios from Thessaly, it served to repudiate Skarga's charges that the Ruthenian religion and culture were mute because the Church Slavonic language had not been codified. The text develops the notion of an existing intimate connection between the Greek and Church Slavonic languages by juxtaposing Greek grammar with Church Slavonic grammar on each page, as if the two languages were "so close as to be considered two aspects of a linguistic unit."[69] By employing the Greek and Church Slavonic languages in the inscriptions of the Berestovo Church, Mohyla was visually countering the accusations of Catholic polemicists and asserting the equivalency of both languages.

Metropolitan Mohyla's donor portrait is set over the arch leading into the sanctuary and under the vaulted canopy of the heavens (fig. 4.10). It shows the Mother of God presenting the kneeling metropolitan to Christ, who sits enthroned as the King of Kings, Lord of Lords, Great Pontiff. To the other side of Christ stands the haloed Prince Volodymyr the Great. Mohyla offers the Berestovo Church to Christ and entreatingly utters: "Lord, accept this church I, unworthy, built [it] in your name and him, who having looked believing, enlighten with the light of your countenance. Hence, your eyes will continually watch over this sanctuary!" Christ responds: "I look upon it, in fulfillment of your will!"[70] Mohyla's work in reforming the Eastern Church, symbolized by the Church of the Savior that he presents to Christ, is juxtaposed with the Christianization efforts of Prince Volodymyr. Many scholars

Figure 4.10. Donor portrait of Metropolitan Petro Mohyla on the east wall of the naos of the Church of the Savior on the Berestovo Hill in Kyiv, Ukraine. Photo by Ivan Vasylovych Krezhenstovskyi. Reproduced by permission from Olenka Z. Pevny.

have pondered the significance of the juxtaposition of Mohyla, an ecclesiastic hierarch, with a secular ruler. Some have suggested that Mohyla may have traced his own lineage back to the age of Prince Volodymyr.[71] Yet other visual and textual evidence shows that Mohyla was clear about the fact that he was an ecclesiastical rather than secular ruler.

An engraving titled *Helykon*, which introduces the first cycle of poems of the 1632 panegyric pamphlet *Eucharisterion: Or Thanksgiving* (Ἐυχαριστήριον: *Albo, Vdiachnost*) shows Mohyla standing on Mount Helicon dressed as archimandrite of the Kyiv Caves Monastery holding the staff of clerical shepherdhood in his right hand, and a branch of wisdom in his left. To his left, a scepter and the cloak fall to the ground representing the abandonment of secular rule.[72] The image simultaneously reminds viewers and asks them to forget Mohyla's secular standing, which is now subsumed under the cloak of his commitment to the church. Moreover, Mohyla's *Euchologion*, published just weeks before his death, includes a sermon on the power that Christ bestows upon the church. In it, Mohyla, reminds readers that God's power is greater than that of any earthly ruler, and that it is bestowed upon the hierarchs of the Orthodox Church. In a further passage, which all but explains the donor portrait in the Berestovo Church, Mohyla tells readers that if they want to access Christ's kingdom, they must fall with faith and repentance at the feet of priests as if they were Christ's feet, because priests are Christ's gatekeepers and his representatives, and what they confer on earth will be approved by Christ-God in heaven.[73]

The Berestovo donor portrait does not posit a direct relationship between the Metropolitan and Prince Volodymyr, but rather it refers to the conditions that preoccupied Mohyla and Kysil in the negotiation of church unity. In his deliberations at the 1629 Church Synod, Kysil bemoaned the ongoing struggle among the "united" and "non-united" Ruthenian-Rus' people by reminding the gathered clerics that the baptism of the entire Ruthenian-Rus' nation occurred in one font—that of the Dnipro waters, six hundred years ago in the time of Prince Volodymyr. By the late sixteenth century, the lineage of Ruthenian-Rus' secular nobility was often traced to the Rurikid dynasty—that is, to Prince Volodymyr and his times.[74] Kysil's genealogy offers a good example: his ancestor was deemed to be Sviatold, a heroic leader associated with Prince Volodymyr.[75] In the context of the 1640s, the emphasis placed on Petro Mohyla and the inclusion of the figure of Prince Volodymyr in the donor fresco should be read against the background of ecclesiastical negotiations that were guided by the nobility and that would bestow patriarchal-like powers on the Kyiv metropolitan. Here, Mohyla is depicted as the head of the Ruthenian-Rus' Church, and Prince Volodymyr stands as the symbolic representative of Ruthenian-Rus' nobility. Together the two figures speak to Mohyla's and Kysil's veiled desire to establish an Eastern Christian Kyivan patriarchate within the framework of the Commonwealth's noble nation and the Universal Church. They also attest to the new political ambitions of the Ruthenian-Rus' Eastern Christian nobility, who came to see the Ruthenian-Rus' lands incorporated into the Polish Crown with the Union of Lublin as a third nation within the Commonwealth. From the late sixteenth century, these Ruthenian-Rus' lands came increasingly to be associated with the name "Ukraine."[76]

Sylvestr Kosiv's *Paterikon*, commissioned by Mohyla and dedicated to Kysil, identifies Kyiv as heaven and the holy brethren of the Caves Monastery as individual planets; the Church of the Savior visually re-creates this imagined ecumenical universe within its walls. Here, engaging images in flexible rhetorical play, Mohyla redefines coexistence in the Polish-Lithuanian Commonwealth from a Ruthenian-Rus' Orthodox perspective.

Mohyla died in January 1647, and his vision of a Universal Church union and a Kyivan patriarchate never materialized. Nevertheless, the Church of the Savior in Berestovo reminds us that the story of the Polish-Lithuanian Commonwealth is a tale of constant transcultural negotiations involving individuals and communities with multiple and fluid identities dispersed across numerous cultural centers. One such early seventeenth-century center was the city of Kyiv, in which a Ruthenian-Rus' cultural identity rooted in the past of Kyivan Rus' was consolidating.

Modern History and the Church of the Savior at Berestovo

Modern academic interest in the medieval beginnings of the Church of the Savior in Berestovo dates to the mid-nineteenth century.[77] However, already in the first half of the seventeenth century, the medieval foundations of this church were identified and used in the early modern restoration of Kyiv carried out under the patronage of Petro Mohyla, the Orthodox metropolitan of Kyiv, Halych, and All Rus'. Whereas in the first half of the seventeenth century, Kyiv was the Orthodox center of Ruthenian-Rus' lands under the jurisdiction of the Polish Crown within the Polish-Lithuanian Commonwealth, in the nineteenth century, Kyiv was part of the Ukrainian lands of the Russian Empire. Political goals informed both the early modern and modern restorations of the church.

In the 1640s, when Metropolitan Mohyla renewed the ruined Berestovo Church, he believed it had been built by Prince Volodymyr the Great on the site of the pagan idol of Perun and on the location of Kyiv's earliest monastic cells. The metropolitan based his knowledge of the history of the Berestovo Church on Rus' and Polish sources. His rebuilding project did not seek to restore the medieval structure to its original appearance, but rather to reenvision Kyiv's historical and cultural past with a view to its present and future. Supported by King Ladislaus IV, Mohyla saw Kyiv as a center of Eastern Christianity in the Commonwealth and saw the Ruthenian-Rus' Eastern Christian Church as having an important role to play in the Universal Church.

In the nineteenth-century Russian Empire, imperial historians saw the Berestovo Church as a relic of an imagined "Holy Rus'" to which all East Slavic peoples belonged. Russian nineteenth-century scholarship on Rus' emphasized that the Rurikid dynasty, the Slavonic language, and the Orthodox religion served to unify the disparate lands of Rus'. Such a vision of the Rus' past was used to justify the formula "Orthodoxy, Autocracy, and

Nationality" that advocated the predominance of a single church, of imperial power, and of the "Great Russian" nation over other Slavic peoples. Basing their work on the evidence found in Rus', Muscovite, and Russian chronicles, nineteenth-century scholars came to date the Berestovo Church to the late eleventh century and to identify the Kyivan prince Volodymyr Monomakh (r. 1113–1125) as its patron.[78] At first, they attributed the frescoes in the Berestovo Church to the medieval Rus' period; soon, however, concurrent architectural studies proved their assumption wrong.[79] It was revealed that only the walls of the barrel-vaulted naos and the adjacent bays date back to the late eleventh and early twelfth centuries, while the east end of the structure—that is, the main sanctuary apse and the two side apses—belonged to the period of Metropolitan Mohyla.[80]

In the Soviet period, the early modern past of the Berestovo Church was ignored and its Rus' inheritance highlighted. In 1947, on the eight-hundredth anniversary of the founding of Moscow by Prince Iurii Dolgorukii (grand prince of Kyiv, 1149–1151), a symbolic sarcophagus was erected in the north bay of the naos in honor of him.[81] A quarter of a century later, the search for Rus' remains in the monument continued. In the 1970s, seventeenth-century representations of prophets and scenes of the Passion cycle were removed from the west wall of the naos to reveal a large medieval Rus' fresco of the *Second Miraculous Catch of Fish*.[82] On the exterior, archaeological excavations cleared the foundations of the earlier Rus' structure and delineated its imprint on the ground, so that visitors could get a sense of the plan and size of the lost medieval structure.[83] To further emphasize the Rus' origins of the Berestovo Church on the church exterior, medieval walls were partially cleared of plaster to expose original brickwork.

Despite attempts to highlight the medieval origins of the Berestovo Church, today it is Metropolitan Mohyla's revival of the interior that is the most visually striking aspect of the monument. Here, late Byzantine-style frescoes of stunning color and rich iconography are framed by a web of Gothic ribs on the sanctuary ceiling. The very juxtaposition of Eastern and Western Christian visual characteristics alerts viewers to an underlying narrative of transcultural negotiation. Nevertheless, no meaningful scholarly assessment of the early modern features of the Berestovo Church has previously been undertaken; in fact, the frescoes of the Berestovo Church remain unpublished.[84] This chapter takes the first step to expose the rich cultural entanglement of early modern Ruthenian-Rus' visual culture as preserved in the Church of the Savior at Berestovo.

Finally, the chapter's analysis also prompts us to realize that Mohyla saw Kyiv not as a periphery or borderland, but as "the center of the universe around which all planets turn." His engagement with medieval Kyivan monuments was not concerned with restoring a dated notion of Orthodoxy, but rather with reinscribing Kyiv as a major center of Ruthenian-Rus' Eastern Christianity in the Commonwealth and in the Universal Church. To this end, in the Church of the Savior at Berestovo, the metropolitan restaged Orthodox imagery in a manner that confounds definitions of tradition and modernity, realigns cultural boundaries, and challenges our expectations of the development of identities.[85] Rather than simply acknowledge diversity, as is often the case in texts emphasizing the Commonwealth's "multiculturalism," the Church of the Savior at Berestovo challenges the very nature of the cultural, political, and ecclesiastical divisions that are assumed to have structured Commonwealth society.

5

Sarmatia Revisited

Maps and the Making of the Polish-Lithuanian Commonwealth

Tomasz Grusiecki

The map of "European Sarmatia" by the Polish physician and cartographer Andrzej Pograbka (d. 1602) was published in Venice in 1570 at a moment of historic change in central and eastern Europe (fig. 5.1). Just one year previously, on July 1, 1569, the nobilities of the Kingdom of Poland and the Grand Duchy of Lithuania had agreed to bind together their composite polities "in perpetuity," forming a confederated political entity that replaced a looser union first forged in 1385. The new body politic is known in the English-language scholarship as the Polish-Lithuanian Commonwealth, but in the original Polish-written document it was described simply as *Rzeczpospolita*, meaning both a well-ordered political community and "something held in common by a wider public," [our] *shared thing—res publica* in the classical rendering, and "common wealth" in the early modern English translation.[1] Strictly speaking, there were still two autonomous polities, the Kingdom of Poland and the Grand Duchy of Lithuania (both of which were composite realms), but their political communities ceded parts of their sovereignty to the Commonwealth, establishing a common Sejm (legislative assembly) and currency. Pograbka's map was the first to appear after the forging of this momentous political alliance, and thus it marks an important milestone in representing the newly formed Commonwealth as an integrable entity.

Figure 5.1. Andrzej Pograbka, *Partis Sarmatiae Europeae quae Sigismundo Augusto Regi Poloniae Potentissimo subiacet, nova descriptio,* 1570, printed in Venice, 68 × 46 cm. Munich, Bayerische Staatsbibliothek, 2 Mapp. 464. Artwork in the public domain; photograph provided by digitale-sammlungen.de/MDZ: Münchener DigitalisierungsZentrum, Digitale Bibliothek; CC BY-NC-SA 4.0.

Pograbka needed to tackle several issues, however, in order to render his cartographic representation of the Polish-Lithuanian territories legible and indelible. For how was it possible to depict a confederated polity on a map, with only mountain ranges and rivers acting as subdivisions of land, and with no internal or external borders added to the picture? What would this polity even be called if its self-proclaimed name referred simply to an idealized system of governance? "Commonwealth" (or its cognates, such as "Republic") did not unambiguously convey the composite character of the Polish-Lithuanian union, and, given that most cartographic depictions of Poland-Lithuania were produced and consumed in western Europe,[2] there was always the danger that the meaning of the toponym "Commonwealth" might have been lost in translation. Indeed, mapmakers tended to use the name of the more powerful partner in the union, Poland, to refer to the entire confederated polity, as is evident in the 1570 edition of Abraham Ortelius's *Theatrum orbis terrarum*. Less frequently, they included the names of both territorial states, as in various editions of Sebastian Münster's *Cosmographia*.[3] For map owners in Poland-Lithuania, the former solution risked irritating the Lithuanian elites, who continued to insist on the legal distinctiveness of the Grand Duchy within the Commonwealth; the latter accommodation entirely ignored the converging aspect of the union.

Pograbka's choice to call the Commonwealth "European Sarmatia" was an answer to these concerns. Rather than entering into the potentially contentious politics of his day, marked by often bitter disagreements over the nature of the union, Pograbka offered a less politicized and simultaneously more inclusive vision of the Polish-Lithuanian lands by mapping them onto cartographic divisions dating back to Ptolemy's treatise *Geographia*, an ancient text written around 150 AD, first printed as a modern illustrated edition with maps in 1477, and still widely read in the sixteenth century.[4] Backed by the authority of this celebrated Greco-Roman geographer, European Sarmatia in Pograbka's map served as an ancient substitute for the lands that lay between the Vistula and the Don, which in the early modern period were inhabited by Poles, Lithuanians, Ruthenians, and Prussians. The term was not only meant to give these otherwise separate peoples a sense of historical continuity and an impetus for greater association between them, but also marked their place firmly among all those other Europeans with a claim to classical heritage. Using an ancient geographical concept and applying it to an early modern context, Pograbka solved the problem of naming the new

Commonwealth, while also claiming for it an allegedly unbroken history anchored in "Sarmatian" antiquity.

As the literary historian Tadeusz Ulewicz (1917–2012) observed in his pioneering study *Sarmacja* (Sarmatia, 1950), a scholarly monograph on the uses and abuses of Ptolemy in premodern Polish historical discourse, Sarmatia is a concept intimately linked to cartographic representation and philological antiquarianism.[5] Its embrace by Polish-based humanists and their patrons from the late fifteenth century onward was an element of a pan-European revival of classical learning, fueled at least in some measure by the early modern elites who attempted to locate their origins in antiquity, vying with each other for the most impressive lineage from an ancient people, ideally recorded by Herodotus, Ptolemy, Tacitus, Julius Caesar, or another Greco-Roman authority. The French, for example, had stories of their supposed descent from the Gauls, Swedes from the Goths, and the Dutch from the Batavians.[6]

Although Ulewicz is mostly interested in early modern perceptions of Sarmatia as a geographical concept flexible enough to include various eastern European peoples and places, he nonetheless asserts that the region's inhabitants were united by "the peculiar, highly characteristic, and irrevocable style of life and a way of thinking" that he refers to as "Sarmatism"—an elusive term of eighteenth-century origin, in the 1950s used primarily as a synonym for Polish Baroque culture.[7] Ulewicz borrows this definition from the art historian Tadeusz Mańkowski (1878–1956), who reintroduced Sarmatism to scholarly attention in a series of studies culminating in *Geneaologia Sarmatyzmu* (Geneaology of Sarmatism), one of the most influential works of Polish historiography, published three years before *Sarmacja*, in 1947.[8] For Mańkowski, Sarmatism is something between a worldview, a lifestyle, and a specific set of attitudes and conventions typified by the formal "orientalization" of Polish material culture in the sixteenth to eighteenth centuries. Thus, the denizens of Sarmatia were not merely an interconnected group of peoples sharing a historical territory, but explicitly a community of shared historical experience, united and living by the same purpose and values. There is, then, an important difference between Ulewicz's Sarmatia as a historical place and Mańkowski's Sarmatism as a cultural formation.

While Ulewicz's Sarmatia is a transnational spatial unit, Mańkowski's Sarmatism is a genealogical account of a specific (modern) nation, Poland, and its direct ancestry from the Sarmatians, an ancient Iranian people originally inhabiting the Pontic Steppe.[9] According to this interpretation, Poland is not only genealogically coherent but also becomes an analogue for the en-

tire Polish-Lithuanian Commonwealth, which in turn becomes a larger version of Poland, a coherent society with one indivisible culture consisting of
Poles and assimilated (polonized) Lithuanians, Ruthenians, and Prussians,
who as a result of Sarmatism's hold over historians' imaginations become,
more or less, regional versions of Poles. Their culture is shared because—as
is argued in a truly circular manner—it is Polish, and therefore Sarmatian,
and therefore "a feature of Old Poland's life and thought."[10] Mańkowski's followers mostly accepted this notion of Sarmatism's assimilatory quality, im-
buing the Commonwealth with a coherent cultural identity allegedly shared
among the noble citizens who partook in "Sarmatian culture," "Sarmatian
art," "Sarmatian portraiture," "Sarmatian ideology," and many other things
"Sarmatian."[11] Sarmatia in this assimilatory projection is a nation in the
making, with a teleological arc of collective memory rooted in self-avowedly
shared traditions, contexts, and historical experiences.

An important aspect of this narrative is how it summons the specter of
orientalism, an assumption that the Polish nobles were aware of the Sarmatians' origins in the "East," somewhere on the Eurasian Steppe; and that the
outpouring of stories supposedly promoting Poland's Sarmatian lineage triggered a process of the orientalization of Polish costume and material culture
in the sixteenth century.[12] This seemingly oriental mode of Sarmatism was, as
stated in the catalog to the first affirmative exhibition of "Sarmatian" decorative arts held at Warsaw's National Museum in 1980, "a specific lifestyle and
its physical manifestation serving as the external expression of Polishness."[13]

Enticing as it is (at least for some Polish nationalists), such a narrow account of Sarmatism is ahistorical, since no citizen of the Polish-Lithuanian
Commonwealth (of which fewer than half were Catholic Poles) would have
applied the notion of Sarmatia to describe the culture, art, portraiture, music,
theater, or belief systems of this vast political union. Certainly cartography,
which provided the impetus for associating Poland-Lithuania with Sarmatia,
offers no grounds for an assimilatory reading. In the Pograbka map (fig. 5.1),
to return to our opening image, Sarmatia is a projection, not a fact. It is a
collection of different political units rather than a single territorial state.
"Ducatus Lithuaniae" (the [Grand] Duchy of Lithuania) is marked as separate from "Polonia Maior" (Greater Poland, Wielkopolska) and "Polonia
Minor" (Lesser Poland, Małopolska), with Prussia, Samogitia, Volhynia, Podolia, and "Russia" (the Ruthenian province) also added to the picture. Thus,
while forming the Polish-Lithuanian Commonwealth—that is, the modern
Sarmatia—these historically distinctive provinces are captioned on the map

as discrete entities. Pograbka's Sarmatia is not a single nation, but a union of different Sarmatian lands. It is first and foremost a geographical container, more akin to Ulewicz's spatial continuum than Mańkowski's account of Sarmatia's genealogically related constituent peoples.

This chapter hence proposes to redirect the discussion of Sarmatia from genealogy to cartography, where it originally came from, in order to yield a new interpretation of this contentious toponym not as a synonym for a Polish-led Commonwealth with a shared language and culture, but rather as a place name acknowledging the heterogeneous character of the Polish-Lithuanian union. The term "Sarmatia" is more capacious than is currently acknowledged; it certainly does not denote a monocultural nation moving toward an ever increasing degree of uniformity. The open-ended potential inherent in Sarmatia makes it less compatible with Mańkowski's cultural determinism and more with Ulewicz's geographical functionalism. While the earlier approach assumes the allegedly full cultural assimilation of the Commonwealth's various ethnolinguistic and confessional communities into the dominant polonizing model, the latter recognizes that the Commonwealth was always a pluralistic realm distinguished by the heterogeneity of its constituent peoples, who needed to be continually convinced of the union's relevance so as to keep the Sarmatian historico-geographical nomenclature meaningful and consequential. Cartography projected a coherent, classically inspired vision for Poland-Lithuania, while simultaneously guarding its composite character. Early modern maps of Sarmatia, therefore, did not merely reflect a commonwealth in the making; they actively participated in its creation and sustenance.

What's in a Name?

The question of the nature of Sarmatian identity has of late become a subject of debate. While scholars of different political bents still uphold received wisdom maintaining that Sarmatism existed in early modernity as a real cultural formation, Jakub Niedźwiedź has recently pointed to the questionable foundations of this claim. Referencing Eric Hobsbawm and Terence Ranger, he argues that Sarmatism is an invented tradition, a Romantic identity discourse that developed in the nineteenth century as a response to a lost political sovereignty, attempting to essentialize Polishness through the lens of an idealized past.[14] It is hard to disagree with Niedźwiedź's reading of Sarmatism as an epistemic construct. Although it might appear as if it were an age-old cultural paradigm, Sarmatism is more accurately a grand narrative of Polish culture that emerged only after the confederate state formation that some cartographers described as European Sarmatia had disappeared from the map.

The term "Sarmatism" appeared for the first time during the Enlightenment, when it served as a slur against the traditionalist nobility, who wanted to preserve the political system that favored their interests over those of other social classes, and who manifested their conservatism in, among other ways, the Ottomanesque costume once popular in Poland-Lithuania, but which by the late eighteenth century had become a historical relic.[15] It was then that the *Monitor*, the newspaper supporting King Stanislaus Augustus's reformist agenda, called the traditionalists "thickheads of sarmatism" (*bałwany sarmatyzmu*), and Franciszek Zabłocki's comedy *Sarmatyzm* (1784) labeled them as a bunch of degenerates stuck in the past.[16] But what the Enlightenment-era critics mock is not so much a particular cultural profile or stylistic predilection as the social and political reactionism of the period, which manifested itself in, among other things, an outdated (early modern) overreliance on classical sources, uncritically repeated and unchallenged, focusing on tradition over progress. The anonymous *Monitor* critic is particularly animated when he announces that Polish has replaced the allegedly unscientific Latin as the language of scholarship in the Enlightenment-era Commonwealth. In doing so, he seems not to notice that Latin had once been the lingua franca of European humanism and science.[17] However, it was the Romantic and post-Romantic writers, particularly Henryk Sienkiewicz (1846–1916), who wrote most vividly of Sarmatism as a cultural formation in their literary descriptions of Old Poland, outlining the country's flamboyant manners, Ottomanesque costume, and bellicose character. They constructed a positive, glorifying vision of a lost Commonwealth, and indeed Sienkiewicz himself was unafraid to confess that he, too, was "a Sarmatian child."[18]

While literary Sarmatism enjoyed its greatest success in the nineteenth century, it was not until the twentieth century that the phenomenon received its first scholarly study. It all began with Mańkowski's *Genealogia Sarmatyzmu* (1947), notably the first monograph to conflate the Ottomanization of Polish-Lithuanian fashions with the emergence and spread of belief in the Commonwealth's genealogical lineage from ancient Sarmatia. His book amalgamated these historical processes, neither of which is critically analyzed, into a teleological model of thinking about Polish history (Mańkowski tellingly treats Lithuania as a Polish province, nearly ignores Ruthenia, and pays no attention to Prussia). In this model, the Commonwealth is an eastern land inhabited by a quintessentially eastern people. Mańkowski goes as far as to assert that Poles "looked to the East as the cradle of their nation."[19] Seeking reasons for the nobility's self-labeling as descendants of the Sarmatians, he assumed that the cultural character of the Commonwealth was determined by its citizens' genealogical predispositions.

This is a specious claim, however, as Mańkowski's argument makes many assumptions that find no confirmation in historical sources. Presupposing that early modern Poles had his modern understanding of the ancient Sarmatians as an Iranian people, and caring little about Lithuanians, Prussians, and Ruthenians, Mańkowski in fact anachronistically applied the philological and archaeological knowledge of his own day to Polish-Lithuanian epistemologies.[20] Although according to Herodotus and Strabo, the Sarmatians were related to the Scythians and inhabited the Pontic Steppe, and while Tacitus compares them to the Persians,[21] none of the key early modern Polish-Lithuanian historical narratives (of which more will follow) explicitly states the Iranian extraction of these peoples, as Mańkowski would have it (and as his acolytes would blindly endorse).

Contrary to Mańkowski's framing of Polish historical memory, early modern chroniclers do not understand Sarmatia in terms of lineage. They emphasize the Poles' long-term presence in Sarmatia, back to antiquity, and argue that Poles were Slavs who cohabited Sarmatia with other peoples. These writers are not interested in taxonomic classification of Sarmatian origins, but rather in a people's connection to a place. Maciej Miechowita (1457–1523), for example, asserts in the *Chronica Polonorum* (Chronicle of the Poles) of 1519 that Poles have always inhabited the same lands: "Poles and all other Slavs, have been living in this kingdom, making their permanent home here, and nowhere else."[22] Marcin Kromer (*Ger.* Martin Cromer) in *Polonia* (1577) is of a similar opinion: "Poles are a Slavic and Sarmatian people,"[23] by which he means that they are related to other Slavic peoples, and that they live in Sarmatia. There is no self-orientalizing genealogical rhetoric in this statement because Sarmatia is a place located in east-central Europe, not an oriental, exotic setting. The author of the often reissued Polish-language *Kronika świata* (World Chronicle, 1550), Marcin Bielski, dates the presence of Sarmatians in Polish-Lithuanian lands to a far more distant past, tracing their origins to one of the sons of Noah: "[Japheth] our Christian [*sic!*] father ... came to this northern country in Europe after the Deluge and multiplied his offspring by the Lord's will."[24] The *Kronika polska, litewska, żmódzka y wszystkiej Rusi* (Chronicle of Poland, Lithuania, Samogitia and All of Ruthenia, 1582) by the Lithuanian-based Pole and Catholic priest Maciej Stryjkowski (1547–1593) confirms this account, qualifying (after Jan Długosz, most notably) that the Lithuanian nobility were descendants of the Roman nobleman Palemon and his five hundred companions, who settled in Lithuania, a Sarmatian land, and gradually adopted the Sarmatian customs and language.[25] The term "Sarmatian" in this context stands for the customs and language of the local people. At no point, however, did early modern Poles or Lithuanians identify themselves with any Middle Eastern or Central Asian people.[26] Mańkowski's "Sarmatism" is then not only an anachronism but also a catalyst for erroneous interpretations of Polish history.

Historical sources before the eighteenth century—including the most "Sarmatian" of them all, Jan Chryzostom Pasek's *Pamiętniki* (Memoirs, probably written in the 1690s)—never mention the term,[27] and Polish historians have an abundance of other designations to describe the Commonwealth's culture, including "early modern," "transcultural," "preindustrial," or even the outmoded "Renaissance" and "Baroque." While eighteenth-century (modern) critics gave us the word, they did not see it as a useful analytical category to make sense of the Commonwealth's historical patterns. For them, Sarmatia was not an ethnic or national community, but a holdover from Renaissance philological discourse. It is unclear whether they understood its cartographic origins, but the Enlightenment-era critics patently read the concept of "Sarmatia" as a classically inspired spatial image, perhaps heuristically useful, but unsuitable to serve their own modernizing goals. Questions of suitability aside, it is then important to remember that the original (early modern) rationale for Sarmatia was to serve as a rhetorical conceit alluding to the continuity of the Commonwealth's ancient borders. The term was picked up from cartography by early modern chronicle writers. In other words, maps come first, and historical narratives of Sarmatia come later—not the other way around.

What to Do with Sarmatia's Heterogeneity

The exploration of Sarmatia as a classical analogue for modern realms took shape at a particularly momentous time: when Renaissance humanists were starting to think, for the first time, with maps in mind.[28] Pograbka was not the first to claim European Sarmatia as a predecessor of Poland-Lithuania. He followed in the footsteps of previous mapmakers and antiquarians,

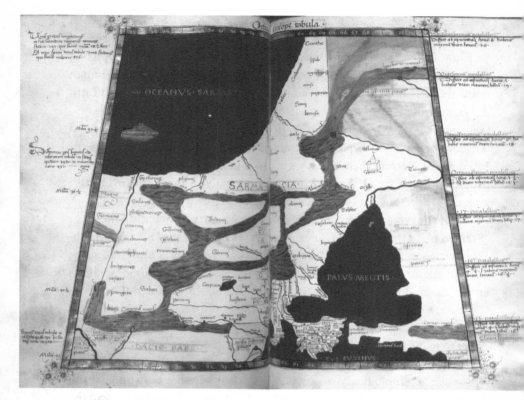

Figure 5.2. Nicolaus Germanus, Eight Map of Europe (Sarmacia Europea), in *Cosmographia Claudii Ptolomaei Alexandrini*, ca. 1460. Manuscript and Archive Division, New York Public Library, Astor, Lenox and Tilden Foundations, 427027. Artwork in the public domain; photograph provided by the New York Public Library Digital Collections, https://digitalcollections.nypl.org/items/510d47da-e68a-a3d9-e040-e00a18064a99; no known copyright.

mostly Italian and German, who invoked Tacitus, Strabo, Pliny, Pomponius Mela, and above all, Ptolemy in referring to northeastern Europe as European Sarmatia.[29] Ptolemy's *Geography* (AD 150), in particular, was becoming the standard reference on geography in the fifteenth and sixteenth centuries, containing both textual and cartographical descriptions of the world known to the ancients.[30] Brought to Florence in undocumented circumstances in the early fifteenth century, probably from Constantinople, *Geography* inspired geometrically driven representations of the known world by providing a method for charting linear depiction of land on a gridded and uniformly scaled surface.[31] But while changing the ways in which land, distance, and location were conceptualized, the translation of Ptolemy also reinforced the classical nomenclature in early modern political geography and established "European Sarmatia" as a standard geographical reference for the combined Polish and Lithuanian lands.[32] By 1550, there were twenty-six editions in various European cities, and thus the diffusion of the idea of "European Sarmatia" owed much to the popularity of Ptolemy's *Geography*.[33]

The first modern rendition of Ptolemy's map covering the territories of the Kingdom of Poland and the Grand Duchy of Lithuania was designed by Cardinal Nicholas of Cusa (1401–1464), often referred to by his Latinized name, Cusanus. We only know it, however, from a later version (fig. 5.2) prepared by the Benedictine friar Nicolaus Germanus (ca. 1420–ca. 1490), which was later to be used in the printed editions of Ptolemy's atlases. The Cusanus-Germanus map depicts a territory roughly corresponding to the early modern Polish-Lithuanian union, but described as *Sarmatia Europea* (European Sarmatia) in direct adherence to Ptolemy's toponymy.[34] Thus, the Roman province of Dacia borders European Sarmatia in the south, the Vistula River in the west, the Baltic Sea (*Oceanus Sarmaticus*) in the north, and the Don (*Tanais*) and the Black Sea (*Palus Meotis*) in the east. Although these are the coordinates from Ptolemy's treatise, Cusanus was likely assisted by a Polish scholar, who supplied locations of towns on a grid of parallels of latitude and meridians of longitude. The scholar probably came from Lesser Poland or Red Ruthenia, given that the urban centers from these lands predominate on the map. A likely candidate is Jan Długosz (1415–1480), canon at Kraków, who met Cusanus in Rome. This hypothesis is further strengthened by the map's inclusion of two localities, Brzeźnica, Długosz's birthplace, and Oleśnica, the family seat of his patron, Zbigniew Oleśnicki (1389–1455), bishop of Kraków.[35]

Długosz is best known for his *Annales seu cronicae incliti regni Poloniae* (Annals or Chronicles of the Famous Kingdom of Poland), one of the earliest chronicles of Polish history, written in the mid-fifteenth century, concurrently with Cusanus's map.[36] This work is one of the earliest to apply the Ptolemaic idea of Sarmatia in the historical narrative of the Polish state. But while he uses the term to define the land, Długosz does not understand it in ethnic terms. He does not treat Sarmatia as the precise equivalent of the modern Polish kingdom, but rather as a description that the Romans used to encapsulate the ethnically diverse ancestors of the current inhabitants of this realm. The author simply states that Poles and Ruthenians had already inhabited their respective lands in antiquity, and since classical writers called this region European Sarmatia, these Slavic peoples were known as Sarmatians in Greek and Roman times.[37]

Długosz does not specify when exactly Poles and Ruthenians settled in east-central Europe, though he hints that before the arrival of Lech and Rus—legendary leaders of the Poles and the Ruthenians, respectively—they lived in Pannonia and later in Slavonia.[38] Despite this acknowledgment of intermingling and coexistence, Długosz is polonocentric in his narrative, treating Ruthenians as the younger cousins of Poles—Rus was not Lech's brother, but his son. The chronicler treats Lithuanians as a people who arrived in Sarmatia after the Slavs, as they had allegedly descended from the Romans.[39] In general, however, he renders Sarmatia as a space of coexistence between different peoples. It might be a space destined to be dominated by the Poles, but it is certainly not an ethnically delineated, closed-off community. It is, then, important to keep in mind that Długosz actively participated in the creation of maps and was likely surrounded by them when writing the *Annales*.[40] As an image of a territory encompassing most of eastern Europe—which largely exceeded the confines of Długosz's Poland, and included not only the Grand Duchy of Lithuania but also Bohemian, Hungarian, Muscovite, and Tatar lands—Sarmatia needed to remain heterogeneous if its historical integrity were to be preserved.

Cartography played a role in propagating this intercultural image of Sarmatia. That Sarmatia did not originally denote an ethnic or political community is evident in two woodcut maps from 1526 by Bernard Wapowski (1450–1535), secretary to King Sigismund I (r. 1506–1548). Published in Kraków by the printer Florian Ungler, this was the first cartographic image of Sarmatia produced in Poland, possibly serving as a double companion map to Długosz's *Annales*.[41] The original maps had long been thought to have perished until they were discovered in the Central Archive of Old Records in Warsaw in 1932 by the Polish librarian Kazimierz Piekarski, who found three fragments in the bindings of accounting books, where Wapowski's maps were used as scrap paper.[42] The maps were later lost during the destruction of Warsaw in 1944, but from descriptions and photographic reproductions (for example, fig. 5.3), we know that the size of these two maps put together was 60 × 90 cm without margins; we also know that they included a grid of latitudes and longitudes, thus implying Ptolemy's influence. The now-lost fragments depicted southern and central Poland, Hungary and the northern Balkans, the Grand Duchy of Lithuania, Crimea, and parts of Muscovy. Clearly, Wapowski's Sarmatia was not a map of the Polish state.

We can additionally infer what territories these maps covered from a privilege dated October 18, 1526, granted to Ungler by Sigismund I. And so

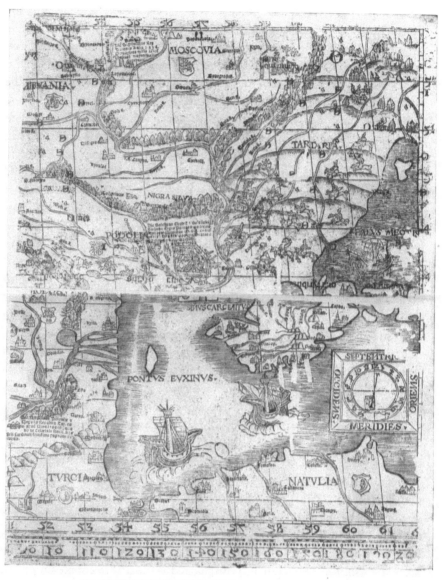

FIG. 8. FRAGMENT OF A PROOF PRINT OF THE MAP OF SOUTHERN SARMATIA BY BERNARD WAPOWSKI
Woodcut made in 1526. This surviving fragment shows the eastern part of the map.
Actual size.

Figure 5.3. Bernard Wapowski, fragment of a proof print of the map of Sarmatia, facsimile (original woodcut made in 1526; lost during World War II), from Karol Buczek, *The History of Polish Cartography from 15th to the 18th Century* (Wrocław: Zakład Narodowy im. Ossolińskich, 1966), figure 9. Photograph provided by Zakład Narodowy im. Ossolińskich; no known copyright.

these maps covered Poland, Hungary, Wallachia, "Turkey" (likely, only the European parts of the Ottoman Empire), "Tartaria" (likely, Crimea and its environs), Muscovy, Prussia, Pomerania, Samogitia, and Lithuania.[43] Another archival clue comes from a letter written by the Lutheran theologian Johann Hess (1490–1547), a resident of Breslau (now Wrocław), on May 11, 1529, to the Nuremberg humanist Willibald Pirckheimer (1470–1530). In this letter, Hess reports that "two maps of Sarmatia and Scythia had been recently published in Kraków; although they are inelegant, they seem useful."[44] Two months later, Hess dispatched another missive (dated July 13) in which he informed Pirckheimer that he was sending him "the second map of Sarmatia" and that he had requested the "first map" from friends in Kraków.[45] The Lutheran reformer Philip Melanchton (1497–1560) was another recipient of Wapowski's "maps of Sarmatia distributed by Hess," evidence of which we find in a letter sent by Melanchton to his "friend" Andrzej Trzecieski the Elder (1497–1547) in October 1529.[46] Wapowski himself calls these lands Sarmatia in a letter sent on December 1, 1530, to the prince-bishop of Warmia (*Ger.* Ermland) Johannes Danticus (*Pol.* Jan Dantyszek; 1485–1548), assuring his addressee that he has shipped "two chorographies of Sarmatian lands" to the Catholic theologian Johannes Eck (1486–1543), as requested.[47] Wapowski treats them in geographical rather than political terms, a sentiment evident in his use of the plural form "lands" in describing Sarmatia's transregional ambit. After all, Wapowski's cartographic works are first and foremost modern editions of Ptolemaic atlases imposing a classical toponym onto the borders of modern territorial states.

For the Polish humanist scholar Maciej Miechowita, writing around the same time, divisions between different lands within Sarmatia remained intact. His widely circulated *Tractatus de duabus Sarmatiis Asiana et Europiana et de contentis in eis* (Treatise on the Two Sarmatias, Asian and European, and What Is Found in Them," first printed in Kraków in 1517) firmly distinguished between the Poles, Lithuanians, Ruthenians, and Muscovites who inhabited the land called *Sarmatia Europea*, and the various Turkic peoples (whom he calls Scythians), who lived east of the Don in the area known as *Sarmatia Asiatica*.[48] Miechowita is often cited as the first to equate European Sarmatia with Poland,[49] but in fact he describes a much wider territorial expanse. His use of the term is not synonymous with the Polish kingdom, but rather alludes only to its potential future expansion to the east and south.[50] As Miechowita was a noted map collector,[51] and his understanding of history and current affairs was shaped by maps, he was well placed to recount the ethnic diversity of (early) modern Sarmatia.

This multicultural framing continued in other treatises, even as they used the idea of Sarmatia as a potential unifier of the diverse peoples inhabiting the lands of the Polish-Lithuanian union.[52] As early as 1521, in his *De vetustatibus Polonorum* (On the Ancient Origins of the Poles), Justus Ludwik Decjusz (*Ger.* Jost Ludwig Dietz), secretary to King Sigismund I, maintained in tautological fashion that Poles, Prussians, Lithuanians, and Ruthenians were all defined as Sarmatians because they inhabited the lands of Sarmatia. Sigismund was thus king of both Sarmatia as a whole and Poland as its constituent part.[53] A perfect example of cartographically inspired imagination shaping real interactions between peoples, Sarmatia offered new potential for connecting regions and integrating its inhabitants.[54] This humanistic interpretation of the coexistence of the four major peoples of Poland-Lithuania was thus paving the way to a shared self-identification for the otherwise distinct nobilities of the Polish and Lithuanian realms. That the royal secretary Decjusz should embrace the idea of uninterrupted historical cohabitation of all Polish-Lithuanian peoples is not surprising. After all, he worked for a Jagiellonian monarch who reigned over all these lands and had a dynastic interest in tying them more closely together.

As maps circulated across Poland-Lithuania and the rest of Europe, their use as a visual counterpart to text-based chronicles and pamphlets was becoming more widespread. The first update to Wapowski's map covering Poland and Lithuania was completed around 1558 by Wacław Grodecki (ca. 1535–1591), a nobleman of Teschen in Silesia (now Cieszyn, Poland), who was then still a student at Leipzig (fig. 5.4).[55] Perhaps due to anxieties over the development of a cohesive ethnic and religious self for an emerging polity, it was more overtly polonocentric than Wapowski's map, as it assumed Poland's dominion over all the lands of the union. After all, the map—first published in Basel in 1562 by Johann Oporinus—is captioned "in praise of Poland" (*in Poloniae laudem*) in the cartouche on the bottom left, thus claiming the historical lands included in Wapowski's apolitical representation as subordinate to the Polish Crown. Grodecki used Długosz's *Chorografia* and Wapowski's designs, either in the original or a copy, to create the most accurate map of Poland and Lithuania to that time,[56] but he departed from the more inclusive logic of Sarmatia. The actual first practical application of the map, however, went against Grodecki's Polish-centered rhetoric. Printed with neither the name of the author nor a date, it was ironically used as a cartographic counterpart to Philip Melanchton's short treatise on the origin of Slavs, published in 1558.[57] Given the context, this version of the map made

Figure 5.4. Wacław Grodecki, *In Poloniae laudem, et tabulae huius commendationem*, facsimile (original printed in 1562 by Johann Oporinus in Basel), from *Monumenta Poloniae Cartographica*, ed. Karol Buczek, vol. 1 (Kraków: Polska Akademia Umiejętności, 1939), Tab. VI. Artwork in the public domain; photograph provided by polona.pl/Biblioteka Narodowa; no known copyright.

much wider claims—about the history of all Slavic peoples—than the stand-alone published map of 1562 dedicated to Sigismund II Augustus of Poland-Lithuania (r. 1548–1572).

But the same map could be employed in different written chorographies (descriptions of regions), serving different purposes. The publication of Grodecki's map at Oporinus's Basel printing house is not without significance, as at the time Oporinus was likely also thinking about publishing the first authorized edition of *Polonia* (Poland), a treatise on the history and geography of Poland-Lithuania by Marcin Kromer, royal secretary and bishop of Warmia.[58] Like Decjusz's *De vetustatibus Polonorum*, Kromer's *Polonia* naturalized Jagiellonian rule by asserting that Poles, Lithuanians, and Prussians were all Sarmatians, a claim laid with the aid of cartography.[59] While Oporinus never published the book—which eventually came out in Cologne in 1577—there is surviving correspondence between Kromer and Oporinus, and between Jan Grodecki (Wacław's brother) and Kromer, which confirms that Kromer thought about including a version of Grodecki's map as an illustration to his work.[60] It was only the third authorized edition of *Polonia*, published in 1589 in Cologne, that included a map to help the reader make sense of the text. Recycled from the 1570 edition of Abraham Ortelius's atlas *Theatrum orbis terrarium* (Theater of the Orb of the World), which itself was based on Grodecki's version published earlier by Oporinus, it served as a visual tool for deriving geographical information.[61] The commissioning of a map specifically to accompany a historical chronicle thus demonstrates that Kromer saw cartography as indispensable in contextualizing his written descriptions of the land and its history; in other words, an account of "Polonia" without its visual counterpart was seen as insufficient in communicating chorographical ideas clearly and effectively.

This brings us back to Pograbka who, despite heavy reliance on Grodecki's designs in his 1570 map (fig. 5.1), nonetheless refrained from calling the lands of the union "Polonia," preferring instead to refer to them by the classical designation "European Sarmatia." According to the dedication in the cartouche, he created this representation to address inaccuracies in the maps of Poland available in Venice at the time. He was probably referring here to a 1562 map by Giacomo Gastaldi, based on maps by Wapowski and Gerard Mercator. Pograbka's map was not innovative in purely cartographical terms. As Kazimierz Kozica has demonstrated, he merely revised Grodecki's 1562 map by adding 161 new localities to the picture.[62] However, Pograbka's key contribution lay in his marrying of the Ptolemaic idea of Sarmatia with the

cartographic projection of Poland in Grodecki's modern map, turning a previously apolitical idea into a community-building exercise.

Published after the 1569 union, Pograbka's work offers a different perspective on the Polish-Lithuanian realms. The map of the union is no longer a collection of territories that forgo their individual identity "in praise
of Poland," as is proclaimed by the cartouche in Grodecki's map, but as a
community of historical lands that together form the "parts of European
Sarmatia, which are under the control of the powerful Polish king Sigismund
Augustus."[63] Although the textual rhetoric of this formulaic account of sovereignty underlines the king's dominion in the Commonwealth, it simultaneously proposes to spread the value-neutral, classically sanctioned umbrella
of European Sarmatia over the newly confirmed Polish-Lithuanian union.
After all, Sigismund II was from a legal point of view not simply the king of
Poland, his most prestigious regal title, but also "by the grace of God, Grand
Duke of Lithuania, Ruthenia, Prussia, Masovia, Samogitia, Livonia, Smolensk, Siveria, and Chernihiv." The visual language of the map is admittedly
polonocentric, as the western parts of the depiction are richer in detail, but it
also respects the legal identity of all the territories of the union, each with its
own historic name and distinct character. Thus, the Commonwealth's visual
identity is celebrated not as a coherent state inhabited by polonized citizens,
but as a geographical entity consisting of separate units that together fill in
the time-honored contours of European Sarmatia. This is not yet a fully united realm, but rather a projected vision of a polity inhabited by diverse peoples
whose shared identity is based on living in a commonwealth whose roots go
back to antiquity. Looking at this cartographic representation, early modern
Polish-Lithuanian viewers of different linguistic and cultural backgrounds
would have seen their regional distinctiveness simultaneously reinforced
and open to reconfiguration, possibly even growing stronger emotive ties
with their fellow "Sarmatians." To paraphrase Richard Helgerson, Pograbka's
map would have allowed them to see the Commonwealth for the first time.[64]
Through this and similar images, an imagined community of "Sarmatia"
was effectively coming into being.[65] Importantly, however, this casting of
political sentiment in cartographic abstraction was merely the beginning
of a process that had still not been completed by the time of the partitions
of the Commonwealth in the late eighteenth century. In this sense, it was not
a reflection of reality.

It is always difficult to gauge the impact of early modern images on
collective identity, but soon after Pograbka's map was published, a change

in the conception of Sarmatia began to take shape. While Marcin Bielski's earlier *Kronika świata* (1551) links Sarmatia only with Poland and Ruthenia (like Długosz's *Annales*), removing Lithuania from the picture altogether,[66] chronicles published in the 1580s push a different narrative. For example, Stryjkowski's *Kronika polska, litewska, żmódzka y wszystkiej Rusi* (1582) provides the first detailed account of Lithuanian history as intimately related to the histories of Poland and Ruthenia. Funded not by the court, but by over thirty Polish-Lithuanian noblemen, Stryjkowski's narrative mixes Polish historiography with the Lithuanian-Ruthenian chronicles (though he omits their anti-Polish character), claiming that the Polish-Lithuanian union connected all the Sarmatian peoples under the aegis of a single polity.[67] Accordingly, Stryjkowski recounts the entangled past of all the Sarmatian nations, focusing on shared heritage and points of historical intersection. *Kronika* had a wide reception in the Commonwealth, and it was popularized throughout Europe by the work of Alessandro Guagnini (*Pol.* Aleksander Gwagnin), an Italian soldier and writer active in Poland, who in 1578 published *Sarmatia Europae descriptio* (A Description of European Sarmatia), a plagiarized version of Stryjkowski's manuscript.[68] Like Stryjkowski, Guagnini included the previously separate Polish, Lithuanian, and Ruthenian histories, uniting them under Sarmatian auspices.

Stryjkowski's account of the connections between all the nations inhabiting the Polish-Lithuanian Commonwealth quickly became a conventional mode of recounting the histories of its by then united peoples. To give a notable example, the Calvinist nobleman Stanisław Sarnicki, who in 1587 published the Latin *Annales, sive de origine et rebus gestis Polonorum et Lithuanorum* (Annals, or, On the Origins and Deeds of Poles and Lithuanians), described the principal peoples of the Commonwealth as having coexisted since the fourteenth century. Although he calls them Sarmatians and claims that the Sarmatians had always inhabited the same lands in northeastern Europe (that would later become Poland-Lithuania),[69] Sarnicki nonetheless treats Polish, Lithuanian, Ruthenian, and Prussian histories separately. This is not a coherent narrative of one Sarmatian people, but rather a history of neighboring Sarmatian nations that had interacted with one another for generations and had only recently united. In Ruthenia and Prussia, similar integrating processes materialized in historical writing, as local chroniclers began to update their nations' histories.[70] Nevertheless, the competing discourses of Lithuanians as allegedly descending from the Romans, Prussians as heirs to Goths, and Ruthenians as the successors of Kyivan Rus' were never fully displaced.[71]

One Sarmatia, Many Sarmatians

Adaptations of classical nomenclature and chorography gave Poles, Lithuanians, Prussians, and Ruthenians a corpus of entangled historical accounts,
which supported a shared political project. Importantly, however, this was
never a homogenizing undertaking. On the contrary, when early modern
chroniclers use the term "European Sarmatia," they do not envision the history of a singular people called Sarmatians, but simply provide a historical
description of an ancient place branded as European Sarmatia by classical
geographers. They are not interested in the genealogy of a people, but rather
in the geographic study of a place. It is a presentist narrative insofar as it is
told from the perspective of early modern scholars serving the interests of
a ruler or noble patrons who laid claim to the historical lands of European
Sarmatia, but regardless of whether a chronicle is produced by a Pole or a
Lithuanian, Sarmatia is a land, not an ethnic community.

Poland-Lithuania would remain a composite polity throughout its existence. It was possible to add Sarmatia to one's sense of self without causing
identity dissonance, since it was not an exclusionary national category, but
a geographical, historiographical, and (only implicitly) political designation
that set the grounds for a shared vision of the union. Thus, when the Ruthenian nobleman Adam Kysil (*Pol.* Kisiel; ca. 1600–1653) delivered a list of Ruthenian grievances at the Sejm of 1641, he called his fellow nobles "Ruthenian
Sarmatians," and addressed his grievances to the "Polish Sarmatians."[72] The
rhetoric of his speech foregrounds a polity that is shared between Poles and
Ruthenians, while also revealing differences between them. They are not a
single, united people, but rather two separate peoples who inhabit a connected geographical, political, and cultural space. Sarmatia in this account is a
space of interconnectivity.

A similar use of the Sarmatian trope occurs in the Catholic clergyman
Stanisław Orzechowski's (1513–1566) often-cited letter to Pope Julius III
(1550–1555), in which he argues against the church's rule of celibacy for priests
(just after his own marriage and subsequent excommunication). As he delivers his tirade, Orzechowski gives the following autobiographical details:
"I am of the Scythian people and of the Ruthenian nation [*gente Scytha, natione Ruthena*]. But I am also of the Sarmatian kind [*modo*], for Rus', which
is my *patria*, is located in European Sarmatia. To the right [of Rus'] there is
Dacia, and to the left is Poland. Before [Rus'] is Hungary, and indeed behind
it is the actual Scythia that turns toward the rising sun."[73] Orzechowski's

self-identification is nothing if not complex. He feels simultaneously Scythian, Ruthenian, and Sarmatian, seeing no conflict between these (seemingly) inconsistent identity claims. But while the earlier two appellations refer to genealogy, it is clear that Orzechowski uses Sarmatia in a geographical sense. He speaks explicitly of location when addressing Sarmatia, while he is Ruthenian "by descent" or "by birth" (Latin *natione*). Just like Kysil, then, he sees himself as a Ruthenian Sarmatian.

But there were also other types of Sarmatians. For example, the seventeenth-century Prussian historian and educator Christoph Hartknoch asserts in his history of Prussia (*Alt- und neues Preussen*, 1684) that "one European Sarmatia, as one common mother, nurtured the Poles and the Lithuanians and the Prussians."[74] These peoples are distinct nations among the denizens of Sarmatia; yet by virtue of living in the same long-inhabited land they are, respectively, Polish, Lithuanian, and Prussian Sarmatians. History affects the present in this account, as current residents owe their country to different Sarmatian ancestors, who are identified as such based on their historical dwelling in Sarmatia. While Hartknoch's reasoning is circular in nature, as he begins with what he is trying to end with, he does not see a logical fallacy in his account. He simply takes the Ptolemaic notion of Sarmatia for granted, and, just like his Polish, Lithuanian, and Ruthenian counterparts, he treats the appellation "Sarmatian" as a geographical reference. Even if the Ptolemaic map of Sarmatia itself had not directly influenced his ideas, Hartknoch assumed an epistemic position that had naturalized Ptolemy's system into a default method in the scholarly investigation of the Commonwealth and its history. The increased circulation of maps in this period promoted an image of Poland-Lithuania—both as a whole and of its constituent lands—that could be shared among the inhabitants of all the historically self-governing lands of this vast political union, giving rise to a sense of collective belonging that nonetheless coexisted with local forms of self-identification. There was one Sarmatia, a geo-body that appeared real, and even historical to its diverse inhabitants,[75] but there were many different kinds of Sarmatians, and it would have crossed nobody's mind to see this as a contradiction.

The repeated self-identification of different inhabitants of the Commonwealth as Sarmatians raises the question of this chapter's purpose. If there was a Sarmatia and even Sarmatians, then why question the relevance of "Sarmatism" for the study of identity and culture in the Commonwealth? Is there any point to this revisionism? The answer lies in the modern appropriation of Sarmatian discourse from cartography to genealogy. It is thus imperative to reveal the anachronism of this reading because "Sarmatism" is not merely an idiosyncratic interpretation of Polish history, but rather a major metanarrative of Polish culture that reinforces polonocentric interpretations of the Commonwealth, which is seen in this model as a "polonized" realm.[76] But although much of the twentieth-century scholarship on Sarmatism has (unwittingly) reproduced the Romantic bias of nineteenth-century national ideology and ignored the inherent diversity of both ancient and early modern Sarmatia, looking back to its cartographic origins reveals an unexplored archive of cosmopolitan thought in the Sarmatian discourse itself.

A critical rereading of early modern accounts of Sarmatia through the lens of cartography makes a positive case for an entangled history of Poles, Lithuanians, Ruthenians, and Prussians as separate but interconnected nations within the Commonwealth. Although Sarmatia was a phantasm conjured up by the early modern followers of Ptolemy and other Greco-Roman geographers, it nonetheless provided a useful classically sanctioned moniker for conceptualizing connections between the elites of Poland-Lithuania in spatial terms. Cartography, then, not only reproduced reality as it appeared in the light of day but also reordered it, constituting a means of thinking about and transforming reality through representation of territory. Poland-Lithuania appeared in this representation as the early modern equivalent of an ancient land, with a similarly heterogeneous population, and thus offering a base for political projections. Since there was a shared past, there must also be a shared future.

While the Commonwealth did not need an ethnic common denominator to function, it was desirable to have a spatial metaphor and a visual trope that could embrace the whole territory of the Commonwealth without homogenizing or dividing its constituent peoples: the Poles, Lithuanians, Ruthenians, and Prussians. The rhetoric of Sarmatia, which reinforces but does not supplant ideas of the Republic or the Commonwealth, foregrounds a polity that is shared between these peoples, while also revealing differences between them.[77] They are not a single united entity, but rather separate peoples with different ancestors who inhabit a connected geographical, political, and cultural space. Polish-Lithuanian "Sarmatians" did not see themselves as connected through lineage and shared ethnic origins, as is traditionally assumed (at least by some Polish scholars), but rather through the exigencies and expectations of living together in a shared polity. This, precisely, is the rhetorical function of Sarmatia: to act as a spatial container of a dualistic polity comprising two composite states and at least four different peoples who all—at least at times—called themselves Sarmatians. The Commonwealth was not a nation-state in the making.[78] Instead, it was a union of diverse peoples who often disagreed (just as Adam Kysil disagreed with the Polish nobility at the Sejm of 1641), but who still saw value in a shared political project that could be mapped onto the geographical contours of ancient Sarmatia.

6

Confessions, Confessionalization, and the Partitions of the Polish-Lithuanian Commonwealth

Richard Butterwick

"I shall not evoke how happy were our ancestors, when they commenced their assemblies with this: *pax inter dissidentes*. Later, from the forgetting of these words, the Commonwealth suffered many disasters." Such was the succinct argument made in the Sejm on April 18, 1791, by Ludwik Gutakowski (1738–1811).[1] He was elected envoy (or member) for Orša (*Pol.* Orsza), a place that symbolizes a rising and falling trajectory. The name still resonates in Belarusian, Lithuanian, Polish, and Ukrainian memories because of the victory won there by the army commanded by Hetman Konstanty Ostrogski (*Ukr.* Kostiantyn Ostrozkyi; *Bel.* Kanstantyn Astroski or Astrožski; *Lit.* Konstantinas Ostrogiškis; ca. 1460–1530)—an Orthodox believer—against the hosts of Muscovy in 1514.[2] More recently, however, nearly all of this district in the northeast of the Grand Duchy of Lithuania had been annexed by the Russian Empire. After the first partition of the Polish-Lithuanian Commonwealth in 1772 the district's sejmik had to meet in the neighboring palatinate of Minsk.

The occasion for Gutakowski's speech was a parliamentary debate on the proposed law on the "Free Royal Towns of the Commonwealth." The enactment of this law, which bestowed far-reaching civil and civic rights on the burghers of royal towns and became an integral part of the Constitution of May 3, 1791, testifies to the vitality of the Commonwealth before its final dismemberment in 1795. However, the law's unanimous acclamation was almost derailed by an unexpected dispute over whether Catholics should have priority over non-Catholics (called "dissidents") for municipal office.[3] While some speakers warned that Protestant or Orthodox "dissidents" represented the interests of foreign powers, others—like Gutakowski—insisted on the Commonwealth's tradition of peaceful coexistence of different religions. This particular controversy, to which we shall later return, highlights the wider problem of confessional factors in the partitions of the Commonwealth.

Elsewhere, I have analyzed this and other debates of the Polish Revolution or Four-Year Sejm (1788–1792) to explain the contested concepts of "tolerance" and "intolerance" in late eighteenth-century Polish discourse.[4] In this chapter, the debate serves to introduce evaluations of the role of confessional diversity in the final and fatal trajectory of the Polish-Lithuanian Commonwealth. For the clashing views articulated during this debate highlight a fundamental disagreement that lies at the heart of this chapter's considerations. Did confessional diversity undermine the Commonwealth by sowing dissension among its citizens, facilitating foreign interference, and so contributing to the loss of its territory and sovereignty? Or was it rather efforts undertaken over several generations to marginalize and intimidate non-Catholics that divided the political community, weakened the civic values that had hitherto sustained it, provoked a significant part of the populace to revolt, and led to the fatal intervention of neighboring powers, supposedly on behalf of their coreligionists and in the name of enlightened "tolerance"?

Posed thus, the alternative discourages dispassionate analysis—the kind that might conclude that both processes could have operated together, asymmetrically interacting in ways that changed over time. At the time of writing, Poland is viscerally riven by its own variant of global culture wars driven by the politics of identity. It has become a staple feature of the Third Republic of Poland's "politics of history" to celebrate the "tolerance" of the old Commonwealth. While for some Polish politicians, commentators, and historians, this has become a defensive retort to charges of Catholic "fanaticism," others have fondly imagined a "multicultural," "multinational," and "multiconfessional" Commonwealth as an antidote to modern ethnolinguistic nationalism, and even as a precursor of the European Union.[5] In fact, the totemic resolution of the 1573 Confederacy of Warsaw (formed by nobles during the perilous interregnum and royal election that followed the extinction in the male line of the Jagiellonian dynasty) amounted to far more than the mere toleration of divergence from a religious norm, but less than an embrace of "diversity." It was an agreement between equal noble citizens, dangerously divided by religion ("dissidentes de religione"), not to persecute each other in any way. The religious freedom of non-nobles was another matter altogether.[6]

The purpose of this chapter is neither to "celebrate diversity," as today's proponents of normative multiculturalism urge us to do, nor to defend the honor of *Polonia semper fidelis*. Instead, it is concerned with the conditions of interconfessional coexistence and their political consequences. It will examine and challenge some assumptions underpinning historians' writing on these topics. Given the emotive nature of the subject, it is all the more important to clarify two things: first, the relationship between "confession" and "culture"—and thus between multiconfessionality and "multiculturalism." The Commonwealth's diverse confessions overlapped with its socially and linguistically framed "cultures" (here used in the anthropological sense: systems of signs, customs, assumptions, and values that enable members of a community to communicate between themselves and to distinguish themselves from other communities). However, religious confessions (and here we shall be concerned with Christian confessions) by no means entailed discrete cultural communities—still less "ethnic" or "national" ones. To take but one example, by the later eighteenth century (and probably much earlier), a cultural chasm separated almost all the peasants of Samogitia, who spoke dialects of Lithuanian, from the great majority of their predominantly Polonophone lords and priests, despite the fact that almost all of them worshiped in the Latin Rite of the Catholic Church. Second, it is now difficult to find historians prepared to state unequivocally either that worsening religious "intolerance" led to the destruction of the Commonwealth, or that religious dissensions weakened it from the outset, and that "betrayal" by "disloyal" dissidents hastened its end.

It is instructive, therefore, to recall the views of the interwar Second Republic of Poland's most prominent historian, Władysław Konopczyński (1880–1952). The prolific "devourer of archives" had a polemical streak and was for a time deeply involved in the right-wing politics of National Democracy (Narodowa Demokracja, ND). He agreed with much of the ND chief ideologue Roman Dmowski's (1864–1939) coruscating verdict on the old Commonwealth and its nobility. In his landmark synthesis of early modern Polish history, first published in 1936, Konopczyński pronounced that "in the confessional century *par excellence*, the sixteenth, religious differences could wreck states as effectively as national and linguistic ones today." He admitted that the 1596 Union of Brest, intended to bring the Orthodox Church in Poland-Lithuania into union with Rome and the Commonwealth's political structures, while retaining the Slavonic liturgy and the married parish clergy, backfired: it had split Eastern Christendom into Uniates and "disuniates" (a pejorative term for those who remained staunchly Orthodox), contributed to revolts by the Zaporizhzhian Cossacks and thence to the loss of the Commonwealth's easternmost lands to Muscovy in the mid-seventeenth century, before putting down deeper roots. Nevertheless, he judged that the relatively peaceful victory of Catholicism over Protestantism, achieved by the early seventeenth century, helped consolidate national unity in the face of external threats. Protestantism, he pronounced, was "fundamentally foreign"; its further advances would have worsened internal dissensions and sucked Poland into the Thirty Years' War. Besides the intrinsic merits of the resurgent Catholic religion, he attributed much of the recovery to the pro-Catholic policies and patronage of Kings Stephen Báthory (r. 1576–1586) and Sigismund III Vasa (r. 1587–1632). He described the later contacts of "dissidents" and "disuniates" with foreign courts with unconcealed distaste, while also lamenting the political fallout of the discriminatory anti-dissident legislation of 1733, 1736, and 1764. Nevertheless, confessional factors were all but absent both from his lacerating summary of the Commonwealth's internal weaknesses and his final conclusion: ultimately, a revitalized Poland was dismembered by its expansionist neighbors.[7]

For some decades it has been all but unknown to find similarly partisan judgments among serious historians. It is common, however, to find passages celebrating the shared civic culture that held the Commonwealth together across confessional and ethnic divisions during its first few decades, while lamenting the later intensification of religious intolerance and its corrosive social and political consequences. Prominent here have been Andrzej Sulima Kamiński and his pupils.[8] One of the clearest statements of the latter case has been made by Wojciech Kriegseisen, an expert on the Commonwealth's Protestant communities:

> The multiconfessional and multicultural Commonwealth of the second half of the sixteenth century was a state in which communities of the heterodox— that is, Protestant and Orthodox—nobles, holding equal rights with Catholics on the basis of the Confederacy of Warsaw of 1573, played a very important political role. However, as a result of the successes of the Counter-Reformation of the sixteenth century and the policy of confessionalization supported by the state authorities in the seventeenth century, the political significance of the heterodox nobility fell away, and in the second half of the seventeenth

century and in the first of the eighteenth century, the ever less numerous heterodox nobles (the Orthodox szlachta disappeared almost entirely) were ever
more frequently considered a "foreign body" and even a threat to the Catholic
state, and subjected to chicanery. Finally, in 1717 and 1735 [sic] their political
and civil rights were restricted. This was the genesis of the dissident affair,
considered one of the efficacious causes of the first partition in 1772, and in
consequence also of the final downfall of the Commonwealth of nobles. . . .

In the eighteenth century, the heterodox, especially Evangelicals, aroused
authentic antagonism, not only because they were perceived as a dangerous
instrument of foreign, above all Prussian and Russian policies. The hostility
to them, growing with the process of the Sarmatization and Catholicization
of Polish culture, had deeper, cultural roots, and the hardening conviction in
social mentality that a Pole was a Catholic was especially dangerous for the
Protestant szlachta, which from the beginning of the eighteenth century was
ever more expressly excluded from the previously supra-confessional noble
community of the "political nation." The refusal to acknowledge the heterodox as equal members of this "nation" and the accompanying fear that they
would appeal to foreign violence, had thus every characteristic of a self-fulfill-
ing prophecy.[9]

Elsewhere, Kriegseisen has expressed himself more ambivalently, and paid
deeper attention to the theory, model, or paradigm of "confessionalization"—a term applicable to the Commonwealth, as I will argue, in a particular variant.[10]

"Confessionalization" in the Commonwealth

In its original adumbration in the context of the principalities and cities
of the sixteenth- and seventeenth-century Holy Roman Empire, "confessionalization" was a two-stage process. First came the doctrinal definition
and organizational differentiation of distinct confessions as a result of the
Protestant Reformations and Catholic (Counter-)Reformation. The second
stage involved the combined efforts of the secular and clerical authorities
to promote and enforce a linked religious, political, and social conformity
among all ranks of the population. The latter phenomenon is linked to
"social disciplining"—a joyless process more poetically described by Peter
Burke, referencing a picture by Pieter Bruegel the Elder, as "the triumph of
Lent."[11] The supposed consequence of these endeavors was the "moderniza-

tion" of state and society during the early modern period. This framework has proved highly influential among historians of early modern Europe, but it has evolved significantly over several decades. One revision has been the growing attention paid to "bottom-up" as well as "top-down" manifestations of greater religious conformity and unity in particular localities, but with greater sensitivity to phenomena that crossed confessional boundaries. Another has been the contesting of the link between "confessionalization" and the neo-Weberian idea of "modernization."[12]

The notion that "confessionalization" might apply to the noble-dominated, ideologically republican, politically decentralized, and religiously plural Polish-Lithuanian Commonwealth has met with understandable skepticism. The element of "modernization" has proved especially problematic, given the profound crisis experienced by the polity, society, and economy from the middle of the seventeenth century onward.[13] Early applications of the model seemed more appropriate in the specific contexts of the Lutheran-dominated and mostly Germanophone cities of Royal Prussia and the vassal Duchy of Courland, than to the Commonwealth as a whole.[14] However, once we accept that "confessionalization" could often proceed (more or less spontaneously) "from below" more effectively than "from above"—allowing us to posit a long-term and ultimately incomplete process and thus to jettison the tired concept of "modernization"—then a strong case can be made for confessionalization in Poland-Lithuania.

Thus understood, "confessionalization" proceeded unevenly, mainly "from below," but encouraged "from above," in different parts of the Commonwealth, reflecting local circumstances.[15] The relative efficacy of the more general causes for the retreat of Protestantism and Orthodoxy, and the recovery and expansion of Catholicism have long been contested (not least between Jesuits and Dominicans, and their respective historians).[16] These reasons include the excellence and availability of Catholic schooling, the sensuality of Catholic worship, the approachability of the heavenly company of interceding saints, the zeal of some of the post-Tridentine bishops, most kings' decided preference for Catholics in their distribution of patronage, the divisions among the Evangelical confessions, their failure to attract petty nobles and to accustom peasants to changes, and in the east, the social prestige of Latin-rite Catholicism vis-à-vis Orthodoxy.[17]

Whatever the proportions and relations between the causes, the effects are clear enough. By the middle of the eighteenth century, about five-sixths of the total population (of at least twelve million) belonged to one or another rite of the Catholic Church. The Latin Rite accounted for slightly more than half of the total population, the Uniate Ruthenian (or Greek) Rite for almost a third, while Catholics of the Uniate Armenian Rite were few in number. Of the rest of the population, almost half were Jews, with much smaller communities of Muslims and Karaites. Non-Catholic Christians were most numerous at the Commonwealth's margins: Protestants in the towns of the western and northern fringes as well as in Courland, and Orthodox clusters in the east.[18] Since the turn of the seventeenth century, the Union had extended its sway toward the Russian frontier, although shifts in religious worship and popular confessional allegiance lagged behind the transfer or foundation of parishes. Moreover, relatively few nobles kept the Ruthenian Rite. Those that did tended to be younger sons who entered the Basilian order of monks and thence creamed off the Uniate bishoprics. This phenomenon contributed to a closer weave between the Uniate hierarchy and the nobility in the eastern reaches, but it did nothing to close the chasm between most lords and their peasants who supposedly belonged to two rites of the same Catholic Church.[19]

The predominance of Catholics of the Latin Rite was especially marked among the "nation" composed of up to three-quarters of a million noble citizens.[20] At the time of the Commonwealth's foundation in 1569–1573, up to a fifth of the nobility adhered to the Evangelical Churches (rising to almost half of the Senate). The majority of these nobles belonged to the Reformed or Calvinist Church, which continued to flourish for several decades. Nevertheless, by the 1620s decline was unmistakable, especially in the Polish Crown. Among the nobility of the Grand Duchy of Lithuania, Protestantism retreated more slowly.[21] By the mid-eighteenth century, the total number of Protestant (mainly Calvinist) noble families had shrunk to several hundred. While the number of remaining Orthodox nobles is unknown, suffice it to say that later eighteenth-century Russian ambassadors despaired of finding respectable and literate citizens among the Orthodox families that still inhabited the Polesian marshlands.[22]

This quantitative trend went hand in hand with the cultural consolidation of an increasingly coherent "Polish nation." In the Grand Duchy of Lithuania, a feeling of being Polish in a broad sense slowly came to coexist seamlessly with the idea of a "Lithuanian nation." The Grand Duchy consolidated its distinct political and legal identity vis-à-vis the Polish Crown at the same time as its nobles increasingly cultivated the Polish language at the expense of Lithuanian and Ruthenian.[23] The conjoined nation's markers included its shared treasures of "golden liberty," deriving from the "jewel" (*klejnot*) of inherited noble status, or the cultivation of a widespread belief in their community's roots in ancient Sarmatia,[24] as well as the evolution of a distinctive national costume proudly worn from Polatsk (*Pol.* Połock) to Poznań.

The cohering national community was also increasingly suffused with a performative Catholicism, with an intense baroque repertoire of pilgrimage, penance, processions, and pomp. The succession of debilitating wars fought by the Commonwealth against Orthodox Muscovites, Protestant Swedes, Brandenburgers and Transylvanians, and Muslim Tatars and Turks, with their prayer-beseeched escapes from imminent calamities, and subsequent votive offerings, gave rise both to the conviction of the special protection of the Virgin Mary as Queen of Poland, and to the idea of the less than fully Polish nature of non-Catholic nobles.[25] Hence the growing acceptance of the harassment of "heretics" by Catholic bishops, the restrictions placed on their right to repair their churches, let alone build new ones, and the partial adjudications of the Catholic-dominated tribunals. In political terms, the final stages were the expulsion of the last Protestant envoy from the Sejm in 1718, a prohibition confirmed formally by laws in 1733 and 1736. The legislation of 1764 added ineligibility to hold the office of *starosta* with judicial responsibilities and accompanying Crown estates (*królewszczyzny*) to their existing exclusion from the legislature.[26]

This process can fairly be called a variant of "confessionalization." The nobles' Commonwealth became permeated by Catholicism, while the institutional Church and its clergy were dominated by noble families and reflected much of their outlook. This kind of confessionalization, more "bottom-up" than "top-down," was perfectly compatible with entrenched mistrust not only of kings, who were always suspected of conspiring against liberty, but also of the corporate privileges of the Catholic clergy. Unlike during the Commonwealth's first decades, by the mid-eighteenth century, anticlericalism went hand in hand with intolerance.[27]

Confessional Strife and the First Partition

Even among those citizens who were relaxed ("latitudinarian" in eighteenth-century English parlance) about doctrinal differences and who lived easily with heterodox persons of various backgrounds, it had long been axiomatic that confessional diversity threatened the unity of the political community. According to the influential arguments of Justus Lipsius (1547–1606), echoed in the Commonwealth by the Jesuit Piotr Skarga (1536–1612) and many others, the heterodox could be tolerated by those of the dominant religion only for the sake of peace, and as briefly and restrictively as possible.[28] Such reasoning, traced back to Jesus's dictum—in a different context: "Every kingdom divided against itself is brought to desolation; and every city or house divided against itself shall not stand" (Matthew 12:25)— remained unexceptionable right across early modern Europe. Toleration was a pragmatically conceded lesser evil, not an ideal to be pursued.[29]

In 1766, the unquestionably enlightened King Stanislaus II Augustus (r. 1764–1795) made the case to Catherine II of Russia (r. 1762–1796) that religious unity was especially important in a republican polity:

> The nature of a free state such as ours is incompatible with even the most limited admission to the legislature of those who do not profess the dominant religion. The more national liberties there are in the constitution of a government, the more necessary are conformity of action and strict and respectful submission to the laws on the part of the citizens admitted to the movement of the machine. Otherwise, an avowed diversity of opinions on a matter as politically essential as religion can only produce frequent fragmentations, which are the most dangerous wherever a sufficiently prompt corrective to transgressions is not provided by a supreme absolute authority entirely concentrated in the person of the sovereign.

Neither the Dutch Republic nor England, he continued, were governed by religious prejudice, but both states excluded nonconformists from their legislatures. Mixed arrangements in the Holy Roman Empire had been forced by the outcome of the Thirty Years' War, and in any case, he argued, the empire was no republic but an association of rival sovereigns.[30]

Catherine II took no heed. She continued intransigently to demand that the Commonwealth restore political equality to heterodox citizens, just as she had done since 1764. However, the Sejm of 1766, stiffened by a philippic from the papal nuncio, once again rejected her demands. In response, the Russian ambassador Nikolai Repnin organized confederacies of non-Catholics and Catholic nobles in the Polish Crown and the Grand Duchy of Lithuania. He then intimidated the Sejm of 1767–1768 into passing everything the empress had demanded. This now included not only legislation greatly expanding the rights of non-Catholic nobles, the Orthodox clergy, and the Protestant-dominated Royal Prussian cities, but a formal Russian guarantee of the Commonwealth's form of government. Even before "Repnin's Sejm" had ended, the Confederacy of Bar was formed in defense of the Catholic faith and nobles' liberty.[31]

The persistent nuisance caused by this ultra-Catholic insurgency, the Russo-Ottoman War it triggered, and the ensuing geopolitical concerns in Berlin and Vienna, all contributed to Catherine's decision, reached toward the end of 1770, for a partial partition of Poland-Lithuania, in order to resolve the impasse as advantageously as possible.[32] The link between the "dissident question" and the first partition of 1772 is therefore a strong one. The amputated Commonwealth had its political and constitutional torso again shackled and "guaranteed" by Russia. Moreover, the tripartite annexation of almost a third of its territory and more than a third of its population set an inviting precedent, should international politics have made further partitions convenient to the court of Saint Petersburg.[33]

So far, the argument expounded by Kriegseisen holds—whether or not one accepts Lord Acton's maxim that "liberty provokes diversity, and diversity preserves liberty."[34] The later sixteenth-century Commonwealth had managed its confessional dissensions well within its shared civic culture, but the overwhelmingly Catholic political community of the first two-thirds of the eighteenth century mismanaged its relations with heterodox nobles (as well as the patricians of Royal Prussia) so badly that it gave the Empress Catherine a pretext to intervene in Polish-Lithuanian affairs. The consequences were catastrophic—not least for the Protestants (burghers and nobles alike) of Royal Prussia, who lost most of their liberties to the Hohenzollern monarchy.[35] The first partition made the Commonwealth more susceptible to being carved up again; nonetheless, the second and third partitions of 1793 and 1795 were not its inevitable consequences.

Explaining the Second and Third Partitions

The Commonwealth's acquired inability to resist invasion was a necessary, but not sufficient condition for its final destruction. The eighteenth-century international system was a perilous environment for weaker states, but it could also operate to prolong their existence. Each of the three partitions of Poland-Lithuania was an event in diplomatic history with its own particular causes.[36] Confessional factors played a much less prominent and very different role in the second and third partitions than in the first. The revised constitutional settlement imposed on the Commonwealth and "guaranteed" by Russia in 1773–1775 pruned the rights of the heterodox compared to the provisions of 1768.[37] It provided for the election of up to three envoys to the Sejm (one from each province: Greater Poland, Lesser Poland, and the Grand Duchy of Lithuania), although none were actually chosen until 1784.[38] By the time of the Four-Year Sejm of 1788–1792, the participation of a handful of Protestant envoys in the legislature provoked no qualms at all. The most prominent of them, General Paweł Grabowski (1759–1794), envoy for Vaŭkavysk (*Pol.* Wołkowysk), was well connected, active, and trusted: he was chosen for the delegation tasked with investigating purported rebellions in the Commonwealth's Ruthenian lands.[39]

Of greater numerical significance was the question of whether to give Catholics priority in urban governance, an issue discussed in the parliamentary debate of April 18, 1791, on a proposed law on the "Free Royal Towns of the Commonwealth"—the case that opened this chapter. Many of the arguments made in the debate against enshrining priority for Catholics in law were based on realistic assessments of how varying local arrangements in urban governance reflected patterns of settlement. For example, some towns along the Commonwealth's border with the Kingdom of Prussia had scarcely any Catholic burghers. Other speakers emphasized that one of the principal purposes of the reform was to boost commerce by attracting immigrants, who might be deterred by confessional discrimination. As one Lithuanian envoy concluded, "persecutions for the sake of religion drove away our inhabitants."[40]

On the other hand, those who supported priority for Catholics appealed to the status of Catholicism as the dominant religion, affirmed by the Cardinal Laws passed on September 2–3, 1790.[41] Fears were voiced that the dissidents would, through their proposed parliamentary plenipotentiaries and long-standing connections with foreign courts, again assail the Commonwealth's dominant religion—this time aided by "eager lovers of novelty."[42] Benedykt Hulewicz (1750–1817) countered Ludwik Gutakowski's evocation of "pax inter dissidentes." Referring to the provisions of the Confederacy of Warsaw, he claimed that only "unhappy necessity" had "forced the Commonwealth to enter into a treaty with the dissidents." Previously, he contended, the maxim had been "unus pastor et unum ovile" (one shepherd and one flock).[43]

Wider political arguments, extending beyond the towns, were also made by those who opposed priority for Catholics. Prince Adam Kazimierz Czartoryski (1734–1823), having stressed his own Catholic credentials and aversion to "heresy," argued: "The spirit of our former intolerance lost us the Ukraine;

the spirit of fresh intolerance brought a foreign guarantee upon us. To what end are we trying to complete this matter, through the granting of justice to towns? So as not to give anyone cause to seek foreign protection; and we shall ruin this intention if this condition is added."[44] Czartoryski's first reference was to the conflicts between Catholicism and Orthodoxy sparked by the 1596 Union of Brest. His second reference was to the events of 1764–1768.

On April 18, 1791, it was the marshal of the Lithuanian parliamentary confederacy, Kazimierz Nestor Sapieha (1757–1798), who finally persuaded the Sejm to exclude any reference to religion from the law on towns. Earlier in the debate he had rejected any reduction in the rights written for the dissidents "by a foreign hand," given that they were willing to renounce the "guarantee" and trust in the offer of the same rights by the sovereign Commonwealth. He could not understand how "the maintenance of the dissidents' privileges could serve foreign courts, which through them [the dissidents] could intrigue in the country."[45]

Just over two weeks later, the first article of the Constitution of May 3, 1791, maintained the status of Roman Catholicism as "the national and dominant religion," first established formally in the Cardinal Laws of September 2–3, 1790, and like those laws, also retained "apostasy" as a crime (without specifying the penalty). However, it expanded the scope of religious freedom by assuring "all people of any confession"—not just those hitherto tolerated—"peace in faith and the protection of government."[46] In contrast, the 1573 Confederacy of Warsaw had explicitly allowed lords to enforce obedience from their peasant subjects in spiritual as well as temporal matters.[47] The religious freedom pledged by the Constitution was also both more and less than the toleration conceded by Joseph II (r. 1765–1790) in the Habsburg Monarchy. The emperor specified the permitted confessions as well as the limitations on public worship, but on the other hand he allowed conversion from Catholicism under certain conditions.[48] In the Commonwealth after May 3, 1791, the only offices implicitly still reserved for Catholics were the kingship and ministries. Even the counterrevolutionary Confederacies of Targowica and Wilno, formed in 1792, who stressed their Catholic credentials within an ultra-republican creed, accepted without demur the decision of Catherine II that confessional matters would be regulated by the settlement of 1773–1775.[49] In short, heterodox citizens' participation in decision making was no longer a problem for the Commonwealth.

On this basis, one could conclude that Catherine II's decisions in 1792–1795 to invade, partition, subject, pacify, and finally annihilate Poland-Lithuania had nothing whatsoever to do with confessional factors, and everything to do with the political and social revitalization of the Commonwealth. This renewal, manifested during the Four-Year Sejm and the Kościuszko Insurrection of 1794, threatened to block the projection of Russian power westward into European affairs. The empress could not tolerate the existence of a Polish-Lithuanian neighbor that was *not* passively subordinated to Russia. The Commonwealth would be resubjected at the earliest opportunity, and—should it prove necessary—eliminated.[50] In 1793, having been disappointed by the chaotic attempts of the counterrevolutionary confederates to quell opposition, Catherine seized vast, fertile, and strategically vital lands at a moment when Austria was in no position to demand compensation in Poland, and when Prussian claims there had been reduced by humiliations in the war against revolutionary France. In 1795, following her armies' defeat of the Kościuszko Insurrection, she was in a prime position to adjudicate rival Austrian and Prussian claims and to help herself to the territories she wanted.[51]

As for Prussia, the territorial appetites of successive Hohenzollerns for the Polish lands that lay between their own dominions are amply documented.[52] Moreover, the often-quoted reaction of the experienced minister Ewald von Hertzberg to the news of the Constitution of May 3—his fear of a "*coup de grâce* to the Prussian monarchy," for a Poland strengthened by a "hereditary throne and a constitution better than the English" could not be prevented from taking back West Prussia and perhaps even East Prussia as well—is sufficient testimony to Berlin's vital interests.[53] These had only temporarily been disguised during the rift with Saint Petersburg in 1788–1791. As regards Austria, in 1772 and 1795 alike, the decisive factor was the court of Vienna's concern not to be left empty-handed, when Saint Petersburg and Berlin made significant gains. It was Catherine II who decided on and chiefly benefited from the second and third partitions.[54]

Confessional Policies of Catherine II and the Sovereign Commonwealth

We should add two important and linked caveats to this generally sound conclusion about the decisive role of geopolitical factors in the Russian-orchestrated destruction of the Commonwealth in 1792–1795. The first was that the leaders of the Polish Revolution and Insurrection pursued a coherent confessional policy, which contributed to the Commonwealth's revitalization. We have so far considered this policy mainly regarding Protestants, but it was principally concerned with the Uniate and Orthodox populace of the Ruthenian lands.[55] The other relates to Catherine II's policies toward the Orthodox Church.

Catherine II's coronation in 1762 was enlivened by a passionate speech by Georgii Konisskii (1717–1795), the bishop of Mahilioŭ (*Pol.* Mohylew), the sole remaining Orthodox see in the Commonwealth. He compared his flock's sufferings to the Egyptian captivity of the Hebrews, and he beseeched the new tsaritsa's protection. The Russian Empire claimed the right to intervene on behalf of the Orthodox Church in the Commonwealth by stretching the provisions of the 1686 treaty of "eternal peace" regarding the protection of Orthodox and Catholic believers in the respective jurisdictions. However, it made only sporadic interventions until the mid-1750s, while Orthodoxy lost ground to the Union. During the following decade, a trio of energetic hierarchs halted and then reversed the trend: Bishop Konisskii, Bishop Hervasii Lintsevskyi (ca. 1700–1769) of Pereiaslav in Left-bank or Russian Ukraine, which claimed jurisdiction on the right bank as well, and Melkhizidek Znachko-Iavorskyi (ca. 1716–1809), the superior of the monastery of Motronyn in the far southeastern corner of Polish Ukraine. Their emissaries sought to persuade Uniate parishioners and priests to "return" to the Orthodox fold, spurring counteractions by the Uniate hierarchy. The success of these rival endeavors depended in part on landowners' attitude to the Union, and in part on the disposition of Russian troops.[56]

Although most of the eighteenth-century rulers of the Russian Empire regarded the Union as a rebellious schism from the Orthodox Church, the protection of Orthodox believers in Poland-Lithuania was not in itself a priority. It could, however, provide a pretext for intervention. On the whole, neither Catherine II nor her predecessors wished to encourage potentially contagious peasant rebellion; it was sometimes useful, however, to remind Polish nobles of the possibility. She and her ministers also realized that improving the conditions for Orthodoxy in the Commonwealth might stimulate peasant flight from the Russian Empire. She therefore authorized the stepping up of pressure against the Uniates only when this coincided with other important interests.[57]

Catherine II, according to her biographers, was little touched by religious faith—assessments have varied from agnosticism to a kind of secularized Protestantism. Nevertheless, she had to devote much time to religious rituals. "Her Court remained knee-deep in holy water," as Simon Dixon puts it. At the uncertain start of her reign, especially, she needed to assert her Orthodox and Russian credentials. The former Princess Sophie Auguste Friderike von Anhalt-Zerbst had taken the imperial throne from her stubbornly Lutheran and Germanophone husband Peter III, while deciding to implement his decision to close many monasteries, especially in Left-bank, Russian Ukraine.[58] So Konisskii would have been encouraged to appeal passionately to the new empress, who could then present herself at home as the pious defender of Orthodoxy while posing abroad as the angel of "tolerance." Konisskii's escalating complaints and demands on behalf of his coreligionists piled pressure on Polish-Lithuanian politicians during the 1760s, and the legislation forced by Russian ambassador Repnin in 1767–1768 named him to chair the mixed court to judge disputes between Catholics and either Protestant or Orthodox plaintiffs. Nevertheless, even Repnin sometimes regarded him as a nuisance. Only in the spring of 1768, when the Confederacy of Bar provoked a massive Cossack and peasant rebellion in Polish Ukraine, originating from the monastery at Motronyn, did Russian forces assist the mass takeover of Uniate parishes.[59]

In 1773, a second wave of Russian military pressure against the Union in the southeast of the Commonwealth ceased once the Sejm had ratified the treaties of the first partition. Uniate parishes in the lands annexed by Russia from the Grand Duchy of Lithuania were generally left in peace until the end of the decade, when the empress again ordered the ratcheting up of the pressure on the Uniate clergy to "return" in retaliation for the insulting refusal of the newly designated Uniate archbishop of Polatsk, Maksymilian Ryllo (ca. 1719–1793), to move to the Russian Empire. She relented when she had obtained the blessing of the Holy See for her prior establishment of a Latin-rite archbishopric of Mahilioŭ for the entire Russian Empire, held by her obedient protégé, Stanisław Siestrzeńcewicz. As Larry Wolff has argued, Catherine's persecutions of the Union were precisely timed to achieve specific political goals. These included the strict subordination of ecclesiastical to political jurisdictions.[60]

One confessional aspect of Catherine's policies toward the Commonwealth had an especially sharp political edge. This was the subordination of the Orthodox Church in Poland-Lithuania to the Holy Synod in Saint Petersburg (which since the reign of Peter the Great had governed the Russian Orthodox Church in the absence of a patriarch of Moscow).[61] The hierarch who tightened this subordination was Viktor Sadkovskii (1741–1803). Formerly chaplain in the Russian embassy in Warsaw, in 1785 he was consecrated bishop of Pereiaslav in Left-bank Ukraine. He resided at Slutsk (Pol. Słuck) in the south of the Grand Duchy of Lithuania, as superior of the local monastery. He busied himself with disciplining a clergy that he believed had become slack—in this respect, he acted analogously to many post-Tridentine Catholic bishops. However, he also arranged for the import of new liturgical books printed in Russia, and ordained pictures of and prayers for the empress in every Orthodox church. He also brought clergy from the Russian Empire to supplement or replace the locals. By this time, the Orthodox parish network was growing again, largely because of the purchase by Catherine's effective coruler, Grigorii Potemkin (1739–1791), who had previously obtained Polish noble status (the *ius indigenatus*) of the latifundium of Smila (*Pol.* Smiła) in the southeast corner of the Polish Crown. This soon became a booming "state within a state," with an overwhelmingly Orthodox population.

Uniate hierarchs and local nobles eventually managed to persuade the king that these were dangerous tendencies. The Polish monarch demanded an oath of allegiance from Sadkovskii, but the latter swore one only in May 1787, after Stanislaus Augustus's summit with Catherine on the River Dnieper (during which journey the king manifested his support for the Union). The text, drafted by Potemkin and Russian grand chancellor Aleksandr Bezborodko (1747–1799), included a promise to respect the rights of the Catholic Church, but did not specifically mention the Ruthenian Rite. Sadkovskii continued unfazed, until early in 1789, with the Four-Year Sejm well under way, panic seized the southeast. Nobles feared that Potemkin's emissaries were fomenting a massive peasant revolt. Catherine and Potemkin did in fact consider this possibility between 1789 and 1791, but each time she decided that she was not obliged by the international situation to risk such a contagious conflagration. In April 1789, Sadkovskii and some of his acolytes were arrested and his monastery was searched for incriminating documents. No proof was found of his inciting rebellion, but much evidence transpired of his drive to impose Russian control on the Orthodox Church in the Commonwealth. This included a threat to destroy the local clergy and their "accursed Lithuanian language."[62]

The panic soon subsided, but the rebellion scare convinced a majority in the Sejm of the need for a coherent confessional policy, especially regarding Ruthenia. One aspect was the raising of the prestige of the Uniate Church, by belatedly and partially realizing a postulate of the Union of Brest—the metropolitan archbishop of all Rus', Teodozy Rostocki (*Ukr.* Teodosy Rostots'kyi; ca. 1725–1805), took his seat in the Senate in 1790. The other aspect was the cutting of the dependency of the Orthodox Church in the Commonwealth on the Holy Synod in Saint Petersburg, and the establishment of an autonomous or autocephalous Orthodox hierarchy and consistory in Poland-Lithuania. This solution was negotiated at a congress held in Pinsk (*Pol.* Pińsk) in the summer of 1791. However, the need felt by the king to keep the Holy See on the side of the Polish Revolution may have delayed its approval until May 21, 1792, when the Sejm overwhelmingly voted for the proposal, in an atmosphere charged by the Russian invasion of the Commonwealth three days earlier. By then it was too late to make any practical difference, but autocephaly was revived during the 1794 Insurrection.

The thinking behind the policy was expressed during the May 1792 debate.[63] As Michał Kochanowski (1757–1832), envoy for Sandomierz, who had negotiated the solution at Pinsk, explained, the point was that "no citizen within Polish borders should be subject to foreign power," and that the country would be most strongly defended when the people of the region "would be led away from seeking spiritual authority abroad."[64] The marshal of the Lithuanian confederacy Kazimierz Sapieha argued that if the choice of bishops was left to the Synod in Saint Petersburg, candidates would be examined "not in virtuous qualities, but in inclination for that power."[65] More idealistically, Stanisław Sołtyk (1753–1831) argued that when the Orthodox tasted "orderly liberty" (*rządna wolność*), they could not be seduced by any foreign power, because "liberty is our greatest secret against any foreign usurpation; it is the strongest defensive wall against neighbors' invasions. Let people speak in different languages; let there be differences between them as regards religion. Freedom, when well understood, and justice, given strictly to everyone, will unite them most swiftly, and will teach one sentiment, the same expressions of their own liberties."[66] Here was a return to the principles on which the Commonwealth had been founded: a civic culture above confessional differences.

The greatest difference, compared to the spirit of 1573, was that this conviction was part of a policy encompassing the burghers, Jews, and peasants, envisioned by Sołtyk's colleague, Crown Vice-Chancellor Hugo Kołłątaj (1750–1812). It involved the harmonization of the curriculum in schools of all confessions, as well as the encouragement of the use of the Polish language except in sacred liturgies, in order to imbue a shared love of a common Fatherland among all of the Commonwealth's inhabitants.[67] It was not an expression of confessional or religious indifference, or indeed the equality of status implied in the 1573 Confederacy of Warsaw. The enshrining of Catholicism as the "dominant religion" in the Cardinal Laws of September 1790 and in the Constitution of May 3, 1791, was not the zenith of confessionalization in the Commonwealth, but a gesture of reassurance to conservative Catholic nobles and clergymen as "deconfessionalization" proceeded.[68] The political community once again learned how to deal with confessional diversity by placing its civic values first. The lesson had been learned about driving the heterodox into the arms of foreign powers. A similar conclusion may be drawn from the debate on the towns with which this chapter commenced, and by the policy adopted toward the Commonwealth's Protestants. Non-Catholic immigrants would be welcomed. Manifestations of joy and gratitude from Evangelical burghers and their pastors, and from prominent Orthodox clergymen and communities, suggest that the policy was well judged.[69] The Uniate hierarchy also appealed to the Ruthenian populace in the face of the Russian invasion.[70]

The sovereign Commonwealth's confessional policy cut at the roots of Russian interference in its affairs. It was also an integral part of the revitalization of the polity. It was not surprising, therefore, that the same Russian declaration that had prompted the approval of the Orthodox hierarchy on May 21 included complaints about the imprisonment and alleged maltreatment of Sadkovskii and other Orthodox priests. A proclamation of April 1793, justifying the annexations accomplished by the second partition, expressed the empress's anger at the "oppressions" suffered by "the towns and provinces belonging to the dominions of Her Imperial Majesty, being her former and rightful inheritance, inhabited and filled with people of one race and tribe and enlightened by the Orthodox Christian faith and professing it to this day."[71] The claim was manifestly false, for all of Catherine's own studies of medieval chronicles, but inconvenient reality could, it seemed to her, be corrected. The following spring and summer, while the Kościuszko Insurrection raged farther west, substantial detachments of the imperial Russian army helped hundreds of parishes in Ukraine and eastern Volhynia to return to the Orthodox fold. Even at this point, however, it is important to emphasize the priority of political over religious factors. It would be several decades before the tsarist regime proceeded to the final liquidation of the Uniate Church within the Russian Empire.[72]

Confessional Consequences of the Partitions

A case could be made that the Russian Empire paid too high a geopolitical price for its annexations of Polish-Lithuanian territory. Not only was the "Polish Question" born, but Austria and especially Prussia were strengthened by their own gains, and in the First World War they brought the Russian Empire to its knees. Conversely, it could also be argued that the two German powers had more to fear from a strengthened Russia on their borders, or else that the partitions initiated a long nineteenth century in which the three monarchies' shared interest in suppressing the "Polish Question" usually helped them to cooperate. The point is moot.

From a long-term confessional perspective, however, the partitions enabled the Orthodox Russian Empire to reverse the expansion of Catholicism (of all rites) in the Ruthenian lands. The exception that proves the rule was Austrian-ruled Galicia, where the Union of Brest finally put down ineradicable roots in a region that had initially resisted it. After 1917 or 1939, depending on the location, the Bolsheviks destroyed the overwhelmingly Latin-rite Catholic Polish-Lithuanian nobility that had survived tsarist rule. Pockets of Roman Catholic and Polish culture (which overlap, although not completely) still cling on in parts of Belarus and Ukraine. Nevertheless, the elimination of Catholic and Polish competition from most of eastern Slavdom has been one of the most lasting and significant consequences of the partitions of the Commonwealth. Another effect, albeit a slow-burning one, has been renewed aggravation in interconfessional and interethnic relations, and the conflation of modern Polish nationalism with fervent Roman Catholicism. In today's idiom, the lands of the old Commonwealth became much less "multicultural" well before the Second World War.

In considering the expansion of a great power, it is worth doing so both from its own perspective and from that of its victims. The same factor—confessional in this case—can be seen to act differently on each side. Without doubt, the entanglement of confessional problems in the Commonwealth and in the Russian Empire generated a series of events that contributed to the first partition, although ultimately that was a politically, not confessionally, driven decision made by Catherine II. The Polish-Lithuanian elite learned the lesson of the dangers of the dependence on foreign powers of marginalized heterodox communities. Consequently, it began to "deconfessionalize" the Commonwealth and rely instead on shared civic values for coherence. This endeavor contributed to the very revitalization of the Commonwealth, which, by openly defying the empress and challenging the geopolitical interests of her empire, triggered the second and third partitions. In the final reckoning, those who attribute a major part in the destruction of the Commonwealth to *either* confessional dissension *or* intolerant "confessionalization" have reversed cause and consequence.[73]

PART II

THE COMMONWEALTH IN MEMORY

7

The Ukrainian Sublime

Nineteenth-Century Polish Visions of the East

Stanley Bill

Since at least the Romantic era, Ukraine has often figured in the Polish imagination as a "theater of atrocity," a place stained blood red by popular violence against Polish Catholic nobles, clergy, and Jewish communities in the seventeenth and eighteenth centuries.[1] In many nineteenth-century representations, after the partitioning of the Polish-Lithuanian Commonwealth, the diverse Ukrainian territories became synonymous with the explosion of religious, social, and ethnic conflict that had contributed to the multicultural union's decline. At the same time, this negative image of Ukraine was complicated by more positive visions emphasizing the harsh beauty of its landscape and peoples, including an idealized image of the wild liberty of Cossack warriors. Some of these images partly mirrored representations of the same historical events in the works of Ukrainian Romantic writers, who depicted them as key moments in a struggle for liberation from Polish Catholic oppression. In Polish-language writing, all these disparate elements came together to form a coherent myth satisfying Romantic fascinations with colorful local culture, national struggle, authentic wildness over civilized finesse, cathartic violence, and a powerful notion of absolute freedom.[2]

In this chapter, I propose to refer to this paradigm simply as the "Ukrainian sublime": an imaginative schema permeating the Romantic works of Antoni Malczewski (1793–1826), Seweryn Goszczyński (1801–1876), Juliusz Słowacki

(1809–1849), and others, but also shaping perhaps the most influential vision of Ukraine in all of Polish culture—Henryk Sienkiewicz's historical novel *With Fire and Sword* (*Ogniem i mieczem*, 1884). These works not only created lasting—and often tendentious—images of Ukraine, but also presented a series of retrospective interpretations of the Commonwealth's ethnic and religious diversity. In a period in which definitions of the "Polish" nation were beginning to shift from political to cultural meanings, Polish-language writers often defined their relation to "the other" through conflict. This dark mode of representing Ukraine was accompanied by the idyllic myth of the "Kresy," or eastern "Borderlands," as an arcadian realm of Polish civilizing action—though even these polonocentric fantasies were increasingly framed through loss.[3]

The question of names and definitions will loom large in this chapter. Many of its key terms have had very different meanings at different points in history. The word "Ukraine" (Ukr. *Ukraïna*; Pol. *Ukraina*)—roughly meaning "borderland"—first began to be widely used in the sixteenth century to describe the Commonwealth's large southeastern palatinates of Kyiv (Kijów), Bratslav (Bracław), and, later, Chernihiv (Czernihów).[4] The ethnonym "Ukrainian" did not then have its modern meaning. The ancestors of today's Ukrainians were variously referred to as Ruthenians, Cossacks, "countrymen" (Ukr. *zemliaki*), the "folk" (Pol. *lud*), or differentiated as speakers of the Ruthenian language or as adherents of Eastern Orthodoxy, and later of the Uniate Church.[5] When the term "Ukrainian" appeared at all, its sense was geographical, and thus could equally apply to Polish Catholic nobles settled in the region. Indeed, the terms "Pole" and "Polish" are arguably just as problematic. Though these terms were used in the periods discussed in this chapter, their meanings were also different from their modern significations—for instance, some Ruthenian nobles and Cossacks came to understand themselves politically as members of the "Polish" nobility.[6] My approach to this complexity will be to prefer the specific terms used in the works under analysis—for instance, "Cossacks" and "Ruthenians"—while sometimes pointing to moments of the early crystallization of modern "Polish" and "Ukrainian" identities in the crucible of intergroup violence.

In philosophy, the quality of the sublime denotes a confrontation of the beholding subject with an unassimilable "other"—usually natural—that threatens it with vast size or violent power. The sublime object poses a physical danger to the subject, while also exceeding its faculties of comprehension or representation. In Polish Romantic and post-Romantic depictions of Ukraine, it is the enormity of the eastern steppe country and the fierce energy of the Cossacks and Orthodox Ruthenian peasantry that overwhelm the representatives of a "Polish" culture often implicitly identified with rational, "Western" civilization and a mission to tame the wild "East." As I will show, representations of the "Ukrainian sublime" suggest the failure of this quasi-colonial mission, as the bastions of "Polish" culture—like the symbolic fortress of Goszczyński's *The Castle of Kaniów* (*Zamek kaniowski*, 1828)—crumble before the elemental "Ukrainian" forces of chaos and bloody rebellion. Though similar depictions of Ukraine are present in Polish-language works from as early as the seventeenth century, it was the Romantics who transformed them into a coherent literary myth aspiring to capture the fundamental "tragedy" of Polish history.[7]

Yet despite the horror of these representations of defeat, the Romantic works, and especially Sienkiewicz's novel, have also exhilarated and inspired generations of Polish readers.[8] The idea of the sublime sheds some light on this paradox, as it precisely combines horror and pleasure, both triggering and defusing the rational subject's anxieties by setting him or her above the irrational expressions of nature's size and power. In this case, as I will argue, the Polish subject often lays claim to its own cultural or moral superiority to wild Ukrainian nature. Crucially, this dimension of the Ukrainian sublime cannot be separated from the political context in which these Polish-language works arose—that is, after the partitioning of the Polish-Lithuanian Commonwealth. From the depths of historical despair, nineteenth-century Polish writers engaged in the construction—and sometimes deconstruction—of compensatory myths of a "civilizing" mission in the east. In short, the Ukrainian sublime offered an aesthetic fantasy of power in the face of historical disempowerment.

At the same time, I will argue, these Polish-language works bear witness to a developing historical confrontation between very different understandings of "Polish" identity: namely, between the inclusive, political forms that had begun to decline in significance along with the demise of the multicultural Commonwealth, and the new cultural or ethnic ideas of nation that were beginning to replace them—or rather to develop alongside them—in the nineteenth century. In many of the works, divisions between Poles, Cossacks, and Ruthenians are fluid or difficult to define, as ethnic, linguistic, and religious identities refuse to synchronize in accordance with the emerging modern national categories. The dangerous Ukrainian "other" that the Polish-language writers depict is not entirely external to their own identity, but rather an inseparable part of its historical heterogeneity.

In these constructions of the Ukrainian sublime, Polish-language writers of the nineteenth century reflected in various ways on intergroup conflict in the multicultural Commonwealth: sometimes showing respect for the autonomy of the "other" (for instance, in the Romantic works of Goszczyński and Słowacki); sometimes with a stronger emphasis on the putative moral and civilizational superiority of the "Polish" subject to what physically overwhelms it (especially in Sienkiewicz's novel). To some extent, I will be tracing a shift across the nineteenth century from the ambivalent Romantics to Sienkiewicz's more overtly compensatory model, perhaps running in parallel with historical shifts in understandings of Polish national identity. Yet the Ukrainian sublime always remains a mode of representation of an "other" that partly inhabits the "self"—at least as a memory of an earlier version of that self. It simultaneously captures the origins of conflict between modern national identities in an incipient phase of their construction and harks back to the mixed early modern identities from which they emerged.

Diversity and Conflict in Early Modern Ukraine

The largest proportion of the former territory of the Polish-Lithuanian Commonwealth today lies within the independent state of Ukraine. Once belonging to the principalities of medieval Rus', the southeastern, "Ukrainian" palatinates of the Commonwealth had been absorbed by Lithuania in the fourteenth century, before being transferred to the Kingdom of Poland— along with the Volhynian palatinate—in the Union of Lublin in 1569. The region was largely inhabited by the ancestors of modern-day Ukrainians: East Slavic Ruthenians adhering to Orthodox Christianity. The ruling Orthodox nobility was of mixed Lithuanian and Ruthenian origin, though many eventually adopted Polish language and culture along with Roman Catholicism after 1569. Catholic nobles from westerly parts of the Kingdom of Poland as well as large Jewish communities also settled in the region. The far southern areas saw frequent raids from the Muslim Tatars of the neighboring Crimean Khanate, which lay beyond a buffer region of "wild fields" partly inhabited by mostly East Slavic, Orthodox bands of Cossacks. The Ukrainian lands thus represented much of the diversity and tension of the multicultural Commonwealth. And it was here that these relations began to unravel.

In 1648, after many smaller rebellions, a major uprising broke out in Ukraine, led by the Cossack Hetman Bohdan Khmelnytsky (ca. 1595–1657). The Cossack rebels were joined by Eastern Orthodox peasants, who rose up against what they may have perceived as a combination of Polish, Catholic, noble, and Jewish oppression.[9] Polish Catholic nobles, clergy, and Jews were killed in large numbers, provoking equally brutal reprisals against Ruthenian peasants. The final outcome of the violence was an agreement between the Cossacks and the tsar of Russia that effectively transferred part of the Commonwealth's Ukrainian territories, including the city of Kyiv, to the tsardom. By the end of the seventeenth century, the Commonwealth was smaller, weaker, and entering what is often retrospectively viewed as a period of terminal decline. In 1768, another mass rebellion of Cossacks and Eastern Orthodox peasantry—the Koliivshchyna—coincided with the Bar Confederation (1768–1772), frequently interpreted as the Polish nobility's last stand against increasing Russian domination of the Commonwealth.[10] The failure of this "first Polish uprising" in 1772 preceded the final partitioning of the Commonwealth out of existence by Russia, Prussia, and Austria.

In this context, Ukraine has often symbolized the failure of the multiethnic, multicultural, multiconfessional Commonwealth. The nature of this failure varies in different interpretations. From the perspective of many later Ukrainian interpreters—perhaps most notably the historian Mykhailo Hrushevsky (1866–1934)—the Commonwealth was always a project of Polish Catholic hegemony over Eastern Orthodox Ukrainians/Ruthenians and Cossacks.[11] Its diversity and tolerance were merely pretexts for the dominance of the Polish nobility, which oppressed the Ukrainian peasantry both economically and religiously. Some Polish and other scholars have supported this view, in recent times using postcolonial theory to present the Polish "mission" in the east as a colonial or imperial enterprise in political, economic, and cultural terms.[12] According to this perspective, Ukraine was a typically colonized "periphery," a vast reservoir of natural and human resources to be exploited by Polish colonial overlords, who exported Ukrainian raw materials to various "centers," either in the Polish heartland or in western Europe.

From this point of view, the "multiculturalism" of the Commonwealth was always of a quasi-imperial kind, whereby one dominant group draws others into a heterogeneous polity nevertheless subject to its own monopolistic political and cultural power.[13] The Cossack uprisings thus embodied a struggle for the liberation of subordinated groups in the Ukrainian lands. The rebellions contributed to the Commonwealth's demise, which—in turn—was a precondition for the formation of the modern Ukrainian nation. The unmaking of an oppressive "multicultural" identity in the Commonwealth allowed for the making of modern Ukrainian identity.[14] At the same time, an early modern "Polish" identity that had once constituted a political category embracing multiple confessions, languages, and ethnicities could also be unmade, or rather remade, into a more homogeneous, ethnic idea.[15]

Other scholars, especially in Poland, have rejected postcolonial interpretations of the Polish presence in Ukraine as simplifications of a more complex set of relations.[16] They argue that there was never an invasion or conquest of Ukraine by Polish forces. The fourteenth-century Lithuanian absorption of former principalities of Rus' was partly consensual, producing a mixed state with both Lithuanian and Ruthenian elements, ruled by mixed Lithuanian-Ruthenian families. Later, when the Ukrainian lands became part of the Kingdom of Poland in 1569, it was some of the Ruthenian elites themselves who had pushed for this outcome. Moreover, the great lord "oppressors" of the Ukrainian principalities, with their enormous estates and private armies, were themselves Ruthenian, descendants of the Orthodox ruling families of Rus', even if they later converted to Roman Catholicism and partly adopted Polish culture. In all these respects, the Polish scholars argue, the history of the Commonwealth was far removed from the colonial conquests of the western European powers in the Global South. Another critique suggests that postcolonial interpretations tend to diminish or elide the agency of Ruthenian elites themselves in the political and cultural development of a composite state.[17]

All these opposing historical interpretations may have some (though not necessarily equal) validity. It is true that the Kingdom of Poland did not originally "conquer" the Orthodox Ruthenian lands, subjugating them to the control and exploitation of a colonial center. There was no single "colonizing" moment. Nevertheless, it is possible to refer to the gradual emergence of a situation with increasingly "colonial" characteristics. The Ruthenian elites had always exploited the labor of the Ruthenian peasantry, but as they adopted the "Polish" religion and language, they cut themselves off culturally as well, exacerbating and "nationalizing" the social divide as they participated in what appeared to be an aggressive campaign of Catholicization, polonization, and "internal colonization."[18] The gradual development of these quasi-colonial relations between the dominant "Poles" and the subordinated Orthodox Ruthenians, who were no longer represented in the body politic, aggravated existing social tensions, which then exploded in bloody rebellions also conditioned by the Cossacks' emergence as a military force willing to identify with, and to defend, the Orthodox faith.

This historical train of events was perhaps not the only possible course for Polish-Ruthenian relations. Indeed, there is a long tradition of lamenting the

failure to institute a truly cooperative and equal union of "three nations"—
the ambition of the unrealized Treaty of Hadiach (*Pol.* Hadziacz, 1658).
Timothy Snyder argues that "Poles" and "Ukrainians" were not doomed to
be enemies.[19] The seventeenth century simply marked the failure of the Commonwealth to reach a compromise with the Cossacks and to form the mooted
Grand Duchy of Ruthenia on the same footing as the Kingdom of Poland and
the Grand Duchy of Lithuania. Other scholars, like Andrzej Kamiński, have
taken a more skeptical view, suggesting that the circumstances of internal
strife in Ukraine and external pressure from Russia militated against such
compromises.[20] Either way, by the beginning of the eighteenth century, the
alternative path of the Hadiach Union had long since been closed, and the
Commonwealth continued to decline—for a variety of reasons—before the
final catastrophe of the partitions.

In the aftermath, the key figures of Polish culture, especially in the
period of Romanticism, focused obsessively on this collective historical
trauma, mythologizing the lost state and even imagining the regaining of
independence as part of an eschatological process. Some of their works included retrospective representations of the key seventeenth- and eighteenth-
century turning points in the unmaking of the multicultural Commonwealth
in the Ukrainian lands. In particular, the Romantic works of the so-called
"Ukrainian school"—a very loose term imposed on diverse authors—depicted both the deconstruction of the old forms of identity and rising conflicts
between groups whose new collective identities were only just beginning
to coalesce. In doing so, they imbued the modern Polish imagination with
ambivalent images of a "sublime" Ukrainian east.

The Romantic Paradigm of the Ukrainian Sublime

From the eighteenth century, the idea of the sublime has referred to the
partly pleasurable aesthetic impression of overwhelmingly large or powerful natural phenomena. The philosophers of the sublime describe a
mixture of fear, horror, or pain with pleasure or exaltation in the mind and
physical senses of the receiver. In the simplest terms, the sublime denotes a
stimulating feeling of being overpowered. Yet this basic characteristic has
manifested itself in multiple variants. Immanuel Kant (1724–1804) argued
that the overpowering of the individual as a physical being made him or
her aware of a much greater power within himself or herself: reason. By
contrast, Edmund Burke (1729–1797) proposed that the human mind was

essentially humbled by its confrontation with an unassimilable "other."[21] As more recent thinkers have highlighted, the sublime thus suggested a failure of representation or the imagination.[22] In summary, the sublime could give a sense of either human "mastery," in the Kantian version, or powerlessness, in Burke's account.

These two dominant eighteenth-century notions of the sublime—both of which would influence Romantic literature—are mostly concerned with the "other" of nature. Yet they are also relevant to Romantic depictions of the cultural "other," especially when that "other" is closely associated with natural wildness and power. Indeed, some scholars have already pointed to the existence of orientalist, colonial, or postcolonial versions of the sublime in representations of a wild cultural "other" that can be mastered—or not—by the rational powers of the colonizer.[23] Depictions of Ukraine in Polish literature of the nineteenth century are filled with this version of the sublime, as the scale and power of both the boundless steppe and the Ukrainian peoples inspire terror or defy representation. In Kant's terms, the Ukrainian land and its inhabitants often appear as both "mathematically" and "dynamically" sublime—that is, immeasurable and unencompassable in both size and power.[24]

In its "mathematical" dimension, the sublime appears in these Romantic works in the archetypal Ukrainian landscape of the steppe, almost invariably characterized as menacingly boundless and formless, evoking melancholic introspection in the beholding subject through its apparent hostility to all human hopes and projects. The empty landscape is crisscrossed only by Cossack riders, who seem to be part of the natural environment, with burial mounds and remnants of past battles as the sole signs of human history, now overgrown and reintegrated into nature. In Malczewski's *Maria: A Ukrainian Tale* (*Maria: powieść ukraińska*, 1825)—a poetic work constituting a sustained metaphorization of Ukraine as limitless space—this image includes the ghosts of a fallen Polish glory or a lost idyll:

> For over the vast fields extends a great silence;
> With no voices of merry nobility or knights,
> Only the wind rustles sadly through the bending stalks;
> Only sighs from the graves and moans from under the grass,
> Of those who sleep on withered wreaths of their former glory.[25]

The characteristic reference here to "silence" also appears in multiple other works, denoting the absence of human voices, language, and culture. This lack of sound is accompanied by a visual void, as in another exemplary description from one of Michał Czajkowski's *Cossack Tales* (*Powieści kozackie*, 1837): "Empty and silent in front of them and behind them—the steppe and the clouds around them. There was no human face to be seen, and no human voice to be heard."[26] The "empty, silent, dead" land of the wandering Ukrainian Cossacks is contrasted with the "beautiful, rich country" of neighboring human settlements, suggesting a fundamental opposition between nature and culture, but also—in Kantian aesthetic terms—between the sublime and the beautiful.[27]

The sublime is also specifically concerned with the insufficiency of the human senses. Multiple works describe the emptiness of the Ukrainian steppe through the incapacity of the "eye" to "rest upon anything." Human sight "wanders" or "roams" across the landscape like a "Ukrainian horse across the steppe without a bit," through a "space" unfettered by any barriers, as Czajkowski describes it in his novel *Wernyhora* (1838).[28] The vastness of the expanse reveals the limits of human perception, as the eye fails to encompass the scale of the space, leading to an "agitation" of the subject also described by Arthur Schopenhauer (1788–1860) in his account of the sublime effect of the similarly empty landscapes of the American prairies.[29] Indeed, this "wasteland" motif was common in Romantic literature across Europe, often featuring a beholding subject trapped in melancholic reflection on the void.[30] Such images dominate the "Ukrainian school" of Polish Romanticism, where the apparent freedom of a limitless space paradoxically creates the impression of a prison.[31]

At the same time, in spite of its emptiness, the Ukrainian landscape also harbors overwhelmingly dynamic natural forces that threaten the very existence of the beholding subject: sudden storms, great rivers filled with deadly rocks, and—as a part of nature—the fierce bands of violent people who tear across it. In *Maria*, the Cossacks are explicitly conflated with the steppe, horses, and darkness in "one wild soul."[32] Orthodox Ruthenian peasants are frequently described with the pejorative collective term *czerń*, suggesting an undifferentiated "black" element, or a backward, uncivilized "rabble." In various works, these frenzied masses destroy the products of "Polish" civilization, butchering men, women, and children in the historical uprisings against Catholic overlords. The Ukrainian steppe roils with blood in manifestations of a dynamic sublime that overwhelms these "Polish" characters—and perhaps the reader—with a sense of "horror" that is central, in particular, to Burke's conception of the sublime.[33]

In multiple works, the violence is specific to the historical "Haidamaky" uprising, or "Koliivshchyna," of 1768, in which Cossacks and Ruthenian peasants turned against Polish Catholic nobles, Roman Catholic clergy, Jews, and Ruthenian Uniates for a mixture of religious, "national," and social reasons.[34] Representations of the rebellion in Polish Romantic literature emphasize the elemental ferocity of the insurgents, who embody a dynamically sublime force of nature: a "dark cloud" (*tuman*) of revolution rolling across Ukraine, as Goszczyński describes them in *The Castle of Kaniów*.[35] Multiple depictions capture the most brutal and perverse forms of intergroup violence, often directed against Polish women and children, signaling both the innocence of the victims and an almost genocidal threat to the reproductive continuity of the group.

In his re-creation of the historical Uman Massacre (1768) in *Wernyhora*, Czajkowski shows Iwan Gonta (*Ukr.* Ivan Honta)—a Cossack defector to the rebel side—killing his own sons because of the "Polish blood" (*lacka krew*) they had supposedly inherited from their mother.[36] He then enjoins the rampant insurgents to "destroy even the fetus in a slain mother's womb" in a frenzy of slaughter of Poles and Jews. In *The Silver Dream of Salomea* (*Sen srebrny Salomei*, 1843), Słowacki constructs multiple scenes of extreme violence and horror, including the forcing of dead puppies into the hacked open womb of a murdered Polish mother.[37] The play depicts a Ukraine bathed in blood, frequently comparing the rebels to irresistible natural forces or reducing them to the status of animals. When the Polish nobleman Gruszczyński charges into the masses of the enemy to avenge his own murdered children, he is overpowered by a "black rabble" (*czerń*) that swarms around him "like ants."[38]

The level of detail and the length of these often poetic descriptions of violence give the impression that these Romantic works almost revel in the bloodshed, exposing the perverse pleasure that intermingles with fear, horror, and pain in various conceptions of the sublime.[39] Kant understands this unexpected enjoyment, or even exaltation, as a consequence of the subject's recognition of his or her own ultimate transcendence of the natural menace. As he explains in his *Critique of Judgment* (*Kritik der Urteilskraft*, 1791), the subject's confrontation with the terrifying forces of nature paradoxically reveals an inner capacity to master the seemingly insurmountable through the faculty of reason.[40] The subject is thus split between the vulnerable "natural being" and the independent "mind," which "has a vocation that wholly transcends the domain of nature."[41] In short, the feeling of the sublime reveals the superiority of the individual subject's rationality over even the most overwhelming expressions of natural power.

In the context of Polish-Ukrainian relations, these aesthetic dimensions of the sublime intersect with the political. In various Polish-language depictions, the overwhelming spaces and brutishness of the Ukrainian lands and their peoples function partly to reveal the transcendent power of "Polish" reason, culture, and language. Accordingly, ideas of "Polishness" and "Ukrainianness" (in both Cossack and Ruthenian variants) overlap with a series of binary oppositions: beautiful versus sublime; reason versus animal instinct; West versus East; ordered estates versus wild fields; culture versus nature; civilization versus barbarism. The Ukrainian sublime inspires horror with its scale, formlessness, frenzy, and violence, while also revealing the civilizing mission that Poles have often imagined for themselves in the east. The Ukrainian lands thus appear as a natural theater for the exercise of the power of "western" rationality—a savage *terra nullius* open to both the ambitions and moral claims of Polish "colonizers."

This idea of a Polish "colonizing" mission in the past had particular piquancy in the post-partition context in which the Polish-Lithuanian Commonwealth no longer existed.[42] As Maria Janion puts it, "Colonized in the nineteenth century by the partitioners, we could be proud that we had once been colonizers."[43] In its aesthetic and philosophical dimensions, this compensatory myth reflects the experience of the Kantian sublime of "mastery." The "Polish" subject perceives—or rather constructs—its own civilizational or moral superiority in the encounter with a seemingly overpowering "other."

In the opening exposition of Michał Grabowski's *Pan Starosta Kaniowski* (1856), the narrator explains that "the Polish magnates . . . had set about colonizing the vast wastes," bringing the fruits of reason to Ukraine—including the Roman Catholic catechism, advanced farming practices, and commerce.[44] Elsewhere, in Słowacki's *Silver Dream of Salomea*, the character of Regimentarz Stempowski, a military commander representing Polish legal authority, refers pointedly to the concepts of "high justice" and "the right [law] of the sword [*prawo miecza*]" as his righteous response to the violence of the rebels. Polish law is the answer to Ukrainian disorder, and the justification for the appropriation of territory: "It is time to show that we Poles are the owners of this land."[45] Admittedly, Słowacki subjects the character of the Regimentarz and the "Poles" more generally to strong ironizing critique, as we shall see. Nevertheless, even in this ambiguous context, the regimenting power of "Polish" reason is revealed—or forged—in confrontation with sublime "Ukrainian" violence.

The Burkean Sublime and the Unassimilable "Other"

Many works of the "Ukrainian school" give only partial expression to the comforting myths of Polish dominion. Written long after the Ukrainian lands were taken from the Commonwealth, their melancholy mood and focus on periods of violent upheaval reflect the ultimate failure of the Polish "civilizing" mission. In the domestic conflicts that weakened the state and opened the way to the triumph of Russian power, the products of "Polish" reason had been swept away (though in fact the Polish landed nobility retained its privileges in the region through part of the nineteenth century under Russian rule). In this sense, the Ukrainian sublime more often appears not in the version of Kantian "mastery," but rather in the Burkean mode of a chastened horror and even humility before the vast and powerful "other." From this perspective, the Polish Romantics often seem to posit the incommensurability of this "eastern" region and its people with the Polish colonizing mission, and perhaps with "western" reason.

In the wake of the Commonwealth's final demise, the Polish Romantics of the "Ukrainian school" looked back to the Koliivshchyna as a moment of catastrophic failure, when the cracks in the multicultural ideal had yet again revealed themselves. In many cases, their message is merely a gloomy recognition that Ukraine had proved to be untamable, as in the melancholic contemplation of the ghostly remnants of Polish glory in Malczewski's *Maria*. In a slightly different vein, Goszczyński's *Castle of Kaniów* gives an allegorical account of a failed "marriage" between Poles and Ruthenians in the eastern lands of the Commonwealth. Against the background of the historical revolt itself, the story tells of a Ruthenian woman, Orlika, who has been forced to marry an abusive Polish husband and eventually kills him before perishing herself. The violent end of this "poor marriage, with the devil as matchmaker" reflects the disintegrating relations between the two peoples in a storm of violence that ultimately destroys both sides.[46] Goszczyński's work thus describes the end of what he calls "Polish Ukraine," with the central image of the destruction of the eponymous castle also symbolic of the overthrow of Polish power and its degenerated civilizing mission. Far from any association with "reason," the brutal Polish lord himself—as in various other works—is but another violent emanation of the Ukrainian sublime.[47]

Such allegories were also bound up with debates about the very nature of the "Polish nation" that were unfolding among opposing émigré camps at the time the Romantics were writing. Many thinkers of the era were committed to the restoration of some version of the old Commonwealth in its multicultural and multiconfessional form, thus espousing a "political" conception of national identity.[48] Yet this dominant idea came into conflict with emerging "ethnic" conceptions, with increasing recognition of separate Ruthenian or Cossack identities, and with a hierarchical framework that privileged the Polish language and Roman Catholicism even within the multicultural version of the imagined community.[49] In this sense, the Romantic writers of the "Ukrainian school"—who belonged to various ideological camps, from the conservatism of Czajkowski to the social radicalism of Goszczyński—were all implicitly grappling with ongoing transformations of what "Polishness" should mean. This process found expression in their representations of the civil wars that had precisely exposed the emerging division between separate "Polish" and "Ukrainian" identities and interests.

As Goszczyński's negative depiction of the abusive Polish husband suggests, many of the Polish Romantics were far from one-sided in their view of this conflict.[50] Even as he continued to believe in the fundamental "Polishness" of Ukraine (though not in any modern ethnic sense), Goszczyński represents the Koliivshchyna rebellion as a form of vengeance for Polish colonial crimes, placing particular emphasis on rape and forced marriage inflicted on Ruthenian women. While broader themes of social inequality and revolution remain central to the work beyond any proto-national concerns, Goszczyński's critique of social relations suggests ethnically framed anxieties over reproduction, endogamy, and male control of women.[51] He also explains in an author's note that the historical punishments meted out to the rebels by the "Polish" authorities were just as brutal as the excesses of the "Ukrainian" mob, thus exacerbating the uprising in a furious cycle of violence between groups.[52]

In his critique of Polish power in the east, Goszczyński's work—among others—is not very far removed from depictions of the same historical events by Ukrainian Romantic writers. Taras Shevchenko (1814–1861) depicts the Koliivshchyna as a just reaction to growing oppression from Polish overlords in his narrative poem *Haidamaky* (1841), which may partly have been a response to Goszczyński's poem and especially to Czajkowski's *Wernyhora*.[53] As in *The Castle of Kaniów*, the theme of Polish men making violent claims on Ruthenian women is prominent, as a young Cossack seeks vengeance on Polish lords who have kidnapped his betrothed. Though Shevchenko's poem occasionally revels in the resulting revolutionary violence—as streams of blood flow across the steppe and cathartic fires sweep away the unjust order—his portrayal of the destruction is ultimately tragic. For the narrator of the poem, the conflict is unnatural and fratricidal: "One's heart aches as these brother Slavs / Tear brother Slavs to bits. / Who is to blame for such a crime? / The Polish Jesuits."[54] According to Shevchenko, Catholic fanatics are at fault, as the forces of the Counter-Reformation have dismantled the Commonwealth's former religious tolerance, applying unbearable pressure on the Orthodox religion in the east.[55] Now both Poles and Ukrainians must pay the price. Goszczyński seems to reach a similar conclusion, arguing in a foreword to his poem that "the intolerance of Catholic priests and the inhumanity of the lords" had provoked the Ruthenian masses.[56]

Ukrainian writers also attacked the distance between the declarative Polish attachment to freedom and the oppressive reality for the Orthodox peasantry and Cossacks. Through their own sufferings and through the violence inflicted on the Polish overlords, the Ukrainian people were to teach their brothers the true meaning of liberty. In Shevchenko's *Haidamaky*, the narrator uses bitter irony to capture the gulf between the Polish ideal and the hypocritical reality: "See the confederates—at torture tense— / Those men who rise in Liberty's defense."[57] The false liberty the Polish noblemen defended meant little more than their own narrow class interests, while the rebels of the Koliivshchyna were fighting for the greater freedom of the masses. This sacrificial process was explicated in more programmatic form in *The Books of the Genesis of the Ukrainian People* (*Knyhy buttia ukrayinskoho narodu*, 1846), written largely by Mykola Kostomarov for the Cyril and Methodius Brotherhood. In direct response to Adam Mickiewicz's *Books of the Polish Nation* (*Księgi narodu polskiego*, 1832), with its pronouncement that "Poland" embodied liberty, Kostomarov exposes the hollowness of such claims about the historical role of the Commonwealth from the perspective of those oppressed within it. Echoing Mickiewicz's language about the three partitioning powers, he accuses both the Polish nobility and Moscow of establishing the most radical systems of slavery and oppression in world history.[58]

Unlike Shevchenko, who never used the word "Ukrainian" as an ethnonym, Kostomarov refers directly to "Ukrainians" and the "Ukrainian nation," thus playing an important part—along with Panteleimon Kulish (1819–1897)—in the development of these modern concepts.[59] Kostomarov posits the Ukrainian nation's embodiment of a more authentic freedom that will deliver on the unfulfilled promise of Poland's claims about itself. Through suffering—both their own and that inflicted as punishment on the Poles—the Ukrainians would make the Poles and all other Slavs truly free.[60] This Ukrainian version of national messianism imagines a utopian future of harmonious relations between Ukrainians, Poles, and Russians in a federated Slavic Union centered in Kyiv. In the same period, Shevchenko's "To the Poles" (*Poliakam*, 1847) focuses more specifically on Ukrainian Cossacks and Poles, painting an idealized past picture of the two peoples living together in freedom, before this putative harmony was shattered by the tyranny of "Latin priests and magnates."[61] The poem then concludes with a messianic anticipation of future concord. Both Poles and Ukrainians had a special calling for liberty, but the Catholic Poles had strayed from the path and needed the Ukrainians to bring them back to it.

A belief in the deeper historical, or even eschatological, meaning of the Polish-Ukrainian conflict also seems to animate Słowacki's *Silver Dream of Salomea*. While Shevchenko, Goszczyński, and others lament the crushing consequences of the Koliivshchyna for both sides, including the loss of self-determination that followed, Słowacki—like Kostomarov—strikes a messianic note. In the case of *The Silver Dream*, critics have focused on the underlying mystical system of the play, according to which the "suffering of bodies" would lead to a purification of souls.[62] In historical context, Słowacki almost seems to view the violence inflicted on Poles in the east as a cathartic punishment for an earlier failure to recognize the independent aspirations of Cossacks and Ruthenians. In various interpretations, the blood spilled on both sides in the play has a sacrificial meaning, as mass suffering accompanies the historical death of the idealized Ukraine of the old Commonwealth and the subsequent birth of two separate nations.[63] According to George Grabowicz, two entirely "new worlds"—Polish and Ukrainian—arise on the ruins of the failed "silver dream" of Ukraine as a harmonious union of the two peoples.[64] In this sense, Słowacki's work captures in mythological form—perhaps unintentionally—a key moment in the development of modern Polish and Ukrainian national identities after the destruction of the early modern ideal of the multicultural Commonwealth. The sublime of horrific physical suffering symbolically confirms the new subjectivities of the two nations.[65]

From a certain "Polish" perspective, the chastening horror of the confrontation with the dynamic sublime of the Ukrainian rebellion—both in Słowacki's play and in history—forces humility in the face of the power of the fully autonomous "other," who cannot be subjugated.[66] Instead of Kantian "mastery" and the compensatory pleasures of a myth of past glory, Słowacki's work suggests a Burkean notion of the limited nature of the self—in this case, the collective self. The colonizing reason and law of the Polish lords cannot subdue, subsume, or transcend the Ukrainian "other," which embodies an autonomous identity with a powerful critical voice, especially in the character of Semenko, the Cossack leader of the rebels.[67] In Słowacki's vision, the violence of the sublime forces recognition of the autonomy of the "other," leading to the possibility of historical progress, the improvement of a decadent nobility, and more just future relations between the two peoples.[68] The untamable power of the sublime is properly apocalyptic, opening up visions of a totally changed reality.[69]

Yet such interpretations ignore a crucial dimension of Słowacki's play: namely, the difficulty of distinguishing between the collective "self" and the "other." In short, the dividing line between "Poles" and "Ukrainians" (Cossacks/Ruthenians) is often difficult to define. Many of the characters exhibit a mixed background or identity, leading the contemporary critic Dariusz Skórczewski to characterize the whole play as a "parade of hybrids."[70] The eponymous Salomea herself has a partly Ruthenian mother; Princess Wiśniowiecka represents a powerful Ukrainian family of the Polish nobility, with its roots in medieval Rus'; and the devious rebel leader Semenko masquerades as a registered Cossack loyal to the Polish Crown. Even the members of the "Polish" Gruszczyński family slaughtered by the rebels have Ruthenian lineage.

The most overt and dramatic example of mixed identity is that of another Cossack, Sawa, a character who identifies with the "Polish" side of the conflict, and who seems intent on extirpating the "Ukrainian" part of his identity. In a postcolonial interpretation of the play, Skórczewski asserts that the Polish "colonial project" has won out in Sawa, forcing him to concede the inferiority of his own "original identity."[71] This analysis assumes a somewhat essentialized conception of an integral ethnic identity, as if the Cossack had been disinherited of an "authentic" native culture by Polish colonial power. Yet Sawa's own self-description suggests a deeper, tragic understanding of the increasingly unviable status of an earlier mixed identity in which each dimension was once just as "authentic" as the other:

> An eagle torn in half,
> With two hearts and beaks;
> A man of a threefold character,
> Of Lach [Pole], Cossack, and the devil.[72]

Sawa's lament reflects his condemnation of what he considers to be the base acts of his Cossack and Ruthenian compatriots. But it also reveals the fate of the old multicultural identities in a new era of intergroup conflict. No longer would it be natural for individuals, especially members of the nobility, to be both "Ruthenian" and "Polish," with religious, cultural, ethnic, linguistic, and political aspects of their identity intertwined in complex ways. Sawa feels that he must now choose between "Polish" and "Ukrainian," or rather "Lach" and "Cossack," sides locked in intractable conflict. In this emerging context, the mixed or "impure" nature of his identity can only bring him suffering, as he pledges his loyalty to the "Polish" side against the "Ukrainian" rebels. He has become the exception in a new reality: no longer a Cossack, but not entirely "Polish"—in the emerging sense—either. Sawa's tragedy is that he remains trapped in what he himself already recognizes to be a rapidly expiring mode of transcultural identity.

In this way, *The Silver Dream of Salomea* captures the central symbolic drama of the Ukrainian sublime as it pertains to collective identity: the violent and traumatic separation of the "self" from an apparently unassimilable "other" that nevertheless remains vestigially attached to it. This drama, in return, reveals the rising conflict in the Romantic era between early modern (transcultural) and modern (ethnic) conceptions of the "Polish" subject. Although many of Słowacki's characters are hybrid combinations of "Polish" and "Ukrainian" dimensions, variously understood, the logic of conflict forces them toward new, monolithic forms of proto-national identity.

Hybrid Identities in Henryk Sienkiewicz's *With Fire and Sword*

The most influential work of what I am calling the "Ukrainian sublime" is Henryk Sienkiewicz's *With Fire and Sword* (*Ogniem i mieczem*, 1884), a historical novel set during the early years of the Khmelnytsky Uprising (1648–1657). The novel draws on most of the key tropes of the earlier Polish Romantic representations of violent uprisings in the Ukrainian lands, including the familiar mathematical and dynamic dimensions of the sublime.[73] In Sienkiewicz's version, the enormous expanse of the Ukrainian lands remains "wild, beautiful, and dangerous," soaked with blood, filled with primitive people, haunted by ghosts and demons. The main distinction is only that the more positive aspects of the Romantic depictions are significantly less prevalent in Sienkiewicz's narrative.

Admittedly, there is still ambivalence—Bohun, the main Cossack antagonist, is not entirely without Romantic appeal—but, overall, Sienkiewicz presents a starker opposition between good and evil, between the noble forces loyal to the Commonwealth and the rabble of Khmelnytsky's brutal Cossacks. This simultaneous imitation and rejection of the Romantic legacy partly reflects Sienkiewicz's position in the wider Positivist movement, which defined itself against Romanticism while still borrowing some of its ideas. However, the Manichaean nature of the "Pole" versus "Cossack" confrontation may also reflect the late nineteenth-century crystallization of new, ethnolinguistic ideas of nation that had not yet emerged at the time of Goszczyński and Słowacki.[74] While Sienkiewicz himself ostensibly shared the Romantics' multicultural, or "political," conception of national identity, his writings reflect with even greater clarity the hierarchical, proto-ethnic assumptions already intertwined with it.[75] *With Fire and Sword*—at least superficially—suggests a sharper division between "Poles" and their ethnic antagonists, drawing on the aesthetics of sublime horror before a vast and powerful enemy defined in cultural and religious terms.

In the symbolic world of the novel, Khmelnytsky and his men manifest themselves as an overwhelming force, "[obscuring] the light of day" and casting a shadow "from sea to sea."[76] In multiple scenes, frenzied Cossacks commit acts of bestial violence, tearing their victims to pieces in a darkness only lit by the hellish light of fires.[77] As in some of the Romantic works, the Eastern Orthodox Ruthenian peasants are described using the pejorative *czerń*, or "black mob."[78] These demonizing depictions have led to numerous controversies among both Polish and Ukrainian scholars over the novel's negative stereotyping of Ukrainians and generally dubious historicity, ethnography, and geography.[79] As early as 1885, the Ukrainian historian Volodymyr Antonovych attacked the novel for its distorted depictions of both Cossacks and Ruthenian peasants.[80] Half a century later, in the 1930s, a debate raged over the work's historical accuracy among Polish historians against the fraught background of Polish-Ukrainian tensions in the interwar Polish Republic.[81]

Insofar as Sienkiewicz's negative depictions reflect the "Ukrainian sublime," they belong to what I have characterized as the Kantian type, whereby a confrontation with the terrifying size and power of "the other" reveals the "Polish" subject's superiority as a moral or rational entity. For example, the narrator describes the Wiśniowiecki (*Ukr.* Vyshnevetsky) magnate family as torchbearers for a putatively "Polish" culture and religion that has "changed [the] gloomy wilderness of the past into a settled country" and "introduced the rule of law and justice."[82] In the end, it is also Jeremi Wiśniowiecki (*Ukr.* Yarema Vyshnevetsky, 1612–1651) who crushes the uprising. As a representative of "Polish" civilization and political authority—though his family's

Ruthenian origins suggest key complexities to which I will shortly return—
he restores order to a wild land, taming its fractious peoples, even if the
historical record would reveal the ultimate failure of this "Polish" mission.

Here, the Kantian sense of "mastery" occasioned by the sublime becomes
a fantasy of political mastery, a glorification of the dying days of the Polish
colonial project in Ukraine, constructed retrospectively for Polish readers
in the late nineteenth century, when the Commonwealth had long since lost
these lands and its own independent existence. Once again, the memories of
Poland's own former status as "colonizer" may compensate for the reality of
Poland as "colonized" in Sienkiewicz's time. As Ryszard Koziołek explains,
Sienkiewicz "drew the reader into the seventeenth century, and in this way
avoided the catastrophe of the Polish state in the eighteenth," thus creating
a "credible myth" for Polish contemporaries "humiliated by the partitions,
and then by early capitalist modernity."[83] Sienkiewicz's historical novels are
a retreat from the present of an "enslaved nation" into a reimagined past that
could serve what he famously called the "strengthening of hearts."

This context of lost independence differentiates Sienkiewicz's Polish quasi-colonial narrative toward Ukraine from the classic western "orientalist"
representations of "the east." The resulting ambivalence reveals itself in a
striking set of gender reversals, as Elżbieta Ostrowska observes. Whereas
western myths about the colonized "other" foreground the gaze of the
western male penetrating the mystery of the exotic female, the Polish male
protagonist of Sienkiewicz's novel, Jan Skrzetuski, is surprisingly bereft of
agency at key moments, especially when trying to save his beloved from the
clutches of the charismatic Cossack, Bohun.[84] This undermining of Polish
masculinity—sometimes accompanied by masculinization of female characters—thus reflects the "emasculating" effects of the colonial context in which
Sienkiewicz was writing.[85] Poland's historical status as both "colonizer" and
"colonized" comes through in these unusual interactions between gender
and ethnicity, which, according to Ostrowska, reveal deep insecurities about
the Polish nation's political and cultural position in Europe.[86]

However, this interpretation tends to essentialize proto-national differences, and thus to elide a much deeper level of ambivalence over the
identity of the "Polish self." Like the earlier Romantic works, Sienkiewicz's
novel often seems to undermine any simple distinctions between "self" and
"other," "Pole" and "Cossack," instead exhibiting hybrid identities in multiple
characters. Ostrowska acknowledges that the novel's "nationalist" mission to
exclude a symbolic "other" is complicated by nostalgia for the more inclusive

political understanding of nation exemplified by the multiethnic Commonwealth. Yet these tensions do not arise only with respect to the body politic,
but in the bodies of the novel's central characters as well. As in Słowacki's
Silver Dream of Salomea, hybridity is not just a quality of a diverse nation,
but also a fundamental characteristic of individual human selves. Even in
Sienkiewicz's apparently simplified representation, the dichotomy between
the civilized Polish subject and savage Cossack or Ruthenian peasant "other"
is sabotaged by nagging uncertainties about identity.

Throughout the novel, characters embody a mixture of backgrounds,
slipping between different identities, speaking multiple languages, or using
a dialect of Polish studded with Ukrainian or Ruthenian expressions, often
incorrectly rendered by Sienkiewicz.[87] On the battlefields that dominate the
story, the two opposing sides have difficulty distinguishing each other. A
prime example of these hybrid forms of identity is the main female character, Helena Kurcewiczówna. Ostrowska describes her as "an ideal Polish
woman," in an interpretation that generations of Polish readers would no
doubt find uncontroversial.[88] Helena's ideal "Polishness" is threatened by the
attentions of "the other man"—the Cossack Bohun—whose ethnic otherness endangers an implicit principle of ethnic endogamy. Ultimately, Helena
fights off these dangerous advances, and—according to Ostrowska—"her
resistance confirms both her ideal femininity as well as her 'Polishness' as an
indestructible and incorruptible idea."[89] But in what way is Helena "Polish"?

Among the earliest descriptions of the character in the novel is the follow-
ing: "Helena was, after all, a Ukrainian woman [*Ukrainka*] of fiery blood."[90]
Of course, the term "Ukrainka" does not denote ethnicity or nationality here.
Helena is a member of the Polish Catholic nobility from the Commonwealth's
"Ukrainian" regions. In the same way, the heroic Polish Catholic nobleman
Michał Wołodyjowski is proud of his regional identity as a member of the
"Ukrainian nobility" (*szlachta ukraińska*).[91] However, these terms are not
entirely devoid of a cultural dimension with implications for identity. Other
descriptions of Helena as a "flower of the steppe" (*kwiat stepowy*) link her
with the Cossack and Ruthenian "people of the steppe" (*lud stepowy*).[92] Like
the Cossacks of Polish Romantic poetry, Helena is a natural emanation of the
sublime emptiness of the Ukrainian land, blooming out of the darkness on
the edge of the civilized world. Later in the novel, the term "Ukrainian" seems
almost to become a quasi-national category—for instance, when "Ukrainian
maidens" (*mołodycie ukraińskie*) are contrasted with "Polish women" (*Lasz-
ki*) in the violent descriptions of Khmelnytsky's Tatar allies murdering and

enslaving civilians after the Battle of Korsun (1648).[93] In this case, the very word "mołodycie" is a Ukrainianism (Ukr. *molodytsia*). The Polish Catholic nobleman Onufry Zagłoba's disguise as a "Ukrainian beggar" (*did ukraiński*) also seems to be a national disguise, with the word "did" (literally, "old man") borrowed from Ukrainian. Elsewhere, the narrator tells of "Ukrainian banditry" (*ukraińskie rozbójnictwo*) in specific reference to the iniquities of the Cossacks and Ruthenian peasantry.[94] Perhaps most interestingly, Bohun, "the other man" who plans to capture Helena, is described as "the very model of Ukrainian beauty—extravagant, colorful and swaggering."[95] Apart from its archetypal Romantic fetishization of Cossack freedom, this description is strikingly similar to characterizations of the "hot-blooded" Helena. Both Helena and Bohun are wild "Ukrainian" beauties. Indeed, only the Cossack witch Horpyna describes Helena—pejoratively—as a *Laszka* at all, bringing Bohun to wish he were a *Lach*, since she might then want him, according to the endogamous principle that he too seems partly to accept.

Yet if Helena is a *Laszka*, then it is not in any modern ethnic sense. Indeed, the narrator emphasizes her predominantly East Slavic lineage: "The Kurtsevichi Bulygi were of an ancient princely stock which used the escutcheon of Kurts, claimed to be from Koryat, but was really from Rurik."[96] Koriat, or Karijotas, was a Lithuanian, son of the grand duke of Lithuania, Gediminas (ca. 1275–1341), one of the last defenders of the traditional pagan religion. Rurik was the legendary Varangian founder of the dynasty that ruled the principalities of Rus'. According to the narrator, Helena's father, Wasyl, only converted to the Latin rite from Orthodoxy in 1629.[97] He was later accused of betraying the army of the Polish king to the Muscovites at Smolensk in 1634, a disgrace that forced him into exile and almost destroyed the family. Helena's "Polishness" is clearly not based on descent. The same applies to the heroically represented character of Jeremi Wiśniowiecki, who—unlike Helena—is a historical figure. The narrator explains that Wiśniowiecki could also trace his roots back to the Gediminid dynastic family of Lithuania, which had intermarried with the old families of Rus', while his mother's side was Orthodox Moldavian.[98] He himself converted to Catholicism as late as 1632, one of the last of the Commonwealth's great Eastern Orthodox lords to do so.

These narratives make clear that religion had become a key marker of identity. Helena Kurcewiczówna and Jeremi Wiśniowiecki are religiously "Polish"—that is, Roman Catholic—and it is this fact, above all, that differentiates them from the Orthodox Cossacks and Ruthenian peasants who share their cultural, geographical, and ethnic background. In the old political sense, they are also "Polish" insofar as this term can be used to denote the mixed noble ruling class. However, in this dimension, they are no more "Polish" than Bohdan Khmelnytsky himself, who specifically stands upon his rights as a "Polish nobleman [*szlachcic polski*]" in the novel.[99] In fact, what the novel reveals—like the Romantic works before it—is the eclipsing of this old political identity by new proto-national ethnic identities partly rooted in religious denomination. The historical Wiśniowiecki/Vyshnevetsky identified as both Roman Catholic and Ruthenian, but—at least in the world of Sienkiewicz's novel, and probably also in history—this identification had become very difficult to sustain. Indeed, Ukrainian chronicles of the time describe such apostates as no longer belonging to the Ruthenian community.[100] By converting to Roman Catholicism, Wiśniowiecki had become a "Pole" in a new, more limited understanding of this term.

Yet even this version of "Polishness" is not the same as modern ethnic variants, and the old hybrid or transcultural forms of identity continued to haunt the new understandings shaped by conflict. This persistent heterogeneity is particularly evident in language. The historical Wiśniowiecki/ Vyshnevetsky spoke both Polish and Ruthenian, among other languages. Many of the characters in Sienkiewicz's novel are similarly multilingual. The Polish of the text is peppered with Ruthenian expressions, especially in the speech of certain characters, but also in the narrator's descriptions. Skrzetuski's men constantly refer to him as *bat'ku* (Ukrainian for "father"). Zagłoba speaks and sings in Ruthenian, as part of his disguise as a Ukrainian *did*, fooling everybody with his dissemblance. When Khmelnytsky's Cossacks disguise themselves as noblemen at royal elections, the narrator emphasizes that nobody can distinguish them from "Poles" by their speech.[101] Identity is a fluid concept in the Ukrainian borderlands, and the many interpretations of Sienkiewicz's novel as a depiction of a "Polish-Ukrainian" conflict rely on assumptions that are not explicitly presented in the work—or, rather, are presented in a way that dismantles their coherence and force.

Accordingly, as in Słowacki's *Silver Dream of Salomea*, the Ukrainian sublime in Sienkiewicz's novel does not manifest itself only in affirmative, self-serving representations of a simple conflict between a rational "Polish" self and an irrational "Ukrainian" other, since the border between them is never entirely clear. Instead, it implies a more unsettling encounter with irrational and violent forces that invade or inhabit the supposedly rational self, at least as an expression of its past. In this context, it is also significant that the novel explicitly describes some of the actions of the Polish forces as just as brutal as those of the Cossacks. The exultant feeling of superiority that Kant describes is impossible here. The wild "Ukrainian" other is kin, an uncanny part of the rational "Polish" subject, inextricably linked to it by both lineage and the political and cultural history of the multicultural Commonwealth.[102] The works of the Ukrainian sublime convey fear, compensatory pleasure, and cautious recognition of an "other" that is not quite separable from the self.

Aesthetics and Identity

The "Ukrainian sublime" is an aesthetic category embodied—or constructed—in works of literature. It does not give specific insight into the real history of Polish/Ruthenian/Cossack encounters in the Ukrainian lands of the Polish-Lithuanian Commonwealth. Instead, it sheds light on the tensions and contradictions of retrospective literary interpretations of a complex history. In nineteenth-century Polish-language representations, the Ukrainian land and its peoples often appear as vast and powerful forces of nature, an inscrutable "other," whose wild violence resists the Polish "civilizing" project. Some Polish Romantic poets joined their Ukrainian contemporaries in critiquing this project, thus expressing recognition of the autonomy of the "other." Other works, especially Sienkiewicz's *With Fire and Sword*, deliver a fantasy of quasi-colonial "mastery" echoing the logic of Kant's version of the sublime, whereby the physical overwhelming of the subject does not preclude its moral superiority. In this regard, the Ukrainian sublime in Polish literature bears similarities to a kind of colonial sublime also present in orientalist works of western Romantic literature.

However, unlike the western orientalizers, the Polish quasi-colonial subject could never define itself in neat separation from the eastern "other." All the works of the Ukrainian sublime, even those indulging in fantasies of Polish power, come up against the fundamental hybridity of identity in the historical periods they describe. In the early modern world of the Polish-Lithuanian Commonwealth, distinctions between groups were not always clear, or ran along lines quite different from those of modern national identifications that were only just beginning to develop in the period in which these retrospective works were being written. This fluidity was also a result of the fact that the Commonwealth was not originally an imperial power in the western European sense. Instead, it had begun as a real—albeit imperfect and unequal—union, in which a capacious early modern version of "Polish" identity developed in dialogue with internal constituencies toward which a quasi-colonial relation would only later emerge.

The "Polish nation" had once been a political construct that potentially included Catholic Poles and Lithuanians, Protestant Germans, and Orthodox Ruthenians. In Ukraine, as many Ruthenian nobles converted to Roman Catholicism and began to use the Polish language, this political "nation" homogenized and crystallized around these new characteristics of "Polishness," separating these nobles from the wider Orthodox population—both Ruthenian peasant and Cossack. With this division came the beginnings of modern distinctions between "Polish" and "Ukrainian" nations, with religious difference forming a key early catalyst. Yet in the world of Słowacki's Cossack Sawa, or Sienkiewicz's Wiśniowiecki, these historically contingent distinctions were still coalescing, even if genuine differences already existed. In the works of the Ukrainian sublime, the embattled Polish subject faces a wild and dangerous "other" to which it is bound by historical, cultural, linguistic, and ethnic ties. These works thus give aesthetic expression to the early moments of a transition from the diversity of the early modern Commonwealth—in which religious, class, and ethnic differences were often not aligned—to a future world of violent conflict between homogenizing modern nations.

8

Imagining the Past and Remembering the Future

Oskar Halecki, Lewis Namier, and the Burden of History

Robert Frost

One would expect people to remember the past and to imagine the future. But in fact, when discoursing or writing about history, they imagine it in terms of their own experience, and when trying to gauge the future, they cite supposed analogies from the past, till, by a double process of repetition, they imagine the past and remember the future.

—Lewis Namier

Imagining the future for the peoples emerging from the wreckage of the great empires of central and eastern Europe at the end of the First World War was no easy task. The German, Austro-Hungarian, and Ottoman Empires were disintegrating before their eyes, while the Bolshevik Revolution had transformed the Russian Empire into an anarchic theater of civil war that posed the most serious challenges of all for the peacemakers who assembled in Paris in January 1919. One thing was clear. In the political chaos created by the collapse of the powers that had partitioned the multicultural Polish-Lithuanian Commonwealth between 1772 and 1795, multiculturalism did not feature on the agendas of those contemplating the reconstruction of a shattered Europe.

The futures imagined by the traumatized peoples of Europe in 1919 were rather different. The subject peoples of Europe's fragmenting empires dreamed of national independence, despite the problems of establishing nation-states in central and eastern Europe, with its kaleidoscope of peoples who had lived together for centuries despite differences in language, culture, and religion. The tide, however, was running firmly in favor of the principle of national independence, and the historic cultural diversity of these regions was seen as a problem by national movements and peacemakers alike.

The Allies had raised expectations by accepting President Woodrow Wilson's Fourteen Points, presented to Congress in January 1918, as the philosophical basis of the coming peace. Although Wilson declared that the principle of self-determination for Europe's peoples was fundamental, the Fourteen Points, issued before the collapse of the German and Austro-Hungarian Empires became manifest, were more cautious, calling instead for "the freest opportunity for autonomous development" for the peoples of Austria-Hungary, and "autonomous development" for the non-Turkish peoples of the Ottoman Empire.

Quite what "autonomous development" might mean was unclear, but as the peoples of central and eastern Europe took matters into their own hands in late 1918, the principle of national self-determination took center stage. Wilson declared to Congress in his Four Principles speech of February 11, 1918, that "the right of small nations and nationalities to determine their allegiances and forms of political life . . . was not a mere phrase, but an imperative principle of action."[1] His allies—Lloyd George, Clemenceau, and Orlando, all of whom had empires or imperial aspirations of their own—were more skeptical concerning the practicalities of implementing this high-minded principle. Wilson was aware of the potential problems: he was careful to stress that the principle of self-determination was not absolute, and that "all well-defined national aspirations shall be accorded the utmost satisfaction that can be accorded them without introducing new or perpetuating old elements of discord and antagonism that would be likely in time to break the peace of Europe and consequently of the world."[2]

Wilson understood that it might be difficult to realize the imagined futures of all the peoples of Europe. Nevertheless, he recognized one "well-defined aspiration." In point thirteen of the fourteen, he called for the establishment of an "independent Poland with free and secure access to the sea." The singling-out of Poland owed something to Wilson's courting of the USA's substantial Polish community, over four million strong,[3] but the main reason was historical. Poland was the only European state to have disappeared in modern times. In the age of the American and French Revolutions, which proclaimed the principle of the sovereignty of the people, Prussia, Russia, and Austria had removed the Polish-Lithuanian Commonwealth from the map against the wishes of its citizens in the partitions of 1772, 1793, and 1795.

Robert Howard Lord, a Harvard historian and author of a 1915 study of the Second Partition, did not doubt the significance of the Polish case. Stating that the "Polish question" was the "most difficult and perplexing of the 'national' problems with which the last century has had to deal," he argued that "no other event in modern times has produced such lasting changes in the map of Europe as did the dismemberment of the Polish Republic, a state . . . whose area very considerably surpassed that of France or Germany today."[4] Lord observed that the Polish question had proved a permanent source of instability. He highlighted the failure of policies of Germanization and Russification, quoting Prince Bernhard von Bülow's view that "the Polish problem is one of the gravest of those confronting Prussia, and one upon which the future of the Empire and the whole German nation depends."[5] Prussia had obtained the largest acquisition of territory it had ever made in 1793; Lord argued that this act constituted "one of the most short-sighted, disastrous, and morally reprehensible transactions in her history."[6]

Thus, the Polish question was a moral question:

> At the present moment, a war which has turned Poland into a second Belgium has once more drawn the horrified attention of the world to this unhappy country. . . . Whatever the outcome of the struggle may be, is it too much to hope that this time Poland will not have suffered in vain; that this time the rights of a nation . . . which has so many claims upon the respect, the sympathy, and the justice of the world, will not go unrecognized; that this time the Polish Question, which has tortured the conscience of Europe for over a century, will finally be set at rest?[7]

Lord's hopes were to be dashed. The independent Poland that emerged after 1918 was only partially the creation of the Paris peacemakers. The wars it fought with its neighbors between 1918 and 1923 gave full play to the "old elements of discord and antagonism" that Wilson had feared, as the eastern lands of the former Commonwealth suffered a brutal cycle of paramilitary violence and civil war.[8] The Poland that emerged from this maelstrom breached in several respects the principles of self-determination, and proved fragile. A mere two decades later, the Polish question was to provide the immediate cause of the most terrible of all European wars, a war in which Poland's suffering was to be greater than anything yet imagined.

This outcome was not entirely the fault of the Paris peacemakers, who could only exert direct influence over Poland's western border. Nevertheless, the Polish question encapsulated the problems that faced them as they struggled to close the lid of the Pandora's box that Wilson had opened in his high-minded attempt to redefine the philosophical basis of the European state system. History mattered to all of the aspirant nations urging their cases in Paris, and in the Polish case, history posed questions that proved all but impossible to answer. For the "Poland" that had disappeared in 1795, as this volume has shown, was a multicultural, multinational republic, not a nation-state. Among the Poles celebrating the declaration of Polish independence on November 11, 1918, there was no consensus about the kind of "Poland" that should rise from the ashes. If "Poland" were to be restored within the borders of 1772, as many believed it should be, then it would have to confront both its multicultural past, and the aspirations of the other peoples of the old Commonwealth.

Remembering the Past

Lord published his classic study two years before the US entered the war. His expertise was soon in demand. He led the East European section of the American Inquiry, an advisory body of experts, from April 1918, and toured Poland as a member of an Interallied Mission in early 1919. In Paris, he chaired the Interallied Commission on Polish Affairs.[9] He was by no means the only historian among the teams of experts assembled by the Great Powers and the aspiring nation-states clamoring for their attention. Hegel's claim that "a nation with no state formation (a mere nation) has, strictly speaking, no history—like the nations that existed before the rise of states and others which still exist in a condition of savagery,"[10] still influenced thinking among the imperial powers, and aspirant nation-states knew they had to demonstrate that they were "proper" nations through claims to a history of statehood and to a national territory in which it had been exercised in the past.

The Great Powers were aware of the problems involved in these claims, and assembled teams of historians to assess them. The Political Intelligence Department of the British Foreign Office employed a dazzling array of historical talent, including James Headlam-Morley (1863–1929), Edwyn Bevan (1870–1973), and Arnold Toynbee (1889–1975). Robert Seton-Watson (1879–1951), the foreign editor of the *Times*, rejected an invitation to join the unit, but traveled privately to Paris, where his expertise on central and southeastern Europe was much in demand.[11]

For the army of historians marching on Paris in 1919, the challenges were considerable. Were all peoples who claimed nationhood really nations? How far were historical claims to territory or the status of nationhood to be accommodated? How were differing historical accounts of peoples who shared a common past and claims to a common territory to be reconciled? How far were historical borders to be respected? Nowhere were the problems more evident than in the case of Poland. This chapter looks at these problems through a consideration of two great Polish historians, Oskar Halecki (1891–1973) and Lewis Namier (1888–1960), exact contemporaries and members of the expert teams informing the Paris negotiations: Halecki as an adviser to the Polish delegation, and Namier as the Polish specialist in the British Political Intelligence Department. Both grew up in the multinational, multicultural Habsburg monarchy, but their very different approaches to the old Commonwealth's multicultural legacy shed light on the serious problems that history posed for the peacemakers.

Namier and Halecki had much in common. Both were, in their different ways, outsiders. Namier was born Ludwik Bernstein vel Niemirowski in Russian Poland, but grew up in a polonized landowning family of Jewish descent in multicultural Habsburg Eastern Galicia, a province that was the focus of endless claims and counterclaims after 1918. A Polish patriot in his youth, he left for England in 1907. He studied at the London School of Economics and Balliol College Oxford, changed his name, became a British citizen, transformed the way in which eighteenth-century British history was understood, and embraced his Jewish heritage by joining the Zionist movement. Halecki moved in the opposite direction. His father, Oskar Alojzy Halecki (1838–1903), a general in the Habsburg army, was a loyal Habsburg subject; his mother, Leopoldina Dellimanić (1856–1943) was Croatian. Born in Vienna, Halecki's first language was German, and he attended the renowned Viennese Schottengymnasium. It was an unusual background for a Polish patriot.

Halecki's father, however, was proud of his Polish-Ruthenian forebears, the Chaleckis, whose estate of Chalcz (*Bel.* Chalč), near Homel (Homiel) in what is now Belarus, remained in the family until 1805. Oskar Alojzy insisted that his son should learn Polish and complete his education at Kraków's Jagiellonian University, where Oskar proved a talented historian, studying under Wiktor Czermak, Wacław Sobieski, and Stanisław Krzyżanowski. To his dismay, Halecki lost out in 1917 to Władysław Konopczyński—another historical adviser to the Polish delegation in Paris—in the competition to fill Krzyżanowski's chair of Polish history; a year later he accepted a chair at the University of Warsaw, where he remained until he fled the Nazis in 1940.[12]

Both men were active commentators during the war. Namier, despite earning a considerable reputation at Balliol, failed to secure a position at the college and was twice denied a fellowship at All Souls by antisemitic prejudice.[13] From 1915, he worked for the Foreign Office, preparing press summaries and briefings on eastern Europe, while supplementing his salary by writing for Seton-Watson's *New Europe*, the *New Statesman*, the *Times*, and the *Manchester Guardian*. Halecki held no official position, but he wrote articles and tracts supporting the Polish cause, including *Das Nationalitäten Problem im alten Polen* (The Nationalities Problem in Old Poland, 1916) and *Polens Ostgrenze im Lichte der Geschichte Ostgaliziens, des Chelmer Landes und Podlachien* (Poland's Eastern Border in the Light of the History of Eastern Galicia, Chełm Region and Podlachia, 1918); in the latter, he was still using the magnificently Habsburg designation Privatdozent Dr. Oskar Ritter von Halecki.

Both men wrote on Polish history, but their perspectives were very different. Namier's primary interests lay in the history of the eighteenth-century British Parliament and England's landed elites. It was in this field that he made his major theoretical contribution to the historical sciences, and it is on this work that his considerable reputation rests.[14] Namier's writings on Polish history were part of a wider project—which never reached fruition—to produce a general history of nineteenth-century Europe. Whereas Namier's work on British history was based on detailed archival research, his writings on Poland were more general. Only in his history of the 1848 revolutions did he draw on a substantial body of published sources, a fact recognized in a review in the *Kwartalnik Historyczny* by Stefan Kieniewicz, who, not realizing that Namier was a Pole, observed that it was unusual for an Anglo-Saxon scholar to use Polish sources.[15] Perhaps Namier permitted himself a wry smile when he read it.

Before 1940, Halecki was as assiduous a source-based historian as Namier. His main focus was on the formation of the Polish-Lithuanian union as a multiethnic, multicultural polity. His doctorate was on the origins of parliamentary culture in the Grand Duchy of Lithuania; his habilitation thesis analyzed the 1569 Union of Lublin, and he wrote important studies of the union's Lithuanian and Ruthenian lands before publishing his definitive history of the Jagiellonian union in 1919–1920.[16]

Both men rejected the narrow, ethnic Polish nationalism that emerged in the late nineteenth century and was embodied in the National Democratic Party, led by Roman Dmowski (1864–1939). Yet Halecki and Namier's views on the multicultural legacy of the Polish-Lithuanian Commonwealth differed greatly. A consideration of their contrasting approaches to that legacy can therefore shed light on the way in which the Commonwealth was remembered and how its legacy complicated the reconstruction of east-central Europe after 1918.

Imagining the Past: Oskar Halecki and the Jagiellonian Idea

Halecki's history of the Jagiellonian union had a political as well as a scholarly motivation. As he wrote in the preface: "The moment at which this history of the Jagiellonian Union appears lends itself twofold to the rendering of deserved homage to the greatest achievement of our ancestors. We are summoned to do so by the 350th anniversary of the Union of Lublin; we are summoned more urgently by current events. If today we feel the need to draw together all nations into one great union, based on the principles of justice and good will, equality and freedom, we should recall a very similar solution, albeit on a more modest scale, several centuries ago in our lands."[17] Halecki was referring to Wilson's proposed League of Nations, which he supported enthusiastically after its establishment. In September 1920, he published a popular guide to the league after accepting nomination by the Bureau for Foreign Propaganda of the Polish Council of Ministers as delegate to the league's Geneva Secretariat.[18] From 1921 to 1924, he served as secretary of the league's International Committee on Intellectual Cooperation, whose members included Albert Einstein, Henri Bergson, and Marie Skłodowska-Curie, and attended international scholarly congresses organized by the league, where his linguistic skills—he was a native German speaker and spoke fluent French and English—were put to good use.[19]

Halecki believed that the history of the Polish-Lithuanian union had contemporary relevance, although he recognized that its multicultural legacy posed problems in a new age in which the "old elements of discord and antagonism" feared by Wilson had already emerged: "If today on these very lands, tribal and social hatreds are rampant, impeding the reconstruction of that which was destroyed by external forces, then faith in a better future can only be inspired by looking into the distant past, and reviving for us all an age of the honorable cohabitation of united nations; of common good fortune and power."[20] Halecki endorsed the federative idea as a viable solution to the problems posed by the intermingling of peoples, nations, religions, and cultures across the lands of the old Commonwealth. For him, as for many Poles, it was clear that the injustice and manifest breaches of international law perpetrated by the partitioning powers should be reversed, and that "Poland" should seek restoration within the borders of 1772. His *History of the Jagiellonian Union* sought to provide historical arguments to buttress the federalist program advocated by followers of Józef Piłsudski (1867–1935), a socialist revolutionary, commander of the Polish Legions during the war, and independent Poland's first head of state.

Halecki, in seeking a historical basis for this vision, appealed to the Jagiellonian idea, a nineteenth-century concept that saw the multicultural Jagiellonian
union as a model for current politics. Halecki argued that it constituted an
ethical force underpinning the union that was relevant to the present: "The
triumph of these moral laws, which have in a miraculous way returned to us
our free Fatherland, justifies the hope that the Jagiellonian Idea, the sacred
heritage of its history, in spite of apparently insurmountable obstacles, can be
realized anew. This idea alone, this return to tradition, can resolve today, as in
the fourteenth or the sixteenth century, the problem of a stable reconstruction
of Eastern Europe."[21] Central to his Jagiellonian idea was Halecki's claim that the
Polish-Lithuanian union was formed not by conquest or dynastic inheritance,
but was based on the free consent of the peoples involved. He countered claims
that the union was merely a form of empire, in which Polish power was extended
over its reluctant neighbors: "[Russian and Ukrainian scholars] have not hesitated to involve themselves in the matter of the union with their tendentious
judgements, trumpeting that [the Lublin union], this watershed in east European history, was an act of violence and force, [whose significance] has been
idealistically falsified by Poles."[22] Halecki rejected this interpretation, arguing
that Poland did not acquire its eastern territories by force, but through mutual
agreement with its neighbors, and stressing that modern ideas of nationality
should not be projected onto the past. The Jagiellonian union was religiously tolerant—a necessity, given Lithuania's substantial Orthodox population—and if
many among the Lithuanian and Ruthenian elites adopted the Polish language
and converted to Catholicism after 1569, this was their own choice, and was
not enforced from above. Moreover, Halecki argued, many Polish peasants who
migrated into the Ruthenian lands assimilated freely to Ruthenian culture.[23]

Halecki was no fantasist, imagining a utopian past of mutual harmony. He
stressed the problems faced by the union, analyzing the often bitter arguments
between Poles and Lithuanians over its nature, and the problems posed by
religion. He welcomed the efforts of the Jagiellons to promote church union
between Catholic and Orthodox—he published a study of the origins of the
1596 Union of Brest, which created the Uniate Church—but was aware of the
problem of treating Orthodox nobles as second-class citizens, an issue that
fueled the civil wars of the 1430s and erupted again to deadly effect in 1648.[24]

Halecki appreciated the problems of applying the Jagiellonian idea in the
present; nevertheless, he maintained his faith in its inspirational force. As he
wrote in 1937: "[Poland] . . . stands on the threshold of a new epoch, living
in closer but more difficult relations than ever before with other nations,

both within its borders and in international relations. It must seek a new idea to inspire it; intuitively, it returns to find it in the old but eternally fresh Jagiellonian Idea."[25] Halecki was a scholar not a politician. His study of the union carefully assessed the agreements that formed it after the 1385 Union of Kreva, which resulted in the marriage of Poland's young queen regnant, Jadwiga (1374–1400), to Ladislaus II Jagiełło (ca. 1351–1434), the pagan grand duke of Lithuania, whose conversion to Catholicism and election to the Polish throne constituted a fundamental turning point in European history. Halecki's assessments of these acts—Vilnius-Radom (1401), Horodło (1413), and Mielnik (1501), and the consummation of the union at Lublin in 1569— are masterly, and remain essential reading.

Yet Halecki provided no blueprint for the realization of the Jagiellonian idea in the very different context of Europe after 1919. In 1937, he observed that "the Jagiellonian Idea remains a magnificent slogan that is loosely interpreted, rather than a closely defined scientific idea." Yet, instead of suggesting how it might be realized, he sought to provide that close scientific definition. This very attempt revealed the idea's shortcomings, however. Halecki defined its essence as the "misterium caritatis," the mystical brotherly love between Poles and Lithuanians that, he claimed, lay at the heart of the 1413 Horodło union.[26] He argued that pressure to form a unitary state "naturally" under Polish rule through the incorporation of Jagiełło's Lithuanian and Ruthenian lands into the Kingdom of Poland, as advanced by various Polish politicians down to 1569, was never constant, "nor was it necessary or possible to realize."[27]

Halecki saw the Lublin union as a triumph, on account of its recognition of the equality and separate statehood of the Grand Duchy of Lithuania within one republic: a unitary state dominated by Poles could never have secured the loyalty of Lithuanians, as the Commonwealth of the Two Nations secured their loyalty after 1569. He fully appreciated the problem that was to bedevil the union: the failure to acknowledge that it contained another nation, the Ruthenians—most of whom were Orthodox in 1569—whose status within the union was not recognized in the same way.[28]

Ultimately, however, for all his empathy with the Lithuanians and Ruthenians, Halecki argued that the union's greatest achievement was its transmission of European, Latin culture, to the east. As a devout Catholic— he developed close contacts with the Vatican and was later involved in the campaign to canonize Queen Jadwiga—he believed that the Poles played a providential role in this historic mission, in a Polish version of manifest destiny. It was through the adoption of Catholicism, argued Halecki, that the pagan Lithuanians raised themselves to be worthy of the equal status that they were accorded in 1569.

Yet the very success of Halecki's civilizing mission among the Commonwealth's elites helped to undermine the union that he saw it as creating. The civic nation formed at Lublin was increasingly Catholic and Polish-speaking. Protestantism spread rapidly among the wealthier and middling nobility across the union after 1550, but its appeal waned, and by the early seventeenth century, Counter-Reformation forces were in full flood. Catholicism became the dominant religion of civic nation as the great Ruthenian families converted to Catholicism following the 1596 Union of Brest, which failed to secure the support of the Ruthenian masses. After 1648, non-Catholics were increasingly excluded from central office and the Sejm. Although active persecution of religious minorities was rare, religious differences established a gulf between the landed elites of the Commonwealth's eastern territories and the Lithuanian- and Ruthenian-speaking peasantry that only widened after 1795.

The Jagiellonian idea, dreamed up in the bleak years when Poland did not exist, was part of an imagined past. The Jagiellons behaved like any other European dynasty, pursuing dynastic claims to assemble a composite polity; their aims were dynastic, and they had no program of fostering closer union in the interests of promoting Western civilization. The dynasty sought to keep Lithuania in a loose relationship with Poland, resisting Polish claims that it had been incorporated into Poland. Closer union at Lublin only came about on account of a dramatic change of heart by the last Jagiellon, the childless Sigismund II Augustus, who feared that the union would founder on his death, leaving Lithuania at the mercy of Ivan IV's Muscovy.

The Jagiellonian idea idealized the republican vision that lay at the heart of the union. For the appeal of the notion of a self-governing civic nation that transcended the Polish, Prussian, Lithuanian, and Ruthenian nations that formed it was considerable. By the late seventeenth century it had produced a governing class that was Polish in language, largely—although never exclusively—Catholic in religion, and hybrid in identity. Despite the use of the term "Sarmatian" to designate the supposed common descent of this civic nation, the sense of history of Lithuanian and Ruthenian nobles was strong enough for many of them to retain ideas of their separate histories and separate identities under the umbrella of the civic nation.[29] Nevertheless, whereas the 1707 Anglo-Scottish union liquidated the ancient and separate kingdoms of England and Scotland to establish the new Kingdom of Great Britain, and the term "British" came to designate the common civic identity of the Scottish and English nations, "Sarmatian" never really established itself in the same way. Increasingly, the term "Pole" came to be used by all the republic's non-Polish citizens without necessarily compromising their separate identities as Prussians, Lithuanians, or Ruthenians. In 1795, "Polish" did not mean what it had come to mean by 1918.

This broad sense of Polishness lingered long after 1795, but by 1918 it had been undermined by the forces of nineteenth-century nationalism. The influence of Herder's claim that nations were defined by language, culture and a common history inspired linguistic nationalist movements among the peoples of the former Commonwealth. In 1855, Adam Czartoryski (1770–1861) could declare, "I am above all a Pole, my whole life gives sufficient proof of that, but I am [also] Ruthenian and Ukrainian," but by 1918 a new, exclusive sense of Polishness had arisen, based on modern ideas of race and ethnicity.[30]

Its foremost spokesman was Dmowski, who proposed a radically different view of the nation and of Polishness from Piłsudski, the Polish Lithuanian whose followers clung to the older concept of a "Polish" civic nation. Dmowski, the son of a stonecutter, championed a new, plebeian nationalism influenced by social Darwinist ideas of national struggle, in which minority groups represented a threat to national cohesion, even where they had adopted the Polish language and Polish culture. Dmowski sought to nationalize the Polish masses in a process of modernization and democratization that would produce a culturally unified modern nation.[31]

Dmowski's concept of Polishness rejected notions of hybridity or dual identity, and the paternalistic nationalism of the noble elites. His malignant antisemitism derived from his fear that the significant Jewish urban population represented an alien element culturally, and a threat to the interests of the Polish middle classes. Yet Dmowski was no fascist. He regarded ethnicity as culturally constructed, a product of history, not a mystical, eternal entity: all nations were composed of different elements and none—least of all the Poles—could claim ethnic purity. Unlike fascists, he advocated "fairness" and "civilized conduct" in the national struggle, and criticized the Nazis for their brutal application of political violence.[32] Finally, he was no Catholic fanatic. The National Democrats originated as a standard nineteenth-century secular, modernist nationalist party suspicious of the Catholic Church. Dmowski had long been an atheist and was only received into the Catholic Church in 1937, two years before his death. Nevertheless, from the 1920s his view that the nation was essentially a cultural construct persuaded him to stress that Catholicism constituted the essence of the Polish nation.[33]

Dmowski saw Germans as a greater threat to the establishment of a Polish nation-state than Russians. Throughout the war he supported the Allies, unlike Piłsudski, whose Polish Legions fought for the Habsburgs. Although Piłsudski ended the war in a German prison and was the first head of the new Polish state in 1918–1919, it was Dmowski, based in London since 1915, who was more acceptable to the Allies, despite his open antisemitism, which frequently upset his British interlocutors, who preferred their own form of covert common-room antisemitism, the sort that had denied Namier his All Souls fellowship.

The National Democrats started from the same premise as Halecki's Jagiellonian idea, but they drew much darker conclusions. Where Halecki embraced the old Commonwealth's multiethnic, multicultural character, conceiving it as the basis for a harmonious federation of autonomous nations under benevolent and progressive Polish leadership, Dmowski saw it as antithetical to the formation of a homogeneous Polish nation. For Lithuanians, Belarusians, and Ukrainians, however, it was hard to distinguish the two versions of Polish nationalism, not least because Piłsudski—himself a Lithuanian of Polish culture—in practice was less committed to the federal idea than his major supporters in the Polish Socialist Party, such as Leon Wasilewski (1870–1936), Tadeusz Hołówko (1889–1931), or Witold Kamieniecki (1883–1964). As he remarked in 1919: "I want to be neither a federalist nor an imperialist, until I can talk about these matters . . . with a gun in my pocket."[34] When he did have a gun in his pocket, and it became clear that Lithuanians, Belarusians, and Ukrainians were uninterested in federation, he acted to ensure that Wilno (Vilnius), the old Lithuanian capital, and Lwów (now Lviv, Ukraine) remained in Polish hands.

Since it was Dmowski who led the Polish mission, the vision of a federation within the 1772 borders had no purchase in Paris. Even Lord, whose favorable attitude toward Poland led Eugeniusz Romer, a geographer and member of the Polish delegation, to quip that he was *nasz Lord* (our Lord), was no supporter of the restoration of the 1772 borders in the case of the Lithuanians, who were not a Slavic people.[35] He was more inclined to accept Polish views on Galicia and Silesia, which provoked an attack on him by Lloyd George, who told Wilson that: "the fate of peoples must be determined by the people themselves, and not by a Dr. Lord, who thinks he knows better than they what they want."[36]

Lloyd George's remark reflected his concern that although Dmowski opposed the restoration of the borders of 1772, since to do so would considerably dilute the Polish nature of the state, his proposed borders were far to the east of what allied statesmen felt were appropriate, and clearly breached Lithuanian and Ukrainian claims for self-determination. Nevertheless, Dmowski spoke a language of nationalism that the Great Powers understood. For the concept of the nation that dominated discussions in Paris had little room for the dual identities so common in the old Commonwealth. Halecki's studies were published in Polish, and could do little to affect the discussions in Paris. Dmowski was more inclined to listen to another of his historical advisers, Konopczyński, a National Democrat, who had no time for the Jagiellonian idea, which he saw as "an abstraction of the post-partition age, dreamed up in a psychological interpretation of highly diverse phenomena ... it was founded on an exceptional conjuncture, when the unbaptized boor Jogaila married Jadwiga, and submitted himself to the direction of sophisticated Polish politicians; his contribution to their common achievement was a huge, sparsely populated, uncultured East, hoping for Polish protection against Muscovy and the Tatars. Such a conjuncture repeats itself at best once every millennium."[37] The peoples of the Commonwealth's eastern lands did not regard themselves as uncultured, and the Jagiellonian idea played no part in the discussions at Paris, where a different conceptualization of Polish nationalism took center stage. Konopczyński's dyspeptic view of the Jagiellonian idea certainly had greater resonance in Lithuania, where historians, led by Adolfas Šapoka (1906–1961), presented the union with Poland as a dark period in Lithuania's history, in which Lithuania's elites abandoned the Lithuanian people and their language, and became Poles.[38] Ukrainians thought no differently. For all Halecki's sympathy toward the Commonwealth's Lithuanian and Ruthenian citizens, his vision was too Catholic and too Polish to arouse anything other than resistance from Poland's former partners in union.

Remembering the Future: Lewis Namier and Polish History

Although Namier grew up in Eastern Galicia as a Polish patriot who admired Piłsudski, he had no time for the Jagiellonian idea, and a far less positive view than Halecki of the Commonwealth and its legacy. On account of his wartime work for the Foreign Office, where he worked with characteristic dedication to persuade the peacemakers not to grant Eastern Galicia, with its majority Ruthenian population, to the new Polish republic, and his publications, both scholarly and journalistic, on Polish history, Namier is regularly accused of polonophobia: Bartłomiej Rusin goes as far as accusing him of "an implacable hatred for Poland."[39]

Namier certainly worked assiduously against any extension of Poland's border to the east. Although within the Foreign Office he was meant to focus on routine summaries of the Polish and Austrian press, he frequently added his own commentaries debunking claims made by Polish politicians and interpolating his own views. He grew more strident in 1915 after Dmowski's arrival in Britain from Petrograd. Dmowski had long believed that Poland was not powerful enough to stand against both Germany and Russia, and initially supported reunification of the Polish lands as an autonomous entity under Russian rule.

The Russians had made vague promises to this end, and Dmowski's stance was welcome to the British government. After the Bolshevik seizure of power in November 1917 and the failure of the Ludendorff offensive in March 1918, Poland's eastern border suddenly became a live issue, and Namier's briefing papers mounted bitter attacks on Dmowski, while Dmowski was reprimanded by the British government for his overtly antisemitic complaints about a man whom he termed in his memoirs "this little Galician Yid."[40]

Namier's briefing-paper polemics landed him in trouble on several occasions, and he was warned about including his own views in what were meant to be press summaries. Arthur Balfour, then foreign secretary, consulted Sir Charles Oman, another distinguished historian, who had examined Namier at Oxford. Oman replied: "He is quite sincere, but very self-centered and disputatious: he used to consider himself as the only authority in England on the Ruthenian question, and to resent anyone else having independent views upon it.... In my opinion [Namier's] criticism ... is written in a spirit of exaggerated hostility, making the worst of the Polish case wherever it is possible to do so."[41] On another occasion, Headlam-Morley reprimanded Namier, telling him: "The Poles have no special monopoly of vice.... [Y]ou are charged with Polish affairs and what people look to you for is not merely criticisms of Poland, but sympathetic advice as to how the Poles can best be helped."[42]

The historian Amy Ng concludes that Namier "singularly failed" to alter the direction of British policy on Poland.[43] Namier was able to circumvent his superiors, however, through his close relationship with Philip Kerr (1882–1940), the private secretary to Lloyd George between 1916 and 1921, and Andrzej Nowak argues that Namier's influence on Lloyd George was decisive.[44] Whether it was sufficient to change the course of British foreign policy is open to doubt, however. Namier's trenchant opinions on Poland may well have influenced Lloyd George, who confronted the ebullient Ignacy Paderewski (1860–1941), the renowned concert pianist and Polish prime minister in June 1919, on the question of the claim to all of Galicia, but Lloyd George, as Larry Wolff points out, was primarily concerned to challenge what he saw as Wilson's overly pro-Polish stance and his willingness to countenance Polish rule over Eastern Galicia despite his attachment to the principle of self-determination.[45] D. W. Hayton also highlights the relationship with Kerr, and agrees that Namier's persistent questioning of the legitimacy of Poland's claims to Eastern Galicia "played a considerable part in shaping prime-ministerial decisions," but in the last analysis Polish rule over Eastern Galicia was determined by force of arms, and the fait accompli was formally recognized by the British government along with its allies in December 1919. This was a bitter blow to Namier, who resigned from the Foreign Office in April 1920 a disillusioned man.[46] He at least did not believe that he had changed the course of British foreign policy.

In the highly charged context of the time, simply to brand Namier as a polonophobe would be to misread his complex, conflicted, and frequently contradictory feelings toward the land of his birth. What is interesting about Namier's writings on Poland is what they reveal about Namier the historian, whose reputation rests primarily on his work in British history. In Linda Colley's view: "The sheer ambition of Namier's approach to European history seems far removed from his scrupulously detailed and archivally based British history, yet in fact there were close intellectual links between these two aspects of his work."[47] This is undoubtedly true at one level, but the argument can only be accepted with reservations. Part of the difference was purely technical. The impact of Namier's great books on British history, *The Structure of Politics at the Accession of George III* (1929) and *England in the Age of the American Revolution* (1930) rested on his prodigious archival research, and the revolutionary approach in which he ignored the pamphlets, speeches, and writings of the great figures of British politics to focus on the ordinary members of the House of Commons, information on whom he zealously uncovered in what he called his paper chases around provincial archives. The copious material he unearthed enabled him to challenge accounts that took seriously the ideas that politicians claimed animated their policies and behavior. He was notoriously suspicious of ideas—which he famously termed "cant" or "flapdoodle"—concentrating instead on the hidden material interests that, so he claimed, ultimately determined political behavior.

He deployed his battery of material facts to demolish the comfortable narratives that had traditionally explained British politics under George III. He was unable to adopt the same approach, however, when he wrote on Polish or European history. The archives of central and eastern Europe were difficult to access, which meant that although Namier was formidably well read, and used an impressive range of printed primary sources in his study of the 1848 revolutions, his writings on European history were not based on Namierite methodology.

This difference posed a problem for Namier. For he believed that "the first and greatest task of a historian is to understand the terms in which men of different age thought and spoke, and the angle from which they viewed life and society."[48] His massive accumulation of archival material enabled him to fulfill this aim in his writings on British history, but in his writings on European history in general, and on Polish history in particular, he showed little inclination to attempt the empathetic approach to the past that he advocates here.

Namier's writings on Europe had a different purpose and a different motivation. His observation that historians imagine the past in terms of their own experience seems particularly apt when considering his approach to Polish history. As Colley observes, his understanding of modern European history was deeply personal and almost Manichaean, while Cairns suggests that "[a] passion and a personal involvement haunts the European writings which is almost entirely missing from the English works."[49]

Underlying this passion lay Namier's conflicted attitude toward his native land. He knew a great deal about Polish history. Although he never studied the subject formally, the private tutors engaged by his father included the socialist Edmund Wieliński (1878–1940), later deputy mayor of Łódź, who was murdered by the Soviets in 1940, and Stanisław Kot (1885–1975), of whom Namier wrote in 1945 as "one of my closest friends."[50] The left-liberal Kot was a distinguished historian of sixteenth-century Poland who rose from his humble birth on a peasant smallholding to become a minister in Władysław Sikorski's government-in-exile during the Second World War.

Namier's early political views were shaped by men such as these, and reflected his upbringing. His Jewish grandparents were fervent Polish patriots. Both his grandfathers fought in the 1863 rising against the Russians. His father, Józef Bernstein vel Niemirowski (1858–1922), was married in a traditional Jewish ceremony, but subsequently, along with Namier's mother Anna, née Sommerstein (1868–ca. 1942), converted to Roman Catholicism. Józef was a Polish patriot in the liberal, Romantic tradition, an erudite man who owned a considerable library, which Kot admired.[51] Namier initially followed this tradition, forming friendships with Marian Kukiel (1885–1973), a soldier, a close ally of Piłsudski, and later a distinguished historian, and August Zaleski (1883–1872), another man of the left who became president of the government-in-exile, whom Namier met at the London School of Economics.

Despite these contacts on the Piłsudski-ite left, after his move to England Namier refused to have anything to do with the grand myths of Polish history that inspired his father and grandfathers in the tradition of Adam Mickiewicz and the Romantics, who saw Poland as the "Christ of the Nations," martyred for the freedom of all. This rejection had much to do with Namier's highly conflicted relationship with his father. Namier hints as much. He was profoundly influenced by Freudianism, and in a revealing essay on human nature in politics he praised the work of Graham Wallas, who in 1908 emphasized the importance of the unconscious mind, adding:

> Since then we have learnt about fixations in both individuals and groups, about psychological displacements and projections, and the externalization of unresolved inner conflicts. A man's relation, for instance, to his father or to his nurse may determine the pattern of his later political conduct or of his intellectual preoccupations without his being in the least conscious of the connexion; and self-deception concerning the origin and character of his seemingly intellectual tenets enables him to deceive others: the intensity of his hidden passion sharpens his mental faculties and may even create the appearances of cold, clear-sighted objectivity.[52]

Namier, who had a close relationship with his nurse Ella, a Moravian German, was clearly writing about himself. All who knew him recall his ability to speak with a passion that was far from hidden despite his nurturing of a persona dedicated to cold, clear-sighted objectivity, and that passion infuses his trenchant briefing papers for the Foreign Office.

Namier had a tempestuous relationship with his father. Here, the historian must be careful. Much of what is known about Namier's relationship with his family derives from what Namier told his biographer, his second wife Julia, late in his life. Some of what he said about Józef is confirmed by testimony from members of the family, who testify to Józef's compulsive gambling and complain that he was a bore, but the negative picture of Józef that stalks the biography's pages cannot be accepted at face value.[53] Józef, it seems was rather too like his son, and Namier himself always recognized the force of his father's intellect. The argumentative Józef relished formal disputations around the family dinner table, where he was perfectly able to match his formidable son.[54]

Whatever the dynamic behind the relationship, Namier rejected much of what his father stood for. Józef had abandoned his Jewish roots and sought to integrate into Polish noble society; his son embraced his Jewish heritage—or at least the secular, Zionist version of Jewishness—after his move to England. Namier's negative view of the Commonwealth's multicultural legacy undoubtedly owed much to his conflict with Józef and a reaction against his parents' attempts to integrate into a community in which their Jewish origins meant that many refused to accept them as true Poles. Banned from speaking Ukrainian, seen as nothing more than a peasant dialect by his parents, Namier developed an affinity with the Ruthenian peasants who worked the family estate, and an animus against the conservative Polish gentry who dominated the Eastern Galician countryside, and to whom political control over the whole province was handed by the Habsburg government in 1868.

Yet Namier's rejection of the class into which he was born ran counter to much that he stood for as a historian and much of what he desired as an individual. One of the most devastating moments in Namier's personal life occurred on the death of his father in 1922, when he discovered that he had been disinherited and that his dream of returning to the family estate of Koszyłowce as owner would not come to pass. That Józef should disinherit him is, perhaps, understandable: Namier had quarreled frequently with his father over the running of the estate; he had abandoned his country and taken up the citizenship of a foreign land; while his public attacks on the Galician gentry had caused his family much pain: even after the family estate was looted and his father beaten by Ukrainian nationalists during the Polish–Ukrainian War, Namier published articles suggesting that such attacks were precisely what one might expect as a consequence of the harsh rule of the Polish gentry.

In contrast, when writing on British history, Namier showed a deep attachment to the landed classes. He was a worshipper of the British Empire, despite a deep-seated aversion to nations that sought to dominate other nations. In a revealing essay on nationalism and liberty, which analyzed French and German nationalism, he wrote: "Thus every nation was exalted above the rest: compensatory dreams of grandeur dreamt by suffering or afflicted nations and uprooted individuals—immature, comparable to the day-dreams of adolescents. Nations unified, regenerated, or resurrected have since proved to be in no way better than other nations—and what remains after the idealistic gilt of nationalism has worn off is the claim to superiority, hence to dominion."[55] Thus, Namier criticized the Hungarians as well as the Poles for imposing dominion over what they regarded as lesser nations, observing that the Magyars were consistently opposed to any federal solution for the Habsburg monarchy that conceded territorial or linguistic rights for Romanians and other "subject" peoples, and criticizing the raising of the Galician Poles to the same status in 1868.[56]

Namier's championing of subject peoples had distinct limits, however. Although he came to reject Piłsudski-ite federalism, he only partially adhered to Wilsonian self-determination, as can be seen from his attitude toward the Ukrainian question. His excoriation of Polish landowners in Eastern Galicia for their treatment of their Ruthenian peasants has understandably won Namier the admiration of historians of Ukraine. Hunczak applauds his sense of "fairness and intellectual integrity," claims that he was "naturally a dedicated supporter of suppressed peoples," and praises him for his rejection of linguistic nationalism, and his recognition that "the relations of groups of men to plots of land, of organized communities to units of territory, form the basic content of political history."[57] Yet when one looks beyond Namier's emotional bond with the Ruthenian peasantry, it emerges that he was no supporter of Ukrainian nationalism. In a 1941 review in the *Times Literary Supplement* of W. E. D Allen's *The Ukraine: A History* (1940), Namier observed that one could read the book carefully without discovering "whether the author considers the 'Ukrainians' to be a separate people or a branch of the Russian nation. That he should not have reached any definite conclusion on this point is evidence of knowledge and of prudence." He sympathized with Allen for having to fend against "certain strained 'interpretations' by modern Ukrainian historians which can only be considered as strongly biased and founded on misunderstanding and as making no contribution to historical truth."[58]

Andrzej Zięba doubts that Namier, despite his regard for Ruthenian peasants, had any interest in Ukrainian culture.[59] Namier's dismissal of Ukrainian nationalism was part of a broader and principled rejection of nationalism as a political ideology. That rejection owed much to personal experience. During his brief period at Lwów University in 1906 there was considerable tension between the National Democrats and Ukrainian nationalists. A third of the students in Lwów were Ukrainians—down from 46 percent before 1868, when the Austrians had handed the university over to Polish control, and its language of instruction became Polish instead of German. During Namier's studies there, the great Ukrainian historian Mykhailo Hrushevsky, who had a chair in Lwów, was writing his multivolume *History of Ukraine-*

Rus', waging a controversial campaign to be allowed to speak Ukrainian at faculty meetings, and supporting Ukrainian students in their clashes with National Democrats.[60]

Namier, uncharacteristically, said nothing to Julia about his experiences in Lwów. It is clear that he fell foul of radical National Democrats, an experience that did much to establish his views on the destructive effects of nationalism. Nevertheless, there is no sign that he had any sympathy with Ukrainian opponents of the National Democrats, or for Hrushevsky and his mission to provide the Ukrainians with a history of their own. Indeed, Namier probably had Hrushevsky in mind when he talked of "strained interpretations" by modern Ukrainian historians. Hrushevsky was in many respects the epitome of the intellectual nationalists that Namier loathed. Kajetan Czarkowski-Golejewski, a Polish Ukrainophile who met Namier in London after 1945, likened his views on the matter to those of the National Democrats: "As for the existence of the Ukrainian nation, [Namier] shares the opinion of our domestic hurrah-nationalists; he simply denied this fact, feeling that these lands ought to belong to Russia."[61] His father would not have agreed on the last point, but Namier's view of the Ukrainian claim to nationhood was closer to that of the Galician gentry than he might have cared to admit.

Nevertheless, his motives for this position should not be equated with those of Dmowski's hurrah-nationalists. For Namier, nationalism was a mystification peddled by posturing intellectuals, whom he saw as the agents of what he termed the "super-national" 1848 revolutions.[62] This position helps explain his attraction to Pan-Slavism, a doctrine that sought to transcend the differences between the Slavic nations under Russian leadership, and his belief that Ukrainians should accept Russian rule. Namier idealized Russia and Russian culture—Dostoevsky was his favorite novelist—and he consistently supported Russian rule over Ukraine and Belarus. Russia was an imperial power, and its nationalism was imperial: Namier, like Russian nationalists then and now, saw Ukrainians and Belarusians as "brother nations" of the Great Russians, which perhaps explains why someone who had been born in the Russian Empire but never experienced the realities of Russian rule seems to have accepted Russia's self-appointed status as a dominant master-nation that he denied to Germans and Poles.

He was similarly indulgent to Britain's imperial ruling class. In a 1915 article written for *Political Quarterly*, and expanded into a short book under the title *Germany and Eastern Europe*, he wrote that "the future for empires, and for the white race, lay outside Europe, with Britain, Russia and the United States. Their mutual relations, their internal development, and their relations to the coloured races will in all probability form the chief contents of the history of the twentieth century."[63] Thus, Namier only had a problem with Poles and Germans when they claimed to have civilizing missions. Being Namier, he had a robust intellectual defense for his position: it was the overt linguistic nationalism of the Germans that he abhorred, while the Poles were charged with oppressing their subject peoples. Nevertheless, his Balliol friends must have sapped Namier's critical faculties considerably for him to claim that "the British did not, in any way, interfere with the cultural development of their subjects."[64]

Such indulgence was not afforded to the Poles. Once again, the contradictory nature of Namier's attitude to Polish history emerges. He identified a change in the Polish concept of nationality during the early modern period, arguing that in the late Middle Ages the Poles had developed "an early form of conscious linguistic nationality," which they had changed as a result of their expansion to the east: "Poland and Lithuania, constitutionally united, became a gentry republic . . . based not on a common language or religion, but on caste: the gentry-nation spoke Polish, White and Little Russian, and Lithuanian; in some western and northern districts also German and Swedish; and it comprised even Moslem Tartars, Armenians, and baptized Jews. Citizenship depended on being of the gentry, or being received into it."[65] This is one of the few passages in which Namier directly addresses the multicultural reality of the old Commonwealth, which was not in practice as all-embracing as he suggests here: Polish was overwhelmingly the lingua franca across the Commonwealth by the seventeenth century, while Muslim Tatars never formed part of the noble nation,[66] although under the Lithuanian statutes if they converted to Catholicism, they could automatically claim noble status, as could baptized Jews.

Despite his abhorrence of linguistic nationalism, Namier did not praise this alternative model, partly because of the Counter-Reformation, which ensured that over time "the overwhelming majority of the gentry nation joined Rome" and became polonized. By detaching themselves from the peasants, the non-Polish nobility of the eastern lands created barriers to "modern development," and the old Commonwealth "might consequently have survived" had it not taken this turn. For this detachment from the peasantry, Namier argued, meant that in the nineteenth century, when this "single-class" community aspired to recover the territorial inheritance of the old Commonwealth, it was "driven into hopeless contradictions and maneu-vers." Although the Polish "gentry-nation" had, within its historic frontiers, "a fuller and freer political life than most Continental nations, and therefore a stronger civic consciousness and patriotism," its attempt to reestablish its free and independent community was doomed to failure, because it had become a social anachronism "and could not be rebuilt on modern foundations."[67]

In this passage, Namier paradoxically comes close to Dmowski's views in implying that the path to modernity was only open to the linguistic nation-alists whom he detested. Its implicit rejection of the Jagiellonian idea must be taken as his final verdict on the old Commonwealth and its multicultural legacy. Apart from his treatment of the 1848 revolutions, most of his writings on Poland took the form either of journalism or briefing papers. In these, he was often focused not on the past, but the future: he was using his histori-cal knowledge selectively to advance the personal causes he endorsed, in a struggle not just against the ethnic nationalism of the National Democrats, but against the liberal nationalism of his father and the class into which he had been born.

Namier's rejection of both forms of Polish nationalism was deeply per-sonal, which is why it is shot through with paradoxes and contradictions. These contradictions suggest what he means by his curious phrase about "remembering the future." Namier remained a Polish patriot, but he could see with great clarity where the policies of the Polish parties at the end of the First World War might lead. He warned, frequently and presciently, of the dangers of including substantial national minorities within the borders of the Polish state. Quite what kind of Poland he envisaged is unclear, and it is possible that, before 1917, he shared the view of his archenemy Dmowski that an autonomous Poland under Russian sovereignty might be the most desirable outcome. Once the Bolshevik Revolution ruled out this possibility, however, it was the future that worried Namier, and he devoted much of his energy in the 1930s to warning of the dangers of Hitler and Nazism, giving full rein to his deep-seated anti-German prejudices. A determined enemy of appeasement, he remembered this future with particular clarity.

The Burden of History

Despite the serried ranks of historians at the Paris Peace Conference, their erudition had little influence on the peace treaties. History was appealed to by nation after aspirant nation, but history played a relatively minor role

when it came to settling actual borders. This is particularly clear with regard to Poland. For in no other case was the problem of discontinuity so
great. The multicultural, ethnically diverse polity that disappeared in 1795
displayed many of the virtues that appealed to liberal nationalists—toleration, a consensual parliamentary system, a civic nation, and a fierce attachment to liberty—but the idea of the nation had changed fundamentally in
its years off the map.

This discontinuity was the fundamental flaw that undermined hopes that
the Jagiellonian idea might provide a template for the future of east-central
Europe. A federation of autonomous nations had in theory the potential to
avoid the problems of national minorities that plagued the interwar Polish
state, and to accommodate the dual—or multiple—identities so common
across the old Commonwealth. A federation was easier to conceive than to
realize, however, not least because, as Namier understood, while memory of
the old Commonwealth remained bright in the nineteenth century, and was
burnished by artists like Jan Matejko (1838–1893) or novelists like Henryk
Sienkiewicz (1846–1916), that world had vanished. Thus, Halecki's Jagiellonian idea, with its idealization of the supposed civilizing mission of the Poles,
had no appeal to the largely peasant populations of the eastern lands. Their
former elites had abandoned them; their new intellectual elites were busy
constructing national literary languages and writing national histories that
defined Polishness as the enemy. Many of these intellectuals, such as the
Ukrainian nationalists Volodymyr Antonovych (1834–1908) and Ivan Franko
(1856–1916) were themselves from polonized gentry families, who chose their
Ukrainian rather than their Polish identities.[68]

In the last analysis, Halecki and Namier were more similar in their out-
looks than their very different attitudes to the history of Poland might suggest. Both abhorred the strident nationalism of Dmowski and his National
Democrats, and both believed in the civilizing missions of what they took to
be higher cultures; the main difference was that Halecki saw Poland's civilizing mission as a positive historical force, whereas Namier emphasized its negative consequences for the non-Polish peoples of the Commonwealth, both
before and after 1795. Namier's rejection of the political culture in which he
was raised owed much to personal experience of the way in which Ukrainians
and Jews were treated by the conservative Polish nobles among whom he was
raised, with whom his parents and grandparents identified, but by whom his
family was never truly accepted. Yet he was happy to endorse the civilizing
mission of the British Empire and of Russia, whether in its Pan-Slavic or—up

to a point—its Soviet incarnations, and dismiss Ukrainian claims to be one of Hegel's historic nations.

The contrasting attitudes of these two historians raise important questions about the legacy of the multicultural Commonwealth. The political union forged between 1385 and 1569, proved eminently adaptable, and capable of attracting support from Poles, Lithuanians, Ruthenians, and Prussians, not least through institutionalizing local self-government and accommodating religious difference. Yet the very success of this concept of union fostered cultural and linguistic homogenization, which detached the elite from those excluded from the civic community of noble citizens. The erosion of the elite's religious diversity saw Protestant, Orthodox, and Uniate nobles marginalized by the triumph of intolerant Counter-Reformation Catholicism. The consequences were all too evident by 1918: they rendered any prospect of the Commonwealth rising like a phoenix from the ashes of the Great War an impossible dream.

Halecki and Namier both grew up in the liberal Polish tradition, but followed very different paths as historians. Halecki remained an idealist, convinced that despite everything, the vision of civic society developed in the multicultural Commonwealth was still relevant. Namier rejected the Romantic tradition that idealized it, but there was something of the Romantic idealist in his veneration of the British political system, despite his hardheaded views concerning the material and careerist motives of eighteenth-century members of Parliament. Although he fought Dmowski every inch of the way between 1915 and 1920, his embracing of the Zionist cause demonstrates that he accepted the basic premise of Dmowski's modernist version of nationalism. He supported the idea of a national homeland for Jews and was by no means opposed to the establishment of an independent Poland, but he believed that it had to be, in Wilson's terms, on lands that were indisputably Polish. He offered no solution, however, to the problem of the mixed populations of the former Commonwealth's eastern territories, beyond denying the Polish majority populations of Wilno and Lwów inclusion in the new Polish republic and abandoning Ukrainians to Russian rule. At least Halecki had a vision that took account of this problem, although his idealized Jagiellonian idea is perhaps an example of what Namier meant when he talked of historians citing supposed analogies from the past to imagine that past and remember the future. The burden of history was too great, however: it was a future impossible to realize in an east-central Europe traumatized by war.

9

Whose Grand Duchy?

Contesting the Multicultural Past in Lithuania and Belarus

Rūstis Kamuntavičius

On August 23, 2020, two weeks after the contested Belarusian presidential elections that resulted in a long-term wave of protests and
unprecedented political turmoil in the country, two former Lithuanian
presidents were among over fifty thousand people who formed a human
chain from Vilnius to the Belarusian-Lithuanian border.[1] The occasion was
the thirty-first anniversary of the Baltic Way demonstration of 1989, an iconic
show of transnational popular protest against Soviet rule, and the Lithuanian
commemorative initiative in 2020 was thus intended as a sign of solidarity
with the Belarusian pro-democracy movement. Yet in the three decades since
the collapse of the USSR, Lithuanian and Belarusian civil societies have perhaps been at odds with each other more than they have been in congenial
agreement. One of the main points of contention has been over which nation
can "rightfully" lay claim to the legacy of the Grand Duchy of Lithuania—a
dispute that, mostly, has been constituted as a zero-sum game.

Whereas both societies seemingly had similar goals in the wake of the
collapse of state socialism—to reconstruct sovereign national identities and
consolidate national memories—the politics of memory in Lithuania and
Belarus have in recent decades been cardinal contrasts. In the Lithuanian
case, national and state narratives have been closely aligned.[2] Although since

approximately the turn of the twenty-first century, there have been pioneering historical treatments of non-ethnic-Lithuanian themes—especially
Polish and Jewish ones—by prominent public intellectuals, the dominant
vision has remained very ethnocentric.[3] The Belarusian case, meanwhile, has
been less consolidated. After a brief period of pluralism until 1994—when
Alexander Lukashenko won the country's first, and to date only free and
fair presidential elections—a neo-Soviet interpretation of the past gained
the backing of the state. It argued that the Belarusian state was a creation of
the October Revolution, and preached historical brotherhood with Russia.[4]
In parallel, a national narrative has also flourished, mostly as the preserve of
the political opposition, although more recently (since approximately 2005)
the state has also mobilized the symbolic capital of this narrative.[5]

The dominance of "national narratives" in place of more "objective" history is especially prominent in the historiography of "smaller" nations whose
very existence has been threatened, as Anthony F. Upton observes.[6] In such
cases, a desire to write history from an impartial perspective with a critical
attitude toward the dominant narrative can often turn scholars into traitors
in the eyes of their own compatriots. Thus, while source-based academic
studies remain normal practice in Belarus and Lithuania, researchers—
whether consciously or unconsciously—often select topics for research and
draw conclusions in line with their respective dominant national narratives.

The memory of multiculturalism illustrates the paradox of the similarities
and differences between the two countries' dominant narratives. In both
Lithuania and Belarus, notwithstanding some specific exceptions,[7] these
narratives have often made symbolic claims to the historical diversity and
"tolerance" of the Grand Duchy of Lithuania (thirteenth century–1795),
depicting it as a country of many nations, religions, and languages. In Lithuania, especially in recent decades, the coexistence of different peoples has
been presented as one of the greatest achievements of "historical Lithuania."
The moment when Gediminas (*Bel.* Hiedzimin, *Pol.* Giedymin; grand duke,
1316–1341) invited western Europeans, mostly artisans from northern Germany, to settle in Lithuania has been regarded as the starting point of the
country's unique diversity.[8] Characteristic is this passage about religious
and cultural tolerance in a history of Lithuania published on behalf of the
Ministry of Foreign Affairs: "The boundaries of tolerance later narrowed in
both Poland and Lithuania, but changes took place slowly and without com-
pulsion, and multiconfessionalism survived right until the twentieth century.
Western Europe's situation in the sixteenth century is characterized by the

St. Bartholomew's Day Massacre in Paris (1572), which became a symbol of religious intolerance in European history. Are all of the aforementioned not enough to conclude that Lithuania, in the mid-sixteenth century, was Europe's cradle of tolerance?"[9] A similar idea has been expressed in an interview by Belarus's former minister of foreign affairs, Uladzimir Makiej: "In Belarusian history, examples of religious or ethnic conflicts, or manifestations of force in relation to neighboring states, are rare. Tolerance, which implies respect for all peoples without exception, acceptance of other cultures and ways of development, and an orientation toward dialogue, are characteristic both of the Belarusian nation as a whole and of its individual representatives."[10] A comparison of the two statements reveals a paradoxical situation whereby both sides agree on the cosmopolitan past while disagreeing at the same time over which modern nation it should symbolically belong to. On the one hand, both claim the Grand Duchy as a multicultural state. On the other hand, they both claim that multicultural state to be "theirs," that is, Lithuanian or Belarusian, respectively. The modern national Lithuanian and Belarusian narratives are in conflict with one another over the fundamental cultural identity of the Grand Duchy. While placing their emphases on different aspects of its history, they mutually accuse each other of attempts to "appropriate the past."[11]

At its core, this conflict over memory centers on dates and places. Belarus and Lithuania cannot agree on whose Grand Duchy it was, in part because they both accent different historical moments, usually when "their" own ethnos dominated the other, while also espousing very different visions of who founded the state and where. On both sides, the rhetoric is often exclusionary and monologic: neither Belarusian nor Lithuanian historians have successfully offered up a vision of convivial coexistence with the other. This chapter examines the most important points of contention, showing that the disputes have spiraled in a positive feedback loop, with each strident disagreement making it less likely that consensus can be reached. A shared understanding of the multicultural history of the Grand Duchy of Lithuania has not yet been reached.

The Thirteenth Century: Who Founded the Grand Duchy?

The dominant contemporary Lithuanian narrative legitimizes the modern nation-state by appealing to the ethnicity of the founders of the Grand Duchy.[12] According to this vision, the Grand Duchy of Lithuania was created by Lithuanians in the thirteenth century as a state that had its core territory in Lithuanian-speaking lands. A starring role in this story is played by Mindaugas (*Bel.* Mindoŭh, *Pol.* Mendog; grand duke, 1236–1263), who established the Lithuanian state in the 1240s and 1250s. In the fourteenth century, this state expanded into ethnically Slavic lands (today's Belarus and Ukraine), but the rulers remained Baltic Lithuanians. The proclamation of the modern Lithuanian Republic on February 16, 1918, drew its legitimacy from this period: it harked back to the legacy of the Grand Duchy, but was limited to the majority Lithuanian-speaking territories that composed only a small area within the former state.

The newborn independent Lithuanian Republic, initially democratic and then from 1926 an autocratic nationalistic regime, invested huge efforts into consolidating the nation and especially its vision of the past. The most important text for this ideological drive was the book *Lietuvos istorija* (The History of Lithuania, 1936), edited by Adolfas Šapoka.[13] This volume was printed in huge editions, and also enjoyed a second life after 1988, when reprints were widely read by Lithuanians eager to know their "true" history after decades of Soviet mythmaking. Šapoka's volume endures as the most influential treatise in Lithuanian historiography.[14] Its impact on both academic historians and the general populace is immense, with its evocative appeal to "find Lithuanians in the history of Lithuania."[15] Curiously, however, the volume has never been translated into any other language, although it is generally accepted that one cannot understand modern Lithuanian interpretations of the past without reading it.

In contrast, the Belarusians did not succeed in creating their own national state in the interwar period, and so could not consolidate a national mnemonic narrative.[16] On the eve of the First World War and especially in the 1920s,[17] when Belarusian historiography was more or less free (before Stalinist terror and Sovietization), nationalist historians did write works that argued for an understanding of the Grand Duchy as the cradle of a Belarusian state. These scholars, however, were never promoted by the Soviet authorities; instead, a Soviet Russocentric concept of history was imposed. According to this official narrative, the Grand Duchy was an oppressive, "foreign" state, in which Lithuanian and Polish noblemen had exploited poor Belarusian peasants. The latter were freed by benevolent Russian rule and emancipated in the nineteenth century during the reforms of Tsar Alexander II. A "genuine" Belarusian state appeared only after the October Revolution: the Belarusian Soviet Socialist Republic.[18] This narrative did not clash with the Lithuanian one, a fact that helped Lithuanians to nationalize and appropriate the legacy of the Grand Duchy.

This situation began to change in the 1980s, when the consolidated Lithuanian-Soviet interpretation was confronted with a reviving Belarusian national imagination. After the collapse of the Soviet Union in 1991, Belarus initially changed its state symbols to those directly related to the Grand Duchy of Lithuania (the white-red-white tricolor and the "Pahonia" coat of arms), while also beginning to revive the Belarusian language and to rewrite its history manuals. Some of the early nationalist histories from the first half of the twentieth century were also reprinted, though these did not have quite the same all-pervading impact as Šapoka's book in Lithuania.[19]

These developments in Belarus prompted a harsh reaction from the side of the Lithuanians, who were shocked by their neighbors' attempts to "steal our history." At the same time, attempts were made to ease the conflict— for example, through bilateral commissions that were created to stimulate dialogue and to seek agreement on common interpretations of the past. At one such meeting in 1992, it was agreed that both sides would call the Grand Duchy of Lithuania a "Lithuanian-Belarusian" or "Belarusian-Lithuanian" state.[20] Also, both countries pledged to refrain from depicting rulers of the Grand Duchy of Lithuania on their national currencies.[21]

From the mid-1990s, the Lukashenko regime's revisionist politics reenthroned the old pro-Soviet narrative, as a result of which the official Belarusian interpretation of the past again diverged from that of Lithuania. Since approximately 2005, however, official Belarusian memory has also instrumentalized the legacy of the Grand Duchy for its own legitimation.[22] The most likely reasons for this turn were geopolitical. Increasing political and economic pressure from Russia sparked serious fears of the loss of Belarusian sovereignty; thus, in order to resist those tendencies, at least ideologically, the regime began to acknowledge the importance of the Grand Duchy in the history of Belarus. This trend was also triggered by the European Union's "Eastern Partnership" program, and designed to improve the relationship between Minsk and Brussels. New history teaching guidelines were written, monuments were erected, such as the statue of the early modern humanist Francysk Skaryna (ca. 1490–ca. 1551) in front of the National Library in Minsk, and the official past of the country was modified in a national mode in an attempt to make Russia more distant, and Lithuania (as well as the rest of Europe) closer. In this way, the previously marginalized Belarusian national narrative started to entrench itself at the institutional level, and was adopted by both the regime and the opposition. This policy of "soft Belarusization" was abruptly abandoned in the aftermath of the 2020 protests in Belarus, when the regime's brutal crackdown led to renewed tensions between Belarus and the EU, while Lukashenko became increasingly reliant on Russia for political and financial support.[23] This shift has been further entrenched by Lukashenko's support of Russia's 2022 invasion of Ukraine and the use of Belarusian territory by Russian forces.

Like the Lithuanian vision of the past, the Belarusian national narrative has paid special attention to the origins of the Grand Duchy. The modern Belarusian national narrative states that the Grand Duchy was created through the joint venture of Baltic (i.e., Lithuanian) and Slavic (i.e., Belarusian) peoples, an idea that follows an earlier tradition.[24] On the other hand, more recent interpretations have moved on from earlier attempts to completely eliminate Lithuanians from this history, which were made in the nineteenth century by the West-Rus'ism tradition and also, on the opposite side of the spectrum, by late Soviet nationalist historians, such as Mikola Jermalovič.[25] This notion of a "Baltic-Slavic alliance" serves to distance Belarus from Russia and endow the Belarusian nation with a historical specificity.

Thus, according to this narrative, Mindaugas, a Lithuanian, was the first ruler, just as in the Lithuanian version. However, for the Belarusian master narrative, the history of the Grand Duchy begins at the point when Mindaugas united his Baltic lands (the southeastern part of modern Lithuania) with the now-Belarusian lands to their south, either in 1248 or approximately 1250.[26] In this way, the core of the newborn state was not entirely Lithuanian, but shared between the Baltic and Slavic peoples and located somewhere on the border between the modern Lithuanian and Belarusian republics. By contrast, the Lithuanian version prefers to start the Grand Duchy in 1236 or the early 1240s.[27] This was the time when Mindaugas consolidated the ethnic Lithuanian lands, including the eastern part of Samogitia, whereas expansion to the Belarusian side happened later. Thus, the Belarusian and Lithuanian versions do not directly contradict each other, but place different accents on when the Grand Duchy was founded.

In addition, the Belarusian narrative has placed particular emphasis on the cultural role of the Slavic population of the early Grand Duchy. According to these interpretations, Belarusians were much more culturally "advanced" and "civilized" than the "barbaric" Lithuanians. This thinking is influenced by fact that the area's Slavs were Christianized in the tenth century and, on the eve of Grand Duchy's foundation, already had cities, monasteries, writing, and their own states with established histories (especially important are the Rus'ian principalities of Polatsk and Turaŭ). Lithuanians, in contrast, remained pagan until the end of the fourteenth century, although this did not prevent them from making important contributions to the polity: according to popular interpretations, they brought vitality and military energy. In short, Belarusians did culture, Lithuanians did war: the Belarusians taught Lithuanians to write (in Belarusian, of course), and to organize the state, whereas the Lithuanians defended the cities and preserved culture against foreign invasions.[28] The Lithuanian side, meanwhile, does not even mention or try to refute this interpretation (presumably because they treat it as nonsense); it is simply absent from Lithuanian historiography.

To complete the picture, the Belarusian narrative posits that the two nations had good, cooperative relations and were not prone to conflict. Mindaugas, a Lithuanian, did not conquer the Belarusian lands, but was invited by the people of Navahrudak to defend them from external enemies. There he found faithful and intelligent allies who helped him and his son Vaišvilkas (alternatively Vaišelga; *Bel.* Vojšalk, *Pol.* Wojsiełk; grand duke 1264–1267) to continue the unification and consolidation of the Grand Duchy. Such a picture is in direct contradiction to the modern Lithuanian interpretation, which treats the ancient Lithuanians as fierce warriors who subjugated their neighbors and were ubiquitously feared.[29] It also raises the issue of where the geographical or notional center of the early Grand Duchy was. If Mindaugas accepted an invitation to rule over the Slavic territories, then the location of the Grand Duchy moves into what is now Belarus by mutual consent. If he conquered those lands, then "ethnic" Lithuania can be seen as the core of the Grand Duchy and the "Belarusian" part as a periphery.

Between Navahrudak and Kernavė: Where Was the First Grand Duke Crowned?

A cornerstone of the Belarusian-Lithuanian confrontation is Mindaugas's coronation. As the first ruler of Lithuania, recognized as such since the interwar period, Mindaugas holds a key position in Lithuanian history. He was also the first and the only king of Lithuania, with all the other rulers of the country who followed him being "only" grand dukes.[30] The problem is that no reliable sources indicate unequivocally where and when the coronation took place. In the public consciousness and historiographic master narratives of the two countries, however, a curious paradox can be observed:

Lithuanians know when Mindaugas was crowned but do not know where, whereas Belarusians know where this happened but cannot pinpoint a date.[31]

There are archival sources from the Middle Ages that indicate 1253 as a likely year of coronation. Unfortunately, neither a month nor a day are recorded. Nevertheless, this gap appears not to pose a problem for Lithuanian memory. In the months following the declaration of Lithuanian independence from the USSR in 1990, the Seimas (Parliament) intensively discussed the question of when Lithuanian statehood was first established and decided to officially commemorate Mindaugas's coronation to represent the historical continuity of Lithuanian statehood. Lithuanian historians were consulted in search of an exact date to mark in the calendar. A professor at Vilnius University, Edvardas Gudavičius, suggested July 6.[32] The Seimas quickly voted to confirm the date and, in spite of obvious errors in the historian's deductions,[33] Lithuania has celebrated that date every year since 1991 as Statehood Day (Valstybės diena).

Belarusian historians, on the other hand, have been less interested in the exact date on which the coronation took place. Instead, they have tended to focus on the place, believing that Mindaugas was crowned in Navahrudak, today a small town in western Belarus.[34] Again, there are no direct sources to prove this assumption. Since approximately the sixteenth century, some interpretations have suggested that Mindaugas was crowned and, later, buried at Navahrudak Castle.[35] Accordingly, this symbolic place has been endowed with all the elements necessary to prove the strong Belarusian fundaments of the history of the Grand Duchy: Navahrudak is held to be the place of coronation, the first capital, and, finally, the place of the first ruler's burial.

Lithuanian historians, however, reject this thesis.[36] One argument focuses on the lack of direct evidence for it, based on historical sources. In addition, there is a strong conviction in Lithuanian historiography that the Lithuanian ruler could neither have had himself crowned nor established a capital in a town outside his patrimonial lands. This belief is strengthened by the circumstance that Navahrudak was ceded to rival Galicia-Volhynia soon after the coronation.[37] The Lithuanian narrative also refuses to treat Navahrudak as Mindaugas's burial place. Since 2015, an alternative site has been advanced, based on indirect evidence: Aglona (Lit. Agluona), a village in eastern Latvia, a region much closer to the Baltic core of modern Lithuania.[38] In short, Navahrudak has been entirely erased from the Lithuanian historical imagination.

Meanwhile, Lithuanians have found their own solutions concerning the first capitals of the Grand Duchy. The Navahrudak hypothesis was rejected as early as the interwar period in favor of Kernavė and Trakai. These local-ities are in the modern Lithuanian Republic, not far away from Vilnius, in ethnographically Lithuanian lands that belonged to the nucleus of Mindau-gas's realm. According to the chronicles, the main castle of Grand Duke Traidenis (*Bel.* Trajdzień, *Pol.* Trojden; 1269/1270–1282) was at Kernavė.[39] This fact is traditionally treated as evidence that it was the first known capital of the Lithuanian state. Later, according to the Lithuanian master narrative, the center of political gravity moved to Trakai. Grand Duke Gediminas is said to have transferred his capital from Trakai to Vilnius in 1323, suggesting that the former was the capital in the meantime. This notion is supported by Lithuanian chronicles written in the fifteenth and sixteenth centuries. The Kernavė–Trakai–Vilnius scheme is explained in every Lithuanian school textbook since Soviet times, but its roots lie in the interwar Lithuanian imagination.[40]

The Fourteenth to the Sixteenth Centuries: How Did the Grand Duchy Evolve?

It has been not an easy task for twentieth-century Lithuanian historiogra-phy, addicted to the cult of language, to prove the Baltic Lithuanian iden-tity of the Grand Duchy. Between the fourteenth and sixteenth centuries, only a negligible minority of the country's political and cultural elites spoke Lithuanian. This historical fact is glaringly obvious and undeniable. Still, Lithuanian historians have found a way around this problem. In the interwar period, the Lithuanian historical imagination constructed a story about energetic Lithuanian warriors who conquered (or acquired through marriage and shrewd politics) vast territories in the Slavic-dominated east (i.e., modern Belarus and Ukraine).[41] The conquerors were, however, unable to hold these lands due to the scarcity of their human resources, and also because, being pagans, they had little chance of assimilating locals who had already been Christians for over two centuries. Therefore, in order to gain native support, they decided not to intervene in the local cultures or social structures. All that was asked of the subjects was that they pay taxes and obey the Lithuanian rulers, who in turn learned to communicate with locals by adopting their language, customs, and, frequently, even religion. This narrative rendered the Grand Duchy a kind of Lithuanian empire, ten times bigger than today's Lithuania, and, moreover, multicultural. The Grand Duke Algirdas (*Bel.* Alhierd; *Pol.* Olgierd; 1345–1377) called himself an em-

peror (*basileus*) and his official title included numerous territories stretching from Samogitia to diverse principalities of Rus'.[42] Since all empires
are multicultural, it was the Lithuanian ethnicity of the ruling elites that
counted the most, not the language they spoke. After 1990, this narrative
was augmented with a comparison of Lithuania to the Frankish state, where
a small group of Germanic Franks conquered and assimilated "downward"
with the local Gauls.[43]

Meanwhile, the Belarusian interpretation of this period is more strongly
based on prosaic everyday history that, in turn, is extremely congenial to
the modern Belarusian vision. Above all, the language question supports
Belarusian claims to the Grand Duchy. The principal written language of
the court, Lithuanian law, and the Lithuanian chronicles was a Chancery
Slavic, written in the Cyrillic alphabet. This lasted until the end of the seventeenth century, when it was almost totally replaced by Polish. Belarusians
call this language Old Belarusian, but it has been given a variety of names
by philologists of different backgrounds, including "Ruthenian," "Chancery
Slavonic," and, simply, the "language of the Lithuanian Chancellery."[44] More
recently, Lithuanian historians and philologists have preferred to use "Ruthenian" (*rusėnų*) instead of Old Belarusian, apparently in order to minimize
the perceived Belarusian influence.[45] Whatever the name, it is impossible
to deny that the written language so widely used in the official life of the
country between the fourteenth and the sixteenth centuries originated from
the Belarusian part of the Grand Duchy and had nothing in common with the
Baltic Lithuanian language. This fact strengthens the claim that Belarusians,
who inhabited the larger part of the country's lands, exerted a decisive cultural and linguistic impact on the Lithuanian elites; that is, the conquerors
gradually lost their identities and, at least from the cultural point of view,
essentially "became Belarusian." Taken to its extreme, this logic is deployed
by a radical minority in support of an idea that Belarusians are in fact the
"true" Lithuanians (*Licviny* or *Litviny* in Belarusian, i.e., the inheritors of the
Grand Duchy, *Litva*), whereas modern Baltic Lithuanians (often referred to
somewhat pejoratively as *Žamojty*, "Samogitians" or *Lietuvisy*, people from
today's *Lietuva* as opposed to historical *Litva*), are descendants of the lower
unassimilated strata of society and, in fact, it was they who stole the name
that "rightfully" belonged to the Belarusians.[46]

The Belarusian national narrative unequivocally states that the period
between the fourteenth and the sixteenth centuries was the "golden age" of
Belarusian religious and cultural life. The culmination of this flourishing was

the first printing house and the first books published in Old Belarusian (from 1522 onward) in Vilnius, the city traditionally held to be the most important center of Belarusian culture (called Vilnia in Belarusian). Up to the moment when the Lithuanian-speaking population accepted the Catholic faith (in around 1400), Orthodox Belarusians are said to have experienced complete freedom and authority of their religion. Furthermore, as mentioned above, the Baltic Lithuanian elites often converted and assimilated. One of the most striking examples was the son of Mindaugas, Vaišvilkas, who became an Orthodox monk. Throughout the fifteenth century, a modus vivendi was found between Catholics and the Orthodox faithful that guaranteed freedom of confession and extensive rights for the Orthodox.

The sixteenth century was a turbulent time, with the Reformation disrupting the balance of power and unleashing a complex set of events in the Grand Duchy. In the middle of the century, many members of the Orthodox elite converted to Protestantism, and by the end of the century many nobles were converting to Catholicism. Those who remained Orthodox were touched by the Union of Brest (1596), which brought the Eastern rite eparchies under the authority of Rome, so that, over the next two centuries, almost all became Uniate Christians. However complicated these developments, the overall result was irrefutable: the Slavs of the Grand Duchy successfully integrated into the ruling elites of the country and did not concede to the Lithuanians in political, cultural, or economic terms. These "successes" can be illustrated by the fact that the greatest intellectual achievement of Lithuanian-Belarusian society, the Lithuanian Statutes (1529, 1566, and 1588), were composed—as Vice-Chancellor of the Grand Duchy Leŭ Sapieha (*Pol.* Lew Sapieha, *Lit.* Leonas Sapiega; 1557–1633) put it—"not in some foreign language, but in our own," that is, in so-called Old Belarusian, and not in Lithuanian, Polish, or Latin.[47]

The question of political dominance is also contested. From the Belarusian perspective, the ancestors of modern Belarusians inhabited the core territory of Lithuania, not a periphery that was annexed by the first Lithuanian rulers.[48] Historical studies of early modern society in the Grand Duchy have argued that the territory that is now Belarus played a central role in the polity between the fourteenth and sixteenth centuries.[49] Especially important nodes in these interpretations are the military victories over the Teutonic Knights at Grunwald (*Bel.* Hrunvaĺd; *Lit.* Žalgiris, *Ger.* Tannenberg; 1410)[50] and over Muscovy at Orša (*Pol.* Orsza; 1514). The Grand Duchy's greatest triumphs in the west and in the east, respectively, have served as symbols of the fight for freedom. The Battle of Orša arouses less conflict between the Lithuanian and Belarusian narratives because it is favorable for both national perspectives. Interpretations of the Battle of Grunwald, however, have differed greatly in terms of how much importance is given to the Belarusian and Lithuanian contributions.[51]

Historical maps and atlases provide another angle on the divergent Lithuanian and Belarusian collective memories.[52] Just after the First World War, the Lithuanian Republic and the Belarusian Soviet Socialist Republic both appeared. Such countries had never existed before. Each of them had their own territories, borders, capital, and other major cities. Both territories were administratively modified at the end of the 1940s, and their borders have remained unchanged to this day in their contemporary successor states. For various reasons—among them technocratic, political, and practical considerations—new identities were expected to fit into these newly established borders. When speaking about the history of Lithuania, only cities, towns, villages, and regions of the Lithuanian Republic could be discussed in history manuals as well as in the works of professional historians; the situation was the same in Belarus. The problem was that the territory of the Grand Duchy embraced both of these countries. Accordingly, the focus was on its Lithuanian-speaking part in Lithuanian historical books, and on its Belarusian part in Belarusian ones. Lithuanians studied the history of Kaunas, Šiauliai, Samogitia, and Aukštaitija, while Belarusians dug into the history of Polatsk, Viciebsk, Minsk, and Hrodna. Yet both historiographies referred to the same entity—the Grand Duchy of Lithuania. As a result, there appeared two different narrations of the same history, based on two different geographical focuses.

In the multicultural puzzle of the Grand Duchy, there were also numerous other peoples (Tatars, Jews, Italians, Germans, and many others) besides the Belarusians and Lithuanians, with the Poles being of particular cultural and political importance. From the time of Jogaila (Bel. Jahaila, Pol. Jagiełło; grand duke 1377–1381 and 1382–1392; king of Poland 1386–1434), Poland and Lithuania were brought into close contact through the dynastic union sealed in 1385. Yet both Lithuanian and Belarusian historiographies have been traditionally characterized by attempts to marginalize any Polish influence. The Union of Krėva (Bel. Kreva, Pol. Krewo) has been treated as a minor act or merely a set of promises, and even serious doubts about its authenticity have been raised.[53] In fact, modern Lithuanian historiography does not use the word "union" to denote any agreement between Poland and Lithuania, with the key exception of the Union of Lublin in 1569. The polonization and close political integration of the Lithuanian elites, especially in the sixteenth century, are generally regarded as national catastrophes for Lithuania, although dissenting voices from some intellectual spheres have been heard, including in recent times.[54] Similarly, historical atlases published in Lithuania in the twentieth century intentionally avoided detailed depictions of Poland, especially in relation to the Grand Duchy under Vytautas the Great (1392–1430).[55] The Belarusian national narrative has likewise tended toward the marginalization of Polish influence, especially before the Union of Lublin. The blossoming of Belarusian culture, book publishing, and civil society in the sixteenth century is understood to have been undermined by Polish influence in later centuries.[56] In these ways, both the Lithuanian and Belarusian interpretations of history have attempted to eliminate other claimants to the common past, in addition to one another.

Toward Dialogue?

The modern Belarusian and Lithuanian master narratives about the Grand Duchy of Lithuania are not value-free attempts to understand the past. Their primary thrust is ideological: both serve as tools of national indoctrination, manipulating the past to forge present-day identity. The sometimes irrational claims and paradoxical differences between the two visions result from their ideological nature.[57]

The Lithuanian national narrative is conservative and defensive in nature; its main task is the preservation of the identity that was shaped during the interwar period and reborn in the 1990s. This story envisages the Grand Duchy as a source of historical Lithuanian glory and a great inspiration for the small nation that exists today. Multiculturalism is referenced here only as a rhetorical device that demonstrates the gracious tolerance and humanism of the Lithuanian tradition, thus consolidating Lithuania's credentials as a European state that has always shared the contemporary values of the European Union and its older member states.[58] On the other hand, this archaic vision of the past contributes to a cultural inferiority complex, because it is at its core a sad story of the devastating and ultimately losing fight against aggressors from both east (Moscow) and west (Germany and Poland), which ended in the ruination of the glorious civilization of pagan Lithuania. It also results in negative and ignorant attitudes toward Lithuania's neighbors, Poland and Belarus in particular, which complicates the country's geopolitical situation and clashes with the positive image of Lithuania as part of a diverse and free Europe. The Lithuanian elites are aware of these shortcomings, but the substantial attempts in recent decades to modify this image of the past into a more open and dialogic construct have not, so far, been successful.

Compared to Lithuania, where there is a broad consensus on the identity and importance of the Grand Duchy, the past in Belarus has often been riven by major divisions between different political actors. More recently, however, a grand narrative based on ancient Baltic-Slavonic cooperation resulting in a "Lithuanian-Belarusian" state called the Grand Duchy of Lithuania is emerging as a common ground on which actors of different political bents can agree—both pro-regime ideologues and nationalist-minded opposition historians. According to this consolidated vision, the historical state was strongly dominated by the Belarusian language and culture in its early modern heyday. Nevertheless, whereas the modern Lithuanian narrative almost totally elides the historical presence of the ancestors of the Belarusians, the Belarusian story has been much more prepared to integrate Baltic Lithuanians into the historical process of state formation. In a way, therefore, it is the Belarusians whose narrative takes multiculturalism in the history of the Grand Duchy more seriously, acknowledging the mixed origins of the state and its culture.

There are two reasons for this difference. First, the Lithuanian historiographical tradition positing the decisive role of Lithuanians in the formation of the state is much older and better established, so it cannot be openly ignored. Second, the Belarusian narrative has had a geopolitical purpose, to redirect the strategic orientation of Belarus westward. Accordingly, it has been supported at different times by both the authoritarian regime and the opposition alike, though, in the aftermath of the 2020 presidential elections and Russia's 2022 invasion of Ukraine, the Lukashenko regime has decisively turned away from its "pro-western" course. Paradoxically, the main barrier to mutual understanding before these radical changes was the hostile attitude of the Lithuanians, who had expressed little readiness to compromise with Belarus on the issue of their shared history.

The Lithuanian and Belarusian narratives are not, as yet, in any kind of dialogue, except at the fringes where a small number of intellectuals and historians have been collaborating on how to resolve the conflicts between the conflicting memory cultures. There are very few translations into Lithuanian of Belarusian history books, and Lithuanian curricula have little space for the history of Belarus.[59] The overall picture is the same in Belarus, with the exception of the *ARCHE* project (a private, opposition-based intellectual journal and publishing house), which has translated into Belarusian a dozen or so important Lithuanian studies on the history of the Grand Duchy.[60] There are also no serious discussions (if any) about shared history manuals.[61] One reason for this reluctance is the language barrier. Though most Lithuanian historians read and understand Russian as well as Belarusian, most other Lithuanians, especially of the younger generation, do not know these languages. On the other side, fluency in Lithuanian among Belarusian counterparts is negligible: only a small number of historians in the country are even able to read Lithuanian texts. The metaphorical gap between the first capitals of the Grand Duchy—Kernavė and Navahrudak—remains unbridgeable, and there are no signs that it will be overcome in the near future.

At the core of this situation is a fundamental misunderstanding of the purpose of history and memory, according to which only one correct description of the past can exist. The belief in one truth, indoctrinated from the times of secondary school, distorts the past. As Jacques Le Goff has warned, "We must reject the establishmentarian cult of history."[62] A broader acceptance of at least these two contradictory narratives about the past of the Grand Duchy—Lithuanian and Belarusian—would contribute to the development of empathy, mutual understanding between the two sides, and better knowledge of the Grand Duchy itself. Unfortunately, such a prospect appears far off on both sides, because to begin to unsee the Grand Duchy in national terms would be to modify a very complex set of identities, geopolitical goals, and future expectations. Yet the multiculturalism of the shared past is undeniable, and the attempts of historians and figures of culture to bring it to light can only become more mainstream with time.

10

Polish-Belarusian Encounters and the Divided Legacy of the Commonwealth

Simon Lewis

In October 2017, in the Swiss town of Solothurn, a minor spat broke out involving Belarusian émigré intellectuals on one side, and the Polish embassy and media on the other. The fifteenth of the month marked the two-hundredth anniversary of the death of General Tadeusz Kościuszko (*Bel.* Tadevuš Kasciuška, 1746–1817) in Solothurn, where the celebrated military leader and statesman had spent his last years in exile. The Association of Belarusians in Switzerland had decided to erect a monument to mark the anniversary, with a plaque featuring the words "to a son of Belarus, from grateful compatriots" in Belarusian and German. Kościuszko was born in a manor in the Grand Duchy of Lithuania in what is now western Belarus (*Bel.* Maračoŭščyna, *Pol.* Mereczowszczyzna).[1] He fought for the independence of the Polish-Lithuanian Commonwealth in the insurrection that he led against Russian forces in 1794, on the eve of the third and final partition (1795).[2] Yet no Belarusian-sponsored monument to the leader existed anywhere, including in Belarus itself—in contrast to the many statues to be found in Poland and elsewhere.[3]

The Polish embassy in Bern, however, protested against the wording of the commemorative shield. Arguing that Kościuszko should be commemorated as a "universal hero for all humanity, not just a 'son of Belarus' or a 'Polish general,'" the Polish representation refused to participate in a joint ceremony with the Belarusian organization and lodged a complaint with the local authorities of Solothurn, who urged the Belarusians to alter the inscription.[4] They did so, albeit reluctantly, and the ceremony went ahead a week later than planned. While the final version of the plaque featured only Kościuszko's name and the dates of his birth and death, as well as the identity of the organization that had placed the monument, the controversial phrase was displayed on a banner during the event. The Lithuanian ambassador and the mayor of Solothurn were guests of honor, but no official Polish delegate attended.

This Swiss episode illustrates the extent to which the Polish-Lithuanian Commonwealth still lives on in contemporary memory, but with its legacy disputed. The memory of its multiculturalism, here embodied synecdochically in the person of Kościuszko, is subject to power gradients and symbolic struggle. The Commonwealth was a pre-national, multiethnic polity; it was multicultural (or "many-cultured") in a "thin" sociological sense of many coexisting ethnic and religious groups.[5] Kościuszko—as an icon of remembrance—was himself *retrospectively* multicultural in that he could never fit neatly into post-Enlightenment national narratives. Nevertheless, it is Polish memory that has most successfully claimed his heritage: Magdalena Micińska calls the myth of the *Naczelnik* ("Commander," as he is informally known in Polish) an "artificially initiated legend which became deep-rooted in the imagination and memory of the [Polish] masses."[6] The revisionist attempt by the Belarusian community to inscribe the Kościuszko canon into a Belarusian narrative was inevitably engaged in an uneven dialogue with the monolithic polonization of the symbol. Belatedly retrofitting the Commonwealth's multicultural heritage into the national realm, the Belarusian activists engaged in a form of pseudo-postcolonial revindicative remembrance.

The Polish response, on the other hand, is interesting for what it did *not* claim: namely, that Kościuszko was clearly and unequivocally Polish. The rhetorical reference to "universalism" reinforces the notion that claims to inclusivity are always discursively situated. As Nina Glick Schiller puts it: "To insinuate that cosmopolitans appreciate otherness is also to take for granted that the cosmopolitan speaks from a position of unequal and superior power—the power to define who and what is different and to grant or not grant the humanity of others."[7] In this particular instance, the power with which the Polish officials declared Kościuszko's cosmopolitan belonging was a nationally inflected one. It was Polish state institutions that had the loudest voice on whether and to what extent the other associated nations would be admitted to the "universal" symbolism of Kościuszko memory. Thus, the legacy of the Polish-Lithuanian Commonwealth emerged on this anniversary as both divided and divisive. It is caught between national and cosmopolitan discourses, between competitive and inclusive memory; moreover, the uneven distribution of perceived legitimacy leads to tensions between different stakeholders. Far from fading into the background in the shadow of other supranational structures, such as the European Union, the multicultural Commonwealth remains a source of both inspiration and contention.[8]

On the Polish-Belarusian axis, where questions of perceived Polish hegemony and Belarusian victimhood have shaped debates over several decades, arguments over the Commonwealth's heritage have often been a lopsided affair, with Belarusian intellectuals advancing claims, but gaining little recognition. In Poland, the nineteenth-century myth of the *Kresy Wschodnie* (Eastern Borderlands), whereby the eastern territories of the former Commonwealth are remembered as bastions of Polishness and a lost arcadia, has created a dominant discourse of Belarus as a subordinate realm in which Belarusians are hardly visible or alternatively feature as a threat to the Polish-speaking (petty) nobility.[9] Belarusian cultural self-affirmation—which has also been counterposed with Russian and Soviet claims on Belarus as part of the "Russian world"—has sought legitimacy in the country's past as part of the Commonwealth, although this picture is complicated by a simultaneous tendency to reject the "Polish" legacy as inimical to Belarusian sovereignty.[10]

This chapter analyzes Polish-Belarusian cultural encounters in the postwar period of the twentieth century and up to the present day, a time during which bilateral relations have been reset: the 1945 Potsdam Agreement settled a new border between the Polish People's Republic and the Belarusian Soviet Socialist Republic, and a Belarusian polity (albeit a constituent republic of the USSR) appeared on the map for the first time. With the majority Belarusian territories no longer forming any part of a Polish state, unlike in the interwar period, cultural and political recognition could finally become aligned—at least potentially.

Direct references to the Commonwealth have not been particularly prominent in Polish-Belarusian cultural exchanges; the Belarusian national narrative has focused more on the Grand Duchy of Lithuania specifically (see chapter 9 in this volume), while the Polish perception of Belarus has often been marginalizing and alienating. Yet the shadow of the Commonwealth is omnipresent as an unspoken bond, a legacy that the Belarusian and Polish national discourses share. The afterlife of the Commonwealth's multiculturalism is espoused precisely in the power play between national cultures, in the often-strained attempts to build dialogue.

This chapter begins with a very brief overview of historical tensions between the Polish and Belarusian national projects, and then examines a literary conversation between two writers active in the late socialist period: the Polish novelist and filmmaker Tadeusz Konwicki (1926–2015) and the Polish-Belarusian writer Sakrat Janovič (*Pol.* Sokrat Janowicz; 1936–2013). Polish cultural representations of Belarus have historically had a dual significance for Belarusian identity. On the one hand, they tend to embody an appropriating stance or an implicit cultural superiority—including, to some extent, in apparent exceptions, such as passages about Belarus in works by Konwicki. On the other hand, writing against and in dialogue with Polish hegemony has given Belarusian writers an impetus for national self-affirmation. This is illustrated by the example of Janovič, who engaged with Konwicki's ideas and sought to carve out a space for Belarus in both Polish and Belarusian imaginings of the legacy of the Commonwealth.

The chapter then examines literary developments of the post-socialist era, including the bilingual literary hoax *The Belarusian Girl* (*Białorusińka/ Bielaruska*; 2003) by an anonymous author writing under the pseudonym Marta Pińska. This erotically charged work of political fiction explores Belarusian-Polish relations through the story of a lesbian love affair, thereby metaphorizing the tensions and contradictory desires of the Polish-Belarusian encounter. Finally, the novel *Sońka* (2014) by the Białystok-born author Ignacy Karpowicz (born 1976) deconstructs center-periphery relations from a Polish perspective through metafictional play. Through its postmodern structure and engagement with Polish-Belarusian entanglement, *Sońka* disavows Polish culture's ability to speak for Belarus's past and present. It decenters Polish hegemony to make room for multicultural memory.

Overall, this chapter shows that Polish-Belarusian literary encounters are often colored by a perceived imbalance in power and legitimacy, whose roots lie in the inequitable distribution of the Commonwealth's heritage in the cultural imagination. Because the Polish-Lithuanian Commonwealth is widely considered to have been "Polish," Belarus's status as one of its successor nations is tacitly disputed. Literary imaginings of Polish-Belarusian relations are a prime site in which these divided legacies are gradually reconfigured.

"The Tragedy of Isolation": Etching Belarus into Polish Memory

The Polish-Belarusian cultural contact zone is colored not only by the memory of the Commonwealth but also by later legacies of Russian and Soviet colonialism, wartime and postwar ethnic cleansing, and post-socialist integration.[11] To necessarily simplify: in the nineteenth and early twentieth centuries, many Polish-speaking intellectuals dreamed of resurrecting the Commonwealth in its entirety, although there was little consensus on the potential status of the cultural minorities such as the Lithuanians and Belarusians. For many Poles, the Belarusian-speaking peasantry were a sub-element of the larger Polish-led nation, with no subjectivity of their own.[12] For a minority of others, especially after the turn of the twentieth century, the legacy of the Commonwealth was to be shared between nations with an equal status: for example, the Stronnictwo Krajowe Litwy i Białorusi (Territorial Party of Lithuania and Belarus), a group of conservative think-ers mainly of the landed nobility based in the territory of the former Grand Duchy of Lithuania, campaigned for the equal enfranchisement of all na-tionalities within a future resurrected Polish-Lithuanian state.[13]

In the aftermath of the Polish–Soviet War of 1919–1921 and the division of the majority Belarusian and Ukrainian territories into regions ruled by Warsaw and Moscow, the developing Belarusian nationalism was subject to the political exigencies of the continued rivalry between Poland and the USSR.[14] In interwar Poland, a multiethnic state in which substantial groups of ethnic minorities struggled for representation, the authorities vacillat-ed between allowing concessions to the Belarusian community (such as Belarusian-language schools) and forcing the closure of Belarusian cultural and political institutions. This tension reflected the rivalry between the social-ist and nationalist camps in Polish politics. After 1927, under the heavy-handed Sanacja regime, it was the repressive approach that picked up pace.[15]

The Second World War and its aftermath constitute in many ways the de-fining historical event through whose prism later Polish-Belarusian contacts can be interpreted. Not only did the combined attacks of Nazi Germany and Stalin's USSR result in extreme demographic changes through the Holocaust and mass deportations; the postwar redrawing of borders and mutual expul-sions to create ethnically homogeneous territories permanently altered the relations between the two cultures. Separate, self-contained Belarusian and Polish republics came into existence for the first time, with only small mi-nority populations remaining on the "wrong" side of the border in both coun-tries.[16] In the postwar period under state socialism, memories of intercultural exchanges and mutual injuries were largely taboo: in Poland, nostalgia for the "lost" territories of the prewar state was generally suppressed in the public realm.[17] In the Belarusian Soviet Socialist Republic (BSSR) a Russocentric master narrative of the past discouraged the exploration of the legacy of the Polish-Lithuanian Commonwealth.[18]

Thus, the postwar period brought to its apex a gradual process that Sakrat Janovič called the "tragedy of isolation" (*tragedia osamotnienia*), that is, the irreversible separation of national identities in the former Polish-Lithuanian Commonwealth from the beginning of the nineteenth century onward, strengthened in particular by Russian expansionism.[19] At the same time, however, cultural dialogues gradually emerged between representatives of the two nations, making the initial contours of shared remembrance discernible: academics such as those based at the Department of Belarusian Studies at the University of Warsaw, founded in 1956, started a scholarly exchange; a prominent popular history of Belarus by Marceli Kosman was published in Polish in 1971;[20] Konwicki and Czesław Miłosz (1911–2004) were among the best-known Polish literary figures whose works touched upon Belarusian themes.

A major role in this development was played by Janovič himself, a Belarusian-speaker from the town of Krynki, located slightly to the west of the post-1945 Polish-Belarusian border. As a Belarusian in Poland and a prominent cultural authority among the country's Belarusian minority, he was well positioned to speak both to Poles about Belarus and to Belarusians in Belarus about Poland, and therefore to act as a cultural conduit between the two countries. Although Janovič began his literary career as a local intellectual writing predominantly in Belarusian for ethnic minority publications in the Białystok region and in the BSSR, in 1973 he published his first book in Polish translation with a Warsaw publisher, followed in subsequent years by several others.[21] In 1987, his landmark essayistic work *Belarus, Belarus* (*Białoruś, Białoruś*), written originally in Polish and explicitly addressed to Polish readers as a corrective to dominant stereotypes about Belarus and Belarusians, appeared to critical acclaim.

Belarus, Belarus was in part a response to Tadeusz Konwicki's use of this phrase in his own book-length essayistic memoir of 1976, *The Calendar and the Hourglass* (*Kalendarz i klepsydra*). Konwicki was a native of the interwar Wilno (Vilnius) region—an area where Belarusian-speakers were numerous, alongside Jews, Lithuanians, and Poles. In a short passage in *The Calendar and the Hourglass*, he riffs with a mixture of irony and nostalgia on the importance of Belarus to him as a writer: "What do I owe to Belarus? I owe it the fact that I still can't write well in Polish. . . . I owe it that nostalgia which grabs me by the hair-tips out of the blue in Warsaw, in Paris or Manhattan.

I owe it that overwhelming anxiety that drives me to keep moving, to keep moving although I am standing still, to go anywhere, to a place I am anxious about reaching, although I have to get there in the end. Belarus, Belarus, why are you called Belarus?"[22] For Konwicki, then, his roots in the multicultural eastern territories of the interwar Polish republic had an ambivalent significance. They defined him and he by no means rejected his past, but a line separated his present-day identity as a metropolitan Polish-language writer from his provincial childhood: "What language did I speak as a child? Was it 'simple talk' [po prostemu, i.e., Belarusian] or 'city-speak' [po miastowemu, i.e., Polish]?"[23] Implicit in this rhetorical question is the fact that he later fully urbanized—and by extension, polonized.

Konwicki's relationship to Belarus was one of both sympathy and distance. On the one hand, he devoted several works to literary commemoration of the prewar Wilno region, thematizing Belarus and giving it presence in the Polish cultural imagination.[24] For instance, in his early novella Marshes (Rojsty; written in 1947, published in 1956), a first-person narrative of participation in an anti-Soviet militia in the years 1944–1945, the narrator readily admits, "We shot at Belarusian peasants whom we suspected of sympathizing or outright collaborating with the Bolsheviks."[25] In another scene, a Belarusian peasant girl is raped by Polish soldiers.[26] The later work Bohin Manor (Bohiń, 1987), a dreamy postmodernist narrative about the author's grandmother in her youth, centers on a romance between Helena Konwicka and a Jew at her family estate "in a Lithuanian village, but even more so a Belarusian one."[27] On the other hand, in Konwicki's vision, Belarus and Belarusians ultimately have little agency: "You didn't etch yourself into people's memories, oh Belarus. You didn't deprive others of their freedom, you didn't conquer their lands, you didn't murder people from behind neighborly bounds. . . . You are too good, too mild, too noble for our times."[28] For Konwicki, Belarus can be little more than a passive victim and object of "mild nostalgia" (łagodna tęsknota).[29] While he was a rare voice on the Polish side of the conversation who attempted to see things otherwise than from a hegemonic polonocentric point of view, Belarus remained for him a land without subjectivity.

Sakrat Janovič was ten years younger than Konwicki and similarly hailed from a region that was highly multicultural before the Second World War: the Polish-Belarusian borderlands near Białystok. In books like Belarus, Belarus, he polemicized with the empathetic and open, yet ultimately Polish view on Belarus voiced by Konwicki and others like him.[30] Janovič's lasting concern was the articulation of Belarusian cultural agency through the ages, a task that gained an added urgency when he wrote for a Polish audience and therefore demanded recognition from the majority culture.[31] Setting out to prove that Belarusians had been makers of their own history and full-fledged members of the Polish-Lithuanian Commonwealth, Janovič gives countless examples of Belarusian (i.e., Ruthenian) political and cultural activity that spanned the territory of the Commonwealth and beyond: from the Latin poet Nicolaus Hussovianus (*Bel.* Mikola Husoŭski, *Pol.* Mikołaj Hussowski, ca. 1480–ca. 1533), who published his *Song about Bison, Its Stature, Ferocity and Hunt* (*Carmen de statura feritate ac venatione bisontis*) in Kraków in 1523—according to Janovič, a "wonderful Latin narrative poem about Lithuania the fatherland"[32]—to twentieth-century authors and academics who were active in preserving the pre-Soviet heritage of the land. Moreover, in the short story collection *The Silver Horseman* (*Srebrny jeździec*, 1984), Janovič gives fictional reinforcement to the myth of a continuous Belarusian past.[33] Comprising three loosely interconnected stories set in the fifteenth century, the nineteenth century, and the postwar present day, the narratives present overtly Belarusian protagonists playing significant roles in the ebb and flow of macro-scale history. In the final story, in which a pair of young siblings uncovers a range of historical artifacts while on holiday, the narrator concludes that further discoveries may "completely change our view of the history of the Belarusians."[34] Janovič thus makes his intention explicit that readers should see Belarusians as agents of history.

However, reclaiming history for a collective rendered "ahistorical" is a fraught enterprise, and the inherent contradictions of "Belarusianizing" the Commonwealth's legacy left their mark on Janovič's prose. He appears to have tacitly recognized as much: "I'm so bloody envious of the Poles for the richness of their culture and history!"[35] For all his desire that Belarus have its "own" autonomous past, he cannot escape the fact that, in the eighteenth and nineteenth centuries, many of the personas he discusses were peripheral figures within the former Commonwealth's culturally polonized society: "As the elites adopted Polish culture, the Belarusian muse, confined to the margins, . . . degenerated into a red-faced simpleton with tastes straight out of a coarse burlesque."[36] Janovič hypercompensates by exaggerating the Belarusian elements of his historical narrative: he Belarusianizes names (e.g., the poet Jan Czeczot, 1796–1847, becomes "Czaczot" [with the stress on the second syllable]; the playwright Wincenty Dunin-Macinkiewicz, 1808–1884, becomes "Vincuk Dunin-Marcinkievicz"); downplays the obscurity of some of his references; and ignores much of the Polish-language output of writers he considers to have contributed to Belarusian culture.

The literary historian Danuta Zawadzka argues that "at the core of [Janovič's] writing lies a many-sided and perverse dependence on Polish narrations."[37] Her postcolonial reading of Janovič's textual memory work finds multiple traces of Bhabhian mimicry:[38] for example, in the very fact of writing in Polish; in the adoption of the characteristically Polish colloquial prose genre of the *gawęda* in nonfictional works such as *Belarus, Belarus*; and in the paradoxical ambivalence of the desire to imitate the Polish model of a linear national history, which both undermines its own emancipatory aim (i.e., copying the model of the center and thereby decentering itself) and threatens the dominant Polish narrative (by creating a Belarusian version within the Polish cultural realm). Thus, two contradictory aims coexist in Janovič's writings: on the one hand, to celebrate the cosmopolitanism of the former Commonwealth, specifically by reviving its Belarusian (also Lithuanian, Ruthenian, and Orthodox) legacy, which has been largely displaced by an ethnocentric Polish viewpoint; and on the other hand, to dilute that same cosmopolitanism by superimposing a national Belarusian framework onto the multicultural past.

It is therefore not surprising that *Belarus, Belarus* has been called both "an anti-Polish work," and a "revolutionary" one that allowed Poles to look at "[their] own history through the eyes of others."[39] Nonetheless, Zawadzka's argument that Janovič's writing is imbued with postcolonial injury is somewhat overstated. While Janovič certainly disapproved of Polish stereotypes about Belarus and its elision from discussions about the Commonwealth, this view did not necessarily translate into a vision of Polish culture as a pseudo-imperial presence in Belarus; his endeavor was hardly a case of the "empire writing back," that is, "abrogating" and "appropriating" the language of colonial power.[40] In his 1993 work *Terra Incognita: Belarus* (*Terra Incognita: Białoruś*), Janovič states explicitly that he harbors a "pride in the beautiful non-Polish past and a simultaneous burning Polish patriotism."[41] An advocate of the Commonwealth legacy in all of its pluralism, he believed in dialogue and mutual interaction, arguing that just as the modern Belarusian classic writers Janka Kupala (1882–1942) and Jakub Kolas (1882–1956) had written under the influence of major Polish writers, so Adam Mickiewicz had read and drawn from Hussovianus's *Carmen de bisonte*.[42] One of Janovič's para-literary legacies was the establishment in 1999 of an annual series of "Trialogues"—moderated discussions between representatives of Belarusian, Polish, and other European cultures. Formally organized by the Villa Sokrates foundation headquartered in Janovič's former family home in Krynki, these gatherings continue to this day, despite Janovič's death in 2013.

Sakrat Janovič, then, made a substantial contribution to a mild Belarusization of the legacy of the Commonwealth within Polish culture. He effectively introduced the notion that not only was Belarus geographically part of a Polish-dominated Commonwealth, but that the Commonwealth had multiple cosmopolitan legacies, among which was a Belarusian thread. His writing did contain elements of revisionist nationalism, for which he was sometimes castigated; but the contradictions within his prose illustrate above all the difficulty of articulating shared remembrance in an era when the separation of nationalities is a fait accompli, with the symbolic distribution of the Commonwealth's legacy heavily weighted in favor of the Polish side. Janovič's self-confessed "envy" of Polish high culture can be read as an admission that only through critical self-reflection can cross-cultural dialogue be initiated; articulating a suppressed Belarusian perspective in any other way would descend into nationalist kitsch. Belarusian identity was undoubtedly important to him, but more as an antidote to homogenizing Polish ethnopolitics than as an end in itself. As he put it in 2001: "More and more often these days I consider myself to be just a writer; I am a Belarusian author only when somebody wants me to be."[43]

A quintessential borderland intellectual, Janovič became a canonical figure neither in Poland nor in Belarus, although his legacy is generally recognized among intellectuals in the Białystok region and in the Belarusian humanities and literary circles. In the meantime, since the collapse of state socialism, the Belarusian minority in eastern Poland has become increasingly assimilated into the dominant Polish culture.[44] Concurrently, the Białystok region has gained something of a (perhaps undeserved) reputation as Poland's hotbed of right-wing integral nationalism and antisemitism, as captured in (and arguably perpetuated by) the journalist Marcin Kącki's book *Białystok: White Power, Black Memory* (*Białystok: Biała siła, czarna pamięć*).[45] The conversation started by Janovič, in other words, has not gained widespread currency, and the legacy of the Commonwealth remains contested. The nostalgic, polonizing myth of the *Kresy* continues to haunt the Polish national imaginary in new ways after the collapse of state socialism—for example, in a growing multiplicity of photography albums, literary memoirs, local memory groups, and political statements.[46] In Belarus, the Grand Duchy of Lithuania has been raised on a pedestal as a golden era of Belarusian statehood, especially (but not only) in opposition circles: the

Polish-Lithuanian Commonwealth has gained in symbolic value, although it is the Lithuanian (and thus partly Belarusian) part that is most revered.[47] To adapt Michael Rothberg's terms, memory on the Polish-Belarusian axis has more often been competitive than multidirectional.[48] The Commonwealth remains a symbolic resource, continually fought over in the aftermath of "the tragedy of isolation."

Theaters of Desire: Metaphors of Domination and Emancipation

Since the authoritarian regime of Alexander Lukashenko came to power in 1994 and consolidated its grip on Belarus, Polish government institutions and civil society have been consistently active in supporting the prodemocratic opposition in its eastern neighbor state. Playing on the symbolism of the Solidarity movement of the 1980s, Polish activists have teamed up with Belarusian cultural figures to declare that they are "Solidarni z Białorusią" (in solidarity with Belarus) at regular concert events held annually under this banner since 2006. After the regime's brutal crackdown in the aftermath of the 2020 protests, Poland and Lithuania have been among the most active supporters of Belarusian civil society—for instance, by accepting large numbers of political émigrés, issuing scholarships to students, and vocally criticizing the excesses of the authoritarian regime.

At the same time, the extent to which political solidarity translates into mnemonic solidarity is open to debate.[49] Belarus continues to have a limited cultural presence in the Polish imagination, featuring above all as the "poor" neighbor still struggling for basic civil rights. This politicized image of the country is visible, for example, in the newspaper reportage of the *Gazeta Wyborcza* correspondent Andrzej Poczobut,[50] or the feature film *Viva Belarus!* (directed by Krzysztof Łukaszewicz, 2012), about a youth activist's struggles against the regime. Alternatively, Belarus remains a place of Polish nostalgia, the object of a touristic gaze that sees its sites as realms of Polish history.[51] While a small number of Polish translations of Belarusian literature have appeared, few if any recent Polish works feature Belarus or Belarusians—in contrast to a plethora of books in various genres on Russia and Ukraine.[52] Thus, in the mainstream Polish cultural imaginary, Belarus is more a poorly understood and somewhat awkward neighbor than a fellow inheritor of the Commonwealth tradition.

The imbalance in symbolic capital between the two countries is also reflected in Belarusian treatments of Poland. Nelly Bekus has studied a set of written texts and films, arguing that they "either sustain a constructed sense of Poland's 'Otherness' or, on the contrary, overcome this Otherness to discover its closeness in order to find a place for Belarus in Europe, alongside Poland."[53] To Belarusian writers and intellectuals, Polish "solidarity" appears tinged with a haughty superiority. This is unsurprising given that Belarusian nationalist thinkers have long considered Poland to be a historical oppressor of the Belarusian people.[54] At the same time, the relatively new development of Polish cultural superiority appearing *desirable*—because it signifies by proxy a form of civic European identity—reveals that Poland's place in the Belarusian imaginary cannot be reduced to a binary choice between oppressor and benefactor. In some representations, relations between the countries take on an erotic hue, as realms of sexual fantasy and domination.

Indeed, one of the literary works analyzed by Bekus is a 2008 short story by Eva Viežnaviec (nom de plume of Sviatlana Kurs, born 1972), "Happiness, Ltd." ("Ahiencyja 'Ščasc'e'"), about a dating agency connecting Polish men with Belarusian women.[55] Told from the point of view of a Belarusian woman who sets up the agency because "marrying West with East is now a noble deed,"[56] the story ironically casts light on the difficult choices facing women in contemporary Belarus; marrying westward entails cultural and sexual objectification, but does come with material benefits. Bekus concludes somewhat optimistically that the story's Belarusian women "agree to forget about the subaltern experience and losses incurred by Belarusian culture and traditions under Polish domination, acquiring, in return, symbolic justification of Belarusian ties to Europe."[57] A different reading, however, would interpret the sacrifices of the Belarusian women not as an admission to "Europe," but as a Girardian "scapegoat effect," defined as "that strange process through which two or more people are reconciled at the expense of a third party who appears guilty or responsible for whatever ails, disturbs, or frightens the scapegoaters."[58] In an ironic gesture, Viežnaviec envisions the androcentric national narratives of Belarus and Poland, embodied in cash-wielding Polish males and absent Belarusian ones, tacitly agreeing on the commodification of Belarusian women—as long as this brings Belarus closer to its western ideal and Poland closer to symbolic rule over its former East. In this story, Belarusian-Polish cultural relations are allegorized as a site of domination, whereby Belarusian women become an object of trade.

Sexual desire also functions as a metaphorical commentary on Polish-Belarusian relations in another work, an intriguing literary experiment titled *The Belarusian Girl* (*Białorusinka/Bielaruska*) by an anonymous author writing under the pseudonym Marta Pińska.[59] Published in 2004 by Sakrat Janovič's Villa Sokrates foundation in Poland, the book presents the same story in two versions: in Polish from one cover and, when flipped over, in Belarusian from the other. The narrative purports to be an originally Polish-language manuscript translated by another person hiding behind a pseudonym, Dziadźka ("Uncle" or "Old Man") Vasiĺ. Yet, as Jan Maksymiuk has shown, linguistic analysis suggests very strongly that the Belarusian text is the original, with the deliberate typological errors in the Belarusian version scarcely providing cover for the occasional awkwardness of the Polish translation.[60] The novella is a first-person narrative told from the point of view of a young Polish woman, who intimately documents her daily experiences during a lengthy sojourn in Minsk; in particular, she reveals the details of a romance with a young Belarusian woman. Thus, *The Belarusian Girl* is a portrait of a Polish view on Belarus as told by a Belarusian author (almost certainly a female one); it is an exercise in role-playing theatrics that reveals far more about Belarusian views of Poland than vice versa.

As Maksymiuk argues, *The Belarusian Girl* is above all a story of female emancipation in the context of the political liberation of the 1990s, both a paean to the era of national "rebirth" (*adradženne*) and a challenge to the male-dominated discourse of that time.[61] The novella's two heroines, the narrator and the unnamed Belarusian woman, experiment sexually with an array of men as well as with each other, and discuss avant garde literature, critical theory, jazz music, and contemporary politics. Between them, they have encounters with a Latvian, a Lithuanian, a "Belarusified" Russian, two Italian men, and a middle-aged American Jew visiting his father's birthplace of Vilnius. The Belarusian woman travels to Bratislava and Prague in addition to the Lithuanian capital. Thus, the Minsk of the 1990s, told through the eyes of a Pole, emerges as a dynamic city with ties to multiple other places, where many different urban subcultures interact. The sexual episodes are described in vivid detail,[62] both in direct first-person narration and the narrator's retelling of other characters' stories; the novella therefore breaks social taboos about homosexuality through its eroticism, giving voice to female sexuality and documenting the self-empowerment of two young intellectuals during a turbulent and carnivalesque time.

Yet *The Belarusian Girl* is also, as its title suggests, a text about nationally inflected desire. The title character is a Belarusian incarnation of a paradigmatic femme fatale. For the narrator, she is never fully attainable, despite their mutual attraction. To emphasize her aloofness, the text refers to her only using the third-person pronoun, often capitalized. Moreover, the narrator expresses jealousy and frustration at several junctures when she sees "Her" with other lovers. That "She" is attractive to the narrator specifically as a Belarusian woman is revealed in the final words of the novella. Pent-up tensions in their relationship are resolved when "She" confesses she has had an abortion, and then moves to Prague to start a new life as a journalist. The narrative concludes with a reconciliatory letter, a rare moment in which "Her" voice is heard directly in prose and without mediation, as "She" expresses a wish to meet again, signing off as *Tvaja Belaruska* ("your Belarusian girl").[63] In this closing gesture, which simultaneously articulates both affection and difference, the ironies of the work come to the fore. The recurrent links between sexual attraction and desired ownership are reversed. Now that their relationship is over, "She" finally claims to be "yours." Moreover, the privileged position of the Pole in Minsk is lightly mocked through the explicit reference to nationality; the unnecessary emphasis on "Her" Belarusianness appears as a dig at Polish exoticization of Belarus and Belarusians.

The Belarusian Girl therefore narrativizes the perceived tensions between a paradigmatically Polish view of Belarus and concomitant Belarusian ressentiment. The historical genealogies of these tensions are not overtly alluded to in the work, but they do surface in minor details. For example, the narrator, who is from Kraków—Poland's historical cultural capital, vaunted by Sakrat Janovič as both a magnet and a curse for Belarusians—claims to prefer Minsk to her hometown, where "every apartment had at least a bit of bourgeois warmth."[64] Despite this self-aware criticism of Kraków's supposed superiority and her willing self-immersion in Belarusian cultural life, the narrator nonetheless reveals an adherence to old stereotypes about Belarus: "When I wanted to return to my description of Belarusian phlegmatism, she scowled that I did not know what I was talking about."[65] Defending Belarusian subjectivity and historical agency, "She" also finds inspiration in the crypt of Niasviž (*Pol.* Nieśwież) castle, where she encounters firsthand the relics of the Lithuanian Radziwiłł family of Commonwealth magnates: "She touched upon a world that was buried somewhere within her, like a sadness at the centuries and bygone ages, like a returning memory, like the continuation of a forgotten legend."[66] The Grand Duchy and Commonwealth inspire "Her" and constitute her identity, whereas the Polish narrator cannot enter this world of remembrance.

"Marta Pińska's" book, then, is in some ways a response to Janovič's *Belarus, Belarus*, although it makes no direct reference to it. While the older writer

presented Belarus to Polish readers, trying, with mixed results, to show that
Belarus had its own autonomous history, the feminist reply metaphorizes
Polish views of Belarus for a (mostly) Belarusian readership, while also referring to a Belarusian "practical past" that can shore up a separate identity.[67]
Through the figure of a Polish woman in love with a Belarusian one, the book
challenges not only social taboos on gender and sexuality but also received
cultural codes about the relationship between the two countries. The rebellious flirtation of the Belarusian woman, as well as the concluding letter's
request to remain friends, emerges from the text as an allegory of Belarus's
consolidated sovereignty and cultural independence. "She" moves to Prague
for a job at Radio Svaboda (Freedom), the name of the Belarusian service of
Radio Free Europe; in doing so, she also appears to declare Belarus's cultural
freedom, as an equal and independent central European nation no longer
caught in the Polish gaze.

Needless to say, however, an obscure Belarusian novella published in the
Polish periphery has had little effect on Polish perceptions of Belarus. Indeed,
the gradual resurgence of conservative nationalism in Poland, confirmed by
the 2015 and 2019 electoral victories for the Law and Justice party (Prawo
i Sprawiedliwość, PiS), led to a political legitimization of pseudo-imperial
claims to the prewar Polish regions now in Belarus, Lithuania, and Ukraine.[68]
This is the political context in which the spat over Tadeusz Kościuszko, with
which this chapter began, unfolded. Recognition of Belarus in Poland clearly
depends more on developments in Poland itself, on the exigencies of internal
culture wars over the meanings of Polish nationhood (civic or ethnic), and on
the legacies of the postwar border shifts that moved Poland "out of" Belarus
and other eastern neighbor states. An important intervention was provided
in 2014 by another writer from the Białystok region, Ignacy Karpowicz, in
his novel *Sońka*.[69]

Metafiction and Memory: Giving Voice to the Voiceless

Sońka is the first mainstream Polish novel to feature a Belarusian protagonist, and an innovative experiment in metafictional narrative as a means
of disrupting established cultural orthodoxies. The work tells the story of
an encounter between the author's alter ego and the titular Sonia, a ninety-
year-old Belarusian woman in a small village on the eastern margins of
Poland, Królowe Stojło. The narrator, a successful playwright based in Warsaw called Igor, is driving through the countryside in the Białystok region

when his car breaks down outside Sonia's house. He steps out to find that in this backwater he has no mobile phone reception, and so he is forced by circumstance to communicate with Sonia, who is out leading her cow to pasture. This unlikely meeting of two contrasting worlds has substantial consequences. Sonia and Igor talk into the night, the old woman seeing in Igor an outlet for the wartime traumas she has kept stored up for decades, and Igor finding in Sonia an inspiring story to turn into his next play.

Sońka, however, is not a linear narrative. The novel's basic structure is a modified Chinese box, with layers of framing complicating the interpretation of the story. At the core is the story of Sonia: a major part of the novel is narrated in her voice, in the first person, and recalls how she was sexually and physically abused by her father as a teenage girl, and how she found refuge during the Second World War in a brief and naive romance with a German soldier called Joachim. Sonia's oral narration is embedded within a third-person narrative that centers on Igor. We see Sonia exclusively through Igor; the subaltern figure of the Belarusian villager can only be mediated through the narrative voice of the Polish writer. Moreover, we also *hear* Sonia through Igor, although this is less obvious because her testimony is rendered in the first person and has a veneer of authenticity. Sonia's text must, however, be a transcription or retelling, because in the framing narration—Igor's story—Sonia speaks to Igor in Belarusian only, while Sonia's own narrative is then rendered in Polish, with some stylizations in transcribed Belarusian. Meanwhile, it remains unclear whether this text is Igor's prose or that of an external author figure (Ignacy Karpowicz).

The relationship between the external author and the character of Igor, himself a writer, is made deliberately and playfully ambiguous. On the one hand, an authorial voice intrudes in the form of an explanatory footnote early on, clarifying the decision to put a Belarusian-Polish glossary at the end. The novel is also typeset in a nonstandard manner, the shifted margins and feigned metatextual notes enhancing the aura of incompleteness and the overdetermined sense of a demiurgical presence shaping the text. On the other hand, the character of Igor is replete with auto-irony, and is manifestly a ghost of the author himself. We quickly learn that Igor is not, in fact, Igor, but Ignacy. Originally from a Belarusian-speaking family in the Białystok region, he left this unglamorous identity behind when he moved to Warsaw: "He cut himself off from himself, acquired the name Igor, a new and better name neatly confirmed by his identity documents."[70] Thus, Igor/Ignacy is split between center and periphery, and Ignacy is Igor's repressed Belarusian past: "Igor had carefully hidden his childhood, painted it over. He was assiduously ashamed of it, had scrupulously forgotten it, erased it and buried it."[71] As the author's ironic self-projection into the novel, Igor/Ignacy is also a kindred spirit to Sonia, a bridge between Polish and Belarusian subjectivities, and a buffer between reality and fiction. He is a postmodern shadow of the Belarusian presence in postwar Poland, or Sakrat Janovič's culturally assimilated literary grandson.

Igor/Ignacy's status as the narrative focal point of the novel has a double meaning, with significant consequences for the novel's interpretation. His fascination with Sonia manifests itself in two contrasting urges. On the one hand, he is irresistibly drawn to her life story; in understanding Sonia and letting her speak through him, he is also effectively digging up and exposing his own suppressed identity. He even slips into Belarusian, letting his guard down before Sonia: "'Ni pamrecie [You won't die],' he said, although he didn't believe his words. It was Ignacy who said this, washed out with shame, repression, and inferiority."[72] Because, as Ignacy, he is an autochthonous member of the borderland community, he can revisit the periphery with authenticity. On the other hand, the end product of his fascination with Sonia is a play, to be staged in Warsaw. Intermeshed with the narration about Igor and Sonia's meeting are digressions detailing Igor's fantasies for the future theater production and even complete pages of script. The desire to "translate" Sonia's biography into a theatrical work for the metropolitan center, however, is inevitably bound up with an urge to sanitize and sensationalize the primary material: "He understood that he had to memorize even more than what Sonia was telling, that he had to harness his memory to a theatrical or novelistic mill, in order to save himself, to finally tell some kind of truth, to fight for something."[73] Igor's urge to "save himself" and "fight for something" emerges as an auto-satirical commentary on the creative process in a borderland setting: the novel openly ridicules Igor's cultural appropriation of Sonia's story. In this way, Sońka's ludic deconstruction of Igor's literary megalomania undermines his narrative authority.

Sońka, in other words, can be read as a metafictional critique of the very possibility of speaking for Sonia—that is, for the marginalized ethnic others who inhabit the borderlands of the Polish nation-state. According to Linda Hutcheon: "The best way to demystify power, metafiction suggests, is to reveal it in all its arbitrariness. . . . In other words, a text can call attention to authority structures in such a way as to subvert the Romantic ideology of the myth of originality that once subtended them."[74] Sonia cannot speak for herself, but the availability of a metropolitan subject who can endow her with a voice is exposed as a narcissistic fantasy of the powerful center, in "all its arbitrariness." The novel effectively denies all narrative authority through its framing structure and dismantling of Igor/Ignacy's subject position. The result is, paradoxically, an empowering of Sonia's peripheral voice: as the sub-altern, she cannot speak, but if Igor cannot do so either, then her experience is no less valid.

Sonia's story conjures up the multiculturalism of prewar Poland and si-multaneously disrupts the dominant myths of Polish memory of the Second World War. The main strand of her narrative—her love affair with Joachim, whom she still refers to as her "true love"—is provocative because it hits a nerve in the collective imaginary: the taboo of consorting with the enemy is exacerbated by her ethnic and gendered marginality. Not only is Sonia a Belarusian in Poland; she is also a woman in a patriarchal community. The affront that her wartime actions constitute to established Polish modes of self-congratulatory remembering of the war are made clear in the fact that the local community continues to exclude her.[75] In one passage, Igor tries to obtain honest assessments of Sonia from her neighbors: "Sońka, said oth-ers, was our punishment for the misdeeds of the war. Our memory, said the drunkest and most reflexive. We're evil, evil, and she was the worst of all of us. The worst, because she didn't regret it."[76] Sonia's story, therefore, exposes the repressed memories of the terrible past. On the one hand, the oblique reference to "misdeeds of the war" implicates locals in the atrocities of the occupation period, including the Holocaust, which features prominently in Sonia's testimony. On the other hand, this passage demonstrates how Sonia is scapegoated as the "worst of all of us." Because of her weak position at the peripheries of Polish society, she is an easy target onto whom those in the community can project their guilt and thereby partially exonerate them-selves. Nonetheless, the novel makes it clear that Sonia is above all a victim. Her juvenile naïveté at the time and her unreliability as a narrator make the claim that Joachim was her "true love" hardly believable: if anything, this brings her victimhood into sharper relief, as a reflection of her manipulability and powerlessness. Sonia testifying to Igor—and by extension, to contem-porary readers—after a seventy-year gap grants her a form of restitution. The suppressed Belarusian thread of Polish war memory is given delayed exposure, and Sonia's subjectivity is finally restored.

Yet *Sońka* is a work that exposes its fictionality and decenters its narrative voices; in such metafictional novels, "meaningful memories do not exist prior to the process of remembering and narrating the past, but . . . are constituted by the active creation of self-narrations."[77] In other words, what remains in the void is writing itself, together with the act of reading. Rather than presenting an authoritative narrative of the past for passive consumption, the novel involves its reader in the remembering process. In Hutcheon's words: "If language . . . constitutes reality (rather than merely reflecting it), readers become the actualizing link between history and fiction."[78] The novel's ending makes the performative nature of reading explicit, as it evolves into a dreamlike allegory in which the boundaries between fiction and history, and between the play within the novel and the novel itself, are further blurred. It features a funeral lament for Sonia, in which the novel's characters interchange dynamically with actors performing Igor's embedded play, chanting the Kaddish, a Hebrew prayer of mourning. Thus, the memory of the Holocaust, witnessed by Sonia, is brought into dialogue with the memory of the Belarusian trace in postwar Polish culture, embodied in Sonia herself. In this suspended reality, the text begins to appeal directly to the reader, breaking the "fourth wall" within the novel's own theatricality. "Just one person is missing for a praying quorum. So that we can finally part with history, that sworn enemy . . . Maybe you are the one we need?"[79] In calling directly upon the (Polish) reader to help "finally part with history" by praying in Hebrew for its Belarusian protagonist, the novel draws lines of mnemonic solidarity between the Belarusian, Jewish, and Polish nodes of remembrance. It insists that memory must be multicultural.

From Isolation to Reconciliation

Tadeusz Konwicki was both right and wrong when he wrote that Belarus had not "etched itself into people's memories." From the perspective of Polish literary discourse, Belarus was indeed a non-place, or, as part of the *Kresy Wschodnie*, merely a peripheral region of the historical Commonwealth that was generally considered Polish. Yet for Belarusians, this claim was of course absurd: Belarus undoubtedly had its own memories and traditions, many of which were closely associated with the legacy of the Polish-Lithuanian Commonwealth. The very fact that a statement such as Konwicki's was possible is a sign that the Commonwealth's legacy and legitimacy have been unevenly distributed in favor of the Poles. Cultural developments in recent decades in both Poland and Belarus have been, in part, aimed at addressing this imbalance.

The question then is: What forms of narration are effective and appropriate in reclaiming multicultural histories, and in facilitating the latter-day recognition of the more marginalized successors to the Commonwealth's heritage? Unilateral Belarusianization of the Commonwealth past antagonizes other successor nations, leading to memory war—as the Kościuszko activists in Switzerland discovered in 2017. The pioneer of Belarusian Commonwealth memory, Sakrat Janovič, trod a more delicate line, writing in Polish about Belarus and emphasizing the many contact points and interactions between Belarusian and Polish historical figures. At the same time, he also tended toward overt Belarusization of the past, his revisionist essentialism and claims to mimetic truth intermixed with his dialogism.

Later literary treatments have been more self-reflexive in their form, using metaphor and innuendo to deconstruct persisting hegemonies. "Marta Pińska" employs an overtly fictional and allegorical narrative, wrapped in the veneer of a feigned back translation. Exploring the Polish-Belarusian contact zone through the prism of sexual desire, *The Belarusian Girl* can be read as an elaborate metaphor on the power relations still at play between the two cultures. The title character enters into a relationship with the Polish narrator, but ultimately asserts her sovereignty and independence while parting on amicable terms. "She" is a symbol of rediscovered subjectivity after Polish-Belarusian union.

Ignacy Karpowicz also empowers a Belarusian voice in *Sońka*, using a metafictional structure to deconstruct the text itself as a site of authority, thereby debunking Polish ethnopolitics and the competence of the Polish center to speak for Belarusians at all. The story of Sonia emerges as a powerful reminder of Poland's multiethnic past and implores readers to engage in hybrid remembrance, connecting the Belarusian, Jewish, and Polish strands of twentieth century history. *Sońka* therefore goes beyond Konwicki's sympathy for the country that "didn't etch itself into people's memories." It suggests the burden is not on Belarus to create memory (for Poles); rather, the shared legacies should be divided equitably between cultures.

Poland and Belarus have a centuries-long history of cultural exchange (though, of course, not as the nation-states of Poland and Belarus), with both modern nations drawing their lineage from the Polish-Lithuanian Commonwealth. This exchange has not always been equitable, and the threads connecting the two cultures have undoubtedly become less dense as a result of Russian and Soviet rule in Belarus. Nonetheless, the activities of the writers analyzed in this chapter give an indication that hybrid zones of contact endure to this day. All three authors examined here in depth bridge the cultural divide. Janovič was a self-identifying Belarusian with Polish citizenship, writing in both languages and vaunting the Belarusian past as a key element of the Commonwealth's legacy. "Marta Pińska's" true identity is unknown, but her novel displays a close familiarity with both cultures and a critical engagement with the historical interactions between them. Karpowicz is another borderland intellectual from eastern Poland, a Pole who is acutely sensitive to the multicultural trace of the historical Belarusian presence in Polish culture and whose novel *Sońka* innovatively allegorizes the imperative to remember prewar multiculturalism. These literary encounters show that, even after the "tragedy of isolation," the legacy of the Commonwealth still binds cultural memory.

11

Jewish Heritage Revival in the Polish-Belarusian-Ukrainian Borderlands and the Myth of Multiculturalism

Magdalena Waligórska, Ina Sorkina, and Alexander Friedman

In recent decades, Jewish heritage has witnessed an unprecedented revival, especially in Poland, but also in the neighboring states of Lithuania,
Belarus, and Ukraine. In Poland, it has gained momentum both in the
cultural sphere, with Jewish culture festivals, museums, and art projects
mushrooming across the country, and in the commercial sector, where the
"Jewish boom" has manifested itself through the proliferation of Jewish heritage tours, Jewish-style restaurants, and the revitalization of historic Jewish
quarters.[1] Although Jews did not constitute the largest ethnic minority in
pre-1939 Poland, it is Jewish heritage that has become *the* synecdoche for the
past multiculturalism of both the interwar Second Polish Republic and the
Polish-Lithuanian Commonwealth. A similar model of a "Jewish revival,"
both commercially successful and politically exploitable, has also begun to
emerge in other countries of the region—particularly in Lithuania, Belarus,
and Ukraine.[2] Yet can we speak of a transnational trend following the same
pattern in the entire region of the former Polish-Lithuanian Commonwealth,
or are these revivalist efforts rather trapped in their distinct national memorial traditions, historical narratives, and political exigencies?

This chapter seeks to investigate the wider political and cultural ramifications of such memory projects in regard to issues of cultural appropriation.
It looks at memorial initiatives that reference the region's multicultural past

in three former shtetls in today's Polish-Ukrainian-Belarusian borderland: a shtetl reconstruction in Biłgoraj (Poland); the state-owned Museum of National Cultures in Iŭje (Belarus); and a project to restore the synagogue of Brody (Ukraine). Comparing different grassroots, private, and state-supported initiatives to preserve the region's multiethnic heritage, we show that a range of commemorative formats have been mobilized, including museums, restoration projects, and simulacra. These projects have been embedded in a variety of discourses, while also evincing different patterns of cooperation between local actors and the Jewish diaspora. However, in each case, we find that national frames of memory—stereotypes, nationally dominant myths, state-backed metanarratives, and so on—are still the most important factor in determining how the multicultural past is remembered and discussed.

A common feature of the towns under scrutiny here is not only the high proportion of the population represented by the Jewish community before 1939 but also the fact that their townsfolk included Catholic Poles, Greek Catholic Ukrainians, Orthodox Belarusians, Tatars, Armenians, Roma, and German minorities.[3] This high ethnic and religious diversity, characteristic of urban centers in this part of East-Central Europe, had a long tradition, shaped by the Polish-Lithuanian Commonwealth's histories of expansion, migration, and urban development. The three towns under scrutiny share this rich history of changing geopolitical allegiances. Before 1795, Iŭje was located in the Grand Duchy of Lithuania, while Biłgoraj and Brody belonged to the Polish Crown. This geography changed in the partition period, when Brody was under Austrian rule, while Iŭje and Biłgoraj became part of the Russian Empire. The three towns returned to the dominion of a single state after the Treaty of Riga in 1921, when they all found themselves within the borders of the Polish Second Republic. Their history of multiethnicity came to a sudden and brutal end in the mid-twentieth century, brought about by the Holocaust, forced migrations, and the change of borders in the aftermath of the Second World War.[4] The area comprising today's western Belarus, western Ukraine, and eastern Poland was also the territory where Aktion Reinhardt and the "Holocaust by bullets" left the most devastating mark.[5] This means not only that the memory of past multiculturalism is inextricably linked to the heritage of atrocity but also that local non-Jewish populations witnessed firsthand the unprecedented brutality of the Nazi-led genocide, and were sometimes implicated in the process: both through participation in locating Jewish fugitives from the ghettos, and, on a truly mass scale, in the takeover of Jewish property in the aftermath of the killing.[6]

To understand the complexity of the position that present-day custodians of Jewish heritage in these locations inhabit, we apply Michael Rothberg's category of the "implicated subject." Transcending the dichotomy of "victims" and "perpetrators," and challenging the figure of the "passive bystander," Rothberg's concept refers to individuals who are either genealogically or structurally implicated in a history of violence and injustice. Implicated subjects "occupy positions aligned with power and privilege without being themselves direct agents of harm; they contribute to, inhabit, inherit, or benefit from regimes of domination but do not originate or control such regimes. An implicated subject is neither a victim nor a perpetrator, but rather a participant in histories and social formations that generate the positions of victim and perpetrator."[7] Rothberg's framework is interesting for our analysis not only because it theorizes the position of "latecomer[s] to the histories of perpetration," offering a mode with which to reflect on the intergenerational impact of trauma, but also because it zeroes in on the long-term effects of violence and injustice, including continuing material benefits and positions of power for the communities privileged by past violence. In Rothberg's vision, "implication" can only occur if historical injustices continue to have an impact on the present: "Implication emerges from the ongoing, uneven, and destabilizing intrusion of irrevocable pasts into an unredeemed present."[8] Applying Rothberg's theoretical framework to post-Holocaust East-Central Europe, we will investigate how material traces of the Jewish past—whether in the curated form of exhibitions, performances, and monuments, or in the unmediated presence of ruins or human remains in the public space—provide points of "intrusion" of traumatic histories into the present, triggering local efforts that both challenge and reproduce positions of privilege resulting from past violence. Looking at revivalist projects that showcase past multiculturalism in Poland, Belarus, and Ukraine, we trace how the celebration of past diversity can—sometimes simultaneously—both lift taboos, bringing a history of wrongdoing into the public space, and constitute a form of control over memorial spaces and narratives.

We look at this phenomenon in a geographical borderland that has been "the most fiercely embattled turf of Central Europe in the twentieth century."[9] It has also been crucial for Polish nationalist discourses, as the mythical locus of the idyllic coexistence of different ethnic groups, and the Polish civilizational frontier, conceptualized, until the early twentieth century, as Antemurale Christianitatis, and the edge of Europe, where Poles "spread civilized behavior into eastern 'wild fields.'"[10] The new borders dividing the three towns since 1945 have reconfigured this borderland, but continue to mark this part of Europe as a space that remains "fiercely embattled" also in the twenty-first century.

Biłgoraj, Poland: The Shtetl Reconstructed

Biłgoraj (Yid. ביללגאריי) has the past of a classic Polish shtetl.[11] The first written record of the town's Jewish community dates back to 1597, and, despite the losses suffered by local Jews in the Khmelnytsky pogroms (1648–1656), Biłgoraj's Jewish life continued to flourish both in the period of the Polish-Lithuanian Commonwealth and after its demise.[12] In the 1800s, the Jewish community expanded rapidly, reaching 42 percent of the town's population by the end of the century.[13] The Jewish stamp on the urban environment was by that time impossible to overlook. After the first wooden synagogue, dating back to the first half of the eighteenth century, was destroyed in a fire, the kehillah commenced, in 1875, the construction of a new brick synagogue, which was to become "the gem of the town."[14]

In the interwar period, the town already had three Jewish cemeteries, a Beys Jakov school, three Jewish banks, an orphanage, and a printing office.[15] By 1921, two-thirds of Biłgorajans were Jewish and the town boasted a vibrant and multifaceted Jewish cultural and political life.[16] This came to an end with the arrival of the German occupying forces on September 16, 1939, and the subsequent launch of deadly anti-Jewish policies. These actions were not only extremely brutal, but also played out to a large extent inside the town, in plain view of the Christian neighbors.[17] Multiple Jewish witnesses reported that when systematic extermination began in 1942, "the whole town was covered with dead bodies and blood was streaming down the streets like in a slaughterhouse."[18] The roads leading out of Biłgoraj were likewise strewn with Jewish corpses.[19] This unmitigated proximity to the killing also created conditions for plunder, extortion, and collaboration on the part of the non-Jewish townsfolk. Sources list not only acts of direct complicity in the killing on the part of the Polish police and local Volksdeutsche but also the participation of civilians, helping to locate Jewish hideouts, searching for fugitive Jews in the surrounding forests, or pillaging Jewish houses.[20] While some of these forms of complicity became subject to postwar prosecution, Rothberg's category of the "implicated subject" helps widen the lens beyond acts of active criminal behavior—making visible the widespread forms of participation in genocidal violence and dispossession that involved whole communities.

All in all, almost 4,000 Biłgorajan Jews lost their lives in Aktion Reinhardt, nearly 500 of them shot in local executions, and another 2,800–3,300 deported to the Bełżec death camp.[21] In the whole district of Biłgoraj, only 274 Jews managed to survive in hiding until the town's liberation by the Red Army in July 1944.[22] In 1945, just 25 Jewish survivors were registered as town residents, with virtually all of them leaving Biłgoraj soon afterward.[23] In this way, the history of Jewish Biłgoraj came to an irrevocable end. And yet, in 2016, Biłgoraj became the only town in postwar Poland that could boast a newly constructed synagogue.

The new synagogue of Biłgoraj is part of an unprecedented urban reconstruction initiative that aims to re-create a typical borderland shtetl in a one-to-one scale. The passion project of a single individual, the local businessman Tadeusz Kuźmiński, the "reconstructed" shtetl is intended as an expression of architectural multiculturalism. Planned to extend across forty hectares of land and to encompass entire streets of wooden houses—together with a mosque, Protestant, Orthodox, and Catholic churches, and a manor house including a museum of the Polish gentry—the still unfinished complex is clearly among the most unusual memorial undertakings in Poland.

The shtetl reconstruction is not the only initiative showcasing the Jewish past in Biłgoraj, which, over the past fifteen years, has come to grapple very intensively with its lost multicultural heritage. Today, Biłgoraj boasts two annual Jewish culture festivals, a museum dedicated to Isaac Bashevis Singer, who spent part of his childhood there, and a number of sites commemorating local Jews, including monuments, murals, and a "park of memory." Town authorities are also planning to honor local Jews with new street names. Moreover, the town's memorial book (*yizkor bukh*), published in 1956 in Israel, appeared in 2009 in Polish translation as just the second such edition to appear in the Polish language.[24]

The "Town of Borderland Cultures" initiative (Pol. *Miasteczko na Szlaku Kultur Kresowych*) is neither a restoration project nor a direct reconstruction of any historic part of prewar Biłgoraj. Instead, gesturing toward the Polish myth of the "Kresy," the Eastern Borderlands Poland lost to the Soviet Union after 1945, it embodies the Polish nostalgia for the lost pre-1939 Second Republic.[25] The synagogue, which, against the rules of shtetl topography, is placed at the center of the market square, is actually a replica of the synagogue in Voŭpa, located over four hundred kilometers northeast of Biłgoraj in today's Belarus (fig. 11.1). This masterpiece of wooden Jewish architecture and preeminent example of the Jewish baroque, destroyed by the Germans during the Second World War, was incorporated into the Biłgoraj project because detailed architectonic documentation of the building still existed, while no archival trace was left of Biłgoraj's own original wooden

Figure 11.1. The reconstructed synagogue of Voŭpa in Biłgoraj, 2015. Photo by Dominika Macocha.

synagogue. The overall layout of the planned complex likewise departs from the historical topography of the town. With the "urban part" structured around two nuclei—a "Jewish market square" and a "Polish market square"—complemented by a picturesque parklike area dotted with wooden church replicas and a manor house, the project's blueprint is an Arcadian potpourri of architectonic gems, rather than a one-to-one reflection of any lived urban experience. It is quite simply a myth of multiculturalism rendered in wood and stone—a vision of harmonious coexistence ready to be inhabited in one-to-one scale.

Yet, despite the inaccuracy of this simulacrum, perched on the edge of a modern town, the project has an undeniable and visceral connection to Biłgoraj's history. Tadeusz Kuźmiński, who conceived the project and supervised it for over a decade until his death in 2020, rooted his vision both in his own childhood memories of Biłgoraj's wooden architecture and in sound historical research. The houses lining the streets of his "borderland town" are all copies of authentic buildings representing the architectural style of the region. To find historical documentation for his vision, he searched the archives, contacted families of survivors, and undertook a four-month study trip across eastern Europe, visiting dozens of open air museums of wooden architecture from Belarus to Montenegro.[26]

Kuźmiński saw his engagement with Jewish heritage as a product of his "fascination with the history of the Polish Jews," but also as a reaction to the pervasive sense of loss in places like Biłgoraj.[27] A Biłgorajan by birth, he grew up in a town where haunting traces of the Jewish absence were omnipresent, and the past, quite literally, intruded on the present. As a child, he would play at the former Jewish cemetery, repurposed after the war into a sports field, where "bones would knock around next to the ball."[28] Bones would continue to resurface there well into the 1970s, when, during construction work on the sports field, pupils were required to collect them from the site in large wooden crates, which were then removed to an unknown location.[29] Throughout Kuźmiński's childhood in the 1960s, shallow graves of victims killed during a fire in 1939 and the later liquidation of the ghetto would often expose human remains. "Wherever there used to be Jewish houses, and people would dig to set new foundations, they would always come across bones," he recounted.[30] Jewish gravestones were also a common sight, often recycled after the war into the foundations of buildings or sidewalks. Some of them paved the driveway into the local vicarage until as late as 2003.[31] When the local Isaac Bashevis Singer Cultural Society was founded in 2005, other Jewish objects began "resurfacing" in the town, finding their way into the hands of the activists. In 2006, for example, the association organized a ritual burial of a Torah scroll, purchased from a local resident who had found it walled in during renovation work at his apartment.[32]

This "intrusion" of the town's traumatic past into the daily life of Biłgorajans—who, over the past seventy years, have been constantly confronted with the physical traces of the Holocaust and the moral consequences of inhabiting a Jewish cemetery—is an important motivation for local memory brokers. For Tadeusz Kuźmiński and like-minded activists, engagement with the town's multicultural past is ultimately also a form of recompense and an attempt to mend a historical injustice in which some ethnic Poles necessarily played a part, however secondary. "We have not yet, as a nation, gone through the process of atonement, through catharsis," Kuźmiński said in an interview. "Polish history is still full of lies, and many facts remain swept under the carpet, but as long as our society does not cleanse itself, [the difficult history] will remain a festering wound."[33]

Kuźmiński had no illusions that confronting his fellow Biłgorajans with their history of "implication" would be an easy task; rather, it would necessarily be a long process requiring "great sensitivity."[34] He hoped, however, that his "Town of Borderland Cultures" could contribute to this reckoning. By offering a space where Poland's lost ethnic diversity could be experienced firsthand, not only through architecture but also through art and cuisine, he wanted to foster curiosity about other cultures and to help overcome prejudice. At the same time, the very act of reconstruction carried for him an ethical dimension of making amends. One of the historic buildings, whose replica he included in his vision, is a wooden Orthodox church from the nearby village of Rudka, burned down by Polish authorities during a wave of anti-Ukrainian reprisals in 1938.[35] The multicultural shtetl, therefore, when brought to completion, will not only visualize the lost heritage of the country's "others," but will also confront visitors with some uncomfortable questions about Polish complicity in its destruction.

The memory of the multicultural heritage of Biłgoraj, brought back to light by the shtetl reconstruction project and the "Festival of Cultures," thus constitutes a challenge to the older narratives that dominated in the post-1945 period. Integrating the story of the town's past multiculturalism and showcasing Jewish heritage as a precious and integral part of the town's legacy, local activists reinscribe Biłgoraj's expunged Jewish past into the public space, making it visible and tangible again. Symbolically "reversing" wartime destruction and postwar efforts to efface "otherness," Biłgoraj's shtetl simulacrum can thus also be read as an endeavor to lift the taboo surrounding the community's implication in the past violence and its long-term benefits.

This potentially transformative effect of the local Jewish heritage revival becomes apparent perhaps most clearly through the backlash it has also provoked. Antisemitic slurs addressed at local memory brokers on the online forum of the local newspaper, hate mail, and minor acts of vandalism are accompanied by more sophisticated and institutional attempts to "neutralize" the local "return" of Jews into the public space.[36] After the town unveiled a "Wall of Memory" in 2016, built with the help of donations from both the Biłgorajan diaspora and the local community, the park area surrounding the memorial became designated as a space for grassroots commemorations, where families of Biłgorajan Jews who do not have a proper tombstone could place a symbolic *matzevah*. The first memorial stele to appear in the park, however, was one sponsored by the state Institute of National Remembrance (Instytut Pamięci Narodowej), commemorating a Catholic family killed by the Germans for assisting Jews in hiding.

By putting the focus on the Polish helpers of Jews, a commendable gesture in itself, the monument reinforces the mainstream Polish narrative of historical benevolence toward Jews and the heroic posture of the whole nation during the Second World War. Placed on the perimeter of the Jewish cemetery, which was leveled in the post-1945 period and built over with a concrete factory, the stele and the message it stands for obscure the very reasons for which the "park of memory" was called to life: the systematic erasure of

Jewishness from the townscape.[37] What is more, by foregrounding a position taken by only a small minority of Poles during the German occupation, it stifles a conversation about the indifference of the majority, not only during the ongoing genocide but also in its aftermath.

Over the past fifteen years, memorial initiatives in Biłgoraj have usually taken place in close cooperation with Jewish partners, including the Association of Biłgoraj Survivors in Israel, the Jewish Historical Institute in Warsaw, and the Warsaw Singer Festival. Both local activists and the town authorities, who have also initiated cooperation with a partner town in Israel, see these contacts as an important resource. But while these networks on the grassroots level have enormous potential and enable memory work that would not be possible without such cooperation, they take place within a web of mostly unacknowledged power relations resulting from historical implication. In other words, non-Jewish Poles, who became custodians of Jewish spaces and artifacts, but also of the memory of the Jewish past, in the aftermath of violence from which they structurally benefited, remain the privileged party in this exchange. It is ultimately in their hands how the Jewish past will be represented locally, as well as what will be left out of the narrative they shape.

For instance, Tadeusz Kuźmiński decided against the idea of reconstructing Biłgoraj's original pre-1939 synagogue, on the grounds that "it was not of exceptional beauty," and that, due to its brick construction, it would not fit into his architectural vision.[38] Some members of the Israeli survivors' association, however, find it a shame that the original synagogue was not reconstructed, pointing out that the shtetl reconstruction project "does not reflect the character of prewar Biłgoraj" and "is not a *Jewish* town."[39] According to Israel Bar-On, head of the association, it is the authentic, historical places that are of principal interest to the Biłgorajan diaspora—those that directly relate to the life of their ancestors.[40] A reconstruction, however accurate, will never carry the same emotional charge as the actual locations where Jewish life took place.

In the fervor of local revivalist activities, such Jewish sensitivities can at times be overlooked. When local activists invited Shmuel Atzmon-Wircer to perform with his Yiddish theater in Szczebrzeszyn, he discovered that the performance was scheduled to take place at the former synagogue—the very place where, in 1940, his grandfather was burned alive while attempting to save a Torah scroll after the Germans set fire to the building.

I came to Szczebrzeszyn and I ask them "where is the performance taking place?" because I remembered Szczebrzeszyn was a small town and didn't really have a stage. They say: "We do have a stage—at the cultural center."...And they drive me to the *synagogue*. I have a look at it, and I say: "Listen, I can't play here. I'm going to have a heart failure!" They say: "But Mr. *Szmulik*, we sold all the tickets, people are waiting for the performance! How can you call it off?" So I said: "You know what, [I'll play] under one condition: there will be a doctor and an ambulance on site."[41]

This negotiation scene encapsulates in a particularly poignant way the power relations at work. The multicultural past is being staged here according to a script prepared by the new custodians of the local Jewish heritage sites, even at the cost of the emotional anguish of a Holocaust survivor, forced to perform at the very site of his grandfather's death. Privilege gained as a result of violence is reproduced in a unilateral and inconsiderate, if also uninformed, decision about the terms and conditions on which representations of the "other" will be generated. The same privilege is at play when the history of the town is written in a way to conveniently occlude certain facts. Thus, on Biłgoraj's local government website, which celebrates Shmuel Atzmon-Wircer as an honorary citizen of the town, we read that he left Poland after 1945 "because of the political situation," while the actual reason—postwar antisemitic violence—remains unarticulated.[42]

The memory of Biłgoraj's past multiculturalism, rooted in the old Commonwealth, while very visible in the town's public space, cultural life, and development agenda, remains highly ambivalent and problematic. It opens a contact zone where different actors meet and negotiate ways of narrating, celebrating, and coping with the town's multiethnic past. Yet, at the same time, it also allows silences, myths, and taboos to persist within the nostalgic frame of harmonious coexistence, colorful diversity, and good neighborly relations—a vision that occludes the underlying power relations, antagonisms, and violence.

Iŭje, Belarus: Symmetrical Multiculturalism and the Myth of Tolerance

Much like Biłgoraj, Iŭje (*Pol.* Iwje, *Yid.* אײװיע) has a long history as a multi-ethnic urban settlement, dating back to the fifteenth century. Alongside its Jewish population, the town was inhabited by Roman Catholics, Orthodox Christians, Muslim Tatars, and an antitrinitarian Christian community of Arians.[43] Tatars, who are believed to have been brought to the area by Grand Duke Vytautas (*Bel.* Vitaŭt, *Pol.* Witold; r. 1392–1430) in the fourteenth century, have shaped the image of the town to this day. The wooden mosque, built in 1882, was the only operating mosque in the entire Belarusian SSR, and remains a landmark of the town, also known as "the Tatar capital of Belarus." By 1938, Iŭje was over three-quarters Jewish, boasting not only a Jewish Tarbut school but also numerous charity organizations, a fire brigade, a football team, a theater, and an orchestra.[44]

The Jewish community of Iŭje almost ceased to exist on May 12, 1942, the day of a mass execution of over 2,500 Jews, shot by the Germans in the nearby forest of Stonievičy.[45] Smaller-scale executions had taken place earlier—for example, in August 1941, when members of Iŭje's Jewish intelligentsia and highly skilled professionals were murdered.[46] After the mass shooting of May 1942, the remaining Jews (around 1,000 of them) were relocated to a fenced ghetto in the northern part of the town, which existed until December 1942.[47]

Around eighty Iŭje Jews managed to survive the Holocaust, either in hiding or by joining partisan groups in the nearby forests.[48] While some took the opportunity to leave the Soviet Union—where Iŭje was located after the war—by enlisting for a "repatriation" scheme relocating them to Poland, and eventually emigrating to the "West," seven Jewish families remained in Iŭje until the breakup of the Soviet Union, only to emigrate to Israel in the early 1990s.[49] Although Jewish life continued in the town after 1944, the survivors' community had to confront postwar dispossession, obliteration of Jewish sites, the demise of Jewish religious traditions, and lingering antisemitism.[50]

In 2009, two decades after the last Jews of Iŭje had departed, the local authorities inaugurated a museum whose goal was to memorialize the town's multiethnic heritage. With a permanent exhibition titled "Under a Common Sky through the Centuries," the Museum of National Cultures, which is one of a kind in Belarus, presents local history through the prism of the town's ethnic and religious diversity. With three exhibition halls devoted to the Christian, Jewish, and Tatar populations, respectively, the museum both departs from a mainstream historical narrative that has for decades, particularly in western Belarus, eclipsed the presence of ethnic "others," and reinforces it by celebrating the myth of Belarus's exceptional tolerance and framing Iŭje's Jews and Tatars as essentially exogenous groups.[51]

The organization and layout of the Iŭje museum not only fails to represent the actual pre-1942 ratio of different ethnic groups inhabiting the town but also labels the section of the exhibition devoted to Christians as that of the "native population." Jews and Tatars, though they feature in the museum's narrative as "Belarusian Jews" and "Belarusian Tatars," appear as essentially non-native, each enclosed in their own separate exhibition space, not unlike in Biłgoraj, where "Polish" and "Jewish" nuclei of the shtetl reconstruction are also spatially divided. Moreover, despite Iŭje's traumatic modern history, marked by genocide, mass migration, and repopulation, the story of its multidenominational and multiethnic past is told exclusively as one of peaceful coexistence and harmony. This story, in which ethnic or religious difference remains marked and placed outside the realm of "nativeness," serves to define the national features of the Belarusian Christian "core" as open, benevolent, and tolerant.[52] In a 2015 feature about the museum, the local newspaper *Iŭjeŭski Kraj* posited that "Iŭje stands out among [other western Belarusian towns] in respect to its religious and national tolerance." The journalist also put forward a hypothesis that the local mosque never closed down in the Soviet period because "local authorities have always focused their ideological work on national consensus among local people, their friendship, [and] respect for their historical roots," promoting a deep sense of patriotism and of attachment to the "shared skies of the Motherland."[53]

The opening of the refurbished Jewish exhibit in 2019 was, likewise, framed in the spirit of interreligious harmony. Reporting on the ceremony, in which Ryhor Abramovič, chief rabbi of the Religious Association of Progressive Judaism in Belarus, invited a local Catholic priest and the head of the Tatar community to read a portion of the Torah, the local newspaper effused that there was "no other place but Iŭje where one could witness anything like this."[54] By idealizing past interethnic relations in the town and inscribing them onto the plane of religious ecumenism, the official narrative of Iŭje's multiculturalism has molded the town's complex history to fit the master frame of Belarusian nationalism as articulated by the Lukashenka regime, while entirely occluding the question of local implication in Holocaust-related violence and dispossession.

This framing is especially evident in the way Iŭje's Museum of National Cultures has inscribed itself into the dominant narrative about the "Great Patriotic War" as a source of Belarusian national identity. Not only is a quarter of its exhibition space devoted to the Second World War, but the decisive impulse to create the museum came on the heels of the preparations for the sixtieth anniversary of the Soviet victory in 1945. Despite the fact that different grassroots initiatives to create a local museum had existed since the 1980s, and that the local Tatar community, along with Iŭje's Jewish diaspora, had been lobbying for a museum that would represent the town's multicultural past for some time, it was only the context of the major Second World War anniversary that allowed the project to gain traction.[55] But while the period between 1939 and 1944 is no doubt crucial to

Figure 11.2. Monument to the friendship and unity between the confessions of the Iŭje region, Iŭje, 2021. Photo by Ina Sorkina.

understanding the history of Iŭje as a shtetl, the museum does not foreground the Second World War as a traumatic caesura that resulted in the town's losing over half of its population. Instead, it celebrates the "Great Patriotic War" as a moment of heroic resistance to the Nazi occupation, focusing on the trope of victory rather than victimhood.[56] This dominant narrative, originating in the Soviet times, is additionally reinforced by the memorial setting that surrounds the museum, most significantly including large busts of Vladimir Lenin and Mikhail Kalinin at its entrance.

The same celebratory message of ethnic diversity and harmony is conveyed by the memorial to four religions, erected at the center of the town's main square in 2012 (fig. 11.2). Consisting of four white, ten-meter-high concrete stelae representing Catholicism, Orthodox Christianity, Islam, and Judaism, the monument visualizes the town's past multiethnicity with the same symmetry we encounter in the museum. The stelae—adorned with the figures of Pope John Paul II, the Virgin Mary, a crescent moon, and a menorah—each point in the direction of a corresponding temple, ostensibly celebrating diversity, inclusiveness, and "friendship" between religions.[57] By creating an image of perfect geometrical balance, accord, and innocence, this imposing structure sanctions the official, sanitized version of the town's history, thus also generating a troubling aporia. Given that the last Jews of Iŭje emigrated in the 1990s, and the town's Jewish heritage has undergone a systematic obliteration and overwriting, the Jewish stela has a radically different significance from the purely indexical remaining three. While its placement in the ensemble suggests continuity and equivalence, it only obscures the loss of the actual religious community and the power relations between the postwar Christian majority in Iŭje and its Jewish "others."

One space where this contradiction between the town's newly rediscovered multicultural heritage and the long-term systematic practices of urban overwriting is most troubling is the former Jewish cemetery. Remaining relatively intact at the end of the war and still in use in the immediate postwar years, it was demolished in the late 1960s to make way for apartment blocks and a bank, while local inhabitants began using the *matzevahs* to pave their backyards. In 2013, the last remaining undeveloped stretch of green was chosen as the location of an open-air memorial installation. Consisting of fourteen massive boulders placed in a circle, "The Wheel of History" is intended to commemorate momentous events in the town's history. With plaques marking the first mention of Iŭje in historical documents (1444) and the granting of town privileges (1742), the installation also attempts to situate local history within the wider perspective of imperial power shifts. Separate boulders thus mark the periods when Iŭje was part of the Polish-Lithuanian Commonwealth (1569–1795), the Russian Empire (1795–1917), interwar Poland (1921–1939), Nazi-occupied territory (1941–1944), and the Soviet Union, respectively. In this monumental town chronicle, the only indirect mention of Jews is a laconic plaque stating that a synagogue was erected in Iŭje in the eighteenth century.[58]

The monument placed on the site of the Jewish cemetery not only reduces the centuries-long history of Jewish settlement to a vague mention that fails to reflect the immense contribution of Jews to the development of the town but also performs an act of overwriting. By remaining silent about the physical location it occupies, it perpetuates and sanctions urban erasure. In effect, the monument replaces the Soviet homogenizing metanarrative of supranational brotherhood and atheism with a brand of multiculturalism firmly anchored in a myth of national benevolence and tolerance that acknowledges diversity only if it does not threaten the positive collective identity of the ethnic or religious majority.

In reality, pre-1939 Iŭje had not one, but three synagogues; yet, while all three buildings survived the war, none regained its function in the postwar period.[59] Converted into a cultural center, a bakery, and a power station, respectively, none of them could be used as a temple for Iŭje's remaining Jewish community. Local Jews, who learned to cope with the situation with a witty dictum that the synagogues still provided the townsfolk with "the most important things: bread, electricity, and culture,"[60] nonetheless painfully felt the sense of exclusion from their former communal spaces. After the dissolution of the Soviet Union, Jewish material heritage continued to undergo systematic destruction. The former synagogue building, repurposed as a power station, was demolished in the 2010s, just before local notables were to visit the town for the harvest festival, while other formerly Jewish houses, appropriated after the war to host public institutions, were likewise left to decay and eventually torn down.[61] This process of deliberate erasure sometimes took a very undisguised form, as when Hebrew characters from the building of the former Tarbut school, now in the possession of the city, were one day removed.

Iŭje's state-sponsored revival of the myth of multiculturalism coexists, therefore, with the continued neglect, marginalization, and erasure of Jewish material traces in the town, as well as with a historical amnesia about the traumatic aspects of the town's history. Dark chapters, especially those concerning the complicity of the local population in anti-Jewish violence and the appropriation of Jewish property, remain taboo. Accordingly, neither the local museum nor the memorial landscape mentions a pogrom that took place in the town in 1923, or the systematic looting of Jewish houses by locals after the mass execution in May 1942.[62] The site of the mass grave in the Stonievičy forest, where the majority of Iŭje's Jews lost their lives, is well marked.[63] However, the fact that local policemen, both Polish and Belarusian, participated in the execution, remains unmentioned.[64] The site has also suffered from repeated acts of desecration by local residents, who, in the postwar period, dug there in search of gold teeth and other valuables.[65]

Another unaddressed issue that complicates the image of harmonious coexistence of Jews and non-Jews in postwar Iŭje is the question of the mass-scale appropriation of Jewish property in the town. Unlike in Biłgoraj, where local Jewish survivors confronted the situation of expropriation for just a brief period of time, before they left the town and eventually emigrated from Poland, surviving Iŭje Jews who remained in the town had to face the sense of injustice and deprivation for decades to come. The postwar status quo, in which Jewish apartments were appropriated by other families, or sequestered by state authorities for other uses, was, as a rule, nearly impossible to reverse. Majsiej Koščar, who survived the Holocaust in the Soviet interior, thus never returned to his ancestral house, even though he held a post in the Soviet administration. Moreover, having located his family's looted furniture, he was forced to buy it back from the postwar owner.[66]

While this "transfer" of Jewish property and the local community's implication in wartime violence remained taboo in the town throughout the postwar period, the past began to "intrude" into the present, quite paradoxically,
at the very moment when local Jewish life was coming to an end. Just as the
last remaining Jewish families of Iŭje were about to emigrate from Belarus in
the early 1990s, a US choreographer, Tamar Rogoff, accompanied by an international cast of dancers and actors, came to the town to create a series of
performances depicting Iŭje's lost Jewish life. The open-air spectacle, staged in
the forest of Stonievičy, ran for three weeks, gathering thousands of spectators
from across Belarus, Lithuania, Estonia, and Russia, and attracting considerable media attention.[67] Though focused on daily shtetl life rather than wartime
violence, Rogoff's performance, casting local Jews as actors, confronted the
local non-Jewish population with a number of uncomfortable issues, including
dispossession.[68] Scenes of Jews entrusting their non-Jewish neighbors with
valuables for safekeeping or burying silverware in the ground—including a
powerful stage set of silver cutlery sticking out of the forest floor just meters
away from the execution site—brought to the surface thorny questions of
loss, appropriation, and the long-term effects of the mass dispossession that
took place in shtetls like Iŭje. The fact that all the props—prewar furniture,
silverware, and so on—came directly from villages surrounding Iŭje added a
troubling layer of authenticity and tension to these theatrical reenactments.[69]
By linking Jewish material possessions directly to the execution site, Rogoff
powerfully visualized Iŭje's structural implication in the mass-scale redistri-
bution of goods and its direct relation to genocidal violence.

It is very telling that this "intrusion" of the shtetl past into the post-
perestroika present coincided in time with another memorial gesture that
provided a strong symbolic counterpoint. In 1994, Iŭje consecrated its
newest temple, an Orthodox church, in a ceremonial opening celebrated
with considerable pomp, with the patriarch of Moscow and all Rus' Alexy
II leading a service attended by nearly the entire town. Tellingly, the new
church was dedicated to Saint Gabriel of Białystok, a boy allegedly murdered
by Jews for ritual purposes in 1690.[70] The cult of Gabriel of Białystok, who
was canonized by the Orthodox Church in 1820 and serves as the patron
saint of children and youth, regained popularity in the 1980s and 1990s, both
in Belarus and Poland.[71] The choice of this controversial patron saint for
the local church did not pass unnoticed. The remaining Iŭje Jews saw the
decision as "nonsensical" and "offensive," fearing that the cult would fuel the
blood libel myth whose consequences they still remembered experiencing

firsthand.[72] Valiancina Koščar (born in 1941) recollects that the myth of Jews drinking Christian blood still circulated in Iŭje in the 1950s, when she was confronted with such stories by her childhood friends.[73] Indeed, blood libel narratives still reverberated locally well into the 1990s.[74] The local Orthodox priest Viačaslaŭ Paškievič, who unabashedly subscribes to the story of Saint Gabriel as a victim of ritual murder, emphasizes, however, that the church received its patron saint by a joint decision of the clergy and the congregation.[75] Iŭje's history of implication, unearthed by Rogoff's performance, promptly triggered a counterreaction, which took the form of an attempt to frame Jews as *perpetrators* of violence. This symbolic reversal, performed in such an ostentatious way in the public space, reveals how the awareness of implicated subjects of their collective, structural implication in past injustice may cause a discomfort demanding relief.

Local strategies of celebrating the myth of past local multiculturalism thus reveal a deep rift within Iŭje's collective memory, where the desire to acknowledge the town's multiethnic heritage conflicts with the need to retain a positive group identity of the current non-Jewish majority.[76] The only way both goals can be achieved is through a narrative of past harmony and symmetrical multiculturalism that both expunges interethnic conflict or violence and glosses over the power relations that determine the conditions in which the story of Iŭje's exceptional tolerance is constructed and disseminated. Thus, public acts of celebrating Jewish heritage as part of Iŭje's colorful multicultural tapestry, seen as a relic of the Grand Duchy of Lithuania, come at the cost of eliding past and present instances of appropriation, willful destruction, and overwriting, as well as questions of the implication of the town's non-Jewish population in the Holocaust and the economic benefits that it generated. While the local authorities seem to appreciate the presence of Jewish actors in the cocreation of the myth of Belarusian benevolence toward Jews, the script into which their efforts are inscribed reveals the sinews of power behind the façade of religious equality and interethnic brotherhood. Historical injustices suffered by local Jews as well as enduring antisemitic prejudice in the town remain banished beyond the self-congratulatory mainstream narrative that reproduces positions of privilege originating in ethnic violence and displacement.

Brody, Ukraine: In the Shadow of the Jewish Ruins

Known since the late eleventh century, the town of Brody (*Yid.* בראָד) belonged to the Kingdom of Poland from 1340. Along with Ukrainians and

Poles, numerous Jews, Greeks, and Armenians settled in this city in the sixteenth and seventeenth centuries. Brody developed into a significant economic center in the Polish-Lithuanian Commonwealth, strengthening its
important position in trade between western and eastern Europe, and attracting the most enterprising Jewish tradesmen and merchants. It was also
the meeting place of the Council of the Four Lands—the highest institution
of Jewish self-administration in the Kingdom of Poland.[77]

In the first partition of Poland, Brody was annexed by Austria and made a
part of the Crown land of Galicia. Due to its position near the border between
Austria and Russia, the shtetl developed into an important Austrian trade
hub, in which Jews played a central role.[78] This, and the fact that Brody had
the highest proportion of Jews in the entire Habsburg Empire (88 percent in
1820; 68.5 percent in 1900) gave the shtetl a reputation as Austria's or Galicia's
"little Jerusalem."[79]

Brody was occupied by the Soviet Union in September 1939, and then, at
the end of July 1941, by Nazi Germany, with parts of the Ukrainian population greeting the German occupiers as "liberators" from Bolshevism.[80] Some
local inhabitants were willing to take part in the National Socialist persecution and annihilation of the Jewish population—for example, as informers
and ghetto guards.[81] Only 150 to 250 of Brody's 9,000 to 10,000 Jews survived
the Holocaust.[82] The heterogeneous, Jewish-dominated shtetl was replaced
by a homogeneous Ukrainian-Soviet provincial city, whose multiethnic and
multiconfessional legacy from Polish-Lithuanian and Austrian times was
rather scorned.

The tragedy of the Jews in Brody played no role in the Soviet culture of
memory after the war: no Holocaust monument was raised in the city until
1994.[83] Information on the participation of locals in Nazi atrocities was mostly
suppressed in the Soviet era, and even after 1991 it is rarely discussed in Brody.
More widespread is the apologetic narrative constructed by Ukrainian emigrants who left Brody for the West after the war that—although the Jews had
supposedly "exploited," "harassed," and "mistreated" the Ukrainian population of Brody in Poland-Lithuania, in Austrian Galicia, and above all during
the short Soviet wartime intermezzo (1939–1941)—numerous Ukrainians
had sheltered and rescued Jews at great risk to their own lives. At the same
time, other Jews—for example, the Jewish Ghetto Police—had denounced
their coreligionists to the Germans. According to this narrative, "ungrateful"
Holocaust survivors were slandering their rescuers as "antisemites" and "col-
laborators" instead of acknowledging the Ukrainians for their noble deeds.[84]

Figure 11.3. The Great Synagogue of Brody, 2021. Photo by Serhii Khomiak, Wikimedia, CC BY-SA 4.0.

In February 1946, a Holocaust survivor from Brody described the situation of the city in a letter to the Israeli literary critic and politician Dov Sadan (1902–1989), who had been born in Brody: "The city of Brody is half in ruins and it is completely deserted. . . . Only the walls of the old synagogue are standing in their splendor. The synagogue looks like the Colosseum from afar. Of the Jews of Brody, only enough for a *minyan* have survived."[85] Built in the 1740s, Brody's richly furnished fortress synagogue reflected the affluence and enhanced self-image of the town's Jewish community.[86] Severely damaged in both world wars, it now fell victim to Soviet antireligious and antisemitic policies.[87]

In the following decades, the Great Synagogue (fig. 11.3) remained Brody's ruined "Colosseum." With only a handful of Jews left in Brody after the war, reusing the synagogue as a house of worship was off the table. However, in the early 1960s, the building was officially recognized as a "monument of architecture," renovated, and used as a storage space and cafeteria. Adventurous locals regarded it as a mysterious place where Jews might have buried their gold and valuables before the German attack on the Soviet Union.[88] The deterioration of the synagogue continued in the meantime, with the local authorities remaining passive and allowing its ongoing decay.

In the 1990s and 2000s, this once major landmark withered into a dump site and public toilet. In 2006, the building's roof collapsed, and the final demise of the Great Synagogue seemed inevitable.[89] However, a growing influx of Western tourists interested in, among other things, the city's Jewish legacy,[90] and the danger of the synagogue's complete destruction, gradually led to a rethink on the part of the town's residents. The Ukrainian "Revolution of Dignity" (Euromaidan, 2013–2014), the early stages of the Russian war against Ukraine (from 2014), and the country's generally pro-Western course spurred an intense interest—especially in the formerly Polish and Austrian Eastern Galicia—in the region's multiethnic and multiconfessional traditions, which were increasingly perceived as "European." The Ukrainian nationalist narrative, widespread in western Ukraine before the "Revolution of Dignity," that the Polish and Jewish cultural legacy was "not Ukrainian" and thus alien, gradually began to give way to a Ukrainian-European narrative that regarded the region's Jewish and Polish history as part of Ukrainian history.[91] The Russian invasion of Ukraine in 2022 will doubtless present another turning point for the reception, and also sheer physical continuity, of Jewish heritage in the war-affected territories, but its concrete impact, at the time of writing, is impossible to predict.

In the years leading up to the 2022 war, the ethnic and religious diversity that Brody had lost in the Second World War—encapsulated in the image of "Galicia's Jerusalem"—was clearly becoming more salient. However, the Polish-Lithuanian period of the city's history, which was so central to the development of Brody's Jewish community, has played only a marginal role in the ongoing memory work, remaining in the shadow of the Austrian epoch, often considered the golden age of Brody.[92] The journalist and author Joseph Roth (1894–1939), who spent his childhood and youth in Brody, and who remains one of the city's most famous Jewish residents, embodies this later period particularly well.[93]

Roth, who left the city of his birth in 1913, has returned to Brody more than a century later as a Jewish-Austrian legend. Recently rediscovered as Brody's "forgotten son," Roth has inspired a series of cultural events intended to increase the attractiveness of Brody as a tourist destination.[94] The museum of local history, which also offers sightseeing tours devoted to the city's Jewish heritage, has even organized a special Joseph Roth tour.[95] In 2019, on the author's 125th birthday and the 80th anniversary of his death, a monument to

Roth was unveiled in Brody.[96] In August of the same year, the international LvivMozArt festival, sponsored mostly by Austrian donors, staged a commemorative concert against the backdrop of the Great Synagogue. Resonating widely in both Ukraine and Austria, the performance drew attention to the desolate condition of the building.[97]

In fact, the impetus to restore the Brody synagogue had begun a few years earlier. A survey conducted by the local nongovernmental organization Kray (Homeland) in 2016 showed that many city residents, especially young people brought up after the collapse of the Soviet Union, regarded the Great Synagogue as an important site and favored its reconstruction.[98] The question of who should defray the substantial associated costs was, however, not addressed in the survey. The standpoint voiced in 2017 by Volodymyr Bulyshyn, the director of Brody's local television station, that the Ukrainian state and the local authorities should restore the Great Synagogue seems not to have found much support in Brody.[99] More widespread in the city was the idea that "affluent Jews" (for example, Ukrainian oligarchs of Jewish descent) or foreign sponsors should take care of the former house of worship, rather than the Ukrainian state, still afflicted by the lasting economic crisis and the war against Russia.[100]

Yet the most vocal advocate of the restoration of the Brody synagogue has been the local activist and professional restorer Volodymyr Kovalchuk, who has described the reconstruction of the temple as his life's mission.[101] In the late 2010s, he began renovation work on the grounds of the synagogue on his own initiative. Both the local and national Ukrainian press reported on his efforts, characterizing him as a "crazy man," "oddball," "visionary," and even as the "Don Quixote of Brody."[102] Kovalchuk was motivated to assume responsibility for the synagogue by what he described as a sense of embarrassment that all foreign guests to Brody could see of the beautiful Great Synagogue was a deteriorated ruin.[103] In Kovalchuk's view, media reports like that of a Swiss television station referring to "a huge ruin in the middle of . . . Joseph Roth's hometown of Brody" damaged the city's reputation.[104]

The motif of collective embarrassment at the Jewish ruin constituting an architectural "blemish" within the townscape could also be read figuratively. The dramatic, decaying structure in the town's center is perhaps the most literal manifestation of the "intrusion" of the past into the present, and a poignant reminder of Brody's unarticulated history of implication. An imposing historic building collapsing in full view of local inhabitants calls for action both in the physical and moral dimensions. As a synecdoche of

Jewish presence, and a visual metaphor of destruction, the ruin also provides material testimony to decades of neglect, desecration, and amnesia regarding the Jewish past.

The complexity of implication that the synagogue ruin brings to light is perhaps best articulated in the chief revivalist's personal Jewish-Ukrainian family history. Kovalchuk's mother Yenta Holdshteyn was born to a well-to-do Jewish family who, wishing to save her from Nazi atrocities, arranged for their Ukrainian domestic worker to adopt her. Under the assumed Ukrainian identity, of Iadviha Kovalchuk, Yenta thus managed to survive the Holocaust as a forced laborer in Hamburg, and returned to Brody in the late 1940s.[105] Rothberg's theory—which stipulates the "coexistence of different relations to past . . . injustices" within a single individual, who can simultaneously occupy the position of "implicated subject" and victim (or perpetrator)—suggests that the categories of perpetrators, victims, and implicated subjects are not rigid "ontological identities," but rather dynamic positions that individuals inhabit in respect to different histories.[106] Volodymyr Kovalchuk's perspective of "complex implication" points both to the region's tangled history of colonization, occupation, and ethnic violence, and to the ambivalent nature of Jewish heritage revival projects in this part of Europe, which usually escape easy labels of self-affirmation, expiation, or exploitation.

Over the past few years, Kovalchuk, assisted by a crew of volunteers, has cleared trees from the synagogue grounds, renovated the doors, and collected trash and dirt from the site. His ongoing efforts, supported by donations from small companies and private persons from Ukraine and Israel, have elicited a range of different responses in the town. While the municipal administration of Brody has supported Kovalchuk by providing trucks to remove the trash, others have spread rumors that the restoration work is only a front for a search for buried Jewish treasures.[107]

While the first grassroots efforts to tap into the narrative of Brody as the "Galician Jerusalem" have begun to generate some interest in the town's Jewish past as a potential tourist attraction, Brody's Jewish heritage revival has a long way to go. While the still absent reckoning with Ukrainian complicity in the Holocaust presents one major obstacle on the way to embracing the Jewish past of the town as part of its history, the heritage of foreign rule adds another layer of complexity.[108] While the period of Austrian rule in Brody played an increasingly important role in the local politics of memory, as an epoch that legitimizes western Ukraine's sense of belonging to the European, or even western European, multicultural, cosmopolitan "civilization," the

Polish-Lithuanian era—not least because of Ukraine's subordinate position in the Commonwealth—has received markedly less attention.

Thus, the Habsburg monarchy, which offered conditions conducive to the rise of Ukrainian nationalism, enjoys the image of a progressive, multi-ethnic, and tolerant polity.[109] In contrast, the Polish-Lithuanian Commonwealth, also perceived through the prism of an interwar Polish rule marked by repressive anti-Ukrainian policies, appears as a more negatively charged period. Partly for this reason, the invocation of the Austrian-Jewish legacy, embodied in particular in the person of Joseph Roth, seems to have enjoyed more popularity among the Ukrainian public than Jewish material heritage, like the Great Synagogue, which dates back to the time of the Polish-Lithuanian Commonwealth and indirectly connotes the Polish yoke.

Myths of Multiculturalism

The working hypothesis informing this chapter is that memory projects showcasing Jewish heritage as a synecdoche of the past multiculturalism of the Polish-Belarusian-Ukrainian borderlands can be conceived of as a response to the "intrusion of the past into the present." In the former shtetls we have investigated, the radical demographic changes and the conditions of structural implication in past interethnic violence have created a situation in which the material heritage of the "other" both fell entirely under the control of the new ethnic majority and remained a "disinherited heritage,"[110] potentially causing dissonance and discomfort to its current "heirs." The unsettling presence of Jewish ruins, resurfacing human remains, collapsing cellars, walled-in objects, and recycled tombstones has thus generated a recent spate of revivalist responses that have often used the topos of multiculturalism both to reproduce and challenge the position of privilege that directly resulted from the "disappearance" of the Jewish majority.

One way in which such projects have helped preserve the position of privilege is by framing the heritage of the "other" as an economic asset for the whole community. The discourses that frame the synagogue in Brody or Bilgoraj's reconstructed shtetl as tourist magnets to stimulate local economies perpetuate the expectation that Jewish material heritage is a resource that the local non-Jewish population can tap into at will and benefit from. Paradoxically, this narrative persists despite the fact that many revivalist enterprises not only generate no financial profit whatsoever but also rely on state subsidies, private donations, and the work of volunteers.

Another way in which the revival of past multiculturalism relates to the "regimes of domination" is the self-protecting function of the myths it generates. The reference to the more distant and idyllic "happy days" of the Polish-Lithuanian Commonwealth, the Grand Duchy of Lithuania, or the Austro-Hungarian Empire thus enables an occlusion of the more recent and painful past marked by interethnic violence. Moreover, the topoi of tolerance, peaceful coexistence, and harmony that constitute this myth help to white-wash the local communities by suggesting that the successor states inherited the principles and values associated, in each respective national imaginary, with the three "historical nations."[111] Focusing on good neighborly relations, as in Iŭje, or showcasing local success stories, such as the literary careers of Joseph Roth or Isaac Bashevis Singer in Brody and Biłgoraj, respectively, the narrative of cultural diversity helps bypass the less harmonious episodes in the local interethnic relations, including antisemitism, collaboration, and expropriation.

While the myth of past multiculturalism doubtless contains an escapist potential, revivalist projects propelled by it can also function as a vehicle for raising awareness about past injustices, or even a means of offering redress. For the founder of the Biłgoraj shtetl reconstruction, Tadeusz Kuźmiński, the act of material reconstruction carried an ethical dimension of "saving" or bringing back to life destroyed gems of Jewish wooden architecture. By including in his design the reconstruction of a local Orthodox church burned down by Polish authorities, Kuźmiński also demonstrated how showcasing multiculturalism does not have to exclude painful chapters from the past, but can both bring them to public attention and offer a mode of recompense.

While the Biłgoraj activists have framed their revivalist involvement as a response to a sense of moral responsibility and a vehicle for "cleansing the nation" and counteracting antisemitism, the actual effectiveness of "mul-ticulturalism light," or popular representations of pre-Holocaust cultural diversity, surely cannot be taken for granted. Whether culture festivals or architectonic reconstructions can move the interested audience to critically reexamine the historical wrongdoing of members of their own group remains an open question. But the fact that such an agenda is even being formulated might point to a change in the perception of Jewish/non-Jewish relations in Poland, where a critical investigation of the implication of members of the national community in anti-Jewish violence has been going on for at least two decades, leaving a mark not only on historiography but also on the collective imagination.[112] While such a reckoning seems absent in the Ukrainian and

Belarusian cases at hand, sweeping generalizations about the introspective and educational agenda of such revivalist projects, or lack thereof, cannot really be made at this point.

What does become apparent from this comparative study, however, is the extent to which local efforts to revive the myth of multiculturalism in Poland, Ukraine, and Belarus are ultimately trapped in national historical narratives and cultures of memory. While for western Ukraine, the legacy of the Habsburg period carries more weight and political significance than the memory of the Polish-Lithuanian Commonwealth, for Belarus's pro-democracy movement—and, up to 2020, official organs as well—the myth of multiculturalism has been linked directly to visions of the Grand Duchy of Lithuania as a predecessor of the Belarusian nation-state and a "historical nation" legitimating the country's aspirations to the European sphere of influence. Since the brutal clampdown on the 2020 protests in Belarus, however, the myth of the Grand Duchy of Lithuania as the golden age of Belarusian statehood has waned from the official narratives crafted by the Lukashenka regime, giving way to the Soviet-era topos of eternal friendship with Russia. Nevertheless, ideas of the Grand Duchy continue to inspire the pro-democracy protest movement.

Reviving the myth of multiculturalism in former shtetls has complex ethical implications for societies that are affected—like Poland, Belarus, and Ukraine—by past ethnic violence. When present-day "implicated subjects" reconstruct, curate, and perform Jewish heritage, they effectively reassert the conditions of power and privilege created by the Holocaust. In such cases, it is the hegemonic majority, often backed by state institutions, that makes decisions about how to represent the "others" and narrate their history in the public space. On the other hand, by creating a link between present-day communities and past ethnic or religious diversity, such projects, perhaps even unintentionally, help to establish the causal connection between the status quo—postwar ethnic homogeneity, absence, destruction, and neglect of multicultural heritage—and the implication of local populations in the historical injustices that have led to it. In some cases, they even offer means of redress, or spaces of critical reflection and dialogue. The legacy of the Commonwealth and its ethnic diversity, whether directly invoked and romanticized, or elided and critically challenged, thus remains fraught with contradictory interpretations for its successor nation-states, providing narratives that can both soothe and unsettle their contemporary inhabitants.

12

A New Multiculturalism in Poland

Memory of the Past and Migration from Ukraine

Ewa Nowicka

Translated by Annamaria Orla-Bukowska

At least it's becoming more colorful in the world. Cultures are blending—
maybe it'll help someone open up toward others.

—Interview, sixty-year-old woman, 2019

In academic and media discussions in Poland, much recent attention has been devoted to the phenomenon of "multiculturalism."[1] Also known as "cultural pluralism," multiculturalism shapes the conditions for an intense and often productive exchange of diverse experiences, views, and values.[2] After years of relative homogeneity, new waves of migration—above all, from Ukraine—are making Poland more culturally diverse today. Yet, as a look back at the premodern Polish-Lithuanian Commonwealth evidences, such diversity is not new in the country's history. More recently, the interwar Polish Republic (1918–1939) was also a multicultural state—before genocide, postwar deportations, and border changes established a more monolithic society after 1945. The multiculturalism of the past encompassed both ethnic and nonethnic categories, including social class and urban/rural divides. Its roots could be found in (proto-)national differences, or in historical, regional, and local patterns.[3] The contemporary type of cultural pluralism, however, is primarily the result of intensive processes of migration, taking place in recent decades in Poland, and across Europe.[4]

The concept of multiculturalism can be understood on two levels. The first focuses on objective categories and descriptions of existing cultural diversity in a society of various nationalities, ethnicities, regionalisms, and other cultural identities. The second encompasses axiological or normative categories accompanying an assessment of that diversity.[5] This means the establishment of rules to shape social behaviors within a framework that sets acceptable boundaries and spheres for cultural differences—some of which may even become attractive or desirable. Attitudes and practices conducive to the maintenance of this normative multiculturalism include the "folklorization" of difference and a sense of the philosophical attractiveness of difference, whereby dissimilarity becomes a source of pleasure or fascination.[6] These presentations are sometimes associated with "boutique," "festive," or "promotional" forms of multiculturalism, often linked with cosmopolitanization and the global availability of products from a wide spectrum of cultures.[7]

Both government policy and general systems of social values play an essential role in the building of a culturally diverse society. Legislatures must update and adapt legal regulations in order to reflect changes in the cultural mix of today's societies.[8] Governments must shape policies toward cultural pluralism that facilitate and encourage communities to cultivate and develop their own identity, culture, language, and historical consciousness. In this sense, multiculturalism means that coexisting, culturally different communities must be ready to interact and to accept diversity. Multiculturalism will therefore be understood here as the peaceful coexistence of culturally distinct groups within a single country—without the necessity of a minority's full assimilation into the majority. The crux of cultural pluralism lies in an integration of different cultures that simultaneously preserves their diversity, thus leading to the creation of a new, holistic society. From this perspective, the assimilation or acculturation of one group into another fundamentally contradicts the idea of multiculturalism.

Despite the relative simplicity of cultural pluralism as a theoretical principle, it does present significant challenges in practice.[9] Alongside the benefits mentioned above, the coexistence of diverse groups can also be a source of social conflict. This was often the case in the multiethnic, multilingual, and multinational Polish-Lithuanian Commonwealth. Indeed, Poland's particular historical experience with various forms of multiculturalism naturally provokes questions as to how and to what degree this experience affects perceptions of the current wave of migration to the country—especially from Ukraine, some of whose territory once formed part of the Commonwealth. These considerations lead us to some of the questions to be addressed in this chapter. Is there a popular memory in contemporary Poland of the cultural diversity of the Polish-Lithuanian Commonwealth, or of the interwar Polish Republic? If so, can such a memory act as a factor contributing to the development of a multicultural Polish society in the twenty-first century? If not, then what other cornerstones can there be for such a process of development?

In trying to answer these questions, the focus will not be on the autochthonous, culturally different groups that have been settled for generations in Poland and that are well integrated with Polish society.[10] Instead, I will be looking among the newly arrived for the leaven of a postmodern cultural diversity—migratory, unrooted, and constructing itself on the basis of wholly different circumstances.

One vital condition for a positive, constructive course in a nascent, contemporary cultural pluralism is the presence of open and tolerant attitudes, rooted axiologically and ideologically in the host society with regard to newcomers. Another prerequisite is an adaptive, acculturative approach among immigrants—that is, their assent to key norms of the host society. For at least thirty years, acceptance of cultural diversity under these conditions has become an ideological norm in Poland, while the failure to support social inclusiveness—both as a political declaration and as an institutional instrument—is subject to condemnation. Yet in mass media and colloquial discourse, Polish society is often perceived as hermetic and mistrustful of all forms of difference. Nevertheless, my own research, and that of other sociologists, delivers a contrasting diagnosis: a readiness to accept immigrants declared by all age cohorts.[11]

Relying primarily on field research data—in-depth interviews with Poles and Ukrainian migrants in Poland—this chapter argues that present-day Poland is developing into a kind of multicultural society. Nevertheless, for the majority of "ordinary" Poles living in an era of migration-based diversity, the extent to which attitudes to the current cultural pluralism draw inspiration from history—including the Polish-Lithuanian Commonwealth's mostly autochthonous diversity—is very limited. Despite historical overtones, the Ukrainians who are entering en masse and often settling down permanently in Poland are building their integrational plans economically and practically, not on memories of the political community of yore. Likewise, their recognition and acceptance by the Poles is gauged more rationally and reflectively.[12]

This chapter focuses on the external and internal factors shaping a new multiculturalism in Poland today.

Contemporary Multiculturalism in Poland

The Republic of Poland legally recognizes thirteen national minorities (referring to groups possessing their "own" nation-state elsewhere), including Lithuanians, Belarusians, Germans, Slovakians, Czechs, Russians, Armenians, and Ukrainians. Recognized ethnic, stateless minorities include Lemkos (Carpatho-Rusyns), Romani groups, Tatars, and Karaites, while Kashubians are the single recognized regional minority. Jews are recognized as both a religious and national minority. Since 2011, the national census permits the declaration of one or two identities; hence, among the members of cultural minorities (officially recognized or not) are Polish citizens who declare a non-Polish national, ethnic, or regional identity.[13]

Minorities are thus defined as culturally distinct from the majority, but autochthonous to Polish lands for at least a hundred years (though most have lived here for much longer). Also significant is that among these officially recognized minorities are groups settled on historically native territories (e.g., Germans, Czechs, Slovaks, Ukrainians, Belarusians, Lithuanians, and Lemkos) as well as groups dispersed more widely across Poland (e.g., Armenians, Jews, and Romani people). These groups have acquainted Polish society with a cultural diversity that can be described as traditional and historically rooted. Each of these recognized national or ethnic minorities is institutionally supported by the Polish state. Among other things, education in the mother tongue, cultural centers, and festivals are all financed from the national budget from funds earmarked for the preservation of the cultural distinctiveness of these minorities. For example, the Warmia-Masuria region in northeastern Poland has a local Commission for National and Ethnic Minority Affairs (Komisja Mniejszości Narodowych i Etnicznych), mostly organized by resident Ukrainians.

Yet Poland's increasing diversity in recent years has not primarily been driven by these autochthonous communities, but rather by new arrivals. At the beginning of 2020, the Central Statistical Office of Poland (Główny Urząd Statystyczny, GUS) conducted its first attempt at estimating the number of foreigners in Poland on the basis of data in administrative registries. The sum total was 2,106,101 people, among whom a clear majority (64.2 percent) were citizens of Ukraine: 1,351,418. Other groups of note were citizens of Belarus (105,404), Germany (77,073), Moldova (37,338), the Russian Federation (37,030), India (33,107), Georgia (27,917), Vietnam (27,386), Turkey (25,049), China (23,838), and assorted other countries (360,541).[14] According to the Public Opinion Research Center (Centrum Badania Opinii Społecznej, CBOS), "an analysis of migration trends indicates that Poland is transforming from a typically emigration country to an emigration-immigration one."[15]

The modern type of multiculturalism is linked to intensive immigration, primarily treated as a supplementary source of labor, as observed across the European continent over the past few decades. The Polish regions in which this phenomenon has begun to develop are, above all, the urban and metro-politan "islands," which offer some forms of supra-cultural community and a sense of belonging.[16] In these locations, from the beginning of the twenty-first century, growing recognition and appreciation of minority groups has led to the organization of various festivals and other events, such as Warsaw's Days of Diversity (Warszawskie Dni Różnorodności), which have enjoyed a high level of interest among local residents. In the Polish case, cultural di-versity has generally not led to the creation of ethnic enclaves composed of a self-isolating group—with the partial exception of Vietnamese and Chinese communities.

In conjunction with these processes, questions have arisen in Poland about the place of immigrants in general society and the nature of their social and cultural rights.[17] An increasing acceptance of the "otherness" rep-resented by migrants in Poland—an axiologically profound transformation of attitudes—does not mean an equal social position for Poles and immi-grants. More broadly, the 2015 migration crisis, which shook Europe and provoked political conflicts within the European Union, destabilized what had appeared to be ideological givens. An awareness of hierarchical relations between immigrants and European citizens surfaced. European countries demanded linguistic, behavioral, and (to some degree) axiological adaptation to the host society. This also affected Polish society to some degree.[18] Di-rectly after 2015, an evident mood swing was registered against migrants and refugees—yet approval quickly rose again to reach 2013 levels. The tremor affected Poland less, due to the much lower numbers of immigrants in the country compared to western European states.

A significant, usually permanent, and negative condition for cultural mi-nority communities is the divide that frequently opens up between them and the sociopolitical majority, thus underlining their difference. Accordingly, a key dimension affecting the general level of integration in a society is the degree of cultural difference between the majority and specific minorities within it. It is generally assumed that the closer two cultures are, the easier and quicker the adaptation of one to the other, though the relatively successful example of the Vietnamese in Poland attests to other mechanisms at work besides the cultural.[19] Every society has political, legal, customary, or axiological factors that—when encroached upon by a culturally different collective—may impede or even preclude integration. Consequently, it is useful to investigate and identify those elements that have the opposite effect. What values, for instance, are so crucial and meaningful within the Polish context that adaptation to them becomes a factor facilitating acceptance in spite of any other differences? These axiological specificities delineate multiculturalism's boundaries, but also provide its best building materials.

Over three decades ago, Jerzy Smolicz—a scholar working on integration processes encompassing a wide variety of ethnic groups in Australia's immigrant society—noticed a practical necessity: all culturally distinct groups must to a certain extent accept and share values that are, de facto, built upon the axiology of the Anglo-Saxon (or, more broadly, European) majority.[20] In Australia, the earliest immigrants considered themselves practically "native," treating later immigrants as minorities. Under such circumstances, the majority can exploit its more advantageous position, demanding that diverse minorities abandon their culture, forcing assimilation, and countering attempts to create a truly multicultural society. Nevertheless, it should be noted that this assimilation need not involve all aspects of a culture or all rules of social coexistence, but rather those that the dominant group perceives as the crucial underpinnings of its value system.

In the present case study, it is worth closely investigating the most important elements of the Polish system of values, as reflected in sociological research.[21] Among the positive statements that Poles most frequently make about immigrants in this research, the following characteristics are frequently lauded:

A strong work ethic and economic independence; self-sufficiency in Polish economic and legal institutions; diligence, energy, or "pulling oneself up by one's own bootstraps";

Competency in peaceful coexistence with the social milieu, a friendly disposition, and readiness to help; and

Cultural similarities (linguistic, religious, historical, etc.), which ensure mutual understanding.

On the one hand, all of the above-listed qualities reveal the limits of Poland's multiculturalism and acceptance of immigrants. On the other, they shine a light on the opportunities for integration into Polish society—and pathways toward this integration—for individuals and communities of diverse nationalities and ethnicities. These parameters are directly relevant to the recent integration of large numbers of Ukrainian immigrants—a culturally familiar group that once lived with Poles in a single political state. But is the cultural pluralism of the past relevant to the emerging multicultural reality of the present?

Rekindling the Historical, or Creating a Contemporary Multiculturalism

Although many institutions, intellectuals, and activists in its successor states treasure the heritage of the Polish-Lithuanian Commonwealth, sociological scrutiny indicates that this memory is significantly thinner in mass consciousness in Poland.[22] In truth, it carries greater weight within certain subpopulations, such as the inhabitants of present-day border regions or among descendants of Poles who once lived on the territory of today's Ukraine, Belarus, and Lithuania before the Second World War. But even where recollections of past pluralism still exist—above all, from the interwar period—this collective memory is insufficient to underpin the creation of a culturally diverse society characterized by mutual acceptance and understanding today.

In fact, the idea of a common past is insupportable for various nationalities due to negative memories they associate with the pluralism of both the multicultural Commonwealth and the interwar Polish state. For this reason, rejection is more common than any desire to return to the previous relationships and communities, seen as more political than cultural. Despite prevailing cultural similarities, non-Polish groups tend to remember the Commonwealth period as a time of Polish domination.[23] Moreover, the interwar period of the twentieth century plays an important role in memory as a time of interethnic conflict in the eastern provinces of the Polish state, where social differences between nationalities provoked discrimination and strife.

Not only the extreme nationalist right, but the vast majority of Polish society—along with most mainstream politicians—have shown little interest in appealing to the multicultural past as a foundation stone for contemporary society. It should also be noted that the forms of religious and cultural tolerance found in the Commonwealth differ significantly from those of contemporary European societies. For example, the Commonwealth's ethnic groups were clearly delineated by legal and social boundaries—divisions unthinkable in a modern democracy.[24]

The historical events of the mid-twentieth century transformed not only the political world. The shifting of Poland's borders westward as a consequence of the Second World War involved the relocation of many thousands of citizens. The repatriation (or arguably impatriation) of the Polish population that had inhabited the prewar eastern provinces (the so-called Kresy Wschodnie, or Eastern Borderlands) led to the creation of a new (and currently vanishing) multiculturalism in the so-called Recovered Lands (Ziemie Odzyskane), previously part of Germany. The new western provinces were settled by Poles not only from areas incorporated into Soviet Belarus, Ukraine, and Lithuania but also from central Poland, especially from the devastated capital. Poles from distant and distinct regions of interwar Poland were now in close cultural contact. Added to the mix were immigrants forcibly resettled from various other countries (e.g., Greek refugees from the 1946–1949 civil war) as well as Polish repatriates from Bosnia or Bukovina. The old, ethnically diverse structures were irrevocably plowed over, leading to a fundamentally reconstructed social consciousness. The historical vision of diversity dissipated, and its popular memory faded.

In the 1990s, new independent states were established on Poland's eastern border—Lithuania, Belarus, and Ukraine—further altering collective memories. On the one hand, a cornerstone of Polish foreign policy has been the maintenance of alliances with these border states, conventionally assigned the role of a buffer zone between Poland and Russia. On the other hand, this policy has been met with various hurdles in practice, including divergent interpretations of historical events and historical figures. In the case of Polish-Ukrainian relations, the cultural, economic, and political dominance of Poles in western Ukraine during the period of the interwar Polish Republic remains a difficult memory for Ukrainians. Furthermore, Polish discourse places a premium on the painful memory of the 1943–1944 massacres of Poles in Volhynia and Eastern Galicia by nationalists from the Ukrainian Insurgent Army (Ukrainska Povstanska Armiia, UPA) as well as other clashes that continued until as late as 1947. The recollection of such negative aspects of historical relations between Poles and Ukrainians are more inclined to discourage than to foster the establishment of positive patterns for a contemporary multicultural society.

It is symptomatic that among the numerous in-depth interviews I conducted with Poles from various social categories, only one respondent viewed the distant past as an appropriate foundation on which to build a positive, stable, and collaborative Polish-Ukrainian relationship today. This respondent was primarily motivated by political reasons: he wanted the grudges and grievances that have been "swept under the carpet" between Poles and Ukrainians to finally see the light of day. He further argued that such a vision could be a practical long-term solution for several nations: "We have to somehow muddle through our feuds. The only hope for both our nations [Poland and Ukraine] is that we come to an agreement and create our own, common state.... The only thing that can be done, in my opinion, is a rather exotic-sounding idea of re-creating the Great Commonwealth—a republic of the nations that lived under its rule."[25]

Even this optimistic enthusiast described his notion as "exotic." We might add that it is totally misaligned with twenty-first-century political conditions. The community of the Commonwealth was rooted in the domination of a specific part of society—something that would be unacceptable for the average Pole today, not to mention for members of other nations who have now been living in sovereign states for decades. The new multiculturalism in Poland is emerging not as a result of grand political visions, but rather as a consequence of the physical mobility of individual people—mostly for economic reasons, though increasingly for political ones as well. The resulting cultural diversity has little in common with that found in the Commonwealth.[26] The latter comprised an ethnic and regional cultural pluralism that was, in general, rooted territorially or in social class.[27] The rising diversity in contemporary Poland is thus not a return to past patterns, but the result of new social processes tied to migration.

In the remainder of this chapter—fundamentally written before the Russian war against Ukraine—I examine the development of a multicultural society in Poland through the prism of the large-scale immigration from Ukraine that had made its mark even before the arrival of two to four million displaced people after February 24, 2022. The focus will be on mutual perceptions and processes of integration to which history is not irrelevant. Indeed, it is no coincidence that Poland's largest immigrant group is territorially and culturally close and has been in firsthand contact with Poles for centuries. Yet my research shows that history and memory are more often burdens to be cast off than resources for the construction of a Polish-Ukrainian multicultural society today.

Methods and Empirical Sources

In my analyses of the development of modern multiculturalism in Poland, I draw on a number of sources, primarily including: (1) empirical data from my own qualitative and quantitative research (interviews conducted with various societal cohorts as well as surveys); (2) available quantitative statistical data (GUS and CBOS); and (3) the findings of other scholars (mainly based in Poland). The core source is a series of qualitative studies based on face-to-face, in-depth interviews. Also significant are nationwide, quantitative surveys regarding attitudes of selected segments of Polish society about immigration to Poland. Most pertinent to the text at hand is a study conducted by my own research team on attitudes toward Ukrainian immigrants to Poland.

Between 2014 and 2016, I conducted a few qualitative studies on the subject of Polish-Ukrainian relations, looking into specific subgroups of Poles. This entailed interviews with a group of Polish citizens who were in some way connected with Ukraine: either descendants of families who had lived in the eastern regions of the interwar Polish Republic before 1945, on what is today Ukrainian territory, or students of Ukrainian philology at the University of Warsaw. The initial research coincided with a politically stormy time in Ukraine (Euromaidan, the annexation of Crimea, and the beginning of the war in Donbas), but also a time of an evident warming in Polish-Ukrainian relations. My subsequent research on Polish attitudes toward migration and migrants took place in 2018 and 2019: 59 individual interviews were conducted with members of an older generation (aged fifty-nine to eighty) and a younger generation (aged twenty-two to thirty), all with higher education and residency in Warsaw. During both research projects, the specific topic of immigrants from Ukraine often surfaced spontaneously.

Here we should note a certain psychological aspect that comes into play when studying a social group as distinct as people enrolled in tertiary education or degree-holding graduates, even if they come from different age categories. Highly educated people manifest a higher internalization of certain norms, such as tolerance and anti-xenophobia. They are more conscious of existing social norms and attitudes that are recognized as important or commendable. Therefore, expressions indicating inclusiveness, broad-mindedness, and approbation of cultural difference and diversity can be treated not only as sincere communication of an underlying attitude but also as a desire to demonstrate such attitudes in the unique self-presentation of a face-to-face interview. Such behavior, of course, delivers valuable information about the desired or obligatory norms in a society.

In seeking answers to questions about the cornerstones of multicultural-ism in Poland today, analysis must be conducted from two complementary perspectives: (1) general research into the attitudes and values of Polish so-ciety; and (2) analysis of the attitudes and aims of immigrants—in this case, Ukrainians—in their specific migration circumstances.

Ukrainian Immigrants in Poland

Before the 2022 influx of Ukrainian war refugees, Ukrainians already consti-tuted more than half of all foreign nationals living in Poland. As mentioned earlier, in 2020 they comprised over 60 percent of the noncitizen population in the country.[28] Their numbers had been systematically rising since the be-ginning of the twenty-first century, not decreasing significantly during the COVID-19 pandemic, and spiking dramatically after the Russian invasions of both 2014 and 2022. Their presence is noticeable and commonplace, dis-tinguished from others mostly due to their native language or their accent in Polish. Many individuals work in sales, banking, construction, and home care, while others are students.[29] Ukrainians are particularly numerous in certain private tertiary education institutions, sometimes even constituting the majority of the student population.

The factors behind the pre-2022 wave of Ukrainian immigrants to Poland were primarily economic in the first instance. Even the small group of young men who came to Poland as a way to avoid military service (after Russia's an-nexation of Crimea in 2014) often found employment, and generally returned home after a while. Poland and Ukraine have vastly different standards of living, as evidenced by GDP comparisons, so emigration to Poland and oth-er European countries is, for many, an escape from fundamental economic challenges and a striving toward a better life. As a consequence, Ukraine had lost about seven million citizens by 2017.[30] According to research done in Ukraine in 2016, 65 percent of those asked wanted to leave their country permanently.[31] Chain migration has also been a factor: one immigrant draws others to follow the same path by establishing optimal routes of action.

Poland also attracts Ukrainians based on a belief in the equal treatment of migrant and Polish workers. According to an ordinance issued in January 2018, migrant worker wages can neither fall below the minimum, nor be lower than those of a Polish worker.[32] In addition, to protect the rights of Ukrainians employed in Poland, the Nationwide Labor Union of Ukrainian Workers (Międzyzakładowy Związek Zawodowy Pracowników Ukraińskich) was established, initiated by both Polish labor unions and a nongovernmental organization, the Poland-Ukraine Sociocultural Association (Stowarzyszenie Społeczno-Kulturalne "Polska-Ukraina"). To serve the linguistic needs of migrant workers, the Polish language is not imposed in many contexts, and access in Ukrainian is often provided in financial, mass media, telecommunications, and other service centers. Various international agreements signed between Poland and Ukraine over the past decade have also stabilized the employment status of Ukrainian workers and their rights to a Polish retirement pension and social services.[33] Overall, the specific functioning of the labor market has been crucial to the development of a new cultural pluralism in Poland.

Aside from those who settle and integrate with Polish society, a much larger percentage of Ukrainians stays briefly, but returns many times over. This leads to a kind of rotational diversity, since part of the group is exchanged, while another is permanently in place. One reason for this practice is the need for a work permit, which is granted for a set period; another reason is that only certain sectors of the labor market are "reserved" for migrant workers. Well-paid professions in Poland are, as in the majority of economically developed countries, accessible to only a small percentage of immigrants, while the vast majority of newcomers are unskilled or manual laborers—sometimes working below, sometimes at the same level of competency as at home.[34] Indeed, despite institutional support, such factors discourage some Ukrainians from putting down roots in Poland. Social and career position can have a detrimental effect on an individual's frame of mind in a new country and environment, especially when the work undertaken is below his or her qualifications, leading to a stagnation of social capital.[35] Individual adaptability to new conditions and a capacity for integration with new people in the country of immigration are keystones for effective functioning in everyday life and at work, thus shaping decisions as to whether to stay or return home.[36]

A study carried out by Agata Górny among students from Ukraine reveals that some plan on remaining in Poland, others plan on going farther west, but a significant proportion plans to follow the cyclical migration described above—dividing their time and lives between Poland and Ukraine. Since women numerically predominate among immigrants from Ukraine, it is mostly this subset that intends to settle permanently.[37] In fact, Ukrainian women began to migrate earlier than men, even before Poland joined the European Union, whereas men began to appear in greater numbers only after the Donbas war broke out, often to evade conscription. The relatively young age of most Ukrainian migrants, especially the men, is propitious for cultural integration and assimilation as well as decisions to stay in Poland.[38] People of Polish ancestry also constitute a certain segment among Ukrainian migrants, many of whom plan to apply for or already hold a "Polish Card" (Karta Polaka), which gives rights to work and study in Poland. Many such individuals foresee a permanent move to Poland—not as Ukrainian immigrants, but as Poles repatriating from abroad who will therefore obtain Polish citizenship more quickly.

The difficult political situation in their homeland as well as the humanitarian and political support lent by the Polish state has created a favorable atmosphere for Polish-Ukrainian relations. This subsequently translates into good contact on a daily basis and an acceptance of both working and studying Ukrainians—despite the still high proportion of Poles declaring an antipathy toward Ukrainians in surveys. On the one hand, the presence of Ukrainians in Poland was seen as beneficial by 38 percent in June 2015,[39] compared to barely 15 percent in 1999 and 26 percent in 2004. On the other hand, CBOS surveys from 2018 through 2020 showed sympathy for Ukrainians rising from 24 percent to 31 percent and then 35 percent of those polled, while antipathy was at 40 percent, 41 percent, and then 33 percent. In short, positive perceptions are rising, a high percentage of those surveyed remain ambivalent (approximately 30 percent), and antipathy is falling, though not radically.[40]

In 2015, complementary research was carried out among Ukrainian students, who were asked to evaluate the attitude of Poles toward other nations.[41] The student responses tended to point to friendliness in contacts with Poles living in cities where these Ukrainians were studying (primarily Kraków and cities in eastern Poland).[42] Crucially, more than half (55 percent) of the surveyed Ukrainian students (women more often than men) declared an intention to remain in Poland upon completion of their degrees. Those Ukrainian students planning to stay in Poland came from the middle class (materially and socially). One-third of those who stated that they would not be returning home—generally those from high status family backgrounds—planned to move to western Europe or the United States. Educational and economic migration to Poland are undertaken much more frequently by people from western Ukraine—a region which, in addition to direct territorial adjacency, has been historically linked to Poland for centuries. It is from this area that many Ukrainian citizens of Polish descent also come to study in Poland.[43]

The outcome of fieldwork in Kraków, Rzeszów, and Przemyśl, surveying a nonrepresentative sample of over six hundred students in 2015 and 2017,[44] reveals that one impetus for viewing Poland as a place for working and studying—apart from any material benefits—is its geographical and cultural proximity. The very fact that there is already a sizable, preexisting group of Ukrainian economic immigrants in Poland provides young Ukrainian newcomers with a sense of security. In this way, the young people have both a substitute sense of home and a country in which it is easier to earn more.[45] Additionally, studying temporarily or settling permanently in Poland is associated with both a rise in social status and a proximity to western culture. Many students also declared themselves pro-EU and pro-NATO, believing that Ukraine will one day be accepted into these institutions.

For Ukrainians, adaptation to Polish social conditions is generally easier than for many other groups. Nevertheless, the process of integration always requires the fulfillment of several conditions: on the one hand, the host country needs to be institutionally prepared for immigration, while on the other, immigrants must possess a degree of preparedness to understand ordinary life in the host society and cope with it practically.[46] Some migrants inevitably lack the social capital and cultural competencies required to adapt to the host country and its cultural codes.[47] This kind of deficiency on the part of the migrant often leads to clustering in emigrant communities, creating enclaves which, in the case of permanent settlement, shape a very different form of multiculturalism. As for Ukrainian immigrants, it can be assumed that some will dissolve to a great extent into Polish society, while others will isolate themselves in some spheres of their lives, thus creating their own distinct segment within the cultural diversity of Polish society.

Mutual Stereotypes and Integration

Two elements play a particularly significant role when creating the conditions for multicultural coexistence. On the one hand, there is the stereotype of the immigrant group that already functions in the host society. On the other hand, there is a warped mirror image—a self-image that the host society assumes immigrants will have of it.[48] With regard to the former, the Polish stereotype of Ukrainians is historically conditioned and deeply inscribed. With regard to the latter, belying Polish expectations, cogitated and reworked past experiences will evolve into the real attitudes Ukrainians have toward Poles.

The stereotypical Polish image of Ukrainians is very clear. Testifying to this is the relatively low proportion of ambivalent responses alongside the constant prevalence of negative over positive opinions when the Polish population is surveyed—as confirmed by the CBOS nationwide polls cited earlier. In surveys conducted regularly since 1993, Polish sympathy toward Ukrainians has persistently been lower (9–16 percent) than antipathy (measured at about 59–66 percent among those sampled).[49] In the year 2000, there was a somewhat affirmative shift: antipathy remained high at 69 percent, but sympathy toward Ukrainians rose to 21.4 percent, with the percentage of those expressing ambivalence falling. As for the Ukrainian opinion envisioned by Poles, the outcome was similar: 20 percent of Poles expected sympathy from Ukrainians, 68 percent expected antipathy, and 16.1 percent held no opinion.[50]

In fact, in a study conducted in 2003 in both Ukraine and Poland, Ukrainians situated Poles in third place (after Germans and Russians) among nations at whose hands Ukrainians had suffered the most. In the same study, Poles remarkably put Ukrainians in first place.[51] During the subsequent decade, however, the Polish attitude toward Ukrainians began to move significantly toward the positive. CBOS research done in February 2014 shows 34 percent of the Polish population expressing sympathy for Ukrainians vis-à-vis an almost equal number, 33 percent, expressing antipathy (26 percent declared ambivalence). A survey done at the beginning of 2015 provided a similar outcome: 36 percent of Poles felt sympathetic toward Ukrainians whereas 40 percent felt antipathetic.[52]

On the whole, Ukrainians have tended to represent one of the least liked neighbors for Poles (alongside Russians and Belarusians), but slight movement toward sympathy (and away from antipathy) is manifest. The nature of the Polish image of Ukrainians is well reflected by a quantitative study of 70 students in 2015. The Polish students applied practically the same number of positive (650, an average of 20 selected by each respondent) and negative (650, an average of 22 selected by each respondent) adjectives to describe Ukrainians. Among the positive traits that the Polish respondents chose, the most common were "cheerful," "hardworking," and "brave." The most often chosen negative traits were "impulsivity," "hostility," "helplessness," and "complaisance." Overall, however, the constellation of positive and negative adjectives does not vary significantly, attesting to the relative durability of the Polish image of Ukrainians.

A study by Joanna Bierówka at tertiary educational institutions with a high percentage of Ukrainians enrolled shows that, while basically exhibiting benevolence toward these peers, Polish students also critique rather trivial features ascribed to customary Ukrainian behavior.[53] Among other things, Poles notice with disapproval a perceived inclination among Ukrainian women to disproportionately apply makeup and inappropriately dress up. In contrast, Ukrainian women describe their Polish counterparts as shabbily dressed and concentrated on comfort. Nevertheless, Ukrainian students favorably rate the attitude of Polish men toward women in comparison with that of Ukrainian men, among whom a higher level of aggression is seen as common. Overall, the study includes only rare descriptions of incidents that could fundamentally alter an overriding sense of friendly relations between Poles and Ukrainians in this milieu.[54]

When it comes to the impression that Ukrainian immigrants have of Polish attitudes toward them, a more negative image emerges. Ukrainians in Poland as economic immigrants believe that Poles maintain a certain distance from them, though usually without outright offense. Attesting to this are the findings of Krzysztof Jurek, whose respondents often point to more positive perceptions among Poles of the countries of western than eastern Europe.[55] In the opinion of those surveyed, Poles have a "superiority complex" and view Ukrainians as people who abuse alcohol and are uncultured, quick-tempered, aggressive, and civilizationally backward. According to Ukrainians, Poles are not interested in Ukraine, and generally do not view post-Soviet states as attractive. One respondent observed: "If somebody is from a western country, then he or she stirs greater curiosity and is more interesting—say from France or Spain. Someone from the East, in turn, is seen as a worse type."[56] In the opinion of the immigrants, the stereotypical Ukrainian is seen in Poland as a poor, improvident, and unenterprising individual: "[Poles] will explain how everything works, how to use each thing, how to turn on the vacuum cleaner, how the dishwasher works—sometimes making a face as if we had no vacuum cleaners in Ukraine or never actually saw one and might break it."[57] Ukrainians also emphasize that the use of the term "ruscy" (Russkies) to describe them is offensive.

In the eyes of Ukrainian immigrants, Poles have an unwelcome tendency to bring up sensitive historical topics, often viewing Ukrainian historical heroes as negative or even criminal figures (e.g., Bohdan Khmelnytsky, Stepan Bandera, etc.). In fact, this impression of Polish perspectives is partly confirmed in my interviews with younger Poles whose families had once lived in what is today's western Ukraine. Their responses called up memories of wartime violence by Ukrainian Insurgent Army ultranationalists against ethnic Poles—accusations then indiscriminately extended to all Ukrainians. One interviewee, whose family had barely escaped death at the hands of UPA, summarized: "The conclusions are the same . . . that UPA is evil and that they are generally worse than Germans or Russians taken together."[58]

Qualitative research done more recently among this select group of the university-educated reveals key changes in the attitudes Poles show toward Ukrainians as well as changes in the content of stereotypes. Political events taking place in Ukraine have had a significant influence on the shift in attitude. Particularly important were the Orange Revolution of 2004 and the Maidan Revolution of 2014, during which Polish society was in solidarity with Ukrainian society in its fight for independence, freedom, and democracy—values that are central to Polish narratives of identity.[59] Nationwide surveys showed that over half (52 percent) of the Polish population felt that Poland, along with the European Union, should support Ukrainians.[60] This supportive mood is reflected in the comments of a Ukrainian woman living in Lublin: "That was an exceptional time. My neighbor was telling me that we [Ukrainians] have to fight for what is ours, just like you Poles. It was like a holiday here. In Lublin, people—Ukrainians and Poles together—were coming together."[61]

Another key influence was Russia's occupation of Crimea and Ukraine's fighting for its eastern borders as of 2014. This aggression led to strong criticism of the former in Polish public opinion and strong support for the latter from the Polish government. Polish political leaders engaged actively in the Ukrainian–Russian conflict. These tragic events for Ukraine paradoxically fortified affirmative and supportive aspects of the Polish stereotype of Ukrainians, who were seen as fighting for sovereignty and democracy against Russia—Poland's eternal enemy as well. As a consequence of these political events, surveys show that Poles now assign more positive traits to Ukrainians, such as courage, determination, diligence, resourcefulness, and so on.

The shifts visible in the survey results are also mirrored by in-depth interview responses. The qualitative study I conducted in 2018–2019 among educated Poles from two distinct generations indicates that economic migrants from Ukraine do not evoke negative associations, even among individuals who are generally critical of social reality. From my perspective, the outlook of more highly educated people, especially from the younger generation, may provide the foundations for the building of a new multicultural ideology in Poland. Due to their leading position in Polish society, this contingent has opinion-making and trendsetting potential. Among both the younger and older generations of educated respondents, Ukrainian migrants can count on understanding and respect, as people trying to improve their lives through hard work rather than aiming to take economic and social advantage of their host country.

The Polish respondents also commented favorably on the perceived placidity of Ukrainians and the absence of political misunderstandings or nationalistic tendencies. A sixty-year-old woman states: "Personally, I do not have anything against migration. I have friends from Ukraine and Belarus who have lived here for quite some time and are already assimilated in Poland. They work, have families, children, and in all that time the issue of nationalism has never been raised. I also work in a company in which many immigrants from Ukraine are employed, and I've never had any problems or misunderstandings with them."[62] Another characteristic appreciated by Poles is Ukrainian immigrants' capacity to adapt to everyday life in Poland. Polish interviewees frequently emphasize Ukrainians' focus on work, economic self-reliance, and social advancement. An additional factor facilitating the harmonious coexistence of Poles and Ukrainians is the perceived closeness of the two cultures, as another interlocutor observes:

It is said that Ukrainians are a nation in a certain way similar to us and that, if some nation is to stream in, then Ukrainians are better who are closer to us in socio-religious thinking than some people living far away who won't be assimilating with Poles. . . . And that is the next thing. The assimilation of these people. When the Chinese stream in, they most often don't mix, don't acclimate. They don't move toward Polishness; they create an enclave of their world, their customs. They are a closed nation. I think, however, that Ukrainians have the potential to blend into the Polish population.[63]

Thus, Ukrainians are seen as a group that assimilates and polonizes—something clearly expected by this woman, with her conviction that Ukrainians have a much higher chance of adapting and assimilating than other nations. Another interviewee—a young man—calls attention to a similarly positive aspect of the migration of Ukrainians to Poland: "They work and do things on our terms and are not a source of violence. . . . Here I speak of persons coming from Ukraine—there isn't something like people being afraid of Ukrainians on the streets. I think that we actually take Ukrainians in rather smoothly because, and this might sound stupid, but they look like us in the sense that there isn't that aspect of an exotic look. I have the impression that our languages are close enough that we can understand each other."[64]

A young woman journalist also places particular emphasis on physical features in the process of integration: "It's that way with Slavic features that no matter where a Ukrainian goes—at least in the region of Poland—he will always be warmly welcomed. He won't be met with any hate speech, but, quite the contrary, will always find a group of friends. Maybe it's precisely because we look similar."[65] A thirty-six-year-old graphic designer also accentuates an evident resemblance: "Many people, for instance, will more easily accept a person from Ukraine, because they look similar, understand the Polish language better, etc."[66]

A student of economics claims that Poles generally have a negative attitude toward immigration into their country, but notes that "when it comes to immigration from Ukraine, then the attitude is as if more favorable."[67] Another young man, who works with people of many different nationalities, praises them all, but principally Ukrainians.[68] A student also working as a waiter explains the entire immigrant situation with sympathy and understanding: "It has always somehow been the same: the migrant simply came usually to earn money. These are ordinary people who emigrate in order to have a better life, to earn money, so that they can somehow do better. They often emigrate, leaving their family in Ukraine to earn money, build a house there. They send [money] to their family, mother, father, and that's how it looks."[69]

A similarity in Ukrainian and Polish worldviews is also highlighted in interview responses: "For sure, such persons—from Ukraine or other countries where there is a similar religion—we more willingly accept [them] than those from Islam who destroy everything and do nothing."[70] A working student of law concludes: "I believe that we should help above all those who are coming precisely from Ukraine. In the first place, let's help our neighbors, those Ukrainians. They understand our culture the best, because they're simply closer."[71]

Along with their generally positive stance toward Ukrainians, my interlocutors also noticed certain negative phenomena connected with migration. Some mentioned the difference in public health systems, including the recent issue of COVID-19 vaccinations; others referred to wage policies applied to foreigners—for instance, state subsidies currently given to employers for non-Polish employees. A twenty-four-year-old working student observed: "The last case [was when] Ukrainians came with their children and all of them were sick with the measles—the other, Polish kids caught it, it goes fast. A second disadvantage is work: we as Poles hold ourselves in high regard; the foreigner starts at a low wage. What does that mean? An employer prefers to hire two Ukrainians and to pay them less than one Pole."[72] From the viewpoint of Polish workers, the large number of immigrant workers is a clear drawback as this lowers wages, thus affecting the Polish labor market.

Other comments highlight an everyday habituation to the presence of Ukrainians in Poland, again often comparing them with less-favorably received groups. A twenty-five-year-old journalist observes that "inasmuch as we've all likely gotten accustomed somehow to the migration from Ukraine and those people from Ukraine, I don't know if we are capable of getting accustomed, for example, to people coming in from such countries as India or Nepal."[73]

All respondents—both older and younger generations—take note of the ubiquity of Ukrainian immigrants in Poland: "Wherever you go, you see a person from Ukraine. You go to a shop—a Ukrainian there; you go to a restaurant, you hear the language. When you begin to get to know another person and confront what you have in your head a bit, with how it really is or with what the other person thinks, it starts to change things in you a bit."[74] This totally new kind of contact between Poles and Ukrainians is shaping normalization and neutrality. In another example, young Ukrainians are appearing at all levels of Polish education, and thus, young Poles (especially the students surveyed) recall even elementary school interactions with the children of Ukrainian immigrants. For their own part, young Ukrainians present the attitudes of Polish schoolchildren toward their Ukrainian peers as friendly—although close friendships and deepened, mutual interests are rarely mentioned.[75]

Affected by their contacts with Ukrainians working and/or studying in Poland, my interlocutors are cognizant of the fact that a lower standard of living and the promise of better earnings are what push Ukrainians into economic migration. From a market perspective, this immigration is understood as a positive phenomenon in a situation wherein the Polish workforce is shrinking. Polish citizens are well aware of this. Many observe that the economy would be in danger of crashing if the country were to lose the Ukrainian workforce, a view justifying consent to the stable presence of Ukrainian immigrants. When considering adaptation to host country conditions, this minority constitutes a significantly smaller problem: their melting into the Polish pot is simpler than in the case of other culturally distant ethnicities.

From my conversations, it is also apparent that Polish migration experiences further influence opinions on Ukrainian migration. Those interviewed in 2018 and 2019 refer to the experiences of Polish economic emigrants to western Europe when looking at the essentially similar immigration of Ukrainians to Poland. Both older and younger interviewees are conscious of the universality and globalized nature of migration, pointing to the economic factors that should facilitate acceptance of migratory tendencies. In their responses, interviewees often underscored that Poland—due to its own history of emigration—needs to take in migrants to make up for massive losses in its labor force to the western, even more economically attractive states of the European Union. Sometimes this entire situation is disapprovingly labeled as a "failure" for Poland: "Now we will be missing that labor force, and an economic crash could begin. This is a completely new situation ahead of us."[76] My interviewees also assume that, as soon as the possibility arises, the Ukrainians working in Poland will head westward.

In summary, changes in the image of the Ukrainian in Polish society show an evident trend toward acceptance, identification of positive traits in the spirit of cultural proximity, and an atmosphere of sympathy and human understanding. These changes have been grounded, on the one hand, in perceptions of core Polish values, and, on the other, in a recognition of demographic changes and the needs of the Polish economy. Old animosities, conflicting memories, and mutual grievances that once precluded peaceful coexistence have retreated into the background—perhaps even more so after Russia's invasion of Ukraine in 2022. In other words, the history of the culturally diverse Polish-Lithuanian Commonwealth and interwar Polish Republic functions more as ballast than as a motor for the development and growing acceptance of difference. In daily interactions between Poles and Ukrainians, therefore, the past is often deliberately avoided so as not to open wounds. In this sense, the shared history of these two nations is dead weight to be jettisoned in order to make way for more positive, constructive relations on a largely pragmatic basis.

The most important factors in the birth of a contemporary multiculturalism in Poland have been entirely new, direct, rational actions, with an accompanying change in attitudes. These, in turn, need to be supported by government policies put into practice to shape a certain form of a culturally pluralistic society. Just as public opinion has changed, so Polish political institutions have adapted to new economic circumstances, facilitating an immigration that has translated into a much higher percentage of foreign workers in Poland today. Ukrainian immigrants have already carved out their significant place in this new reality. My interviewees refer to a continued need to regulate and manage the institutional aspects of immigration, long-term settlement, and, consequently, multiculturalism as state policy in Poland—a consciously managed phenomenon including, for example, the education system of a diverse society.[77]

An Immigratory Multiculturalism

Despite the fact that Poles and Ukrainians lived in the same multinational, multilingual, and multiconfessional political entities for centuries, little of that legacy remains today for most people in their daily interactions. In the twentieth century, both peoples experienced two world wars—the last of which unraveled earlier social orders, radically shifted borders, and relocated populations. As a consequence, both societies—and especially Poland—became more ethnically homogeneous. Only along the borderlands have traces of the old type of cultural pluralism lingered. In those regions, a traditional interethnic coexistence persists, full of tensions and sometimes conflicts, supported by legally guaranteed rights for national and ethnic minorities to nurture features of their uniqueness.

Yet it is not these peripheral lands that constitute the keystone for the development of a modern multicultural society in Poland. The crucial role here is played by recent immigrants from Ukraine, whose numbers were already in excess of 1.3 million people even before the 2022 refugee influx. Their presence has introduced elements of a real cultural diversity to Poland, leading to a shift in attitudes and a greater degree of mutual acceptance and understanding. In this way, a form of multiculturalism is taking shape on two levels in Poland: through the emergence of factual diversity and through an axiological change in social consciousness. Despite all the historical controversies and mutual accusations, it is precisely immigrants from Ukraine who are already building—and will no doubt continue to build—the foundations of a new cultural pluralism in Poland.

Polish-Ukrainian grievances and antipathies have still remained firmly in place. This is confirmed by surveys on Polish attitudes toward other nations, in which Ukrainians and Russians have ranked high on the list of disliked nations for decades. This impression is also echoed by the opinions of Ukrainian immigrants, who resent a Polish sense of civilizational superiority made palpable in the way they feel they are treated. These impediments are rooted in a shared multinational, multicultural past that sometimes created conflict—even if memory of the premodern Commonwealth is buried by both Poles and Ukrainians deep in the archives of history. Indeed, the national identity of Ukrainians—as in the case of Lithuanians and Belarusians—is partly built in opposition to Polishness. Today, these nations have their own independent states, and have no desire to renew past types of relations with Poles.

The positive, constructive factors that dominate in Polish-Ukrainian relations under the current conditions of economic immigration include:

> Linguistic and cultural similarities, which facilitate Ukrainian immigrant adaptation precisely in Poland;
>
> Territorial proximity to home, which simplifies the logistics of journeys in both directions;
>
> Ease of finding employment in Poland due to demand in several sectors of the labor market;
>
> Involvement of the Polish government as well as private businesses in facilitating linguistic communication, providing economic buffers, and arranging visas for immigrants from Ukraine; and
>
> Poland's membership in the EU as a guarantee of specific rights.

Several of these factors are deeply rooted in a shared history. In particular, the cultural proximity that many Poles notice and approve of among Ukrainian immigrants—especially when compared with other groups—is a direct result of centuries of close contact, for better or for worse. Nevertheless, it appears that what counts most in the decisions of Ukrainian immigrants to Poland is pragmatism—not the historical past, from which they have often cut themselves off. In everyday life and everyday contacts between Poles and Ukrainians, at work or at university, both sides try hard to avoid historical topics, with their accompanying tensions and conflicts. Among Poles, there is a strong awareness that friendly relations with Ukrainians depend upon evasion of this shared history. Leaving the past behind, relations for the future are being built upon pragmatic choices and ordinary, everyday practices.

Editors' Afterword

Russia's full-scale onslaught against Ukraine from February 24, 2022, has created a profound humanitarian crisis throughout Europe, with at an estimated fourteen million people displaced from their homes by war. Over three million of those crossed the Polish border in the first three months of the conflict, and Polish civil society has been widely lauded for its outpouring of solidarity as the country that has accepted and supported the largest number of refugees. As was shown earlier in this chapter, Russian military aggression has since 2014 acted as a catalyst for the warming of relations between ordinary Poles and Ukrainians, and the renewed invasion appears to have consolidated this mutual friendship further. Throughout the country, Poles have mobilized to house and assist people fleeing the war, and Polish institutions and organizations have been instrumental in creating infrastructure to support the refugees. In line with the observations made throughout this chapter, it is unlikely that memories of the Commonwealth per se have played a prominent role in motivating this spontaneous self-organization. However, if even a small portion of those displaced persons stay in Poland in the mid- to long term, adding to the over 1.3 million Ukrainians already present, the character of the country's multiculturalism is likely to evolve further, increasingly taking the form of a "biculturalism," as Ukrainians come to massively outnumber other minority groups. Whether the historical memory of centuries of coexistence can still be used as a symbolic instrument to foster integration and understanding remains to be seen.

NOTES

Introduction

1. On the history of Poland-Lithuania before 1569, see, in particular, Robert Frost, *The Oxford History of Poland-Lithuania*, vol. 1: *The Making of the Polish-Lithuanian Union, 1385–1569* (Oxford: Oxford University Press, 2015).

2. *Unia Lubelska (1569)*, http://www.agad.gov.pl/unia%20lubelska/uni_lub.html, accessed May 1, 2022.

3. The equivalent in modern Lithuanian is *Abiejų Tautų Respublika*, although the Polish loan word "Žečpospolita" is also used for reasons explained below.

4. Jakub Olszewski, *Żałoba po śmierci naiasnieyszey Konstanciey krolowey polskiey xiężny Litewskiey, w kościele kathedralnym wileńskim 19 Jul. r.p. 1631 wystawiona* (Vilnius: Typis Academicis Soc. Iesv., 1631), cited in Artūras Tereškinas, *Imperfect Communities: Identity, Discourse and Nation in the Seventeenth-century Grand Duchy of Lithuania* (Vilnius: Lietuvių literatūros ir tautosakos institutas, 2005), 31.

5. Tomasz Kamusella, *The Un-Polish Poland, 1989 and the Illusion of Regained Historical Continuity* (Cham: Palgrave Macmillan, 2017), 18. The author explains that he has "exempted Jews, Armenians and Tatars from the qualification of inverted commas. At that time, in Poland-Lithuania none of the three groups was defined through language but exclusively by religion". (19).

6. See, e.g., Józef Andrzej Gierowski, *The Polish-Lithuanian Commonwealth in the XVIIIth Century: From Anarchy to Well-Organised State* (Kraków: Nakładem Polskiej Akademii Umiejętności, 1996), 24–41; Andrzej K. Link-Lenczowski and Mariusz Markiewicz, eds., *Rzeczpospolita wielu narodów i jej tradycje: materiały z konferencji "Trzysta lat od początku unii polsko-saskiej. Rzeczpospolita wielu narodów i jej tradycje," Kraków 15–17 IX 1997* (Kraków: Towarzystwo Wydawnicze Historia Iagellonica, 1999); Andrzej Sulima Kamiński, *Historia Rzeczypospolitej wielu narodów, 1505–1795: Obywatele, ich państwa, społeczeństwo, kultura* (Lublin: Instytut Europy Środkowo-Wschodniej, 2000); and Michał Kopczyński and Wojciech Tygielski, eds., *Pod wspólnym niebem: Narody dawnej Rzeczypospolitej* (Warsaw: Muzeum Historii Polski, 2010). See also Karin Friedrich and Barbara Pendzich, eds., *Citizenship and Identity in a Multinational Commonwealth: Poland-Lithuania in Context, 1550–1772* (Leiden: Brill, 2009).

7. For chapter-length summaries on individual groups, see Kopczyński and Tygielski, *Pod wspólnym niebem*. Kopczyński and Tygielski divide the ethnic communities of the Commonwealth into three groupings: the "locals," i.e., the Poles, Lithuanians, and Ruthenians (Belarusians and Ukrainians); the "assimilated," i.e., the Jews, Germans, Tatars, Armenians, Karaites, and Roma; and the "newcomers," i.e., the Italians, Scots, and Mennonites. This work is also available in English as Michał Kopczyński and Wojciech Tygielski, eds., *Under a Common Sky: Ethnic Groups of Commonwealth of Poland and Lithuania*, trans. William F. Hoffman (New York: PIASA Books and the Polish History Museum, 2017).

8. See, among others: Nataliia Starchenko, "Liublinska Uniia iak resurs formuvannia kontseptu politychnoho 'Narodu Ruskoho' (1569–1648)," *Ukrainskyi istorychnyi zhurnal* 2 (2019):

4–45; and Jerzy Borzecki, "The Union of Lublin as a Factor in the Emergence of Ukrainian National Consciousness," *Polish Review* 41, no. 1 (1996): 37–61.

9. Juliusz Bardach, *O dawnej i niedawnej Litwie* (Poznań: Wydawnictwo Naukowe UAM, 1988), 202; and Michał Kopczyński, "Wstęp," in Kopczyński and Tygielski, *Pod wspólnym niebem*, 11.

10. See, e.g., Jan Kozik, *Ukraiński ruch narodowy w Galicji w latach 1830–1848* (Kraków: Wydawnictwo Literackie, 1973); Ryszard Radzik, *Między zbiorowością etniczną a wspólnotą narodową: Białorusini na tle przemian narodowych w Europie Środkowo–Wschodniej XIX stulecia* (Lublin: Wydawnictwo Uniwersytetu Marii Curie-Skłodowskiej, 2000); Timothy Snyder, *The Reconstruction of Nations: Poland, Ukraine, Lithuania, Belarus, 1569–1999* (New Haven, CT: Yale University Press, 2003), 15–132; Pavel Tereshkovich, *Etnicheskaia istoriia Belarusi XIX–nachala XX v.: V kontekste Tsentral'no-Vostochnoi Evropy* (Minsk: BGU, 2004); and Simon Lewis, *Belarus—Alternative Visions: Nation, Memory and Cosmopolitanism* (Abingdon: Routledge, 2019), 27–52.

11. Adam Teller, "Jews in the Polish–Lithuanian Economy (1453–1795)," in *The Cambridge History of Judaism*, vol. 7, ed. Jonathan Karp and Adam Sutcliffe (Cambridge: Cambridge University Press, 2017), 579.

12. Royal Prussia was an autonomous province of the Polish Crown and then the Commonwealth, established after the Second Peace of Thorn (1466), remaining an integral part of the Commonwealth until the Partitions. See esp. Karin Friedrich, *The Other Prussia: Royal Prussia, Poland and Liberty, 1569–1772* (Cambridge: Cambridge University Press, 2000). Livonia was part of the Grand Duchy of Lithuania from 1561, and under the agreements of the Union of Lublin became a joint domain of the Polish Crown and Grand Duchy as the Duchy of Livonia. The Duchy of Livonia existed until 1621, when a significant part of its territory was ceded to Sweden. Thereafter, the remaining area was governed jointly by the Polish Crown and Grand Duchy as the Livonian palatinate (*Województwo inflanckie*), also known informally as "Polish Livonia" (*Inflanty Polskie*). See esp. Krzysztof Zajas, *Absent Culture: The Case of Polish Livonia* (Frankfurt am Main: Peter Lang, 2013).

13. On the identity entanglements of the German-speaking members of the nobility, see Friedrich, *Other Prussia*, 147–70; Karin Friedrich "Citizenship in the Periphery: Royal Prussia and the Union of Lublin 1569," in Friedrich and Pendzich, *Citizenship and Identity*, 49–69.

14. Kamiński, *Historia Rzeczypospolitej wielu narodów*, 17, 14.

15. See, e.g., Jerzy Tomaszewski, *Rzeczpospolita Wielu Narodów* (Warsaw: Czytelnik, 1985).

16. Kamusella, *Un-Polish Poland*, 1–14.

17. Kamiński dedicates his book to "the Belarusian, Lithuanian, Polish and Ukrainian reader." Kamiński, *Historia Rzeczypospolitej wielu narodów*, 9.

18. See, e.g., chapter 9 in this volume; and Mathias Niendorf, *Das Großfürstentum Litauen: Studien zur Nationsbildung in der Frühen Neuzeit (1569–1795)* (Wiesbaden: Harassowitz Verlag, 2006), 9–21.

19. Andrzej Leder, *Prześniona rewolucja* (Warsaw: Wydawnictwo Krytyki Politycznej, 2014), 53.

20. On "Noblemen's Commonwealth," see, e.g., Andrzej Wyczański, *Polska Rzeczą Pospolitą szlachecką* (Warsaw: PWN, 1991); and Gierowski, *Polish-Lithuanian Commonwealth in the XVIIIth Century*. Quotation from Jerzy Lukowski, *Liberty's Folly: The Polish-Lithuanian Commonwealth in the Eighteenth Century, 1697–1795* (London: Routledge, 1991), 9.

21. Richard Butterwick, *The Constitution of 3 May 1791: Testament of the Polish-Lithuanian Commonwealth* (Warsaw: Polish History Museum, 2021), 127–28.

22. Alfredas Bumblauskas, *Wielkie Księstwo Litewskie: Wspólna historia, podzielona pamięć* (Warsaw: Bellona, 2013), 290.

23. Andrei Portnov, "Izobretaia Rech' Pospolituiu," *Ab Imperio* 1 (2007), 46.

24. Kamusella, *Un-Polish Poland*, 2–5.

25. See, e.g., Stefan Rohdewald, *"Vom Polocker Venedig": kollektives Handeln sozialer Gruppen einer Stadt zwischen Ost- und Mitteleuropa (Mittelalter, frühe Neuzeit, 19. Jh. bis 1914)* (Stuttgart: Steiner, 2005); and David Frick, *Kith, Kin, and Neighbors: Communities and Confessions in Seventeenth-Century Wilno* (Ithaca, NY: Cornell University Press, 2013). Andrzej Romanowski, *Wschodnim pograniczem literatury polskiej: Od średniowiecza do oświecenia* (Kraków: Universitas, 2018).

26. Natalia Jakowenko, *Historia Ukrainy od czasów najdawniejszych do końca XVIII wieku,* trans. Ola Hnatiuk and Katarzyna Kotyńska (Lublin: Instytut Europy Środkowo-Wschodniej, 2000); Jarosław Hrycak, *Historia Ukrainy 1772–1999: narodziny nowoczesnego narodu,* trans. Katarzyna Kotyńska (Lublin: Instytut Europy Środkowo-Wschodniej, 2000); Hienadź Sahanowicz, *Historia Białorusi: Od czasów najdawniejszych do końca XVIII wieku,* trans. Hubert Łaszkiewicz (Lublin: Instytut Europy Środkowo-Wschodniej, 2002); and Zachar Szybieka, *Historia Bialorusi: 1795–2000,* trans. Hubert Łaszkiewicz (Lublin: Instytut Europy Środkowo-Wschodniej, 2002). The aforementioned Kamiński, *Historia Rzeczypospolitej wielu narodów* is also part of this series. A two-volume history of Lithuania was planned, but appears to have never been published.

27. See, e.g., Ziemowit Szczerek, *Przyjdzie Mordor i nas zje, czyli Tajna historia Słowian* (Kraków: Korporacja Ha!art, 2013); and Ziemowit Szczerek, *Tatuaż z tryzubem* (Wołowiec : Wydawnictwo Czarne, 2015). Żanna Słoniowska, *Dom z witrażem* (Kraków: Znak Literanova, 2015).

28. See, e.g., Žanna Niekraševič-Karotkaja, *Šmatmoŭnaja litaratura Belarusi ŭ kantekscie aktualnych litaraturaznaŭčych kancepcyj* (Minsk: Belaruski dziaržaŭny ŭniversitėt, 2015). See also chapter 9 in this volume, especially the concluding section.

29. See, e.g., Starchenko, "Liublinska Uniia yak resurs"; and Nataliia Yakovenko, *Narys istorii seredniovichnoi ta ranniomodernoi Ukrainy* (Kyiv: Krytyka, 2009).

30. See, e.g., Rūstis Kamuntavičius, *Gudijos istorija Baltarusijos istorija* (Vilnius: MELC, 2021).

31. See, e.g., Friedrich and Pendzich, *Citizenship and Identity*; Frost, *Oxford History of Poland-Lithuania*, vol. 1; Butterwick, *Constitution of 3 May 1791*; and Richard Butterwick, *The Polish-Lithuanian Commonwealth, 1733–1795: Light and Flame* (New Haven, CT: Yale University Press, 2021).

32. See, e.g., Andrej Kotljarchuk, *Making the Baltic Union: The 1655 Federation of Kedainiai between Sweden and the Grand Duchy of Lithuania* (Saarbrücken: VDM Verlag Dr. Müller, 2008); Dariusz Kołodziejczyk, *The Crimean Khanate and Poland-Lithuania: International Diplomacy on the European Periphery (15th–18th Century), A Study of Peace Treaties Followed by an Annotated Edition of Relevant Documents* (Leiden: Brill, 2011); and Michal Wasiucionek, *The Ottomans and Eastern Europe: Borders and Political Patronage in the Early Modern World* (London: I. B. Tauris, 2020).

33. Natalia Nowakowska, ed., *Remembering the Jagiellonians* (Abingdon: Routledge, 2019). At least two more volumes are expected to result from the Jagiellonians Project, a five-year multidisciplinary research project based at the University of Oxford between 2013 and 2018 (https://www.jagiellonians.com/).

34. For a recent publication of selected essays from an international conference that also

discussed both the history and memory of the Commonwealth, see Andrzej Chwalba and Krzysztof Pomorski, eds., *The Polish-Lithuanian Commonwealth: History, Memory, Legacy* (New York: Routledge, 2021).

35. "Multiculturalism," *Stanford Encyclopedia of Philosophy*, last modified September 9, 2020, https://plato.stanford.edu/entries/multiculturalism/; Luís Cordeiro Rodrigues, "Multiculturalism," *Internet Encyclopedia of Philosophy*, https://iep.utm.edu/multicul/, accessed February 1, 2022.

36. Edward A. Tiryakian, "Assessing Multiculturalism Theoretically: E Pluribus Unum, Sic et Non," *International Journal on Multicultural Societies* 5, no. 1 (2003): 20–39.

37. John R. Baldwin, Sandra L. Faulkner, and Michael L. Hecht, "A Moving Target: The Illusive Definition of Culture," in *Redefining Culture: Perspectives across the Disciplines*, ed. John R. Baldwin, Sandra L. Faulkner, Michael L. Hecht, and Sheryl L. Lindsley (London: Routledge, 2005), 23–26.

38. Clifford Geertz, *The Interpretation of Cultures: Selected Essays* (New York: Basic Books, 1973), 5; and A. L. Kroeber and Clyde Kluckhohn, *Culture: A Critical Review of Concepts and Definitions—The History of Human Culture, Its Role in Social Sciences* (Cambridge, MA: The Museum, 1952), 181.

39. Kevin Avruch, *Culture and Conflict Resolution* (Washington, DC: United States Institute of Peace Press, 1998), 17–18.

40. Edward Said, *Culture and Imperialism* (London: Vintage Books, 1994), xxix.

41. William H. Sewell Jr., "The Concept(s) of Culture," in *Beyond the Cultural Turn: New Directions in the Study of Society and Culture*, ed. Victoria E. Bonnel and Lynn Hunt (Berkeley: University of California Press, 1999), 52.

42. On "two-layered identity," see Juliusz Bardach, *O Rzeczpospolitą Obojga Narodów* (Warsaw: Krajowa Agencja Wydawnicza, 1998), 56. On "captured in the formula," see, e.g., Adam Świątek, *Gente Rutheni, natione Poloni: Z dziejów Rusinów narodowości polskiej w Galicji* (Kraków: Księgarnia Akademicka, 2014).

43. Jacob T. Levy, *The Multiculturalism of Fear* (Oxford: Oxford University Press, 2000), 127.

44. Will Kymlicka, *Multicultural Citizenship: A Liberal Theory of Minority Rights* (Oxford: Oxford University Press, 1995).

45. Frank E. Sysyn, "Seventeenth-Century Views on the Causes of the Khmel'nyts'kyi Uprising: An Examination of the 'Discourse on the Present Cossack or Peasant War,'" *Harvard Ukrainian Studies* 5, no. 4 (December 1981), 439. "Lach" is a derogatory term for a Pole.

46. Frost, *Oxford History of Poland-Lithuania*, 1:460.

47. Bogdan Walczak and Agnieszka Mielczarek, "Prolegomena historyczne: wielojęzyczność w Rzeczypospolitej Obojga Narodów," *Białostockie Archiwum Językowe* 17 (2017): 255–68.

48. Bardach, *O Rzeczpospolitą Obojga Narodów*, 49–54.

49. Agnieszka Pasieka, "How Pluralism Becomes Hierarchical? Debating Pluralism in Contemporary Poland," *Sprawy Narodowościowe* 43 (2013): 53–73; and Agnieszka Pasieka, *Hierarchy and Pluralism: Living Religious Difference in Catholic Poland* (Basingstoke: Palgrave Macmillan, 2015).

50. Tiryakian, "Assessing Multiculturalism Theoretically," 24; and Eva-Maria Asari, Daphne Halikiopoulou, and Steven Mock, "British National Identity and the Dilemmas of Multiculturalism," *Nationalism and Ethnic Politics* 14, no. 1 (2008): 10–11.

51. Steven Vertovec, "Towards Post-Multiculturalism? Changing Communities, Conditions and Contexts of Diversity," *International Social Science Journal* 61, no. 199 (2010), 84.

52. See Johannes Feichtinger and Gary B. Cohen, eds., *Understanding Multiculturalism: The Habsburg Central European Experience* (New York: Berghahn Books, 2014), 4; Gary B. Cohen, "Nationalist Politics and the Dynamics of State and Civil Society in the Habsburg Monarchy, 1867–1914," *Central European History* 40, no. 2 (2007): 241–78; and Rok Stergara and Tamara Scheer, "Ethnic Boxes: The Unintended Consequences of Habsburg Bureaucratic Classification," *Nationalities Papers* 46, no. 4 (2018): 575–91.

53. Homi Bhabha distinguishes between a normative notion of cultural *diversity* and a more deconstructive idea of *difference*. The former involves "containment," whereby "a transparent norm is constituted, a norm given by the host society or dominant culture, which says that 'these other cultures are fine, but we must be able to locate them within our own grid.'" The articulation of difference, on the other hand, is subversive in its affirmation of a decentered subject position and its rupture of the symbolic unity of nationhood. See Jonathan Rutherford and Homi Bhabha, "The Third Space: Interview with Homi Bhabha," in *Identity, Community, Culture, Difference*, ed. Jonathan Rutherford (London: Lawrence and Wishart, 1990), 208.

54. Paul W. Knoll, "Religious Toleration in Sixteenth-Century Poland: Political Realities and Social Constraints," in *Diversity and Dissent: Negotiating Religious Difference in Central Europe, 1500–1800*, ed. Howard Louthan, Gary B. Cohen, and Franz A. J. Szabo (New York: Berghahn Books, 2011), 42.

55. The first line of Mickiewicz's verse epic *Pan Tadeusz, czyli ostatni zajazd na Litwie* (Paris: Aleksander Jełowicki, 1834). See chapter 8 in this volume and Dariusz Szpoper, *Sukcesorzy Wielkiego Księstwa: myśl polityczna i działalność konserwatystów polskich na ziemiach litewsko-białoruskich w latach 1904–1939* (Gdańsk: Arche, 1999); Aliaksandr Smalianchuk, *Pamizh kraevastsiu i natsyianal'nai ideiai: Polski rukh na belaruskikh i litouskikh ziamliakh, 1864–1917h.* (Hrodna: Hrodzenski Dziarzhauny Universitet, 2001); and Simon Lewis, "Cosmopolitanism as Subculture in the Former Polish-Lithuanian Commonwealth," in *Identities In-Between in East-Central Europe*, ed. Jan Fellerer, Robert Pyrah, and Marius Turda (New York and London: Routledge, 2019), 149–69.

56. See, e.g., Jerzy Tomaszewski, *Rzeczpospolita wielu narodów* (Warsaw: Czytelnik, 1985); Brian Porter-Szűcs, *Poland in the Modern World: Beyond Martyrdom* (Chichester: Wiley-Blackwell, 2014), 126–43; Paul Brykczynski, *Primed for Violence Murder: Antisemitism, and Democratic Politics in Interwar Poland* (Madison: University of Wisconsin Press, 2016); and Kathryn Ciancia, *On Civilization's Edge: A Polish Borderland in the Interwar World* (Oxford: Oxford University Press, 2021).

57. Czesław Miłosz, *Szukanie ojczyzny* (Kraków: Znak, 1992), 28.

58. See, e.g., Will Kymlicka, "Multiculturalism: Success, Failure, and the Future," in *Rethinking National Identity in the Age of Migration: The Transatlantic Council on Migration*, ed. Bertelsmann Stiftung and Migration Policy Institute (Gütersloh: Verlag Bertelsmann Stiftung, 2012), 37–45; and Richard T. Ashcroft and Mark Bevir, "British Multiculturalism after Empire: Immigration, Nationality, and Citizenship," in *Multiculturalism in the British Commonwealth: Comparative Perspectives on Theory and Practice*, ed. Richard T. Ashcroft and Mark Bevir (Berkeley: University of California Press, 2019), 25–45.

59. Elizabeth Buettner, *Europe after Empire: Decolonization, Society, and Culture* (Cambridge: Cambridge University Press, 2016), 324.

60. Kymlicka, "Multiculturalism," 34.

61. According to Stephen Small, this phrase is "an assertion and slogan common among activist people of color, Black and non-Black, in England from the 1970s." Stephen Small, *20 Questions and Answers on Black Europe* (The Hague: Amrit, 2018), 11.

62. Paul Gilroy, *After Empire: Melancholia or Convivial Culture?* (London: Routledge, 2004), 2–3.

63. On the Benin Bronzes, see especially Dan Hicks, *The Brutish Museums: The Benin Bronzes, Colonial Violence and Cultural Restitution* (London: Pluto Press, 2020).

64. See, e.g., Patricia M. Mazón and Reinhild Steingröver, eds., *Not So Plain as Black and White: Afro-German Culture and History, 1890–2000* (Rochester, NY: University of Rochester Press, 2005); Fatima El-Tayeb, *European Others: Queering Ethnicity in Postnational Europe* (Minneapolis: University of Minnesota Press, 2011); Peo Hansen and Stefan Jonsson, *Eurafrica: The Untold History of European Integration and Colonialism* (London: Bloombury, 2014); Kalypso Nicolaïdis, Berny Sèbe, and Gabrielle Maas, eds., *Echoes of Empire: Memory, Identity and Colonial Legacies* (London: I. B. Tauris, 2015); Buettner, *Europe after Empire*; David Olusoga, *Black and British: A Forgotten History* (London: Pan Macmillan, 2016); Natasha A. Kelly, *Afrokultur: "der raum zwischen gestern und morgen"* (Münster: UNRAST, 2016); Gurminder Bhambra and John Narayan, eds., *European Cosmopolitanism: Colonial Histories and Postcolonial Societies* (London: Routledge, 2017); and Olivette Otele, *African Europeans: An Untold History* (London: Hurst, 2020).

65. See Snyder, *Reconstruction of Nations.*

66. Michael Fleming, "From Homogenisation to 'Multiculturalism': Socialist and Postsocialist Nationality Policy and Practice in Poland (1944–2010)," *Historia Contemporánea* 45 (2012): 519–44.

67. Such visions are often well-intentioned, and, in their scholarly versions, not without nuance. See, e.g., Leszek Korporowicz, Sylwia Jaskuła, Małgożata Stefanovič, and Paweł Plichta, eds. *Jagiellonian Ideas: Towards Challenges of Modern Times* (Kraków: Jagiellonian Library, 2017).

68. Agnieszka Pasieka, "Wielokulturowość po polsku: Polityka wielokulturowości jako mechanizm umacniania polskości," *Kultura i Społeczeństwo* 57, no. 3 (2013): 129–55.

69. See Andrzej Nowak, "Czy Polska była imperium? Rozmowa z Romanem Szporlukiem," *Od Imperium do Imperium: Spojrzenia na historię Europy Wschodniej* (Kraków: Arcana, 2004), 337–55.

70. See, e.g., Daniel Beauvois, "Mit 'kresów wschodnich,' czyli jak mu położyć kres," in *Polskie mity polityczne XIX i XX wieku*, ed. Wojciech Wrzesiński (Wrocław: Wydawnictwo Uniwersytetu Wrocławskiego, 1994), 93–105; and Bogusław Bakuła, "Colonial and Postcolonial Aspects of Polish Discourse on the Eastern 'Borderlands,'" trans. Tadeusz Z. Wolański, in *From Sovietology to Postcoloniality: Poland and Ukraine from a Postcolonial Perspective*, ed. Janusz Korek (Huddinge: Södertörns högskola, 2007), 41–59; Hanna Gosk, "Polski dyskurs kresowy w niefikcjonalnych zapisach międzywojennych: Próba lektury w perspektywie 'postcolonial studies,'" *Teksty Drugie* 6 (2008): 20–33; Robert Traba, "Kresy: miejsce pamięci w procesie reprodukcji kulturowej," in *Polska wschodnia i orientalizm*, ed. Tomasz Zarycki (Warsaw: Scholar, 2013), 146–70; Paweł Ładykowski, "Poland and Its Eastern Neighbours: A Postcolonial Case Study," *Baltic Journal of European Studies* 5, no. 1 (2014): 109–32; and Tomasz Zarycki, *Ideologies of Eastness in Central and Eastern Europe* (London: Routledge, 2014), 115–51.

71. See, e.g., Jan Sowa, *Fantomowe ciało króla* (Kraków: Universitas, 2011); Dangiras Mačiulis and Darius Staliūnas, *Lithuanian Nationalism and the Vilnius Question, 1883–1940* (Marburg: Verlag Herder-Institut, 2015); Dorota Michaluk, "Okres Rzeczypospolitej Obojga Narodów w dziejach Białorusi w ocenie białoruskiej historiografii XIX i początku XX wieku," in *Tożsamość—pamięć historyczna—idee: Przemiany narodowościowe i społeczne na Litwie i*

Białorusi w XIX i na początku XX wieku, ed. Dorota Michaluk (Warsaw: DiG, 2016), 43–72; Andrii Portnov, *Poland and Ukraine: Entangled Histories, Asymmetric Memories* (Berlin: Forum Transregionale Studien, 2020); and Georgiy Kasianov, *Memory Crash: The Politics of History in and around Ukraine, 1980s–2010s* (Budapest: Central European University Press, 2022), 319–49.

72. Dirk Uffelmann, "Theory as Memory Practice: The Divided Discourse on Poland's Postcoloniality," in *Memory and Theory in Eastern Europe*, ed. Uilleam Blacker, Alexander Etkind, and Julie Fedor (New York: Palgrave Macmillan, 2013), 104–6.

73. Magdalena Waligórska, *Klezmer's Afterlife: An Ethnography of the Jewish Music Revival in Poland and Germany* (Oxford: Oxford University Press, 2013), 274.

74. On "multidirectional" memory, see Michael Rothberg, *Multidirectional Memory: Remembering the Holocaust in the Age of Decolonization* (Stanford, CA: Stanford University Press, 2009).

75. Kristina Sabaliauskaitė, *Silva Rerum* (Vilnius: Baltos Lankos, 2008); *Silva Rerum II* (Vilnius: Baltos Lankos, 2011); *Silva Rerum III* (Vilnius: Baltos Lankos, 2014); and *Silva Rerum IV* (Vilnius: Baltos Lankos, 2016).

76. Kristina Sabaliauskaitė, *Silva Rerum*, trans. Izabela Korybut-Daszkiewicz (Kraków: Znak, 2015); *Silva Rerum II*, trans. Izabela Korybut-Daszkiewicz (Kraków: Wydawnictwo Literackie, 2018); and *Silva Rerum III*, trans. Kamil Pecela (Kraków: Wydawnictwo Literackie, 2021).

1: How Jewish Is the History of the Polish-Lithuanian Commonwealth?

1. "Odsłonięto pomnik Romana Dmowskiego" (PAP), *Wiadomości*, November 11, 2006, https://wiadomosci.wp.pl/odslonieto-pomnik-romana-dmowskiego-6037524950385281a.

2. "Skini, policja i antyfaszyści. Konflikt trwa od lat," *Gazeta Wyborcza*, November 9, 2012, https://warszawa.wyborcza.pl/warszawa/56,34862,10624511,Skini__policja_i_antyfaszysci__Konflikt_trwa_od_lat.html.

3. Kasia Narkowicz and Konrad Pędziwiatr, "From Unproblematic to Contentious: Mosques in Poland," *Journal of Ethnic and Migration Studies* 43, no. 3 (2017): 444, 446. See also chapter 3 in this volume.

4. Sebastian Conrad, *What Is Global History?* (Princeton, NJ: Princeton Unviersity Press, 2017), 3.

5. Władysław Smoleński, *Stan i sprawa Żydów polskich w XVIII wieku* (Warsaw: Nakład Księgarni Celsa Lewickiego i Spółki, 1876), 5–6.

6. Raphael Mahler's estimates, based on a census of 1764–1765, have been widely accepted by scholars. See Raphael Mahler, *Yidn in amolikn Poyln in likht fun tsifern: di demografishe un sotsyal-ekonomishe strukturfun* (Warsaw: Yidish bukh, 1958).

7. Gershon David Hundert, *Jews in Poland-Lithuania in the Eighteenth Century: A Genealogy of Modernity* (Berkeley: University of California Press, 2004), 21. See also Gershon Hundert, "An Advantage to Peculiarity? The Case of the Polish Commonwealth," *AJS Review* 6 (1981): 21–38; Gershon Hundert, "Re(de)fining Modernity in Jewish History," in *Rethinking European Jewish History*, ed. Jeremy Cohen and Moshe Rosman (Oxford: Littman Library, 2009). See also Shaul Stampfer's work on Jewish demography: Shaul Stampfer, "Gidul Ha-ukhlusiyah ve-hagirah be-yahadut polin-lita be-'et ha-ḥadashah," in *Kiyum ve-shever: yehude polin le-dorotehem*, ed. Yisrael Bartal and Israel Gutman (Jerusalem: Merkaz Zalman Shazar, 1997); Jacob Goldberg, "On the Study of Polish-Jewish History," in *Studies in the History of the Jews in Old Poland*, ed. Adam Teller (Jerusalem: Magnes Press, 1998) ; Shaul Stampfer, "The 1764 Census of Lithuanian Jewry and What It Can Teach Us," *Papers in Jewish Demography 1993* (1997). See

also Zenon Guldon and Waldemar Kowalski, "The Jewish Population of Polish Towns in the Second Half of the 17th Century," in Teller, *Studies in the History of the Jews.*

8. Hundert, "Re(de)fining Modernity in Jewish History," 135.

9. Moshe Rosman, *How Jewish Is Jewish History?* (Oxford: Littman Library of Jewish Civilization, 2007), 37.

10. Moshe Rosman, "How Polish Is Polish History?" in Imaginations and Configurations of Polish Society: From the Middle Ages through the Twentieth Century, ed. Yvonne Kleinmann, Jürgen Heyde, Hüchtker Dietlind, Dobrochna Kalwa, Joanna Nalewajko-Kulikov, Katrin Steffen, and Tomasz Wiślicz (Göttingen: Wallstein Verlag, 2017), 19–34.

11. Natalia Aleksiun, *Conscious History : Polish Jewish Historians before the Holocaust* (London: Littman Library of Jewish Civilization, 2021).

12. See, e.g., Feliks Kiryk and Henryk Samsonowicz, eds., *Dzieje Sandomierza* (Warsaw: Polskie Towarzystwo Historyczne, 1993), 1:244–346, 2:20; Jacek Kaczor, "Kahał ostrowiecki w XVII–XVIII wieku," in *Żydzi wśród chrześcijan w dobie szlacheckiej Rzeczypospolitej*, ed. Waldemar Kowalski and Jadwiga Muszyńska (Kielce: Akademia Świętokrzyska, 1996), 63–64; and Jadwiga Muszyńska, "Ludność żydowska w Książu Wielkim w końcu XVIII wieku," in Kowalski and Muszyńska, *Żydzi wśród chrześcijan*, 69–76; and Stefan Gąsiorowski, *Chrześcijanie i Żydzi w Żółkwi w XVII i XVIII Wieku* (Kraków: Polska Akademia Umiejętności, 2001), 130, 146, 151, etc. See also Dariusz Rolnik, "Żydzi Czasów Rzeczypospolitej Stanisławowskiej w Polskiej Literaturze Pamiętnikarskiej XVIII–XIX w.," in *Staropolski Ogląd Świata: Problem Inności*, ed. Filip Wolański (Toruń: Wydawnictwo Adam Marszałek, 2007). Even publications issued by the Jewish Historical Institute have occasionally slipped into language referring to the "law of Moses"; see, e.g., Zofia Borzymińska, *Dzieje Żydów w Polsce: Wybór Tekstów Źródłowych, XIX Wiek* (Warsaw: Żydowski Instytut Historyczny, 1994).

13. See, e.g., essays in Feliks Kiryk, ed., Żydzi w Małopolsce: Studia z dziejów osadnictwa i życia społecznego (Przemyśl: Południowo-Wschodni Instytut Naukowy, 1991).

14. I have discussed the question of "diaspora" as applied to Jews in the Polish-Lithuanian Commonwealth in Magda Teter, "Jews in the Polish-Lithuanian Commonwealth: An Embedded Diaspora," in *The Oxford Handbook of the Jewish Diaspora*, ed. Hasia R. Diner (New York: Oxford University Press, 2021).

15. Kim D. Butler, "Defining Diaspora, Refining a Discourse," *Diaspora: A Journal of Transnational Studies*, no. 2 (2001), 190–91. Menachem Stern offers a definition of "Diaspora" in the latest edition of *Encyclopedia Judaica*. Here "the word Diaspora . . . is used in the present context for the voluntary dispersion of the Jewish people as distinct from their forced dispersion . . . Galut." Accordingly, the term could only be applied "to the period of the First Temple, the Second Temple, and that subsequent to the establishment of the State of Israel." Menachem Stern, "Diaspora," in *Encyclopedia Judaica*, 2nd ed., 5:637.

16. See, e.g., Khachig Tölölyan, "Rethinking Diaspora(s): Stateless Power in the Transnational Moment," *Diaspora: A Journal of Transnational Studies*, no. 1 (1996): 3–36; Jon Stratton, "(Dis)placing the Jews: Historicizing the Idea of Diaspora," *Diaspora: A Journal of Transnational Studies*, no. 3 (1997): 301–29; Butler, "Defining Diaspora"; Denise Eileen McCoskey, "Diaspora in the Reading of Jewish History, Identity, and Difference," *Diaspora* 12, no. 3 (2003): 387–418.

17. Barbara Kirshenblatt-Gimblett, "Spaces of Dispersal," *Cultural Anthropology* 9, no. 3 (1994), 339.

18. Adam Kaźmierczyk, *Żydzi w dobrach prywatnych: w świetle sądowniczej i administracyjnej praktyki dóbr magnackich w wiekach XVI–XVIII* (Kraków: Uniwersytet Jagielloński, Katedra Judaistyki, 2002), 8.

19. See, e.g., Passover haggadot and seventeenth-century documents discussing ceremonial and philanthropic links with Jewish communities in the land of Israel, in Israel Halpern, ed., *Pinkas va'ad arb'a arazot* (Jerusalem: Mosad Bialik,1945), 459, no. 870; 464–65, no. 884.

20. Moshe Rosman has recently called for a transnational approach to Jewish history that would connect Jewish communities beyond the political boundaries of non-Jewish states. See Moshe Rosman, "Jewish History across Borders," in Cohen and Rosman, *Rethinking European Jewish History*. Several scholars in recent decades have made a strong case for thinking about Jews, and Polish Jews in particular, as—to use Moshe Rosman's phrase—"*of* their countries and not just *in* them" (Rosman, "Jewish History across Borders," 23).

21. See, e.g., Kiryk and Samsonowicz, *Dzieje Sandomierza*, 2/1:170. See also Kiryk, *Żydzi w Małopolsce*, 13.

22. This tension is very much present, for example, in Stefan Gąsiorowski's book on Jews in Żółkiew. See Gąsiorowski, *Chrześcijanie i Żydzi w Żółkwi*.

23. Maria Bogucka and Henryk Samsonowicz, *Dzieje miast i mieszczaństwa w Polsce przedrozbiorowej* (Wroclaw: Zakład Narodowy im. Ossolińskich, 1986), 157, 159–60; and Władysław Rusiński, ed., *Dzieje Kalisza: Praca zbiorowa* (Poznań: Wydawnictwo Poznańskie,1977), 90. See also Kiryk, *Żydzi w Małopolsce*, 13.

24. Kiryk and Samsonowicz, *Dzieje Sandomierza*, 2/1:163.

25. Kiryk and Samsonowicz, *Dzieje Sandomierza*, 2/1:170.

26. See, e.g., Gąsiorowski, *Chrześcijanie i Żydzi w Żółkwi* .

27. Bogucka and Samsonowicz, *Dzieje miast*, 359.

28. See, for instance, the work of Maria Cieśla and Tomasz Wiślicz, such as Maria Cieśla, "Żydowscy Celnicy w Wielkim Księstwie Litewskim w XVII–XVIII Wieku," *Studia Judaica* 19, no. 2 (2016): 229–49; and Tomasz Wiślicz, *Zelman Wolfowicz i jego rządy w starostwie drohobyckim w połowie XVIII w.* (Kraków: Universitas, 2020).

29. Conrad, *What Is Global History?* 3. See also chapter 3 in this volume, and Rosman, "How Polish Is Polish History?"

30. Antonio Maria Graziani, *Antonii Mariae Gratiani a Burgo S. Sepulchri Episcopi Amerini De Vita Joannis Francisci Commendoni Cardinalis Libri Quatuor* (Parisiis: apud Sebastianum Mabre-Cramoisy regis typographum, via Jacoba sub Ciconiis, 1669); and Antonio Maria Graziani and Esprit Flèchier, *La vie du Cardinal Jean Francois Commendon* (Paris: Chez Sebastien Mabre-Cramoisy, Imprimeur du Roi, 1671).

31. See Hundert, *Jews in Poland-Lithuania*, 7—although note 8 contains some bibliographical inaccuracies. Graziani and Flèchier, *La vie du Cardinal Jean Francois Commendon*, 207. The 1694 French dictionary defined *citoyen* as "bourgeois, habitant d'une cité" (a burgher, inhabitant of a city). *Le Dictionnaire de l'académie Françoise, dedié au Roy. Tome Premier. A–L* (Paris: Jean Baptiste Coignard, 1694). *Dictionnaires d'aurtefois*, http://artfl-project.uchicago.edu/node/17, accessed March 18, 2016.

32. On the question of marginality, see Moshe Rosman, "An Innovative Tradition," in *Cultures of the Jews: A New History*, ed. David Biale (New York: Schocken Books, 2002). Hundert, *Jews in Poland-Lithuania*. For other accounts, see, for example, Papal Nuncio Luigi Lippomano, who laments the impossibility of implementing in Poland the 1555 papal bull *Cum Nimis Absurdum*, which had established the Roman ghetto just the year prior, reporting that Jews in Poland "receive unbelievably many favors, and all these lords and palatines are their strong defenders." Henricus Damianus Wojtyska and Aloisius Lippomano, eds., *Aloisius Lippomano (1555–1557)*, *Acta Nuntiaturae Polonae*, vol. 3/1 (Rome: Institutum Historicum Polonicum Romae, 1993), 276–78. On Lippomano in Poland, see Magda Teter, *Sinners on Trial: Jews and Sacrilege after the*

Reformation (Cambridge, MA: Harvard University Press, 2011), ch. 5. See also Teter, "Jews in the Polish-Lithuanian Commonwealth."

33. On the differences between the Crown and the Grand Duchy, see Maria Cieśla, "Sharing a Commonwealth: Polish Jews or Lithuanian Jews?," *Gal-'Ed* 24 (2015): 15–44.

34. Adam Kaźmierczyk, *Rodzilem się Żydem . . . : Konwersje Żydów w Rzeczypospolitej XVII–XVIII wieku* (Kraków: Księgarnia Akademicka, 2015), 11.

35. Leon Matwijowski, *Prawo ormiańskie w dawnej Polsce* (Lwów: Ksiegarnia Książka Aleksander Mazzucato, 1939).

36. Jakub Goldberg, "Żydowski Sejm Czterech Ziem w społecznym i politycznym ustroju dawnej Rzeczypospolitej," in *Żydzi w dawnej Rzeczypospolitej,* ed. Andrzej Link-Lenczowski (Wrocław: Ossolineum, 1991), 44–58; and Moshe Rosman, "The Authority of the Council of Four Lands Outside of Poland," in *Polin: Social and Religious Boundaries in Pre-Modern Poland,* ed. Adam Teller and Magda Teter (Oxford: Littman Library of Jewish Civilization, 2010). For an example of perceptions of the Council as an autonomous, "independent" body, see Halpern, *Pinkas va'ad arb'a araẓot.* Moshe Altbauer examines the vocabulary used in Jewish texts to describe Jewish autonomous institutions, demonstrating their rootedness in the Polish context. See Shmuel Ettinger, "The Council of Four Lands," in *The Jews in Old Poland, 1000–1795,* ed. Antony Polonsky, Jakub Basista, and Andrzej Link-Lenczowski (London: I. B. Tauris, Institute for Polish-Jewish Studies, 1993), 93–109; and Moshe Altbauer, "O języku dokumentów związanych z samorządem żydowskim w Polsce," in Link-Lenczowski, *Żydzi w Dawnej Rzeczypospolitej.*

37. Anatol Leszczyński, "Nazewnictwo organów samorządu żydowskiego w dawnej Rzeczypospolitej do 1764 r.," in Link-Lenczowski, *Żydzi w dawnej Rzeczypospolitej;* Goldberg, "Żydowski Sejm Czterech Ziem." For documents related to the Council of Four Lands preserved in Polish archives, see Jakub Goldberg and Adam Kaźmierczyk, *Sejm Czterech Ziem: Źródła* (Warsaw: Wydawnictwo Sejmowe, 2011).

38. The order was not exactly the same, if for no other reason than that the Jewish community in Lithuania had their own council, the *va'ad medinat lita.* For an example of the order of the Council of Four Lands, see Goldberg and Kaźmierczyk, *Sejm Czterech Ziem,* no. 74. For the *takkanot,* ordinances of the Council of Lithuania, see Simon Dubnow, ed., *Pinkas ha-medinah: o pinkas va'ad ha-kehilot ha-rashiyot bi-medinat lita, kovets takkanot u-fesakim mi-shenat 383 'ad shenat 521* (Berlin: 'Ayanot, 1925).

39. Goldberg and Kaźmierczyk, *Sejm Czterech Ziem,* nos. 29, 34, 35, 56, 60, 226.

40. For the use of the distinction between "in" and "of," see Moshe Rosman's work, including Rosman, "An Innovative Tradition," 524; and Rosman, "Jewish History across Borders," 23.

41. Cieśla, "Sharing a Commonwealth." On the Council of Lithuania, the *Va'ad Medinat Lita,* see Anna Michałowska-Mycielska, *Sejm Żydów litewskich (1623–1764)* (Warsaw: Wydawnictwo Akademickie "Dialog," 2014); Anna Michałowska-Mycielska, *The Council of Lithuanian Jews, 1623–1764* (Warsaw: Wydawnictwo Akademickie "Dialog," 2016). For the ordinances of the council, see Dubnow, *Pinkas ha-medinah.*

42. Murray Jay Rosman, *The Lords' Jews: Magnate-Jewish Relations in the Polish-Lithuanian Commonwealth During the Eighteenth Century* (Cambridge, MA: Harvard University Press, 1990), 186.

43. Archiwum Państwowe, Kraków at Wawel (APK-Wawel), Varia 11, "juramentum seniorum Judaeorum noviter electorum," for 1633 on 403–5; for 1634 on 509–11.

44. Goldberg and Kaźmierczyk, *Sejm Czterech Ziem,* no. 60.

45. Goldberg and Kaźmierczyk, *Sejm Czterech Ziem,* no. 64.

46. Cieśla, "Żydowscy celnicy w Wielkim Księstwie Litewskim," 246.

47. Cieśla, "Żydowscy celnicy w Wielkim Księstwie Litewskim," 249.

48. Adam Teller, "The Shtetl as an Arena for Polish-Jewish Integration in the Eighteenth Century," *Polin* 17 (2004): 25–40.

49. Kiryk and Samsonowicz, *Dzieje Sandomierza*, 2/1:131–59.

50. Kiryk and Samsonowicz, *Dzieje Sandomierza*, 2/1:144–47. On the role of Jews in trade in the eighteenth century, see Rosman, *Lords' Jews*.

51. Kiryk and Samsonowicz, *Dzieje Sandomierza*, 2/1:146–47.

52. Kiryk and Samsonowicz, *Dzieje Sandomierza*, 2/1:150.

53. Gąsiorowski, *Chrześcijanie i Żydzi w Żółkwi*, esp. ch. 3–4.

54. In Poznań, restrictions were rather strict. See Archiwum Państwowe, Poznań (APP), Akta m. Poznania, I 2250 "Akta luźne dot. Sporów m. Poznania z żydami 1537–1688, 1717," 76–79; 1610, "Lustratio et revisio domorum per Judaeous . . . possessorum," 107–11; 1617, "Decretum SS Sigismundi 3 anno 1617 contra Judaeos ultra numerorum domorum." See also Adam Teller, *Ḥayim Be-ẓavta: Ha-Rov'a Ha-Yehudi Shel Poznan Ba-Maḥaẓit Ha-Rishonah Shel Ha-Me'ah Ha-Shev'a 'Esreh* (Jerusalem: Magnes Press, 2003). Similar restrictions were issued in Sandomierz.

55. On the social and religious topography of Wilno (now Vilnius), see David A. Frick, *Wilnianie: Żywoty siedemnastowieczne* (Warsaw: Przegląd Wschodni, 2008); and David A. Frick, *Kith, Kin, and Neighbors: Communities and Confessions in Seventeenth-Century Wilno* (Ithaca, NY: Cornell University Press, 2013).

56. Archiwum Państwowe, Przemyśl (APPrzem), Akta m. Przemyśla Scabinalia Officiosa (1639–1642), 284–85. On Przemyśl, see Jacek Krochmal, *Krzyż i menora: Żydzi i Chrześcijanie w Przemyślu w latach 1559–1772* (Przemyśl: Towarzystwo Przyjaciół Nauk w Przemyślu, 1996).

57. Filip Sulimierski, Bronisław Chlebowski, and Władysław Walewski, *Słownik geograficzny Królestwa Polskiego i innych krajów słowiańskich*, vol. 9 (Warsaw: Wydawnictwa Artsytyczne i Filmowe, 1975 [1880]), 800–803.

58. Jacob Goldberg, ed., *Jewish Privileges in the Polish Commonwealth: Charters of Rights Granted to Jewish Communities in Poland-Lithuania in the Sixteenth to Eighteenth Centuries*, 3 vols. (Jerusalem: Israel Academy of Sciences and Humanities, 1985–2001), 2:70.

59. Abraham Getter, "Dzieje Żydów w Sandomierzu do pierwszej połowy XVIII-ego wieku" (masters thesis, Żydowski Instytut Historyczny, 1930s), 14, 17, 86.

60. Kiryk and Samsonowicz, *Dzieje Sandomierza* 2/1: 25; and Melchior Buliński, *Monografija miasta Sandomierza* (Warsaw: Drukarnia F. Czermińskiego i S. Niemiery, 1879), 140. See, esp., Getter, "Dzieje Żydów," 14–15, 22.

61. Kiryk and Samsonowicz, *Dzieje Sandomierza*, 2/1:199. On Joachim and his family, see Getter, "Dzieje Żydów," 32–38.

62. See, e.g., APP, Akta m. Poznania, Acta Consularia I 35 (1617–1623), 1031–39, also 1176–80.

63. APP, Akta m. Poznania, I 2250: 5, a 1565 agreement between the City Council and the Jewish community that Jews would remove mud (*błoto*) from their streets; pp. 174–76, a 1627 complaint that Jews did not maintain the city walls in their neighborhood and were discarding feces and waste in inappropriate places, causing smells. On Poznań, see also Teller, *Ḥayim Be-ẓavta*. See also, for example, the 1682 privileges for Biłgoraj in Goldberg, *Jewish Privileges*, 2:23–24, and for Janowiec, 2:69–72. See also APPrzem, Akta m. Przemyśla 590, 29–32, 63–64.

64. "A chcąc miasto nasze Kazimierz zrujnowane a ruinis resuscitare do dawnej przywieść perfekcyi." Goldberg, *Jewish Privileges*, 1:119–22.

65. Hundert, "Re(de)fining Modernity in Jewish History," 135.

66. Goldberg, *Jewish Privileges*, 2:26. On Żołkiew, see Gąsiorowski, *Chrześcijanie i Żydzi w Żółkwi*. See also Magda Teter, *Jews and Heretics in Catholic Poland: A Beleaguered Church in the Post-Reformation Era* (Cambridge: Cambridge University Press, 2006), ch. 2 and 5.

67. "Ponieważ miasto Lwów w województwie ruskim antemurale Regni primo furori od nieprzyjaciela Krzyża S. resistit, tedy paternam nostram curam do kontynuowania fortyrfik-acji jego do namowey z wielmożnymi hetmanami." Anna Michałowska-Mycielska, *Sejmy i sejmiki koronne wobec Żydów: Wybór tekstów źródłowych* (Warsaw: Wydawnictwo Uniwersytetu Warszawkiego, 2006), 98.

68. "Żydzi miejscy i przedmiejscy, more antique do pomocy około armaty po wałach obse-quentes być mają." Michałowska-Mycielska, *Sejmy i sejmiki koronne wobec Żydów*, 98.

69. Jakub Goldberg and Adam Kaźmierczyk, *Sejm Czterech Ziem: Źródła* (Warsaw: Wydawnictwo Sejmowe, 2011), no. 13. On Jews in trade, see Teller, "Shtetl as an Arena"; Rosman, *Lords' Jews*; and Gershon David Hundert, "The Role of the Jews in Commerce in Early Modern Poland-Lithuania," *Journal of European Economic History* 16, no. 2 (1987): 245–75.

70. On economic relations between Jews and the Catholic Church, see Yehudit Kalik, "Patterns of Contact between the Catholic Church and the Jews in the Polish-Lithuanian Commonwealth: Jewish Debts," in Teller, *Studies in the History of the Jews*; Yehudit Kalik, "Ha-Knesiyyah Ha-Katolit Ve-Ha-Yehudim Be-Mamlekhet Polin-Lita Ba-Me'ot Ha-17–18" (PhD diss., Hebrew University, 1998); Yehudit Kalik, "Economic Relations between the Catholic Church and Jews in the Polish-Lithuanian Commonwealth during the Seventeenth and Eighteenth Centuries," *Gal-Ed* 23 (2012): 15–36; Henryk Samsonowicz, "The Agreement between the Bishop of Płock and the Jews of Ostrow Mazowiecka in 1721," in Teller, *Studies in the History of the Jews*; and Jakub Goldberg, "Jak Ksiądz z Żydem zakładali manufakturę żelazną w Wielkopolsce: O Przedsiębiorstwach żydowskich w Przemyśle polskim w XVIII w.," in *The Jews in Poland*, ed. Andrzej Paluch (Kraków: Jagiellonian University, 1992). On the Jews and the Catholic Church in Poland, see also Teter, *Jews and Heretics*. For an example, see also Muzeum Miasta Jarosławia, Akta m. Jarosławia 66, Księga wójtowsko-ławnicza, 147r–147v.

71. Archiwum Kurii Metropolitalnej, Cracow, MS. Acta Episcopalia 90, document "Conservationis Judaeorum in Bonis Spiritualis contra Parochem Gołaszowiensis et Mielczensis," folio 271.

72. This may have required cooperation with secular authorities.

73. See, e.g., Israel Halpern and Israel Bartal, eds., *Pinkas va'ad arb'a arazot* (Jerusalem: 1989), takanah 639 of 1739. See also Moshe Rosman, "The Indebtedness of the Lublin Kahal in the Eighteenth Century," in Teller, *Studies in the History of the Jews*.

74. Adam Teller, *Money, Power, and Influence in Eighteenth-Century Lithuania: The Jews on the Radziwiłł Estates* (Stanford, CA: Stanford University Press, 2016), originally published in Hebrew in 2006 as *Kesef, koaḥ ve-hashpa'ah*.

75. Archiwum Państwowe, Lublin (APL), Akta m. Lublina, Consularia 209, "sub lege Moysi," e.g., 54, 56, 175, but on 150 "sub supersitione Judaismi."

76. For examples of signatures in Hebrew, see several documents in Muzeum Miasta Jarosławia, Akta m. Jarosławia 66, Księga wójtowsko-ławnicza, 147r–147v; APP, Księgi Grodzkie Poznańskie W. 13, Akta sądu wojewodzińskiego 1732–1740; see also APK-Wawel, Acta Castrensus Palatinatus Cracoviensis, Castrensia Cracoviensia 481 on 493–94.

77. APL, Akta m. Lublina, Acta consularia 208, 12r–13r, 25v.

78. See, e.g., APK-Wawel, Acta Castrensus Palatinatus Cracoviensis: Castrensia Cracoviensia, Relationes 90.

79. See, e.g., APL, Akta m. Chełma 1 and 2; and Akta m. Sawina 3 and 4.

80. APP, Księgi Grodzkie Poznańskie W. 13, Akta sądu wojewodzińskiego 1732–1740, 76–77.

81. On Poland, see Magda Teter, *Jews and Heretics in Catholic Poland: A Beleaguered Church*

in the Post-Reformation Era (Cambridge: Cambridge University Press, 2006), ch. 4; Magda Teter, "'There Should Be No Love between Us and Them': Social Life and Bounds of Jewish and Canon Law in Early Modern Poland," in Teller and Teter, *Polin*.

82. Yosef Kaplan, *An Alternative Path to Modernity: The Sephardi Diaspora in Western Europe* (Leiden: Brill, 2000), 105. See also Teter, "Jews in the Polish-Lithuanian Commonwealth."

83. APL, Akta m. Lublina, Acta Consularia 209, 218v–219.

84. Benjamin Aaron ben Abraham Slonik, *Mas'at Binyamin: ve-hem she'elot u-teshuvot* (Kraków: M. N. Meisels, 1632), no. 86. This responsum was censored in some later editions, either by replacing "Christians" with "Ishmaelim" (Muslims), or by being entirely removed, as it was in the 1894 Vilna edition. See also Teter, *Jews and Heretics*; Teter, "'There Should Be No Love,'" 260–61; and Teter, "Jews in the Polish-Lithuanian Commonwealth."

85. See Solomon Luria, *She'elot u-teshuvot*, no. 72. See also, Edward Fram, *Ideals Face Reality: Jewish Law and Life in Poland, 1550–1655* (Cincinnati, OH: Hebrew Union College Press, 1997), 30.

86. Slonik, *Masa'at Binyamin*, no. 30.

87. Magda Teter, *Blood Libel: On The Trail of an Antisemitic Myth* (Cambridge, MA: Harvard University Press, 2020), 203. Sebastian Śleszkowski, *Odkrycie zdrad, złośliwych ceremoniy, taiemnych rad, praktyk szkodliwych Rzeczypospolitey y wszystkich zamysłów żydowskich,* (Brunsbergae: In Officina typographica Georgij Schonfels, 1621), unnumbered.

88. *Arkhiv iugo-zapadnoi Rossii* (Kyiv: Universitetskaia Tipografiia, 1869), vol. 1, p. 5: 267–70. For the English translation by Magda Teter at the Early Modern Workshop in 2006, see "Two Cases of Apostasy in Dubno 1716: Jews, Christians, and Family Life," www.earlymodern.org., accessed March 10, 2023.

89. See Kaźmierczyk, *Rodziłem się Żydem*. See also Edward Fram and Magda Teter, "Apostasy, Fraud, and the Beginning of Hebrew Printing in Cracow," *AJS Review* 30, no. 1 (2006): 31–66; Teter, *Jews and Heretics in Catholic Poland*, 64–66; Magda Teter, "The Legend of Ger Zedek of Wilno as Polemic and Reassurance," *AJS Review* 29, no. 2 (2005): 237–63; and Magdalena Teter, "Jewish Conversions to Catholicism in the Polish-Lithuanian Commonwealth of the Seventeenth and Eighteenth Centuries," *Jewish History* 17, no. 3 (2003): 257–83.

90. For another telling example, see the trial of Szmul Dubiński, in Adam Kaźmierczyk, ed. *Żydzi Polscy 1648–1772: Źródła*, vol. 6 (Kraków: Uniwersytet Jagielloński Katedra Judaistyki, 2001), 147–51, 169–71. For the English translation of the trial, see Magda Teter, "The Early Modern Inn as a Space for Religious and Cultural Exchange," Early Modern Workshop 2012, www.earlymodern.org., accessed March 10, 2023. Also discussed in Teter, "Jews in the Polish-Lithuanian Commonwealth."

91. Goldberg, "On the Study of Polish-Jewish History," 9.

2: Multiconfessionalism and Interconfessionality

1. David Frick, *Kith, Kin, and Neighbors: Communities and Confessions in Seventeenth-Century Wilno* (Ithaca, NY: Cornell University Press, 2013), 85–86.

2. Frick, *Kith, Kin, and Neighbors*, 87.

3. Frick, *Kith, Kin, and Neighbors*, 88.

4. Natalia Nowakowska, *King Sigismund of Poland and Martin Luther: The Reformation before Confessionalization* (Oxford: Oxford University Press, 2018), 68.

5. Joanna Kostylo, "Commonwealth of All Faiths: Republican Myth and the Italian Diaspora in Sixteenth-Century Poland-Lithuania," in *Citizenship and Identity in a Multinational Commonwealth: Poland-Lithuania in Context, 1550–1772*, ed. Karin Friedrich and Barbara M. Pendzich (Leiden: Brill, 2009), 172–205.

6. Inge Lukšaitė, *Reformacija Lietuvos Didžiojoje Kunigaikštystėje ir Mažojoje Lietuvoje. XVI a. trečias dešimtmetis–XVII a. pirmas dešimtmetis* (Vilnius: Baltos lankos, 1999), 271–307.

7. Wojciech Świeboda, *Innowiercy w opiniach prawnych uczonych polskich w XV wieku: Poganie, zydzi, muzulmanie* (Kraków: Societas Vistulana, 2013), esp. 105–9.

8. [John Peyton], *A Relation of the State of Polonia and the United Provinces of that Crown Anno 1598*, ed. C. H. Talbot (Rome: Elementa ad Fontium Editiones XIII, 1965), f. 42v–43. See also see Sebastian Sobecki, "John Peyton's A Relation of the State of Polonia and the Accession of King James I, 1598–1603," *English Historical Review* 129 (2014): 1079–97.

9. Andrzej Frycz Modrzewski, *De Republica Emendanda: O poprawie Rzeczypospolitej*, ed. Stanisław Bodniak (Warsaw: PIW, 1953), part 4, "O kościele," ch. 6, 406–8; in contrast, see Piotr Skarga, "Kazanie trzecie," in *Kazania sejmowe*, ed. Janusz Tazbir and Mirosław Korołko (Wrocław: Zakład Narodowy im. Ossolińskich, 1995), 54–55. On early modern national stereotypes, see Stanisław Kot, "Właściwości narodów," in *Polska złotego wieku a Europa. Studia i szkice*, ed. H. Barycz (Warsaw: PIW, 1987), 761–66.

10. For the Holy Roman Empire, see Kaspar von Greyerz and Kim Siebenhüner, eds., *Religion und Gewalt: Konflikte, Rituale, Deutungen, 1500–1800* (Göttingen: Vandenhoeck & Ruprecht, 2006), 354–60.

11. Józef Kazimierski, "Z dziejów Węgrowa w XV–XVII wieku," *Rocznik Mazowiecki* 3 (1970): 267–82; and Almut Bues, ed., *Die Aufzeichnungen des Dominikaners Martin Gruneweg (1562–ca. 1618) über seine Familie in Danzig, seine Handelsreisen in Osteuropa und sein Klosterleben in Polen*, 4 vols. (Wiesbaden: Harrassowitz, 2008), 1:290.

12. Frick, *Kin, Kith, and Neighbors*, 415.

13. Thomas Kaufmann, "Transkonfessionalität, Interkonfessionalität, binnenkonfessionelle Pluralität," in *Transkonfessionalität, Interkonfessionalität, binnenkonfessionelle Pluralität: Neue Forschungen zur Konfessionalisierungsthese*, ed. Kaspar von Greyerz et al. (Gütersloh: Gütersloher Verlagshaus, 2003), 9–15.

14. Markus Friedrich, "Katholische Mission in protestantischer Deutung: Heidenbekehrung als interkonfessionelles Thema des frühen 18. Jahrhunderts," in *Polycentric Structures in the History of World Christianity*, ed. Klaus Koschorke and Adrian Hermann (Wiesbaden: Harrassowitz, 2014), 271–72.

15. Susan Karant-Nunn, "Changing One's Mind: Transformations in Reformation History from a Germanist's Perspective," *Renaissance Quarterly* 58, no. 4 (2005):, 1124.

16. Henryk Litwin, *Napływ szlachty polskiej na Ukrainę 1569–1648* (Warsaw: Semper, 2000); and Marzena Liedke, "Rody Ruskie w elicie politycznej Wielkiego Księstwa Litewskiego w XVI–XVIII wieku," in *Społeczeństwo Staropolskie. Seria Nowa, I: Społeczeństwo a Polityka*, ed. Andrzej Karpiński (Warsaw: DIG, 2008), 137–62.

17. On the problematic nature of the concept, see Wojciech Kriegseisen, *Between State and Church: Confessional Relations from Reformation to Enlightenment; Poland—Lithuania—Germany—Netherlands* (Frankfurt: Peter Lang, 2016), 15–28.

18. Janusz Tazbir, *A State without Stakes: Religious Toleration in Reformation Poland-Lithuania* (New York: Kościuszko Foundation, 1973).

19. Nicholas Terpstra, *Religious Refugees in the Early Modern World: An Alternative History of the Reformation* (Cambridge: Cambridge University Press, 2015), 15–17; and Andrew Pettegree, "The Politics of Toleration in the Free Netherlands, 1572–1620," in *Tolerance and Intolerance in the European Reformation*, ed. Ole Peter Grell and Robert Scribner (Cambridge: Cambridge University Press, 1996), 182–98.

20. Jolanta Dworzaczkowa, *Bracia Czescy w Wielkopolsce w XVI i XVII wieku* (Warsaw:

Semper, 1997), 28; and Oskar Halecki, *Zgoda Sandomierska 1570 r.: Jej geneza i znaczenie w dziejach reformacyi Polskiej za Zygmunta Augusta* (Warsaw: Anczyca i spółki, 1915). See Maciej Ptaszyński, "Between Marginalization and Orthodoxy: The Unitas Fratrum in Poland in the Sixteenth Century," *Journal of Moravian History* 14, no. 1 (Spring 2014): 1–29.

21. Confoederatio Generalis Warsaviensis 1573, in *Volumina Legum* II, ed. Jozafata Ohryzki [Saint Petersburg: n.p. 1859] (repr. Warsaw: Wydawnictwo Artystyczne i Filmowe, 1980), 124 (§ 841).

22. Kęstutis Daugirdas, "Rezeption der Theologie Calvins im Großfürstentum Litauen und Königreich Polen," in *Calvin und Calvinismus: Europäische Perspektiven,* ed. Irene Dingel and Hermann Selderhuis (Göttingen: Vandenhoeck & Ruprecht, 2011), 157.

23. Kolja Lichy, "Reden als Aushandeln: Rhetorik und Zeremoniell auf dem polnisch-litauischen Sejm zu Beginn der Wasa-Zeit," in *Politische Redekultur in der Vormoderne: Die Oratorik europäischer Parlamente in Spätmittelalter und Früher Neuzeit,* ed. Jörg Feuchter and Johannes Helmrath (Frankfurt am Main: Peter Lang, 2008), 149–72.

24. David Frick, *Wilnianie: Żywoty siedemnastowieczne* (Warsaw: Uniwersytet Warszawski, 2007). More recently, see Tomasz Kempa, *Konflikty wyznaniowe w Wilnie od początku reformacji do końca XVII wieku* (Toruń: Wydawnictwo Naukowe Uniwersytetu Mikołaja Kopernika, 2016).

25. Kazimierz Bem, *Calvinism in the Polish-Lithuanian Commonwealth, 1548–1648: The Churches and the Faithful* (Leiden: Brill, 2020), 172.

26. Bem, *Calvinism in the Polish-Lithuanian Commonwealth,* 156, 172, 38–39, and 73–76.

27. Robert Knecht, *The French Civil Wars, 1562–1598* (Harlow: Longman, 2000)

28. Cited in Tadeusz Wasilewski, "Tolerancja religijna w Wielkim Księstwie Litewskim w XVI–XVII wieku," *Odrodzenie i Reformacja w Polsce* 19 (1974):,120, alluding to the 1572 Saint Bartholomew's Day massacre.

29. Hugo Grotius to Izrael Jaski in Gdańsk, see Stanisław Kot, "Grotius a Polska," in Kot, *Polska złotego wieku,* 597.

30. Heinz Schilling, "Die Konfessionalisierung im Reich," *Historische Zeitschrift* 246 (1988): 1–45; and Wolfgang Reinhard, "Reformation, Counter-Reformation, and the Early Modern State: A Reassessment," *Catholic Historical Review* 75 (1989):, 383–84.

31. For a critical assessment, see Jörg Deventer, "'Confessionalization': A Useful Theoretical Concept for the Study of Religion, Politics and Society in Early Modern East-Central Europe?" *European Review of History—Revue européenne d'Histoire* 11, no. 3 (2004): 403–25; and Bahlcke and Strohmeyer, eds., *Konfessionalisierung in Ostmitteleuropa: Wirkungen des religiösen Wandels im 16. und 17. Jahrhundert in Staat, Gesellschaft und Kultur* (Stuttgart: Franz Steiner Verlag, 1999), esp. the introduction, 7–10.

32. Maciej Ptaszyński, "The Polish-Lithuanian Commonwealth," in *A Companion to the Reformation in Central Europe,* ed. Howard Louthan and Graeme Murdock (Leiden: Brill), 40–67.

33. See, among others, Evamaria Engel, "Die Wirkungen der Reformation in Danzig," *Zeitschrift für Ostforschung* 42 (1993): 195–206; and Maciej Ptaszyński, *Reformacja w Polsce a dziedzictwo Erazma z Rotterdamu* (Warsaw: Wydawnictwa Uniwersytetu Warszawskiego, 2018), 96–158.

34. Marian Pawlak, *Studia uniwersyteckie młodzieży z Prus Królewskich w XVI–XVIII w.* (Toruń: UMK, 1988), 114 and table 9 in the appendix.

35. Jacek Wijaczka, *Albrecht von Brandenburg-Ansbach (1490–1568): Ostatni mistrz zakonu Krzyżackiego i pierwszy książę w Prusiech* (Olsztyn: Wydawnictwo Littera, 2010), esp. 78–115.

36. Jacek Wijaczka, *Asverus von Brandt, 1509–1559: Życie i działalność dyplomatyczna w służbie księcia Albrechta pruskiego* (Kielce: WSP, 1996)

37. Karin Friedrich, "Die Reformation in Polen-Litauen," in *Polen in der europäischen Geschichte: Ein Handbuch in vier Bänden*, vol. 2, *Frühe Neuzeit*, ed. H. J. Bömelburg (Stuttgart: Hiersemann, 2011), 127.

38. Michael G. Müller, *Zweite Reformation und städtische Autonomie im Königlichen Preußen: Danzig, Elbing und Thorn in der Epoche der Konfessionalisierung 1557–1660* (Berlin: Akademie Verlag, 1997), 42–44.

39. *Acta Tomiciana* [AT], ed. Władysław Pociecha et al., 18 vols. (AT 1–13, Poznań: Biblioteka Kórnicka, 1852–1915; AT 14–17, Poznań: Wyd. PAN, 1952–1966; AT 18, Poznań: Biblioteka Kórnicka, 1999), here: AT 7, no. CXIII, 356–57 ; also AT 8, no. XIII, 31; AT 8, no., XLIII, 62; AT 7, no. LXXXVI, 318, "his tumultibus ac erroribus."

40. *Acta Tomiciana* 7, 249–50.

41. Stanisław Hosius, *Confession, Das ist: Ein Christliche Bekantnuß Des Catholischen Glaubens oder vil mehr ain auszlegung solcher Bekantnuß, wölche die Vätter der Provintzen Gnesen und Lewenburg im Königreich Polen auff dem Synodo zu Petricovien auffgericht im jar des Herren geburt MDLI. Confessio Catholicae Fidei Christianae* (Ingolstadt: Weissenhorn, 1560), 2 vols., cited in Kolja Lichy, "Against Luther's 'Satanism'? Catholic Reform and Lutheran Reformation in East-Central Europe," in *The Luther Effect in Eastern Europe: History—Memory—Culture*, ed. Joachim Bahlcke et al. (Munich: Oldenbourg Verlag, 2017), 83.

42. Mirosław Korolko, *Klejnot wolnego sumienia: Polemika wokół konfedercji warszawskiej w latach 1573–1658* (Warsaw: Instytut Wydawniczy PAX, 1974), 192.

43. Urszula Augustyniak and Wojciech Sokołowski, eds., *"Spisek Orleański" w latach 1626–1628* (Warsaw: PWN, 1990). For the impact of the Swedes, see Robert I. Frost, *The Northern Wars, 1558–1721* (Harlow: Longman, 2000), 114–28.

44. Archiwum Państwowe w Toruniu Kat. II, no. 13. 32, "Briefe und Miscellen aus verschiedenen Städten nach Thorn," November 5, 1681, 6–8. See the use of such stereotypes as explored in Jan S. Bystroń, *Megalomania narodowa* [1935], repr. (Warsaw: Książka i Wiedza, 1995), 175–78.

45. Müller, *Zweite Reformation*, esp. 191–220.

46. Mariusz Brodnicki, *Nauczanie filozofii w Gdańskim Gymnasium Akademickim do połowy XVII wieku* (Gdańsk: Wydawnictwo Athenae Gedanenses, 2012).

47. Aleksander Klemp, "Skład wyznaniowy i społeczny szlachty protestanckiej w Prusach Królewskich (druga połowa XVII–druga połowa XVIII wieku)," in *Szlachta i ziemiaństwo na Pomorzu w dobie nowożytnej XVI–XX wieku*, ed. Jerzy Dygdała (Toruń: TNT, 1993), 55.

48. Katarzyna Cieślak, "Luterańska sztuka kościelna w Gdańsku, 1540–1703," in *Protestantyzm i protestanci na Pomorzu*, ed. Jan Iluk and Danuta Mariańska (Gdańsk: Typos, 1987), 63–77.

49. Sławomir Kościelak, "Dzieje wyznaniowe Prus Królewskich XVI–XVIII wieku," in *Prusy Królewskie: Społeczeństwo, kultura, gospodarka, 1454–1772*, ed. Edmund Kizik (Gdańsk: Muzeum Narodowe w Gdańsku, 2012), 238.

50. Bem, *Calvinism in the Polish-Lithuanian Commonwealth*, 45.

51. Müller, *Zweite Reformation*, 224–25, 230–33.

52. Krzysztof Mikulski, "Obcy w oblężonej twierdze protestantyzmu: portret zbiorowy katolików Toruńskich w II połowie XVII i w XVIII wieku," in *Rzeczpospolita wielu wyznań: Materiały z międzynarodowej konferencji: Kraków 18–20 listopada 2002*, ed. Adam Kaźmierczyk et al. (Kraków: Księgarnia Akademicka, 2004), 294–310.

53. Marian Biskup, ed., *Historia Torunia*, vol. 3: *Między barokiem i oświeceniem, 1660–1793* (Toruń: TNT, 1996), 104–6.

54. Sławomir Kościelak, *Katolicy w protestanckim Gdańsku od drugiej połowy XVI do końca XVIII wieku* (Gdańsk: Wydawnictwo Uniwersytetu Gdańskiego, 2012).

55. Henryk Łowmiański, *Studia nad początkami społeczeństwa i państwa litewskiego*, 2 vols. (Wilno: Nakład Towarzystwa Przyjaciół Nauk, 1931–1932).

56. Ingė Lukšaite, "Die reformatorischen Kirchen Litauens bis 1795," in *Die reformatorischen Kirchen Litauens: Ein historischer Abriss*, ed. Arthur Hermann and Wilhelm Kahle (Erlangen: Martin-Luther-Verlag, 1998), 39. See also Lukšajtė, *Reformacija Lietuvos Didžiojoje Kunigaikštystėje*, esp. 338–401.

57. Lukšaite, "Die reformatorischen Kirchen," 41.

58. Vaclovas Vaidava, "Über die Beziehungen zwischen Žemaitija und Herzogtum Preußen im 16. Jahrhundert," *Annaberger Annalen* 4 (1996): 93–106.

59. Marzena Liedke, "Bezowocne starania: Korespondencja Jana Kalwina z Zygmuntem Augustem, Jakubem Uchańskim, Janem Tarnowskim i Mikołajem Radziwiłłem Czarnym," in *Ewangelicyzm Reformowany w pierwszej Rzeczypospolitej: Dialog z Europą i wybory aksjologiczne w świetle literatury i piśmiennictwa XVI–XVII wieku*, ed. Dariusz Chemperek (Warsaw: Wydawnictwa Uniwersytetu Warszawskiego, 2015), 17–56, esp. 35–40.

60. Ptaszyński, "Polish-Lithuanian Commonwealth," 54.

61. Jacek Wijaczka, "Reformacja w miastach prywatnych w koronie w XVI wieku," *Roczniki dziejów społecznych i gospodarczych* 77 (2016): 379–406.

62. Matthias Niendorf, *Das Großfürstentum Litauen: Studien zur Nationsbildung in der Frühen Neuzeit (1569–1795)* (Wiesbaden: Harrassowitz, 2006), 126–27.

63. Henryk Lulewicz, "Skład wyznaniowy senatorów świeckich Wielkiego Księstwa Litewskiego za panowania Wazów," *Przegląd Historyczny* 68, no. 3 (1977), 425–32; Ambroise Jobert counts fifteen Protestants, eight Orthodox, and one Catholic. See Ambroise Jobert, *De Luther à Mohila: la Pologne dans la crise der la Chrétienté 1517–1648* (Paris: Institut des Études Slaves, 1979), 322.

64. Marzena Liedke and Piotr Guzowski, eds., *Akta Synodów Prowincjonalnych Jednoty Litewskiej 1626–1637* (Warsaw: Semper, 2011), ix.

65. Urszula Augustyniak, "Non de fide, sed de securitate pacis: Wiara i polityka ewangelików w Rzeczypospolitej w latach 1631–1632," *Odrodzenie i Reformacja w Polsce* 44 (2004): 71–98.

66. See, e.g., Świętosław Orzelski, *Bezkrólewia ksiąg ośmioro 1572–1576: Scriptores Rerum Polonicarum* 22, ed. Eduardus Kuntze [1592] (Cracoviae: Sumptibus Academiae Litterarum Gebethner et Wolf, 1917.

67. *Volumina Legum* II, 124 (§ 841).

68. *Statut Wielkiego Xięstwa Litewskiego naprzód za Nayasnieyszego Hospodara Króla Jegomości Zygmunta III w Krakowie w roku 1588: Drugi raz w Wilnie 1619 roku . . . Teraz zas piąty raz ze szcześliwie panuiącego Naiasnieyszego Króla Jegomości Augusta Trzeciego przedrukowany* (Wilno: Drukarnia Societatis Jesu, 1744), 62–65.

69. Henryk Wisner, *Najjasniejsza Rzeczpospolita: Szkice z dziejów Polski szlacheckiej XVI–XVII wieku* (Warsaw: PIW, 1978), 41–43.

70. Based on archives of noble tribunals in Małopolska that no longer exist, see Marek Wajsblum, *Ex regestro arianismi: Szkice z dziejów upadku protestantyzmu w Małopolsce* (Kraków: Nakł. Towarzystwa Badań nad dziejów Reformacji w Polsce, 1937). Tomasz Kempa, *Wobec Kontrreformacji: Protestanci i prawosławni w obronie swobód wyznanionwych w Rzeczypospolitej w końcu XVI i w pierwszej połowie XVII wieku* (Toruń: Adam Marszałek, 2007), 468, 503. During the 1645 Sejm, Protestant grievances focused on tribunal judgments breaching Protestant immunities.

71. Stanisław Karnkowski, *Epistolae illlustrium virorum in tres libros digestae* (Cracoviae, 1578), cited in Robert Kościelny, *Problem Tolerancyjności Kontrreformatorów w Rzeczypospolitej na przełomie XVI i XVII wieku* (Szczecin: Wydawnictwo Naukowe Uniwersytetu Szczecińskiego, 1997), 93.

72. Kriegseisen, *Between State and Church*, 28–29.

73. See Urszula Augustyniak, *Testamenty ewangelików reformowanych w Wielkim Księstwie Litewskim w XVI–XVIII wieku* (Warsaw: Semper, 2014).

74. Unlike Poland, Lithuania did not experience an "execution movement" in the 1560s, led by the lower nobility and directed against the domination of magnate families. See Antoni Mączak, *Rządzący i rządzeni: Władza i społeczeństwo w Europie wczesnonowożytnej* (Warsaw: Semper, 2002), 114–15.

75. Niendorf, *Das Großfürstentum*, esp. 130–31.

76. Mariusz Kowalski, *Księstwa Rzeczpospolitej: Państwo magnackie jako Region Polityczny* (Warsaw: PAN-IgiPZ, 2013), 120.

77. *Volumina Legum* II, 124 (§ 842)."Spiritual or secular" relates to lands and population; see Józef Siemieński, *"Rebus" w konfederacji warszawskiej r. 1573* (Warsaw: Nakład Towarzystwa Naukowego Warszawskiego, 1927).

78. Müller, "Der Consensus Sandormiriensis," 397–407.

79. Biblioteka PAN w Kórniku rkps 325, p. 579, cited in Wisner, *Najjasniejsza Rzeczpospolita*, 150.

80. Bem, *Calvinism in the Polish-Lithuanian Commonwealth*, 196–221.

81. Hans-Jürgen Bömelburg, "Konfessionspolitische Deutungsmuster und konfessionsfundamentalistische Kriegsmotive in Polen-Litauen um 1600: Durchsetzung und Grenzen in einer multikonfessionellen Gesellschaft," in *Konfessioneller Fundamentalismus: Religion als politischer Faktor im europäischen Mächtesystem um 1600*, ed. Heinz Schilling (Berlin: De Gruyter Oldenbourg, 2007), 299.

82. Lulewicz, "Skład wyznaniowy," 440.

83. Deimantas Karvelis, "Przymus wyznaniowy w 'księstwie birżańskim' u schyłku XVI i w pierwszej połowie XVII wieku," in *Litwa w epoce Wazów*, ed. Wojciech Kriegseisen and Andrzej Rachuba (Warsaw: Neriton, 2006), 261.

84. Bem, *Calvinism in the Polish-Lithuanian Commonwealth*, 104–12.

85. Augustyn Mieleski-Rotundus blamed the "licence" among citizens on "poorly understood freedom of religion." See "Letter by Augustyn Rotundus to Andrzej Wolan, 10 December 1571," in Andrzej Wolan, *De Libertate politica, sive civili: O wolnosci Rzeczypospolitej albo slacheckiej*, ed. Maciej Eder and Roman Mazurkiewicz, transl. Stanisław Dubingowicz (Warsaw: Neriton, 2010), 263.

86. Waldemar Kowalski, "From the 'Land of Diverse Sects' to National Religion: Converts to Catholicism and Reformed Franciscans in Early Modern Poland-Lithuania," *Church History* 70, no. 3 (2001): 482–526.

87. Janusz Tazbir, "Bracia polscy w Zabłudowie i Dojlidach: Z dziejów arianizmu na Podlasiu," *Odrodzenie i Reformacja w Polsce* 52 (2008): 5–25. See also Karol Żojdź, *Jan Mierzeński: Klient i rezydent Bogusława Radziwiłła w latach 1656–1665* (Oświęcim: Napoleon V, 2012), 90–95.

88. Michał Gochna, *Porządki jako największe i najlepsze: Bogusław Radziwiłł w dziejach Węgrowa—rola magnata w funkcjonowaniu miasta prywatnego* (Węgrów: Tow. Miłośników Ziemi Węgrowskiej, 2016), 6, 130.

89. Ptaszyński, *Reformacja*, 64–66.

90. Janusz Tazbir, *Reformacja w Polsce: Szkice o ludziach i doktrynie* (Warsaw: Książka i Wiedza, 1993), esp. 106–27, 235–52; Karin Friedrich, "Konfessionalisierung und politische Ideen in Polen-Litauen (1570–1650)," in *Konfessionalisierung in Ostmitteleuropa*, ed. Bahlcke et al., 249–66; on Belarus, see Hienadź Sahanowicz, *Historia Białorusi do końca XVIII wieku* (Lublin: Instytut Europy Środkowo-Wschodniej, 2001), 188.

91. Orzelski, *Bezkrólewia ksiąg ośmioro*, 339.

92. Stefania Ochmann-Staniszewska, *Sejmy z lat 1615 i 1616* (Wrocław: Ossolineum, 1970), 98.

93. Frost, *Oxford History of Poland-Lithuania*, 1:114.

94. Ewa Dubas-Urwanowicz, "Dylematy wyznaniowe magnaterii litewsko-ruskiej w XVI–XVII w.," in *Rzeczpospolita wielu wyznań: Materiały międzynaraodowej konferencji Kraków 8 Listopada 2002*, ed. Adam Kaźmierczak et al. (Kraków: Księgarnia Akademicka, 2004), 80.

95. Wojciech Kriegseisen, *Stosunki wyznaniowe w relacjach państwo-kościół między reformacją a oświeceniem: Rzesza Niemiecka, Niderlandy Północne, Rzeczpospolita polsko-litewska* (Warsaw: Semper, 2010), 422.

96. Kriegseisen, *Stosunki wyznaniowe*, 427.

97. Alfons Brüning, *Unio non est Unita—Polen-Litauens Weg im Konfessionellen Zeitalter (1569–1648)* (Wiesbaden: Harrassowitz, 2008), 249–50.

98. Wiktor Czermak, "Sprawa równouprawienia katolików i schizmatyków na Litwie (1432–1563)," *Rozprawy Akademii Umiejętności, Wydział Historyczny-Filozoficzny*, series 2, vol. 19 (1903): 353–55.

99. Kriegseisen, *Stosunki wyznaniowe*, 429.

100. Dubas-Urwanowicz, "Dylematy," 82.

101. Tomasz Kempa, *Konstanty Wasyl Ostrogski, wojewoda kijowski i marszałek ziemi wołyńskiej* (Toruń: UMK, 1997)

102. Bem, *Calvinism in the Polish Lithuanian Commonwealth*, 259–63.

103. Archiwum Główne Akt Dawnych (AGAD, Warsaw), AR IV, kop. 63, Bogusław Radziwiłł to Anna Maria, October 4–November 5, 1665, 1–39, passim; Sławomir Augusiewicz, "Stryj i bratanica: O małżeństwie Anny Marii i Bogusława Radziwiłłów," in *Między Barokiem a Oświeceniem*, ed. Stanisław Achremczyk (Olsztyn: Ośrodek Badań Naukowych im. Wojciecha Kętrzyńskiego, 2006), 356–72.

104. Borys A. Gudziak, *Crisis and Reform: The Kyivan Metropolitanate, the Patriarchate of Constantinople, and the Genesis of the Union of Brest* (Cambridge, MA: Harvard University Press, 1998), esp. 79–88.

105. Michael V. Dmitriev, "L'Union de Brest (1595–1596), les Catholiques, les orthodoxes: un malentendu?" in *Stosunki międzywyznaniowe w Europie środkowej i wschodniej w XIV–XVII wieku*, ed. Marian Dygo et al. (Warsaw: DIG, 2002), 39–60.

106. A. G. Welykyj, ed., *Documenta Unionis Berestensis eiusque autorum (1590–1600)* (Rome: PP. Basiliani, 1970), nos. 138–45. See Dmitriev, "L'Union de Brest," 56; Brüning, *Unio non est Unitas*, 275; and Gudziak, *Crisis and Reform*, 251–53.

107. Moyhla, cited in Brüning, *Union non est Unitas*, 248. See also Frank Sysyn, *Between Poland and Ukraine: The Dilemma of Adam Kysil* (Cambridge, MA: Harvard University Press, 1985), 122. Liudmila Charipova called Mohyla's institution "a Western-oriented establishment in an Orthodox environment." See Liudmila V. Charipova, *Latin Books and the Eastern Orthodox Clerical Elite in Kiev, 1632–1780* (Manchester: Manchester University Press, 2006), 176. See also chapter 4 in this volume.

108. Leszek Ćwikla, *Polityka władz państwowych wobec Kościoła prawosławnego i ludności prawosławnej w Królestwie Polskim,Wielkim Księstwie Litewskim oraz Rzeczypospolitej Obojga narodów w latach 1344–1795* (Lublin: KUL, 2006), 218.   ·

109. For a definition, supported by case studies of multiconfessional coexistence, see Thomas Max Safley, ed., *A Companion to Multiconfessionalism in the Early Modern World* (Leiden: Brill, 2011).

110. Leszek Jarmiński, *Bez użycia sił: Działalność protestantów w Rzeczypospolitej u schyłku XVI wieku* (Warsaw: Semper, 1992), 233–42.

111. Tomasz Kempa, "Animatorzy współpracy protestancko-prawosławnej w okresie kontrreformacji," in *Rzeczpospolita państwem wielu narodowości i wyznań: XVI–XVIII wiek*, ed. Tomasz Ciesielski and Anna Filipczak-Kocur (Warsaw: DIG, 2008), 323.

112. Kempa, *Wobec kontrreformacji*, 197–209.

113. Rafał Degiel, *Protestanci i prawosławni: Patronat wyznaniowy Radziwiłłów birżańskich nad Cerkwią prawosławną w księstwie słuckim w XVII w.* (Warsaw: Neriton, 2000), 18–20.

114. AGAD AR IV, no. 56, p. 59, December 9, 1663, to Jan Mierzeński, from Königsberg.

115. Degiel, *Protestanci i prawosławni*, 100–103.

116. Kempa, "Animatorzy," 335–36.

117. AGAD AR II, no. 741, 803–08; AGAD, AR VIII, 713, S. 74–162v.; and Urszula Augustyniak, "Stosunek ewangelików reformowanych (kalwinistów) do innych wyznań w świetle akt synodów Jednoty Litewskiej z lat 1611–1686," in Dygo et al., *Stosunki międzywyznaniowe*, 87.

118. Antoni Mironowicz, *Prawosławie i unia za panowania Jana Kazimierza* (Białystok: Orthdruk, 1997), 266 (my translation).

119. Edmund Kotłubaj, *Życie Janusza Radziwiłła* (Wilno: M. Mindelsohn, 1859), 375. Letter of March 20, 1655 to Krzysztof Dowgiałło Stryżka.

120. Cited after Liedke and Guzowski, ed., *Akta Synodów* of 1616, in Augustyniak, "Stosunek," 88.

121. Lulewicz, "Skład wyznaniowy," 440, argues against Kosman, who supports the thesis of Orthodoxy as a "peasant religion."

122. Lulewicz, "Skład wyznaniowy," 443.

123. Cited in Degiel, *Protestanci i prawosławni*, 23.

124. Lilia Zabolotnaia, "The Riddles, Myths and Facts concerning Maria (Lupu) Radziwiłł's Last Will and Testament," *Istorija / History* Lietuvos Edukologijos Universitetas 97, no. 1 (2015): 5–25.

125. Wioletta Zielecka-Mikołajczyk, *Prawosławni i unici w Rzeczypospolitej XVI–XVIII wieku wobec życia i śmierci w świetle testamentów* (Warsaw: Neriton, 2012), 57–58; Tadeusz Wasilewski, "Walka o spadek po księżnej Marii Wołoszce, wdowie po Januszu Radziwille w latach 1660–1690," in *Miscellanea Historico-Archivistica 3: Radziwiłłowie XVI–XVIII wieku: W kręgu polityki i kultury*, ed. Edward Potkowski et al. (Warsaw: Archiwum Główne Akt Dawnych, 1999), 291–308.

126. Andrzej S. Kamiński, "Przestrzenie obywatelskie w wieloetnicznej, wielowyznaniowej i wielokulturowej Rzeczypospolitej," in *Lex est Rex in Polonia et in Lithuania: Tradycje prawnoustrojowe Rzeczypospolitej—doświadczenie i dziedzictwo*, ed. Adam Jankiewicz (Warsaw: DIG, 2011), 85–98.

127. Dariusz Kuźmina, *Wazowie a Kościół w Rzeczypospolitej* (Warsaw: Oficyna Wydawnicza ASPRA-JR, 2013), 241–44. For the denial of a seat in the Chamber, see Bogusław Radziwiłł, *Autobiografia*, ed. Tadeusz Wasilewski (Warsaw: PIW, 1979), 149.

128. Kowalski, "From the 'Land of Diverse Sects'"; and Bem, *Calvinism in the Polish-Lithuanian Commonwealth*, 165–95.

3: Encounters with Islam within the Commonwealth's Borders and Beyond

1. For a representative view, see Perry Anderson, *Lineages of the Absolutist State* (London: NLB, 1974), 279–98.

2. Peter Haldén, "From Empire to Commonwealth(s): Orders in Europe 1300–1800," in *Universal Empire: A Comparative Approach to Imperial Culture and Representation in Eurasian History*, ed. Peter Fibiger Bang and Dariusz Kołodziejczyk (Cambridge: Cambridge University Press, 2012), 280–303.

3. For instance, the term "multiculturalism" appears in the title of a project headed by Jeremy Jones and devoted to medieval Sicily, which has won funding from the European Research Council: *Documenting Multiculturalism: Co-existence, Law and Multiculturalism in the Administrative and Legal documents of Norman and Hohenstaufen Sicily, c. 1060–c. 1266*. Its authors declare that by focusing on multilingual legal documents and adopting a bottom-up perspective, they aim at reconstructing the "topsy-turvy world of Normal Sicily," whose realities often challenge our received wisdom; see http://krc.orient.ox.ac.uk/documult/, accessed November 24, 2020).

4. Adam Moniuszko, "Changes in the Legal Culture of Lithuanian Tatars from the Sixteenth to the Eighteenth Century," in *Crossing Legal Cultures*, ed. Laura Beck Varela, Pablo Gutiérrez Vega, and Alberto Spinosa (Munich: Martin Meidenbauer, 2009), 187.

5. See Karen Barkey, *Empire of Difference: The Ottomans in Comparative Perspective* (Cambridge: Cambridge University Press, 2008), 110; Dariusz Kołodziejczyk, "Khan, Caliph, Tsar and Imperator: The Multiple Identities of the Ottoman Sultan," in Bang and Kołodziejczyk, *Universal Empire*, 175–93; and Eleni Gara, "Conceptualizing Interreligious Relations in the Ottoman Empire: The Early Modern Centuries," *Acta Poloniae Historica* 116 (2017), 73–75.

6. See Dariusz Kołodziejczyk, *The Crimean Khanate and Poland-Lithuania: International Diplomacy on the European Periphery (15th–18th Century); A Study of Peace Treaties Followed by Annotated Documents* (Leiden: Brill, 2011), 5, with further references to the works by Stefan Maria Kuczyński and Feliks Šabul'do.

7. Heath W. Lowry, *The Nature of the Early Ottoman State* (Albany: State University of New York Press, 2003), 56–57. This argument, formulated as a polemic with the still powerful vision of Paul Wittek, who in 1938 depicted early Ottomans as Muslim holy warriors, has been later softened by the author, who has nonetheless maintained his point that the portrait of early Ottoman rulers as pious Sunni Muslims is mainly the product of late fifteenth-century Ottoman historiography.

8. Kołodziejczyk, *Crimean Khanate and Poland-Lithuania*, 7–13. Numerous Tatars found themselves under Lithuanian rule not as a result of immigration, but rather of the extension of Lithuanian territory toward the Black Sea in the last decades of the fourteenth century. However, by the sixteenth century their descendants had either migrated to Crimea, adopted Christianity, or been resettled to the north, joining the Muslim settlements in present-day Belarus and Lithuania.

9. *Et Thartari quidem in Poloniam translati, deposito gentilitatis errore, fidem Christi professi sunt, et unus populus cum Polonis iungendo invicem matrimonia, effecti. Hi vero, qui in Lithuania resederant, secta spurcissimi detinentur Machmeti, atque in uno angulo terrae Lithuaniae a Withawdo Duce locati, suis moribus, suoque detestando ritu vivunt*; see, *Joannis Długossii seu Longini canonici Cracoviensis Historiae Polonicae libri XII*, vol. 3: *Libri IX., X.*, ed. A. Przeździecki (Kraków: "Czas," 1876), 523. See also Michael Połczyński, "Seljuks on the Baltic: Polish-Lithuanian Muslim Pilgrims in the Court of Ottoman Sultan Süleyman I," *Journal of Early Modern History* 19 (2015), 21.

10. Conflicting national(ist) traditions regarding the memory of this battle are reflected even in the toponymy. It has been remembered as the Battle of Grunwald, Tannenberg, and Žalgiris in the Polish and Belarusian, German, and Lithuanian historiographies, respectively. See also chapter 9 in this volume.

11. See Dariusz Kołodziejczyk, "Entre l'*antemurale Christianitatis* et la raison d'État: L'idée de Croisade en Pologne aux XVe et XVIe siècles," in *L'Europe centrale au seuil de la modernité: Mutations sociales, religieuses et culturelles; Autriche, Bohême, Hongrie et Pologne, fin du XVIe–milieu du XVIe siècle*, ed. Marie-Madeleine de Cevins (Rennes: Presses universitaires de Rennes, 2010), 19–26.

12. Jan Tyszkiewicz, *Tatarzy na Litwie i w Polsce: Studia z dziejów XIII–XVIII w.* (Warsaw: Państwowe Wydawnictwo Naukowe, 1989), 222–54, 274–75.

13. Stanisław Kryczyński, "Tatarzy litewscy: Próba monografii historyczno-etnograficznej," *Rocznik Tatarski* 3 (1938), 184–85; Tyszkiewicz, *Tatarzy na Litwie i w Polsce*, 286–89; Andrzej Drozd, "Meczety i parafie muzułmańskie na ziemiach Rzeczypospolitej," in *Meczety i cmentarze Tatarów polsko-litewskich*, ed. Andrzej Drozd, Marek M. Dziekan, and Tadeusz Majda (Warsaw: Res Publica Multiethnica, 1999), 26–29; and Artur Konopacki, *Życie religijne Tatarów na ziemiach Wielkiego Księstwa Litewskiego w XVI–XIX wieku* (Warsaw: Wydawnictwa Uniwersytetu Warszawskiego, 2010), 98–119. According to Andrzej Zakrzewski, the total number of mosques that functioned in Poland-Lithuania throughout the early modern period (albeit not simultaneously) may have reached between thirty and fifty (Andrzej Zakrzewski, "Meczet w Wielkim Księstwie Litewskim—prawo a praktyka," in *Pro bono Reipublicae: Księga jubileuszowa Profesora Michała Pietrzaka* [Warsaw: LexisNexis, 2009], 149).

14. Following the Lithuanian model, Tatar warriors were also settled in the surroundings of the ruler's castles in Mazovia and the Palatinate of Lublin, both of which belonged to the Polish Crown (though Mazovia was only fully incorporated into Poland in 1526). See Konopacki, *Życie religijne Tatarów*, 30–31. However, there is no evidence that they were formally authorized to openly perform the rites of their religion. It is worth noting that all the settlements with ancient mosques and Muslim cemeteries that can be visited in present-day Poland and are proudly exhibited to tourists as the proof of ancient Polish multiculturalism, including Kruszyniany, Bohoniki, and Studzianka, are situated in the lands that had originally belonged to the Grand Duchy of Lithuania.

15. In the Polish scholarly literature, they are referred to as *Tatarzy hospodarscy*, "the lord's Tatars"; the term derives from the Ruthenian title of the Lithuanian grand duke—*hospodar*—who granted lands to the Tatars in return for their service.

16. Stanislav Dumin, "Tatarskie kniaz'ia v Velikom kniazhestve litovskom," *Acta Baltico-Slavica* 20 (1989): 7–49. The most picturesque genealogy, preserved in a marriage contract from 1781, traces its holder's ancestry back to Aurangzeb, Babur, and Timur, although a present-day scholar observes that it might have been invented by the aristocratic patroness of the bride, Barbara Sanguszko, who was known for her literary ambitions; see Andrzej Zakrzewski,"Powstanie przekonania o szlachectwie Tatarów litewskich," in *Święte księgi judaizmu, chrześcijaństwa i islamu w słowiańskim kręgu kulturowym: Prace dedykowane Profesorowi Czesławowi Łapiczowi*, vol. 2: *Księgi wyznawców judaizmu i islamu: Historia—socjologia—sztuka*, ed. Monika Krajewska, Joanna Kulwicka-Kamińska, and Arleta Szulc (Toruń: Wydawnictwo Naukowe Uniwersytetu Mikołaja Kopernika, 2016), 46.

17. The conditions of military service, both for the Tatars and for Christian nobles, underwent subsequent changes, and the requirement that the royal call to *levée en masse* (*pospolite ruszenie*) be authorized by the Sejm was introduced in Lithuania only in the late sixteenth century. Yet it is generally true that Tatars were called to arms more frequently, their mobilization required fewer formalities and less time, and their units maintained military valors longer than those of ordinary Christian nobles; see Andrzej Zakrzewski, "Służba wojskowa Tatarów w Wielkim Księstwie Litewskim (XVI–XVIII w.): Chorągwie ziemskie," in *Istorijos akiračiai*, ed. A. Dubonis, Z. Kiaupa, and E. Rimša (Vilnius: Lietuvos Istorijos Institutas, 2004), 127–42.

18. Jacek Sobczak, "Czy tatarska ludność Litwy należała do stanu szlacheckiego," *Przegląd Historyczny* 77 (1986): 467–80; see also Jacek Sobczak, *Położenie prawne ludności tatarskiej w Wielkim Księstwie Litewskim* (Warsaw: Państwowe Wydawnictwo Naukowe, 1984), 81–97.

19. Andrzej Zakrzewski, "Czy Tatarzy litewscy rzeczywiście nie byli szlachtą?" *Przegląd Historyczny* 79 (1988): 573–80; see also Zakrzewski, "Powstanie przekonania," 47.

20. Kołodziejczyk, *Crimean Khanate and Poland-Lithuania*, 242, 459, 564–65; Sobczak, *Położenie prawne ludności tatarskiej*, 75; Konopacki, *Życie religijne Tatarów*, 39.

21. Zakrzewski, "Powstanie przekonania," 48.

22. Czyżewski, whose pamphlet was issued in Vilnius in 1617, lamented that immediately after the bishop's death as many as four mosques were constructed by the Tatars in and around Vilnius and Trakai. See Piotr Czyżewski, *Alfurkan tatarski prawdziwy na czterdzieści części rozdzielony*, ed. Artur Konopacki (Białystok, 2013), 76 (20 in the original edition); Andrzej Zakrzewski, "Rzeczpospolita XVI–XVIII w.: państwem Tatarów?" in *Rzeczpospolita państwem wielu narodowości i wyznań: XVI–XVII wiek*, ed. T. Ciesielski and A. Filipczuk-Kocur (Warsaw: Wydawnictwo DiG, 2008), 229.

23. Andrzej Zakrzewski, "Struktura społeczno-prawna Tatarów litewskich w XV–XVIII wieku: Próba nowego ujęcia," in *Inter Orientem et Occidentem: Studia z dziejów Europy Środkowowschodniej ofiarowane Profesorowi Janowi Tyszkiewiczowi w czterdziestolecie pracy naukowej*, ed. Tadeusz Wasilewski (Warsaw: Wydawnictwo DiG, 2002), 129–30.

24. Andrzej Zakrzewski, "Osadnictwo tatarskie w Wielkim Księstwie Litewskim: aspekty wyznaniowe," *Acta Baltico-Slavica* 20 (1989), 139; and Zakrzewski, "Meczet w Wielkim Księstwie Litewskim," 145–46.

25. See Rossitsa Gradeva, "Ottoman Policy towards Christian Church Buildings," in *Rumeli under the Ottomans, 15th–18th Centuries: Institutions and Communities* (Istanbul: Isis Press, 2004), 339–68.

26. The term "dżemiat" was derived from Arabic جماعة and Turkish *cema'at*.

27. Zakrzewski, "Osadnictwo tatarskie," 140–41; Andrzej Zakrzewski, "Muslim Charity in the Polish-Lithuanian Commonwealth," *Acta Poloniae Historica* 87 (2003), 92.

28. *Akty izdavaemye Vilenskoiu kommissieiu dlia razbora drevnikh aktov*, vol. 31: *Akty o Litovskikh tatarakh* (Vilnius: Tipografiia Russkiĭ Pochin, 1906), 185. See also Zakrzewski, "Osadnictwo tatarskie," 145.

29. Zakrzewski, "Rzeczpospolita XVI–XVIII w," 224.

30. Kołodziejczyk, *Crimean Khanate and Poland-Lithuania*, 37.

31. Kołodziejczyk, "Entre l'*antemurale Christianitatis* et la raison d'État," 23–25.

32. "Zdanie sprawy o Tatarach litewskich, przez jednego z tych Tatarów złożone sułtanowi Sulejmanowi w roku 1558," ed. A. Muchliński (Vilnius: Teka Wileńska, 1858). The Polish translation is accompanied by an Arabic-script edition of the original text in Ottoman Turkish, titled *Risale-i Tatar-i Leh* ("The Treatise of Polish Tatars"). It was preserved in an eighteenth-century manuscript that is not extant today. In recent years, the authenticity of the report has been questioned by Stephen Rowell and Il'ia Zaitsev, who both accuse Muchliński of making it up and suggest that he had been motivated by Polish nationalism and a desire to idealize ancient Polish tolerance. According to Rowell, the very title of the report is anachronous, since the Tatars were Lithuanian and not Polish, and it rather reflects the nineteenth-century wording of members of the Polish intelligentsia who—like Muchliński—treated Lithuania as a part of historical Poland. See Stephen Rowell, "Lietuva, tėvyne mūsų? Tam tikrų XVI a. LDK raštijų pavyzdžiai," in *Senosios raštijos ir tautosakos sąveika: kultūrinė Lietuvos Didžiosios Kunigaikštystės patirtis*, ed. R. Repšienė (Vilnius: Lietuvių literatūros ir tautosakos institutas, 1998), 123–37. Although this point

is important, it nonetheless ignores the Ottoman audience for which the memorandum was produced. In the Ottoman chancery language, both Lithuania and Poland appeared as one unified kingdom that was termed *Lehistan* or *vilayet-i Leh* ("Poland"). Only the Crimean khans, whose relations with Lithuania predated those with Poland, distinguished between the two states, although even in their chancery language Lithuania was eventually subsumed into the "Polish Commonwealth" (*Leh cumhuri*). See a document from 1742 in Kołodziejczyk, *Crimean Khanate and Poland-Lithuania*, 1001–8. Zaitsev also observes that the report's language deviates from the Ottoman court style and has no analogy in the sixteenth-century Lithuanian Tatar literary tradition, finding the rendering of Nowogródek/Navahrudak as Yenişehir (literally "New Town") in the Turkish text suspicious (Il'ia Zaitsev, "Antonii Mukhlin'skii i 'Risale-ii Tatar-i Lekh' ('Traktat o pol'skikh tatarakh' ili 'Traktat pol'skogo professora'?)," in *Fal'sifikatsii istochnikov i natsional'nye istorii: Materialy kruglogo stola* [Moscow: IV RAN, 2007], 23–24). The latter doubts can be dismissed by invoking the Tatar author's non-Ottoman background, the recent reappraisal of the literature of Lithuanian Tatars (see below), and the fact that Slavic toponyms were often replaced with Turkish synonyms in Ottoman sources. As a matter of fact, the village of Sorok Tatary was also recorded in the *Risale* as Kırk Tatar (literally "Forty Tatars"), and this last form can also be found in seventeenth-century Arabic-script documents drawn up by Lithuanian Tatars (see Henryk Jankowski, "The Tatar Name of Sorok Tatary / Keturiasdešimt Totorių Discovered," in *Orientas Lietuvos Dzidžiosios Kunigaikštijos visuomenės tradicijoje: totoriai ir karaimai*, ed. T. Bairašauskaitė, H. Kobeckaitė, and G. Miškinienė [Vilnius: Vilniaus universiteto leidykla, 2008], 147–59). By far the least convincing is the argument that Muchliński's Polish nationalism was the driving force behind his supposed forgery. As the *Risale*'s author expressed his hope that the Ottoman sultan would conquer Poland and convert its inhabitants to Islam, while beautiful Polish women would fill the sultan's harem ("Zdanie sprawy o Tatarach litewskich," 14, 25 [Polish translation]; *Risale*, ٩١ , ٠١ [Turkish original]), if we were to attribute this text to Muchliński and believe that he used it to extol the ancient Polish toleration toward Muslims and the latter's reciprocal loyalty, then the author must simultaneously be accused of a kind of cuckold masochism.

33. Połczyński, "Seljuks on the Baltic," 2–3.

34. On Rustem's conciliatory policy in Central Europe at the time when the Porte was engaged in military confrontation with Spain in the Mediterranean, see Andrzej Dziubiński, *Stosunki dyplomatyczne polsko-tureckie w latach 1500–1572 w kontekście międzynarodowym* (Wrocław: Fundacja na rzecz Nauki Polskiej, 2005), 218–19. Połczyński erroneously maintains that the Ottomans regarded Poland-Lithuania as a hostile infidel territory, described as the "domain of war" (*dar al-harb*), whereas in fact Poland belonged to the "domain of treaty" (*dar al-'ahd*), especially after Suleyman concluded an "eternal treaty" with Sigismund I, in 1533, and then renewed it with his son and successor, Sigismund II Augustus, in 1553. See Dariusz Kołodziejczyk, "La Res Publica polono-lituanienne était-elle le vassal de l'Empire ottoman?" in *Studies in Oriental Art and Culture in Honour of Professor Tadeusz Majda*, ed. A. Parzymies (Warsaw: Dialog, 2006), 125–36.

35. On the prospects of the conquest or peaceful Islamization of Poland-Lithuania voiced in the *Risale*, see Połczyński, "Seljuks on the Baltic," 25–29.

36. Dariusz Kołodziejczyk, *Ottoman-Polish Diplomatic Relations (15th–18th Century): An Annotated Edition of 'Ahdnames and Other Documents* (Leiden: Brill, 2000), 125.

37. Warsaw, Archiwum Główne Akt Dawnych, Archiwum Koronne Warszawskie, Dział Tureckie, karton 71, teczka 269, no. 500; published in facsimile, along with an eighteenth-century French translation by Antoni Crutta and a Polish translation by Stanisław Szahno-Romanowicz, in Jan Tyszkiewicz, "Pismo sułtana Murada III do Zygmunta III z roku 1591 w

sprawie Tatarów litewskich," *Studia Źródłoznawcze* 30 (1987), 86, 88–89, 91, 95–96. The relevant fragment in Ottoman Turkish reads: *gerekdir ki name-i hümayun . . . vusul buldukda . . . taife-i mezbure bayram ve cum'a namazı kılmak içün münasib olan mahalde cami'-i şerif bina edüb* ("It is necessary that when [my] imperial letter arrives, a noble Friday mosque be built in a suitable site so that the aforementioned community may perform prayers on the occasion of religious feasts as well as Friday prayers"). The names of Ottoman sultans are indeed invoked in the Tatar prayers from the seventeenth and eighteenth centuries that have been preserved in Polish translations recorded in the Arabic script; see Andrzej Drozd, *Arabskie teksty liturgiczne w przekładzie na język polski XVII wieku: Zagadnienia gramatyczne na materiale chutb świątecznych* (Warsaw: Wydawnictwo Akademickie Dialog, 1999), 42–45.

38. Drozd, "Meczety i parafie muzułmańskie," 28, 30; and Zakrzewski, "Osadnictwo tatarskie," 151.

39. Sobczak, *Położenie prawne ludności tatarskiej*, 107, 110; and Zakrzewski, "Osadnictwo tatarskie," 151.

40. Czyżewski, *Alfurkan tatarski*; see also Sobczak, *Położenie prawne ludności tatarskiej*, 106; and Zakrzewski, "Osadnictwo tatarskie," 150.

41. Artur Konopacki, "Komentarz krytyczny," in Czyżewski, *Alfurkan tatarski*, 6–11.

42. Czyżewski, *Alfurkan tatarski*, 79–82.

43. Konopacki, *Życie religijne Tatarów*, 79.

44. Stanisław Kryczyński, "Bej barski: Szkic z dziejow Tatarów polskich w XVII w.," *Rocznik Tatarski* 2 (1935), 259; and Zakrzewski, "Osadnictwo tatarskie," 139.

45. Kryczyński, "Bej barski," 266–300. For articles on the Lithuanian Tatars in the Polish-Ottoman treaties of 1672, 1676, and 1678, see Kołodziejczyk, *Ottoman-Polish Diplomatic Relations*, 494, 497, 499, 502, 509, 516, 521–22, 525, 530–31, 539.

46. See Mariusz Kaczka and Dariusz Kołodziejczyk, eds., *Turecki pasza i szlachta: korespondencja osmańskiego gubernatora Chocimia Iliasza Kołczaka paszy ze szlachtą Rzeczypospolitej z lat 1730–1739* (Warsaw: Narodowy Instytut Polskiego Dziedzictwa Kulturowego za Granicą Polonika, 2020).

47. Dariusz Kołodziejczyk, "Rola islamskiego sąsiedztwa w kulturze i polityce Rzeczypospolitej," in *Rzeczpospolita wielu wyznań*, ed. Adam Kaźmierczyk, Andrzej Link-Lenczowski, Mariusz Markiewicz, and Krystyn Matwijowski (Kraków: Księgarnia Akademicka, 2004), 442–43. On the literary genre known as *kitabs*, see Czesław Łapicz, "Zawartość treściowa kitabu Tatarów litewsko-polskich," *Acta Baltico-Slavica* 20 (1989): 169–91; Henryk Jankowski and Czesław Łapicz, "Przedmowa" and "Wstęp," in *Klucz do raju: Księga Tatarów litewsko-polskich z XVIII wieku* (Warsaw: Dialog, 2000), 7–55; Andrzej Drozd, "Piśmiennictwo Tatarów polsko-litewskich (XVI–XX w.): Zarys problematyki," in Andrzej Drozd, Marek Dziekan, and Tadeusz Majda, *Piśmiennictwo i muhiry Tatarów polsko-litewskich* (Warsaw: Res Publica Multiethnica, 2000), 12–37; Joanna Kulwicka-Kamińska and Czesław Łapicz, "Co wiemy o najstarszym datowanym rękopisie Tatarów Wielkiego Księstwa Litewskiego? (*Kitab z 1631 r.*—transliteracja, ortografia, przekład, komentarze)," *Slavistica Vilnensis* 62 (2017): 79–95; and Shirin Akiner, *Religious Language of a Belarusian Tatar Kitab: A Cultural Monument of Islam in Europe. With a Latin-Script Transliteration of the British Library Tatar Belarusian Kitab (OR 13020) on CD-ROM* (Wiesbaden: Harrassowitz Verlag, 2009).

48. Andrzej Zakrzewski, "Tatarzy litewscy wobec władzy państwowej, od epoki wczesnonowożytnej po koniec wieku XX," in Bairašauskaitė, Kobeckaitė, and Miškinienė, *Orientas Lietuvos Dzidžiosios Kunigaikštijos visuomenės tradicijoje*, 15.

49. *Tarih binde doksan sekizinci yılında mübarek Muharrem ayında tamam oldı Minske*

şehrinde; Andrzej Drozd, "Koran staropolski: Rozważania w związku z odkryciem tefsiru mińskiego z 1686," *Rocznik Biblioteki Narodowej* 36 (2004), 248 (the present transcription slightly deviates from the one provided by Drozd; I cordially thank Andrzej Drozd for sending me the photograph of the relevant page).

50. Drozd, "Koran staropolski," 247; Urjasz/Uriasz is a Polish form of Uriah. On the popularity of names derived from the Old Testament among the Lithuanian Tatars, especially in the seventeenth century, see Andrzej Zakrzewski, "Niektóre aspekty położenia kulturalnego Tatarów litewskich w XVI–XVIII w.," in *Wilno-Wileńszczyzna jako krajobraz i środowisko wielu kultur,* ed. E. Feliksiak (Białystok: Towarzystwo Literackie im. Adama Mickiewicza, Oddział Białostocki, Filia Uniwersytetu Warszawskiego w Białymstoku, 1992), 115–16.

51. Drozd, "Koran staropolski," 241–42.

52. Andrzej Drozd, "O twórczości literackiej Tatarów w dobie staropolskiej," *Przegląd Orientalistyczny* (2017), 22, 26. Still, there are some arguments supporting the thesis that the translation, or at least parts of it, might be dated earlier. Apart from some archaisms visible in the Polish text, there is evidence provided by an Ottoman chronicler, Ibrahim Peçevi (died ca. 1650). In his description of the Astrakhan campaign of 1569, Peçevi devoted a paragraph to the Tatars who had settled in Muscovy and Poland-Lithuania, invoking a testimony by Musa, a steward (*kethüda*) of Iskender Pasha, the commander of the Ottoman campaign against Poland in 1620. Having fallen prisoner, Musa spent over ten years in Polish captivity and became acquainted with several local Tatars. He later recalled that "even though they still copy the glorious Koran in the Arabic script, if they want to translate it, they do it in the language of the Polish infidels" (*hatta Kur'an-i 'azimi yine 'arabi hatt ile yazarlar ve tefsir etseler Leh keferesi lisanıyla tefsir ederler*); *Tarih-i Peçevi,* vol. 1 (Istanbul, 1283/1866), 472. See also Antoni Muchliński [Mukhlinskii], *Izsliedovanie o proiskhozhdenii i sostoianii Litovskikh" tatar"* (Saint Petersburg: Tipografiia Eduarda Veimara, 1857), 32, 60–61; and Cengiz Orhonlu, "Lipkalar," *Türkiyat Mecmuası* 16 (1971), 63.

53. Until the discovery of the Minsk manuscript, the two oldest known translations of the Koran into Polish were dated 1723 and 1725. Whereas the manuscript of 1686 only contains a partial Polish translation, the translations in the latter two manuscripts are complete (see Drozd, "Koran staropolski," 238). On the *tefsir* of 1725 that is today held in London, see also Glyn Munro Meredith-Owens and Alexander Nadson, "The Byelorussian Tartars and Their Writings," *Journal of Byelorussian Studies* 2, no. 2 (1970), 158–59, 169–71.

54. Drozd, "Koran staropolski," 244–45.

55. Drozd, "Koran staropolski," 242.

56. Drozd, "Koran staropolski," 244.

57. Andrzej Drozd, "Wpływy chrześcijańskie na literaturę Tatarów w dawnej Rzeczypospolitej: Między antagonizmem a symbiozą," *Pamiętnik Literacki* 88 (1997), 10–11; and Jankowski and Łapicz, "Wstęp," 24.

58. Drozd, "Wpływy chrześcijańskie," 13–14.

59. Drozd, "Wpływy chrześcijańskie," 11, 18–19.

60. Drozd, "Wpływy chrześcijańskie," 16, 20, 28.

61. Drozd, "Wpływy chrześcijańskie," 12, 15, 29–30.

62. See Jankowski and Łapicz, "Wstęp," 17–18.

63. Drozd, "Wpływy chrześcijańskie," 5–6, 8; Zakrzewski, "Rzeczpospolita XVI–XVIII w.," 226; Jankowski and Łapicz, "Wstęp," 25; and Jankowski, "Tatar name of Sorok Tatary," 159.

64. Andrzej Zakrzewski observes that the transition from Ruthenian to Polish as the first-choice language among Lithuanian Tatars was delayed by about twenty or thirty years in comparison to the local Christian nobles, and that this transition was more rapid among the

Tatarzy hospodarscy (see above on this term) than among other Tatars. He also provides some interesting statistics: among 346 signatures left by Lithuanian Tatars on various extant documents in the years 1560–1792, the ratio of Arabic script to Cyrillic script and Latin script was 45:54:1 in the years 1560–1599; 27:41:32 in the years 1600–1649; 33:2:64 in the years 1650–1699; 15:0:85 in the years 1700–1749; and 9:0:91 in the years 1750–1792. See Zakrzewski, "Niektóre aspekty położenia kulturalnego Tatarów litewskich," 107–13, 119.

65. Drozd, "Wpływy chrześcijańskie," 4, 7, 33; and Drozd, "O twórczości literackiej Tatarów," 24–25.

66. See Raoul Motika, "Adam Neuser: Ein Heidelberger Theologe im Osmanischen Reich," in *Arts, Women and Scholars: Studies in Ottoman Society and Culture; Festschrift Hans Georg Majer*, ed. Sabine Prätor and Christoph Neumann (Istanbul: Simurg, 2002), 2:535.

67. On Bobowski, also known under his Latin pen name Bobovius and under his Muslim name Ali Ufki, see Hannah Neudecker, "From Istanbul to London? Albertus Bobovius' Appeal to Isaac Basire," in *The Republic of Letters and the Levant*, ed. Alastair Hamilton, Maurits H. Van den Boogert, and Bart Westerweel (Leiden: Brill, 2005), 175–96; Agata Pawlina, "The Pole Who Translated the Bible for the Turks," *Polish Journal of Biblical Research* 15, no. 2 (2016): 31–37; and Agnieszka Ayşen Kaim, *Ludzie dwóch kultur: Wybrane przypadki transgresji kulturowej Polaków w Imperium Osmańskim w XVII, XVIII i XIX wieku* (Warsaw: Instytut Slawistyki Polskiej Akademii Nauk, 2020), 92–164.

68. Martin W. Lewis and Kären E. Wigen, *The Myth of Continents: A Critique of Metageography* (Berkeley: University of California Press, 1997), 146.

69. For numerous examples of this genre, see Jerzy Nosowski, *Polska literatura polemiczno-antyislamistyczna XVI, XVII i XVIII w.: wybór tekstów i komentarze* (Warsaw: Akademia Teologii Katolickiej, 1974), 2 vols.; Piotr Tafiłowski, *"Imago Turci": Studium z dziejów komunikacji społecznej w dawnej Polsce (1453–1572)* (Lublin: Wydawnictwo Uniwersytetu Marii Curie-Skłodowskiej, 2013); and Wołodymyr Pyłypenko, *W obliczu wroga: Polska literatura antyturecka od połowy XVI do połowy XVII wieku* (Oświęcim: Napoleon V, 2016).

70. See Dariusz Kołodziejczyk, "Stosunki dawnej Rzeczypospolitej z Turcją i Tatarami: Czy naprawdę byliśmy przedmurzem Europy?" *Praktyka Teoretyczna* 4 (2017), 17–18, 28–31.

71. Andrzej Zakrzewski, "Szklany sufit litewskich Tatarów w XVIII stuleciu," in *Kintančios Lietuvos visuomenė: struktūros, veikėjai, idėjos; Mokslinių straipsnių rinkinys, skirtas prof. habil. dr. Tamaros Bairašauskaitės 65-mečio sukakčiai*, ed. Olga Mastianica, Virgilijus Pugačiauskas, and Vilma Žaltauskaitė (Vilnius: Lietuvos Istorijos Institutas, 2015), 33.

72. Kryczyński, "Tatarzy litewscy," 93.

73. In a preface to the new edition of his book, Richard White recalls the success of the first edition, which brought many scholars to question whether his model fit into their areas of study, be it "Africa, Asia, South America, Australia, New Zealand, and more." See Richard White, "Preface to the Twentieth Anniversary Edition," in *The Middle Ground: Indians, Empires, and Republics in the Great Lakes Region, 1650–1815* (Cambridge: Cambridge University Press, 2011), xi. It is telling that he did not list Europe among his examples, perhaps because this continent is still regarded as culturally homogeneous and equipped with central governments too strong to allow for "middle grounds."

74. Gara, "Conceptualizing Interreligious Relations," 88–89.

75. Zakrzewski, "Tatarzy litewscy wobec władzy państwowej," 16.

76. *Zazhyvshy pryiatel' susedei svoikh khrestiianskogo i bisurmanskogo rozhaiu do sebe . . .*; see *Akty izdavaemye Vilenskoiu kommissieiu*, vol. 31, 335; also quoted in Zakrzewski, "Rzeczpospolita XVI–XVIII w.," 229, albeit under an erroneous date.

77. Zakrzewski, "Rzeczpospolita XVI–XVIII w.," 229–30. Admittedly, this phenomenon did not apply to all. Some Polish-Lithuanian Tatars chose emigration to the Ottoman Empire, but their departure might have hastened the assimilation of those who stayed behind.

78. Andrzej Drozd, "The Decade of Exploration of the Polish-Lithuanian Tatars' Epigraphy: Results and Perspectives," *Rocznik Orientalistyczny* 62 (2009), 27. The banner has not been preserved, but is depicted in a watercolor painting made in 1690 by Olof Hoffman and today preserved in the Armémuseum in Stockholm. For a description and picture, see Jacek Gutowski, *Broń i uzbrojenie Tatarów* (Warsaw: Res Publica Multiethnica, 1997), 68 and 133 (no. 93).

79. Zakrzewski, "Powstanie przekonania," 48–50.

80. See Zakrzewski, "Tatarzy litewscy wobec władzy państwowej," 20.

81. By way of analogy, one might point to the interrelation between the legal position of Yugoslavia's Muslims and shifts in the foreign policy of Josip Broz Tito, especially after the Bandung Conference of 1955.

82. According to Poland's 2011 National Population and Housing Census, 1,828 Polish citizens declared their belonging to the Tatar ethnic minority. See "Tatarzy," in *Mniejszości Narodowe i Etniczne*, https://www.gov.pl/web/mniejszosci-narodowe-i-etniczne/tatarzy, accessed November 24, 2020.

4: Art and Transcultural Discourse in the Ukrainian Lands of the Polish-Lithuanian Commonwealth

1. *Paterikòn abo Zywoty SS. Oycow Pieczarskich, Obszyrnie Słowieńskim ięzykiem przez Swiętego Nestora Zakonnika y Látopiscá Ruskiego przedtym nápisány, Teraz záś z Græckich, Łáćińskich, Słowiáńskich y Polskich Pisárzow obiásniony y krocey podány*, Przez Wielebnego w Bogu Oyca Silvestra Kossowa, Episkopá Mśćisłáwskiego, Orszáńskiego y Mohilewskiego. W Kiiowie, w Drukarni S. Lawry Pieczarskiey Roku, 1635, 10. Reprint in "The *Paterikon* of Syl'vestr Kosov," in *Seventeenth-Century Writings on the Kievan Caves Monastery*, intro. Paulina Lewin (Cambridge, MA: Harvard University Press, 1987), 14; for a modern Ukrainian translation of the text, see Nataliia Sinkevych, *Paterykon Silvestra Kosova: pereklad ta doslidzhennia pamiatky* (Kyiv: Vydavets Oleh Filiuk, 2013).

2. The Church of the Savior is dedicated to the Transfiguration of Christ (Matthew 17:1–8; Mark 9:2–8; Luke 9:28–36).

3. In the Commonwealth, inhabitants of what are today Belarusian and Ukrainian lands were referred to as Rus' in Slavonic or as Ruthenians in Latin; they wrote in Chancery Ruthenian, Church Slavonic, Polish, Latin, and sometimes in Greek, and were associated mainly, though not exclusively, with Eastern Christianity. In this essay, I use the hyphenated designation Ruthenian-Rus' to refer to the East Slavic inhabitants of the Polish-Lithuanian Commonwealth. The hyphenated term acknowledges both the distinct Rus' origins of the lands in question and their situatedness in the Latin-oriented Commonwealth.

4. On Petro Mohyla, see Stepan Golubev, *Kievskii mitropolit Petr Mogila i ego spodvizhniki (Opyt tserkovno-istoricheskago izsliedovaniia)*, 2 vols. (Kiev: Tip. G. T. Korchak-Novitskago / Tip. S. V. Kul'zhenko, 1883–1898); and Arkadii Zhukovskyi, *Petro Mohyla i pytannia iednosty tserkov* (1969; repr., Kyiv: Mystetstvo, 1997). Ihor Ševčenko's, "The Many Worlds of Peter Mohyla," *Harvard Ukrainian Studies* 8, no. 1/2 (1984): 9–44 has been especially influential in my analysis of the Church of the Savior in Berestovo.

5. I use the adjectives "united" and "non-united" to refer to the two communities of Ruthenian-Rus' Eastern Christians that came into existence in the Commonwealth after the Union of Brest. I use the designations "Uniate" and "Orthodox" to refer to the two Eastern Christian

Churches of the Commonwealth after the Polish king's formal recognition of the "non-united" hierarchy in 1633. This decision is arbitrary, as the process of legalisation of the "non-united" church was gradual, and, in 1620, a hierarchy of the "non-united" Ruthenian-Rus' Church was consecrated, though not formally recognized, in the Commonwealth. See Yury P. Avvakumov, "Caught in the Crossfire: Toward Understanding Medieval and Early Modern Advocates of Church Union," in *Stolen Churches or Bridges to Orthodoxy? Pathways for Ecumenical and Inter-religious Dialogue*, ed. Vladimir Latinovic and Anastacia K. Wooden (Cham: Palgrave Macmillan, , 2021), 19–40; and Yury P. Avvakumov, "Western 'Confessions' and Eastern Christianity," in *The Cambridge History of Reformation Era Theology, c. 1475–c.1650*, ed. Nelson H. Minnich and Kenneth Appold (Cambridge: Cambridge University Press, forthcoming). I would like to thank Professor Avvakumov for sharing his work with me prior to publication. On the legal status of the "non-united" church, see Vasilii Alekseevich Bednov, *Pravoslavnaia tserkov' v Pol'she i Litve po "Volumina Legum"* (1908; repr., Minsk: Luchi Sofii, 2002), 127–205.

6. I thank Ihor Teslenko for bringing Kysil's unique status as an Orthodox senator from the Kingdom of Poland to my attention. See Kazimierz Chodynicki, *Kościół prawosławny a Rzeczpospolita Polska: zarys historyczny, 1370–1632* (Warsaw: Pałac Staszica, 1934), 470; Eugeniusz Janas and Witold Kłaczewski, eds., *Urzędnicy województw kijowskiego i czernihowskiego XV–XVIII wieku. Spisy*, (Kórnik: Biblioteka Kórnicka, 2002), 30, 158; and Henryk Lulewicz, "Skład wyznaniowy senatorów świeckich Wielkiego Księstwa Litewskiego za panowania Wazów," *Przegląd Historyczny* 68, no. 3: 427.

7. On Kysil, see Frank E. Sysyn, *Between Poland and Ukraine: The Dilemma of Adam Kysil, 1600–1653* (Cambridge, MA: Harvard University Press, 1985).

8. See Evgenij Francevič Šmurlo, *Le Saint-Siège et l'Orient orthodoxe russe, 1609–1654* (Prague: Orbis, 1928), part 2, 164.

9. Richard Slimbach, "The Transcultural Journey," *Frontiers: The Interdisciplinary Journal of Study Abroad* 11 (2005): 205–30.

10. Homi K. Bhabha, *The Location of Culture* (London: Routledge Classics, 1994), xi, xv.

11. The text of the seventeenth-century *Paterikon* relies on the Second Cassian Redaction (1462) of the medieval prototype. For a critical edition of the medieval text, see Dmytro I. Abramovych, ed., *Kyievo-Pecherskyi Pateryk*, in *Das Paterikon des Kiever Höhlenklosters*, ed. Dmitrij Tschiżewskij [Dmytro Chyzhevskyi] (1930, repr., Munich: Eidos Verlag, 1964). On the text in the early modern context, see Iurii A. Isichenko, *Kyievo-Pecherskyi pateryk u literaturnomu protsesi kintsia XVI–pochatku XVII stolittia na Ukraini* (Kyiv: Naukova dumka, 1990), and Sinkevych, *Paterykon*, 19–214.

12. I follow the periodization of the Ukrainian language put forth in George Shevelov, *A Historical Phonology of the Ukrainian Language* (Heidelberg: Carl Winter, 1979), 40. Language was an important but not determining marker of cultural identification in the early modern Ruthenian-Rus' lands. See Giovanna Brodgi Bercoff, "Plurilinguism and Identity: Rethinking Ukrainian Literature of the Seventeenth Century," in *Ukraine and Europe: Cultural Encounters and Negotiations*, ed. Giovanna Brogi Bercoff, Marko Pavlyshyn, and Serhii Plokhy (Toronto: University of Toronto Press, 2017), 45–71.

13. "*Paterikon* of Syl'vestr Kosov," 3.

14. Natalia Sinkevych, "The 1635 *Paterykon* by Sylvestr Kossov: Its Purpose, Originality, Sources and Interpretations," *Jahrbücher für Geschichte Osteuropas* 64 (2016): 181–88. Sinkevych specifically mentions the Chronicles of John Skylitzes (d. after 1101) and John Zonaras (twelfth century).

15. "*Paterikon* of Syl'vestr Kosov," 18–19.

16. On Mohyla's renovation of churches, see Golubev, *Kievskii mitropolit Petr Mogila,*

2:411–59; A. Zhukovskyi, *Petro Mohyla*, 94–96; N. T. Pugacheva, "Ideino-polemicheskii smysl restavratsionnoi deiatel'nosti Petra Mogily," in *Chelovek i istoriia v srednevekovoi filosofskoi mysli russkogo, ukrainskogo i belorusskogo narodov*, ed. V. S. Gorskii (Kyiv: Naukova dumka,1987), 132–39; P. Trotskii, "Vozobnovlenie drevnikh kievskikh khramov mitropolitom Petrom Mogiloiu," *Kievskie eparkhial'nye vedomosti*, no. 9, May 1, 1864, 261–81.

17. See Liudmila V. Charipova, "Peter Mohyla and St. Volodimer: Is There a Symbolic Link?" *Slavonic and East European Review* 80, no. 3 (July 2002): 439–58. On the existence of a chapel dedicated to Volodymyr erected by Mohyla, but resting on very speculative evidence, see Nadiia Nikitenko, "Volodymyrskyi memorial u Sofii Kyivskii chasiv Petra Mohyly," in *Petro Mohyla: bohoslov, tserkovnyi i kul'turnyi diach*, ed. A. Kolodnyi, V. Nichyk, and V. Klymov (Kyiv: Dnipro, 1997), 159–66.

18. Evgenii Bolkhovitinov, "Opisanie Kievo-Sofiiskogo sobora i kievskoi ierarkhii," in *Yevhenii Bolkhovitinov, Vybrani pratsi z istorii Kieva*, ed. Tetiana Anan'eva (Kyiv: Lybid, 1995), 60–61. For the English translation of the inscription, see Charipova, "Peter Mohyla and St. Volodimer," 443.

19. Simon Ditchfield, "Text before Trowel: Antonio Bosio's *Roma sotterranea* Revisited," *Studies in Church History* 33 (1997), 344.

20. Reprinted in Afanasii Kal'nofoiskyi, "The Teraturgema of Afanasij Kal'nofojskyj," in *Seventeenth-Century Writings on the Kievan Caves Monastery*, xxiv–xxvii, 117–326.

21. "The *Paterikon* of Syl'vestr Kosov," 14.

22. On Mohyla, see Golubev, *Kievskii mitropolit Petr Mogila*, and Zhukovskyi, *Petro Mohyla*. For further bibliography, see P. V. Holobytckyi, N. I. Moiseienko, and Z. I. Chyzhniak, eds., *Petro Mohyla (1596–1647): bibliohrafichnyi pokazhchyk* (Kyiv: Natsionalna Akademiia Nauk Ukrainy, 2003).

23. See Ludmila V. Charipova, *Latin Books and the Eastern Orthodox Clerical Elite in Kiev, 1632–1780* (Manchester: Manchester University Press, 2006), 49–54. On Jesuit schooling in Ukraine, see Tetiana Shevchenko, *Yezuitske shkilnytstvo na ukrainskykh zemliakh ostannoi chverty XVI–seredyny XVII st.* (Lviv: Svichadlo, 2005).

24. Zhukovskyi, *Petro Mohyla*, 164–75.

25. Zhukovskyi, *Petro Mohyla*, 176–78.

26. The text was first published in Greek. See Ševčenko, "Many Worlds of Peter Mohyla," 24n20; and Zhukovskyi, *Petro Mohyla*, 154–63. In 1645, the text was published in Middle Ukrainian in Kyiv.

27. For the Russian version of the inscription, see N. I. Petrov, *Drevniaia stenopis' v kievskoi Spasskoi na Berestove tserkvi* (Kiev: Tip. I. I. Gorbunova, 1908), 282–83.

28. Prizri s" nebes, Bozhe, i posieti vinograd" sei, ego zhe nasadi desnitsa Tvoia!" See *Drevnosti rossiiskago gosudarstva, Otdelenie I: Al'bom* (Moscow: Tip. Aleksandra Semena, 1849), no. 86.

29. On Jeremiah II, see Borys A. Gudziak, *Crisis and Reform: The Kyivan Metropolitanate, the Patriarchate of Constantinople and the Genesis of the Union of Brest* (Cambridge, MA: Harvard Ukrainian Research institute, 2001), 168–205.

30. On the Union of Brest, see Gudziak, *Crisis and Reform*, 225–30 and appendix 3, 263–72. See also Serhii Plokhy, *The Cossacks and Religion in Early Modern Ukraine* (Oxford: Oxford University Press, 2004), 76–77.

31. See Bednov, *Pravoslavnaia tserkov' v Pol'she i Litve*, 127–205.

32. On the gradual renewal of the "non-united" Ruthenian-Rus' hierarchy in the 1620s, see Plokhy, *Cossacks and Religion*, 111–23.

33. Sysyn, *Between Poland and Ukraine*, 68–69.

34. See Augustinus Theiner, ed., *Vetera Monumenta Poloniae et Lithuaniae Gentiumque Finitimarum Historiam Illustrantia* (Rome:Typis vaticanis, 1863), vol. 3, 399–401; *Arkhiv Iugo-Zapadnoi Rossii* (Kiev: Universitetskaia tipografiia, 1861), part 2, vol 1., no. 18, 208–14; and Golubev, *Kievskii mitropolit Petr Mogila*, 1:528–32 and appendix, 503.

35. On the new union, see Sysyn, *Between Poland and Ukraine*, 117–28; Šmurlo, *Saint-Siège*, part 1, 96–125 and part 2, 111–16; and Mikolaj Andrusiak, "Sprawa patriachatu kijowskiego za Władysław IV," in *Prace historyczne w 30-lecie działalności profesorskiej Stanisława Zakrzewskiego* (Lwów: Komitet Byłych Uczni z Zasiłkiem Ministerstwa, 1934), 271–76.

36. Quoted in Mykhailo Hrushevskyi, *History of Ukraine-Rus'*, vol. 8, ed. F. E. Sysyn and M. Yurevich, trans. M. D. Olynyk (1922; Alberta: Canadian Institute of Ukrainian Studies Press, 2002), 337.

37. Such an idea floated around Uniate circles since the late 1620s. See Krypiakevych, "Novyi materiialy do istorii soboriv 1629," *Zapysky NTSh* 116 (1913): 7.

38. Denis Zubritskii, *Letopis l'vovskogo Stavropigial'nogo bratstva* (1850, repr. Lviv, 1926), 60–61. For a Ukrainian translation of this text, see Denys Zubrytskyi, *Khronika Stavropihiis'koho bratstva*, trans. Ivan Svaryk (Lviv: Apriori, 2011), esp. 137–78.

39. *Akty otnosiashchiesia k istorii Iuzhnoi i Zapadnoi Rossii, sobrannye i izdannye Arkheograficheskoiu komissieiu* (St. Petersburg: Tipografiia Kulisha, 1861), vol. 3, documents no. 2 and 3, pp. 4–8.

40. Hrushevskyi, *History of Ukraine-Rus'*, 8:339–40. See *Akty IuZ Rossii* (1861), vol. 3, documents no. 2 and 3, pp. 4–8.

41. On Mohyla's and Kysil's Orthodoxy and attitude toward the Roman Church, see Zhukovskyi, *Petro Mohyla*, 151–89, and Sysyn, *Between Poland and Ukraine*, 117–28.

42. See *Documenta Ponificum Romanorum Historiam Ucrainae illustrantia*, ed. A. G. Welykyj (Romae: PP. Basiliani, 1953), 1:530–32.

43. For the text of the *Sententia*, see Šmurlo, *Saint-Siège*, part 2, 159–69 and 173–77. For a discussion of the document and its authorship, see A. H. Velykyi, "Anonimnyi proekt Petra Mohyly po ziedynenniu ukrainskoi tserkvy 1645 r.," *Analecta Ordinis S. Basilii Magni*, ser. 2, sec. 2, vol. 4 (10) (Romae: PP. Basiliani, 1963), 484–97. For a Ukrainian translation of the *Sententia*, see Zhukovskyi, *Petro Mohyla*, 142–64.

44. Sysyn, *Between Poland and Ukraine*, 122–23.

45. Hrushevskyi, *History of Ukraine-Rus'*, 8:342.

46. Velykyi, "Anonimnyi proekt Petra Mohyly," 484–97.

47. For Petro Mohyla's testament, see "Zapovit Mytropolyta Petra Mohyly," in Zhukovskyi, *Petro Mohyla*, 291–98. Various items commissioned specifically for this church further disclose its importance for the metropolitan. These include a silver cross, chalice, and reliquary, as well as a Bible printed in Lviv. Golubev, *Kievskii mitropolit Petr Mogila*, 2:449–50.

48. Kraków, Princes Czartoryski Library, Manuscript Division, no. 1657, folios 325–31. For a Ukrainian translation of the document, see Iurii A. Mytsyk, "Dva publitsystychni traktaty pro prychyny Natsionalno-vyzvolnoi viiny ukrainskoho narodu seredyny XVII st.," in *Ukrainskyi istorychnyi zhurnal* 6 (1999), 128–34.

49. See V. I. Tymofiienko, ed., *Istoriia ukrainskoi arkhitektury* (Kyiv: Tekhnika, 2003), 114–91; Piotr Krasny, "Odbudowa kijowskiej cerkwi Spasa na Berestowie przez metropolitę Piotra Mohyłę a problem nawrotu do gotyku w architekturze sakralnej Rusi koronnej w XVII wieku," *Biuletyn Historii Sztuki* 62, no. 3–4 (2000): 337–61; K. J. Czyżewski and M. Walczak, "O średniowiecznych wzorach nowożytnych kościołów z kaplicami in modum crucis na

ziemiach Rzeczypospolitej," in *Sztuka dawnej ziemi chełmskiej i województwa belskiego*, ed. P. Krasny (Kraków: Universitas, 1999), 25–37; and S. Jurczenko, "Krzyżowe kościoły Ukrainy w pierwszej polowie XVII w.," *Biuletyn Historii Sztuki* 57 (1995): 283–94.

50. Kraków, Princes Czartoryski Library, Manuscript Division, no. 1657, folios 325–31. For a Ukrainian translation of the document, see Mytsyk, "Dva publitsystychni traktaty," 130.

51. Anna Różycka-Bryzek, *Freski bizantyńsko-ruskie fundacji Jagiełły w kaplicy Zamku Lubelskiego* (Lublin: Muzeum Lubelskie w Lublinie, 2000), and Anna Różycka-Bryzek, *Bizantyńsko-ruskie malowidła w kaplicy Zamku Lubelskiego* (Warsaw: Państwowe Wydawnictwo Naukowe, 1983).

52. See Miroslaw Kruk, "Malowidła *Graeco opere* fundacji Jagiellonów jako postulat unii państwowej i kościelnej oraz jedności Kościoła," in *Między teologią a duszpasterstwem powszechnym na ziemiach Korony doby przed trydenckiej: Dziedzictwo średniowiecza i wyzwania XV–XVI wieku*, ed. Wacław Walecki (Warsaw: Wydawnictwo Uniwersytetu Warszawskiego, 2017), 152–55.

53. The use of both Gothic and Byzantine elements within an ecclesiastical foundation is not necessarily indicative of the peaceful coexistence of Western and Eastern Christianity in a given region. See Myroslav Kruk, "Istoricheskie i religioznye konteksty fundatsii Iagellonami t.n. Rus(s)ko-vizantiiskikh fresok v katolicheskikh khramakh pol'shi," in *Religiia i Rus', XV–XVIII vv.*, ed. A. V. Doronin (Moscow: Politicheskaia entsiklopediia, 2020), 52–92.

54. Fraterkulius', "Pamiatnik" drevniago pravoslaviia v" Liublinie—pravoslavnyi khram" i sushchestvovavshee pri nem" bratstvo. Ar. Lonshinov'. Varshava 1883 goda," *Kievskaia starina* (1883) vol. 7 (September and October): 292.

55. Sysyn, *Between Poland and Ukraine*, 99–101. See also Golubev, *Kievskii mitropolit Petr Mogila*, vol. 2, part 2, 9–11, 168–69, 205–6.

56. On the position of the Crown, see Jaroslaw Pelenski, "The Incorporation of the Ukrainian Lands of Old Rus' into Crown Poland (1569): Socio-Material Interest and Ideology—A Reexamination," in *American Contributions to the Seventh International Congress of Slavists (Warsaw, 21–27 August 1973), vol. 3: History*, ed. Anna Cienciala (The Hague: Mouton, 1973), 38–44. For the texts of the Kyivan restitution privilege, see Władysław Semkowicz and Stanisław Kutrzeba, eds., *Akta Unji Polski z Litwą. 1385–1791* (Kraków: Polska Akademia Umiejętności i Towarzystwo Naukowe Warszawskie, 1932), 309–19. On the viewpoint of the Ruthenian-Rus' nobility, see Natalia Yakovenko, "Topos 'ziednanykh narodiv' u panehirykakh kniaziam Ostrozkym i Zaslavskym (bilia vytokiv ukrainskoi identychnosti)," in Natalia Yakovenko, *Paralelnyi svit: Doslidzhennia z istorii uiavlen v Ukraini XVI–XVII st.* (Kyiv: Krytyka, 2002), 231–69.

57. Nataliia Starchenko, "Liublinska Uniia iak resurs formuvannia kontseptu politychnoho 'Narodu Ruskoho' (1569–1648)," *Ukrainskyi istorychnyi zhurnal* 2 (2019): 4–45. See also, Frank Sysyn, "Regionalism and Political Thought in Seventeenth-Century Ukraine: The Nobility's Grievances at the Diet of 1641," *Harvard Ukrainian Studies* 6, no. 2 (1982): 167–90.

58. See Plokhy, *Cossacks and Religion*, esp. 145–75; and Nataliia Yakovenko, "'In libertate nati sumus': zhyttievi stratehii ukrainskoi shliakhty i pravoslavnykh iierarkhiv naperedodni ta v pershe desiatylittia kozatskykh voien (1638–1658)," in Nataliia Yakovenko, *Dzerkala identychnosti: Doslidzhennia z istopii uiavlehta idei v Ukraini XVI–pochatku XVIII stolittia* (Kyiv: Laurus, 2012), 371–96.

59. *Kronika Macieja Stryjkowskiego* (Warsaw: Nakład Gustawa Leona Glüksberga, 1846), vol. 1, book 4, 132.

60. See Frank E. Sysyn, "Concepts of Nationhood in Ukrainian History Writing, 1620–1690," *Harvard Ukrainian Studies* 10, no. 3/4 (1986): 393–97; Oleksii Tolochko, "'Rus' ochyma

'Ukrainy': v poshukakh samoidentyfikatsii ta kontynuitetu," *Suchasnist* 1 (1994): 111–17; and NataliaYakovenko, "Latyna na sluzhbi kyievo-rus'kii istorii," *Paralelnyi svit: Doslidzhennia z istorii uiavlen ta idei v Ukraini XVI–XVII st.* (Kyiv: Krytyka, 2002), 270–95.

61. See Maria Grazia Bartolini, "From Icon to Emblem: The Relationship of Word and Image in Lazar Baranovych's *Truby sloves propovidnykh na narochityia dni prazdnikow* (1674)," *Slavonic and East European Review* 96, no. 2 (2016): 202–42; Maria Grazia Bartolini, "'Judging a Book by Its Cover': Meditation, Memory and Invention in Seventeenth-Century Ukraine," *Canadian Slavonic Papers* 59, no. 1–2 (2017): 21–55; and Maria Ivanova and Michelle R. Viise, "Dissimulation and Memory in Early Modern Poland-Lithuania: The Art of Forgetting," *Slavic Review* 76, no. 1 (Spring 2017): 98–121.

62. See Paul Devos, "Une passion grecque inédite de S. Pierre d'Alexandrie, et sa traduction par Anastase le Bibliothécaire," *Analecta Bollandiana* 83 (1965): 167–77; Gabriel Millet, "La vision de Pierre d'Alexandrie," in *Mélanges Charles Diehl: Études sur l'histoire et sur l'art de Byzance, vol. 2, Art* (Paris: Librairie Ernst Leroux, 1930), 99–114; and Silas Koukiaris, "The Depiction of the Vision of Saint Peter of Alexandria in the Sanctuary of Byzantine Churches," *Zograf* 35 (2011): 63–71.

63. For the inscription, see Petrov, *Drevniaia stenopis'*, 281.

64. P. Zhukovich, *Materialy dlia istorii kievskogo i l'vovskogo soborov 1629 goda* (St. Petersburg: tip. Imp. Akad. nauk, 1911), 17. English translation from Sysyn, *Between Poland and the Ukraine*, 61.

65. For the inscription, see Petrov, *Drevniaia stenopis'*, 267.

66. For the inscription, see Petrov, *Drevniaia stenopis'*, 268–70, and Vera Chentsova, "Grecheskaia ktitorskia nadpis' XVII v. v kievskoi tserkvi Spasa na Berestove," in *Drevniaia Rus': Voprosy medievistiki* 3, no. 65 (2016), 112–13.

67. The original text is available as "O edinstve tserkvi Bozhei Petra Skargi 1577 goda" in *Istoricheskaia biblioteka izdavaemaia Arkheograficheskoiu kommissieiu*, vol. 7, *Pamiatniki polemicheskoi literatury v zapadnoi Rusi* (St. Petersburg: Tipografiia A.M. Kotomina, 1882), vol. 2, cols. 223–526, esp. col. 485–86. The English translation of the relevant passage cited here is from David A. Frick, "Meletij Smotryc'kyj and the Ruthenian Language Question," *Harvard Ukrainian Studies* 9, no. 1/2 (1985), 29–30.

68. See Olexa Horbatsch, ed., *Adelphotes: Die erste gedruckte griechisch-kirchenslavische Grammatik, L'viv-Lemberg 1591* (Frankfurt am Main: Peter Lang, 1973).

69. Iaroslav Isaievych, *Voluntary Brotherhoods: Confraternities of Laymen in Early Modern Ukraine* (Edmonton: Canadian Institute of Ukrainian Studies Press, 2006), 208–9.

70. For the Russian translation of the inscription, see Petrov, *Drevniaia stenopis'*, 286–87.

71. Ševčenko, "Many Worlds of Peter Mohyla," 36–38.

72. Natalia Pylypiuk, "*Eucharisterion, Albo, Vdjačnost*: The First Panegyric of the Kiev Mohyla School; Its Content and Historical Context," *Harvard Ukrainian Studies* 8, no. 1/2 (1984): 45–70. For the image, see Zhukovskyi, *Petro Mohyla*, 76.

73. *Trebnik of Peter Mogyla* [1646], British Library, EAP556/1/7/1, https://eap.bl.uk/archive-file/EAP556-1-7-1, 727–55, esp. 727–28, 754–55.

74. Yakovenko, "Topos 'ziednanykh narodiv,'" 244.

75. Natalia Yakovenko, "Kyiv pid shatrom Sventoldychiv: mohylianskyi panehiryk 1646 roku *Tentoria venienti*," in Yakovenko, *Dzerkala identychnosti*, 293–314.

76. On the usage of "Ukraine," see Serhii Plokhy, *The Origins of the Slavic Nations: Premodern Identities in Russia, Ukraine, and Belarus* (Cambridge: Cambridge University Press, 2006), 316–20.

77. The Berestovo Church was restored in 1863–1865. See N. I. Petrov, *Istoriko-topograficheskie ocherki Drevnego Kieva* (Kiev: Tipografiia Imperatorskago Univesiteta sv. Vladimira,1897), 73.

78. The nineteenth-century scholars who first ascribed the Berestovo Church to Prince Volodymyr Monomakh were Petr A. Lashkarev and Pavel Lebedintsev. See Alina Kondratiuk, "Rozpysy tserkvy Spas an Berestovi doby Petra Mohyly: problematyka i perspektyvy doslidzhennia," *Studii mystetstvoznavchi* 4 (2008): 41–55.

79. Mikhail Karger, *Drevnii Kiev, vol. 2, Pamiatniki Kievskogo zodchestva X–XIII vv.* (Moscow: Izdatel'stvo Akademii Hauk SSSR, 1961), 377–78.

80. Kondratiuk, "Rozpysy tserkvy Spas an Berestovi," 41–42.

81. The inscription on the sarcophagus outlines the details of its installation in the Berestovo Church.

82. Grygorii Logvin, "Vozvrozhdennye freski XI–XII veka," *Iskusstvo* 8 (1971): 64–68.

83. Karger, *Drevnii Kiev*, 383–91; and Iurii Asieiev and Viktor Kharlamov, "Novi doslidzhennia tserkvy Spasa na Berestovi," in *Arkheolohiia Kyieva: doslidzhennia i materialy: Zbirnyk naukovykh prats* (Kyiv: Nukova dumka, 1979), 84–90.

84. For some of the available publications on the seventeenth-century imagery that usually focus on stylistic analysis, on the identity of the artists who may have worked on the church, and take the form of short notices, see Kondratiuk, "Rozpysy tserkvy Spas an Berestovi."

85. An adaptation of a line from Bhabha, *Location of Culture*, 3.

5: Sarmatia Revisited

1. Stanisław Kutrzeba and Władysław Semkowicz, eds., *Akta unji Polski z Litwą, 1385–1791* (Kraków: Nakładem Polskiej Akademji Umiejętności, 1932), 358; Felicia Roşu, *Elective Monarchy in Transylvania and Poland-Lithuania, 1569–1587* (New York: Oxford University Press, 2017), 8–9; and Anna Grześkowiak-Krwawicz, "Respublica and the Language of Freedom: The Polish Experiment," in *A Handbook to Classical Reception in Eastern and Central Europe*, ed. Zara Martirosova Torlone, Dana LaCourse Munteanu, and Dorota Dutsch (Oxford: Wiley-Blackwell, 2017), 179–89.

2. Pograbka's map, for example, was printed in Venice, the unquestioned epicenter of European cartography in the 1560s and 1570s. See Karol Buczek, *The History of Polish Cartography from the 15th to the 18th Century*, trans. Andrzej Potocki (Amsterdam: Meridian, 1982); Michael J. Mikoś, "Monarchs and Magnates: Maps of Poland in the Sixteenth and Eighteenth Centuries," in *Monarchs, Ministers, and Maps: The Emergence of Cartpography as a Tool of Government in Early Modern Europe*, ed. David Buisseret (Chicago: University of Chicago Press, 1992), 168–81; Maria Juda, "Mapy ziem polskich w dawnej typografii europejskiej," *Studia Źródłoznawcze* 41 (2003): 45–63; Jarosław Łuczyński, "Ziemie Rzeczypospolitej w kartografii europejskiej XVI wieku (Próba ustalenia filiacji map wydanych drukiem)," *Polski Przegląd Kartograficzny* 41, no. 2 (2009): 128–44; Kazimierz Kozica, "The Map of the Polish-Lithuanian Commonwealth by Andrzej Pograbka Published in Venice in 1570 in the Niewodniczański Collection 'Imago Poloniae' at the Royal Castle in Warsaw—Museum," in *Proceedings of the 12th ICA Conference Digital Approaches to Cartographic Heritage, Venice, April 26–28, 2017*, ed. Evangelos Livieratos (Thessaloniki: AUTH CartoGeoLab, 2017), 10–14; and David Woodward, *Maps as Prints in the Italian Renaissance: Makers, Distributors and Consumers* (London: British Library, 1996), 4–5.

3. Peter van der Krogt, "The Map of Russia and Poland in Dutch Atlases of the Sixteenth and Seventeenth Centuries," in *Maps in Books of Russia and Poland Published in the Netherlands to 1800*, ed. Paula van Gestel-van het Schip et al. (Houten: Hes & De Graaf, 2011), 113–31; and Andrzej Michał Kobos, "Tomasz Niewodniczański (1933–2010) i jego zbiory," *Prace Komisji Historii Nauki PAU* 11 (2012): 149–97.

4. On the Polish-Lithuanian union, see Robert I. Frost, *The Oxford History of Poland-Lithuania*, vol. 1 (Oxford: Oxford University Press, 2015), 405–94. On Ptolemy, see Benjamin Weiss, "The Geography in Print, 1475–1530," in *Ptolemy's Geography in the Renaissance*, ed. Zur Shalev and Charles Burnett (London: Warburg Institute, 2011), 91–120.

5. Tadeusz Ulewicz, *Sarmacja: Studium z problematyki słowiańskiej XV i XVI w.* (Kraków: Wydawnictwo Studium Słowiańskiego Uniwersytetu Jagiellońskiego, 1950).

6. Henri Estienne, *Traité de la conformité du langage françois avec le grec* (Geneva, 1565); Kristoffer Neville, "History and Architecture in Pursuit of a Gothic Heritage," in *The Quest for an Appropriate Past in Literature, Art and Architecture*, ed. Karl A. E. Enenkel and Konrad Adriaan Ottenheym (Leiden: Brill, 2018), 619–48; and K. A. E. Enenkel and Koen Ottenheym, *Ambitious Antiquities, Famous Forebears: Constructions of a Glorious Past in the Early Modern Netherlands and in Europe*, trans. Alexander C. Thomson (Leiden: Brill, 2019).

7. Ulewicz, *Sarmacja*, 136.

8. Tadeusz Mańkowski, *Genealogia sarmatyzmu* (Warsaw: Towarzystwo Wydawnicze Łuk, 1947).

9. Mańkowski, *Genealogia sarmatyzmu*, 18.

10. Aleksander Brückner, "Sarmatyzm," in *Encyklopedia staropolska* (Warsaw: Trzaska, Evert i Michalski, 1939), 2:451–53.

11. Tadeusz Chrzanowski, *Wędrówki po Sarmacji europejskiej: Eseje o sztuce i kulturze staropolskiej* (Kraków: Znak, 1988); Janusz Tazbir, *Kultura szlachecka w Polsce: rozkwit—upadek—relikty* (Poznań: Wydawnictwo Poznańskie, 1998), 132–52; Mariusz Karpowicz, *Sztuka oświeconego sarmatyzmu: Antykizacja i klasycyzacja w środowisku warszawskim czasów Jana III*, 2nd ed. (Warsaw: PWN, 1986); Tadeusz Dobrowolski, "Cztery style portretu 'sarmackiego,'" *Zeszyty Naukowe Uniwersytetu Jagiellońskiego* 45 (1962): 83–85; Janusz Tazbir, "Polish National Consciousness in the Sixteenth to the Eighteenth Century," *Harvard Ukrainian Studies* 10, no. 3/4 (1986), 318; Stanisław Cynarski, "Sarmatyzm—ideologia i styl życia," in *Polska XVII wieku: państwo, społeczeństwo, kultura*, ed. Janusz Tazbir (Warsaw: Wiedza Powszechna, 1969), 220–43; Władysław Tomkiewicz, "W kręgu kultury sarmatyzmu," *Kultura* 30 (1966); Maria Bogucka, *The Lost World of the "Sarmatians": Custom as the Regulator of Polish Social Life in Early Modern Times* (Warsaw: Polish Academy of Sciences, Institute of History, 1996); and Krzysztof Koehler, *Palus sarmatica* (Warsaw: Muzeum Historii Polski, 2016).

12. Tadeusz Chrzanowski, "Orient i orientalizm w kulturze staropolskiej," in *Orient i orientalizm w sztuce*, ed. Elżbieta Karwowska (Warsaw: PWN, 1986), 43–69; and Paulina Banas, "Persische Kunst und polnische Identität," in *Sehnsucht Persien: Austausch und Rezeption in der Kunst Persiens und Europas im 17. Jahrhundert & Gegenwartskunst aus Teheran*, ed. Axel Langer (Zurich: Scheidegger & Spiess, 2013), 118–35.

13. *Decorum życia Sarmatów w XVII i XVIII wieku: Katalog pokazu sztuki zdobniczej ze zbiorów Muzeum Narodowego w Warszawie* (Warsaw: Muzeum Narodowe, 1980), 7.

14. Jakub Niedźwiedź, "Sarmatyzm, czyli tradycja wynaleziona," *Teksty Drugie*, no. 1 (2015): 46–62; Eric Hobsbawm, "Inventing Traditions," in *The Invention of Tradition*, ed. Eric Hobsbawm and Terence Ranger (Cambridge: Cambridge University Press, 1983), 1–14. On Sarmatism as as a real cultural formation, see Jacek Kowalski, *Sarmacja: obalanie mitów: Podręcznik bojowy* (Warsaw: Zona Zero, 2016); Ewa Thompson, "Sarmatism, or the Secrets of Polish Essentialism," in *Being Poland: A New History of Polish Literature and Culture since 1918*, ed. Tamara Trojanowska, Joanna Niżyńska, and Przemysław Czapliński (Toronto: University of Toronto Press, 2018), 3–29; and Jan Sowa, "Spectres of Sarmatism," in Trojanowska, Niżyńska, and Czapliński, *Being Poland*, 30–47.

15. Dirk Uffelmann, "Importierte Dinge und imaginierte Identität: Osmanische 'Sarmatica' im Polen der Aufklärung," *Zeitschrift für Ostmitteleuropa-Forschung* 65, no. 2 (2016): 193–214.

16. *Monitor Warszawski*, no. 30, 1765, 234; Franciszek Zabłocki, *Sarmatyzm: Komedya w pięciu aktach* (Lwów: nakł. i dr. Wilhelma Zukerkandla, 1905).

17. *Monitor Warszawski*, no. 30, 1765, 234.

18. Maciej Gloger, "Teologia Polityczna Henryka Sienkiewicza," in *Sienkiewicz Ponowoczesny*, ed. Bartłomiej Szleszyński and Magdalena Rudkowska (Warsaw: Wydawnictwo IBL PAN, 2019), 372.

19. Mańkowski, *Genealogia sarmatyzmu*, 97.

20. For a modern account, see Tadeusz Sulimirski, *The Sarmatians* (London: Thames and Hudson, 1970).

21. Herodotus, *Histories*, ed. Carolyn Dewald, trans. Robin Waterfield (Oxford: Oxford University Press, 1998), 4.110–17; Strabo, *Geography*, trans. Horace Leonard Jones, vol. 7 (Cambridge, MA: Harvard University Press, 1995), 3.17; and Tacitus, *La Germanie*, trans. Jacques Perret (Paris: Société d'Édition Les Belles Lettres, 1983), ch. 17.

22. "Poloni . . . et omnia genera slavorum, post diluvium in hanc aetatem in suis sedibus et connatis regnis permanent, et non aliunde supervenerunt." Quoted in Ulewicz, *Sarmacja*, 59.

23. Marcin Kromer, *Polska: czyli o położeniu, ludności, obyczajach, urzędach i sprawach publicznych Królestwa Polskiego księgi dwie*, trans. Stefan Kazikowski (Olsztyn: Pojezierze, 1977), 15.

24. "Ociec nasz krześcijański . . . w ten tu kraj północny przyszedł do Europy po potopie i rozmnożył potomstwo swoje według Pańskiej wolej." Marcin Bielski, *Kronika Polska* (Kraków, 1551), 154v.

25. Maciej Stryjkowski, *Kronika polska, litewska, zmodźka, y wszystkiej Rusi Kijowskiej . . .* (Königsberg, 1582), 74.

26. Even Wojciech Dembołęcki, a Franciscan who conflates ancient Poles with the Scythians, reduces Polish antiquity to a necessary ethnographic prelude to the Christian era. In his account, the Eastern past has no bearing on the present, however, and is implied only to deduce Poles' alleged origin from Seth (whom Dembołęcki calls "Scyth"), the third son of Adam and Eve, and thus to claim that Polish was the language spoken in the Garden of Eden. See Wojciech Dembołęcki, *Wywod iedynowłasnego panstwa swiata, w ktorym pokázuie X. W. Debolecki . . . ze nastárodawnieysze w Europie Krolestwo Polskie, lubo Scythyckie . . . y . . . ze język słowieński pierwotny jest ná świećie* (Warsaw: J. Rossowski, 1633), 27–45.

27. Jan Chryzostom Pasek, *Pamiętniki*, ed. Jan Czubek (Kraków: Polska Akademia Nauk, 1929), http://wolnelektury.pl/katalog/lektura/pamietniki.

28. Katharina N. Piechocki, *Cartographic Humanism: The Making of Early Modern Europe* (Chicago: University of Chicago Press, 2019), 12.

29. Pomponius Mela, *Description of the World*, trans. Frank E. Romer (Ann Arbor: University of Michigan Press, 1998), 110.

30. Patrick Gautier Dalché, "The Reception of Ptolemy's Geography (End of the Fourteenth to Beginning of the Sixteenth Century)," in *Cartography in the European Renaissance*, ed. David Woodward, vol. 3, *The History of Cartography* (Chicago: University of Chicago Press, 2007), 320–21; and Buczek, *History of Polish Cartography*, 25–27.

31. Dalché, "Reception of Ptolemy's Geography," 285–90; Zur Shalev, "Main Themes in the Study of Ptolemy's Geography in the Renaissance," in Shalev and Burnett, *Ptolemy's Geography in the Renaissance*, 7–9; Alexander Jones, "Ptolemy's Geography: A Reform That Failed," in Shalev and Burnett, *Ptolemy's Geography in the Renaissance*, 15–30; and Katharina N. Piechocki, "Erroneous Mappings: Ptolemy and the Visualization of Europe's East," in *Early Modern Cul-*

tures of Translation, ed. Karen Newman and Jane Tylus (Philadelphia: University of Pennsylvania Press, 2015), 81. For a recent critique of the notions of improved cartographic projection and the supposed novelty of the coordinate system, which were traditionally associated with the so-called Ptolemaic revolution, see Sean Roberts, *Printing a Mediterranean World: Florence, Constantinople, and the Renaissance of Geography* (Cambridge, MA: Harvard University Press, 2013), 36–44.

32. Bożena Modelska-Strzelecka, *Odrodzenie Geografii Ptolemeusza w XV w.: tradycja kartograficzna* (Wrocław: Polskie Towarzystwo Geograficzne, 1960); Jadwiga Bzinkowska, *Od Sarmacji do Polonii: studia nad początkami obrazu kartograficznego Polski* (Kraków: Nakł. Uniwersytetu Jagiellońskiego, 1994), 13–25; Lucyna Szaniawska, *Sarmacja na mapach Ptolemeusza w edycjach jego "Geografii"* (Warsaw: Biblioteka Narodowa, 1993); and Anthony Grafton, *New Worlds, Ancient Texts: The Power of Tradition and the Shock of Discovery* (Cambridge, MA: Belknap Press of Harvard University Press, 1992), 1–10.

33. See Henry Newton Stevens, *Ptolemy's Geography: A Brief Account of All the Printed Editions down to 1730* (Amsterdam: Meridian, 1973), 14–25, 106–8.

34. Claudius Ptolemy, *Geography*, trans. Edward Luther Stevenson (New York: New York Public Library, 1932), book 3, ch. 5.

35. Buczek, *History of Polish Cartography*, 26.

36. The work was never published in full, but it circulated widely throughout early modernity. Hans-Jürgen Bömelburg, *Polska myśl historyczna a humanistyczna historia narodowa (1500–1700)*, trans. Zdzisław Owczarek (Kraków: Universitas, 2011), 64.

37. Jan Długosz, *Roczniki czyli kroniki sławnego Królestwa Polskiego* (Warsaw: PWN, 1961), 137.

38. Długosz, *Roczniki czyli kroniki*, 94, 164–65.

39. Długosz, *Roczniki czyli kroniki*, 286.

40. Bzinkowska, *Od Sarmacji do Polonii*, 23–24.

41. Bzinkowska, *Od Sarmacji do Polonii*, 34.

42. Buczek, *History of Polish Cartography*, 32. They are, however, reproduced in Buczek's book from pre–Second World War facsimiles.

43. "Sigismundus etc. Manifestum facimus tenore praesentium universis, quia cum famatus Florianus, civis et calcographus Cracoviensis, duas tabulas cosmographiae, particulares, alteram videlicet nonnulla loca regni nostril Poloniae et etiam Hungariae ac Valachiae, Turciae, Tartariae, et Masoviae [Moscoviae ?], alteram vero ducatus Prussiae, Pomeraniae, Samogithiae et magni ducatus nostril Lithuaniae continentem, per venerabilem Bernardum Vapowski, cantorem ecclesiae cathedralis Cracoviensis, secretarium nostrum." Published by Jan Ptaśnik, ed., *Monumenta Poloniae typographica XV et XVI saeculorum*, vol. 1 (Lwów: Ossolineum, 1922), 119–20, no. 287.

44. "Cracovia Poloniae nuper dedit tabulas duas Sarmatiae et Scythiae, licet inelegantes, tamen, me iudice, non inutiles. Si te illarum tenet ardot habendi, non deero tuo desiderio." Johann Heumann, ed., *Documenta literaria varii argumenti* (Altorf, 1758), 119.

45. "Tabulam Sarmatiae secundo tibi mitto, nam hanc unicam ad manum nunc habui, pro prima scripsi Cracoviensibus amicis, habebis et illam. Quod Ptolemaeum viderit, fert graviter." Heumann, *Documenta literaria*, 79.

46. Bernhard Willkomm, "Beiträge zur Reformationsgeschichte aus Drucken und Handschriften der Universitätsbibliothek in Jena," *Archiv für Reformationsgeschichte* 9, no. 3 (1911/1912): 246–47. See also Paweł Matwiejczuk, ed., *Melanchtoniana polonica*, (Berlin and Warsaw: CBH PAN and Muzeum Historii Polski, 2022).

328 Notes to Pages 126–131

47. "D. Joannes Eckius, a me per literas poposcit, Corographias duas terre Sarmatiae, que opera mea in luce prodierunt, quas nune in eo fasciculo transmitto." Fragment of the letter published in Ludwik Birkenmajer, *Mikołaj Kopernik: Studya nad pracami Kopernika oraz materyały biograficzne* (Kraków: Akademia Umiejętności, 1900), 455. Original in Cod. Ms. Ups. H. 154, list Nr. 39.

48. Maciej z Miechowa, *Opis Sarmacji Azjatyckiej i Europejskiej oraz tego, co się w nich znajduje*, ed. Henryk Barycz, trans. Tadeusz Bieńkowski (Wrocław: Zakład Narodowy im. Ossolińskich, 1972), 28.

49. Mańkowski, *Genealogia sarmatyzmu*, 17.

50. Piechocki, *Cartographic Humanism*, 78.

51. Leszek Hajdukiewicz, *Biblioteka Macieja z Miechowa* (Wrocław: Zakład Narodowy im. Ossolińskich, 1960), 70, 154.

52. J. Kłoczkowski, "Polacy a cudzoziemcy w XV wieku," in *Swojskość i cudzoziemszczyzna w dziejach kultury polskiej*, ed. Zofia Stefanowska (Warsaw: PWN, 1973), 57; Chrzanowski, "Orient i orientalizm," 45; Mańkowski, *Genealogia sarmatyzmu*; and Ulewicz, *Sarmacja*.

53. Jost Ludwig Dietz, *De vetustibus Vetustatibus Polonorum* (Kraków: Hieronymus Vietor, 1521), 2.

54. Kłoczkowski, "Polacy a cudzoziemcy w XV wieku," 57; and Chrzanowski, "Orient i orientalizm," 45. See also Mańkowski, *Genealogia sarmatyzmu*; Tomas Venclova, "Mit o początku," *Teksty* 4 (1974): 104–16; and Ulewicz, *Sarmacja*.

55. Karol Buczek, "Wacław Grodecki," *Polski Przegląd Kartograficzny* 11, no. 43 (1933), 80.

56. Łuczyński, "Ziemie Rzeczypospolitej w kartografii Europejskiej," 134.

57. Buczek, *History of Polish Cartography*, 41.

58. Roman Marchwiński, "Kromer a Grodecki: Podstawy kartograficzne kromerowskiej Polonii," *Acta Universitatis Nicolai Copernici: Historia* 16, no. 114 (1980), 139.

59. Kromer, *Polska*, 15.

60. Buczek, "Wacław Grodecki," 84–85.

61. Buczek, "Wacław Grodecki," 83.

62. Buczek, *History of Polish Cartography*, 45; Zsolt G. Török, "Renaissance Cartography in East-Central Europe, ca. 1450–1650," in Woodward, *Cartography in the European Renaissance*, 3:1816–20, 1833–34.

63. "Partis Sarmatiae Europeae quae Sigismundus Augusto Regi Poloniae Potentissimo subiacet."

64. See Richard Helgerson, *Forms of Nationhood: The Elizabethan Writing of England* (Chicago: University of Chicago Press, 1992), 114.

65. The term "imagined community" is Benedict Anderson's. See Benedict Anderson, *Imagined Communities: Reflections on the Origin and Spread of Nationalism* (London: Verso, 1991), 6.

66. Bielski, *Kronika Polska*, 155, 191–191r, 225–26. See also Bömelburg, *Polska myśl historyczna*, 178.

67. Maciej Stryjkowski, *Kronika*, vol. 1 (Warsaw, 1846), xv and xl; Bömelburg, *Polska myśl historyczna*, 589.

68. Stryjkowski claims his manuscript was stolen by Guagnini. Bömelburg, *Polska myśl historyczna*, 590.

69. Stanisław Sarnicki, *Annales*, 1582, unpaginated. See also Bömelburg, *Polska myśl historyczna*, 239.

70. Bömelburg, *Polska myśl historyczna*, 594–655.

71. Albertus Koialovicius-Wijuk, *Historiae Lithuanae pars prior de rebus Lithuanorum ante susceptam Christianam religionem conjunctionemque . . . cum Regno Poloniae* (Danzig, 1650); Venclova, "Mit o Początku," 104–16; Tazbir, "Polish National Consciousness"; Frank E. Sysyn, "Concepts of Nationhood in Ukrainian History Writing, 1620–1690," *Harvard Ukrainian Studies* 10, no. 3/4 (1986): 393–423; Frank E. Sysyn, "The Cossack Chronicles and the Development of Modern Ukrainian Culture and National Identity," *Harvard Ukrainian Studies* 14, no. 3/4 (1990): 593–607; and Karin Friedrich, *The Other Prussia: Royal Prussia, Poland and Liberty, 1569–1772* (Cambridge: Cambridge University Press, 2006), 103–8.

72. After Frank E. Sysyn, "Regionalism and Political Thought in Seventeenth-Century Ukraine: The Nobility's Grievances at the Diet of 1641," *Harvard Ukrainian Studies* 6, no. 2 (1982): Appendix, 186. See also chapter 4 in this volume.

73. "Sum gente Scytha, natione Ruthena utroque autem modo Sarmata, quod ea Rusia, quae mihi patria est, in Sarmatia Europae sit posita dextra habens Daciam, sinistra Poloniam, ante illam est Ungaria, post vero Scythia vergit ad orientem solem." Letter of Stanisław Orzechowski to Pope Julius III, 1551, in *Humanizm i Reformacja w Polsce: Wybór źródeł dla ćwiczeń uniwersyteckich*, ed. Ignacy Chrzanowski and Stanisław Kot (Lwów, Warsaw, and Kraków, 1927), 328.

74. Christophorus Hartknoch, *Alt- und neues Preussen* (Frankfurt and Leipzig, 1684), 101.

75. For the concept of "geo-body," see Thongchai Winichakul, *Siam Mapped: A History of the Geo-Body of a Nation* (Honolulu: University of Hawai'i Press, 1994), 16.

76. For recent examples, see Kowalski, *Sarmacja*; and Thompson, "Sarmatism."

77. For recent studies in English on Polish-Lithuanian republicanism, see Frost, *Oxford History of Poland-Lithuania*; Roşu, *Elective Monarchy*; and Dorota Pietrzyk-Reeves, *Polish Republican Discourse in the Sixteenth Century* (Cambridge: Cambridge University Press, 2020).

78. See Andrzej Sulima Kamiński, *Historia Rzeczypospolitej Wielu Narodów 1505–1795: Obywatele, ich państwa, społeczeństwo, kultura* (Lublin: Instytut Europy Środkowo-Wschodniej, 2000).

6: Confessions, Confessionalization, and the Partitions of the Polish-Lithuanian Commonwealth

1. MS Diary, April 18, 1791, Archiwum Główne Akt Dawnych, Warsaw: Archiwum Sejmu Czteroletniego (hereafter: ASC), vol. 17, fol. 283v. All translations are the author's, unless otherwise indicated.

2. Ostrogiškis/Ostrogski/Ostrozkyi is the patron of the joint Lithuanian-Polish-Ukrainian brigade established in 2016.

3. See Richard Butterwick, *The Polish Revolution and the Catholic Church: A Political History* (Oxford: Oxford University Press, 2012), 243–46.

4. Richard Butterwick, "Discourses of Tolerance and Intolerance at the Four Years' Sejm (1788–1792)," in *The Polish-Lithuanian Commonwealth: History, Memory, Legacy*, ed. Andrzej Chwalba and Krzysztof Zamorski (New York: Routledge, 2021), 256–72.

5. See, e.g., President Bronisław Komorowski's foreword to the catalog of the exhibition organized by the Museum of Polish History at the Royal Castle in Warsaw in 2012, *Pod wspólnym niebem: Rzeczpospolita wielu narodów, wyznań, kultur (XVI–XVIII w.) / Under a Common Sky: The Commonwealth of Many Nations, Religions and Cultures (16th–18th c.)* (Warsaw: Muzeum Historii Polski, 2012), 7–8. The following foreword (*Under a Common Sky*, 9–12), by the directors of the Museum and the Castle, Robert Kostro and Andrzej Rottermund, respectively, acknowledges the positive power of such myths when based on research.

6. *Volumina Legum*, vol. 2 (St. Petersburg: Jozafat Ohryzko, 1859), 124. The text of the Confederacy of Warsaw is also available at https://agad.gov.pl/?page_id=966, accessed November

26, 2020. On interregna and royal elections see Felicia Roşu, *Elective Monarchy in Transylvania and Poland-Lithuania, 1569–1587* (Oxford: Oxford University Press, 2017).

7. Władysław Konopczyński, *Dzieje Polski nowożytnej*, 2nd ed. (Warsaw: PAX, 1986), 1:184–86, 205–6 (quotations), 2:116–19, 166–73, 182–87, 253–54. Compare Roman Dmowski, *Myśli nowoczesnego Polaka* [1903], 12th ed. (Wrocław: Wydawnictwo Nortom, 2002), 26–33. See Piotr Biliński, *Władysław Konopczyński 1880–1952* (Kraków: Ośrodek Myśli Politycznej, 2017), and chapter 8 in this volume. For the causes and consequences of the Union of Brest, see Borys A. Gudziak, *The Kyivan Metropolitanate, the Patriarchate of Constantinople, and the Genesis of the Union of Brest* (Cambridge, MA: Harvard University Press, 2001); Serhii Plokhy, *The Cossacks and Religion in Early Modern Ukraine* (Oxford: Oxford University Press, 2001); Andrzej Gil and Ihor Skoczylas, *Kościoły Wschodnie w państwie polsko-litewskim w procesie przemian i adaptacji: Metropolia Kijowska w latach 1458–1795* (Lublin: Instytut Europy Środkowo-Wschodniej, 2014); and Alfons Brüning, *Unio non est unitas: Polen-Litauens Weg im konfessionellen Zeitalter (1569–1648)* (Wiesbaden: Harrasowitz Verlag, 2008).

8. See, e.g., Andrzej Sulima Kamiński, *Historia Rzeczypospolitej wielu narodów 1505–1795* (Lublin: Instytut Europy Środkowo-Wschodniej, 2000), 9–22, 45–47, 67–93, 107–11, 125–29, 134, 174–77, 206–11; and Karin Friedrich, "Introduction: Citizenship and Identity in an Early Modern Commonwealth," in *Citizenship and Identity in a Multinational Commonwealth: Poland-Lithuania in Context, c. 1550–1772*, ed. Karin Friedrich and Barbara M. Pendzich (Leiden: Brill, 2009), 1–16.

9. Wojciech Kriegseisen, "Dysydenci i dyzunici w Rzeczypospolitej epoki stanisławowskiej," in *Stanisław August i jego Rzeczpospolita: Dramat państwa, odrodzenie narodu. Materiały z wykładów*, ed. Angela Sołtys and Zofia Zielińska (Warsaw: Arx Regia, 2013), 51, 57.

10. Wojciech Kriegseisen, *Between State and Church: Confessional Relations from Reformation to Enlightenment: Poland—Lithuania—Germany—Netherlands*, trans. Bartosz Wójcik (Frankfurt am Main: Peter Lang, 2016); and Wojciech Kriegseisen, "Toleration, or Church-State Relations? The Determinant in Negotiating Religions in the Modern Polish-Lithuanian Commonwealth," trans. Tristan Korecki, *Acta Poloniae Historica* 107 (2013): 83–99.

11. Peter Burke, *Popular Culture in Early Modern Europe*, 3rd ed. (London: Routledge, 2009), ch. 8, "The Triumph of Lent: The Reform of Popular Culture," 289–334.

12. See, among others, Heinz Schilling, "Confessionalization in the Empire. Religious and Societal Change in Germany between 1555 and 1620," in *Religion, Political Culture and the Emergence of Early Modern Society: Essays in German and Dutch History* (Leiden: Brill, 1992), 205–45; Wolfgang Reinhard, "Was ist katholische Konfessionalisierung?" in *Die katholische Konfessionalisierung*, ed. Wolfgang Reinhard and Heinz Schilling (Münster: Aschendorff Verlag, 1995), 419–52; Thomas A. Brady Jr., "Historical Definitions: Confessionalization: The Career of a Concept," in *Confessionalization in Europe: Essays in Honor and Memory of Bodo Nischan*, ed. John M. Headley, Hans J. Hillebrand, and Anthony J. Papalas (Ashgate: Aldershot, 2004), 1–20; Ute Lotz-Heumann, "The Concept of 'Confessionalization': A Historiographical Paradigm in Dispute," *Memoria y Civilización* 4 (2001), 93–114; R. Po-chia Hsia, *Social Discipline in the Reformation: Central Europe, 1550–1750* (New York: Routledge, 1989); Heinrich Richard Schmidt, "Sozialdisziplinierung? Ein Plädoyer fur das Ende des Etatismus in der Konfessionalisierungsforschung," *Historische Zeitschrift* 265 (1997): 639–82; Marc R. Forster, *Catholic Revival in the Age of the Baroque: Religious Identity in Southwest Germany, 1550–1750* (Cambridge: Cambridge University Press, 2001); and Kaspar von Greyerz et al., eds., *Interkonfessionalität—Transkonfessionalität—binnenkonfessionelle Pluralität: Neue Forschungen zur Konfessionalisierungsthese* (Gütersloh: Gütersloher Verlagshaus, 2003).

13. In her extended introduction to her anthology *Państwo świeckie czy księże? Spór o rolę duchowieństwa katolickiego w Rzeczypospolitej w czasach Zygmunta III Wazy: Wybór tekstów* (Warsaw: Wydawnictwo Semper, 2013), 122–28, Urszula Augustyniak, who generally follows Kriegseisen's line on confessionalization, takes issue with his view that "the lack of modernising processes may have been the price paid by the Commonwealth for denominational equality. The passing of the Sandomierz Agreement and the Warsaw Confederation blocked confessionalisation, since equal rights is fundamentally incompatible with the idea of the confessional state" (Kriegseisen, *Between State and Church*, 451 [in the 2010 Polish original, 537]). She denies the potential for "modernization" in a Catholic clergy that prioritized its own corporate privileges, and she criticizes the characterization of its critics as an anti-modernizing force.

14. See, among others, Michael G. Müller, *Zweite Reformation und städtische Autonomie im Königlichen Preußen: Danzig, Elbing und Thorn in der Epoche der Konfessionalisierung* (Berlin: Akademie Verlag, 1997); Michael G. Müller, "'Late Reformation' and Protestant Confessionalization in the Major Towns of Royal Prussia," in *The Reformation in Eastern and Central Europe*, ed. Karin Maag (Ashgate: Aldershot, 1997), 192–210; Almut Bues, "Konfesjonalizacja w Księstwie Kurlandii: Przypadek wyjątkowy w skali Rzeczypospolitej?" in *Rzeczpospolita wielu wyznań*, ed. Adam Kaźmierczyk et al. (Kraków: Księgarnia Akademicka, 2004), 47–63; Anja Moritz, Hans-Joachim Müller, and Mathias Pohlig, "Konfesjonalizacja Rzeczypospolitej szlacheckiej w XVII i XVIII wieku?" *Kwartalnik Historyczny* 108, no. 1 (2001): 37–46; Alfons Brüning, "Confessionalization in the *Slavia Orthodoxa* (Belorussia, Ukraine, Russia)?—Potential and Limits of a Western Historiographical Concept," in *Religion and the Conceptual Boundary in Central and Eastern Europe*, ed. Thomas Bremer (Basingstoke: Palgrave Macmillan, 2008), 66–97.

15. These processes can be studied in detail at the urban level: see, e.g., David Frick, *Kith, Kin and Neighbors: Confessions and Conflicts in Seventeenth-Century Wilno* (Ithaca, NY: Cornell University Press, 2013); and Tomasz Kempa, *Konflikty wyznaniowe w Wilnie od początku reformacji do końca XVII wieku* (Toruń: Wydawnictwo Naukowe Uniwersytetu Mikołaja Kopernika, 2016).

16. Piotr Stolarski, "Dominican-Jesuit Rivalry and the Politics of Catholic Renewal in Poland, 1564–1648," *Journal of Ecclesiastical History* 62, no. 2 (2011): 255–72.

17. See, among others, Janusz Tazbir, *Szlachta i teologowie: Szkice z dziejów polskiej kontrreformacji* (Warsaw: Wiedza Powszechna, 1987), 15–30, 268–99; and Janusz Małłek, "Wewnętrzne przyczyny regresu Reformacji w Polsce," in *Opera selecta*, vol. 4 (Toruń: Wydawnictwo Naukowe Uniwersytetu Mikołaja Kopernika, 2012), 76–85.

18. See Cezary Kuklo, *Demografia Rzeczypospolitej przedrozbiorowej* (Warsaw: Wydawnictwo DiG, 2009), 211–14, 222–24; Richard Butterwick, "How Catholic Was the Grand Duchy of Lithuania in in the Later Eighteenth Century?" *Central Europe* 8, no. 2 (2010): 123–45; Bogumil Szady, *The Geography of Religious and Confessional Structures in the Crown of the Polish Kingdom in the Second Half of the Eighteenth Century*, trans. Alicja Adamowicz (Berlin: Peter Lang, 2019).

19. On Uniate expansion, see, among others, Barbara Skinner, *The Western Front of the Eastern Church: Uniate and Orthodox Conflict in 18th-Century Poland, Ukraine, Belarus, and Russia* (DeKalb: Northern Illinois University Press, 2009); and Gil and Skoczylas, *Kościoły Wschodnie*, 217–389.

20. Emanuel Rostworowski, "Ilu było w Rzeczypospolitej obywateli szlachty?" *Kwartalnik Historyczny* 94, no. 3 (1987): 3–40.

21. Kazimierz Bem, *Calvinism in the Polish Lithuanian Commonwealth 1548–1648: The Churches and the Faithful* (Leiden: Brill, 2020). See also chapter 2 in this volume.

22. See Wojciech Kriegseisen, *Ewangelicy polscy i litewscy w epoce saskiej (1696–1763): Sytuacja prawna, organizacja i stosunki międzywyznaniowe* (Warsaw: Wydawnictwo Semper, 1996), 55–56.

23. Jūratė Kiaupienė, *Between Rome and Byzantium: The Golden Age of the Grand Duchy of Lithuania's Political Culture; Second Half of the Fifteenth Century to First Half of the Seventeenth Century*, trans. Jayde Will (Boston: Academic Studies Press, 2020), makes a strong case for a politically distinct Lithuanian national identity, which evolved both before and after 1569.

24. See chapter 5 in this volume, which places the Sarmatian myth firmly within its Renaissance European context.

25. Tazbir, *Szlachta i teologowie*, 217–67. Wojciech Kriegseisen, "Protestant Providentialism in the Commonwealth of Nobles: A Critical View on Sarmatism," trans. Anna Kijak, *Kwartalnik Historyczny* 128, English-language edition no. 5 (2021): 5–43, proposes a distinction between an earlier, inclusive "Renaissance Sarmatism," in which non-Catholic citizens could participate as equals, and a later, "decadent," exclusionary "Baroque Sarmatism."

26. See Wojciech Kriegseisen, "Between Intolerance and Persecution: Polish and Lithuanian Protestants in the 18th Century," *Acta Poloniae Historica* 73 (1996): 13–27.

27. Janusz Tazbir, "Staropolski antyklerykalizm," *Kwartalnik Historyczny* 109, no. 3 (2002): 13–22; Mariusz Markiewicz, "Problem antyklerykalizmu w czasach saskich," in Kaźmierczyk et al., *Rzeczpospolita wielu wyznań*, 341–47; and Augustyniak, *Państwo świeckie czy księże?* 7–128.

28. Kriegseisen, *Between State and Church*, 210–19, 459–65, 504–5, 532–34; and Karin Friedrich, "Konfessionalisierung und politischen Ideen in Polen-Litauen (1570–1650)," in *Konfessionalisierung in Ostmitteleuropa: Wirkungen des religiösen Wandels im 16. und 17. Jahrhundert in Staat, Gesellschaft und Kultur*, ed. Joachim Bahlcke and Arno Strohmeyer (Stuttgart: Franz Steiner Verlag, 1999), 249–65.

29. See, in comparative perspective, Jean Berenger, *Tolérance ou paix de religion en Europe centrale: 1415–1792* (Paris: Honoré Champion, 2000); and Heinz Schilling, "Die 'acceptation de la diversité' im Europa der frühen Neuzeit und im Rahmen der Europäischen Union: Die deutschen Religionsvergleiche von 1555 und 1648 in europäisch vergleichender Perspektive," in *Ausgewählte Abhandlungen zur europäischen Reformations- und Konfessionsgeschichte* (Berlin: Duncker & Humblot, 2002), 32–47. I am indebted to Igor Kąkolewski for this reference.

30. Stanisław August to Catherine II, October 5, 1766, *Correspondance de Stanislas-Auguste et ses plus proches collaborateurs (1764–1796)*, ed. Zofia Zielińska (Kraków: Arcana, 2015), 92–96; quoted in Richard Butterwick, *The Polish-Lithuanian Commonwealth, 1733–1795: Light and Flame* (New Haven, CT: Yale University Press, 2020), 101.

31. The most rigorous account of the political aspects of the "dissident question" is now Zofia Zielińska, *Polska w okowach "systemu północnego" 1763–1766* (Kraków: Arcana, 2012), 53–55, 98–99, 154–56, 162–67, 245–51, 392–95, 400–407, 440–54, 472–591, 667–70. At several points, the author details the dissidents' lobbying. She does not, however, consider the reasons *why* they sought foreign protection. On the latter stages, see George T. Lukowski, *The Szlachta and the Confederacy of Radom 1766–1767/68: A Study of the Polish Nobility* (Rome: Institutum Historicum Polonicum Romae, 1977). For accessible discussions in comparative perspective, see Michael G. Müller, "Toleration in Eastern Europe: The Dissident Question in Eighteenth-Century Poland-Lithuania," in *Toleration in Enlightenment Europe*, ed. Ole Peter Grell (Cambridge: Cambridge University Press, 1999), 212–29; and Jerzy T. Lukowski, "The Papacy, Poland, Russia and Religious Reform, 1764–8," *Journal of Ecclesiastical History* 39, no. 1 (1988): 66–92.

32. Dorota Dukwicz, "The Internal Situation in the Polish-Lithuanian Commonwealth (1769–1771) and the Origins of the First Partition (in the Light of Russian Sources)," *Acta Poloniae Historica* 103 (2011): 67–84.

33. Robert Howard Lord, *The Second Partition of Poland* (Cambridge, MA: Harvard University Press, 1915), 64.

34. Quoted after Krzysztof Łazarski, "Freedom, State and 'National Unity' in Lord Acton's Thought," in Friedrich and Pendzich, *Citizenship and Identity in a Multinational Commonwealth*, 269.

35. See Hans-Jürgen Bömelburg, *Zwischen polnischer Ständegesellschaft und preußischem Obrigkeitsstaat: Vom Königlichen Preußen zu Westpreußen (1756-1806)* (Munich: Oldenbourg, 1995); and Karin Friedrich, *The Other Prussia: Royal Prussia, Poland and Liberty, 1569-1772* (Cambridge: Cambridge University Press, 2000).

36. Three good overviews are: Michael G. Müller, *Die Teilungen Polens: 1772, 1793, 1795* (Munich: C. H. Beck, 1984); Tadeusz Cegielski and Łukasz Kądziela, *Rozbiory Polski: 1772–1793–1795* (Warsaw: Wydawnictwa Szkolne i Pedagogiczne, 1990); and Jerzy Lukowski, *The Partitions of Poland: 1772, 1793, 1795* (Harlow: Longman, 1999).

37. *Volumina Legum*, vol. 8 (St. Petersburg: Jozafat Ohryzko, 1860), 27, 47–50.

38. On Nuncio Giovanni Archetti's efforts to prevent their election and avoid recognizing their rights to be elected, see Larry Wolff, *The Vatican and Poland in the Age of the Partitions: Diplomatic and Cultural Encounters at the Warsaw Nunciature* (Boulder, CO: Columbia University Press, Eastern European Monographs, 1988), 117–39.

39. Richard Butterwick, *Polska Rewolucja a Kościół katolicki 1788-1792*, trans. Marek Ugniewski, 2nd ed. (Kraków: Arcana, 2019), 401, 413, 427, 655–56, 723, 841.

40. Tomasz Wawrzecki, envoy for Brasław, MS Diary, ASC vol. 17, fol. 292v.

41. *Volumina Legum*, vol. 9 (Kraków: Nakładem Akademji Umiejętności, 1889), 203.

42. *Głos Jaśnie Wielmożnego Jmci Pana Antoniego Leduchowskiego woiewodzica i posła woiewództwa czerniechowskiego na sessyi seymowey dnia 18. kwietnia 1791. r. miany*, s.l.d.

43. MS Diary, ASC vol. 17, fols. 286v-87v. Hulewicz, envoy for Volhynia, was a notorious libertine, and the king later told him he had been goading the bishops for fun. See Butterwick, *Polska Rewolucja*, 708. Hulewicz was also a client of Szczęsny Potocki, the Commonwealth's richest magnate, who opposed the Sejm's rejection of Russian tutelage.

44. MS Diary, ASC vol. 17, fols. 287v-88r. Czartoryski, who had long since turned down a chair in the Senate, was envoy for Lublin.

45. MS Diary, ASC vol. 17, fols. 295r-95v; *Głos Jaśnie Oświeconego Xięcia Jmci Sapiehy generała artyleryi y marszałka konfederacy W. X. Lit: posła z woiewództwa brzeskiego lit: na dniu 18. kwietnia 1791. roku miany* (Warsaw: Zawadzki, n.d.).

46. *Konstytucja 3 Maja 1791 na podstawie tekstu Ustawy Rządowej z Archiwum Sejmu Czteroletniego*, ed. Anna Grześkowiak-Krwawicz (Warsaw: Muzeum Łazienki Królewskie and Archiwum Główne Akt Dawnych, 2018), 62.

47. *Volumina Legum*, vol. 2, 124.

48. T. C. W. Blanning, *Joseph II* (Harlow: Longman, 1994), 72–76; and Derek Beales, *Joseph II*, vol. 2, *Against the World, 1780–1790* (Cambridge: Cambridge University Press, 2009), 168–213.

49. Władysław Smoleński, *Konfederacya targowicka* (Kraków: Gebether i spółka, 1903), 27.

50. Isabel de Madariaga, *Russia in the Age of Catherine the Great* (New Haven, CT: Yale University Press, 1981), 430.

51. The most convincing accounts of these events and their causes remain Lord, *Second Partition*; and Lord, "The Third Partition of Poland," *Slavonic Review* 3 (1924/25): 481–98.

52. For Frederick William II, see Lord, *Second Partition*. For his predecessors, see Władysław Konopczyński, *Fryderyk Wielki a Polska*, 2nd ed. (Kraków: Universitas, 2010);

Stanisław Salmonowicz, *Fryderyk Wielki*, 3rd ed. (Wrocław: Zakład Narodowy im. Ossolińskich, 1996), 86–122; Klaus Zernack, "Negative Polenpolitik als Grundlage deutsch-russischer Diplomätie in der Machtpolitik des 18. Jahrhunderts," in *Russland und Deutschland*, ed. Uwe Liszkowski (Stuttgart: Ernst Klett Verlag, 1974), 144–59; and Hans-Jürgen Bömelburg, *Friedrich II. zwischen Deutschland und Polen: Ereignis-und Erinnerungsgeschichte* (Stuttgart: Alfred Kröner Verlag, 2011).

53. Ewald von Hertzberg to Girolamo Lucchesini, May 12, 1791, *Źródła do dziejów drugiego i trzeciego rozbioru Polski*, ed. Bronisław Dembiński (Lwów: Towarzystwo do Popierania Nauki Polskiej, 1902), 451; and Emanuel Rostworowski, *Ostatni król Rzeczypospolitej.: Geneza i upadek Konstytucji 3 maja* (Warsaw: Wiedza Powszechna, 1966), 231, 238.

54. Lord, *Second Partition*, xvi.

55. Richard Butterwick, "Deconfessionalization? The Policy of the Polish Revolution towards Ruthenia, 1788–1792," *Central Europe* 6, no. 2 (2008): 91–121.

56. M[aria] Cecylia Łubieńska, *Sprawa dysydencka 1764–1766* (Warsaw: Gebethner i Wolff, 1911), 7–16, 73–82, 176–84; Edward Likowski, *Dzieje Kościoła Unickiego na Litwie i Rusi w XVIII i XIX wieku uważane głównie ze względu na przyczyny jego upadku*, 2nd ed., 2 vols. (Warsaw: Gebethner i Wolff, 1906), 1:84–88, 128–35; Skinner, *Western Front*, 105–11; Sofia Senyk, "Religious Conflict in Dnepr Ukraine in the 18th Century," *Orientalia Christiana Periodica* 73, no. 1 (2007): 5–59; Zielińska, *Polska w okowach*, 21–30, 441, 591; and Lukowski, "Papacy," 79–81.

57. Larry Wolff, *Disunion within Union: The Uniate Church and the Partitions of Poland* (Cambridge, MA: Harvard University Press, 2019), 72–73; and Madariaga, *Russia in the Age of Catherine the Great*, 196–200, 510–15.

58. Simon Dixon, *Catherine the Great* (London: Profile Books, 2009), 3–22, 26–28, 48–52, 79–80, 149–52, 160, 165–66, 190, 284–85, 312 (quotation, 149); Simon Dixon, *Catherine the Great* (Harlow: Longman, 2001), 116–18; and Madariaga, *Russia in the Age of Catherine the Great*, 5–6, 111–22, 199, 503.

59. Likowski, *Dzieje Kościoła Unickiego*, 1:84–124, 135–44; Barbara Skinner, "Borderlands of Faith: Reconsidering the Origins of a Ukrainian Tragedy," *Slavic Review* 64, no. 1 (2005): 88–116; Skinner, *Western Front*, 131–43; and Zielińska, *Polska w okowach*, 392–97, 400–404, 441–49, 575, 585.

60. Wolff, *Disunion within the Union*, 21–49.

61. This and the following two paragraphs are based on Likowski, *Dzieje Kościoła Unickiego*, 1:192–220, 228–34; Eugeniusz Sakowicz, *Kościół prawosławny w Polsce w epoce Sejmu Wielkiego 1788–1792* (Warsaw: Warszawska Metropolja Prawosławna, 1935); Aleksy Deruga, "Kościół prawosławny a sprawa 'buntu' w 1789 roku we wschodnich województwach Rzeczypospolitej," *Ateneum Wileńskie* 13, no. 2 (1938): 175–269; Kamil Paździor, "Dopuszczenie metropolity unickiego do senatu w 1790 r.: Studium z polityki wyznaniowej Sejmu Czteroletniego," *Nasza Przeszłość* 91 (1999): 241–67; Kamil Paździor, "Polityka Sejmu Czteroletniego wobec kościołów wschodnich" (PhD diss., Uniwersytet Śląski, Katowice, 2000); Skinner, *Western Front*, 178–94; Vadzim Anipiarkou, "K voprosu o tom, pochemu konfessional'nii faktor ne stal opredeliaiushchim vo vtorom razdele Rechi Pospolitoi," *Orientalia Christiana Cracoviensia* 9 (2017): 41–66; and Butterwick, *Polska Rewolucja*, 156–62, 390–416, 426–29, 541–42, 548–55, 582–96, 606–9, 829–30, 839–57.

62. Quoted after Aleksy Deruga, review of Sakowicz, *Kościół prawosławny*, in *Ateneum Wileńskie* 11 (1936), 542. Deruga believed that the "accursed" language was Polish (because Sadkovskii had to use Polish to communicate), but he was probably referring to Ruthenian.

63. Paździor, "Polityka Sejmu Czteroletniego," 373–80; and Butterwick, *Polish Revolution*, 307–11.

64. MS Diary, ASC vol. 24, fols. 70v–71r.

65. MS Diary, ASC vol. 24, fol. 72r.

66. *Głos Stanisława Sołtyka posła z woiewodztwa krakowskiego, orderow polskich kawalera, na sessyi seymowey dnia 21. Maia 1792. miany, s.l.d.*

67. See Kamil Paździor, "Edukacja jako narzędzie polityki wyznaniowej Sejmu Wielkiego wobec innowierców," *Nasza Przeszłość* 100 (2003): 329–66.

68. *Pace* Urszula Augustyniak, *History of the Polish-Lithuanian Commonwealth: State—Society—Culture,* trans. Grażyna Waluga and Dorota Sobstel (Frankfurt am Main: Peter Lang, 2015), 168, 205.

69. Butterwick, *Polska Rewolucja,* 711–12, 843, 853.

70. Bishop Porfiriusz Skarbek Ważyński issued such a pastoral letter in Ruthenian after May 22, 1792: Archiwum Państwowe w Lublinie, Chełmski Konsystorz Greckokatolicki [1525] 1596–1875 [1905], sygn. 5. I am indebted to Igor Kąkolewski for this reference.

71. Proclamation quoted after Wojciech Kriegseisen, "Katarzyna II jako mediewistka: Przyczynek do genezy drugiego rozbioru," *Kwartalnik Historyczny* 111, no. 3 (2004), 132.

72. Wolff, *Disunion within the Union,* 65–75; see also Likowski, *Dzieje Kościoła Unickiego,* 1: 241–57; and Skinner, *Western Front,* 196–225.

73. *Pace* Kriegseisen, *Between State and Church,* 592.

7: The Ukrainian Sublime

1. Maria Janion and Maria Żmigrodzka, *Romantyzm i historia* (Warsaw: Państwowy Instytut Wydawniczy, 1978), 128. I warmly thank Andrii Portnov and Tomasz Hen-Konarski for their very helpful comments and suggestions on a draft of this chapter.

2. Alina Witkowska, "Dziko—pięknie—groźnie czyli Ukraina romantyków," *Teksty Drugie* 32, no. 2 (1995): 20–30.

3. Bogusław Bakuła, "Colonial and Postcolonial Aspects of Polish Borderlands Studies: An Outline," *Teksty Drugie* 1, Special Issue (2014), 97; and Daniel Beauvois, *Trójkąt ukraiński: Szlachta, carat i lud na Wołyniu, Podolu i Kijowszczyźnie 1793–1914,* trans. Krzysztof Rutkowski (Lublin: Wydawnictwo Uniwersytetu Marii Curie-Skłodowskiej, 2011), 8–13.

4. Paul Robert Magocsi, *A History of Ukraine: The Land and Its Peoples,* 2nd ed. (Toronto: University of Toronto Press, 2010), 189; and Serhii Plokhy, *The Gates of Europe: A History of Ukraine* (New York: Basic Books, 2015), 71–72.

5. Serhiy Bilenky, *Romantic Nationalism in Eastern Europe: Russian, Polish and Ukrainian Political Imaginations* (Stanford, CA: Stanford University Press, 2012), 79–87.

6. David A. Frick, "'Foolish Rus': On Polish Civilization, Ruthenian Self-Hatred, and Kasijan Sakovyč," *Harvard Ukrainian Studies* 18, no. 3/4 (December 1994), 213.

7. George C. Grabowicz, "The History of Polish-Ukrainian Literary Relations: A Literary and Cultural Perspective," in *Poland and Ukraine, Past and Present,* ed. Peter J. Potichnyj (Edmonton: Canadian Institute of Ukrainian Studies, 1980), 116.

8. Czesław Miłosz, *The History of Polish Literature,* Updated ed. (Berkeley: University of California Press, 1983), 311.

9. See Frank E. Sysyn, "Seventeenth-Century Views on the Causes of the Khmel'nyts'kyi Uprising: An Examination of the 'Discourse on the Present Cossack or Peasant War,'" *Harvard Ukrainian Studies* 5, no. 4 (December 1981): 430–66; and Frank E. Sysyn, "The Khmel'nyts'kyi Uprising: A Characterization of the Ukrainian Revolt," *Jewish History* 17, no. 2 (2003): 115–39.

10. See Barbara Skinner, "Borderlands of Faith: Reconsidering the Origins of a Ukrainian Tragedy," *Slavic Review* 64, no. 1 (Spring 2005): 88–116.

11. See, e.g., Mykhailo Hrushevsky, *History of Ukraine-Rus'*, vol. 7, ed. Serhii Plokhy and Frank E. Sysyn, trans. Bohdan Strumiński (Edmonton: Canadian Institute of Ukrainian Studies Press, 1999), i–lvi. See also Nicholas Chirovsky, *An Introduction to Ukrainian History*, *Vol. 2: The Lithuanian-Rus' Commonwealth, the Polish Domination, and the Cossack-Hetman State* (New York: Philosophical Library, 1989), 289. More recently, Ukrainian historians have taken different views of the Commonwealth. See Polina Verbytska, "What History Do Young Ukrainians Need Today? Reinterpretation of the Image of the Polish-Lithuanian Commonwealth in Contemporary Ukrainian Historiography and History Education," *Polish Review* 65, no. 1 (2020): 66–73; Natalia Yakovenko, *Narys istorii seredniovichnoi ta ranniomodernoi Ukrainy* (Kyiv: Krytyka, 2009); and Andrii Portnov, *Poland and Ukraine: Entangled Histories, Asymmetric Memories* (Berlin: Forum Transregionale Studien, 2020).

12. Among others, see Jan Sowa, *Fantomowe ciało króla: Peryferyjne zmagania z nowoczesną formą* (Kraków: Universitas, 2011); and Maria Janion, *Niesamowita słowiańszczyzna: Fantazmaty literatury* (Kraków: Wydawnictwo Literackie, 2006), 165–79. See also Beauvois, *Trójkąt ukraiński*.

13. Edward A. Tiryakian, "Assessing Multiculturalism Theoretically: E Pluribus Unum, Sic et Non," *International Journal on Multicultural Societies* 5, no. 1 (2003), 24.

14. See Roman Szporluk, "Ukraine: From the Imperial Periphery to a Sovereign State," in *Russia, Ukraine, and the Breakup of the Soviet Union* (Stanford, CA: Hoover Institution Press, 2000), 361–95; Bilenky, *Romantic Nationalism in Eastern Europe*, ix–x, 253; and Frank E. Sysyn, "The Khmel'nyts'kyi Uprising and Ukrainian Nation-Building," *Journal of Ukrainian Studies* 17, no. 1–2 (1992): 141–70.

15. Bilenky, *Romantic Nationalism in Eastern Europe*, ix–x.

16. See Hieronim Grala, "Was the Polish-Lithuanian Commonwealth a Colonial State?," *Polish Quarterly of International Affairs* 4 (2017): 125–50; Jan Kieniewicz, "O perspektywę dla Polski," in *Perspektywy postkolonializmu w Polsce, Polska w perspektywie postkolonialnej: Debaty Artes Liberales*, vol. 10, ed. Jan Kieniewicz (Warsaw: Wydział Artes Liberales, 2016), 69–86; and Wiktoria Kudela-Świątek and Adam Świątek, "W pułapce kolonializmu . . . Ukraińcy w Galicji Wschodniej—kolonizowani czy kolonizatorzy?" *Historyka* 42 (2012): 191–213.

17. Ihor Ševčenko, "Poland in Ukrainian History," in *Ukraine between East and West: Essays on Cultural History to the Early Eighteenth Century* (Edmonton: Canadian Institute of Ukrainian Studies, 1996), 127.

18. Czesław Miłosz, *Native Realm: A Search for Self-Definition*, trans. Catherine S. Leach (Berkeley: University of California Press, 1981), 14. See also Alexander Etkind, *Internal Colonization: Russia's Imperial Experience* (Cambridge: Polity Press), 2011.

19. Timothy Snyder, *The Reconstruction of Nations: Poland, Ukraine, Lithuania, Belarus, 1569–1999* (New Haven, CT: Yale University Press, 2003), 116–17.

20. Andrzej Kamiński, "The Cossack Experiment in Szlachta Democracy in the Polish-Lithuanian Commonwealth: The Hadiach (Hadziacz) Union," *Harvard Ukrainian Studies* 1, no. 2 (June 1977), 194–97.

21. Vanessa L. Ryan, "The Physiological Sublime: Burke's Critique of Reason," *Journal of the History of Ideas* 62, no. 2 (2001): 265–79.

22. Jean-François Lyotard, "Answering the Question: What Is Postmodernism?" in *The Postmodern Condition: A Report on Knowledge*, trans. Geoff Bennington and Brian Massumi (Minneapolis: University of Minnesota Press, 1984), 78; and Thomas Weiskel, *The Romantic Sublime: Studies in the Structure and Psychology of Transcendence* (Baltimore: Johns Hopkins University Press, 1986), 23.

23. See Marc Gotlieb, "The Orientalist Sublime," in *The Deaths of Henri Regnault* (Chicago: University of Chicago Press, 2016), 39–67; Christine Battersby, *The Sublime, Terror, and Human Difference* (London: Routledge, 2007); and Philip Dickinson, "Postcolonial Romanticisms? The Sublime and Negative Capability in Joseph Conrad's *Heart of Darkness* and J. M. Coetzee's *Waiting for the Barbarians*," *Postcolonial Text* 3, no. 1 (2007).

24. See Immanuel Kant, *Critique of Judgment*, trans. Werner S. Pluhar (Indianapolis: Hackett, 1987).

25. Antoni Malczewski, *Marya: powieść ukraińska* (Sanok: Nakład i Druk Karola Pollaka, 1855), 2. Literal translation my own. Unless otherwise noted, all subsequent translations are also my own.

26. Michał Czajkowski, "Attaman Kunicki," in *Pisma*, vol. 3, *Powieści kozackie i gawędy* (Lipsk: F. A. Brockhaus, 1863), 83.

27. Kant, *Critique of Judgment*, 98–99.

28. Michał Czajkowski, *Pisma*, vol. 2, *Wernyhora* (Lipsk: F. A. Brockhaus, 1862), 2.

29. Arthur Schopenhauer, *The World as Will and Representation*, vol. 1, trans. E. F. J. Payne (New York: Dover, 1969), 203.

30. Weiskel, *Romantic Sublime*, 26.

31. Grzegorz Czerwiński, "The Steppe as a Metaphysical Prison of Death: Despair and the Absurd in Antoni Malczewski's 'Maria,'" *Zeitschrift für Slavische Philologie* 67, no. 2 (2010): 313–34.

32. Malczewski, *Marya*, 3.

33. Edmund Burke, *A Philosophical Enquiry into the Origin of Our Ideas of the Sublime and Beautiful* (New York: Oxford University Press, 1990), 53.

34. See Zenon E. Kohut, "Myths Old and New: The Haidamak Movement and the Koliivshchyna (1768) in Recent Historiography," *Harvard Ukrainian Studies* 1, no. 3 (1977): 359–78.

35. Seweryn Goszczyński, *Zamek kaniowski: Powieść* (Kraków: Nakładem Krakowskiej Spółki Wydawniczej, 1925), 95.

36. Czajkowski, *Pisma*, 2:117.

37. Juliusz Słowacki, *Sen srebrny Salomei: Romans dramatyczny w pięciu aktach* (Wrocław: Zakład Narodowy imienia Ossolińskich, 2009), 62.

38. Słowacki, *Sen srebrny Salomei*, 98.

39. Lyotard, "Answering the Question," 77.

40. Kant, *Critique of Judgment*, 120–21.

41. Kant, *Critique of Judgment*, 128.

42. See Bogumił Jasinowski, "Podstawowe znaczenie kresów południowo-wschodnich w budowie polskiej psychiki i świadomości narodowej," *Pamiętnik Literacki* 33, no. 1/4 (1936), 218.

43. Janion, *Niesamowita słowiańszczyzna*, 170.

44. Edward Tersza [Michał Grabowski], *Pan Starosta Kaniowski: Obraz powieściowo-historyczny w trzech rozdziałach* (Warsaw: Drukarnia Gazety Codziennej, 1856), 5.

45. Słowacki, *Sen srebrny Salomei*, 65, 83.

46. Goszczyński, *Zamek kaniowski*, 151.

47. Goszczyński, "Kilka słów o Ukrainie i rzezi humańskiej," in *Zamek kaniowski*, 154. On the symbol of the castle, see also Anna Kurska, "Seweryn Goszczyński wobec przeszłości, czyli o 'Zamku kaniowskim,'" *Prace Polonistyczne* 58 (2003): 19–35.

48. Andrzej Walicki, *Philosophy and Romantic Nationalism: The Case of Poland* (Oxford: Clarendon Press, 1982), 1–5.

49. Bilenky, *Romantic Nationalism in Eastern Europe*, 178–81.

50. See Józef Łobodowski, "A Polish View of Polish-Ukrainian Influences," in Potichnyj, *Poland and Ukraine*, 103.

51. Goszczyński, *Zamek kaniowski*, 87–88.

52. Goszczyński, *Zamek kaniowski*, 98.

53. Grabowicz, "History of Polish-Ukrainian Literary Relations," 119.

54. Taras Shevchenko, "The Haydamaks," in *The Poetical Works of Taras Shevchenko: The Kobzar*, trans. C. H. Andrusyshen and Watson Kirkconnell (Toronto: University of Toronto Press, 1964), 99.

55. Shevchenko, "Haydamaks," 99.

56. Goszczyński, "Kilka słów o Ukrainie i rzezi humańskiej," 155.

57. Shevchenko, "Haydamaks," 80.

58. Mykola Kostomarov, *Knyhy buttia ukrainskoho narodu* (Lviv: Naklad Vydavnytstva Novi shliakhy, 1921), 17.

59. Bilenky, *Romantic Nationalism in Eastern Europe*, 78–79; and David Saunders, "Mykola Kostomarov (1817–1885) and the Creation of a Ukrainian Ethnic Identity," *Slavonica* 7, no. 1 (2001): 7–24.

60. Kostomarov, *Knyhy buttia ukrainskoho narodu*, 21–22.

61. Taras Shevchenko, "To the Poles," in *Kobzar*, trans. Peter Fedynsky (London: Glagoslav, 2013), 304.

62. See Maria Janion, "Romantyczna wizja rewolucji," in *Problemy polskiego romantyzmu*, Series 1, ed. Maria Żmigrodzka and Zofia Lewinówna (Wrocław: Zakład Narodowy im. Ossolińskich, 1971), 193.

63. Stanisław Makowski, "'Hajdamacy' Tarasa Szewczenki i 'Sen srebrny Salomei,'" *Warszawskie Zeszyty Ukrainoznawcze* 6–7 (1998), 170.

64. George G. Grabowicz, "Mit Ukrainy w 'Śnie srebrnym Salomei,'" *Pamiętnik Literacki* 78, no. 2 (1987), 39–40.

65. See also Magdalena Ciechańska, "Ciało cierpiące i ontologiczne strzępy człowiecze w *Śnie srebrnym Salomei* Juliusza Słowackiego," *Annales Universitatis Paedagogicae Cracoviensis: Studia Historicolitteraria* 20 (2020), 205.

66. Słowacki may have loosely drawn on eyewitness accounts of the Koliivshchyna. See Alina Kowalczykowa, *Słowacki* (Warsaw: Wydawnictwo Naukowe PWN 1999), 374.

67. Dariusz Skórczewski, "'Sen srebrny Salomei,' czyli parada hybryd," *Pamiętnik Literacki* 102, no. 1 (2011), 71–72. Grabowicz, "Mit Ukrainy," 43.

68. Janion and Żmigrodzka, *Romantyzm i historia*, 135–39.

69. See Weiskel, *Romantic Sublime*, 42.

70. Skórczewski, "'Sen srebrny Salomei.'" See also Edward Kasperski, "Dramat pogranicza polsko-ukraińskiego (o Śnie srebrnym Salomei Juliusza Słowackiego)," in *Szkoła ukraińska w romantyzmie polskim: Szkice polsko-ukraińskie*, ed. Stanisław Makowski, Urszula Makowska, and Małgorzata Nesteruk (Warsaw: Wydział Polonistyki Uniwersytetu Warszawskiego, 2012), 383.

71. Dariusz Skórczewski, *Teoria—literatura—dyskurs: Pejzaż postkolonialny* (Lublin: Wydawnictwo Katolickiego Uniwersytetu Lubelskiego Jana Pawła II, 2013), 273.

72. Słowacki, *Sen srebrny Salomei*, 65.

73. On the direct influence of Juliusz Słowacki's depictions of Ukraine on Sienkiewicz's work, see Tadeusz Bujnicki, "Wpływ Słowackiego na Sienkiewiczowski obraz Ukrainy w Trylogii," in *Słowacki i Ukraina*, ed. Maria Woźniakiewicz-Dziadosz (Lublin: Wydawnictwo UMSC, 2003), 69–84.

74. See Brian Porter, *When Nationalism Began to Hate: Imagining Modern Politics in Nineteenth-Century Poland* (Oxford: Oxford University Press, 2000), 43–75, 189–200.

75. Ryszard Koziołek, "Modernizowanie Sienkiewicza, Review of: Maciej Gloger, *Sienkiewicz nowoczesny*, Bydgoszcz 2010," *Pamiętnik Literacki* 3 (2012), 234.

76. Henryk Sienkiewicz, *With Fire and Sword*, trans. Jeremiah Curtin (London: J. M. Dent, 1898), 181.

77. Sienkiewicz, *With Fire and Sword*, 129–31.

78. Elżbieta Ostrowska, "Desiring the Other: The Ambivalent Polish Self in Novel and Film," *Slavic Review* 70, no. 3 (Fall 2011), 511.

79. For recent studies on the historical basis of the novel and its geographical inaccuracies, respectively, see *Zeszyty Historyczne* 16 (2017), and Maria Joanna Biela, "Błędy geograficzne w 'Ogniem i mieczem' Sienkiewicza," *Pamiętnik Literacki* 31, no. 1–4 (1934): 472–74.

80. See Volodomyr Antonovych, "Polsko-russkie otnosheniia XVII v. v sovremennoi polskoi prizme (po povodu povesti G. Senkevicha 'Ogniom i miechom')," in *Moia spovid* (Kyiv: Lybid, 1995). See also Olena Chemodanova, "Z dziejów ukraińskiej recepcji 'Ogniem i mieczem,'" *Wiek XIX: Rocznik Towarzystwa Literackiego im. Adama Mickiewicza* 49, no. 7 (2014): 249–60.

81. See Olgierd Górka, *Ogniem i Mieczem a rzeczywistość historyczna* (Warsaw: Wydawnictwo Obrony Narodowej, 1986); and Andrzej Tadus, "Wokół międzywojennego sporu o historyczność 'Ogniem i mieczem,'" *Pamiętnik Literacki* 76, no. 3 (1985): 175–96.

82. Sienkiewicz, *With Fire and Sword*, 288–89.

83. Ryszard Koziołek, *Sienkiewicz's Bodies: Studies of Gender and Violence* (Frankfurt am Main: Peter Lang, 2015), 348.

84. Ostrowska, "Desiring the Other," 523.

85. See also Dariusz Skórczewski, "Polska skolonizowana, polska zorientalizowana: Teoria postkolonialna wobec 'Innej Europy,'" *Porównania* 6 (2009): 95–105.

86. Ostrowska, "Desiring the Other," 523.

87. Tetiana Czuża, "'Żywioł ruski' w 'Ogniem i mieczem' Sienkiewicza w XIX-wiecznej krytyce," in *Henryk Sienkiewicz i chrześcijaństwo: Idee—obrazy—konteksty*, ed. Anna Janicka and Łukasz Zabielski (Białystok: Książnica Podlaska im. Łukasza Górnickiego, 2017), 222.

88. Ostrowska, "Desiring the Other," 516.

89. Ostrowska, "Desiring the Other," 516.

90. Henryk Sienkiewicz, *Ogniem i mieczem* (Kraków: Wydawnictwo Greg, 2013), 46.

91. Sienkiewicz, *Ogniem i mieczem*, 370.

92. Sienkiewicz, *Ogniem i mieczem*, 452.

93. Sienkiewicz, *Ogniem i mieczem*, 142.

94. Sienkiewicz, *Ogniem i mieczem*, 23.

95. Sienkiewicz, *Ogniem i mieczem*, 43.

96. Sienkiewicz, *With Fire and Sword*, 45. See also see Sienkiewicz, *Ogniem i mieczem*, 38, 57.

97. Sienkiewicz, *With Fire and Sword*, 45.

98. Sienkiewicz, *With Fire and Sword*, 32.

99. Sienkiewicz, *Ogniem i mieczem*, 369.

100. Sysyn, "Seventeenth-Century Views," 460–61.

101. Sienkiewicz, *Ogniem i mieczem*, 369.

102. Maria Janion refers to the repressed, "uncanny" East Slavic dimensions of Polish identity. See Janion, *Niesamowita słowiańszczyzna*.

8: Imagining the Past and Remembering the Future

Epigraph source: Lewis Namier, "Symmetry and Repetition," in *Conflicts: Studies in Contemporary History* (London: Macmillan, 1942), 69–70.

1. Woodrow Wilson, Address to Congress, February 11, 1918. http://www.gwpda.org/1918/wilpeace.html, accessed August 5, 2021. See Larry Wolff, *Woodrow Wilson and the Reimagining of Eastern Europe* (Stanford, CA: Stanford University Press, 2021), Kindle edition, 79 of 287.

2. Woodrow Wilson, Address to Congress.

3. Wolff, *Woodrow Wilson*, 122–23 of 287.

4. Robert Howard Lord, *The Second Partition of Poland: A Study in Diplomatic History* (New York: AMS Press, 1915), 3–4.

5. Lord, *Second Partition of Poland*, 5.

6. Lord, *Second Partition of Poland*, 497.

7. Lord, *Second Partition of Poland*, 6.

8. See Jochen Böhler, *Civil War in Central Europe, 1918–1921: The Reconstruction of Poland* (Oxford: Oxford University Press, 2018).

9. Clarence Henry Haring, "Robert Howard Lord," *Proceedings of the Massachusetts Historical Society*, Third Series 71 (October 1953–May 1957), 387; and Wiktor Sukiennicki, *East Central Europe during World War I: From Foreign Domination to National Independence* (Boulder, CO: East European Monographs, 1984), 2:902–3.

10. Georg Friedrich Wilhelm Hegel, *Philosophy of Mind*, trans. William Wallace (New York: Cosimo Classics, 2008), 150.

11. Erik Goldstein, *Winning the Peace: British Diplomatic Strategy, Peace Planning, and the Paris Peace Conference 1916–1920* (Oxford: Oxford University Press, 1991), 58–80.

12. Piotr Biliński, *Władysław Konopczyński, 1880–1952: Człowiek i dzieło* (Kraków: Ośrodek Myśli Politycznej, 2017), 117–19; and Andrzej Maciej Brzeziński, *Oskar Halecki a Liga Narodów: Poglądy i działalność* (Łódź: Uniwersytet Łódzki, 2016), 36.

13. Namier always denied that antisemitism was the reason, but the evidence is clear. See D. W. Hayton, *Conservative Revolutionary: The Lives of Lewis Namier* (Manchester: Manchester University Press, 2019), 41–42.

14. For a comprehensive appraisal of Namier's legacy, see Linda Colley, *Namier* (London: Weidenfeld & Nicolson, 1989).

15. Lewis Namier, *1848: The Revolution of the Intellectuals* (London: Oxford University Press, 1944). Review by Stefan Kieniewicz, *Kwartalnik Historyczny* 56 (1948), 186.

16. Oskar Halecki, *Ostatnie lata Świdrygiełły i sprawa wołyńska za Kazimierza Jagiellończyka* (Kraków: Gebethner, 1915); Oskar Halecki, *Przyłączenie Podlasia, Wołynia i Kijowszczyzny do Korony w roku 1569* (Kraków: Gebethner, 1915); Oskar Halecki, *Unia lubelska: wykład habilitacyjny wygłoszony na Uniwersytecie Jagiellońskim 10 grudnia 1915 r.* (Kraków: Czas, 1916); and Oskar Halecki, *Dzieje Unii Jagiellońskiej*, 2 vols. (Kraków: Akademia Umiejętności, 1919–1920).

17. Halecki, *Dzieje Unii Jagiellońskiej*, vol. 1, xi.

18. Oskar Halecki, *Liga Narodów* (Poznań: Księgarnia św. Wojciecha, 1920).

19. Brzeziński, *Oskar Halecki*, 51.

20. Halecki, *Dzieje Unii Jagiellońskiej*, vol. 1, xi.

21. Halecki, *Dzieje Unii Jagiellońskiej*, vol. 1, xii.

22. Halecki, *Union of Lublin*, 5.

23. Halecki, *Das Nationalitäten Problem*, 17, 21, 25, 27, 32, 65, 75.

24. Oskar Halecki, *From Florence to Brest (1439–1596)* (Rome: Sacrum Poloniae Millennium, 1958).

25. Oskar Halecki, "Idea Jagiellońska," *Kwartalnik Historyczny* 51, no. 2 (1937), 510.

26. Halecki, "Idea Jagiellońska," 493.

27. Halecki, "Idea Jagiellońska," 508.

28. Royal Prussians also conceived of themselves as a nation: see Karin Friedrich, *The Other Prussia: Royal Prussia, Poland and Liberty, 1569–1772* (Cambridge: Cambridge University Press, 2000).

29. See chapter 5 in this volume on the idea of "Sarmatia."

30. Adam Czartoryski, quoted by S. Kalembka, "Les territoires de l'est dans la pensée politique polonaise de 1831 à 1870," in *Les Confins de l'Ancienne Pologne: Ukraine, Lituanie, Bélorussie XVIe–XIXe siècles*, ed. Daniel Beauvois (Lille: Septentrion, 1988), 150.

31. Andrzej Walicki, "The Troubling Legacy of Roman Dmowski," *East European Politics and Societies* 14, no. 1 (2000), 14–15.

32. Walicki, "Troubling Legacy of Roman Dmowski," 15–18.

33. Brian Porter-Szűcs, *Faith and Fatherland: Catholicism, Modernity, and Poland* (Oxford: Oxford University Press, 2011), 179–83.

34. Quoted by Böhler, *Civil War*, 5–6.

35. Wolff, *Woodrow Wilson*, 117, 189–90.

36. Quoted by Wolff, *Woodrow Wilson*, 218.

37. Władysław Konopczyński, "O idei jagiellońskiej," in *Umarli mówią. Szkice historyczno-polityczne* (Poznań: Wielkopolska Księgarnia Nakładowa Karola Rzepeckiego, 1929). http://www.omp.org.pl/stareomp/indexfo32.html?module=subjects&func=viewpage&pageid=615, accessed August 9, 2021.

38. See Adolfas Šapoka, *Lietuva ir Lenkija Jogailos laikais* (Kaunas, 1935); and Adolfas Šapoka, *Lietuva ir Lenkija po 1569 m. Liublino unijos* (Kaunas, 1938).

39. Bartłomiej Rusin, "Lewis Namier, the Curzon Line, and the Shaping of Poland's Eastern Frontier," *Studia z Dziejów Rosji i Europy Środkowo-Wschodniej* 48 (2013), 15. For more measured views, see Hayton, *Conservative Revolutionary*, 70–131; Paul Latawski, "The Dmowski-Namier Feud, 1915–1919," *Polin* 2 (1987): 37–49; and Amy Ng, *Nationalism and Political Liberty: Redlich, Namier, and the Crisis of Empire* (Oxford: Oxford University Press, 2004), ch. 2, 3.

40. Hayton, *Conservative Revolutionary*, 89.

41. Quoted by Hayton, *Conservative Revolutionary*, 93.

42. Quoted by Ng, *Nationalism*, 127.

43. Ng, *Nationalism*, 113.

44. Andrzej Nowak, *Pierwsza zdrada Zachodu: 1920—Zapomniany Appeasement* (Warsaw: Wydawnictwo Literackie, 2015), 241–45.

45. Wolff, *Woodrow Wilson*, 210–11 of 287.

46. Nowak, *Ostatnia zdrada*, 261; and Hayton, *Conservative Revolutionary*, 122.

47. Colley, *Namier*, 14.

48. Quoted by Colley, *Namier*, 58.

49. John Cairns, "Sir Lewis Namier and the History of Europe," *Historical Reflections/ Réflexions Historiques* 1, no. 1 (June/juin 1974), 11.

50. Quoted by Ng, *Nationalism*, n41, 57.

51. Hayton, *Conservative Revolutionary*, 23; and Julia Namier, *Lewis Namier: A Biography* (London: Oxford University Press, 1971), 29.

52. Lewis Namier, "Human Nature in Politics," in *Personalities and Powers* (London: Hamish Hamilton, 1955), 2.

53. Andrzej Zięba, "Historyk jako produkt historii, czyli o tym, jak Ludwik Bernstein

przekształcał się w Lewisa Namiera," in *Historyk i historia (studia dedykowane pamięci Prof. Mirosława Frančicia)*, ed. Adam Walaszek and Krzysztof Zamorski (Kraków: Historia Jagiellonica, 2005), 155–56.

54. Julia Namier, *Lewis Namier*, 47.

55. Namier, "Nationality and Liberty," in *Vanished Supremacies: Essays on European History 1815–1918* (London: Penguin, 1958), 60.

56. Namier, "Nationality and Liberty," 68–69.

57. Taras Hunczak, "Sir Lewis Namier and the Struggle for Eastern Galicia," *Harvard Ukrainian Studies* 1, no. 2 (June 1977), 199, 201. The quote is from Lewis Namier, *England in the Age of the American Revolution* (London: Macmillan, 1930), 20.

58. Namier, "Two Books on Eastern Europe," in *Conflicts*, 174, 176.

59. Zięba, "Historyk," 163.

60. Robert Frost, "Ukraine-Rus' and Poland-Lithuania, 1300–1569," in Mykhailo Hrushevsky, *History of Ukraine-Rus'*, vol. 4, *Political Relations in the Fourteenth to Sixteenth Centuries*, ed. Frank Sysyn, Robert Frost, and Yaroslav Fedoruk (Toronto: Canadian Institute of Ukrainian Studies Press, 2017), lii, lxi.

61. Quoted by Zięba, "Historyk," 170.

62. Namier, *1848*, 3.

63. Quoted by Hayton, *Conservative Revolutionary*, 71–72.

64. Lewis Namier, *In the Margin of History* (Macmillan: London, 1939), 88.

65. Namier, "Nationality and Liberty," 70.

66. See chapter 3 in this volume.

67. Namier, "Nationality and Liberty," 70–71.

68. See Yaroslav Hrytsak, *Ivan Franko and His Community* (Cambridge, MA: Academic Studies Press, 2019).

9: Whose Grand Duchy?

1. "Lithuanians Form Human Chain to Back Democracy in Belarus," *Washington Post*, August 23, 2020, https://www.washingtonpost.com/politics/lithuanians-form-human-chain-to-back-democracy-in-belarus/2020/08/23/91ebaf58-e576-11ea-bf44-0d31c85838a5_story.html.

2. The convergence of state and nation in Lithuania was noted by Czesław Miłosz (1911–2004), the only literary Nobel laureate who was born and spent his youth in Lithuania. He coined the term "philological nation" to name the phenomenon of twentieth-century Lithuania. In other words, the state is understood through the category of the nation, which, in turn, is perceived through a cultural and historical actor—the language. See Czesław Miłosz, *Szukanie Ojczyzny* (Kraków: Znak, 1992), 38.

3. Although historians are clustered in dozens of places all over the country, there are three main centers of historical studies and research in Lithuania: the Lithuanian Institute of History, Vilnius University, and Vytautas Magnus University. The best-known and most influential historians include Alvydas Nikžentaitis, Alfredas Bumblauskas, and Egidijus Aleksandravičius, who have contributed to numerous research projects as well as to the popularization of history (e.g., through TV shows) and public activities to foster knowledge of the multicultural legacy of Lithuania (e.g., the Polish-Lithuanian J. Giedroyć Forum and the Grand Duchy of Lithuania Institute). The ethnocentric nature of the modern Lithuanian historic narrative has been commented on in multiple studies conducted by Lithuanian historians over the past dozen years; see, e.g., Egidijus Aleksandravičius, "XIX a. Lietuvos pasakojimo likimas po 1990 m.: tarp funkcionalumo ir inercijos," in *Tautiniai naratyvai ir herojai Vidurio Rytų Europoje po 1989 m.* (Vilnius: Versus Aureus, 2015), 541–616.

4. For an exhaustive study dedicated to the analysis of the transformations of the Belarusian historiography through the nineteenth and the twentieth centuries, see Rainer Lindner, *Historiker und Herrschaft: Nationsbildung und Geschichtspolitik in Weißrußland* (Munich: R. Oldenbourg, 1999).

5. Popularized by the self-educated historian Mikola Jermalovič (1921–2000), the national narrative was reborn with new energy in Belarus around 1990. Jermalovič was followed by numerous academic historians, ranging from more radical nationalizers like Aleś Kraŭcevič to more ideologically moderate historians like Viačaslaŭ Nasievič: Aleksander Krawcewicz, *Powstanie Wielkiego Księstwa Litewskiego* (Białystok: Wydawnictwo Wyższej Szkoły Ekonomicznej, 2003); and Viačaslaŭ Nasievič, *Bielarusy: stanaŭliennie etnasu i nacyjanalnaja ideja* (Smolensk: Inbielkuĺt, 2015). On the contestation between the two principal narratives of Belarusian nationhood, see especially Nelly Bekus, *Struggle over Identity: The Official and the Alternative "Belarusianness"* (Budapest: Central European University, 2010).

6. Anthony F. Upton, "History and National Identity: Some Finnish Examples," in *National History and Identity: Approaches to the Writing of National History in the North-East Baltic Region, Nineteenth and Twentieth Centuries*, ed. M. Branch (Helsinki: Finnish Literature Society, 1999), 160–64.

7. Since the second half of the nineteenth century, the ideology of so-called West-Rus'ism flourished in this part of the Russian Empire and continued to be visible in the Russocentric ideology of Soviet "brotherhood" between Russia, Belarus, and Ukraine. These narratives argued that the Grand Duchy was a Russian state. Although multiculturalism was not fully negated by this narrative, it generally took a culturally homogeneous approach to the region's past. The phenomenon of West-Rus'ism and its relation to Belarus has been analyzed by the Belarusian historian Andrej Cichamiraŭ. See Andrzej Tichomirow, "West-Rus'ism and the Politics of Memory in Today's Belarus," *Belarusian Review* 25, no. 4 (2013); and Andrej Cichamiraŭ, "Zachodnieruskaja ideja jak dasliedčyckaja prabliema: ci byla jana alternatyvaj dlia Bielaruskaj idei?" in *Belarus' v evropeiskom kontekste: aktual'nye diskussii o natsiostroitel'stve*, ed. Ol'ga Shparaga and Ales' Smolenchuk (Vilnius: EGU, 2014), 89–104.

8. The letters of Gediminas have received special attention in Lithuania, as shown, for example, by a sumptuous reedition of the letters: *Gedimino laiškai* (Vilnius: Vaga, 2003). In both countries, the rule of Gediminas is interpreted in terms of the advance of the tradition of "tolerance." For a prominent Belarusian example, see I. N. Bokhan and S. N. Temushev, *Istoriia Belarusi: 6 klass, 2 chast'*, trans. V. M. Ivanova and I. V. Letunovich (Minsk: Izdatel'skii tsentr BGU, 2016), 53.

9. Alfonsas Eidintas, Alfredas Bumblauskas, Antanas Kulakauskas, and Mindaugas Tamošaitis, *The History of Lithuania* (Vilnius: Eugrimas, 2013), 80–81. The book has been translated into several major languages and distributed as one that illustrates the Lithuanian national point of view.

10. "Stat'ia Ministra inostrannykh del Belarusi V. Makeia v zhurnale 'Belaruskaia dumka'" (mart–aprel' 2017 g.), http://mfa.gov.by/press/smi/c0099b5a53b2c1db.html, accessed December 11, 2020. Translated by the author.

11. The Belarusian-Lithuanian memory conflict is by no means unique in the East-Central European region. The nature and the specificity of such conflicts have been discussed in numerous studies, e.g., Egidijus Aleksandravičius, ed., *The Construction of National Narratives and Politics of Memory in the Central and Eastern European Region after 1989* (Kaunas: Vytautas Magnus University, 2014).

12. This point of view can be encountered in most Lithuanian history books, from Adolfas

Šapoka, ed., *Lietuvos istorija* (Kaunas, 1936) to the aforementioned Eidintas et al., *History of Lithuania*.

13. Šapoka, *Lietuvos istorija*.

14. For editions and reprints of Šapoka's book, see: 1936 (Kaunas, the first and the second modified editions); 1950 (Fiellbach & Württemberg, 3rd ed.); 1981 (reprint in Chicago); and reprints in Lithuania, 1988, 1989, 1999, 2016, 2017, and 2020.

15. On Šapoka's influence, see Simonas Strelcovas, "Konferencija, skirta Adolfo Šapokos 100-osioms gimimo metinėms paminėti," *Lietuvos istorijos metraštis*, no. 1 (2007), 187–88 (Vilnius: Lietuvos istorijos institutas, 2006). Lithuanian historiography of the twentieth century was often underpinned by the claim that the country's history had previously been constructed by foreigners and for foreigners. The slogan "to find Lithuanians in history" was most explicitly declared by Šapoka, who was later followed by other generations of historians.

16. On the difficult history of the Belarusian national movement, see Per Anders Rudling, *The Rise and Fall of Belarusian Nationalism: 1906–1931* (Pittsburgh, PA: University of Pittsburgh Press, 2015).

17. The first influential interpretation of Belarusian history that created conceptual fundaments for other independent and, especially, anti-Soviet histories of the country was Vaclaŭ Lastoŭski's *Karotkaja historyja Bielarusi* (Vilnius: Drukarnia Marcina Kuchty, 1910). Usievalad Ihnatoŭski was one of the most influential authors, with more than thirty publications on the history of Belarus. The most prominent was *Karotki narys historyi Belarusi* (five editions since 1919), which served as a textbook in the 1920s.

18. For an example of a consolidated version of the "Soviet-type" Belarusian narration concerning the Grand Duchy of Lithuania, see Vladimir Terent'evich Pashuto, *Obrazovanie Litovskogo gosudarstva* (Moscow: AN SSSR, 1959).

19. For example, Lastoŭski's *Karotkaja historyja* was reprinted (Minsk: Univiersiteckaje, 1992); Mitrafan Doŭnar-Zapoĺski's *Historyja Belarusi*, completed in 1925 but never previously published, was also issued (Minsk: Bielaruskaja encyklapiedyja im. Pietrusia Broŭki, 1994).

20. Krawcewicz, *Powstanie Wielkiego Księstwa Litewskiego*, 58. Such terms were also commonly used in early Belarusian nationalist historiography. See Simon Lewis, "The Jagiellonians in Belarus: A Gradual Release of Memory," in *Remembering the Jagiellonians*, ed. Natalia Nowakowska (New York: Routledge, 2018), 163–68.

21. One of the official participants of Belarusian-Lithuanian discussions of the early 1990s, Edvardas Gudavičius, related this story to the author of this chapter.

22. Estimates of when exactly the regime started to "Belarusianize" its ideology vary, from around 2001 to 2010. See Vladimiras Snapkovskis, "Pagrindiniai Baltarusijos Respublikos istorijos politikos raidos etapai ir tendencijos," in *Lietuvos ir Baltarusijos istorijos politika*, ed. Justinas Dementavičius, Alvydas Jokubaitis and Raimundas Lopata (Vilnius: Vilniaus universiteto leidykla, 2016), 12–55; Jovita Pranevičiūtė-Neliupšienė, "Forming National Identity and Building Loyalty to the State: A Backbone to Regime Stability?" in *Belarusian Regime Longevity: Happily Ever After . . .* (Vilnius: Vilnius University Press, 2014); Fabian Burkhardt, "Concepts of the Nation and Legitimation in Belarus," in *Politics and Legitimacy in Post-Soviet Eurasia*, ed. Martin Brusis, Joachim Ahrens, and Martin Schulze Wessel (London: Palgrave Macmillan, 2015), 148–71; and Lewis, "Jagiellonians in Belarus," 172–79.

23. The results of the August 9, 2020, presidential elections were not recognized by the European Union or other western democracies, and Belarus was placed under sanctions in response to the widespread police violence against civilian demonstrators. The Lukashenko regime remained in power with support from Russia, and even allowed Russian troops to invade Ukraine from bases on the Belarusian-Ukrainian border in February 2022.

24. For example, in the interwar period, Uladzimir Pičeta wrote about the Grand Duchy as a Lithuanian and Russian (Belarusian) state. See Vladimir Picheta, *Belorussiia i Litva XVI–XVI v.* (Moscow: Izdatel'stvo Akademii Nauk SSSR, 1961).

25. One of the most famous repudiations of Jermalovič was made by the Lithuanian historian Edvardas Gudavičius in a fierce comment on the Belarusian historian's text on the origins of the Grand Duchy. See Mikola Jermalovič, *Pa sliadach adnaho mifa* (Minsk: Navuka i technika, 1991); and Edvardas Gudavičius, "Following the Tracks of a Myth," *Lithuanian Historical Studies*, no. 1 (1996): 38–58 (Vilnius: Lietuvos istorijos institutas, 1996).

26. The date 1248 is suggested by Kraŭcevič. See Krawcewicz, *Powstanie Wielkiego Księstwa Litewskiego*, 130. Though not widely accepted by Belarusians, its impact remains strong, and other scholars start the history of the Grand Duchy at a date hovering around 1250, e.g., Bokhan and Temushev, *Istoriia Belarusi*, 2.

27. For 1236, see Šapoka, *Lietuvos istorija*, 50. The 1240s have been unanimously accepted as the period of the Grand Duchy's foundation in Lithuanian historiography since the 1990s. Eidintas et al., *History of Lithuania*, 29.

28. The peaceful cooperation and mutual interests of both nations (Lithuania and Belarus) is a dominant trend in Belarusian historiography from the 1990s onward. The first and most important text was written by Kraŭcevič: see Aliaksandr Kraŭcevič, *Stvarennie Vialikaha Kniastva Litoŭskaha* (Minsk: Bielaruskaja navuka, 1998). Its Polish translation (2003) helped spread the concept in the region (see Krawcewicz, *Powstanie Wielkiego Księstwa Litewskiego*). The incarnation of this concept in Belarus can be observed in modern history manuals. See Bokhan and Temushev, *Istoriia Belarusi*, 7–10.

29. Throughout the twentieth century, until the 1990s, the dominant belief in Lithuania was that the Grand Duchy had been formed as a response to the aggressiveness of its neighbors: Poland, Kyivan Rus', and the Teutonic Order. The most representative illustration of this tendency is Šapoka, *Lietuvos istorija*. From the end of the twentieth century, a new conception appeared, emphasizing the aggression of the Lithuanians, who united in order to make their war expeditions more effective. This thinking is found in most of modern Lithuanian historiography, e.g., Alfredas Bumblauskas, *Senosios Lietuvos istorija* (Vilnius: R. Paknio leidykla, 2005).

30. The issue of the ruler's title has been a source of many public and scholarly discussions, especially in recent decades. This was caused by lasting Lithuanian and Polish tensions over shared history. In the historiography of the region, which was traditionally dominated by Polish scholarship, it has been an established truth that a kingdom is a more prestigious and powerful unit than a grand duchy, with Poland being a kingdom and Lithuania "only" a grand duchy. The conflict that ensued between Poland and Lithuania in the 1920s strongly contributed to the exaltation of rulers who became (Mindaugas) or were close to becoming (Vytautas the Great, 1392–1430) kings of Lithuania. Although the geopolitical situation changed many times through the twentieth century, the tendency toward the "kingdomization" of Lithuania remains strong even today. One of the most recent contributions to the discussion as to whether the rulers of the grand duchy were kings or grand dukes decides in favor of the former: see Algimantas Bučys, *Lietuvių karaliai ir Lietuvos karalystė de facto ir de jure Viduramžių Europoje* (Vilnius: Alio, 2018).

31. Rūstis Kamuntavičius, "History of the Grand Duchy of Lithuania: Interpretations of Young Belarusians and Lithuanians," in Aleksandravičius, *Construction of National Narratives*, 75–98.

32. Edvardas Gudavičius, *Lietuvos europėjimo keliais: istorinės studijos* (Vilnius: Aidai, 2002), 333–36.

33. The Lithuanian historian Tomas Baranauskas has collected all the existing arguments proving that the coronation could not have happened on July 6. He suggests that the coronation could have taken place in June, as one of several possibilities. One of his popular articles on the problem is "Kada iš tiesų turėtume švęsti Mindaugo karūnavimo dieną?" *Respublika*, July 5, 2012.

34. Bokhan and Temushev, *Istoriia Belarusi*, 11.

35. Uladzimir Kananovich, "Heroes and Villains: Politics and Historical Memory in Late Medieval East Europe; The Case Study of the Land of Navahrudak," *Russian History* 43 (2016): 22–67. The castle at Navahrudak was destroyed in the seventeenth and eighteenth centuries, and now stands as a ruin, adding to the opacity (and perhaps also the romanticism) of the myth.

36. Though some historians of the first half of the twentieth century cautiously discussed Navahrudak as a possible place of coronation (e.g., Zenonas Ivinskis), there is not a single mention of Navahrudak as a capital of the grand duchy in a text by a Lithuanian historian since the last decades of the twentieth century.

37. Such arguments are used in popular educational literature for children, positing that Navahrudak could not have been a capital of Lithuania "regardless of what Belarusians try to claim." For a typical example, see Evaldas Bakonis, *Vaikams apie senąsias Lietuvos sostines* (Kaunas: Šviesa, 2009). Belarusian historians argue that Navahrudak was ceded to the neighboring rival in 1254 for political and military reasons only. Moreover, within four years the peace agreement was broken, and the city returned to Mindaugas's state.

38. "Agluonoje atidengtas paminklas baltiškai karališkai šeimai—Karaliui Mindaugui ir Karalienei Mortai," http://urm.lt/lv/lt/naujienos/agluonoje-atidengtas-paminklas-baltis-kai-karaliskai-seimai-karaliui-mindaugui-ir-karalienei-mortai, accessed December 16, 2020.

39. Edvardas Gudavičius, *Lietuvos istorija: Nuo seniausių laikų iki 1569 metų* (Vilnius: Lietuvos rašytojų sąjungos leidykla, 1999), 74.

40. Šapoka, *Lietuvos istorija*.

41. Šapoka, *Lietuvos istorija*.

42. At the end of the twentieth century, the comparison of the Grand Duchy in the fourteenth and fifteenth centuries to an empire was backed by influential academics and gained wide support in Lithuania. A key publication in this development was a book by a professor at Vilnius University, which was published in Lithuanian (2009) and translated into both Belarusian (2016) and English: Zenonas Norkus, *An Unproclaimed Empire: The Grand Duchy of Lithuania; From the Viewpoint of Comparative Historical Sociology of Empires* (London: Routledge, 2018).

43. The comparison of Lithuania to the Frankish state is a concept most intensively supported and promoted by the influential historian Edvardas Gudavičius and his follower Alfredas Bumblauskas. See Alfredas Bumblauskas, "Lietuvos Didžiosios Kunigaikštijos paveldo 'dalybos' ir 'Litva/Letuva' distinkcijos konceptas," in *Lietuvos Didžiosios Kunigaikštijos tradicija ir paveldo "dalybos"* (Vilnius: Vilniaus universiteto leidykla, 2008), 60.

44. The term "Old Belarusian language" is widely accepted in Belarusian academic and educational literature. See V. A. Voronin, A. A. Skep'ian, A. V. Matsuk, and O. V. Kravchenko, *Istoriia Belarusi: 7 klass* (Minsk: Izdatel'skii tsentr BGU, 2017), 40. The Lithuanian point of view is summarized in a representative encyclopedia article: Olegas Poliakovas, "Slavų kanceliarinė kalba," in *Visuotinė lietuvių enciklopedija*, https://www.vle.lt/Straipsnis/slavu-kance-liarine-kalba-87565, accessed December 16, 2020.

45. Scholarly arguments used by Lithuanians are based on the notion that only one language for East Slavonic people existed until the seventeenth century.

46. See Bumblauskas, "Lietuvos Didžiosios," 15–66.

47. See Obrashchenie podkantslera VKL L'va Sapegi k sosloviiam Velikogo kniazhestva Litovskogo po sluchaiu priniatiia Statuta VKL (1588 g.), http://starbel.by/statut/sapeh2.htm, accessed April 5, 2021. Characteristically, the Third Lithuanian Statute has never been translated into the Lithuanian language (a project directed by the author of this chapter was launched in 2017, and aims at publishing a translation in the near future; see www.3statutas.lt). Modern Lithuanian national narratives have not treated it as a part of their identity, whereas in Belarus it has acquired a canonical status.

48. The search for "genuine" Belarusian lands has intensified in recent decades. Two extensive studies have been produced as a result: see Oleg Łatyszonek, *Od Rusinów Białych do Białorusinów* (Białystok: Wydawnictwo Uniwersytetu w Białymstoku, 2006); and Alieś Biely, *Chronika Bielaj Rusi* (Smolensk: Inbielkuĺt, 2013).

49. Not questioned in Belarusian historiography, this idea has also been supported by some Lithuanian historians. See Rimvydas Petrauskas, *Lietuvos diduomenė XIV a. pabaigoje–XV a.: sudėtis, struktūra, valdžia* (Vilnius: Aidai, 2003).

50. See also Dariusz Kołodziejczyk, chapter 3 in this volume.

51. On the Battle of Grunwald in the national narratives and official histories of the region, see Dangiras Mačiulis, Rimvydas Petrauskas, and Darius Staliūnas, *Kas laimėjo Žalgirio mūšį? Istorinio paveldo dalybos Vidurio ir Rytų Europoje* (Vilnius: Mintis, 2012); and Hienadź Sahanovič, *Hrunvaĺd u bielaruskaj historyi: Sproba razboru palityčnaha mifa* (Minsk: Miedysont, 2015).

52. Rūstis Kamuntavičius, "Interpretacje przeszłości: Litewskie, polskie i bialoruskie mapy historyczne," *Przegląd wschodni* 13, no. 3 (51) (2014): 913–48.

53. Jūratė Kiaupienė, ed., *1385 m. rugpjūčio 14 d. Krėvos aktas* (Vilnius: Lietuvos istorijos institutas, 2002); and Jonas Dainauskas, *Lietuvos bei lietuvių krikštas ir 1387-ieji metai* (Chicago: Vydūno fondas, 1991).

54. The tradition of catastrophe can be illustrated by the chapter title "The Lublin Tragedy" in a book by the eminent Lithuanian medievalist Edvardas Gudavičius. See Gudavičius, *Lietuvos istorija*, 634.

55. Kamuntavičius, "Interpretacje przeszłości," 913–48.

56. Rajner Lindner, *Historyki i ŭlada: Nacyjatvorčy praces i histaryčnaja palityka ŭ Bielarusi XIX–XX st.*, trans. Liavon Barščeŭski (Minsk: Neŭski prasciah, 2003), 453–59.

57. The thesis has also been supported in a recently defended PhD dissertation: Valius Venckūnas, "LDK paveldo dalybų naratyvai Lietuvos ir Baltarusijos politinėje komunikacijoje XXI a. pradžioje" (PhD diss., Vilniaus universitetas, 2021).

58. The European Union has encouraged multicultural and borderland studies. This support has contributed to scholarly interest in such topics as Vilnius as a borderland city (the figure of the poet Tomas Venclova has been very important here: see Tomas Venclova, *Vilnius: A Personal History* [Riverdale-on-Hudson: Sheep Meadow Press, 2009]) and Belarus as a country of crossroads (e.g., A. Smolenchuk, A. Kravtsevich, and S. Tokt', *Belorusy: natsiia pogranich'ia* [Vilnius: EGU, 2011]). Though clearly visible, the real impact of EU policy on these developments has not yet been assessed or thoroughly analyzed.

59. In 2017, the author of this chapter launched the project www.gudija.lt, the only Lithuanian journal dedicated to Belarusian history and contemporary issues. As a result of this project, the first history of Belarus in the Lithuanian language has been published: Rūstis Kamuntavičius, *Gudijos istorija Baltarusijos istorija* (Vilnius: MELC, 2021).

60. See www.arche.by. See, e.g., Zianonas Norkus, "Vialikaje Kniastva Litoŭskaje uu

paraŭnaĺnaj histaryčnaj sacyjaliohii imperyjaŭ," trans. Raman Maladziašyn, *ARCHE*, no. 11 (110) (2011): 260–300; and Rymvidas Piatraŭskas, *Litoŭskaja znać u kancy XIV–XV st.: Sklad—struktura—ulada*, trans. Aleś Mikus (Smolensk: Inbielkuĺt, 2014).

61. A successful example of such a joint initiative from elsewhere is the German-Polish collaboration that yielded the bilingual multivolume study: *Deutsch-polnische Erinnerungsorte* (Paderborn: Ferdinand Schöningh, 2012–15) / *Polsko-niemieckie miescja pamięci* (Warsaw: Scholar, 2015–2016), vols. 1–4, ed. Hans-Henning Hahn and Robert Traba, and vol. 5, ed. Peter Oliver Loew and Robert Traba. A less successful example is a Polish-Russian project to produce school textbooks, http://www.polska-rosja.eu. Though the project has been implemented and the materials have been published, they have not yet been accepted by Polish or Russian societies; moreover, the leader of the project on the Polish side, Mirosław Filipowicz was dismissed from his position as director of the Institute of East-Central Europe in Lublin.

62. Jacques Le Goff, *History and Memory* (New York: Columbia University Press, 1992), 215.

10: Polish-Belarusian Encounters and the Divided Legacy of the Commonwealth

1. The eighteenth-century Grand Duchy of Lithuania included the vast majority of present-day Belarusian territory.

2. He also fought on the US side in the American War of Independence, rising to the rank of brigadier general in the Continental Army. For an English-language biography, see Alex Storozynski, *The Peasant Prince: Thaddeus Kosciuszko and the Age of Revolution* (New York: St. Martin's Press, 2009).

3. Partly as a consequence of the Solothurn incident, the country's first full-size statue of Kościuszko was erected in Maračoŭščyna in 2018. See "Śviata jadnáńnia: jak adkryvali pieršy ŭ Bielarusi pomnik nacyjanaĺnamu heroiu Kaściušku," *Radio Svaboda*, May 12, 2018, https://www.svaboda.org/a/29222865.html. This does not mean, however, that there was previously no commemoration of the general in Belarus. The manor house in which he was born is an interesting example. It was destroyed during the Second World War when the territory was under German occupation, after which the area became part of the Belarusian Soviet Socialist Republic in 1945. While no public commemorative initiatives were undertaken for most of the Soviet era, in 1987 a small memorial plaque was placed, which was replaced by a larger one in 1999. In 2004, after archaeological excavations were conducted to reveal the house's original foundations, it was reconstructed in situ and opened as the Tadeusz Kościuszko Museum.

4. The quote is from "Informacja MSZ w związku z odsłonięciem pomnika Tadeusza Kościuszki w Solurze," Official Website of the Embassy of the Republic of Poland in Bern, October 11, 2017, https://berno.msz.gov.pl/pl/aktualnosci/informacja_msz_w_zwiazku_z_odslonieciem_pomnika_tadeusza_kosciuszki_w_solurze. According to Aliaksandr Sapieha, the president of the Association of Belarusians in Switzerland, the Polish embassy ignored his emails for eight months. "Staršynia Asacyjacyi bielarusaŭ Švajcaryi nazvaŭ niapraŭdaju tlumačeńne MZS Poĺšy nakont pomnika Kaściušku," *Radio Svaboda*, October 11, 2017, https://www.svaboda.org/a/28786776.html.

5. On these two different understandings of multiculturalism, see the introduction to this volume.

6. Magdalena Micińska, "The Myth of Tadeusz Kościuszko in the Polish Mind (1794–1997)," *European Review of History: Revue européenne d'histoire* 5, no. 2 (1998), 191. See also Maria Janion and Maria Żmigrodzka, *Romantyzm i historia* (Warsaw: Państwowy Instytut Wydawniczy, 1978), 250–73.

7. Nina Glick Schiller, "Whose Cosmopolitanism? And Whose Humanity?" in *Whose Cos-*

mopolitanism? Critical Perspectives, Relationalities and Discontents, ed. Nina Glick Schiller and Andrew Irving (New York: Berghahn Books, 2015), 32.

8. In the early 1990s, it was far from clear that the Polish-Lithuanian Commonwealth would not become obsolete, as "nothing more than a historical memory." See Stephen R. Burant and Voytek Zubek, "Eastern Europe's Old Memories and New Realities: Resurrecting the Polish-Lithuanian Union," *East European Politics and Societies* 7, no. 2 (1993), 393. While the example of the Kościusko monument illustrates conflict over memory, it should not be ignored that the shared heritage of the Commonwealth has also been a source of several cross-border cooperation projects. For a book-length study of Polish state assistance to Belarus and Ukraine, see Paulina Pospieszna, *Democracy Assistance from the Third Wave: Polish Engagement in Belarus and Ukraine* (Pittsburgh, PA: University of Pittsburgh Press, 2014). There are also numerous student exchange projects, academic cooperation initiatives, and media collaborations such as the Polish state-funded television station for Belarus, BELSAT. Especially in the wake of the brutal crackdown on civil society after the rigged presidential election on August 9, 2020, Poland, Lithuania, and Ukraine (at least until the beginning of the Russian full-scale invasion in February 2022) have all been prominent supporters of Belarusian civil society.

9. On the myth of the *Kresy*, see, e.g., Daniel Beauvois, "Mit 'kresów polskich,' czyli jak mu położyć kres," in *Polskie mity polityczne XIX i XX wieku*, ed. W. Wrzesiński (Wrocław: Wydawnictwo Uniwersytetu Wrocławskiego, 1994), 93–106; Bogusław Bakuła, "Kolonialne i postkolonialne aspekty polskiego dyskursu kresoznawczego (zarys problematyki)," *Teksty drugie* 6 (2006): 11–33; German Ritz, "Kresy polskie w perspektywie postkolonialnej," in *(Nie)obecność: Pominięcia i przemilczenia w narracjach XX wieku*, ed. Hanna Gosk and Bożena Karwowska (Warsaw: Elipsa, 2008), 115–32; Robert Traba, "Kresy: miejsce pamięci w procesie reprodukcji kulturowej," in *Polska wschodnia i orientalizm*, ed. Tomasz Zarycki (Warsaw: Scholar, 2013), 146–70; and Małgorzata Głowacka-Grajper, *Transmisja pamięci: Działacze "sfery pamięci" i przekaz o Kresach Wschodnich we współczesnej Polsce* (Warsaw: Wydawnictwo Uniwersytetu Warszawskiego, 2016). On nineteenth- and early twentieth century representations of Belarus and Belarusians in Polish-language culture, see Simon Lewis, *Belarus—Alternative Visions: Nation, Memory and Cosmopolitanism* (New York: Routledge, 2019), 40–41. There were also, of course, prominent Polish intellectuals who argued against the narrative of Polish hegemony, such as the interwar politician Leon Wasilewski (1870–1936), who in his book *Litwa i Białoruś: przeszłość, teraźniejszość, tendencje rozwojowe* (Kraków: Spółka Nakładowa Książka, 1912) gave a detailed overview of the history of Belarus and Lithuania as important and autonomous regions of the Commonwealth; and the postwar émigré scholar Juliusz Mieroszewski, who in his essay "Rosyjski 'Kompleks Polski' i obszar ULB," *Kultura*, no. 9/324 (1974): 3–14, argued that Polish claims on its eastern neighbors expressed the "purest form of traditional Polish imperialism" (7).

10. See also the introduction to this volume.

11. I use the term "cultural contact zone" in the sense coined by Mary Louise Pratt: "social spaces where cultures meet, clash and grapple with each other, often in contexts of highly asymmetrical relations of power, such as colonialism, slavery, or their aftermaths." Mary Louise Pratt, "Arts of the Contact Zone," *Profession* (1991), 34.

12. I explore some major trends in Polish, Belarusian, and Russian thought in this period in Lewis, *Belarus—Alternative Visions*, ch. 1.

13. For a concise statement of the group's aims, see Konstancja Skirmuntt, *Stronnictwo Krajowe Litwy i Białorusi*, in her *Kartki polityczne ze spraw krajowych w prasie wileńskiej, 1905–1907: Przedruki z "Kurjera Litewskiego" i "Vilniaus Žinios"* (Warsaw: J. Cotty, 1907). For a detailed

history of the movement, see Dariusz Szpoper, *Sukcesorzy Wielkiego Księstwa: myśl polityczna i działalność konserwatystów polskich na ziemiach litewsko-białoruskich w latach 1904–1939* (Gdańsk: Arche, 1999). See also Simon Lewis, "Cosmopolitanism as Subculture in the Former Polish-Lithuanian Commonwealth," in *Identities in-Between in East-Central Europe*, ed. Jan Fellerer, Robert Pyrah, and Marius Turda (New York: Routledge, 2019), 149–69. The *Krajowcy* movement was in many ways similar to the conservative ideology of *Landespatriotismus* in the Habsburg Empire—thanks are due to Maciej Janowski for this observation.

14. Per Anders Rudling, *The Rise and Fall of Belarusian Nationalism, 1906–1931* (Pittsburgh, PA: University of Pittsburgh Press, 2015).

15. The Sanacja (Sanation) regime came to power after the May 1926 coup d'état by Józef Piłsudski (1867–1935) and turned Poland into a semi-authoritiarian state until the outbreak of the Second World War. Although Piłsudski had earlier been an advocate of empowerment of ethnic minorities within Poland, the country's politics in his last years of rule became increasingly nationalistic. On the Belarusian minority in interwar Poland, see Rudling, *Rise and Fall*, ch. 7; and Eugeniusz Mironowicz, "Białorusini w Polsce (1919–2009)," in *Białorusini*, ed. Teresa Zaniewska (Warsaw: Wydawnictwo Sejmowe, 2010), 10–15.

16. Unlike the People's Republic of Poland, the Belarusian Soviet Socialist Republic was not an independent state. However, as a republic of the USSR it had its own seat at the UN (as did the Ukrainian SSR), which gave it a semblance of sovereignty.

17. See, e.g., Głowacka-Grajper, *Transmisja pamięci*, 1–2; Christoph Kleßmann and Robert Traba, "Kresy und Deutscher Osten: Vom Glauben an die historische Mission—oder Wo liegt Arkadien?" in *Deutsch-Polnische Erinnerungsorte*, vol. 3, ed. Hans Henning Hahn and Robert Traba (Paderborn: Ferdinand Schöningh, 2012), 37–70.

18. Lewis, *Belarus—Alternative Visions*, ch. 2; Simon Lewis, "The Jagiellonians in Belarus: a Gradual Release of Memory," in *Remembering the Jagiellonians*, ed. Natalia Nowakowska (New York: Routledge, 2018), 170–72.

19. Sokrat Janowicz, *Białoruś, Białoruś* (Warsaw: Iskry, 1987), 119.

20. The department was founded as the Center for Belarusian Philology, and has been called the Department of Belarusian Studies since 2005. Marceli Kosman, *Historia Białorusi* (Wrocław: Zakład Narodowy im. Ossolińskich, 1979).

21. The first book is Sokrat Janowicz, *Wielkie Miasto Białystok* (Warsaw: Iskry, 1973). For the others, see, e.g., Sokrat Janowicz, *Samosiej* (Warsaw: Ludowa Spółdzielnia Wydawnicza, 1981); and Sokrat Janowicz, *Srebrny Jeździec* (Warsaw: Czytelnik, 1984).

22. Tadeusz Konwicki, *Kalendarz i klepsydra*, 2nd ed. (Warsaw: Czytelnik, 1982), 23–24. All translations are my own, unless otherwise indicated.

23. Konwicki, *Kalendarz i klepsydra*, 24.

24. See also Marek Zaleski, "Idylliczny Konwicki," in *Kresy: Dekonstrukcja*, ed. Krzysztof Trybuś, Jerzy Kałążny, and Radosław Okulicz-Kozaryn (Poznań: Wydawnictwo Poznańskiego Towarzystwa Przyjaciół Nauk, 2007), 289–302.

25. Tadeusz Konwicki, *Rojsty* (Warsaw: Czytelnik, 1956), 29.

26. This negative depiction of anticommunist military units resonates well with the Stalinist ideology of the time.

27. Tadeusz Konwicki, *Bohiń* (Warsaw: Czytelnik, 1987), 26.

28. Konwicki, *Kalendarz i klepsydra*, 24–25.

29. Konwicki, *Kalendarz i klepsydra*, 24–25.

30. Like Konwicki who considered Belarus passive and "mild," the other preeminent Lithuanian-born postwar Polish writer Czesław Miłosz wrote, "Belarusians were never fortunate

and they were given a choice, like a caught fish, between a frying pan and a fire, i.e. between polonization and russification." Janovič dismissed this claim as the "run-of-the-mill opinion of the average Polish intellectual in the interwar years." Janowicz, *Białoruś, Białoruś*, 82. (Miłosz quote originally from his *Rodzinna Europa* [Paris: Instytut Literacki, 1981], 52.)

31. As Charles Taylor argues: "Our identity is partly shaped by recognition or its absence, often by the misrecognition of others, and so a person or group of people can suffer real damage, real distortion, if the people or society around them mirror back to them a confining or demeaning or contemptible picture of themselves." See Charles Taylor, "The Politics of Recognition," in Charles Taylor et al., *Multiculturalism: Examining the Politics of Recognition*, ed. Amy Gutmann (Princeton, NJ: Princeton University Press, 1994), 25.

32. Janowicz, *Białoruś, Białoruś*, 11.

33. The Polish edition of this work was an amended version of a Belarusian book published in 1978 in Minsk (*Siarebrany jazdok*); the Belarusian edition, however, contained only the title story and some short sketches. The Polish reworking of the publication changed the book significantly, rendering it a more complex collection with a linear chronology. This shows, once again, that addressing a Polish readership made "packaging" Belarus's history as a unitary whole a more important task. For more detail, see Danuta Zawadzka, "Wynajdywanie tradycji: O prozie historycznej Sokrata Janowicza," in *Sokrat Janowicz: Pisarz transgraniczny; Studia, Wspomnienia, Materiały*, ed. Grażyna Charytoniuk-Michiej, Katarzyna Sawicka-Mierzyńska, and Danuta Zawadzka (Białystok: Trans Humana, 2014), 103–6.

34. Janowicz, *Srebrny jeździec*, 136.

35. Janowicz, *Białorus, Białoruś*, 92.

36. Janowicz, *Białorus, Białoruś*, 68.

37. Zawadzka, "Wynajdywanie tradycji," 98.

38. See Homi Bhabha, "Of Mimicry and Man: The Ambivalence of Colonial Discourse," *October* 28 (1984): 125–33.

39. Quotes: Elżbieta Dąbrowicz, "Naród w jednej osobie," in Charytoniuk-Michiej, Sawicka-Mierzyńska, and Zawadzka, *Sokrat Janowicz*, 26–27; and Adam Michnik, cited in Dąbrowicz, "Naród w jednej osobie," 21.

40. Bill Ashcroft, Gareth Griffiths, and Helen Tiffin, *The Empire Writes Back: Theory and Practice in Post-Colonial Literatures* (London: Routledge, 1989).

41. Sokrat Janowicz, *Terra Incognita: Białoruś* (Białystok: Niwa, 1993), 43.

42. Janowicz, *Białoruś, Białoruś*, 12–13.

43. Sokrat Janowicz, "Dilemmas of Creativity: The Belarusan Writer in Post-war Poland," trans. Wojtek Kość, *Central European Review* 95, no. 3 (March 2001), http://www.ce-review.org/01/9/janowicz9.html.

44. Andrzej Sadowski, Maciej Tefelski, and Eugeniusz Mironowicz, "Polacy i kultura polska z perspektywy mniejszości białoruskiej w Polsce," in *Kultura dominująca jako kultura obca: Mniejszości kulturowe a grupa dominująca w Polsce*, ed. Janusz Mucha (Warsaw: Oficyna Naukowa, 1999), 54–91; and Elżbieta Czykwin, "Białoruska mniejszość narodowa: Problem asymilacji w kontekście stygmatu społecznego," in Zaniewska, *Białorusini*, 29–46.

45. Marcin Kącki, *Białystok: Biała siła, czarna pamięć* (Wołowiec: Czarne, 2015). For criticism, see Danuta Zawadzka, Katarzyna Niziołek, and Kataryzyna Sawicka-Mierzyńska, "Dyskusja: Oto czym jesteśmy/jesteście—zrozumieć Białystok (na marginesie książki Marcina Kąckiego *Białystok. Biała siła, czarna pamięć*)," *Pogranicze: Studia Społeczne* 26 (2015): 169–84.

46. For analysis, see, e.g., Andrei Tichomirov, "'Kresy' kak simptom: zametki na poliakh pol'skikh zhurnalov," *Historians.in.Ua*, September 2, 2013, http://www.historians.in.ua/index.

php/en/avtorska-kolonka/834-andrei-tykhomyrov-kresy-kak-symptom-zametky-na-poliakh-polskykh-zhurnalov; Paweł Ładykowski, "Poland and Its Eastern Neighbours: A Postcolonial Case Study," *Baltic Journal of European Studies* 5, no.1 (2014): 109–32; and Paweł Cywiński, "Kresy: Między winą a powinnością," *Kontakt* 28 (2015): 32–37. I have analyzed elsewhere some recent trends that complicate the picture of ubiquitous nostalgia: Simon Lewis, "Border Trouble: Ethnopolitics and Cosmopolitan Memory in Recent Polish Cinema," *East European Politics and Societies and Cultures* 33, no. 2 (2019): 522–49.

47. Marharyta Fabrykant and Renee Buhr, "Small State Imperialism: The Place of Empire in Contemporary Nationalist Discourse," *Nations and Nationalism* 22, no. 1 (2016): 103–22; and Lewis, "Jagiellonians in Belarus." See also chapter 9 in this volume.

48. Michael Rothberg, *Multidirectional Memory: Remembering the Holocaust in the Age of Decolonization* (Stanford, CA: Stanford University Press, 2009), 5.

49. On "mnemonic solidarity," see Jie-Hyun Lim and Eve Rosenhaft, eds., *Mnemonic Solidarity: Global Interventions* (Cham: Palgrave Macmillan, 2021). A separate debate could be held on whether political solidarity *needs to* translate into mnemonic solidarity. On this, see, e.g., Jerzy Jedlicki, "Heritage and Collective Responsibility," in *The Political Responsibility of Intellectuals*, ed. Ian Maclean, Alan Montefiore, and Peter Winch (Cambridge: Cambridge University Press, 1990), 53–76. Thanks to Maciej Janowski for this reference.

50. See also his book, Andrzej Poczobut, *System Białoruś* (Gliwice: Helion, 2013). Poczobut was arrested and imprisoned by the Lukashenko regime in March 2021. He was sentenced in February 2023 to eight years in prison for "actions directed at harming the country's national security, distributing materials containing such calls, and inciting hatred."

51. See, e.g., Tomasz Krzywicki, *Szlakiem Adama Mickiewicza po Nowogródczyźnie, Wilnie i Kownie: Przewodnik* (Pruszków: Rewasz, 1998); Marek A. Koprowski, *Białoruś—uparte trwanie polskości* (Toruń: Wydawnictwo Adam Marszałek, 2006); and Katarzyna Węglicka, *Białoruskie ścieżki: Gawędy kresowe* (Warsaw: Książka i Wiedza, 2006).

52. Notable translations of Belarusian literature include the anthologies: Małgorzata Buchalik and Katarzyna Kotyńska, eds., *Białoruś: Kraina otoczona wysokimi górami* (Olsztyn: Borussia, 2004); Lawon Barshcheuski and Adam Pomorski, eds., *Nie chyliłem czoła przed mocą: Antologia poezji białoruskiej* (Wrocław: KEW, 2008); and Emilia Walczak, ed., *Wschód wolności: Antologia współczesnej literatury białoruskiej* (Bydgoszcz: Miejskie Centrum Kultury, 2020). Single-work translations have also appeared, such as Ihar Babkou, *Adam Kłakocki i jego cienie*, trans. Małgorzata Buchalik (Warsaw: Oficyna 21, 2008); Artur Klinau, *Mińsk: Przewodnik po Mieście Słońca*, trans. Małgorzata Buchalik (Wołowiec: Czarne, 2008); and Natalka Babina, *Miasto ryb*, trans. Małgorzata Buchalik (Poznań: Rebis, 2010). Several of Svetlana Alexievich's books have also appeared in Polish translation, issued by the Czarne publishing house; she is probably the best-known Belarusian author in Poland (as in most other countries). On the presence of Russia and Ukraine in contemporary Polish literature, see, e.g., Magdalena Marszałek and Matthias Schwartz, "Imaginierte Ukraine: Zur kulturellen Topographie in der polnischen und russischen Literatur," *Osteuropa* 11 (2004): 75–86; Monika Bednarczuk, "Imperial Legacies in Contemporary Polish Travel Writing," in *Postcolonial Slavic Literatures after Communism*, ed. Klavdia Smola and Dirk Uffelmann (Frankfurt am Main: Peter Lang, 2016), 347–72; and Przemysław Czapliński, *Poruszona mapa: Wyobraźnia geograficzno-kulturowa polskiej literatury przełomu XX i XXI wieku* (Kraków: Wydawnictwo Literackie, 2017), 12–180. More recently on Ukraine, see esp. works by Ziemowit Szczerek and Żanna Słoniowska (see the introduction to this volume). On earlier literary imaginings of Ukraine, see chapter 7 in this volume.

53. Nelly Bekus, "Constructed 'Otherness'? Poland and the Geopolitics of Contested Belarusian Identity," *Europe-Asia Studies* 69, no. 2 (2017), 243.

54. See Lewis, "Jagiellonians in Belarus."

55. Eva Viežnaviec, "Ahiencyja 'Ščasc'e,'" in her *Šliach drobnaj svolačy* (Minsk: Lohvinaŭ, 2008), 101–15.

56. Viežnaviec, "Ahiencyja 'Ščasc'e,'" 102.

57. Bekus, "Constructed 'Otherness'?" 252.

58. René Girard, "Mimesis and Violence: Perspectives in Cultural Criticism," in *The Girard Reader*, ed. James G. Williams (New York: Crossroad Herder, 1996), 11.

59. Marta Pińska, *Białorusinka/Bielaruska* (Krynki: Villa Sokrates, 2004).

60. Jan Maksimiuk, "Pieršy adradženski," in his *Slovy ŭ holym poli: Bielaruskaja litaratura 1990-ch u snach, uspaminach i fotazdymkach* (Minsk: Lohvinaŭ, 2011), 105–13.

61. Maksimiuk, "Pieršy adradženski," 111–13.

62. This is probably a main reason why the book was published under a pseudonym, to protect the author from accusations of indecency and pornography.

63. Pińska, *Białorusinka/Bielaruska*, 98. Quotes from this work are cited from the Belarusian-language side of the book.

64. Pińska, *Białorusinka/Bielaruska*, 15.

65. Pińska, *Białorusinka/Bielaruska*, 34.

66. Pińska, *Białorusinka/Bielaruska*, 51.

67. Hayden White, *The Practical Past* (Evanston, IL: Northwestern University Press, 2014).

68. For instance, a campaign to decorate the centenary edition Polish passports in 2018 controversially included sites of memory located in Ukraine and Lithuania; see Lewis, "Border Trouble," 522–24. In 2017, the Polish foreign minister Witold Waszczykowski pointedly refused to enter the National Museum of the Victims of Occupational Regimes in Lviv, after asking its director whether Poland was an occupational regime and receiving an affirmative reply; the Ukrainian museum director Ruslan Zabiliy later commented that the entire maneuver was likely to have been an intentionally staged political provocation. "Holovi MZS Polshchi ne spodobalas u Lvovi vidpovid pro okupatsiiu," *Radio Svoboda*, November 5, 2017, https://www.radiosvoboda.org/a/news/28836165.html.

69. Ignacy Karpowicz, *Sońka* (Kraków: Wydawnicto Literackie, 2014). In addition to the novel, *Sońka* was adapted for the stage by Karpowicz himself, premiering in March 2015 at the Teatr Dramatyczny in Białystok. An audiobook was also produced, with the same Belarusian actress Sviatlana Anikiej voicing the title role. Here, however, I will only discuss the text of the original printed book.

70. Karpowicz, *Sońka*, 73.

71. Karpowicz, *Sońka*, 24

72. Karpowicz, *Sońka*, 71.

73. Karpowicz, *Sońka*, 59.

74. Linda Hutcheon, *Narcissistic Narrative: The Metafictional Paradox* (New York: Methuen, 1984), xvi.

75. On Polish mythologization of the Second World War, see, e.g., Lech M. Nijakowski, "Fighting for Victim Status: Polish Debates on Genocide and the Collective Memory of World War II," in *World War II and Two Occupations: Dilemmas of Polish Memory*, ed. Anna Wolf-Powęska and Piotr Forecki (Frankfurt am Main: Peter Lang, 2016), 39–60. On war memory in Belarus, see Lewis, *Belarus—Alternative Visions*, ch. 2, 3, and 5.

76. Karpowicz, *Sońka*, 70.

77. Birgit Neumann, "The Literary Representation of Memory," in *A Companion to Cultural Memory Studies*, ed. Astrid Erll and Ansgar Nünning (Berlin: de Gruyter, 2010), 338.

78. Hutcheon, *Narcissistic Narrative*, xiv.

79. Karpowicz, *Sońka*, 197.

11: Jewish Heritage Revival in the Polish-Belarusian-Ukrainian Borderlands and the Myth of Multiculturalism

1. Ruth E. Gruber, *Virtually Jewish: Reinventing Jewish Culture in Europe* (Berkeley: University of California Press, 2002); Erica T. Lehrer, *Jewish Poland Revisited: Heritage Tourism in Unquiet Places* (Bloomington: Indiana University Press, 2013); and Magdalena Waligórska, *Klezmer's Afterlife: An Ethnography of the Jewish Music Revival in Poland and Germany* (Oxford: Oxford University Press, 2013).

2. Magdalena Waligórska, "Jewish Heritage and the New Belarusian National Identity Project," *East European Politics and Societies and Cultures* 20, no. 10 (2015): 1–28; Sarunas Liekis "The Revitalisation of Jewish Heritage in Vilnius," in *Reclaiming Memory: Urban regeneration in the Historic Jewish Quarters of Central European Cities*, ed. Monika Murzyn-Kupisz and Jacek Purchla (Kraków: International Cultural Centre, 2009), 247–59; Elena Zaslavskaia, "Vitalii Chernoivanenko: Issledovanie evreiskoi istorii Ukrainy dolzhno byt sopriazheno s mezhnatsionalnym ukrainsko-evreiskim dialogom," vaadua.org, February 2016, http://vaadua.org/news/vchernoivanenko-issledovanie-evreyskoy-istorii-ukrainy-dolzhno-byt-sopryazheno-s, accessed December 30, 2020.

3. Biłgoraj's Jewish population amounted to 60 percent of the total population of over 8,000 as of 1939; Iŭje had a Jewish majority exceeding 75 percent of the town's 5,000 inhabitants; and, in Brody, Jews made up 55 percent of a population of 18,000. See Alina Skibińska, "Powiat biłgorajski," in *Dalej jest noc: Losy Żydów w wybranych powiatach okupowanej Polski*, vol. 1, ed. Barbara Engelking and Jan Grabowski (Warsaw: Stowarzyszenie Centrum Badań nad Zagładą Żydów, 2018), 196; Shmuel Spector, ed., *The Encyclopedia of Jewish Life before and during the Holocaust* (New York: New York University Press, 2001) 201–2, 830.

4. Robert Frost, *The Oxford History of Poland-Lithuania*, vol. 1 (Oxford: Oxford University Press, 2015).

5. Timothy Snyder, *Bloodlands: Europe between Hitler and Stalin* (New York: Basic Books, 2010); Christian Gerlach, *Kalkulierte Morde Die deutsche Wirtschafts- und Vernichtungspolitik in Weißrußland 1941 bis 1944* (Hamburg: Hamburger Edition HIS, 2013); and Ilia Altman, *Zhertvy nenavisti: Kholokost v SSSR. 1941–1945 gg.* (Moscow: Fond Kovcheg, 2002).

6. Jan Grabowski and Dariusz Libionka, *Klucze i kasa: O mieniu żydowskim w Polsce pod okupacją niemiecką i we wczesnych latach powojennych 1939–1950* (Warsaw: Stowarzyszenie Centrum Badań nad Zagładą Żydów, 2014); Martin Dean, *Collaboration in the Holocaust: Crimes of the Local Police in Belorussia and Ukraine, 1941–44* (New York: St. Martin's Press, 2003); Barbara Engelking, *Jest taki piękny słoneczny dzień: Losy Żydów szukających ratunku na wsi polskiej 1942–1945* (Warsaw: Stowarzyszenie Centrum Badań nad Zagładą Żydów, 2011); Engelking and Grabowski, *Dalej jest noc*, 2018; and Jan Grabowski, *Na posterunku: udział polskiej policji granatowej i kryminalnej w zagładzie Żydów* (Wołowiec: Czarne, 2020).

7. Michael Rothberg, *The Implicated Subject: Beyond Victims and Perpetrators* (Stanford, CA: Stanford University Press, 2019), 1.

8. Rothberg, *Implicated Subject*, 9.

9. Jochen Böhler, *Civil War in Central Europe 1918–1921: The Reconstruction of Poland* (Oxford: Oxford University Press, 2018), 191.

10. Kathryn Ciancia, *On Civilization's Edge: A Polish Borderland in the Interwar World* (New York: Oxford University Press, 2020), 74,

11. Paweł Sygowski, "Żydzi w Biłgoraju w XIX wieku w świetle materiałów archiwalnych (1810–1875)," in *Biłgoraj, czyli raj: Rodzina Singerów i świat, którego już nie ma*, ed. Monika Adamczyk-Grabowska and Bogusław Wróblewski (Lublin: Wydawnictwo Uniwersytetu Marii Curie-Skłodowskiej, 2005), 37.

12. Henryk Gmiterek, "Żydzi biłgorajscy w okresie przedrozbiorowym," in Adamczyk-Grabowska and Wróblewski, *Biłgoraj, czyli raj*, 22; Abraham Kronenberg, ed., *Zagłada Biłgoraja: Księga Pamięci* (Gdańsk: Słowo Obraz Terytoria, 2009), 23; and Nathan Hannover, *Jawen Mezula: Schilderung des polnisch-kosakischen Krieges und der Leiden der Juden in Polen während der Jahre 1648–1653* (Hannover: Im Selbstverlage des herausgebers, 1863).

13. Adam Kopciowski, "Żydzi w Biłgoraju na przełomie XIX i XX wieku," in Adamczyk-Grabowska and Wróblewski, *Biłgoraj, czyli raj*, 82.

14. Kronenberg, *Zagłada Biłgoraja*, 39.

15. Kronenberg, *Zagłada Biłgoraja*, 38–40, 71–99.

16. See Skibińska, "Powiat biłgorajski," 196.

17. Skibińska, "Powiat biłgorajski," 22–23; and Jan Mikulski "Myśli, wspomnienia, uwagi, refleksje . . . ," unpublished manuscript (Biłgoraj, 1970).

18. Izrael Gajst, "Żydzi biłgorajscy pod okupacją," in Kronenberg, *Zagłada Biłgoraja*, 189.

19. Skibińska, "Powiat biłgorajski," 295.

20. Skibińska, "Powiat biłgorajski," 260–61, 294; Grabowski, *Na posterunku*; and Gajst "Żydzi biłgorajscy pod okupacją," 191, 193–94, 197, 199, 218. Acts of collaboration of local inhabitants are also graphically described in the depositions made by Jewish witnesses in the postwar trial. See Sąd Okręgowy w Zamościu, "Akta w sprawie: Kulesza Franciszek i inni," Archives of the Institute of National Remembrance in Lublin, LU 327/31.

21. A small group was also deported to the Majdanek concentration camp. See Skibińska, "Powiat biłgorajski," 372–80.

22. Skibińska, "Powiat biłgorajski," 368.

23. Data from May 1945. See Skibińska, "Powiat biłgorajski," 365.

24. Kronenberg, *Zagłada Biłgoraja*.

25. The myth of the "Kresy" entails a strong polonizing gaze on these eastern territories, which are seen as inherently Polish, despite the fact that in many areas ethnic Poles made up only a fraction of the population (for example, in the regions of Polesie and Volhynia). The term "Kresy" also connotes the Polish "civilizing mission" in these territories, which Polish state authorities launched in the interwar period. See Ciancia, *On Civilization's Edge*.

26. Tadeusz Kuźmiński, personal interview with Magdalena Waligórska, June 27, 2020.

27. Tadeusz Kuźmiński, personal interview with Magdalena Waligórska, July 11, 2020.

28. Kuźmiński, interview, July 11, 2020.

29. The operation of clearing the bones from beneath the sport court took place around 1978. Artur Bara, interview with Magdalena Waligórska, July 15, 2020.

30. Kuźmiński, interview, July 11, 2020.

31. "Cmentarz żydowski w Biłgoraju," *Virtual Shtetl*, https://sztetl.org.pl/pl/miejsco-wosci/b/1911-bilgoraj/114-cmentarze/7515-cmentarz-zydowski-w-bilgoraju-ul-konopnick-iej-2123, accessed August 27, 2020.

32. Bara, interview, July 15, 2020.

33. Kuźmiński, interview, July 4, 2020.

34. Kuźmiński, interview, July 4, 2020.

35. Mirosława Papierzyńska-Turek, *Między tradycją a rzeczywistością: Państwo wobec prawosławia 1918–1939* (Warsaw: PIW, 1989).

36. Among the acts of vandalism was the destruction of a mural portraying Isaac Bashevis Singer and the writing of antisemitic graffiti on one of the monuments and the "Wall of Memory." Bara, interview, July 15, 2020; "Antysemityzm czy zwykły wandalizm," *Biłgorajska.pl* https://bilgorajska.pl/aktualnosc,3045,0,0,0,Antysemityzm-czy-zwykly-wandalizm.html, accessed August 31, 2020.

37. Zuzanna Brzozowska and Andrzej Trzciński, "Cmentarze żydowskie w Biłgoraju," in Adamczyk-Grabowska and Wróblewski, *Biłgoraj, czyli raj*, 114–15.

38. Kuźmiński, interview, July 4, 2020.

39. Quotes from, respectively, Dalia Bar, personal interview with Magdalena Waligórska, August 25, 2020, and Israel Bar-On, personal interview with Magdalena Waligórska, July 13, 2020.

40. Bar-On, interview, July 13, 2020.

41. Shmuel Atzmon-Wircer, personal interview with Magdalena Waligórska, July 1, 2020.

42. "Samuel Atzmon-Wircer," https://www.bilgoraj.pl/page/470/samuel-atzmon-wircer.html, accessed September 6, 2020.

43. Valieryj Šabliuk, "Iŭje," in *Encyklapiedyja historyi Bielarusi*, vol. 3. (Minsk: BelEn, 1996), 510.

44. The Jews in Iŭje made up 76 percent of the local population in 1938. "*Ive: Istoricheskaia spravka*," Yad Vashem, https://netzulim.org/R/Const/Yad/75righteous/content/places/popup/ivie.htm?height=450&width=565. For more on Iŭje's Jewish history, see Ina Sorkina, "Iwie—karta dziedzictwa kulturowego," https://shtetlroutes.eu/pl/iwie-karta-dziedzictwa-kulturowego/, accessed November 12, 2020.

45. Smilovitskii, *Katastrofa evreev*, 179.

46. "Cmentarz żydowski w Iwiu," *Virtual Shtetl*, https://sztetl.org.pl/en/towns/i/1513-iwie/116-sites-of-martyrdom/46290-cmentarz-zydowski-w-iwiu-miejsce-egzekucji-i-grob-zbiorowy, accessed August 27, 2020.

47. Smilovitskii, *Katastrofa evreev*, and Mikhail (Elimelekh) Melamed, oral history interview, https://iremember.ru/memoirs/partizani/melamed-mikhail-elimelekh-aleksandrovich/, accessed December 20, 2020.

48. Melamed, oral history interview.

49. Tamara Baradach, personal interview with Ina Sorkina, July 8, 2020.

50. "Kogda steny zaplakali: Istoriia Tsili Iofan," Yad Vashem, https://www.yadvashem.org/ru/education/testimony-films/cyla-yoffan.html, accessed September 13, 2020; and Valiancina Koščar, personal interview with Ina Sorkina, October 16, 2020.

51. Iŭjeŭski Muzej Nacyjanalnykh Kultur, https://ivye-museum.by/, accessed April 29, 2022.

52. The same spirit fills the local historiography, which focuses entirely on peaceful coexistence of all the ethnic groups inhabiting the region. See *"Pamiać" Iŭjeŭski rajion* (Minsk: BELTA 2002); and the collections of conference papers *Z historyi viakoŭ i pakalienniaŭ Iŭjeŭskaha kraju* (Hrodna: HrDU, 1999), and *Iŭjeŭskaja ziamlia—suzorje narodaŭ, relihij i kultur* (Hrodna: JurSaPrynt, 2013).

53. Viera Hulidava, "Nie ŭ Rym darohi ŭsich liudziej viaduć, a viaduć jany ich u . . . Iŭje," *Iŭjeŭski kraj*, June 19, 2015, https://ivyenews.by/novosti/kultura/1751-ne-rym-darogi-sikh-ly-udzej-vyaduts-vyaduty-yany-ikh-u-i-e.html, accessed October 10, 2020.

54. V. Gulidova (Viera Hulidava), "Ekspozitsiia pod zvezdoi Davida," *Iŭjeŭski kraj*, November 30, 2019, https://ivyenews.by/novosti/obshchestvo/6085-ekspozitsionnyj-zal-prinyal-pervykh-posetitelej.html, accessed October 13, 2020.

55. Baradach, interview, July 8, 2020.

56. This perspective is perfectly in tune with mainstream Belarusian historiography, which marginalizes the Holocaust, focusing on the heroic victory of the Red Army. See Per Anders Rudling, "'For a Heroic Belarus!' The Great Patriotic War as Identity Marker in the Lukashenka and Soviet Belarusian Discourses," *Nationalities Affairs* 32 (2008): 43–62; David Marples, *"Our Glorious Past": Lukashenka's Belarus and the Great Patriotic War* (Stuttgart: Ibidem Verlag, 2014); and Magdalena Waligórska, "Remembering the Holocaust on the Fault Lines of East and West-European Memorial Cultures: The New Memorial Complex in Trastsianets, Belarus," *Holocaust Studies* 24, no. 3 (2018): 329–53.

57. The monument bears an official dedication "to the friendship and unity between the confessions of the Iŭje region."

58. Baradach, interview, July 8, 2020.

59. As of 2020, one of the former synagogue buildings hosts a gym and the other one a shop. The third synagogue building was demolished.

60. Iľja Koščar, personal interview with Ina Sorkina, October 16, 2020.

61. Baradach, interview, July 8, 2020.

62. On the 1923 pogrom, see Ina Sorkina, "Novyja krynicy pa historyi Iŭja," in *Iŭjeŭskaja ziamlia*, 91. On looting, see Tamara Baradach, personal interview with Ina Sorkina, October 20, 2020.

63. The memorial at the site was erected in 1957. It bore an inscription referring to the victims as "Jews," and not the customary "Soviet citizens." In 1989, the memorial was renovated and expanded.

64. "Kogda steny zaplakali."

65. Baradach, interview, July 8, 2020. For a similar account, see also Leon Segal, *Tears of a Hero: The Amazing Story of Rubin and Ida Segal* (N.p., 2005), 53.

66. Baradach, interview, July 8, 2020.

67. Special buses were provided to bring interested audiences, free of charge, from Belarus, Russia, Lithuania, and Estonia. Tamar Rogoff, personal interview with Magdalena Waligórska, November 17, 2020; and Sharyn Korey "On the Streets, In the Forest," *Contact Quarterly* 32, no. 1 (Winter/Spring 2007): 26–32.

68. Tamar Rogoff and Daisy Wright, dir., *Summer in Ivye*, Tamar Rogoff Performance Projects, 2002.

69. Tamar Rogoff, personal interview with Magdalena Waligórska, November 22, 2020.

70. Gabriel of Białystok, together with Saint Athanasius and Saint Macarius, belong to the group of "Belarusian" holy martyrs, dating back to the seventeenth century, who symbolize the struggle of the "Belarusian" Orthodox community with other denominations. Anton Miranovič (Mironowicz), Pravaslaŭnaja Bielaruś (Białystok: Belaruskae Histaryčnae Tavarystva, 2009), 195. For the discussion of the contemporary cult of Saint Gabriel, see the theme issue of *Societas/Communitas: Polityki Pamięci* 2 (2009).

71. The relics of Saint Gabriel were transferred from Hrodna to Białystok in 1992. See Joanna Tokarska-Bakir, *Legendy o krwi: Antropologia przesądu* (Warsaw: WAB, 2008), 243–44, 297, 324.

72. Baradach, interview, July 8, 2020.

73. Koščar, interview, October 16, 2020.

74. Baradach, interview, October 16, 2020. See also the results of anthropological research from the area of Lida in Anna Engelking, *Kołchoźnicy: Antropologiczne studium tożsamości wsi białoruskiej przełomu XX i XXI wieku* (Toruń: Wydawnictwo Naukowe Uniwersytetu Mikołaja Kopernika, 2012), 583–603.

75. Viačaslaŭ Paškevich, personal interview with Ina Sorkina, September 24, 2020.

76. John C. Turner, "Towards a Cognitive Redefinition of the Social Group," in *Social Identity and Intergroup Relations*, ed. Henri Tajfel (Cambridge: Cambridge University Press, 1982), 34.

77. "Brody," *Elektronnaia evreiskaia Entsiklopediia*, https://eleven.co.il/diaspora/communities/10761/; Börries Kuzmany, "Brody Always on My Mind: The Mental Mapping of a Jewish City," *East European Jewish Affairs* 43, no. 2 (2013), 163–65; Börries Kuzmany, *Brody: eine galizische Grenzstadt im langen 19. Jahrhundert* (Cologne: Böhlau, 2011), 319–20; and Nathan Michael Gelber, "Brody: 'Jerusalem of Austria,'" in *An Eternal Light: Brody, in Memoriam (Ukraine)*, ed. Aviv (New York: JewishGen, 2018), 27–70, https://www.jewishgen.org/yizkor/brody/bro050.html, accessed September 1, 2020. See also chapter 1 in this volume.

78. Kuzmany, *Brody*, 253–58.

79. On the percentage of Jews, see Kuzmany, *Brody*, 125, 126, 345; and on "little Jerusalem," see Gelber, "Brody"; and Kuzmany, "Brody Always on My Mind," 166.

80. Iaroslav J. Chumak, ed., *Brody i Bridshchyna: Istorichno-memuranyi zbirnyk* (Toronto: Shevchenko Scientific Society, 1988), 85, 86.

81. For some examples, see Testimony of Pepa Braun, born in Brody in 1913, Archive of the Jewish Historical Institute in Warsaw (AJHI), 31/2281; Testimony of Zofia Szwarc, born in Brody in 1929, AJHI, 301/5439; and Testimony of Helena Kurc, born in Mikołajew near Brody in 1907, AJHI, 301/5716.

82. Spector, *Encyclopedia of Jewish Life: A–J*, 202; and Kuzmany, "Brody Always on My Mind," 166.

83. Vasyl Strylchuk, *Brody: Halytskyy Yerusalym* (Brody: Brody Historical and Local History Museum, 2015).

84. Chumak, *Brody i Bridshchyna*, 371, 372, 385.

85. David Davidowitz, "The Synagogue of Brody," in Meltzer, *Eternal Light*.

86. Davidowitz, "Synagogue of Brody," 167; and Andrey Korchak, "Brodovskie sinagogi kontsa XVI–nachala XVIII vv.," in *Tirosh—trudy po iudaike*, vol. 9, ed. Mikhail A. Khlenov et al. (Moscow: Sefer, 2009), 69–71.

87. Korchak, "Brodovskie sinagogi," 73; and Kuzmany, "Brody Always on My Mind," 167.

88. Korchak, "Brodovskie sinagogi," 74; and Nina Polishchuk, "'Velyka' synahoha u Brodach," *RISU: Relihiinyi turyzm*, May 15, 2014, https://risu.org.ua/ua/relig_tourism/religious_region/56098/, accessed September 3, 2020.

89. Korchak, "Brodovskie sinagogi," 74.

90. Kuzmany, "Brody Always on My Mind," 168; and Halyna Tereshchuk, "Brody—misto, iakym chodyv Balzak, Franko, Rot," *Radio Free Europe / Radio Liberty (Ukrainian Service)*, June 14, 2013, https://www.radiosvoboda.org/a/25015371.html, accessed September 4, 2020.

91. See, e.g., Bohdan Cherkes and Svitlana Linda, "The Public Space and the Revival of Multicultural Identity in the City of Lviv," *Architectural Studies* 2, no. 2 (2016): 75–84.

92. Ruslan Danyluck, personal interview with Alexander Friedman, July 31, 2020.

93. David Bronsen, *Joseph Roth: Eine Biographie* (Cologne: Kiepenheuer & Witsch, 2018), 21–54.

94. Volodymyr Bulyshyn, "Shchto nam robyty z 'chuzhoiu spadshchynoiu,'" *Bridski visti*, January 2017, 2.

95. On sightseeing tours, see Vasyl Strylchuk, *Brody: Davni chramy* (Brody: Brody Historical and Local History Museum, 2015). On the Roth tour, see Vasyl Strylchuk, *Brody: Misto Yozefa Rota* (Brody: Brody Historical and Local History Museum, 2015).

96. Maksim Suchanov, "V Brodach otkryli biust vydaiushchemusia zemliaku—pisateliu Iozefu Rotu," *Chadashot*, September 2019, http://ww.hadashot.kiev.ua/content/v-brodah-otkryli-byust-vydayushchemusya-zemlyaku-pisatelyu-yozefu-rotu, accessed September 3, 2020.

97. "Stsena festyvaliu 'LvivMozart' hotova pryymaty hostey!" *TV Brody online*, August 2, 2019, https://www.youtube.com/watch?v=gPmAfYeclps&feature=youtu.be&fbclid=IwAR3k-2pENofpXUPiulgrh2_WjS5ZdonzKCclhcQgZQDxXSwFidLiGmN1d_ho, accessed September 5, 2020.

98. Liubomir Bilo, "Chy vvazhaete Vy Brody istorychno pryvablyvym mistom?" *Bridski visti*, August 2016, 2. See also Liubomyr Lysonin, "Prymara velychnoy sporudy," *Bridski visti*, April 2017, 3.

99. Bulyshyn, "Shchto nam robyty z 'chuzhoiu spadshchynoiu.'"

100. Ruslan Danyluck, personal interview with Alexander Friedman, July 31, 2020, and August 10, 2020; Volodymyr Kovalchuk, personal interview with Ruslan Danyluck, December 26, 2020; and Vasyl Strylchuk, personal interview with Rusland Danyluck, December 29, 2020.

101. Valentyna Samchenko, "Pomizh zvukiv Motsartiv u Lvovi," *Ukraina moloda*, July 24, 2019, 10; Mykola Shot, "Lviv polonyla klasychna muzyka," *Uriadovyy kurer*, August 14, 2019, 32; "Oksana Lyniv eröffnete mit beeindruckendem Joseph Roth-Gedenkkonzert," *Kleine Zeitung*, August 5, 2019, https://www.kleinezeitung.at/kultur/festspiele/5669666/LvivMozArtFestival_Oksana-Lyniv-eroeff-nete-mit-beeindruckendem, accessed September 5, 2020; and "Joseph Roth-Gedenkkonzert eröffnete LvivMozArt-Festival," *Salzburger Nachrichten*, August 5, 2019, https://www.sn.at/kultur/allgemein/joseph-roth-gedenkkonzert-eroeffnete-lvivmozart-festival-74393509, accessed September 5, 2020.

102. Volodymyr Kovalchuk, personal interview with Alexander Friedman, August 28, 2020; and Kovalchuk, interview, December 26, 2020.

103. Iuliia Gavrilova, "Restavrator iz Lvovskoi oblasti v odinochku spasaet trekhsot-letniuiu sinagogu," *Komsomolskaia pravda v Ukraine*, December 27, 2018, https://kp.ua/life/627273-restavrator-yz-lvovskoi-oblasty-v-odynochku-spasaet-trekhsotletnuiui-synahohu, accessed September 5, 2020; and Oksana Dudar, "Don Kikhot iz Brodov, ili kak v odinochku spasat isoricheskoe nasledie," *Chadashot*, February 2019, http://hadashot.kiev.ua/content/don-kikhot-iz-brodov-ili-kak-v-odinochku-spasat-istoricheskoe-nasledie, accessed September 6, 2020.

104. Judith Wipfler, "Auf der Suche nach verwischten jüdischen Spuren in der Ukraine," *srf.ch*, September 18, 2014, https://www.srf.ch/kultur/gesellschaft-religion/auf-der-suche-nach-verwischten-juedischen-spuren-in-der-ukraine, accessed September 6, 2020.

105. "I odin v pole voin: v odinochku spasti zdanie brodskoi sinagogi pytaetsia Vladimir Kovalchuk," http://vaadua.org/news/i-odin-v-pole-voin-v-odinochku-spasti-zdanie-brodskoy-sinagogi-pytaetsya-vladimir-kovalchuk, accessed September 6, 2020; and "Chto proizoshlo s sinagogoi v Brodach i Vladimirom Kovalchukom: Prodolzhenie istorii," http://vaadua.org/news/chto-proizosh lo-s-sinagogoy-v-brodah-i-vladimirom-kovalchukom-prodolzhenie-istorii, accessed September 6, 2020.

106. Rothberg, *Implicated Subject*, 8.

107. Dudar, "Don Kikhot iz Brodov."

108. For recent critical Ukrainian historiography addressing the question of complicity in anti-Jewish atrocities, see Iuriy Radchenko (Yurii Radchenko), "Ukrainska politsiia ta Kholokost na Donbasi," *Ukraina Moderna* 24 (2017): 64–121; Yurii Radchenko, "'We Emptied Our Magazines into Them': The Ukrainian Auxiliary Police and the Holocaust in Generalbe-zirk Charkow, 1941–1943," *Yad Vashem Studies* 41 (2013), 63–98; Yurii Radchenko, "'Ukrainische Hilfspolizei' i Kholokost na territorii general-betsirka Chernigov, 1941–1943," *Forum noveishei vostochnoevropeiskoi istorii i kultury, Russkoe izdanie* 1 (2013): 297–321; and Marta Havryshko, "Women's Voices: Jewish Rape Survivors' Testimonies in Soviet War Crimes Trials," in *If This Is a Woman: Studies on Women and Gender in the Holocaust*, ed. Denisa Nešťáková, Katja Grosse-Sommer, and Borbala Klacsmann (Boston: Academic Studies Press, 2021), 221–42.

109. For the development of Ukrainian nationalism under Austrian rule, see Timothy Snyder, *The Reconstruction of Nations: Poland, Ukraine, Belarus 1596–1999* (New Haven, CT: Yale University Press, 2003), 122–32.

110. J. E. Tunbridge and G. J. Ashworth, *Dissonant Heritage* (Chicherster: Wiley, 1996), 21.

111. For the concept of "historical nation," see Eric Hobsbawm, *Nations and Nationalism since 1780: Programme, Myth, Reality* (Cambridge: Cambridge University Press, 1990), 73–75.

112. A milestone for the debate on Polish complicity in anti-Jewish violence was the publication of Jan T. Gross's *Neighbors* (Princeton, NJ: Princeton University Press, 2001), which brought the events of the pogrom in Jedwabne in 1941 to popular attention.

12: A New Multiculturalism in Poland

1. This chapter was written under the auspices of the OPUS 12 research project "'Polacy i inni' trzydzieści lat później" ("'Poles and Others' Thirty Years On"). Agreement UMO-2016/23/B/HS6/03874 was enacted on August 4, 2017, signed by Collegium Civitas with the National Science Centre of Poland (NCN).

2. Anna Śliz, *Wielokulturowość: stygmat współczesnego świata? Próba analizy socjologicznej* (Opole: Uniwersytet Opolski, 2017), 22–30; Will Kymlicka, "Multicultural Odysseys," *Ethnopolitics* 6, no. 4 (December 2007): 585–97; and Will Kymlicka, review of *Political Theory and Australian Multiculturalism*, ed. Geoffrey Brahm Levey (Oxford: Berghahn Books, 2008), *Journal of International Migration and Integration/Revue de l'integration et de la migration internationale* 10, no. 4 (November 2009): 477–78.

3. Janusz Mucha, "Wielokulturowość etniczna i nieetniczna," *Sprawy Narodowościowe* 14, no. 5 (1999): 41–50.

4. Jacek Schmidt, "Imigrant w polskiej przestrzeni miejskiej, czyli długa droga do wielokulturowości i multikulturalizm," *Rozwój Regionalny i Polityka Regionalna* 31 (2015): 67–74. See also Michał Buchowski and Katarzyna Chlewińska, *Tolerance of Cultural Diversity in Poland and Its Limitations* (San Domenico di Fiesole: European University Institute, 2012), 345–48, https://cadmus.eui.eu/handle/1814/24381.

5. See also the introduction to this volume.

6. Regarding the folklorization of difference, see Agnieszka Pasieka, "'Czy Łemkowie chodzą w dżinsach?' Wielokulturowość w Polsce jako kapitał i jako obciążenie," *Pogranicze: Studia Społeczne* 20 (2012): 35–52. Regarding its attractiveness, see Ewa Nowicka, "Wprowadzenie: Inny jako obcy," in *Religia a obcość*, ed. Ewa Nowicka (Kraków: Nomos, 1991), 9–25.

7. Stanley Fish, "Boutique Multiculturalism, or Why Liberals Are Incapable of Thinking about Hate Speech," *Critical Inquiry* 23, no. 2 (1997), 38, http://www.jstor.org/stable/1343988; and Gordon Mathews, *Global Culture/Individual Identity* (London: Routledge, 2000).

8. Kamila Dolińska, "Dwie odsłony wielokulturowości a problem społecznego doświadczania różnicy," in *Wielokulturowość: Konflikt czy Koegzystencja*, ed. Anna Śliz and Marek Szczepański (Warsaw: IFiS PAN, 2011), 99–120.

9. Dolińska, "Dwie odsłony wielokulturowości," 99–120.

10. This includes Ukrainians native to Poland who are Polish citizens from birth.

11. Ewa Nowicka and Sławomir Łodziński, "Better Migrants, Worse Migrants: Young, Educated Poles Look at New Incomers to Poland," *Władza Sądzenia* 18 (2020), http://wladzasadzenia.pl/2020/18/better-migrants-worse-migrants-young-educated-poles-look-at-new-incomers-to-poland.pdf; Ewa Nowicka and Sławomir Łodziński, "Odcienie obcości: Wyniki sondażu 'Polacy i Inni 30 lat później': Analiza porównawcza (1988, 1998, 2018)," *Kultura i Społeczeństwo* 64, no. 3 (2020): 169–98, https://doi.org/10.35757/KiS.2020.64.3.9.

12. Marek Okólski and Dominik Wach, "Immigration and Integration Policies in the Absence of Immigrants," in *Relations between Immigration and Integration Policies in Europe*, ed. Maciej Duszczyk, Marta Pachocka, and Dominika Pszczółkowska (London: Routledge, 2020), 146–72; and Marta Pachocka, Konrad Pędziwiatr, Karolina Sobczak-Szelc, and Justyna Szałańska, "Reception Policies, Practices and Responses: Poland—Country Report" (2020), https://doi.org/10.5281/zenodo.3727093.

13. For instance, the regional minority of Silesians continues to go unrecognized officially, but their identity can be and is written into the census.

14. GUS, *Populacja cudzoziemców w Polsce w czasie COVID-19*, June 4, 2020, 1.

15. CBOS, *Praca obcokrajowców w Polsce: Komunikat z badań, nr 5* (Warsaw: Centrum Badań Opinii Społecznych, January 2020), 3.

16. Regarding the phenomenon of urban, cultural enclaves, see Schmidt, "Imigrant w polskiej przestrzeni miejskiej," 67–74. Regarding a sense of communal belonging, see Agata Górny, Sabina Toruńczyk-Ruiz, and Aleksandra Winiarska, "Wprowadzenie," in *Po sąsiedzku z różnorodnością: Interakcje w miejskich przestrzeniach lokalnych z perspektywy różnych grup mieszkańców*, ed. Agata Górny, Sabina Toruńczyk-Ruiz, and Aleksandra Winiarska (Warsaw: Scholar, 2018), 8–11.

17. Małgorzata Molęda-Zdziech, Marta Pachocka, and Dominik Wach, "Immigration and Integration Policies in Poland: Institutional, Political and Social Perspectives," in *Local Integration of Migrants Policy: European Experiences and Challenges*, ed. Jochen Franzke and Jose Ruano de la Fuente (Cham: Palgrave Macmillan, 2021), 169–99; and Mikołaj Pawlak, "Polityki publiczne wobec migracji," in *Nauki o polityce publicznej: Monografia dyscypliny*, ed. J. Kwaśniewski (Warsaw: Instytut Profilaktyki Społecznej i Resocjalizacji UW, 2018), 288–311.

18. Sławomir Łodziński, "Equal and More Equal: Ethnic Communities and Polish Public Policy 1989–2018," in *Identity Strategies of Stateless Ethnic Minority Groups in Contemporary Poland* ed. Ewa Michna and Katarzyna Warmińska (Cham: Springer, 2020), 4–6.

19. Found in numerous studies, such as Teresa Halik, Ewa Nowicka, and Wojciech Połeć, *Dziecko wietnamskie w polskiej szkole: Zmiana kulturowa i strategie przekazu kultury rodzimej w zbiorowości Wietnamczyków w Polsce* (Warsaw: Wydawnictwo ProLog, 2006); and Teresa Halik and Ewa Nowicka, *Wietnamczycy w Polsce* (Warsaw: Wydawnictwo UW, 2002).

20. Jerzy Smolicz, "Core Values and Cultural Identity," *Ethnic and Racial Studies* 4, no. 1 (1981): 75–90.

21. Nowicka and Łodziński, "Better Migrants, Worse Migrants"; and Nowicka and Łodziński, "Odcienie obcości."

22. Regarding the heritage of the Commonwealth, see esp. chapters 9, 10, and 11 in this volume. Regarding Polish collective memory of it, see, e.g., CBOS, *Świadomość historyczna Polaków: Komunikat z badań, nr 68* (Warsaw: Centrum Badań Opini Społecznych, April 2016).

23. See the introduction to this volume.

24. See esp. chapters 1, 2, and 3 in this volume.

25. Interview 6, 2014, conducted by Ewa Nowicka. Interviews are numbered and accompanied by the year in which they were conducted.

26. Buchowski and Chlewińska, *Tolerance of Cultural Diversity*, 345–48.

27. Mucha, "Wielokulturowość etniczna i nieetniczna," 41–43.

28. GUS, *Populacja cudzoziemców w Polsce w czasie COVID-19*, June 4, 2020.

29. See Joanna Konieczna-Sałamatin, "Konkurencja, zagrożenie, czy ratunek dla gospodarki? Postawy Polaków wobec imigrantów," *Studia Socjologiczno-Polityczne: Seria Nowa* 1, no. 10 (2019): 61–82.

30. Anita Adamczyk, "Imigracja zarobkowa do Polski: Casus Ukraińców (2014–2017)," *Środkowoeuropejskie Studia Polityczne* 2 (2018): 115–35.

31. Adamczyk, "Imigracja zarobkowa do Polski," 117.

32. MM, "Ukraińcy w Polsce wcale nie zarabiają gorzej od Polaków: Często wręcz przeciwnie," *Forbes*, May 28, 2018, https://www.forbes.pl/gospodarka/zarobki-ukraincow-w-polsce-2018/5f9rd4r.

33. Adamczyk, "Imigracja zarobkowa do Polski," 122–25.

34. Iza Chmielewska, Grzegorz Dobroczek, and Adam Panuciak, *Obywatele Ukrainy pracujący w Polsce: raport z badania* (Warsaw: Departament Statystyki NBP, 2018).

35. Paweł Kaczmarczyk and Joanna Tyrowicz, "Migracje osób z wysokimi kwalifikacjami," *Biuletyn FISE* 4 (2008): 9–10; and Sylwia Galanciak and Bohdana Huriy, "Nowe media a rekonstrukcja kapitału społecznego migrantów ukraińskich na polskim rynku pracy," *Studia Migracyjne–Przegląd Polonijny* 46, no. 2 (2020): 153–75.

36. Izabela Grabowska-Lusińska and Ewa Jaźwińska, "Mobilność przestrzenna, społeczna i kariery zawodowe migrantów: Cele, problemy i podejścia badawcze," *Studia Migracyjne–Przeglad Polonijny* 38, no. 2 (2012): 71–104.

37. Agata Górny, "All Circular but Different: Variation in Patterns of Ukraine-to-Poland Migration," *Population, Space and Place* 23, no. 8 (November 2017), https://doi.org/10.1002/psp.2074; and Agata Górny and Ewa Jaźwińska, "Ukraińskie migrantki i migranci w aglomeracji warszawskiej: Cechy społeczno-demograficzne i relacje społeczne," CMR Working Papers 115, no. 173 (2019).

38. Górny and Jaźwińska, "Ukraińskie migrantki i migranci."

39. CBOS, *Przybysze z bliska i z daleka, czyli o imigrantach w Polsce: Komunikat z badań, nr 93* (Warsaw: Centrum Badań Opini Społecznych, June 2015).

40. CBOS, *Stosunek do innych narodów: Komunikat z badań, nr 30* (Warsaw: Centrum Badań Opinii Społecznych, March 2021).

41. CBOS, *Przybysze z bliska i z daleka*, June 2015.

42. Piotr Długosz, "Integracja ukraińskich studentów podejmujących naukę w Polsce," *Studia Migracyjne-Przegląd Polonijny* 44, no. 2 (2018): 67–92.

43. Marcin Gońda, "Mobilność edukacyjna w sytuacji migracji do korzeni: przypadek młodej polskiej diaspory ze Wschodu," *Studia Migracyjne-Przegląd Polonijny* 1, no. 163 (2017): 229–58, http://www.kbnm.pan.pl/images/pdf/SM_PP_1_2017/Studia-Migracyjne-1-17-11Goda.pdf; and Krystyna Gomółka, "Przeciwdziałanie nielegalnej emigracji na granicy polsko-rosyjskiej w dobie członkostwa Polski w Unii Europejskiej," *Annales Universitatis Mariae Curie-Skłodowska, sectio K–Politologia* 24, no. 2 (2017): 75–87.

44. Długosz, "Integracja ukraińskich studentów."

45. Długosz, "Integracja ukraińskich studentów."

46. Kaczmarczyk and Tyrowicz, "Migracje osób z wysokimi kwalifikacjami," 9–10; and Piotr Sztompka, *Kapitał społeczny: Teoria przestrzeni międzyludzkiej* (Kraków: Znak, 2016).

47. Galanciak and Huriy, "Nowe media a rekonstrukcja kapitału społecznego."

48. Ewa Nowicka and Magdalena Majewska, *Obcy u siebie: Luteranie warszawscy* (Warsaw: Oficyna Naukowa, 1993).

49. CBOS, *Stosunek do innych narodów*, March 2021.

50. CBOS, *Stosunek do innych narodów*, March 2021.

51. Joanna Konieczna-Sałamatin, "Konkurencja, zagrożenie, czy ratunek dla gospodarki? Postawy Polaków wobec imigrantów," *Studia Socjologiczno-Polityczne: Seria Nowa* 1 (2019): 61–82.

52. CBOS, *Przybysze z bliska i z daleka*, June 2015.

53. Joanna P. Bierówka, "Opinie studentów ukraińskich na temat ich integracji akademickiej," *Państwo i Społeczeństwo* 16, no. 1 (2016): 199–213.

54. Bierówka, "Opinie studentów ukraińskich."

55. Krzysztof Jurek, "Stereotypy na temat Ukraińców funkcjonujące w Polsce," in *Imigranci z Ukrainy w Polsce: Potrzeby i oczekiwania; reakcje społeczne, wzywania dla bezpieczeństwa*, ed. Michał Lubicz Miszewski (Wrocław: Wydawnictwo AWL, 2018), 31–42.

56. Jurek, "Stereotypy na temat Ukraińców," 34.

57. Jurek, "Stereotypy na temat Ukraińców," 36.

58. Interview 3, 2014, conducted by Ewa Nowicka.

59. Maryana Prokop, "Stereotyp Ukraińca w Polskim tygodniku 'Polityka' oraz stereotyp Polaka na łamach 'Dzerkało Tyżnia–Ukraina,'" *Warmińsko-Mazurski Kwartalnik Naukowy* 3 (2013): 47–66.

60. CBOS, *Stosunek do protestów na Ukrainie: Komunikat z badań, nr 21* (Warsaw: Centrum Badań Opinii Społecznych, February 2014).

61. Interviewee cited in Krzysztof Jurek, "Stereotypy na temat Ukraińców funkcjonujące w Polsce," in Miszewski, *Imigranci z Ukrainy w Polsce*, 35.

62. Interview s23, 2019, conducted by Ewa Nowicka. Interviews are numbered and accompanied by the year in which they were conducted. An "s" at the beginning indicates a respondent from the older generation; "m" indicates a respondent from the younger generation.

63. Interview s30, 2019.

64. Interview m1, 2019.

65. Interview m4, 2019.

66. Interview m14, 2019.

67. Interview m3, 2019.

68. Interview m6, 2019.

69. Interview m7, 2019.

70. Interview m7, 2019.

71. Interview m19, 2020.

72. Interview m9, 2019.

73. Interview m12, 2019.

74. Interview m12, 2019.

75. Długosz, "Integracja ukraińskich studentów," 67–92.

76. Interview s17, 2019.

77. See Tadeusz Lewowicki, "Cztery spojrzenia na wielokulturowość i edukację międzykulturową," *Pogranicze: Studia Społeczne* 17 (2011), 28–38; John W. Berry and Colleen Ward, "Multiculturalism," in *The Cambridge Handbook of Acculturation Psychology*, ed. David L. Sam and John W. Berry (Cambridge: Cambridge University Press, 2016), 441–63; and Halik, Nowicka, and Połeć, *Dziecko wietnamskie w polskiej szkole*.

CONTRIBUTORS

Stanley Bill is professor of Polish studies and the director of the Slavonic Studies Section at the University of Cambridge. He works on twentieth-century Polish literature and culture and on contemporary politics in Poland. He is the author of *Czesław Miłosz's Faith in the Flesh: Body, Belief, and Human Identity* (Oxford, 2021) and coeditor of *The Routledge World Companion to Polish Literature* (Routledge, 2021). He has also published articles, among others, on populism and civil society in Poland, postcolonial theory in the Polish context, legacies of Polish Romanticism, and the works of Czesław Miłosz, Bruno Schulz, and Fyodor Dostoevsky. His translation of Miłosz's novel *The Mountains of Parnassus* was published by Yale University Press in 2017. He is the founder and editor-at-large of the news and opinion website *Notes from Poland*.

Richard Butterwick is professor of Polish-Lithuanian history at the School of Slavonic and East European Studies, University College London and principal historian of the Polish History Museum in Warsaw. In 2014–2020 he held the chair of European Civilization at the College of Europe, Natolin, Warsaw. His research clusters at the interface between politics, ideas, culture, and religion in the Polish-Lithuanian Commonwealth in the age of Enlightenment. Among his publications are the books *Poland's Last King and English Culture: Stanisław August Poniatowski 1732–1798* (Oxford, 1998), *The Polish Revolution and the Catholic Church 1788–1792* (Oxford, 2012), *The Polish-Lithuanian Commonwealth 1733–1795: Light and Flame* (Yale, 2020), and *The Constitution of 3 May 1791: Testament of the Polish-Lithuanian Commonwealth* (Polish History Museum, 2021).

Alexander Friedman is a historian of the Holocaust, specializing in the (post-)Soviet territory, especially Belarus and Ukraine. He holds a PhD from the University of Saarland (2009). His focus lies on National Socialism, Nazi war crimes, history of Jews and Roma in Eastern Europe, and propaganda. He has published extensively on the Holocaust and Nazi crimes in the oc-

cupied territories of the Soviet Union as well as on questions of collective
memory, representations of the past in popular culture, and urban history
of Eastern Europe. He is currently a coinvestigator in the research project
"Mapping the Archipelago of Lost Towns: Post-Holocaust Urban Lacunae in
the Polish-Belarusian-Ukrainian Borderlands" (Gerda Henkel Foundation,
2020–2023).

Karin Friedrich is professor of early modern European history at the University of Aberdeen. Previously she lectured at the School of Slavonic and East
European Studies, University College London (1995–2004). She has received
several awards and fellowships (AHRC, Leverhulme, Gerda Henkel Stiftung,
Institute for European History Mainz, among others), a guest professorship
at the Free University Berlin, and has been an elected member of the Council
of the Royal Historical Society. She is currently president of the German
History Society, UK. Her publications include *The Other Prussia: Poland,
Prussia and Liberty, 1454–1772* (Cambridge, 2000, Polish translation, 2006);
The Cultivation of Monarchy and the Rise of Berlin: Brandenburg-Prussia 1700
(with Sara Smart, Routledge, 2010); and *Brandenburg-Prussia, 1466–1806:
The Rise of a Composite State* (Palgrave Macmillan, 2011). Other publications
focus on the history of political ideas, religion, the Enlightenment in Central
Europe, and the history of social elites in Poland-Lithuania. She is currently
preparing a political biography of the Lithuanian magnate Bogusław Radziwiłł (1620–1669) for Routledge.

Robert Frost holds the Burnett Fletcher Chair of History at the University
of Aberdeen. He wrote his doctoral dissertation at the School of Slavonic
and East European Studies, University College of London under the supervision of Norman Davies, a revised version of which was published as *After
the Deluge: Poland-Lithuania and the Second Northern War, 1655–1660* (Cambridge, 1993). He taught at King's College London from 1987, and published
his second book, *The Northern Wars: War, State and Society in Northeastern
Europe, 1558–1721* (Longman, 2000). He moved to Aberdeen in 2004, and is
currently writing a three-volume history of the Polish-Lithuanian Union
for Oxford University Press. Volume 1, *The Making of the Polish-Lithuanian
Union, 1385–1569* (Oxford, 2015) won the Pro Historia Polonorum Prize for
the best foreign-language book on Polish history published between 2012
and 2017. He has recently published *The Polish Portrait of Bonnie Prince Charlie* (Palgrave/Springer, 2022).

Tomasz Grusiecki is assistant professor of early modern art history at Boise State University. His research focuses on visual and material culture in the Polish-Lithuanian Commonwealth, centering on topics that connect past and present, including early modern proto-nationalism, globalization, cultural entanglement, and perceptions of selfhood and alterity. He has published on these subjects in the *Art Bulletin, Slavonic and East European Review*, and the *Journal of Early Modern History*, among others. He has recently completed his first book, *Transcultural Things and the Specter of Orientalism in Early Modern Poland-Lithuania* (Manchester, forthcoming). He is a coinvestigator on the AHRC-funded research project, "Connected Central European Worlds, 1500–1700" (2021–2023).

Rūstis Kamuntavičius is associate professor of history and the head of the Czesław Miłosz Center at Vytautas Magnus University in Kaunas, Lithuania. He is the director of the Institute of the Grand Duchy of Lithuania, which organizes research on the history and legacy of the Grand Duchy of Lithuania, and acts to promote the notion of a common past among Lithuanians, Poles, Belarusians, and Ukrainians. His main fields of scholarly interest include: (1) historical relations between Lithuania and Western European countries since the Middle Ages; and (2) history, politics, culture, and national narratives of Lithuania, Poland, and Belarus. He is the creator and editor of www .gudija.lt—the first and only Lithuanian website dedicated to Belarus (news, analysis, and history).

Dariusz Kołodziejczyk is professor of history at the University of Warsaw, where he has been employed since 1988. He has held numerous visiting fellowships, including at: the Harvard University Ukrainian Research Institute; Nahost-Institut an der Universität München; Hokkaido University; Collège de France; and Stanford University. He is a member of the Academia Europaea and an honorary member of the Turkish Historical Society (TTK). He has been president of the CIEPO (Comité International des Etudes Pre-Ottomanes et Ottomanes) since 2018. His book-length publications include: *Ottoman-Polish Diplomatic Relations (15th–18th Century): An Annotated Edition of 'Ahdnames and Other Documents* (Brill, 2000); *Defter-i Mufassal-i Eyalet-i Kamaniçe: The Ottoman Survey Register of Podolia (ca. 1681)* (Harvard Ukrainian Research Institute, 2004); *The Crimean Khanate and Poland-Lithuania International Diplomacy on the European Periphery (15th–18th Century)* (Brill, 2011); and *Universal Empire: A Comparative Approach to Imperial*

Culture and Representation in Eurasian History (ed. with Peter Fibiger Bang; Cambridge, 2012).

Simon Lewis is associate professor of East and Central European cultural history at the University of Bremen. He completed his PhD at Cambridge in 2014 and has held research posts at the University of Oxford, the University of Warsaw, Freie Universität Berlin, and the University of Potsdam. He was appointed to his current position in January 2020. His research interests include memory studies, postcolonialism, and comparative literature, with a focus on the written and visual cultures of Belarus, Poland, Russia, and Ukraine. He has published articles on diverse aspects of the cultural history of East-Central Europe, and is a coauthor of *Remembering Katyn* (Polity Press, 2012). His monograph is *Belarus—Alternative Visions: Nation, Memory and Cosmopolitanism* (Routledge, 2019). He also coedited (with Jeffrey K. Olick, Joanna Wawrzyniak, and Małgorzata Pakier) *Regions of Memory: Transnational Formations* (Palgrave Macmillan, 2022).

Ewa Nowicka is a sociologist, social anthropologist, the former head of the Department of Social Anthropology at the Institute of Sociology, University of Warsaw (2001–2013), and currently a professor at Collegium Civitas in Warsaw. She deals with issues of familiarity and strangeness ("us" and "them"), intercultural contact, the emergence of new nations in Siberia and the Balkan Peninsula (Aromanians), the Polish minority in former republics of the USSR, and minority groups (including Ukrainians and Roma) in Poland and Central and Eastern Europe.

Olenka Z. Pevny is associate professor of early Slavic and Ukrainian studies at the University of Cambridge. She is a cultural historian who specializes in the visual culture of Rus', Ruthenian, and Ukrainian lands, and is especially interested in the complexity and impact of cultural discourse on the imagining of past and the formulation of present identities, as well as on preservation and restoration practices and policies. Her published articles cover the visual culture of medieval Rus', early modern Ruthenia, the Cossack Hetmanate, and the Russian Empire, as well as Soviet and independent Ukraine. Before coming to Cambridge, she was asssociate professor of Byzantine studies at the University of Richmond and a curator at the Metropolitan Museum of Art.

Ina Sorkina is a historian of Belarus, particularly the Hrodna region. Her main fields of expertise are Jewish history and shtetl history. She holds a PhD from the Belarusian Academy of Sciences in Minsk (1998). She has authored *Miastechki of Belarus at the End of 18th–First Half of 19th Century* (EHU, 2010), among others. She has also led multiple field expeditions in Belarus in co-operation with Warsaw's POLIN Museum of the History of Polish Jews and Jewish Historical Institute. She is currently a coinvestigator in the research project "Mapping the Archipelago of Lost Towns: Post-Holocaust Urban Lacunae in the Polish-Belarusian-Ukrainian Borderlands" (Gerda Henkel Foundation, 2020–2023).

Magda Teter is professor of history and the Shvidler Chair of Judaic Studies at Fordham University. She is the author of *Jews and Heretics in Catholic Poland* (Cambridge, 2006); *Sinners on Trial* (Harvard, 2011), which was a finalist for the Jordan Schnitzer Prize; *Blood Libel: On the Trail of an Antisemitic Myth* (Harvard, 2020); and dozens of articles in English, Hebrew, Italian, and Polish. Her book *Blood Libel* won the 2020 National Jewish Book Award, The George L. Mosse Prize from the American Historical Association, and the Bainton Prize from the Sixteenth Century Society. Her book *Christian Supremacy: Reckoning with the Roots of Antisemitism and Racism* is forthcoming from Princeton University Press in 2023. She is the recipient of prestigious fellowships, including from the John Simon Guggenheim Memorial Foundation, the Harry Frank Guggenheim Foundation, and the Radcliffe Institute for Advanced Studies at Harvard University. She has served as the coeditor of the *AJS Review* and as the vice president for Publications of the Association for Jewish Studies and is currently the president of the American Academy for Jewish Research.

Magdalena Waligórska is a cultural historian and sociologist based at the Center for Anthropological Research on Museums and Heritage in the Department of European Ethnology of Humboldt University in Berlin, where she is currently leading a research group "Mapping the Archipelago of Lost Towns: Post-Holocaust Urban Lacunae in the Polish-Belarusian-Ukrainian Borderlands" (funded by the Gerda Henkel Foundation, 2020–2023). Her fields of interest include contemporary Polish and Belarusian history, nationalism and national symbols, Jewish heritage and popular culture, Jewish/non-Jewish relations, music and identity, and memory studies. She has published extensively on Jewish culture, Jewish–non-Jewish relations and nationalism, including in *East European Politics and Societies, Holocaust Studies, East European Jewish Affairs*, and *Jewish Cultural Studies*. She is the author of *Klezmer's Afterlife: An Ethnography of the Jewish Music Revival in Poland and Germany* (Oxford, 2013) and *Cross Purposes: Catholicism and the Political Imagination in Poland* (Cambridge, 2022).

INDEX

Note: Page references in *italics* refer to figures.